Fundamentals of Taxation

2010

Ana Cruz
Miami Dade College

Michael Deschamps
MiraCosta College

Frederick Niswander
East Carolina University

Debra Prendergast
Northwestern College

Dan Schisler
East Carolina University

Jinhee Trone
Santa Ana College

McGraw-Hill
Irwin

McGraw-Hill Irwin

FUNDAMENTALS OF TAXATION 2010

Published by McGraw-Hill/Irwin, a business unit of The McGraw-Hill Companies, Inc., 1221 Avenue of the Americas, New York, NY, 10020. Copyright © 2010, 2009, 2008, 2008 by The McGraw-Hill Companies, Inc.

Some ancillaries, including electronic and print components, may not be available to customers outside the United States.

This book is printed on acid-free paper.
2 3 4 5 6 7 8 9 0 DOW/DOW 0

ISBN   978-0-07-337967-8
MHID   0-07-337967-0
ISSN   1933-8066

Vice president and editor-in-chief: *Brent Gordon*
Editorial director: *Stewart Mattson*
Publisher: *Tim Vertovec*
Director of development: *Ann Torbert*
Development editor II: *Daryl Horrocks*
Vice president and director of marketing: *Robin J. Zwettler*
Marketing director: *Sankha Basu*
Associate marketing manager: *Dean Karampelas*
Vice president of editing, design and production: *Sesha Bolisetty*
Project manager: *Dana M. Pauley*
Lead production supervisor: *Carol A. Bielski*
Lead designer: *Matthew Baldwin*
Senior photo research coordinator: *Jeremy Cheshareck*
Media project manager: *Balaji Sundararaman, Hurix Systems Pvt. Ltd.*
Typeface: *10/13 Times New Roman*
Compositor: *Laserwords Private Limited*
Printer: *R. R. Donnelley*

www.mhhe.com

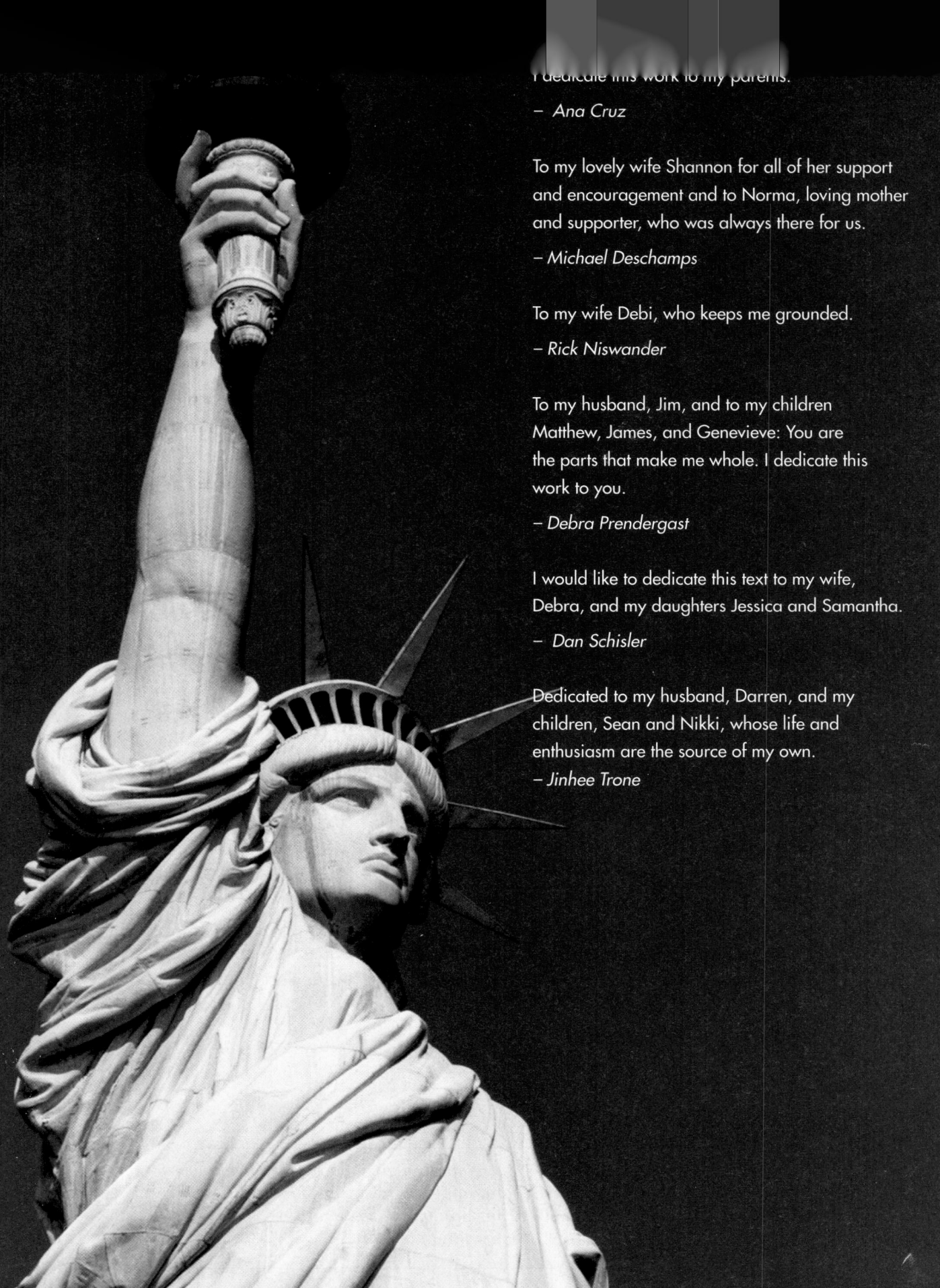

I dedicate this work to my parents.

– Ana Cruz

To my lovely wife Shannon for all of her support and encouragement and to Norma, loving mother and supporter, who was always there for us.

– Michael Deschamps

To my wife Debi, who keeps me grounded.

– Rick Niswander

To my husband, Jim, and to my children Matthew, James, and Genevieve: You are the parts that make me whole. I dedicate this work to you.

– Debra Prendergast

I would like to dedicate this text to my wife, Debra, and my daughters Jessica and Samantha.

– Dan Schisler

Dedicated to my husband, Darren, and my children, Sean and Nikki, whose life and enthusiasm are the source of my own.

– Jinhee Trone

A Monumental New Approach to Teaching Tax

Fundamentals of Taxation 2010

Fundamentals of Taxation 2010

Cruz
Deschamps
Niswander
Prendergast
Schisler
Trone

www.mhhe.com/cruz2010

President Abraham Lincoln and the Republican-controlled Congress of 1861 imposed the first federal income tax eight months after South Carolina seceded from the Union, sparking the start of the American Civil War. The Revenue Act of 1861 included the first income tax statute in the country's history, but it was a flat tax rate. Just a year later the Revenue Act of 1862 changed the income tax to the progressive tax rate that we are familiar with today.

In 1862 the marginal tax rates were 3% on income between $600 and $10,000 and 5% on income above $10,000. When adjusted for inflation, $600 in 1862 is the equivalent of $13,259 in 2008, and $10,000 is the equivalent of $220,993. Due to the exorbitant cost of the war, income tax rates were raised just two years later to 5% on income between $600 and $5,000, 7.5% on income between $5,000 and $10,000, and 10% tax on income above that.

Because the income tax was first introduced to fund Civil War military operations, it was allowed to expire once the war ended. Citizens lived income tax–free until the Revenue Act of 1913 made the income tax permanent—52 years after it was first introduced.

To train tomorrow's tax preparers to handle the complex U.S. tax law, *Fundamentals of Taxation*'s author team has devised **four primary teaching advantages**.

Easy for my students to read and follow. **Definitely a great book for individuals who will be involved with tax preparation.** *After taking a course using this book, a student could easily handle the preparation of a tax return.*
— Andrea M. Murowski, Brookdale Community College

1 First, we organize the text to **closely follow IRS tax forms**. We introduce students to standard IRS forms early and reinforce their use throughout the text. **Actual tax forms are incorporated throughout the text**, giving students the opportunity to understand the principles behind tax law while they learn how to work with clients to obtain the information they will need to complete tax forms.

2 Second, we **illustrate the proper reporting of tax issues**. We present a tax issue, discuss the legal requirements, illustrate the proper tax form placement, and show the completed form in the text. By effectively leading the student through each issue, we demonstrate how tax form preparation is the result of a careful process that balances legal knowledge with practical experience using tax forms.

3 Third, we **integrate an individual income tax software package** into the text that is used in examples. We instruct students how to use the software to complete returns using sample "taxpayers" who appear from chapter to chapter. An important consideration in writing the textbook was to allow instructor flexibility. You can choose to rely heavily on the software, you can incorporate the software only after you cover the law and the reporting, or you can deemphasize the software component. This flexible approach allows you to structure your taxation course the way you want to.

4 Fourth, we supplement the text with **citations of relevant tax authorities** such as the Internal Revenue Code, Treasury regulations, revenue rulings, revenue procedures, and court cases. These citations are almost always provided in **footnotes**. Thus you and your students can easily use, or not use, the footnote material.

Ana Cruz

Dr. Ana Cruz is chair of the Business Department at Miami Dade College, Wolfson Campus, where she utilizes her extensive experience in the areas of general business, management, accounting, and taxes. She has worked in the service, retailing, and manufacturing industries, as well as in the federal government sector, where she served as a field examiner for the Internal Revenue Service. Dr. Cruz, a certified public accountant, has published several articles in business journals and has received the Southeast Banking Corporation Foundation Endowed Teaching Chair (1998) and the Wolfson Senior Foundation Endowed Teaching Chair (2002). Her latest recognition was being named Professor of the Year for the State of Florida by the Council for Advancement and Support of Education and the Carnegie Foundation (2005).

How Does Cruz Form a Better Understanding of Tax?

Forms-Based Approach

Examples of completed tax forms demonstrate how tax theory covered in the text translates to real returns.

Appendix B includes comprehensive problems for 1040 Schedules A, C, D, and E. These longer problems include both easy and difficult schedules to test students' comprehension of a range of topics covered across multiple chapters.

Incorporation of real-world tax returns into the text for electronic as well as manual preparation forces students to learn hands-on skills.

Fundamentals of Taxation features an integrated tax software package from TaxACT, one of the leading tax preparation software companies in the market today. Students are instructed in the practical applications of tax software, with exercises that teach how software can be used to prepare all types of tax returns.

Sample "taxpayers" are used throughout the book, in varying situations, to give students full exposure to the many types of tax preparation challenges they will face. This exposure allows students to **make the connection** between the **tax law,** the **software inputs,** and the **tax output** on the appropriate tax forms.

Fundamentals of Taxation also provides the instructor with the flexibility needed in an individual income tax course. Each chapter can be used **with or without the tax software,** depending on the objectives of an individual instructor's course.

TaxACT features **in-depth form instructions** that supplement the textbook material, making it easier than ever to integrate software into the classroom. Students are provided with the latest tax forms via the **Automatic Update Wizard**, so that at the start of the semester each student will be prepared to work with the most up-to-date information available. With over **120 tax forms**, **schedules, and worksheets,** TaxACT is sure to have the course materials you will need throughout the semester.

Be sure to visit **www.TaxACT.com** today for more information.

I currently use TaxACT for my tax practice and I like your choice.
— Natasha Librizzi, Milwaukee Area Technical College

Michael P. Deschamps

Michael P. Deschamps received a bachelor of science degree in accounting, graduating magna cum laude from the University of San Diego, where he served as the chapter president for Beta Alpha Psi, the international accounting honor society. After working in public accounting and obtaining his CPA license, he returned to San Diego State University, where he earned a master's degree in taxation and a certificate in financial planning. In addition, he earned his Enrolled Agent certificate in 2004. He is currently a professor of accounting at MiraCosta College in Oceanside, CA, and previously was a tenured professor of accounting and financial services at Chaffey College, where he also served as the program coordinator for six years, developing a highly regarded tax program. He is an active member of Teachers of Accounting at Two Year Colleges (TACTYC) and was a presenter at the 2006 and 2007 national conventions. He has published articles in both local and national publications and has given presentations on tax issues to a variety of organizations.

How Does Cruz Better Prepare My Students?

Tax Your Brain

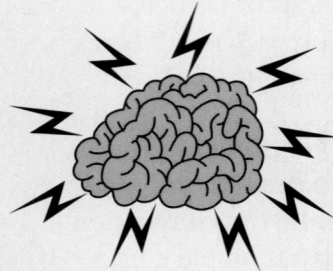

The Tax Your Brain feature is designed to work with the examples in the text to reinforce the understanding of key concepts. Students are given information in an example and then are asked to apply what they have learned to a different situation.

TAX YOUR BRAIN

Use the information in Example 2-1, but assume that Mary and Peter each earned $20,000 from their university employment. Who is entitled to the dependency exemption?

ANSWER

No one. The joint tax return of Mary and Peter would show a tax liability. Thus the Jeffersons cannot claim the dependency exemption because Mary and Peter do not meet the joint return test. Mary and Peter would not receive the dependency exemption either. The IRS deems that the person or persons filing a tax return are not dependents. Mary and Peter would, however, each be entitled to a personal exemption on their joint tax return. Note that the answer would be the same even if Mary and Peter filed separate returns.

By asking students to think critically about theories and concepts, while supplying the answer right after the question, the Tax Your Brain examples provide another opportunity for hands-on experience.

I use examples like this all of the time in my classes as a way to help students **apply concepts** *learned to various situations.*
— Joyce Griffin, Kansas City Kansas Community College

I think these are at a good point in the discussion to not only **make the student think** *but also to force the teacher to allow them to digest the topic.*
— Bill Kryshak, University of Wisconsin–Stout

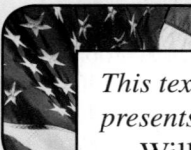

This text is straightforward, **logically organized, and student centered** *and presents fundamental tax concepts in a clear and concise manner.*
— William Lloyd, Lock Haven University

From Shoebox to Software

The From Shoebox to Software examples in each chapter help students understand how they start with a mass of paper provided by a client and proceed to a completed tax return using tax software. The student can actually see the jump from the theoretical tax world to practical application.

*Most importantly, **students learn how to apply** what they learned by preparing tax returns at the end of the chapter, and the bonus is they learn how to use tax software. In 16 weeks, **students would have prepared over 30 tax returns.** This is what attracts students to enroll in the course. It not only meets their requirement for their course of study—they walk away with a life skill.*
— Lolita M. Lockett,
Florida Community
College at Jacksonville

From Shoebox to Software — Two Comprehensive Examples

We now introduce two new taxpayers.

YIMING CHOW
The first taxpayer is Yiming Chow, who is single and lives at 456 Maple Avenue, Somewhere, OH 45678. His SSN is 111-11-1111. During 2008, Mr. Chow received a W-2 from his employer, a 1099-INT from the local financial institution, and a 1099-DIV associated with a mutual fund investment. He also received a 1099-G from the State of Ohio for a $57 tax refund pertaining to tax year 2007. Mr. Chow did not itemize his deductions in 2007. All of these documents are shown in Exhibit 3-9.

Open the tax software. Go to the File pull-down menu and click on New Return. Go through the process to start a new return, and then click on the Forms icon to bring up the list of available forms. Open a Form 1040 to input the basic name, address, and social security number information for Mr. Chow. He is eligible to file Form 1040A, and we will use that form after you enter his personal information.

Now enter the information from the various tax forms into the tax software using the applicable forms in the Documents Received section. Note that you do not need to enter any information concerning the tax refund. Mr. Chow did not itemize deductions in 2007, so you do not need to report his tax refund as income.

Once you have entered the appropriate information, click on Form 1040A. Line 15 should be $41,688. Line 27, taxable income, should be $32,738. Mr. Chow's tax liability on line 28 is $4,515. Because Mr. Chow has wage income and dividend income, you may find it instructive to calculate the tax liability by hand to see if you get the same answer. Because Mr. Chow had $5,070 withheld from his wages, his refund is $555, as shown on lines 44 and 45a.

Make sure you save Mr. Chow's return for use in later chapters.

MR. AND MRS. RAMIREZ
The second taxpayer is the married couple, Jose and Maria Ramirez. They live at 1234 West Street, Mytown, GA 33333. They have three children, Arturo, Benito, and Carmen, born in 1996, 1998, and 2000, respectively. The children lived in the household during the entire year. The SSNs are as follows:

Jose 222-22-2222, Maria 333-33-3333
Arturo 222-22-0001, Benito 333-33-0001, Carmen 444-44-0001

Mr. Ramirez received a W-2 from his employer, a 1099-INT from the financial institution, and a 1099-DIV from his stockbroker. He also received a 1099-G from the State of Georgia for a $645 tax refund. The taxpayer itemized deductions last year and you have determined that the entire refund is taxable.

All of the Ramirezes' documents are shown in Exhibit 3-10.

Open the tax software. Go to the File pull-down menu and click on New Return. Go through the process to start a new return, and then click on the Forms icon to bring up the list of available forms. Open a blank Form 1040 to input the basic name, address, and social security number information for Mr. and Mrs. Ramirez. Use the Dependent Worksheet in the Worksheet section to enter information for the children.

The Ramirezes must file Form 1040 because the state tax refund. For now, we will assume that the couple will take the standard deduction.

Now enter the information from the various tax forms into the tax software using the applicable forms in the "Documents Received" section.

Because you do not have tax return information for tax year 2007, you need to provide information concerning the tax refund. Enter in the system that the full amount of the refund is taxable.

Once you have entered the appropriate information, the total income and the AGI of the taxpayer should be $106,962. After subtracting a standard deduction of $10,900 and personal exemptions of $17,500 ($3,500 per individual), taxable income should be $78,562.

Tax on line 44 should be $12,293. The tax software automatically calculated a $3,000 child tax credit on line 52. We will discuss credits later in the text. The credit reduces the Ramirezes' tax liability to $9,293. Because the taxpayer had withholding of $10,218, the Ramirezes' return should show a refund of $925 on lines 72 and 73a.

Make sure you save the Ramirezes' tax return for use in later chapters. These will be running demonstration problems throughout the text.

The simulation of real-world situations in each Shoebox example helps students become professional tax preparers. Their first day of work is far less stressful because it is not the first time they have seen a Form 1040 or a Schedule D. They are far more productive because they know where to start and how to complete the work.

Frederick Niswander

Dr. Frederick (Rick) Niswander is dean of the College of Business and the W. Howard Rooks Distinguished Professor at East Carolina University. He holds a doctor of philosophy degree from Texas A&M University and a bachelor of science in business administration degree from Idaho State University. He has taught introductory financial accounting, international accounting, intermediate accounting, and a graduate accounting course that encompasses taxation, financial, and governmental accounting. Prior to obtaining his doctorate and joining the ECU faculty in 1993, he was the chief financial officer of a privately held real estate company in Phoenix, Arizona, for eight years. Dr. Niswander has been a CPA in North Carolina since 1994 and in Arizona since 1981. He is a member of the North Carolina Association of CPAs, the American Institute of Certified Public Accountants, and the American Accounting Association. He is also the immediate past chairman of the NCACPA, an 11,000-member statewide CPA organization.

How Does Cruz Provide a Clear Path to Student Success?

Clear Objectives for Your Students

of without the footnotes. If you would like to become familiar with the IRS and other tax authority, the footnotes are a very good place to start exp...

Learning Objectives

When you have completed this chapter, you should be able to master the following Learning Objectives (LO):

LO 1. Understand progressive, proportional, and regressive tax structures
LO 2. Understand the concepts of average and marginal tax rates as well as a simple income tax formula.
LO 3. Understand the components of a 1040EZ income tax return.
LO 4. Determine tax liability in instances when a 1040EZ return is appropriate.
LO 5. Understand the types of tax authority and how they interrelate (Appendix A).

Learning income tax return preparation requires constant reinforcement and practice. The authors have set up Fundamentals of Taxation to provide an easy-to-follow format starting with a list of learning objectives, which are then repeated throughout the book where the related material appears.

Concept Checks are mini-quizzes that test understanding of each objective.

CONCEPT CHECK 2-2—LO 2

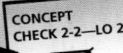

1. Even though you are in the process of getting a divorce, you can file as married filing jointly. True or False?
2. The social security number of the taxpayer's spouse must be shown on the taxpayer's tax return when filing married filing separately. True or False?
3. A surviving spouse who qualified as married filing jointly when the spouse died can file as a qualifying widow(er) for the next two years as long as the surviving spouse pays for more than half the cost of keeping up a household and does not remarry. True or False?

LO 2: Be able to calculate the health savings account deduction.	• A health savings account (HSA) is a tax-exempt savings account used to pay for qualified medical expenses. • To be eligible for an HSA, the taxpayer must be self-employed or an employee (or spouse) of an employer with a high deductible health plan. • Distributions from an HSA are tax free as long as they are used to pay for qualified medical expenses.
LO 3: Determine the deduction for moving expenses.	• If someone moves due to a change in employment, certain expenses related to moving may be deducted. • The costs of moving goods and people from the old residence to the new residence are considered suitable expenses. • The deductibility of moving expense is subject to *both* time and distance tests.

A summary of the learning objectives appears at the end of each chapter, providing a quick reference chart for students as they prepare for exams.

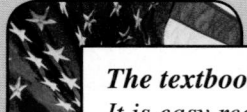

The same learning objectives are also referenced in the end-of-chapter material next to each discussion question, multiple-choice question, and problem.

Problems **LO 1** 43. What are some of the limitations concerning deductibility of student loan interest? Be specific and comprehensive.

LO 1 44. Discuss the characteristics of an eligible educational institution as it relates to the deductibility of student loan interest.

Robust and Relevant End-of-Chapter Material

Fundamentals of Taxation offers a robust selection of end-of-chapter material.

LO 3 14. In January 2007, Jeff incurred $1,200 of moving expenses when he moved from Des Moines to Detroit. When he moved, he had no job but found one a week after moving. He stayed on that job for two months, changed to another job for four months, and changed again to a long-term position that he held for the remainder of the year. What is the amount of moving expense deduction Jeff can report in 2007, if any?

Discussion questions test the basic concepts of each chapter. Students supply short answers to a variety of questions covering each of the major concepts in the chapter.

Tax Return Problems incorporate the TaxACT software and encourage students to apply a range of concepts they have learned throughout the chapter. All Tax Return Problems can also be done by hand. The authors indicate which forms are needed for each problem.

Multiple-Choice Questions

26. (Introduction) *For* AGI, or above-the-line, deductions:
   a. Are determined by the taxpayer.
   b. Are set by statute.
   c. Increase tax liability.
   d. Are reported in Schedule A.

27. (Introduction) *For* AGI, or above-the-line, deductions:
   a. Increase AGI.
   b. Reduce tax credits.
   c. Are only available for MFJ.
   d. Can reduce overall tax liability.

Tax Return Problem 2 In February 2008, Phillip and Barbara Jones and their two dependent children, who are both over 17, moved from Chicago to Albuquerque, a distance of 1,327 miles. The children's names are Roger and Gwen. The move was a result of a job transfer for Phillip. The distance from their old home to Phillip's old office was 30 miles. Barbara quit her job in Chicago and decided to perform volunteer work for a year before seeking further employment. Phillip and Barbara incurred expenses of $4,550 to the moving company (which included $320 for furniture storage), hotel charges of $450, meals of $112 en route from Chicago to Albuquerque, and $422 of hotel charges in Albuquerque while waiting a week for their new house to be completed, which was located on 7432 Desert Springs Way. Phillip, but not Barbara, was employed in the new location throughout the year. Phillip's social security number is 555-66-5555, Barbara's is 555-55-4444, Roger's is 666-11-2222 and Gwen's is 666-22-3333.
Phillip is an attorney for a national law firm; his W-2 contained the following information:

Wages (Box 1) = $124,220.45
Federal W/H (Box 2) = $ 30,565.12

Multiple-choice questions complement the discussion questions as an alternative way to quickly test a variety of learning objectives. The questions range from easy to more complex computational multiple choices.

Debra Prendergast

Dr. Debra Prendergast has a doctor of philosophy degree in public policy from the University of Illinois at Chicago, a master's of business administration degree from Governors State University, and a bachelor of arts degree in business administration with a concentration in accounting from Saint Xavier University in Chicago. She is a licensed and practicing certified public accountant in Illinois and a certified management accountant. She began her professional accounting career as a management advisory services consultant with Grant Thornton before taking a position as the controller for a corporation in Chicago. To spend more time with her family, she left her controller position in 1988 and began teaching accounting at Northwestern College, a private two-year college. In 2008 Dr. Prendergast became the Dean of Educational Programs at Northwestern College. She serves as an officer on the board of Teachers of Accounting at Two Year Colleges (TACTYC) and is on the Precertification Education Executive committee of the AICPA.

How Does the Cruz Package Provide Complete Support?

Instructor Resources

Fundamentals of Taxation authors Cruz, Deschamps, Niswander, Prendergast, Schisler, and Trone know that every component of the learning package must be integrated and supported by strong ancillaries. Critical to any successful ancillary package is author involvement. For this reason, the author team writes all instructor resources that accompany *Fundamentals of Taxation*.

Instructor's Resource Manual

This manual provides for each chapter (1) a chapter summary that highlights the key points of each learning objective, (2) a brief topical and lecture outline, (3) ethics cases, (4) suggestions for group, Internet, and other class exercises to supplement the material in the book.

Solutions Manual

The Solutions Manual includes detailed solutions for every discussion question, exercise, problem, and case in the text.

Testbank

Fundamentals of Taxation's comprehensive Testbank contains more than 900 multiple-choice questions, problems, and essay questions.

PowerPoint® Slides

The PowerPoint presentations serve as a visual representation of the learning objectives and key points in each chapter. The slides are available at the Online Learning Center (OLC).

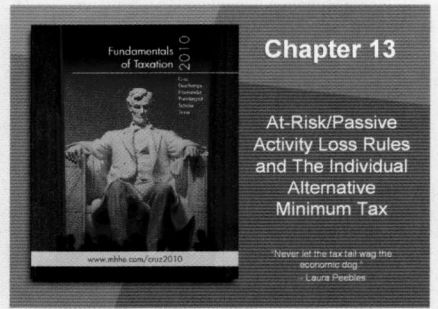

Fundamentals of Taxation 2010

Chapter 13

At-Risk/Passive Activity Loss Rules and The Individual Alternative Minimum Tax

"Never let the tax tail wag the economic dog."
— Laura Peebles

www.mhhe.com/cruz2010

*Complete, practical, and hands-on coverage of the material. The text is well laid-out **student friendly** with great practice quizzes and examples and **very good instructor resources**.*
— John Striebich, Monroe Community College

Online Learning Center (OLC)
www.mhhe.com/cruz2010

The Online Learning Center (OLC) that
accompanies *Fundamentals of Taxation* provides
a wealth of extra material for both instructors and
students. With content specific to each chapter
of the book, the Cruz OLC is available to help
students tackle a wide range of topics. It does
not require any building or maintenance on your
part and is ready to go the moment you and your
students type in the URL.

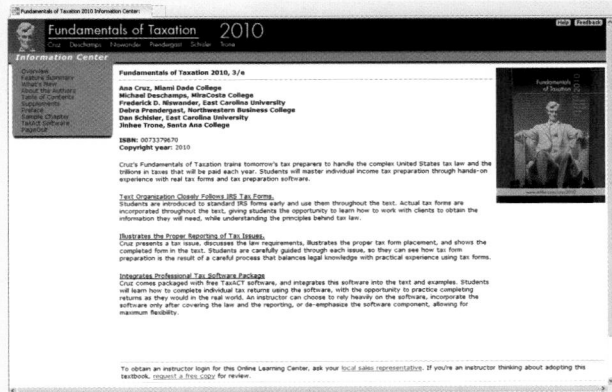

As students study, they can refer to the OLC for such benefits as:

- Self-grading multiple-choice quizzes.
- Electronic flashcards.
- PowerPoint® presentations.

- Links to professional resources.
- Tax law updates.

A secure Instructor Resource Center stores your essential course materials to save
you prep time before class. The Instructor's Manual, Solutions Manual, PowerPoint®
presentations, Testbank, and sample syllabi are just a couple of clicks away. You will
also find useful packaging information about other available supplements.

Dan Schisler

Dr. Dan Schisler is currently the chair of the Accounting Department at East
Carolina University. He holds a doctor of philosophy degree from Memphis State
University, a master's degree in accounting—tax concentration from Auburn
University, and a bachelor of science degree in accounting from Southeastern
Louisiana University. In addition to public accounting experience with Peat
Marwick Main & Co, Dr. Schisler has published numerous articles in national
academic and practitioner journals such as *Journal of the American Taxation
Association*, *Advances in Taxation*, and *Accounting Horizons*. He teaches tax
and accounting at the graduate and undergraduate levels at East Carolina,
where he has been recognized for teaching excellence by numerous teaching
awards at the department, school, and university levels. Dr. Schisler holds CPA
certificates in North Carolina and Louisiana.

A Monumental Development Effort

Acknowledgments

Writing a textbook is always a collaborative effort among authors, the publisher, authors' families, and instructors. The professors listed here contributed their time and insight to help this new edition launch successfully. By attending focus groups, reviewing selected chapters, reading through the whole manuscript, and reviewing page proofs, they contributed careful observations that enabled us to make significant improvements. Each person contributed something different— either a well-deserved criticism or a helpful word of encouragement. We sincerely appreciate their help and professionalism:

Sandy Augustine, *Hilbert College*

Felicia Baldwin, *Richard J. Daley College*

Rick Blumenfeld, *Sierra College*

Sara Bottomley, *Indiana Business College*

Jerold K. Braun, *Daytona State College*

Madeline Brogan, *Lone Star College—North Harris*

Joy Bruce, *Gaston College*

Vickie Campbell, *Cape Fear Community College*

Amy Chataginer, *Mississippi Gulf Coast Community College*

Marilyn Ciolino, *Delgado Community College*

Judy Daulton, *Piedmont Technical College*

Ken Dennis, *San Diego City College*

Brenda S. Fowler, *Alamance Community College*

Debbie Gahr, *Waukesha County Tech College*

Drew M. Goodson, *Central Carolina Community College*

Joyce Griffin, *Kansas City Kansas Community College*

Peggy Helms, *Wayne Community College*

Keith Hendrick, *DeKalb Technical College*

Merrily Hoffman, *San Jacinto College*

Becky Knickel, *Brookhaven College*

William Kryshak, *University of Wisconsin–Stout*

Natasha Librizzi, *Milwaukee Area Tech–Milwaukee*

Susan Logorda, *Lehigh Carbon Community College*

Diane Marker, *University of Toledo*

Mike Metzcar, *Indiana Wesleyan University*

Tom Nagle, *Northland Pioneer College*

Ron O'Brien, *Fayetteville Tech Community College*

William Padley, *Madison Area Technical College*

Cindy Phipps, *Lake Land College*

John S. Ribezzo, *Community College of RI*

Kari Smoker, *Saint John Fisher College*

Barbara Squires, *Corning Community College*

John Striebich, *Monroe Community College*

Lana Tuss, *Chemeketa Community College*

Bob Votruba, *Henry Ford Community College*

Jean Wells-Jessup, *Howard University*

Many thanks, also, to the reviewers who helped us develop the successful 2009 edition:

Donna Ascenzi, *Bryant & Stratton College*

Felicia Baldwin, *Richard J. Daley College*

Amy D. Bentley, *Tallahassee Community College*

Margaret Black, *San Jacinto College*

Vickie Boeder, *Madison Area Technical College–Watertown*

Anna Boulware, *St. Charles Co. Community College*

Teresa Brown, *Penn Valley Community College*

Amy Chataginer, *Miss. Gulf Coast Community College–Gulfport*

Marilyn Ciolino, *Delgado Community College*

John Daugherty, *Pitt Community College*

Judy Daulton, *Piedmont Technical College*

Patricia Davis, *Keystone College*

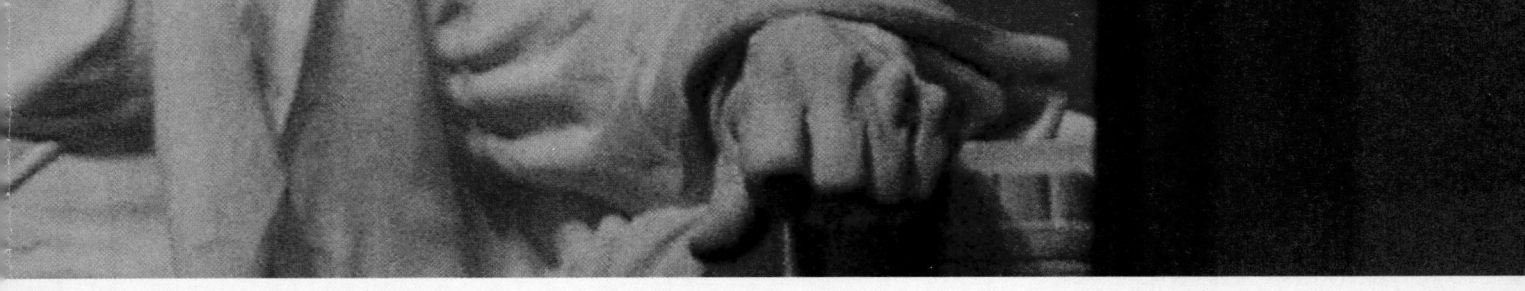

Peggy DeJong, *Kirkwood Community College*

Ken Dennis, *San Diego City College*

Norris Dorsey, *California State University*

Jose Duenas, *Texas State Tech College*

Debbie Gahr, *Waukesha County Technical College*

Drew M. Goodson, *Central Carolina Community College*

Joyce Griffin, *Kansas City Kansas Community College*

Keith Hendrick, *De Kalb Technical College*

Merrily Hoffman, *San Jacinto College*

Carol Hutchinson, *Asheville-Buncombe Tech*

Benjamin W. Johnson, *Oakland City University*

Joseph Kabacinski, *D'Youville College*

Dieter M. Kiefer, *American River College*

Bill Kryshak, *University of Wisconsin–Stout*

Jennifer Lesure, *Ivy Tech Community College of Indiana*

Natasha Librizzi, *Milwaukee Area Technical College–Milwaukee*

Bill Lloyd, *Lock Haven University of Pennsylvania*

Lolita Lockett, *Florida Community College at Jacksonville*

Kim Miller, *Tri-State University*

Jennie L. Mitchell, *St. Mary of the Woods College*

Andrea M. Murowski, *Brookdale Community College*

Michelle Nickla, *Ivy Tech Community College of Indiana*

Jon Nitschke, *Montana State University–Great Falls*

Tracie Nobles, *Austin Community College*

Ron O'Brien, *Fayetteville Tech*

Louis O. Okonkwo, *Manatee Community College*

William A. Padley, *Madison Area Technical College*

Deanne Pannell, *Pellissippi State Tech*

Cynthia L. Phipps, *Lake Land College*

La Vonda Ramey, *Schoolcraft College*

Patrick Rogan, *Cosumnes River College*

Sheryl H. Rogers, *Ogeechee Technical College*

Luis Sanchez, *Sierra College*

Warren Smock, *Ivy Tech Community College of Indiana*

Dawn Stevens, *Northwest Mississippi College*

John Striebich, *Monroe Community College*

Teresa Thamer, *Brenau University*

Hong Trebesh, *Lansing Community College*

Alan Viersen, *MiraCosta College*

Tonya Waters, *Western Piedmont Community College*

Mary Ellen Wells, *Alvernia College*

Barbara Wergeles, *State Fair Community College*

Lloyd White, *Clover Park Technical College*

Tim Whited, *National College*

Jane Wiese, *Valencia Community College*

Jinhee Trone

Jinhee Trone is the chair of business administration and professor of accounting at Santa Ana College. She received a bachelor of science degree in business administration from California State University of Los Angeles. A licensed CPA in California, she has taught various tax and financial and managerial accounting courses at Santa Ana College. Prior to academics, she was an audit manager for the Los Angeles office of Ernst & Young, LLP, and a financial and management consultant.

We greatly appreciate the accuracy-checking work completed by Patrice Johnson (University of Georgia) and Teressa Farough. Their attention to detail has greatly influenced the accuracy of the 2010 edition. Many thanks also go to Kim Watkins (East Carolina University), who assisted in the preparation of the tax forms used throughout the book.

We also appreciate the expert attention given to this project by the staff at McGraw-Hill/Irwin, especially Stewart Mattson, editorial director; Tim Vertovec, publisher; Daryl Horrocks, developmental editor; Dean Karampelas, marketing manager; Dana Pauley and Erika Jordan, project managers; Balaji Sundararaman, media product manager; Matt Baldwin, lead designer; and Carol Bielski, production supervisor.

Ana Cruz

Debra Prendergast

Michael Deschamps

Dan Schisler

Rick Niswander

Jinhee Trone

Assurance of Accuracy

Dear Colleague,

As textbook authors, and more importantly, as instructors of taxation, we recognize the great importance placed on accuracy—not only in the book you are now holding, but in the supplements as well. With this in mind, we have taken the following steps to ensure that *Fundamentals of Taxation* is error-free:

1. We received detailed feedback from dozens of instructor reviews. Each review contributed in significant ways to the accuracy of the content.
2. Each of us wrote, reviewed, and carefully checked the end-of-chapter material.
3. Multiple accuracy checkers reviewed each chapter and its accompanying end-of-chapter material.
4. A copy editor checked the grammar of the final manuscript.
5. A proofreader reviewed each page to ensure that no errors remained.
6. Our Solutions Manual and Testbank were created by the authors and reviewed by independent accuracy checkers.

Given the steps taken above, we have the utmost confidence that you and your students will have a great experience using *Fundamentals of Taxation*.

Sincerely,

Ana Cruz
Mike Deschamps
Rick Niswander
Dan Schisler
Debra Prendergast
Jinhee Trone

CHANGES IN *FUNDAMENTALS OF TAXATION,* 2010 EDITION

For the 2010 edition of *Fundamentals of Taxation,* the Cruz author team has spent considerable time making careful revisions to the textbook and its supplements. These specific enhancements have been made in the 2010 edition:

- All chapters and tax forms have been updated for new tax law, making them current through September 2009. Other updates beyond September can be found at the book's Online Learning Center: www.mhhe.com/cruz2010.

- An independent accuracy checker read every page of the book and the solutions manual to ensure that there were no errors. Each tax return problem, exhibit, and example was carefully checked to make sure that the calculations and form references were accurate.

- In addition, in the Testbank, every multiple-choice question, true/false question, and problem was checked for accuracy by an independent reviewer.

- At the book's Online Learning Center, source documents for all tax return problems and comprehensive problems are now included.

- For all chapters and comprehensive problems, social security numbers and addresses are now included where needed.

- In Chapter 2, coverage of children of divorced or separated parents has been expanded to include a new explanation of the revocation of a release of claim.

- Changes to 2009 unemployment compensation exemptions have been added to Chapter 3. Also, changes for qualified higher education expenses in 2009 have been added below Example 3-12.

- Concept Check 4-4 has been expanded to include an additional requirement. Also, 2009 changes to the Health Savings Account deduction have been added.

- Significant coverage of the National Disaster Relief Act is now included in the Limitation on Personal Casualty Losses section of Chapter 5. New coverage of investment scam losses has been added. In the State and Local Taxes section, new coverage of changes in the excise sales tax has been added, along with a new question (13) in the end-of-chapter material.

- In Chapter 7, new explanations for adjusted basis have been added in Learning Objective 1. Also, under Capital Gain Rates, more detail has been added for the 25% bracket; more detail and examples have also been added for recapture provisions and depreciation.

- More detail has been added to the rental expenses and passive activities sections of Chapter 8.

- Chapter 9 has been revised to correspond with changes to the Hope credit and the addition of two new credits (Making Work Pay and Government Retiree). Concept Check 9-9 has been added.

- Changes to the payroll wage withholding tables as a result of the American Recovery and Reinvestment Act of 2009 (ARRA), including changes to Form 941, are covered in Learning Objectives 1 and 2 of Chapter 10.

- Changes to the required minimum distributions for retirees as a result of the Worker, Retiree, and Employer Recovery Act of 2008 are covered in Learning Objective 5 of Chapter 11.

AS WE GO TO PRESS

This book is completed in mid-October and printed in early December. We picked that publication date to provide you a book that is as up-to-date as possible. A consequence of using that time frame is that Congress or the IRS may change some aspect of the tax law (especially around year-end or election time) that will affect the material in this book. Thus we provide this page to inform you of items that change at the last minute. You can also go to our Web site for changes that occur even later.

Ana Cruz
Michael Deschamps
Rick Niswander
Debra Prendergast
Dan Schisler
Jinhee Trone

Contents

Chapter 13
At-Risk/Passive Activity Loss Rules and the Individual Alternative Minimum Tax   13-1

Chapter 14
Partnership Taxation   14-1

Chapter 15
Corporate Taxation   15-1

Fundamentals
of Taxation

2010

Introduction to Taxation, the Income Tax Formula, and Form 1040EZ

This chapter introduces the federal tax system and presents a broad overview of the tax formula. We begin with a wide-angle look at the U.S. tax system and the three types of tax rate structures. We introduce a simplified income tax formula using Form 1040EZ as a guide.

Throughout the entire text, the footnotes generally provide citations to the Internal Revenue Code (IRC) and other tax law or regulations. You can read this text either with or without the footnotes. If you would like to become familiar with the IRC and other tax authority, the footnotes are a good place to start exploring.

Learning Objectives

When you have completed this chapter, you should understand the following learning objectives (LO):

LO 1. Understand progressive, proportional, and regressive tax structures.

LO 2. Understand the concepts of marginal and average tax rates as well as a simple income tax formula.

LO 3. Understand the components of a Form 1040EZ income tax return.

LO 4. Determine tax liability in instances when a Form 1040EZ return is appropriate.

LO 5. Understand the types of tax authority and how they interrelate (Appendix A).

INTRODUCTION

The federal government enacted the first federal income tax in 1861 as a method to finance the Civil War. Prior to that time, federal tax revenues came primarily from excise taxes and duties on imported goods. Once the war was over, Congress repealed the income tax. Congress again passed a federal income tax in 1894 to broaden the types of taxes and to increase federal revenues. However, in 1895 the Supreme Court held that the federal income tax was unconstitutional. That ruling resulted in the Sixteenth Amendment to the Constitution in 1913:

Sixteenth Amendment to the Constitution of the United States of America

The Congress shall have power to lay and collect taxes on incomes, from whatever source derived, without apportionment among the several States, and without regard to any census or enumeration.

TABLE 1-1
Type and Number of Individual Tax Returns

Source: IRS Publication 1304 (Fall 2008), Table A, and *IRS Statistics of Income Bulletins* (Fall 2007, 2006, and 2005).

Type of Tax Return	2006	2005	2004	2003
Form 1040 returns	83,805,545	81,497,559	80,603,689	80,420,043
Form 1040A returns	32,018,556	31,326,141	30,572,631	29,631,494
Form 1040EZ returns	22,570,653	21,548,977	21,049,722	20,372,089
Total returns	138,394,754	134,372,678	132,226,042	130,423,626
Returns electronically filed (included in figures above)	80,095,643	73,471,852	68,380,152	61,154,815

The Sixteenth Amendment provides the underlying legal and statutory authority for the administration and enforcement of individual income taxes. Congress has promulgated tax law that is the primary source of information for what is, and is not, permitted. That tax law is the Internal Revenue Code (IRC). The IRC covers taxation of individuals, corporations, and partnerships, as well as other tax rules. Appendix A in this chapter discusses the types of tax laws, regulations, and court cases that compose what we refer to as *tax authority.* The material in Appendix A is of particular importance to students who want to be involved in tax planning, tax research, and other tax-related activities that require an understanding of taxes beyond a fill-in-the-forms level.

Currently the federal government collects revenue from various types of taxes. The largest revenue generators are the individual income tax, social security tax, corporate income tax, federal gift and estate tax, and various excise taxes. This text focuses on the largest revenue generator for the federal government: the individual income tax.[1] In tax year 2006, the federal government collected $1 trillion in income tax on $8.0 trillion of gross income ($5.6 trillion of taxable income) as reported on 138.4 million individual tax returns.[2] Table 1-1 presents a breakdown of the number and type of individual tax returns filed for 2003 through 2006.

One major criticism of the current tax system is the complexity of the law and the length of the forms. However, taxpayers filed more than 54 million returns using the two easiest forms—Forms 1040A and 1040EZ. We will introduce you to Form 1040EZ in this chapter. Complexity in the tax system is not necessarily bad. Taxpayers often do not realize that many provisions that require use of the more complex tax forms are deduction or credit provisions that actually *benefit* the taxpayer. This text will help you understand the tax system's complexity, the rationale behind some of the complexity, and how to complete a tax return effectively.

TAX RATE STRUCTURES
LO 1

The study of taxation must begin with a basic understanding of rate structures and the tax system. We will discuss three different types of tax rate structures:

- Progressive rate structure.
- Proportional rate structure.
- Regressive rate structure.

Each of these rate structures is present in the tax collection system at the local, state, or federal level. Taxing authorities use one or more of these structures to assess most taxes.

Progressive Rate Structure

With a *progressive structure,* the tax rate increases as the tax base increases. The tax rate is applied to the tax base to determine the amount of tax. The most obvious progressive tax

[1] The last two chapters are an overview of partnership and corporate taxation.
[2] *IRS Statistics of Income Bulletin* 28, no. 2 (Fall 2008), Table 2.

TABLE 1-2
Individual Income Tax Rate Brackets for Married Taxpayers for Tax Year 2009

Taxable Income	Tax Rate
Up to $16,700	10%
$16,701–$67,900	15%
$67,901–$137,050	25%
$137,051–$208,850	28%
$208,851–$372,950	33%
Over $372,950	35%

in the United States, and the focus of this text, is the federal income tax. Table 1-2 illustrates the progressive rate structure of the individual income tax for married taxpayers who file joint returns.

The federal income tax is progressive because the tax rate gets larger as the taxable income (tax base) increases. For very low taxable income, the tax rate is 10% per dollar of income, and for very high taxable income, the tax rate is 35% per dollar.

EXAMPLE 1-1

Mary and George are married, file a joint federal tax return, and have taxable income of $210,000. Their tax liability is

$16,700 × 10% =	$ 1,670.00
($67,900 − $16,700) × 15% =	7,680.00
($137,500 − $67,900) × 25% =	17,287.50
($208,850 − $137,050) × 28% =	20,104.00
($210,000 − $208,850) × 33% =	379.50
Total tax liability	$47,121.00

Note from Example 1-1 that as the tax base (taxable income) increases, the tax rate per dollar of income gets progressively larger, rising from 10% to 33%.

TAX YOUR BRAIN

On average, how much income tax did Mary and George pay on their taxable income, and how do you interpret your answer?

ANSWER

Mary and George had an average tax rate of 22.4% calculated as their tax liability of $47,121 divided by their taxable income of $210,000. This means that, on average, for each dollar of taxable income, Mary and George paid a little over 22 cents to the federal government for income tax.

Table 1-3 provides some additional evidence of the progressivity of the U.S. tax system. The average tax rates in Table 1-3 confirm that the individual income tax is indeed a progressive tax.

TAX YOUR BRAIN

How can the average tax rate in the $15,000 to $30,000 group be slightly less than the under $15,000 group even though the tax rates are progressively higher for the $15,000 to $30,000 group?

ANSWER

The main reason is that the $15,000 to $30,000 group is more likely to be married and/or have children when compared to the under $15,000 group. If the taxpayers have children, they are eligible for special tax credits such as the child care credit and child tax credit. These credits reduce the amount of tax otherwise owed. In addition, married taxpayers pay less in tax than unmarried taxpayers do for a given level of income.

TABLE 1-3 **Individual Income Tax Returns from 2006, Number of Tax Returns, Taxable Income (in thousands), Total Tax Liability (in thousands), and Average Tax Rate by Ranges of Adjusted Gross Income**

Item	Ranges of Adjusted Gross Income					
	Under $15,000	$15,000 to under $30,000	$30,000 to under $50,000	$50,000 to under $100,000	$100,000 to under $200,000	$200,000 or more
Number of returns	37,807,391	29,599,716	24,839,017	29,995,325	12,088,423	4,064,884
Taxable income	$35,149,188	$250,951,098	$550,046,279	$1,404,139,379	$1,181,233,605	$2,157,630,896
Total income tax liability	$3,297,415	$22,657,535	$59,802,597	$184,462,766	$209,381,101	$544,318,726
Average tax rate*	9.38%	9.03%	10.87%	13.14%	17.73%	25.23%

*The average tax rate is total tax liability divided by taxable income.
Source: *IRS Statistics of Income Bulletin* 28, no. 2 (Fall 2008), Table 2.

Proportional Rate Structure

With a proportional tax structure, the tax *rate* remains the same regardless of the tax base. The popular name for a proportional tax is a *flat tax*. The most common flat or proportional taxes in existence in the United States are state and local taxes levied on either property or sales. For example, a local sales tax could be 6% on the purchase of a new car. Regardless of whether the price of the car (the tax base) was $15,000 or $80,000, the tax rate would still be 6% and the taxpayer would pay either $900 or $4,800 in sales tax, depending on the car purchased.

Another proportional tax is the Medicare tax. This tax pays for medical expenses for individuals over age 65. The rate is 2.9% of every dollar of wage income or self-employment income. Thus a doctor will pay Medicare tax of $14,500 on the $500,000 of income from her medical practice (2.9% × $500,000), and a golf professional will pay $2,900 from his $100,000 tournament winnings (2.9% × $100,000). Although the doctor pays more total tax, the *rate* of tax is the same for both the doctor and the golf professional.

In recent years, there have been numerous political movements to replace the current progressive tax system with a flat tax. One plan called for a 17% flat tax on income. Compared to the current system, the 17% flat tax would result in an increase in tax liability for taxpayers with income of less than $100,000 and a substantial decrease in tax liability for taxpayers with income of more than $100,000 (see Table 1-3).

Regressive Rate Structure

With a regressive tax, the rate decreases as the tax base increases. The social security tax is the most common regressive tax. The rate for social security taxes is 6.2% (12.4% for self-employed taxpayers) on the first $106,800 of wages in tax year 2009. Once wages exceed the $106,800 ceiling, social security taxes cease. Thus the rate drops (from 6.2% to 0%) as the tax base increases.

CONCEPT CHECK 1-1—LO 1

1. The three types of tax rate structures are _____ , _____ , and _____ .
2. The tax rate structure for which the tax rate remains the same for all levels of the tax base is the _____ rate structure.
3. The federal income tax system is an example of a _____ tax structure.

MARGINAL TAX RATES AND AVERAGE TAX RATES
LO 2

Newspaper and magazine articles often discuss taxes and use the terms *average tax rate* and *marginal tax rate*. These two terms are not interchangeable; they mean very different things.

The average tax rate is the percentage that a taxpayer pays in tax given a certain amount of taxable income. The marginal tax rate represents the proportion of tax that he or she pays on the last dollar (or more accurately, the *next* dollar) of taxable income.

Let us assume that Ben and Martha have taxable income of $38,440 and file an income tax return as a married couple. Using the tax rates in Table 1-2, their tax liability is

$16,700 × 10% =	$1,670
($38,440 − $16,700) × 15% =	3,261
Total tax liability	$4,931

If you refer to Table 1-2, you will see that, for a married couple, each dollar of taxable income between $16,700 and $67,900 is taxed at a rate of 15%. In other words, if Ben and Martha earned an additional $100 of taxable income, they would owe the federal government an additional $15. Thus their marginal tax rate (the rate they would pay for an additional dollar of income) is 15%.

Conversely, the average rate is the percentage of total tax paid on the entire amount of taxable income. Ben and Martha have taxable income of $38,440 on which they had a tax liability of $4,931. Their average rate is 12.8% ($4,931/$38,440). The average rate is, in effect, a blended rate. Ben and Martha paid tax at a 10% rate on some of their taxable income and at a 15% rate on the rest of their income. Their average rate is a mixture of 10% and 15% that, in their case, averages out to 12.8%.

TAX YOUR BRAIN   For Ben and Martha, the marginal rate was larger than the average rate. Is that always the case?

ANSWER

No. When taxable income is zero or is within the lowest tax bracket (from $0 to $16,700 for married couples), the marginal rate will be equal to the average rate. When taxable income is more than the lowest tax bracket, the marginal rate will always be larger than the average rate.

A SIMPLE INCOME TAX FORMULA
LO 2

Taxpayers must annually report their taxable income, deductions, and other items to the IRS. Taxpayers do so by filing an income tax return. In its most simplified form, an individual income tax return has the following components:

Income
− Permitted deductions from income
= Taxable income
× Appropriate tax rates
= Tax liability
− Tax payments and tax credits
= Tax refund or tax due with return

Although many income tax returns are complex, the basic structure of every tax return follows this simplified form. For many taxpayers, this simplified formula is sufficient. For

example, most individuals who receive all their income from an hourly or salaried job have a tax return that conforms to this basic structure. In later chapters, we will expand on this tax formula, and we will provide more information about complexities in our tax laws. However, for this chapter, the simplified version is appropriate.

CONCEPT CHECK 1-2—LO 2 	1. The marginal tax rate is the rate of tax imposed on the next dollar of taxable income. True or false? 2. What is the marginal tax rate for a married couple with taxable income of $69,510? 3. Average tax rate and marginal tax rate mean the same thing. True or false? 4. Complex tax returns do not follow the basic (or simplified) income tax formula. True or false?

THE COMPONENTS OF FORM 1040EZ
LO 3

Taxpayers must annually report their income, deductions, tax liability, and other items to the federal government. They do so by filing a tax return. Taxpayers may file Form 1040, Form 1040A, or Form 1040EZ (listed in order from detailed to simple). The return selected and filed generally depends on the complexity of the tax situation of the individual taxpayer.

A taxpayer who has a simple tax structure may be eligible to file the least complex individual income tax return—the 13-line Form 1040EZ, shown in Exhibit 1-1.

To use Form 1040EZ, a taxpayer must meet all of the following criteria:

- File the return as either single or married filing jointly.
- Be under age 65 and not blind.
- Have no dependents.
- Have total taxable income under $100,000.
- Have income only from wages, salary, tips, unemployment compensation, or taxable interest income of $1,500 or less.
- Claim no tax credits except for the Earned Income Credit.

Let us review the components of the simplified tax formula and the restrictions for filing Form 1040EZ. We will refer to the line numbers from the form in much of the discussion.

CONCEPT CHECK 1-3—LO 3 	1. Almost all taxpayers can file Form 1040EZ. True or false? 2. Max, who is 74 years old and single, is eligible to file Form 1040EZ if his taxable income is under $100,000. True or false? 3. Erma, a 28-year-old single taxpayer with no dependents, has wage income of $40,000. She is eligible to file Form 1040EZ. True or false?

Filing Status

To use Form 1040EZ, a taxpayer must be either single or married and file a joint return with his or her spouse. Other filing categories that may apply to taxpayers include married filing separately, head of household, or qualifying widow(er). We explain these additional categories and expand our discussion of filing status in Chapter 2.

For purposes of this chapter, we will assume the taxpayer is either single or married filing a joint return.

Income

To use Form 1040EZ, taxpayers can have income only from wages, salary, tips, interest of $1,500 or less, and unemployment compensation.

EXHIBIT 1-1

Form **1040EZ**	Department of the Treasury—Internal Revenue Service **Income Tax Return for Single and Joint Filers With No Dependents** (99) **2009**	OMB No. 1545-0074

Label (See page 9.)

Use the IRS label.

Otherwise, please print or type.

Presidential Election Campaign (see page 9) ▶

L A B E L H E R E

Your first name and initial | Last name

If a joint return, spouse's first name and initial | Last name

Home address (number and street). If you have a P.O. box, see page 9. | Apt. no.

City, town or post office, state, and ZIP code. If you have a foreign address, see page 9.

Your social security number

Spouse's social security number

▲ You **must** enter your SSN(s) above. ▲

Checking a box below will not change your tax or refund.

Check here if you, or your spouse if a joint return, want $3 to go to this fund . . ▶ ☐ **You**   ☐ **Spouse**

Draft as of 07/08/2009

Income

Attach Form(s) W-2 here.

Enclose, but do not attach, any payment.

You may benefit from filing Form 1040 or 1040A. See *Before You Begin* on page 4.

1 Wages, salaries, and tips. This should be shown in box 1 of your Form(s) W-2. Attach your Form(s) W-2. | **1**

2 Taxable interest. If the total is over $1,500, you cannot use Form 1040EZ. | **2**

3 Unemployment compensation in excess of $2,400 per recipient and Alaska Permanent Fund dividends (see page 11). | **3**

4 Add lines 1, 2, and 3. This is your **adjusted gross income.** | **4**

5 If someone can claim you (or your spouse if a joint return) as a dependent, check the applicable box(es) below and enter the amount from the worksheet on back.

☐ **You**   ☐ **Spouse**

If no one can claim you (or your spouse if a joint return), enter $9,350 if **single**; $18,700 if **married filing jointly.** See back for explanation. | **5**

6 Subtract line 5 from line 4. If line 5 is larger than line 4, enter -0-. This is your **taxable income.** ▶ | **6**

Payments, Credits, and Tax

7 Federal income tax withheld from Form(s) W-2 and 1099. | **7**

8 Making work pay credit (see worksheet on back). | **8**

9a **Earned income credit (EIC)** (see page 12). | **9a**

b Nontaxable combat pay election. | **9b**

10 Add lines 7, 8, and 9a. These are your **total payments.** ▶ | **10**

11 **Tax.** Use the amount on **line 6 above** to find your tax in the tax table on pages 28 through 36 of the instructions. Then, enter the tax from the table on this line. | **11**

Refund

Have it directly deposited! See page 17 and fill in 12b, 12c, and 12d or Form 8888.

12a If line 10 is larger than line 11, subtract line 11 from line 10. This is your **refund.** If Form 8888 is attached, check here ▶ ☐ | **12a**

▶ **b** Routing number | ▶ **c** Type: ☐ Checking   ☐ Savings

▶ **d** Account number

Amount you owe

13 If line 11 is larger than line 10, subtract line 10 from line 11. This is the **amount you owe.** For details on how to pay, see page 18. ▶ | **13**

Third party designee

Do you want to allow another person to discuss this return with the IRS (see page 19)? ☐ **Yes.** Complete the following. ☐ **No**

Designee's name ▶ | Phone no. ▶ | Personal identification number (PIN) ▶

Sign here

Joint return? See page 6.

Keep a copy for your records.

Under penalties of perjury, I declare that I have examined this return, and to the best of my knowledge and belief, it is true, correct, and accurately lists all amounts and sources of income I received during the tax year. Declaration of preparer (other than the taxpayer) is based on all information of which the preparer has any knowledge.

Your signature | Date | Your occupation | Daytime phone number

Spouse's signature. If a joint return, **both** must sign. | Date | Spouse's occupation

Paid preparer's use only

Preparer's signature ▶ | Date | Check if self-employed ☐ | Preparer's SSN or PTIN

Firm's name (or yours if self-employed), address, and ZIP code ▶ | EIN | Phone no.

For Disclosure, Privacy Act, and Paperwork Reduction Act Notice, see page 35. | Cat. No. 11329W | Form **1040EZ** (2009)

(continued)

Version A, Cycle 5

Form 1040EZ (2009)   Page **2**

Worksheet for Line 5 — Dependents who checked one or both boxes

Use this worksheet to figure the amount to enter on line 5 if someone can claim you (or your spouse if married filing jointly) as a dependent, even if that person chooses not to do so. To find out if someone can claim you as a dependent, see Pub. 501.

A. Amount, if any, from line 1 on front . . . . _____

    +   300.00 Enter total ▶   **A.** _____

B. Minimum standard deduction . . . . **B.** _____950.00

C. Enter the **larger** of line A or line B here . . . . **C.** _____

D. Maximum standard deduction. If **single,** enter $5,700; if **married filing jointly,** enter $11,400 . . . . **D.** _____

E. Enter the **smaller** of line C or line D here. This is your standard deduction . . . . **E.** _____

F. Exemption amount.
- If single, enter -0-.
- If married filing jointly and —
—both you and your spouse can be claimed as dependents, enter -0-.
—only one of you can be claimed as a dependent, enter $3,650.

    F. _____

G. Add lines E and F. Enter the total here and on line 5 on the front . . . . **G.** _____

(keep a copy for your records)

If you did not check any boxes on line 5, enter on line 5 the amount shown below that applies to you.
- Single, enter $9,350. This is the total of your standard deduction ($5,700) and your exemption ($3,650).
- Married filing jointly, enter $18,700. This is the total of your standard deduction ($11,400), your exemption ($3,650), and your spouse's exemption ($3,650).

Worksheet for Line 8 — Making work pay credit

Use this worksheet to figure the amount to enter on line 8 if you (or your spouse if filing a joint return) **cannot** be claimed as a dependent on another person's return.

Before you begin: √ If you can be claimed as a dependent on someone else's return, you **do not** qualify for this credit.
√ If married filing jointly, include your spouse's amounts with yours when completing this worksheet.

1a. **Important.** See the instructions on page 12 if your wages include pay for work performed while an inmate in a penal institution; or a scholarship or fellowship grant not reported on Form W-2.

Do you (and your spouse if filing jointly) have 2009 wages of more than $6,451 ($12,903 if married filing jointly)?

☐ **Yes.** Skip lines 1a through 3. Enter $400 ($800 if married filing jointly) on line 4 and go to line 5.

☐ **No.**   Enter your earned income (see instructions) . . . . . **1a.** _____

b. Nontaxable combat pay included on line 1a (see instructions) . . . . **1b.** _____

2. Multiply line 1a by 6.2% (.062) . . . . **2.** _____

3. Enter $400 ($800 if married filing jointly) . . . . **3.** _____

4. Enter the **smaller** of line 2 or line 3 (unless you checked "Yes" on line 1a) . . . . . . **4.** _____

5. Enter amount from line 4 on front . . . . **5.** _____

6. Enter $75,000 ($150,000 if married filing jointly) . . . . **6.** _____

7. Is the amount on line 5 more than the amount on line 6?

☐ **No.**   Skip line 8. Enter the amount from line 4 on line 9 below.

☐ **Yes.** Subtract line 6 from line 5 . . . . **7.** _____

8. Multiply line 7 by 2% (.02) . . . . **8.** _____

9. Subtract line 8 from line 4. If zero or less, enter -0- . . . . **9.** _____

10. Did you (or your spouse, if filing jointly) receive an economic recovery payment in 2009? You may have received this payment if you received social security benefits, supplemental security income, railroad retirement benefits, or veterans disability compensation or pension benefits (see instructions).

☐ **No.**   Enter -0- on line 10.

☐ **Yes.** Enter the total of the economic recovery payments received by you (and your spouse, if filing jointly). **Do not** enter more than $250 ($500 if married filing jointly) . . . **10.** _____

(keep a copy for your records)

11. **Making work pay credit.** Subtract line 10 from line 9. If zero or less, enter -0-. Enter the result here and on Form 1040EZ, line 8. . . . . **11.** _____

Mailing return

Mail your return by **April 15, 2010.** Use the envelope that came with your booklet. If you do not have that envelope or if you moved during the year, see the back cover for the address to use.

Form **1040EZ** (2009)

Many of the IRS tax forms used throughout the text have the word "Draft" and a date printed at an angle across the form (see Exhibit 1-1). The IRS creates and modifies tax forms during the tax year. These forms are in draft form until they have obtained final approval within the IRS and by the federal Office of Management and Budget. The IRS distributes the forms internally, to tax professionals, and to tax software companies. By doing so, the IRS seeks comments to catch errors or to improve the form. Final approval usually occurs on a rolling basis between mid-October and mid-December. Once the form has received final approval, the "Draft" label is removed and taxpayers can use the final form as they prepare their tax returns.

This text went to press in late October, when most IRS forms were available only in draft form. By the time you read this, final forms will be available on the IRS Web site (www.irs.gov) and in your tax software.

Wages, Salaries, and Tips (1040EZ, line 1)

Wages, salaries, and tips are the major source of gross income for most taxpayers. In fact, for millions of Americans, these items are their only source of income. Individuals receive wages, salaries, and tips as "compensation for services."[3] This category is quite broad and encompasses commissions, bonuses, severance pay, sick pay, meals and lodging,[4] vacation trips or prizes given in lieu of cash, fringe benefits, and similar items.[5]

Employees receive wages and related income from their employers. Income received as a self-employed individual (independent contractor) does not meet the definition of wages and is reported on Schedule C.[6]

Wages include tips.[7] Employees receiving tip income must report the amount of tips to their employers.[8] They use IRS Form 4070 for that purpose. Large food and beverage establishments (those at which tipping is customary and that employ more than 10 employees on a typical business day) must report certain information to the IRS and to employees.[9] These employers must also allocate tip income to employees who normally receive tips. You can find more information about reporting tip income in IRS Publication 531, available on the IRS Web site at www.irs.gov.

Taxpayers classified as employees who receive compensation will receive a Form W-2 from their employer indicating the amount of wage income in box 1, "Wages, tips, and other compensation." This amount is reported on line 1 of Form 1040EZ.

An example of a Form W-2 is shown in Exhibit 1-2.

Taxable Interest (1040EZ, line 2)

Interest is compensation for the use of money with respect to a bona fide debt or obligation imposed by law (such as loans, judgments, or installment sales). Interest received by or credited to a taxpayer is taxable unless specifically exempt.[10] Interest paid is often deductible.[11] This section covers interest received.

For individuals, interest income is most often earned in conjunction with savings accounts, certificates of deposit, U.S. savings bonds, corporate bonds owned, seller-financed mortgages, loans made to others, and similar activities.

[3] IRC § 61(a)(1).

[4] Unless excluded under IRC § 119.

[5] Reg. § 1.61-2 and Reg. § 1.61-21.

[6] See Chapter 6.

[7] IRC § 3401(f).

[8] IRC § 6053(a).

[9] IRC § 6053(c).

[10] IRC § 61(a)(4).

[11] Interest paid in conjunction with a trade or business is covered in Chapter 6. Personal interest paid is in Chapters 4 and 5.

EXHIBIT 1-2

a Employee's social security number		Safe, accurate, FAST! Use IRS e-file	Visit the IRS website at www.irs.gov/efile.
OMB No. 1545-0008			

b Employer identification number (EIN)	1 Wages, tips, other compensation	2 Federal income tax withheld
c Employer's name, address, and ZIP code	3 Social security wages	4 Social security tax withheld
	5 Medicare wages and tips	6 Medicare tax withheld
	7 Social security tips	8 Allocated tips
d Control number	9 Advance EIC payment	10 Dependent care benefits
e Employee's first name and initial Last name Suff.	11 Nonqualified plans	12a See instructions for box 12
	13 Statutory employee ☐ Retirement plan ☐ Third-party sick pay ☐	12b
	14 Other	12c
		12d
f Employee's address and ZIP code		

15 State Employer's state ID number	16 State wages, tips, etc.	17 State income tax	18 Local wages, tips, etc.	19 Local income tax	20 Locality name

Form **W-2** Wage and Tax Statement   **2009**   Department of the Treasury—Internal Revenue Service

Copy B—To Be Filed With Employee's FEDERAL Tax Return.
This information is being furnished to the Internal Revenue Service.

EXHIBIT 1-3

☐ CORRECTED (if checked)

PAYER'S name, street address, city, state, ZIP code, and telephone no.	Payer's RTN (optional)	OMB No. 1545-0112	
	1 Interest income $	**2009** Form **1099-INT**	**Interest Income**
	2 Early withdrawal penalty $		
PAYER'S federal identification number	RECIPIENT'S identification number	3 Interest on U.S. Savings Bonds and Treas. obligations $	**Copy B For Recipient**
RECIPIENT'S name		4 Federal income tax withheld $	5 Investment expenses $	This is important tax information and is being furnished to the Internal Revenue Service. If you are required to file a return, a negligence penalty or other sanction may be imposed on you if this income is taxable and the IRS determines that it has not been reported.
Street address (including apt. no.)		6 Foreign tax paid $	7 Foreign country or U.S. possession	
City, state, and ZIP code		8 Tax-exempt interest	9 Specified private activity bond interest	
Account number (see instructions)		$	$	

Form **1099-INT**   (keep for your records)   Department of the Treasury - Internal Revenue Service

Generally, interest income is determined based on the interest rate stated in the documents associated with the transaction. Some exceptions exist, and some interest income is nontaxable. These items are discussed in Chapter 3.

Normally, taxpayers will receive a Form 1099-INT that will report the amount of interest earned (see Exhibit 1-3). The amount in box 1 is reported on Form 1040EZ, line 2.

EXHIBIT 1-4

☐ CORRECTED (if checked)				
PAYER'S name, street address, city, state, ZIP code, and telephone no.	**1** Unemployment compensation $	OMB No. 1545-0120 2**009** Form **1099-G**		**Certain Government Payments**
	2 State or local income tax refunds, credits, or offsets $			
PAYER'S federal identification number	RECIPIENT'S identification number	**3** Box 2 amount is for tax year	**4** Federal income tax withheld $	**Copy B** **For Recipient**
RECIPIENT'S name		**5** ATAA payments $	**6** Taxable grants $	This is important tax information and is being furnished to the Internal Revenue Service. If you are required to file a return, a negligence penalty or other sanction may be imposed on you if this income is taxable and the IRS determines that it has not been reported.
Street address (including apt. no.)		**7** Agriculture payments $	**8** Box 2 is trade or business income ▶ ☐	
City, state, and ZIP code		**9** Market gain $		
Account number (see instructions)				
Form **1099-G**		(keep for your records)		Department of the Treasury - Internal Revenue Service

Unemployment Compensation (1040EZ, line 3)

Federal and state unemployment compensation benefits are taxable.[12] The rationale behind taxing these payments is that they are a substitute for taxable wages. Unemployment benefits are reported to recipients on Form 1099-G in box 1 (see Exhibit 1-4). The amount in box 1 is reported on line 3 of Form 1040EZ. For tax year 2009 (only), taxpayers can exclude up to $2,400 of unemployment compensation from income.

Citizens of Alaska also report any Alaska Permanent Fund dividends they receive on line 3 of Form 1040EZ.

Permitted Deductions from Income (line 5)

On Form 1040EZ, the only permitted deduction from income is on line 5. Although not labeled as such, this deduction is actually a combination of a standard deduction and a personal exemption. We will explain these two items in more detail in Chapter 2. For purposes of this chapter, the line 5 deduction is either $9,350 if the taxpayer is single or $18,700 if the taxpayer is filing a return as married.

Taxable Income (1040EZ, line 6)

Taxable income is the wages, interest, and unemployment income on lines 1 through 3 minus the permitted deduction on line 5. Taxable income is the tax base used to determine the amount of tax.

CONCEPT CHECK 1-4—LO 3

☑

1. Only certain types of income can be reported on Form 1040EZ. They are _____ _____ .
2. Unemployment compensation is reported to the taxpayer on a Form _____ .
3. To be able to use Form 1040EZ, a taxpayer must be either filing status _____ or filing status _____ .

CALCULATION OF TAX (FORM 1040EZ, LINE 11)
LO 4

We will now skip ahead to line 11, total tax. (Later we will come back to lines 7 through 10.)

The total amount of tax liability on Form 1040EZ is determined based on the amount of taxable income (line 6). Taxpayers could calculate their tax using the tax rate schedule shown

[12] IRC § 85(a).

in Table 1-2 (or a similar one if the taxpayer were single). However, that method can be a bit complicated and can result in calculation errors. To make things easier, the IRS has prepared tax tables that predetermine the amount of tax liability for taxable incomes of up to $100,000. Remember that taxpayers must have total taxable income of less than $100,000 to use Form 1040EZ; otherwise they must use Form 1040A or 1040.

The tax tables applicable for tax year 2009 are printed in Appendix D of this text. Please refer to the 2009 tax tables when reviewing the examples and when working the problems at the end of this chapter.

Line 11 represents the total amount the taxpayer must pay to the government for the tax year. As we will see when we discuss lines 7 through 10, the taxpayer has likely already paid all or most of this liability.

EXAMPLE 1-2	Art is a single taxpayer and has taxable income of $42,787. Referring to the tax table, his income is between $42,750 and $42,800. Reading across the table to the Single column gives a tax (for Form 1040EZ, line 11) of $6,881.

EXAMPLE 1-3	Joe and Marsha are married and are filing a joint tax return. They have taxable income of $45,059. In the tax table, their income is between $45,050 and $45,100. Their corresponding tax liability is $5,926.

Notice the effect of a differing filing status. Art had lower taxable income than did Joe and Marsha, but Art's tax liability was higher. All other things being equal, for equivalent amounts of taxable income, the highest tax will be paid by married persons filing separately, followed by single persons, then heads of household, and finally by married persons filing jointly. There are two exceptions to this general observation. The first is that, at low levels of taxable income, tax liability will be the same for all groups. The second is that married persons filing separately and single persons will have equal tax liability at taxable income levels up to $68,525.

In the preceding examples, we used the tax tables in Appendix D of this text to determine the amount of tax liability. If we calculated the amount of tax using the tax rate schedules provided on the inside cover of this text (or in Table 1-2 for married taxpayers), we would have computed a slightly different number.

EXAMPLE 1-4	Bill and Andrea Chappell, a married couple, have taxable income of $48,305. Using the tax tables, their tax liability is $6,414. Using the tax rate schedule in Table 1-2 (and printed on the inside front cover of this text), their tax liability is

Tax on $16,700 × 10%	$1,607.00
Tax on ($48,305 − $16,700) × 15%	4,740.75
Total tax	$6,410.75

Here the difference between the two numbers is $3.25. There will usually be a slight difference between the amount of tax calculated using the tax tables and the amount calculated using the tax rate schedules. The reason is that the tax rate schedules are precise, whereas the tax tables determine tax liability in $50 increments. In fact, the amount of tax liability shown in the tax tables represents the tax due on taxable income exactly in the middle of the $50 increment (as an exercise, check this out for yourself). Thus a taxpayer with taxable income in the lower half of the increment (like Bill and Andrea in the example) will pay a little extra in tax while someone in the upper end of the increment will pay a little less.

Form **1040EZ**	Department of the Treasury—Internal Revenue Service **Income Tax Return for Single and Joint Filers With No Dependents** (99) **2009**				OMB No. 1545-0074

Label (See page 9.)

Use the IRS label.

Otherwise, please print or type.

Presidential Election Campaign (see page 9) ▶

L A B E L H E R E	Your first name and initial **Ed**	Last name **Davidson**	Your social security number **123-45-6789**
	If a joint return, spouse's first name and initial **Betty**	Last name **Davidson**	Spouse's social security number **123-45-6780**
	Home address (number and street). If you have a P.O. box, see page 9. **456 Main Street**	Apt. no.	You **must** enter your SSN(s) above. ▲
	City, town or post office, state, and ZIP code. If you have a foreign address, see page 9. **Anywhere, NC 27890**		Checking a box below will not change your tax or refund.

Check here if you, or your spouse if a joint return, want $3 to go to this fund . . ▶ ☐ **You**   ☐ **Spouse**

Income

Attach Form(s) W-2 here.

Enclose, but do not attach, any payment.

You may benefit from filing Form 1040 or 1040A. See *Before You Begin* on page 4.

1	Wages, salaries, and tips. This should be shown in box 1 of your Form(s) W-2. Attach your Form(s) W-2.	1	53,766
2	Taxable interest. If the total is over $1,500, you cannot use Form 1040EZ.	2	372
3	Unemployment compensation in excess of $2,400 per recipient and Alaska Permanent Fund dividends (see page 11).	3	
4	Add lines 1, 2, and 3. This is your **adjusted gross income.**	4	54,138
5	If someone can claim you (or your spouse if a joint return) as a dependent, check the applicable box(es) below and enter the amount from the worksheet on back. ☐ **You** ☐ **Spouse** If no one can claim you (or your spouse if a joint return), enter $9,350 if **single;** $18,700 if **married filing jointly.** See back for explanation.	5	18,700
6	Subtract line 5 from line 4. If line 5 is larger than line 4, enter -0-. This is your **taxable income.** ▶	6	35,438

Payments, Credits, and Tax

7	Federal income tax withheld from Form(s) W-2 and 1099.	7	4,111
8	Making work pay credit (see worksheet on back).	8	800
9a	**Earned income credit (EIC)** (see page 12).	9a	
b	Nontaxable combat pay election. 9b		
10	Add lines 7, 8, and 9a. These are your **total payments.** ▶	10	4,911
11	**Tax.** Use the amount on **line 6 above** to find your tax in the tax table on pages 28 through 36 of the instructions. Then, enter the tax from the table on this line.	11	4,479

Refund

Have it directly deposited! See page 17 and fill in 12b, 12c, and 12d or Form 8888.

12a	If line 10 is larger than line 11, subtract line 11 from line 10. This is your **refund.** If Form 8888 is attached, check here ▶ ☐	12a	432
▶ b	Routing number	▶ c Type: ☐ Checking ☐ Savings	
▶ d	Account number		

Amount you owe

13	If line 11 is larger than line 10, subtract line 10 from line 11. This is the **amount you owe.** For details on how to pay, see page 18. ▶	13	

Third party designee

Do you want to allow another person to discuss this return with the IRS (see page 19)? ☐ **Yes.** Complete the following. ☐ **No**

Designee's name ▶	Phone no. ▶	Personal identification number (PIN)

Sign here

Joint return? See page 6.

Keep a copy for your records.

Under penalties of perjury, I declare that I have examined this return, and to the best of my knowledge and belief, it is true, correct, and accurately lists all amounts and sources of income I received during the tax year. Declaration of preparer (other than the taxpayer) is based on all information of which the preparer has any knowledge.

Your signature	Date	Your occupation	Daytime phone number
Spouse's signature. If a joint return, **both** must sign.	Date	Spouse's occupation	

Paid preparer's use only

Preparer's signature ▶	Date	Check if self-employed ☐	Preparer's SSN or PTIN
Firm's name (or yours if self-employed), address, and ZIP code ▶		EIN	
		Phone no.	

For Disclosure, Privacy Act, and Paperwork Reduction Act Notice, see page 35.   Cat. No. 11329W   Form **1040EZ** (2009)

(continued)

(concluded)

Version A, Cycle 5

Form 1040EZ (2009)

Page **2**

Worksheet for Line 5 — Dependents who checked one or both boxes

Use this worksheet to figure the amount to enter on line 5 if someone can claim you (or your spouse if married filing jointly) as a dependent, even if that person chooses not to do so. To find out if someone can claim you as a dependent, see Pub. 501.

A. Amount, if any, from line 1 on front . . . .   +   300.00   Enter total ▶   **A.** _____

B. Minimum standard deduction . . . . **B.** _____950.00_____

C. Enter the **larger** of line A or line B here . . . . **C.** _____

D. Maximum standard deduction. If **single**, enter $5,700; if **married filing jointly**, enter $11,400 . . . . **D.** _____

E. Enter the **smaller** of line C or line D here. This is your standard deduction . . . . . **E.** _____

F. Exemption amount.
- If single, enter -0-.
- If married filing jointly and —
  —both you and your spouse can be claimed as dependents, enter -0-.
  —only one of you can be claimed as a dependent, enter $3,650.

}   **F.** _____

G. Add lines E and F. Enter the total here and on line 5 on the front . . . . **G.** _____

(keep a copy for your records)

If you did not check any boxes on line 5, enter on line 5 the amount shown below that applies to you.
- Single, enter $9,350. This is the total of your standard deduction ($5,700) and your exemption ($3,650).
- Married filing jointly, enter $18,700. This is the total of your standard deduction ($11,400), your exemption ($3,650), and your spouse's exemption ($3,650).

Worksheet for Line 8 — Making work pay credit

Use this worksheet to figure the amount to enter on line 8 if you (or your spouse if filing a joint return) **cannot** be claimed as a dependent on another person's return.

Before you begin: √   If you can be claimed as a dependent on someone else's return, you **do not** qualify for this credit.
           √   If married filing jointly, include your spouse's amounts with yours when completing this worksheet.

1a. **Important.** See the instructions on page 12 if your wages include pay for work performed while an inmate in a penal institution; or a scholarship or fellowship grant not reported on Form W-2.

     Do you (and your spouse if filing jointly) have 2009 wages of more than $6,451 ($12,903 if married filing jointly)?

     ☒ **Yes.** Skip lines 1a through 3. Enter $400 ($800 if married filing jointly) on line 4 and go to line 5.

     ☐ **No.** Enter your earned income (see instructions) . . . . . **1a.** _____

b. Nontaxable combat pay included on line 1a (see instructions) . . . . **1b.** _____

2. Multiply line 1a by 6.2% (.062) . . . . . . **2.** _____

3. Enter $400 ($800 if married filing jointly) . . . . **3.** _____

4. Enter the **smaller** of line 2 or line 3 (unless you checked "Yes" on line 1a) . . . . . . **4.** _____800_____

5. Enter amount from line 4 on front . . . . . . **5.** _____54,138_____

6. Enter $75,000 ($150,000 if married filing jointly) . . . . **6.** _____150,000_____

7. Is the amount on line 5 more than the amount on line 6?

     ☒ **No.** Skip line 8. Enter the amount from line 4 on line 9 below.

     ☐ **Yes.** Subtract line 6 from line 5 . . . . **7.** _____

8. Multiply line 7 by 2% (.02) . . . . **8.** _____

9. Subtract line 8 from line 4. If zero or less, enter -0- . . . . . **9.** _____800_____

10. Did you (or your spouse, if filing jointly) receive an economic recovery payment in 2009? You may have received this payment if you received social security benefits, supplemental security income, railroad retirement benefits, or veterans disability compensation or pension benefits (see instructions).

(keep a copy for your records)

     ☒ **No.** Enter -0- on line 10.

     ☐ **Yes.** Enter the total of the economic recovery payments received by you (and your spouse, if filing jointly). **Do not** enter more than $250 ($500 if married filing jointly) . . **10.** _____0_____

11. **Making work pay credit.** Subtract line 10 from line 9. If zero or less, enter -0-. Enter the result here and on Form 1040EZ, line 8. . . . . **11.** _____800_____

Mailing return

Mail your return by **April 15, 2010.** Use the envelope that came with your booklet. If you do not have that envelope or if you moved during the year, see the back cover for the address to use.

Form **1040EZ** (2009)

Total Payments (1040EZ, line 10)

Line 10 is the sum of the tax withholding from line 7 and the credits on lines 8, 9a, and 9b.

Tax Refund (line 12a) or Tax Due with Return (line 13)

Compare the amount owed (line 11) with the total amount paid (line 10). Excess payment results in a refund; excess remaining tax liability means the taxpayer must pay the remaining amount owed when filing the return.

A taxpayer who is entitled to a refund can elect to (a) receive a check or (b) have the refund deposited directly in the taxpayer's bank account by supplying account information on lines 12b, c, and d.

In many ways, a tax return is the document a taxpayer uses to "settle up" with the IRS after a tax year is over. On it, the taxpayer reports income and deductions, the amount of tax, and the tax already paid. The refund (line 12a) or tax due (line 13) is simply the balancing figure required to make total net payments equal to the amount of total tax liability.

Individual income tax returns must be filed with the IRS no later than April 15 of the following year. Thus tax returns for calendar year 2009 must be filed (postmarked) no later than April 15, 2010. If April 15 falls on a weekend, taxpayers must file by the following Monday. Taxpayers can receive a six-month extension to file their return if they file Form 4868 no later than April 15. Any remaining tax liability is still due by April 15—the extension pertains only to the tax return, not the tax due.

EXAMPLE 1-5	Nora, who is single, has determined that her total tax liability for 2009 is $4,486. In 2009 her employer withheld $4,392 from Nora's paychecks. When Nora files her return, she will need to enclose a check for $94. Thus Nora's total payment for tax year 2009 is $4,486 ($4,392 withholdings plus $94 paid with her return), which is equal to her total liability for 2009.

EXAMPLE 1-6	Todd and Ellen, a married couple, determined that their total tax liability for 2009 is $8,859. In 2009 Ellen's employer withheld $5,278 from her paycheck and Todd's employer withheld $3,691. Todd and Ellen will receive a refund of $110 ($5,278 + $3,691 − $8,859). Thus Ellen and Todd's total payment for tax year 2009 is $8,859 ($5,278 and $3,691 of withholdings minus the $110 refund), which is equal to their total liability for 2009.

CONCEPT CHECK 1-6—LO 3	1. Taxpayers pay all of their tax liability when they file their tax returns. True or false? 2. Bret's tax liability is $15,759. His employer withheld $16,367 from his wages. When Bret files his tax return, will he be required to pay or will he get a refund? _____. What will be the amount of payment or refund? _____ 3. An Earned Income Credit will increase the amount of tax liability. True or false?

Appendix A

TAX AUTHORITY

LO 5

Throughout this text, there are many references to "tax authority." As a beginning tax student, you need to understand what tax authority is. The best definition of *tax authority* is that the term refers to the guidelines that give the taxpayer not only guidance to report taxable income correctly but also guidelines and precedent for judicial decisions concerning conflicts between the IRS and the taxpayer. There are three types of primary tax authority:

Statutory sources

Administrative sources

Judicial sources

TABLE 1-4
Legislative Process of U. S. Tax Laws

- U.S. House of Representatives Ways and Means Committee.
- Voted on by the House of Representatives.
- U.S. Senate Finance Committee.
- Voted on by the Senate.
- Joint Conference Committee (if differences between the House and Senate versions).
- Joint Conference bill voted on by the House of Representatives and the Senate.
- If the bill passes the House and Senate—signed or vetoed by the president of the United States.
- If signed—incorporated into the Internal Revenue Code.

Statutory Sources of Tax Authority

The ultimate statutory tax authority is the Sixteenth Amendment to the U.S. Constitution. By far the most commonly relied-upon statutory authority is the Internal Revenue Code (IRC). Congress writes the IRC. Changes to it must pass through the entire legislative process to become law. Table 1-4 shows the legislative process for tax laws.

Typically federal tax legislation begins in the Ways and Means Committee of the House of Representatives (although bills can start in the Senate Finance Committee). A tax bill passed by the House is sent to the Senate for consideration. If the Senate agrees to the bill with no changes, it sends the bill to the president for a signature or veto. If, as is more likely, the Senate passes a bill different from the House, both houses of Congress select some of their members to be on a Joint Conference Committee. The committee's goal is to resolve the conflict(s) between the House and Senate versions of the bill. Once conflicts are resolved in the Conference Committee, both the House and the Senate vote on the common bill. If passed by both bodies, the bill goes to the president and, if signed, becomes law and part of the Internal Revenue Code.

Each enacted law receives a public law number. For example, Public Law 99-272 means the enacted legislation was the 272nd bill of the 99th Congress (the January 2009 to December 2011 legislative years of the Congress represent the 111th congressional session).

Throughout the legislative process, each taxation committee (Ways and Means, Senate Finance, and the Joint Conference Committee) generates one or more committee reports that note the "intent of Congress" in developing legislation. These committee reports can provide courts, the IRS, and tax professionals guidance as to the proper application of enacted tax law. The public law number of the bill is used to reference committee reports. Public Law 99-272 would have a House Ways and Means Committee report, a Senate Finance Committee report, and possibly a Joint Conference Committee report.[14]

The IRS publishes the congressional reports in the *IRS Cumulative Bulletin. Cumulative Bulletins* are in most libraries in the government documents section. The reports are also on various governmental Internet sites. Use an Internet search engine to help you find these sites. *Cumulative Bulletins* for the last five years are available on the IRS Web site (www.irs.gov).

The IRC is organized by subtitle, as shown in Table 1-5.

TABLE 1-5
Subtitles of the Internal Revenue Code

Subtitle	Subject
A	Income taxes
B	Estate and gift taxes
C	Employment taxes
D	Excise taxes
E	Alcohol and tobacco taxes
F	Procedure and administration
G	Joint Committee on Taxation
H	Presidential election campaign financing
I	Trust funds

---

[14] Not all bills have committee reports from each house of Congress. If there are no conflicts between the House and Senate, additional committee reports are not necessary. Such an outcome is unusual.

Most of this text pertains to subtitle A of the IRC (income taxes). The IRC is hundreds of pages in length. An excerpt from the IRC follows:

IRC §61. Gross Income Defined
General Definition.—Except as otherwise provided in this subtitle, gross income means all income from whatever source derived, including (but not limited to) the following items:
Compensation for services, including fees, commissions, fringe benefits, and similar items;
Gross income derived from business;
Gains derived from dealings in property;
Interest;
Rents;
Royalties;
Dividends;
Alimony and separate maintenance payments;
Annuities;
Income from life insurance and endowment contracts;
Pensions;
Income from discharge of indebtedness;
Distributive share of partnership gross income;
Income in respect of a decedent; and
Income from an interest in an estate or trust.

The major national tax publishers such as Research Institute of America (RIA) and Commerce Clearing House (CCH) publish the IRC in bound versions and on their respective Web sites. The IRC can also be located on numerous tax Internet sites, although students are cautioned that the content of most generic Web sites is often not up to date (RIA and CCH are current).

CONCEPT CHECK 1-7—LO 5

1. The committee charged with considering tax legislation in the House of Representatives is called the _____ Committee.
2. The most commonly relied-on statutory authority is _____ .
3. All tax legislation must pass both the House of Representatives and the Senate and be signed by the president of the United States in order to become law. True or false?

As authorized by Congress, the president of the United States enters into tax treaties. Thus treaties between the United States and other countries are also statutory tax authority.

A problem with the IRC is that it is usually extremely broad and sometimes difficult to apply to specific tax situations. Because of this limitation, administrative and judicial tax authorities have evolved.

Administrative Tax Authority

The Internal Revenue Service (IRS), a division of the U.S. Treasury Department, develops administrative tax authority. The tax authority created by the IRS is, in effect, the IRS's interpretation of the IRC. Table 1-6 presents a list of the major IRS administrative authorities. These are the rulings or interpretations of the IRS at the national level. Each region of the IRS also publishes several authoritative guidelines.

TABLE 1-6
Examples of Administrative Authority (in order of strength of authority, from highest to lowest)

Type of Administrative Authority	Example of Typical Research Citation
IRS Regulations (Treasury Regulations)	Reg. § 1.351-1
Revenue Rulings	Rev. Rul. 80-198, 1980-2 CB 113
Revenue Procedures	Rev. Proc. 87-32, 1987-2 CB 396
Private Letter Rulings	PLR 8922063
IRS Notices	Notice 97-69, 1997-2 CB 331

Treasury Regulations

IRS Regulations are by far the strongest administrative authority. Regulations are the IRS's direct interpretation of the IRC. There are four types of IRS Regulations (listed in order of strength of authority, high to low):

Legislative Regulations: The IRS writes these regulations under a direct mandate by Congress. Legislative Regulations actually take the place of the IRC and have the full effect of law.

General or Final Regulations: The IRS writes these regulations under its general legislative authority to interpret the IRC. Most sections of the IRC have General Regulations to help interpret the law.

Temporary Regulations: These regulations have the same authority as General Regulations until they expire three years after issuance. The IRS issues Temporary Regulations to give taxpayers immediate guidance related to a new law. Temporary Regulations are noted with a "T" in the citation (for example, Reg. §1.671-2T).

Proposed Regulations: These regulations do not have the effect of law. The IRS writes Proposed Regulations during the hearing process leading up to the promulgation of General Regulations. The purpose of the Proposed Regulations is to generate discussion and critical evaluation of the IRS's interpretation of the IRC.

Regulations are referred to (or cited) by using an IRC subtitle prefix, the referring code section, and the regulation number. For example, Reg. §1.162-5 refers to the prefix (1) denoting the income tax subtitle, IRC section 162, and regulation number 5. Here are some examples of regulation subtitle prefixes:

1. Income Taxes (Reg. §1.162-5).
20. Estate Tax (Reg. §20.2032-1).
25. Gift Tax (Reg. §25.2503-4).
31. Employment Taxes (Reg. §31.3301-1).
301. Procedural Matters (Reg. §301.7701-1).[15]

Like the IRS, the national publishers (RIA and CCH) publish and sell paperback and hardbound versions of IRS regulations. You can also find regulations on a number of tax Internet sites including the IRS's Web site (www.irs.gov).

Revenue Rulings and Revenue Procedures

Revenue Rulings (Rev. Rul.) and Revenue Procedures (Rev. Proc.) are excellent sources of information for taxpayers and tax preparers. When issuing a Revenue Ruling, the IRS is reacting to an area of the tax law that is confusing to many taxpayers or that has substantive tax implications for numerous taxpayers. After many taxpayers have requested additional guidance on a given situation, the IRS may issue a Rev. Rul. The Rev. Rul. lists a factual situation, the relevant tax authority, and the IRS's conclusion as to the manner in which taxpayers should treat the issue.

Revenue Procedures (Rev. Proc.), on the other hand, are primarily proactive. Through a Rev. Proc., the IRS illustrates how it wants something reported. Often the IRS provides guidelines or safe harbors to help taxpayers follow the law as interpreted by the IRS. For example, after the Tax Reform Act of 1986, the allowable depreciation methods were drastically changed. The IRS issued Rev. Proc. 87-56 and 87-57 to help taxpayers and preparers properly calculate and report depreciation expense under the new rules.

---

[15] Various other prefixes are used in specific situations. When dealing with income taxes, however, the first (1) is used most often.

The citations for Revenue Rulings and Revenue Procedures indicate the year of the ruling or procedure and a consecutive number (reset to 1 each year). For example, Rev. Proc. 87-56 was the 56th Revenue Procedure issued in 1987. Revenue Rulings and Procedures are in the *Cumulative Bulletins* published by the IRS.

Other IRS Pronouncements

Other pronouncements issued by the IRS include Private Letter Rulings (PLRs) and IRS Notices. Each of these has limited authority. The IRS issues PLRs when a taxpayer requests a ruling on a certain tax situation. The PLR is tax authority only to the taxpayer to whom it is issued, although it does indicate the thinking of the IRS.

When there is a change in a rate or allowance, the IRS issues an IRS Notice. For example, if there is a change to the standard mileage rate for business travel from 34 cents a mile to 36 cents a mile, the IRS will issue an IRS Notice to publicize the change.

In addition to the administrative authority discussed in this section, the IRS also publishes various other sources of information that can benefit taxpayers such as Technical Advice Memorandums and Determination Letters.

CONCEPT CHECK 1-8—LO 5

1. Administrative tax authority takes precedence over statutory tax authority. True or false?
2. IRS Revenue Procedures are applicable only to the taxpayer to whom issued. True or false?
3. The administrative tax authority with the most strength of authority is _____.

Judicial Tax Authority

The tax laws and regulations are complex. There can be differences of opinion as to how a taxpayer should report certain income or whether or not an item is a permitted deduction on a tax return. When conflict occurs between the IRS and taxpayers, it is the job of the court system to settle the dispute. The rulings of the various courts that hear tax cases are the third primary tax authority.

Figure 1-1 depicts the court system with regard to tax disputes. Three different trial courts hear tax cases: (1) the U.S. Tax Court, (2) the U.S. District Court, and (3) the U.S. Court of Federal Claims. Decisions by the Tax Court and the district courts may be appealed to the U.S. Court of Appeals and then to the Supreme Court. U.S. Court of Federal Claims cases are appealed to the U.S. Court of Appeals—Federal Claims, and then to the Supreme Court.

The Tax Court hears most litigated tax disputes between the IRS and taxpayers. The Tax Court is a national court with judges that travel throughout the nation to hear cases. Judges hear tax cases in major cities several times a year and are tax law specialists.

FIGURE 1-1
Court System for Tax Disputes

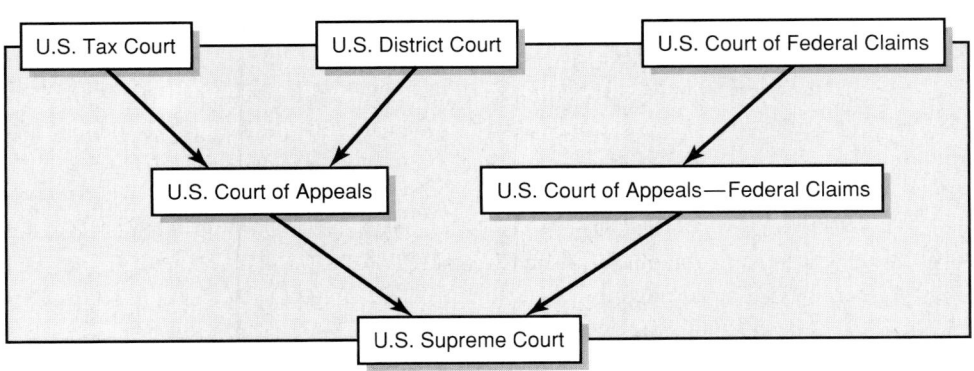

The court system becomes involved when a taxpayer and the IRS do not agree. Typically the IRS assesses the taxpayer for the tax the IRS believes is due. The taxpayer then needs to decide whether to go to court to contest the IRS's position and, if so, determine a court venue. One major advantage the taxpayer has when filing a petition with the Tax Court is that the taxpayer does not need to pay the IRS's proposed tax assessment prior to trial. With the other two judicial outlets (the district court and the Court of Federal Claims), the taxpayer must pay the government and then sue for a refund.

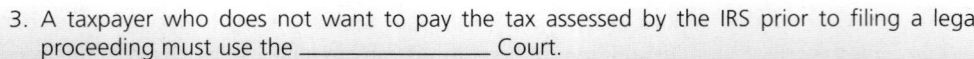

CONCEPT CHECK 1-9—LO 5

1. The U.S. Supreme Court does not accept appeals of tax cases. True or false?
2. A taxpayer who does not agree with an assessment of tax by the IRS has no recourse. True or false?
3. A taxpayer who does not want to pay the tax assessed by the IRS prior to filing a legal proceeding must use the _____ Court.

Appendix B

GETTING STARTED WITH TAXACT

This text includes a CD that contains the TaxACT tax preparation software for individual income tax returns. Throughout this text, we provide examples and end-of-chapter questions and problems that you can solve using tax software.

The tax return problems can be completed either by hand using the tax forms available in this text and on the IRS Web site or by using the TaxACT software bundled with the text. Your instructor will tell you how to prepare the problems. If you are using the tax software, this section will help you get started.

Many tax software products are on the market. They are all similar. Because of that, except for this chapter, we have purposefully written the text in a "software-neutral" manner. What we discuss for TaxACT will generally apply to any individual income tax product you would be likely to use.

The following information will help you get started using the TaxACT software:
- Install TaxACT on your computer according to the instructions provided with the CD.
- Double-click on the TaxACT icon to run the program.
- When you first start TaxACT, the program will ask you a number of questions that you will skip or respond with "Cancel." Subsequent times you start the software it may ask about state tax software. Respond with "Cancel."
- You will eventually arrive at the Home screen.

The TaxACT software allows the user to input tax information in two formats. One is the Interview Method (called QnA). With this method, the computer asks a series of questions that guides the user through the issues pertaining to his or her tax return. This method is active when the program starts and is sometimes helpful for individuals preparing a tax return who know very little about taxes.

The second method is the Forms Method. With it, the user selects the appropriate tax form or input form and types the correct information onto the appropriate line or lines. This method is suited to those who have some familiarity with the tax forms and how they interact. Using this text, you will quickly reach the necessary level of familiarity.

We will exclusively use the Forms Method throughout the text. We do this for three reasons. First, we strongly believe that when preparing taxes, the user needs to understand the forms

that are needed, how they interact, and where the numbers come from and go to. Otherwise it is like memorizing only one way to get to work—if something changes, the individual is totally lost. Second, in the text, we often focus on one or two forms at a time, not an entire tax return (except for the comprehensive examples). The QnA method is not designed to zero in on a form or two—instead it guides a user through an entire return. Third, the QnA method makes assumptions that are sometimes difficult to change.

Other tax software uses similar QnA (interview) or Forms approaches. No matter what software you end up using after you graduate from school, the basic approach and input methodology found in TaxACT will be the same from program to program.

To get the program into the proper input method and to get it ready to accept data, you need to click on the Forms icon on the toolbar, toward the top of the page in the middle.

When you want to start a new "client," perform the following steps:

1. Click on the File pull-down menu at the upper left.
2. Click on New Return.
3. The system will ask you whether you want to order a state tax product. Click Continue.
4. The system will ask you whether you want to import information from last year's return. Respond Cancel.

Now click on the Forms icon to get to the Forms Method.

The TaxACT system is a highly complex computer program. The software recognizes that information "starts" on a certain form or schedule and then is carried forward to other forms or schedules. For example, the name and address of the taxpayer are initially entered on Form 1040. TaxACT automatically transfers these data to other forms that require that information.

As you use the TaxACT software, you will notice that most numerical information is in either a green or blue color. Green numbers are numbers that you can enter directly on the form you are working on. Blue numbers are calculated on (or derived from) another form or worksheet. If you click on a blue number, you can then click on the Folder icon and go to the supporting form or worksheet.

If you click on a blue number and try to enter a figure, the software will warn you that you are trying to alter a calculated value. You can then choose to go to the supporting schedule, or you can choose to override the value. The software strongly advises you *not* to enter information directly but to go to the appropriate supporting form. We concur. Until you have a much better understanding of how tax software works (or unless we specifically tell you otherwise), you should use the supporting schedules. If you fail to do so, you can get unanticipated results that may create an erroneous return. This can occur, for example, when the software transfers a number to two or more follow-up forms. If you change the number on one of the follow-up forms but not on the other(s), you will have an erroneous return.

Important note: Preliminary versions of tax software are generally issued in October with final versions coming out around January. Software vendors want to make sure you are using the most up-to-date versions of their software and tax forms. If you are using a preliminary version of the software, the vendors require you to get an updated version before you can print any tax forms. Before TaxACT will allow you to print out a tax return, you need to update your software. Make sure you have an Internet connection, go to the online drop-down menu, and select Program Updates and then Federal. The update process is automatic.

Finally, we use a number of example "taxpayers" that will reappear off and on throughout the text (the Davidsons introduced in this chapter are an example). Note two important things about these taxpayers. First, they are entirely fictional. They are constructed for illustrative purposes only and do not represent any existing taxpayers. Second, because we will also use the example taxpayers in later chapters (some more often than others), it is important that you save the tax return information in the TaxACT software. That way, you do not have to rekey the data later.

Summary

LO 1: Understand progressive, proportional, and regressive tax structures.

- Taxes are levied by multiplying a tax rate (the rate of tax) by a tax base (the amount taxed).
- Progressive: The tax rate increases as the tax base increases.
- Proportional: The tax rate remains the same regardless of the tax base.
- Regressive: The tax rate decreases as the tax base increases.

LO 2: Understand the concepts of marginal and average tax rates as well as a simple income tax formula.

- The marginal tax rate is the proportion of tax paid on the next dollar of income.
- The average tax rate is the percentage of total tax paid on the amount of taxable income.
- The simple tax formula is

  Income
      − Permitted deductions from income

  = Taxable income
  × Appropriate tax rates

  = Tax liability
  − Tax payments and tax credits

  = Tax refund or tax due with return

LO 3: Understand the components of a Form 1040EZ income tax return.

- Must meet six criteria to be eligible to file Form 1040EZ.
- Major components of Form 1040EZ return are filing status, wage income, taxable interest income, unemployment compensation, permitted deductions, taxable income, tax liability, tax payments, earned income credit, and amount owed or refund.

LO4: Determine tax liability in instances when a Form 1040EZ return is appropriate.

- Tax liability is determined with reference to the tax tables issued by the IRS (and printed in Appendix D of this text).
- Tax liability can also be determined by using the tax rate schedules printed on the inside front cover of this text.

LO 5: Understand the types of tax authority and how they interrelate (Appendix A).

- Statutory tax authority is the Internal Revenue Code and committee reports from appropriate congressional committees.
- Administrative tax authority is issued by the IRS. It includes
  - IRS Regulations.
  - Revenue Rulings.
  - Revenue Procedures.
  - Private Letter Rulings.
  - IRS Notices.
- Judicial tax authority is developed by the courts as a result of court cases between taxpayers and the IRS.

Discussion Questions

1. (Introduction) Give a brief history of the income tax in the United States.

2. (Introduction) For tax year 2006, what proportions of individual income tax returns were filed on a Form 1040EZ, Form 1040A, and Form 1040? What proportion were electronically filed?

LO 1 3. Name the three types of tax rate structures and give an example of each.

LO 1 4. What is a *progressive tax*? Why do you think the government believes it is a more equitable tax than, say, a regressive tax or proportional tax?

LO 1 5. What type of tax is a sales tax? Explain your answer.

LO 1 6. What is the definition of *tax base,* and how does it affect the amount of tax levied?

LO 1 7. What type of tax rate structure is the U.S. federal income tax? Explain your answer.

LO 1 8. A change to a 17% flat tax could cause a considerable increase in many taxpayers' taxes and a considerable decrease in the case of others. Explain this statement in light of the statistics in Table 1-3.

LO 1 9. Explain what is meant by *regressive tax*. Why is the social security tax considered a regressive tax?

LO 2 10. Define and compare these terms: *average tax rate* and *marginal tax rate.*

_____

_____

_____

LO 3 11. What is meant by *compensation for services*? Give some examples.

_____

_____

_____

LO 3 12. What is the definition of *interest*?

_____

_____

_____

LO 3 13. What federal tax forms do taxpayers normally receive to inform them of the amount of wages and interest they earned during the year?

_____

_____

_____

LO 3 14. Explain why unemployment compensation is taxable.

_____

_____

_____

LO 3 15. What is the amount of the permitted deduction for single and married taxpayers who use Form 1040EZ?

_____

_____

_____

LO 3, 4 16. What is the most common way taxpayers pay their income tax liability during the year?

_____

_____

_____

Multiple-Choice Questions

LO 1 17. A tax rate that decreases as the tax base increases is an example of what kind of tax rate structure?
  a. Progressive.
  b. Proportional.
  c. Regressive.
  d. Recessive.

LO 1 18. A tax rate that decreases as the tax base decreases is an example of what kind of tax rate structure?
  a. Progressive.
  b. Proportional.

    c. Regressive.

    d. Recessive.

LO 1 19. Jake earned $15,000 and paid $1,500 of income tax; Jill earned $40,000 and paid $3,000 of income tax. The tax rate structure they are subject to is

    a. Progressive.

    b. Proportional.

    c. Regressive.

    d. Recessive.

LO 1 20. Margaret earned $15,000 and paid $1,500 of income tax; Mike earned $40,000 and paid $4,000 of income tax. The tax rate structure they are subject to is

    a. Progressive.

    b. Proportional.

    c. Regressive.

    d. Recessive.

LO 1 21. Which of the following is an example of a regressive tax?

    a. Federal income tax.

    b. State and local taxes levied on property.

    c. Sales tax.

    d. Social security tax.

LO 1 22. Which of the following is an example of a progressive tax?

    a. Federal income tax.

    b. State and local taxes levied on property.

    c. Sales tax.

    d. Social security tax.

LO 2 23. Jennifer and Paul have taxable income of $68,135 and the following tax liability:

$16,700 × 10% =	$1,670.00
($67,900 − $16,700) × 15% =	7,680.00
($68,135 − $67,900) × 25% =	58.75
Total tax liability	$9,408.75

Their marginal tax rate is

    a. 10%.

    b. 15%.

    c. 25%.

    d. 13.8%.

LO 2 24. Jennifer and Paul have taxable income of $68,135 and the following tax liability:

$16,700 × 10% =	$1,670.00
($67,900 − $16,700) × 15% =	7,680.00
($68,135 − $67,900) × 25% =	58.75
Total tax liability	$9,408.75

Their average tax rate is

    a. 10%.

    b. 15%.

    c. 25%.

    d. 13.8%.

LO 3   25. Which of the following would disqualify a taxpayer from filing Form 1040EZ?

    a. The taxpayer is married.

    b. The taxpayer is age 66.

    c. The taxpayer received unemployment compensation.

    d. The taxpayer had adjusted gross income (line 4 of Form 1040EZ) of $101,000.

LO 3   26. The most complex individual income tax return is a Form

    a. 1040.

    b. 1040A.

    c. 1040C.

    d. 1040EZ.

LO 3   27. Wage income is reported to a taxpayer on a Form

    a. W-2.

    b. 1099-G.

    c. 1099-W.

    d. 1099-INT.

LO 3   28. Interest income is reported to a taxpayer on a Form

    a. W-2.

    b. W-2-INT.

    c. 1099-G.

    d. 1099-INT.

LO 3   29. On Form 1040EZ, the amount of the permitted deduction from income for taxpayers filing a joint return is

    a. $1,500.

    b. $9,350.

    c. $18,700.

    d. $28,050.

LO 3   30. Elizabeth determined her tax liability was $3,942. Her employer withheld $3,492 from her paychecks during the year. Elizabeth's tax return would show

    a. A refund of $450.

    b. A refund of $3,492.

    c. Tax due of $450.

    d. Tax due of $3,942.

LO 4   31. Sandra, a single taxpayer, has taxable income of $86,937. Using the tax tables, her tax liability is

    a. $14,106.

    b. $16,584.

    c. $18,059.

    d. $18,062.

LO 4 32. A married taxpayer has taxable income of $77,381. You have calculated tax liability using the tax tables and using the tax rate schedules. What can you say about the two figures?

    a. Tax liability determined using the tax tables will be more than tax liability determined using the tax rate schedules.

    b. Tax liability determined using the tax tables will be less than tax liability determined using the tax rate schedules.

    c. Tax liability determined using the tax tables will be the same as tax liability determined using the tax rate schedules.

    d. The answer cannot be determined with the information provided.

LO 3, 4 33. Eddie, a single taxpayer, has W-2 income of $42,487. Using the tax tables, his tax liability is

    a. $4,134.

    b. $4,551.

    c. $5,536.

    d. $6,806.

LO 3, 4 34. Arno and Bridgette are married and have combined W-2 income of $93,455. They received a refund of $522 when they filed their taxes. How much income tax did their employers withhold during the year?

    a. $10,547.

    b. $11,591.

    c. $15,222.

    d. $16,266.

Problems

LO 1 35. Using the information in Table 1-3, determine the average amount of taxable income per tax return, rounded to the nearest dollar, for each of the ranges of taxable income provided.

LO 1 36. Using the information in Table 1-3, determine the amount of average income tax liability per tax return, rounded to the nearest dollar, for each income range provided.

LO 1 37. Use the information in Table 1-3. If the federal tax system was changed to a proportional tax rate structure with a tax rate of 17%, calculate the amount of tax liability for 2006 for all taxpayers. How does this amount differ from the actual liability?

LO 2   38. What is the income tax formula in simplified form?

_____

_____

_____

LO 3   39. What six criteria must a taxpayer meet in order to file Form 1040EZ?

_____   _____

_____   _____

_____   _____

LO 3   40. When taxpayers file a tax return, they will either pay an additional amount or receive a refund of excess taxes paid. Briefly explain how this "settling up" process works. Why might a taxpayer pay too much during the year?

_____

_____

_____

LO 4   41. Cameron is single and has taxable income of $42,443. Determine his tax liability using the tax tables and using the tax rate schedule. Why is there a difference between the two amounts?

_____

_____

_____

LO 4   42. Havel and Petra are married, will file a joint tax return, and meet the requirements to file Form 1040EZ. Havel has W-2 income of $31,931, and Petra has W-2 income of $32,783. What is their tax liability? Determine their tax liability using both the tax tables and the tax rate schedule.

_____

_____

_____

LO 2, 4   43. Determine the tax liability, marginal tax rate, and average tax rate in each of the following cases. Use the Form 1040EZ tax tables to determine tax liability.

   a. Single taxpayer, taxable income of $21,690:

   Liability = _____ Marginal = _____ Average = _____

   b. Single taxpayer, taxable income of $36,288:

   Liability = _____ Marginal = _____ Average = _____

LO 2, 4   44. Determine the tax liability, marginal tax rate, and average tax rate in each of the following cases. Use the Form 1040EZ tax tables to determine tax liability.

   a. Married taxpayers, taxable income of $36,288:

   Liability = _____ Marginal = _____ Average = _____

   b. Married taxpayers, taxable income of $97,335:

   Liability = _____ Marginal = _____ Average = _____

LO 2, 4   45. Determine the tax liability, marginal tax rate, and average tax rate in each of the following cases. Use the Form 1040EZ tax tables to determine tax liability.

    a. Married taxpayers, taxable income of $21,690:

        Liability = _____ Marginal = _____ Average = _____

    b. Single taxpayer, taxable income of $97,335:

        Liability = _____ Marginal = _____ Average = _____

LO 4   46. Use the tax rate schedules to determine the tax liability for each of the cases in Problems 43, 44, and 45.

    a. Liability for 43*a* = _____ 43*b* = _____

    b. Liability for 44*a* = _____ 44*b* = _____

    c. Liability for 45*a* = _____ 45*b* = _____

LO 3, 4   47. The W-2 income of Sandra, a single taxpayer, was $67,443. Using the tax tables, determine Sandra's tax liability.

_____

_____

LO 3, 4   48. The W-2 incomes of Betty and her husband Ronald were $32,922 and $30,139, respectively. If Betty and Ronald use a filing status of married filing jointly, determine their tax liability using the tax tables.

_____

_____

LO 3, 4   49. Sheniqua, a single taxpayer, had taxable income of $63,914. Her employer withheld $13,274 in federal income tax from her paychecks throughout the year. Using the tax tables, would Sheniqua receive a refund or would she be required to pay additional tax? What is the amount?

_____

_____

LO 3, 4   50. Xavier and his wife Maria have total W-2 income of $95,558. They will file their tax return as married filing jointly. They had a total of $11,117 withheld from their paychecks for federal income tax. Using the tax tables, determine the amount of refund or additional tax due upon filing their tax return. Indicate whether the amount is a refund or additional tax.

_____

_____

Discussion Questions Pertaining to Appendix A (LO 5)

51. Discuss the concept of *tax authority*. How does tax authority help taxpayers and tax preparers report tax items properly?

_____

_____

_____

52. What are the three types of tax authority? Who issues each type?

_____

_____

_____

53. Discuss the concept of *statutory tax authority*. Why is there a need for additional types of authority when statutory authority is the law?

_____

_____

_____

54. What is the legislative process concerning tax laws? Where does tax legislation often begin?

_____

_____

_____

55. What are committee reports, and how can they help the taxpayer or tax preparer?

_____

_____

_____

56. What is the purpose of a Joint Conference Committee? Its reports are considered more important or carry weight that is more authoritative. Why?

_____

_____

_____

57. Explain what is meant by *Public Law 100-14.*

_____

_____

_____

58. What is administrative authority, and who publishes it?

_____

_____

_____

59. What is a Proposed Regulation? Can a taxpayer rely on a Proposed Regulation as authority on how to treat a certain tax item?

_____

_____

_____

60. Can a taxpayer rely on a Temporary Regulation as authority on how to treat a certain tax item? If so, how long is a Temporary Regulation valid?

_____

_____

_____

61. Differentiate between a General Regulation and a Legislative Regulation. Which one is the stronger tax authority?

_____

_____

_____

62. Where are Revenue Rulings and Revenue Procedures found? When might a Revenue Ruling be useful to a taxpayer? When might a Revenue Procedure be useful to a taxpayer?

_____

_____

_____

63. In what courts are disputes between the IRS and a taxpayer heard?

_____

_____

_____

64. What are the advantages of petitioning the Tax Court versus other trial courts?

_____

_____

_____

65. When would a taxpayer want to sue the government in a district court versus the Tax Court?

_____

_____

_____

66. If a taxpayer loses a case against the IRS in one of the three trial courts, does the taxpayer have any avenue for appeals?

_____

_____

_____

67. After the court of appeals, does a taxpayer have any additional avenue for appeals? If so, what are the taxpayer's probabilities of receiving an appeal after the court of appeals? Why?

_____

_____

_____

68. Why might a district court's opinion regarding a tax decision be more likely to be reversed on appeal?

_____

_____

_____

69. (Longer answer) What is a Treasury Regulation? What are the four types of regulations and how do they differ?

_____

_____

_____

70. (Longer answer) What is the difference between a Revenue Ruling and a Revenue Procedure? How does the level of authority of a ruling or procedure compare with regulations and statutory authority?

_____

_____

_____

Multiple-Choice Questions Pertaining to Appendix A (LO 5)

71. Which of the following are primary sources of tax authority?

    a. Statutory sources.

    b. Administrative sources.

    c. Judicial sources.

    d. All of the above.

72. Which of the following is a statutory source of tax authority?

    a. Internal Revenue Code.

    b. Regulations.

    c. Revenue Rulings.

    d. Tax Court decision.

73. Which of the following types of IRS Regulations have the greatest strength of authority?

    a. General or Final Regulations.

    b. Legislative Regulations.

    c. Proposed Regulations.

    d. Temporary Regulations.

74. Which of the following refers to an income tax regulation?

    a. Reg. §1.162-5.

    b. Reg. §20.2032-1.

    c. Reg. §25.2503-4.

    d. Reg. §31.3301-1.

75. Which of the following trial courts hear tax cases?

    a. U.S. Tax Court.

    b. U.S. district courts.

    c. U.S. Court of Federal Claims.

    d. All of the above.

Tax Return Problems

Use your tax software to complete the following problems. If you are manually preparing the tax returns, you will need a Form 1040EZ for each problem.

Tax Return Problem 1   Brenda Peterson is single and lives at 567 East Street, Beantown, MA. Her SSN is 333-44-5555. She worked the entire year for Applebee Consulting in Beantown. Her Form W-2 contained information in the following boxes:

$$\text{Wages (box 1)} = \$61{,}292.05$$
$$\text{Federal W/H (box 2)} = \$\ 9{,}851.12$$
$$\text{Social security wages (box 3)} = \$61{,}292.05$$
$$\text{Social security W/H (box 4)} = \$\ 3{,}800.10$$
$$\text{Medicare wages (box 5)} = \$61{,}292.05$$
$$\text{Medicare W/H (box 6)} = \$\ \ \ \ 888.73$$

She also received two Forms 1099-INT. One was from First National Bank of Beantown and showed interest income of $537.39 in box 1. The other Form 1099-INT was from Baystate Savings and Loan and showed interest income of $281.70 in box 1.

Prepare a Form 1040EZ for Brenda.

Tax Return Problem 2

Jin Xiang is single and lives at 2468 North Lake Road in Lakeland, MN. Her SSN is 444-55-6666. She worked the entire year for Lakeland Automotive. The Form W-2 from Lakeland contained information in the following boxes:

Wages (box 1) = $36,239.27
Federal W/H (box 2) = $ 4,611.80
Social security wages (box 3) = $36,239.27
Social security W/H (box 4) = $ 2,246.83
Medicare wages (box 5) = $36,239.27
Medicare W/H (box 6) = $ 525.47

On the weekends, Jin worked at Parts-Galore, a local auto parts store. The Form W-2 from Parts-Galore contained information in the following boxes:

Wages (box 1) = $9,167.02
Federal W/H (box 2) = $ 348.39
Social security wages (box 3) = $9,167.02
Social security W/H (box 4) = $ 568.36
Medicare wages (box 5) = $9,167.02
Medicare W/H (box 6) = $ 132.92

Jin also received a Form 1099-INT from Minnesota Savings and Loan. The amount of interest income in box 1 of the Form 1099-INT was $51.92.

Prepare a Form 1040EZ for Jin.

Tax Return Problem 3

Jose and Maria Suarez are married and live at 9876 Main Street, Denver, CO. Jose's SSN is 555-66-7777 and Maria's SSN is 555-66-8888.

For the first five months of the year, Jose was employed by Mountain Mortgage Company. The Form W-2 from Mountain Mortgage contained information in the following boxes:

Wages (box 1) = $32,019.51
Federal W/H (box 2) = $ 4,822.89
Social security wages (box 3) = $32,019.51
Social security W/H (box 4) = $ 1,985.21
Medicare wages (box 5) = $32,019.51
Medicare W/H (box 6) = $ 464.28

Jose was laid off from his job at Mountain Mortgage and was unemployed for three months. He received $1,000 of unemployment insurance payments. The Form 1099-G Jose received from the state of Colorado contained $1,000 of unemployment compensation in box 1 and $75 of federal income tax withholding in box 4.

During the last four months of the year, Jose was employed by First Mountain Bank in Denver. The Form W-2 Jose received from the bank contained information in the following boxes:

Wages (box 1) = $19,820.20
Federal W/H (box 2) = $ 2,397.14
Social security wages (box 3) = $19,820.20
Social security W/H (box 4) = $ 1,228.85
Medicare wages (box 5) = $19,820.20
Medicare W/H (box 6) = $ 287.39

Maria was employed the entire year by Blue Sky Properties in Denver. The Form W-2 Maria received from Blue Sky contained information in the following boxes:

Wages (box 1) = $51,728.05

Federal W/H (box 2) = $ 6,408.82

Social security wages (box 3) = $51,728.05

Social security W/H (box 4) = $ 3,207.14

Medicare wages (box 5) = $51,728.05

Medicare W/H (box 6) = $ 750.06

The Suarezes also received two Forms 1099-INT showing interest they received on two savings accounts. One Form 1099-INT from the First National Bank of Northeastern Denver showed interest income of $59.36 in box 1. The other Form 1099-INT from Second National Bank of Northwestern Denver showed interest income of $82.45 in box 1.

Prepare a Form 1040EZ for Mr. and Mrs. Suarez.

We have provided selected filled-in source documents on our Web site at www.mhhe.com/cruz2010.

TABLE 2-1
Line-by-Line
Comparison of Form
1040 and Form 1040A

Description	Form 1040 Line Location	Form 1040A Line Location	Chapter Where Discussed
Filing Status	1–5	1–5	1, 2
Exemptions	6a–d	6a–d	1, 2
Gross Income			
Wages, salaries, and tips	7	7	1, 3
Taxable and nontaxable interest	8a/b	8a/b	1, 3
Ordinary and qualified dividends	9a/b	9a/b	3
Taxable refunds of state/local taxes	10	—	3
Alimony received	11	—	3
Business income/loss (Schedule C)	12	—	6
Capital gain/loss (Schedule D)	13	10	7
Other gains/losses (Form 4797)	14	—	7
IRA distributions	15a/b	11a/b	11
Pension distributions	16a/b	12a/b	11
Rentals, partnerships, etc. (Schedule E)	17	—	8, 13
Farm income/loss (Schedule F)	18	—	—
Unemployment compensation	19	13	1, 3
Social security benefits	20a/b	14a/b	3
Other income	21	—	3
Total Income	22	15	
Deductions for Adjusted Gross Income			
Educator Expenses	23	16	4
Certain business expenses	24	—	—
Health savings account deduction	25	—	4
Moving expenses	26	—	4
Half of self-employment tax	27	—	4
SEP, SIMPLE, and other retirement plans	28	—	11
Self-employed health insurance	29	—	4
Penalty on early withdrawal of savings	30	—	4
Alimony paid	31a	—	4
IRA deduction	32	17	11
Student loan interest deduction	33	18	4
Tuition and Fees deduction	34	19	4
Domestic production activities	35	—	—
Total *for* AGI deductions	36	20	
Adjusted Gross Income (AGI)	37	21	
Itemized or Standard Deduction*	40a*	24a	2, 5
Increase in Standard Deduction Sch. L	40b	24b	5
Personal Exemptions	42	26	2
Taxable Income	43	27	
Regular Income Tax	44	28	1, 2
Alternative Minimum Tax (AMT)	45	(in line 28)	13
Tax Credits			
Foreign tax credit	47	—	9
Child and dependent care	48	29	9
Elderly and disabled	53	30	9
Education credits	49	31	9
Retirement savings contributions credit	50	32	9
Child tax credit	51	33	9
Miscellaneous other credits	52 & 53	—	—
Total Credits	54	34	—
Income Tax Subtotal	55	35	
Other Taxes			
Self-employment tax	56	—	6
Unreported social security tax	57	—	—
Tax on retirement plans	58	—	11
Advance earned income credits	59	36	9
Household employment taxes	59	—	10
Total Tax before Payments (tax liability)	60	37	

(continued)

TABLE 2-1
(concluded)

Description	Form 1040 Line Location	Form 1040A Line Location	Chapter Where Discussed
Payments			
Withholding	61	38	1, 2, 10
Estimated tax payments	62	39	2
Making work pay and government retiree credits, Sch. M	63	40	9
Earned income credit	64a	41a	2, 9
Additional child tax credit	65	42	2, 9
Refundable education credit	66	43	9
First-time homebuyer credit	67	—	—
Amount paid with extension	68	—	2
Excess social security tax withheld	69	—	2
Other miscellaneous payments	70	—	—
Total payments	71	44	—
Overpayment	72	45	—
Amount of refund	73a	46a	1, 2
Amount owed	75	48	1, 2
Estimated tax penalty	76	49	

*Only itemized deductions are permitted on Form 1040.

A taxpayer should use the form that is right for him or her. For example, a taxpayer who is single or married and has only wage income can use any of the three forms (although Form 1040EZ is the most logical). However, a taxpayer who has dividend income cannot use Form 1040EZ—because taxpayers cannot report dividend income on that form—but could use either Form 1040A or Form 1040. Similarly, if a taxpayer needs to itemize deductions or has self-employed business income, Form 1040 is the only appropriate form.

In the remainder of the chapter, we will discuss some basic topics that pertain to both Form 1040A and Form 1040.

Adjusted Gross Income (Form 1040A, line 21 or Form 1040, line 37)

Before we begin to discuss some of the items introduced on Form 1040A or 1040, we need to introduce the concept of *Adjusted Gross Income* (AGI). The tax code defines AGI as gross income minus a list of permitted deductions.[1] In practice, calculation of AGI is simple: Just subtract all of the *for* AGI deductions (summarized on Form 1040A line 20 or Form 1040 line 36) from total income (shown on Form 1040A line 15 or Form 1040 line 22). *For* AGI deductions are deductions that a taxpayer can take prior to calculating AGI.

AGI is an extremely important concept. Many deductions and credits are determined with reference to it. Furthermore, when a taxpayer's AGI exceeds certain levels, certain tax benefits are reduced or eliminated. We will refer to AGI throughout this text.

CONCEPT CHECK 2-1—LO 1

1. When preparing a tax return, you should always use Form 1040. True or false?
2. The concept of Adjusted Gross Income (AGI) is important because many deductions and credits reported on the tax return are computed based on the amount shown as AGI. True or false?

[1] The permitted deductions are given in IRC § 62(a).

FILING STATUS (FORMS 1040A AND 1040, LINES 1–5)
LO 2

The amount of tax liability depends on many factors, including the filing status of the taxpayer(s). Because of individual circumstances, taxpayers file their returns as one of the following: (1) Single, (2) Married Filing Jointly, (3) Married Filing Separately, (4) Head of Household, or (5) Qualifying Widow(er) with dependent child. Taxpayers must choose the filing status that is appropriate for them. We discuss each of these classifications next.

Single

Individuals use a filing status of single if they are not married and if they do not qualify as either head of household or qualifying widow(er). Marital status is determined on the last day of the tax year.

For purposes of this section, individuals also are single if a divorce or separate maintenance decree was legally executed on or before December 31 of the tax year.

Married Filing Jointly

A couple that is legally married on the last day of the tax year can file one joint tax return that combines all income, deductions, and credits of both spouses.[2] It does not matter if only one spouse earns all of the income. The marital status of a couple is determined under the laws of the state in which they reside. If a spouse dies during the year, the surviving taxpayer can file a joint return if the couple was married on the date of death and the surviving spouse has not remarried as of December 31 of the tax year.

As stated in the section for single status, a person who is legally separated from his or her spouse under a decree of divorce or separate maintenance is not considered married.[3] However, couples in the process of obtaining a divorce (that is not yet final) can file a joint return.

If either spouse is a nonresident alien at any time during the year, generally that person cannot file a joint return. This is because the non-U.S. income of a nonresident spouse is not taxable in the United States. However, if both spouses agree to subject their worldwide income to U.S. taxation, they can file a joint return.

Married Filing Separately

A married couple can elect to file two separate returns rather than one joint return.[4] Only in unusual circumstances is it advantageous for a married couple to file separate returns rather than a joint return.

A taxpayer who files as married filing separately must show the name and social security number of his or her spouse on Form 1040 or Form 1040A. (See Exhibits 2-1 and 2-2.) Additionally, if one taxpayer itemizes deductions, the other spouse must also itemize even if his or her itemized deductions are less than the standard deduction. The standard deduction can be taken only if both of them choose the standard deduction. For a more detailed discussion of this topic, see the sections about standard deductions later in this chapter and about itemized deductions in Chapter 5.

Head of Household

To qualify as head of household, a taxpayer must be unmarried at the end of the tax year, be a U.S. citizen or resident throughout the year, not be a qualifying widow(er), and maintain a household that is the principal place of abode of a *qualifying person* for more than half of

---

[2] IRC § 7703(a)(1) and IRC § 6013(a).

[3] IRC § 7703(a)(2).

[4] IRC § 1(d).

EXHIBIT 2-3   Who Is a Qualifying Person for Filing as Head of Household?[1]

IF the person is your ...	AND ...	THEN that person is ...
qualifying child (such as a son, daughter, or grandchild who lived with you more than half the year and meets certain other tests)[2]	he or she is single	a qualifying person, whether or not you can claim an exemption for the person.
	he or she is married **and** you can claim an exemption for him or her	a qualifying person.
	he or she is married **and** you cannot claim an exemption for him or her	not a qualifying person. [3]
qualifying relative [4] who is your father or mother	you can claim an exemption for him or her[5]	a qualifying person.[6]
	you cannot claim an exemption for him or her	not a qualifying person.
qualifying relative [4] other than your father or mother (such as a grandparent, brother, or sister who meets certain tests)	he or she lived with you more than half the year, **and** he or she is related to you in one of the ways listed under *Relatives who do not have to live with you* in Chapter 3 **and** you can claim an exemption for him or her [5]	a qualifying person.
	he or she did not live with you more than half the year	not a qualifying person.
	he or she is not related to you in one of the ways listed under *Relatives who do not have to live with you* in Chapter 3 and is your qualifying relative only because he or she lived with you all year as a member of your household	not a qualifying person.
	you cannot claim an exemption for him or her	not a qualifying person.

[1]A person cannot qualify more than one taxpayer to use the head of household filing status for the year.
[2]The term "qualifying child" is defined in Chapter 3. **Note.** If you are a noncustodial parent, the term "qualifying child" for head of household filing status does not include a child who is your qualifying child for exemption purposes only because of the rules described under *Children of divorced or separated parents* under *Qualifying Child* in Chapter 3. If you are the custodial parent and those rules apply, the child generally is your qualifying child for head of household filing status even though the child is not a qualifying child for whom you can claim an exemption.
[3] This person is a qualifying person if the only reason you cannot claim the exemption is that you can be claimed as a dependent on someone else's return.
[4]The term "qualifying relative" is defined in Chapter 3.
[5]If you can claim an exemption for a person only because of a multiple support agreement, that person is not a qualifying person. See *Multiple Support Agreement* in Chapter 3.
[6]See *Special rule for parent* for an additional requirement.

Caution: See the text of this chapter for the other requirements you must meet to claim head of household filing status.

Source: IRS Publication 17.

the year. Temporary absences, such as attending school, do not disqualify the person under this section.

Also to qualify as maintaining a household, a taxpayer must pay for more than half the cost of keeping up a home for the year. These costs include rent or mortgage payments, real estate taxes, home insurance, utilities, maintenance and repair, and food eaten in the home. Nonqualifying costs are personal expenditures such as clothing, medical costs, transportation costs, and the like.[5]

A special rule allows a taxpayer's parents to live in a household separate from that of the taxpayer and still permits the taxpayer to qualify for head of household status. However, the taxpayer must pay for more than half of the cost of the household where the parents live.

To understand the definition of a qualifying person for head of household filing status, refer to Exhibit 2-3, from IRS Publication 17. Notice that a *qualifying relative* who is a dependent only because this person lived with the taxpayer for the entire year is not a qualifying person for head of household.

[5] Reg. § 1.2-2(d).

Qualifying Widow(er) with Dependent Child

If a spouse dies during the tax year, the surviving spouse usually can file a joint return. For the two tax years following the death of a spouse, the surviving spouse may be eligible to file as a qualifying widow(er) if all the following conditions are satisfied:

- The taxpayer was eligible to file a joint return in the year the spouse died.

- The taxpayer did not remarry before the end of the tax year in question.

- The taxpayer paid more than half the cost of keeping up a household (see the "Head of Household" section for costs that qualify).

- The household was the principal place of abode for the entire year (except for temporary absences) of both the taxpayer and a child, stepchild, or adopted child who can be claimed as a dependent by the taxpayer (see the rules concerning dependents given later).

   This filing status is also called *surviving spouse.*[6]

CONCEPT CHECK 2-2—LO 2

1. Even though you are in the process of getting a divorce, you can file as married filing jointly. True or false?
2. The social security number of the taxpayer's spouse must be shown on the taxpayer's tax return when filing as married filing separately. True or false?
3. A surviving spouse who qualified as married filing jointly when the spouse died can file as a qualifying widow(er) for the next two years as long as the surviving spouse pays for more than half the cost of keeping up a household and does not remarry. True or false?

PERSONAL EXEMPTIONS (FORMS 1040A AND 1040, LINES 6A–B)
LO 3

In computing taxable income, taxpayers can deduct an exemption amount from AGI for each personal and dependency exemption.[7] The taxpayer receives an exemption for himself or herself, his or her spouse, and each dependent.[8] Dependency exemptions are explained in the next section.

   The exemption amount is subject to annual adjustment for inflation. For 2009 the exemption amount is $3,650 per individual.

   Someone can be claimed as an exemption only once. If a taxpayer is claimed as a dependent on another return, no personal exemption is allowed on the taxpayer's return. This may occur, for example, when a dependent child must file his or her own return because of earnings from a part-time job. The child cannot claim a personal exemption on his or her own return because the parents can claim him or her as a dependent on their return.

CONCEPT CHECK 2-3—LO 3

1. If you file a tax return with your spouse, you can claim a total of $7,300 for personal exemptions. True or false?

---

[6] IRC § 2(a).

[7] IRC § 151.

[8] IRC § 151(b) and IRC §151(c).

DEPENDENCY EXEMPTIONS (FORMS 1040A AND 1040, LINE 6C)
LO 4

Dependents are listed on line 6c of Forms 1040A and 1040, and line 6d shows the total number of personal and dependency exemptions claimed by the taxpayer. The existence and number of dependents affect the determination of total tax liability in areas such as personal and dependency exemptions, child credits, and filing status.

The amount on line 26 (Form 1040A) or line 42 (Form 1040) represents the number of exemptions (from the box on line 6d) multiplied by the exemption amount ($3,650 in 2009).

Beginning in 2005, a taxpayer can claim a dependency exemption if the person is *a qualifying child or a qualifying relative* and the person meets all of the following tests:

1. Dependent taxpayer test.
2. Joint return test.
3. Citizen or resident test.

The dependent taxpayer test means that if an individual can be claimed as a dependent by someone else, then the taxpayer cannot claim a dependency exemption for that person. This is the case even if the person is a qualifying child or qualifying relative of the taxpayer.

For the joint return test, the taxpayer cannot claim a dependency exemption for someone who files a joint return with his or her spouse.[9] However, if the dependent files a joint return simply to claim a refund (that is, if there is no tax liability on the joint return and there would be no tax liability on separate returns), then a dependency exemption is allowed.[10]

EXAMPLE 2-1

Mary is the daughter of Joseph and Iris Jefferson. Mary married Peter Young in January 2009. The Youngs are both 18 years old, are full-time students at State University, and have lived, for the entire year, with the Jeffersons, who paid for all the living expenses of both Mary and Peter. Mary and Peter both work part-time at the university, and each earned $1,000 during the year, from which their employer withheld income taxes. The Youngs had no other sources of income, and they filed a joint tax return for 2009. Assume that, in all respects other than the joint return test, the Jeffersons can claim Mary and Peter as dependents. In this case, the Jeffersons will receive the dependency exemption for Mary and Peter. Even though Mary and Peter filed a joint return, it was solely to claim a refund. The tax liability on a joint return would be zero, and if they filed separate returns, there would still be no liability.

TAX YOUR BRAIN

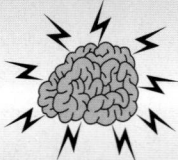

Use the information in Example 2-1, but assume that Mary and Peter each earned $20,000 from their university employment. Who is entitled to the dependency exemption?

ANSWER

No one. The joint tax return of Mary and Peter would show a tax liability. Thus the Jeffersons cannot claim the dependency exemption because Mary and Peter do not meet the joint return test. Mary and Peter would not receive the dependency exemption either. The IRS deems that the person or persons filing a tax return are not dependents. Mary and Peter would, however, each be entitled to a personal exemption on their joint tax return. Note that the answer would be the same even if Mary and Peter filed separate returns.

---

[9] IRC § 152(b)(2).
[10] Rev. Rul. 54-567, Rev. Rul. 65-34.

An individual meets the citizen or resident test if the person is (a) a U.S. citizen, resident, or national, (b) a resident of Canada or Mexico, or (c) an adopted child of the taxpayer if the child is a member of the taxpayer's household all year and the taxpayer is a U.S. citizen or national.[11]

Recall that to claim someone as a dependent, the individual must meet the three tests noted above, *and* the individual must be either a qualifying child or a qualifying relative. We will define those terms next.

Qualifying Child

A person is a qualifying child if he or she meets *all five* of the following tests:

1. Relationship test.
2. Age test.
3. Residency test.
4. Support test.
5. Special test for qualifying child of more than one taxpayer.

Relationship Test

The relationship test is met if the dependent is *one* of the following:

- Child or descendant of child (grandchild or great-grandchild).
- Stepchild.
- Eligible foster child.
- Brother, sister, half-brother, half-sister, stepbrother, or stepsister, or a descendant of them.[12]

A child includes an adopted child and includes a child placed for adoption in the taxpayer's household by an authorized adoption agency even if the adoption is not finalized.[13] Cousins are not included in the definition of qualifying child.

Age Test

At the end of the tax year, the child must be *one* of the following:

- Under the age of 19.
- Under the age of 24 and a full-time student. A full-time student is a person who was in school full-time during any part of each of five calendar months during the calendar year.
- Totally and permanently disabled regardless of age.

Beginning in 2009, the child must be younger than the person claiming the dependency.

Residency Test

The child must live with the taxpayer for more than half of the year to meet this requirement. Temporary absences are exceptions to this rule if the absences are due to education, vacation, illness, or military service.

Support Test

The child must not provide more than half of his or her support. The definition of *support* is broad. It "includes food, shelter, clothing, medical and dental care, education, and the like."[14] Items such as medical insurance premiums, child care, toys, gifts, and vacations have been found to be includable in support, whereas life insurance premiums have been excluded. A scholarship is not counted as support if it is received by, and used in support of, a child (including stepchild, foster child, adopted child, or child placed for adoption) who is a full-time student at an educational institution.[15]

[11] IRC § 152(b)(3).
[12] IRC § 152(c)(2).
[13] Reg § 1.152-2(c)(2).
[14] Reg. § 1.152-1(a)(2)(i).
[15] IRC § 152(F)(5).

EXHIBIT 2-4
When More Than One Person Files a Return Claiming the Same Qualifying Child (Tie-Breaker Rule)

IF more than one person files a return claiming the same qualifying child and . . .	THEN the child will be treated as the qualifying child of the. . .
only one of the persons is the child's parent,	parent.
two of the persons are parents of the child and they do not file a joint return together,	parent with whom the child lived for the longer period of time during the year.
two of the persons are parents of the child, they do not file a joint return together, and the child lived with each parent the same amount of time during the year,	parent with the highest adjusted gross income (AGI).
none of the persons are the child's parent,	person with the highest AGI and having an AGI higher than the highest AGI of any parent of the child.

Source: IRS Publication 17.

For items paid for in cash, support is the amount paid. For noncash items such as lodging, use the fair market value of the item to determine the amount of support.

Special Test for Qualifying Child of More Than One Taxpayer

If a child meets the other four tests and can be a qualifying child for more than one taxpayer, only one individual can claim the exemption. The IRS lets you decide who the taxpayer claiming the exemption should be. However, if you cannot make a decision, the IRS will use the tie-breaker rule as shown in Exhibit 2-4 (from IRS Publication 17).

Child of Divorced or Separated Parents

In most cases, a child of divorced or separated parents will be the qualifying child of the parent with custody. However, the child will be deemed to be the qualifying child of the noncustodial parent if all the following tests are met:

- The child has been in the custody of either or both parents for more than half of the year.
- Either or both parents provided more than half the child's support.
- The parents are (a) divorced or legally separated, (b) separated under a written separation agreement, or (c) living apart at all times during the last six months of the year.
- The decree or separation agreement for 2009 states that the noncustodial parent can claim the child as a dependent, or the custodial parent signs a written document specifying that the child will not be claimed as a dependent.

Beginning after July 2, 2008, Form 8332 or a similar form must be used to revoke a release of claim to exemption that was previously released to the noncustodial parent. Additionally, if the custodial parent gives notice of revocation in 2009, the revocation takes effect in tax year 2010.

CONCEPT CHECK 2-4—LO 4

1. What are the five specific tests you need to meet to claim someone as a qualifying child?

2. To meet the age test, a child who is not disabled must be _____ or _____ if a full-time student.

Qualifying Relative

A person is a qualifying relative if he or she meets *all four* of the following tests:

1. Not a qualifying child test.
2. Relationship or member of household test.
3. Gross income test.
4. Support test.

The four tests are discussed in the next paragraphs.

Not a Qualifying Child Test

If a child is your qualifying child or the qualifying child of another taxpayer, he or she cannot be your qualifying relative.

Relationship or Member of Household Test

The person either must be a member of the taxpayer's household for the entire year *or* must be related to the taxpayer in *one* of the following ways:

- Child or descendant of child (grandchild or great-grandchild).
- Stepchild.
- Eligible foster child.
- Brother, sister, half-brother, half-sister, stepbrother, or stepsister, or a descendant of them.
- Father or mother.
- Brother or sister of parents.
- Son-in-law, daughter-in-law, father-in-law, mother-in-law, brother-in-law, or sister-in-law.

Note that if someone is related to the taxpayer (as indicated in the preceding list), it is not necessary that the person live with the taxpayer for the entire year or, actually, any part of the year. But it may be difficult to meet the support test if the individual does not live in the household.

Gross Income Test

The dependent must *not* have gross income equal to or greater than the amount of the exemption. The amount of the exemption is subject to annual adjustment for inflation. For tax year 2009, the exemption amount is $3,650.

For purposes of this test, gross income does not include certain items such as tax-exempt interest, the nontaxable portion of social security benefits, and the nontaxable portion of a scholarship or fellowship.

Support Test

The taxpayer must provide over 50% of the dependent's support.[16] Recall that the definition of support was explained in the "Qualifying Child" section.

In practice, a taxpayer must determine how much was paid for the support of the dependent (regardless of who paid it) and then determine whether the taxpayer provided over half of that support.

If several dependents receive the benefits of an item of support, allocate the cost of the item to the dependents on a pro rata basis unless the taxpayer can show that a different allocation is appropriate.[17] Money received by a dependent and spent by him or her counts as support. Examples include wages from a part-time job or social security benefits paid to a dependent.

Do not confuse the issue of what expenditures qualify for support with the issue of who paid for the expenditures. These are different but related concepts. Confusion can arise because sometimes it is easier to determine the total amount of support by reference to where the money came from rather than by creating an itemized list of support paid on behalf of an individual.

The support test has two exceptions. The first occurs when several persons provide for more than half the support of someone, but no one person meets the 50% threshold.[18] If each person in the group would be able to claim the individual as a dependent (absent the support test) and no one person in the group furnished more than half of the individual's support, then one of the persons in the group who provided more than 10% of the support can claim the dependent with the agreement of the other persons in the group. Such a multiple support agreement must

---

[16] IRC § 152(a).
[17] Rev. Rul. 64-222, 1964-2 CB 47.
[18] IRC § 152(d)(3).

be in writing; taxpayers use Form 2120 for this purpose. Each person who meets the 10% test but who will not be claiming the dependency exemption must fill out Form 2120. The taxpayer who will receive the exemption must file all the Forms 2120 with his or her return.

If someone is the subject of a multiple support agreement over a number of years, it is not necessary that the same individual claim the dependency exemption each year.

EXAMPLE 2-2

Lisa, Monique, Terry, Robert, and Angie provided all the support for Donald in the following percentages:

Lisa (friend)	30%
Monique (neighbor)	5%
Terry (son)	40%
Robert (son)	10%
Angie (daughter)	15%

Initially you need to determine the members of the group who could claim Donald as a dependent, absent the support test. These are Terry, Robert, and Angie, who are Donald's children (Lisa and Monique cannot claim Donald because he does not meet the relationship test). Next determine whether Terry, Robert, and Angie (as a group) contributed more than 50% of Donald's support. In this case, they contributed 65%. If a multiple support agreement is prepared, either Terry or Angie would be entitled to claim Donald as a dependent. Robert is not entitled to the exemption because he did not contribute *more* than 10% of Donald's support.

TAX YOUR BRAIN

Using Example 2-2, assume that Donald had a part-time job that provided 25% of his support. The other five people provided the remaining 75% of Donald's support in the same proportions given. Which person(s) would be entitled to the dependency exemption for purposes of a multiple support agreement?

ANSWER

No one would be entitled to the dependency exemption. We previously determined that only Terry, Robert, and Angie would have been entitled to claim Donald as a dependent, absent the support test. These three people must supply over half of Donald's support. Here the three individuals contributed only 48.75% of Donald's support (65% of the 75% not paid by Donald). Thus no one can claim Donald as a dependent.

The second exception to the 50% support test is the case of a child of divorced or separated parents. If the child is not a qualifying child, he or she can be treated as a qualifying relative of the noncustodial parent if the following are true:

• The child has been in the custody of either or both parents for more than half the year.

• Either or both parents provided more than half the child's support.

• The parents are (1) divorced or legally separated, (2) separated under a written separation agreement, or (3) living apart at all times during the last six months of the year.

• The decree or separation agreement for 2009 states that the noncustodial parent can claim the child as a dependent, or the custodial parent relinquishes the dependency exemption to the noncustodial parent by signing a written agreement to that effect.[19] However, the agreement is not binding on future tax years.

The preceding tests do not apply if the support of the child is determined based on a multiple support agreement.

---

[19] IRC § 152(e)(2).

**CONCEPT
CHECK 2-5—LO 4**

1. You must meet one of these four tests to be a qualifying relative: not a qualifying child test, relationship or member of household test, gross income test, and support test. True or false?
2. A qualifying relative can earn up to $5,700 for the year 2009. True or false?

Phaseout of Exemption Deduction

Taxpayers receive deductions, credits, or other benefits for many items reported on an individual tax return. Once the AGI of the taxpayer exceeds certain amounts, the tax law restricts the benefit of some of these deductions and credits. A few examples of items that have AGI limitations include personal and dependency exemptions, itemized deductions, the earned income tax credit, the child care credit, the child credit, and deductibility of IRA contributions.[20] Often the law permits the benefit for AGI below a specified dollar amount, reduces the benefit as AGI increases, and eliminates the benefit entirely when AGI exceeds a higher figure. For some items, a certain AGI threshold represents the dividing line between fully receiving a benefit and not receiving it at all. AGI thresholds differ depending on filing status and on the deduction, credit, or other benefit in question.

The allowed deduction for personal and dependency exemptions is subject to phaseout. The AGI limits are subject to annual inflation adjustments. Thresholds in effect for 2009 are as follows:

Filing Status	Lower AGI Threshold	Personal and Dependency Exemptions Reduced When AGI Exceeds
Married filing separately	$125,100	$186,350
Single	166,800	289,300
Head of household	208,500	331,000
Married filing jointly	250,200	372,700
Qualifying widow(er)	250,200	372,700

For each $2,500 ($1,250 for married filing separately), or a portion thereof, by which a taxpayer's AGI exceeds the lower threshold, the deduction for exemptions must be reduced by 2% of the personal and dependency exemption. When AGI exceeds the higher number, the exemption deduction is $2,433(2/3 of $3,650).

EXAMPLE 2-3

Tom and Esther are married and have three children who qualify as dependents. Without regard to their AGI, their personal and dependency exemption deduction is $18,250 ($3,650 × 5) in year 2009. If their AGI is below $250,200, they will receive the full benefit of the deduction, and if their AGI exceeds $372,700, they will receive an exemption deduction of $2,433. Their deduction will be reduced by $365 ($18,250 × 2%) for each AGI increment of $2,500 (or portion thereof) above $250,200. Assume Tom and Esther's AGI is $263,500. Their allowed exemption deduction is

AGI	$263,500
Less lower AGI threshold	250,200
Excess	13,300
	÷2,500
Number of $2,500 increments	5.32
Rounded up	6
Multiply by their reduction amount per increment	× $365
Reduction required before the 2/3	$ 2,190

[20] These items are discussed in detail in subsequent chapters.

Thus the exemption deduction for Tom and Esther is $17,520 ($18,250 − $730) for tax year 2009. The $2,190 reduction is limited to a loss of ⅔ of the exemption amount ($2,190 − $1,460).

STANDARD DEDUCTION (FORM 1040A, LINE 24a OR FORM 1040, LINE 40a)
LO 5

Taxpayers can subtract a standard deduction from AGI.[21] Taxpayers may alternatively elect to subtract itemized deductions and should do so if their itemized deductions are larger than the standard deduction amount.[22] Note that taxpayers who elect to itemize their deductions cannot use Form 1040A—that form permits taxpayers to use only standard deductions.

The standard deduction is the sum of the basic standard deduction and the additional standard deduction.[23] Both components depend on filing status and are subject to annual adjustment for inflation. The basic standard deduction for tax year 2009 is as follows:

Filing Status	Basic Standard Deduction
Single	$ 5,700
Married filing jointly	11,400
Married filing separately	5,700
Head of household	8,350
Qualifying widow(er)	11,400

Taxpayers who either are 65 or older or are blind can claim an additional standard deduction. Taxpayers who are both 65 or older and blind get two additional standard deductions. Note that blind taxpayers are entitled to the additional standard deduction regardless of their age. The additional standard deductions for taxpayers who are 65 or older or blind are

Filing Status	Tax Year 2009
Single	$1,400
Married filing jointly	1,100
Married filing separately	1,100
Head of household	1,400
Qualifying widow(er)	1,100

In addition for 2008 and 2009 taxpayers who do not itemize can take an additional standard deduction amount for real property taxes and other items. These additional items are reported on Schedule L and are discussed in Chapter 5.

EXAMPLE 2-4

Flora is 57 years old, single, and blind. She is entitled to a standard deduction of $7,100 ($5,700 + $1,400). If she were 69 instead of 57, she would have a standard deduction of $8,500 ($5,700 + $1,400 + $1,400).

EXAMPLE 2-5

Peter and Sarah are married and have an eight-year-old dependent child who is blind. Peter and Sarah are entitled to a standard deduction of $11,400. This example illustrates that the additional standard deduction applies only to the taxpayer and the spouse, if any. Dependents do not affect the standard deduction computation.

[21] IRC § 63(c).
[22] We discuss itemized deductions in Chapter 5.
[23] IRC § 63(c)(1).

The standard deduction is zero in any of the following instances:

- A married couple files separate returns and one spouse itemizes deductions. In this case, the other spouse must also itemize.
- A taxpayer is a nonresident alien.
- A taxpayer files a return for a period of less than 12 months because of a change in accounting period.

When a taxpayer can be claimed as a dependent on the tax return of another individual, the basic standard deduction for the taxpayer is limited to the greater of (1) $950 or (2) the taxpayer's earned income plus $300, but not more than the amount of the basic standard deduction.[24] Earned income is generally income from work or the efforts of the taxpayer. Salaries and wages are the most common type of earned income.

Congress enacted the preceding rule to prevent taxpayers from shifting income to their children or other dependents. For example, a couple could give a child a bond that pays interest of $3,500 per year. Without the rule, the entire $3,500 interest income would be tax-free because the basic standard deduction for any filing status exceeds the amount of income. With the rule in place, the standard deduction for the child would be $950.

The standard deduction increases, in effect, for the wages of the dependent person. This permits children, for example, to work a part-time summer job for some extra spending money but not have to pay income taxes.

EXAMPLE 2-6	Linda's parents can claim her as a dependent on their tax return. In 2009 her only source of income was a part-time job in a local store where she earned $2,500 during the year. Linda's standard deduction is $2,800, which is the greater of (a) $950 or (b) $2,500 + $300. As a result, Linda would owe no income tax on her wages.

EXAMPLE 2-7	In 2009 Charles received $1,100 of interest income from a local bank. The interest was his only source of income for the year. His standard deduction is $950, which is the greater of (a) $950 or (b) $0 + $300.

CONCEPT CHECK 2-6—LO 5	1. What is the amount of the standard deduction in each of the following cases?
	    a. The taxpayer is single, 41 years of age, and blind.
	    b. The taxpayer is head of household, 35 years of age, and not blind.
	    c. The taxpayers are married filing jointly, the husband is 67 and the wife is 61 years of age, and neither is blind.

TAX DUE TO IRS
LO 6

It is important to learn how to compute the amount of tax and arrive at the total liability amount. We illustrate some steps to help you determine these two items before we discuss tax payments.

[24] IRC § 63(c)(5). The dollar value given in (1) is for tax year 2009 and is adjusted annually for inflation.

2-20 Chapter 2 *Expanded Tax Formula, Forms 1040A and 1040, and Basic Concepts*

Amount of Tax (Form 1040A, line 28 or Form 1040, line 44)

Most taxpayers determine the amount of tax by looking up the applicable tax due in a tax table.

The tax tables used in the preparation of Form 1040A or 1040 are in Appendix D of this text. As you can see, there are columns for (1) Single, (2) Married Filing Jointly, (3) Married Filing Separately, and (4) Head of Household. The Qualifying Widow(er) filing status uses the same column as Married Filing Jointly.

EXAMPLE 2-8

A taxpayer has taxable income of $71,330. Referring to the tax tables, we can see that the amount of tax for line 28 (Form 1040A) or line 44 (Form 1040) would be $14,019 for a single person, $10,206 for a married couple filing jointly or a qualifying widow(er), $12,684 for head of household, or $14,103 for a married couple filing separately.

The tax tables stop at taxable income of less than $100,000. Taxpayers with taxable income of $100,000 or more must use the tax rate schedules provided on the inside front cover of this text. Recall that the IRS uses tax rate schedules to create the tax tables according to the midpoint of each $50 range.

Total Tax Liability (Form 1040A, line 37 or Form 1040, line 60)

This line represents the total amount the taxpayer must pay to the government for the tax year.

Tax Payments (Form 1040A, lines 38–43 or Form 1040, lines 61–70)

Taxpayers must pay the amount of tax indicated on the total tax line (line 37 on Form 1040A or line 60 on Form 1040). Normally, taxpayers pay some or all of their tax liability prior to the due date of the tax return. Most commonly, taxpayers make payment through income tax withholding and quarterly estimated tax payments, although other payment methods are also possible.

Income Tax Withholding (Form 1040A, line 38 or Form 1040, line 61)

When certain taxable payments are made to individuals, the payer must retain (withhold) a proportion of the payment otherwise due and remit the amount withheld to the U.S. Treasury. The withheld amount represents an estimate of the amount of income tax that would be due for the year on the taxable payment. The IRS credits withholding to the account of the appropriate taxpayer. Withholding reduces the amount otherwise due the IRS on the due date of the return.

For most taxpayers, withholding comes from two sources. First, when an employer pays a salary or wages to an employee, the employer is required to retain part of the amount otherwise due the employee and to pay the retained amount, for the benefit of the employee, to the federal government. The amount retained is the payroll tax withholding, which is a part of virtually every pay stub in the country.[25] Employers report the total amount withheld from the earnings of an employee on a Form W-2 given to each employee shortly after the end of the calendar year.

Second, income tax withholding can also occur when a taxpayer receives interest, dividends, rents, royalties, pension plan distributions, and similar payments. In certain circumstances, payers are required to withhold a portion of the payment and remit it to the government. The concept is similar to that used for wage payments. Payers report the amount of the total payment and the amount withheld on a Form 1099 provided to the taxpayer. Pension plan distributions are the most common payment requiring or permitting withholding.

---

[25] Chapter 10 discusses payer rules associated with determining and remitting withholding taxes, social security tax, and Medicare tax.

Estimated Tax Payments (Form 1040A, line 39 or Form 1040, line 62)

Taxpayers must pay their tax liability throughout the tax year, not at the time they file their tax return. If taxes withheld approximate the total tax liability for the year (the situation for most taxpayers), no estimated payments are due. However, a taxpayer who has income that is not subject to withholding may be required to make estimated payments during the year.[26] Failure to do so may subject the taxpayer to an underpayment penalty.[27]

Taxpayers must make periodic payments based on the *required annual payment,* which is defined as the lesser of 90% of the tax shown on the return or 100% of the tax shown on the return for the preceding year.[28] Payments are equal to 25% of the required annual payment and are due on April 15, June 15, September 15, and January 15. For taxpayers with prior year AGI over $150,000, the 100% figure increases to 110%.

As noted previously, failure to make required estimated payments will subject the taxpayer to a potential underpayment penalty plus interest. However, taxpayers are not assessed a penalty if the difference between the tax shown on the return and the amount of tax withheld for wages is less than $1,000.[29]

Exhibit 2-5 is a flowchart from IRS Publication 17 that illustrates the decision process associated with determining whether estimated payments are required.

EXHIBIT 2-5   Do You Have to Pay Estimated Tax?

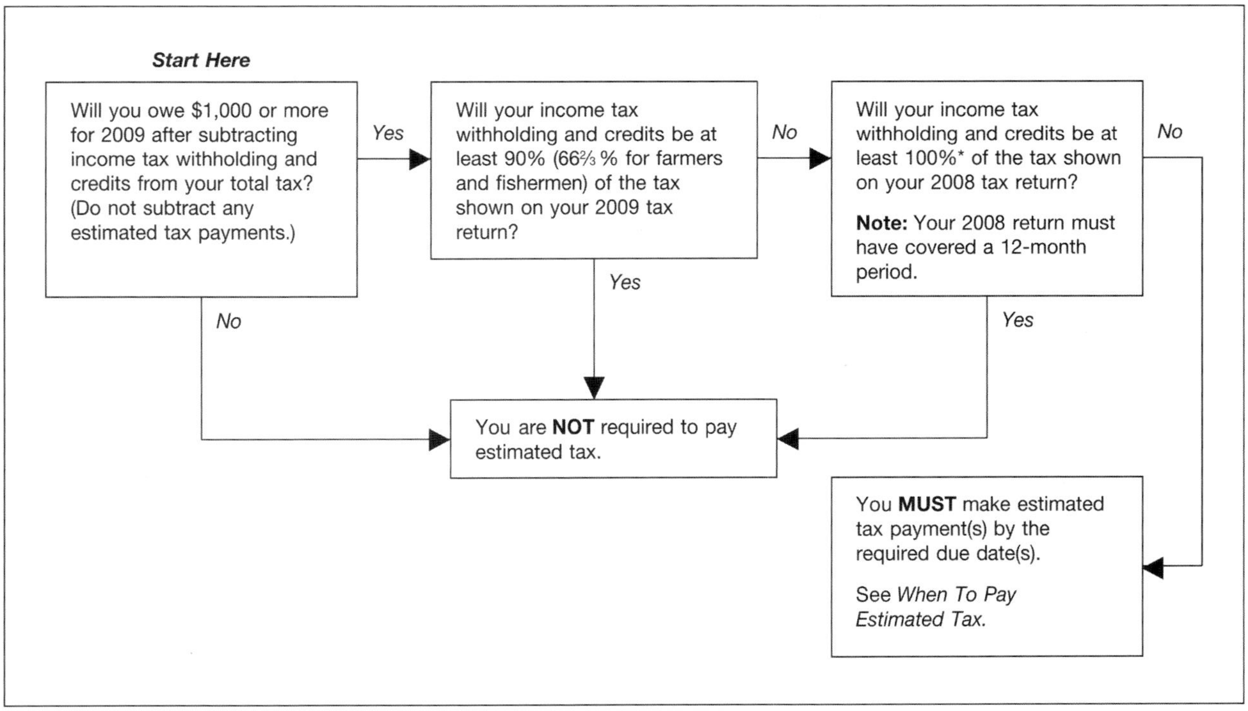

* 110% if less than two-thirds of your gross income for 2008 and 2009 is from farming or fishing and your 2008 adjusted gross income was more than $150,000 ($75,000 if your filing status for 2009 is married filing a separate return).

Source: IRS Publication 17.

[26] IRC § 6654(d).
[27] IRC § 6654(a).
[28] IRC § 6654(d)(1)(B).
[29] IRC § 6654(e)(1).

EXAMPLE 2-9

Janice, who is single, had taxable income of $40,000 in 2009 and had a total tax liability for the year of $6,194. During 2010 she will work only part-time, earn $25,000, and have income tax withholding of $4,100. She receives additional income from selling paintings. Based on her expected painting sales and wage earnings, she expects her tax liability for 2010 will be $6,830. To avoid an underpayment penalty, Janice must make estimated tax payments during 2010. Janice's required annual payment is $6,147, which is the lower of (a) 90% of $6,830 (the tax expected to show on her 2010 return) or (b) $6,194 (the amount of her 2009 liability). Because she expects to have taxes of $4,100 withheld from her paycheck, she must pay the remaining $2,047 ($6,147 − $4,100) in estimated payments during 2010. She must pay the amount in four equal installments of $511.75 on the dates indicated previously. Note that if Janice's 2010 tax liability actually turns out to be exactly $6,830, she will still owe $683 ($6,830 liability minus withholding of $4,100 minus estimated payments of $2,047) when she files her 2010 tax return.

TAX YOUR BRAIN

Assume that Janice's year 2010 wage income will be $50,000 (she worked full-time) and she will have $8,300 withheld from her wages. Also assume that she expects to sell a large number of paintings and that she estimates her total 2010 tax liability will be $18,000. To avoid an underpayment penalty, does Janice need to pay estimated payments during 2010 and, if so, how much must she pay?

ANSWER

Janice does not need to make any estimated payments. Her required annual payment is $6,194, which is the lower of (a) 90% of $18,000 (the estimate of her 2010 tax liability) or (b) $6,194 (her tax liability for 2009). Because her estimated tax withholdings are $8,300, she is not obligated to make estimated payments. She will need to pay the remaining $9,700 ($18,000 − $8,300) no later than April 15, 2011.

Other Payments (Form 1040A, lines 40–43 or Form 1040, lines 63–70)

Taxpayers with earned income (wages, salaries, tips, or earnings from self-employment) below certain limits are entitled to a tax credit.[30] Usually credits are shown on lines 29–33 (1040A) or 47–53 (Form 1040), but the earned income credit is reported in the payments section. The amount of this credit is calculated on Schedule EIC and is reported on line 41a (Form 1040A) or 64(a) (Form 1040). We cover the EIC in Chapter 9.

Employers are required to withhold FICA (social security and Medicare) taxes from wages paid to employees. However, once wages paid to an individual employee exceed a certain limit ($106,800 in 2009), social security withholding ceases.[31] Each employer calculates the FICA withholding without regard to other employers. However, the employee simply needs to reach the limit during the calendar year. Thus an employee who works for more than one employer can have excess social security taxes withheld from his or her paychecks. Excess social security taxes are a payment toward income taxes due and are reported on Form 1040, line 69. Note that the $106,800 wage limitation is determined per taxpayer, not per tax return. Someone who has excess social security taxes withheld cannot use Form 1040A.

Qualifying taxpayers can receive a child tax credit. This credit is reported in the credits section on line 33 (Form 1040A) or line 51 (Form 1040). In certain circumstances, taxpayers can receive an additional child tax credit beyond the amount reported in the credits section. This additional credit is on line 42 or 65 on Form 1040A or 1040, respectively. We discuss the child tax credit in Chapter 9.

---

[30] IRC § 32.

[31] The limitation amount is adjusted annually based on the national average wage index. Go to www.ssa.gov for future limitation amounts. This only applies to social security and not Medicare, which has no limit on the amount of earnings.

A taxpayer may request an automatic six-month extension of time to file his or her tax return.[32] Extending the time to file the return does not extend the time to pay the applicable tax. As a result, if a taxpayer filing an extension determines that he or she owes additional tax, the payment must accompany the extension request (Form 4868). The additional payment is on Form 1040, line 68. Taxpayers paying additional tax with an extension request cannot use Form 1040A.

Taxpayers can use Form 1040, line 70, to claim certain other payments (Form 1040A cannot be used). Farmers and fishermen may be entitled to a refund of federal fuel taxes paid on fuel that was not used in a motor vehicle on the highway (such as fuel used in a farm tractor or a commercial fishing boat). The total from Form 4136 is on line 70. Certain undistributed long-term capital gains (Form 2439) and certain health insurance credits (Form 8885) are also reported on this line. The last two items are unusual.

New for 2009 are the making work pay and government retiree credits and the refundable education credit, which are reported on lines 40 or 63 and lines 43 or 66 on forms 1040A and 1040, respectively.

Tax Refund (Form 1040A, line 46a or Form 1040, line 73a) or Tax Due with Return (Form 1040A, line 48 or Form 1040, line 75)

Compare the amount owed with the total amount paid (line 37 versus line 44 on Form 1040A or line 60 versus line 71 on Form 1040). Excess payment results in a refund; excess remaining tax liability means the taxpayer must pay the remaining amount owed when filing the return.

A taxpayer who is entitled to a refund can elect to (1) receive a check, (2) have the refund deposited directly in his or her bank account, or (3) apply the excess to next year's tax return. The taxpayer who selects the direct deposit option must supply account information on lines 46b through d on Form 1040A or lines 73b through d on Form 1040.

The estimated tax penalty shown on line 49 (1040A) or 76 (1040) comes from Form 2210 and is a result of paying insufficient tax amounts throughout the year. We discuss the penalty in the following section.

CONCEPT CHECK 2-7—LO 6

1. Use the tables in Appendix D of the text to determine the tax amounts for the following situations:
   a. Single taxpayer with taxable income of $34,640.
   b. Married taxpayers filing jointly with taxable income of $67,706.
2. What is the limit on the FICA (social security) amount for 2009?

INTEREST AND TAX PENALTIES
LO 7

Failure to adhere to the tax law can subject a taxpayer to IRS assessments for penalties and interest. Although the IRS can assess a number of different penalties, it assesses only a few to individual taxpayers. In this section, we discuss the most common civil and criminal penalties applicable to individuals. We provide details on the following penalties:

- Interest charged on assessments.
- Failure to file a tax return.
- Failure to pay tax.
- Failure to pay estimated taxes.
- Substantial understatement of tax liability (accuracy-related penalties).
- Fraud penalties.
- Erroneous claim for refund or credit penalty.

[32] IRC § 6081.

From Shoebox to Software

The amount of federal tax withholding is the amount in box 2 of Form W-2 plus the amount in box 4 of all Forms 1099 received (1099-MISC, 1099-B, 1099-INT, etc.). Taxpayers may have multiple W-2 and 1099 forms. Information from W-2s and 1099s is entered into the appropriate forms in the Documents Received section of the tax return software. The software will automatically sum the various documents and will place the total on line 61. The tax preparer should check the amount on line 61 to ensure that all appropriate documentation was correctly entered.

Amounts for estimated payments will come from canceled checks or worksheets prepared when determining the appropriate payment amounts. You enter appropriate amounts in the tax software on a supporting schedule. The software utilizes this supporting schedule to record amounts paid during the year for federal and state estimated tax payments.

The Earned Income Credit and the additional child tax credit are from Schedule EIC and Form 8812, respectively.

A taxpayer who files Form 4868, Application for Automatic Extension of Time to File U.S. Individual Income Tax Return, must pay any additional tax owed with that form. The amount paid should be included on line 68 (Form 1040 only). If the tax software is used to prepare Form 4868, the amount on line 10 (amount paid) will normally be transferred to line 68. Otherwise you must directly enter any additional payment onto line 68. Retain the canceled check or other evidence of payment.

Tax preparers should determine whether excess social security taxes have been withheld when total wages (Form 1040 or 1040A, line 7) exceed the social security limit ($106,800 in 2009) and the taxpayer has received multiple Forms W-2. The tax software will automatically calculate this amount from W-2s entered into the W-2 worksheets.

Entries on line 70 (Form 1040 only) are relatively unusual. Figures come from Forms 2439, 4136, and 8885.

Interest Charged on All Assessments

Many taxpayers are under the false impression that filing a tax return extension also delays the payment of any remaining tax liability. An extension is an extension of time to file, *not* an extension of time to pay. The amount of unpaid tax liability is still due on April 15 for individual taxpayers. If the taxpayer still owes tax after April 15, the IRS assesses interest based on the remaining amount owed. The IRS charges interest on all nonpayments, underpayments, and late payments of tax. The rate charged is the federal short-term rate plus 3 percentage points.[33] Rates are set quarterly. Here are the annualized rates of interest on assessments for the past several years:

Time Period	Percentage Rate
Jan. 1, 2009, to Mar. 31, 2009	5%
Oct. 1, 2008, to Dec. 31, 2008	6
July 1, 2008, to Sept. 30, 2008	5
Apr. 1, 2008, to June 30, 2008	6
Jan. 1, 2008, to Mar. 31, 2008	7
July 1, 2007, to Dec. 31, 2007	8
July 1, 2006, to June 30, 2007	8
Oct. 1, 2005, to June 30, 2006	7
Apr. 1, 2005, to Sept. 30, 2005	6
Oct. 1, 2004, to Mar. 31, 2005	5
July 1, 2004, to Sept. 30, 2004	4
Apr. 1, 2004, to June 30, 2004	5
Oct. 1, 2003, to Mar. 30, 2004	4
Jan. 1, 2003, to Sept. 30, 2003	5

[33] IRC § 6621(a)(2).

Failure to File a Tax Return

A taxpayer who does not file a tax return by the due date of the return, plus extensions, must pay a failure to file penalty. The penalty for failure to file is 5% of the amount of tax due on the return if the failure is less than one month. For each additional month or fraction of a month, the IRS adds an additional 5% penalty, up to a maximum of 25%. Any income tax return not filed within 60 days of its due date is subject to a minimum penalty of the lesser of $135 or the amount of tax required on the return. If failure to file is due to fraud, the penalty is 15% per month, up to a maximum of 75%.[34] The IRS calculates the penalty on the tax liability shown on the return reduced by any payments made by withholding, estimated payments, or credits.

EXAMPLE 2-10	Fred was extremely busy during April and forgot to file his tax return by April 15. He did not file an extension. Fred finally filed his tax return on June and had a remaining tax liability of $2,000. Fred has a $200 failure to file penalty, calculated as follows:

Underpayment	$2,000
Penalty per month or fraction thereof (2 months × 5%)	10%
Failure to file penalty	$ 200

If a taxpayer can show the delay in filing was due to a reasonable cause, the IRS could agree to abate (forgive) the penalty. Reasonable cause occurs when the taxpayer shows that he or she exercised ordinary business care and prudence in providing for payment of his or her liability but, nevertheless, either was unable to pay the tax or would suffer an undue hardship if he or she paid on the due date.[35]

The IRS makes the abatement determination case by case based on the facts and circumstances of the particular situation.

Failure to Pay Tax

The failure to pay and the failure to file penalties are interrelated. The failure to pay penalty is 0.5% of the tax shown on the return for each month (or fraction of a month) the tax is unpaid, up to a maximum of 25%.[36]

However, the failure to file penalty (discussed earlier) is reduced by the failure to pay penalty when both apply. This means that the maximum monthly penalty is 5% when both penalties apply. The IRS will also abate the failure to pay penalty if the taxpayer can show a reasonable cause for not paying. If the taxpayer filed a proper extension to file his or her tax return, the IRS will presume a reasonable cause exists when both of the following conditions apply:

- The amount due with the tax return is less than 10% of the amount of tax shown on the tax return.

- Any balance due shown on the tax return is paid with the return.

EXAMPLE 2-11	Assume the same facts as in Example 2-10. However, Fred filed a proper automatic six-month extension to file his return. Thus his new due date is October 15. If the $2,000 owed by Fred is less than 10% of the amount of tax on the return, then there is no failure to pay penalty. There is also not a failure to file penalty because Fred obtained an extension of time to file.

[34] IRC§ 6651(f).
[35] Reg. § 301.6651-1(c).
[36] IRC § 6651(a)(2).

EXAMPLE 2-12   Assume the same facts as in Example 2-11 except that Fred does not file his tax return until December 1 and the $2,000 tax due is more than 10% of his total tax shown on the return. In this case, Fred would be subject to both the failure to file penalty and the failure to pay penalty. Because the return was due on October 15, the failure to *file* penalty runs from October 15 to December 1 (two months of penalty). Because the $2,000 is more than 10% of the total tax, the failure to *pay* penalty runs from April 15 to December 1 (eight months of penalty).

The calculations are as follows:

Failure to pay	Underpayment	$2,000
	.5% for 8 months	4%
	Failure to pay penalty	$ 80
Failure to file	Underpayment	$2,000
	5% for 2 months	10%
	Failure to file penalty	$ 200
Less failure to pay penalty		
for the months when both apply (2 months × .5% × $2,000)		($20)
	Adjusted failure to file	$ 180

Fred must pay $2,260 ($2,000 + $80 + $180) in taxes and penalties (plus interest) when the return is filed.

Penalty for Failure to Pay Estimated Income Tax

Normally individuals pay income taxes throughout the tax year, not just in April when they file their returns. Taxpayers whose primary income is wages or salary make tax payments through employer withholding. However, taxpayers who earn a large portion of their income from sources other than wages may have little or no income tax withheld.[37]

These taxpayers must pay estimated tax payments throughout the year on a quarterly basis. The quarterly payments are due on April 15, June 15, September 15, and January 15. The IRS will impose an estimated tax penalty on taxpayers who do not pay enough estimated tax.[38]

To avoid this penalty, the taxpayer must pay during the year, either through withholding or estimated payments, a minimum of the following:

- 90% of the current year's tax liability.
- 100% of the prior year's tax liability if the taxpayer's AGI in the prior year is less than $150,000.

If the taxpayer's prior year AGI is more than $150,000, the percentage for the prior year rule increases to 110%.[39]

No estimated tax penalty applies if the tax due after withholding or estimated payments is less than $1,000. The IRS calculates the penalty on a per quarter basis using the same rate at which it charges interest (the short-term federal rate plus 3 percentage points).

Taxpayers use Form 2210 to calculate the failure to pay estimated tax penalty. The tax software automatically calculates the amount of underpayment penalty, if any.

Accuracy-Related Penalties

On a return when negligence or any substantial understatement of income occurs, the IRS will assess a penalty equal to 20% of the tax due.[40]

---

[37] Self-employment and investment income are discussed in Chapters 6 and 3, respectively.

[38] Even taxpayers subject to withholding may be required to make estimated payments if nonwage income is sufficiently large.

[39] IRC § 6654(d)(1)(C).

[40] IRC § 6662.(a)

Negligence includes any failure to make a reasonable attempt to comply with the provisions of the IRC. The negligence also includes any careless, reckless, or intentional disregard for tax authority. The IRS may waive the negligence penalty if the taxpayer makes a good-faith effort to comply with the IRC. If the taxpayer were to take a position contrary to established law, the filing of Form 8275R (the form used to disclose a contrary position) can help avoid the negligence penalty. The 20% penalty also applies when the taxpayer has substantially understated his or her income tax. *Substantial understatement* occurs when the understatement is either

- More than 10% of the tax required to be shown on the return.
- $5,000 or more.[41]

The IRS may reduce the amount of the understatement subject to the 20% penalty if the taxpayer has substantial tax authority for his or her tax treatment.[42] Substantial authority exists only if the weight of tax authority supporting the taxpayer's treatment is substantial in relation to the tax authority supporting the IRS's position.

Fraud Penalties

The IRS can impose a 75% penalty on any portion of understatement of tax that is attributable to fraud.[43] Although the IRC does not define *fraud,* the courts provide a comprehensive definition. One court defined it as intentional wrongdoing with the purpose of evading tax.[44] Another court said it is the intent to conceal, mislead, or otherwise prevent the collection of tax.[45] If any underpayment is due to fraud, the IRS assesses the 75% penalty.[46]

Fraud on a tax return can also lead to criminal charges. Criminal penalties apply only to tax evasion (attempt to evade or defeat tax), willful failure to collect or pay tax, and willful failure to file a return. The IRS can assess criminal penalties in addition to civil penalties. Possible criminal penalties include the following:

- **Any person who willfully attempts to evade or defeat any tax:** The charge is a felony punishable by fines of not more than $100,000 or imprisonment of not more than five years or both.[47]

- **Any person who fails to collect, account for, and pay over any tax:** The charge is a felony punishable by fines of not more than $10,000 or imprisonment of not more than five years or both.[48]

- **Any person who willfully fails to pay estimated tax or other tax and file a return:** The charge is a misdemeanor punishable by fines of not more than $25,000 or imprisonment of not more than one year or both.[49]

Penalty for Erroneous Claim for Refund or Credit

A 20% penalty could be assessed by the IRS on the disallowed amount of the claim if the claim for refund or credit of income filed is found to be excessive. An amount for a claim is classified as "excessive" if the claim amount exceeds the amount of the allowable claim. This penalty does not apply if the fraud or the accuracy-related penalty has been assessed.

---

[41] IRC § 6662(d)(1)(A).

[42] IRC § 6662(d)(2)(B).

[43] IRC § 6663.

[44] *Mitchell v. Comm.,* 118 F2d 308 (5th-CA 1941).

[45] *Stoltzfus v. U.S.,* 398 F2d 1002 (3rd-CA 1968).

[46] IRC § 6663(b).

[47] IRC § 7201.

[48] IRC § 7202.

[49] IRC § 7203.

CONCEPT CHECK 2-8—LO 7

1. A taxpayer filed an automatic extension before April 15 but sent no money to the IRS. He then filed his return by June 2 and paid the amount due of $3,000. What are the amounts for the failure to file a tax return penalty and the failure to pay penalty?
2. Fraud on a tax return can also lead to criminal charges. True or false?

Summary

LO 1: Describe the expanded tax formula and the components of the major sections of Form 1040A and Form 1040.

- Forms 1040A and 1040 are more complex than Form 1040EZ.
- The taxpayer must use the form that is right for him or her.
- Adjusted Gross Income (AGI) is gross income minus a list of permitted deductions.
- Many deductions and credits are determined with reference to AGI.

LO 2: Determine the proper filing status.

- There are five filing statuses.
- Single: not married as of the last day of the year.
- Married Filing Jointly: legally married on the last day of the year; the marital status is determined by state law.
- Married Filing Separately: married but elect to file separately. The standard deduction can be taken only if both take it.
- Head of Household: unmarried at the end of the year and must maintain a household for a qualifying person for more than half the year.
- Qualifying Widow(er) with Dependent Child: eligible to file a joint return the year the spouse died, unmarried, and paying more than half the cost of a household that was the principal place of residence of the taxpayer and child for the year.

LO 3: Calculate personal exemptions.

- Personal exemptions are for the taxpayer and spouse.
- The amount of the personal exemption for 2009 is $3,650 (subject to annual inflation adjustment).
- No personal exemption is allowed on a taxpayer's return if he or she can be claimed as a dependent on another return.

LO 4: Calculate dependency exemptions.

- Must meet the following: dependent taxpayer test, joint return test, and citizen or resident test.
- Must be a qualifying child or a qualifying relative.
- A qualifying child must meet five tests: relationship test, age test, residency test, support test, and special test for qualifying child of more than one taxpayer.
- A qualifying relative must meet four tests: not a qualifying child test, relationship or member of household test, gross income test, and support test.

LO 5: Determine the standard deduction.

- Standard deduction for each filing status: single— $5,700; Married Filing Jointly—$11,400; married filing separately—$5,700; Head of Household—$8,350; and Qualifying Widow(er)—$11,400.
- The amount of standard deduction increases for people who are age 65 and/or blind.
- Dependent taxpayers are limited to the higher of $950 or the taxpayer's earned income plus $300. Limited to the basic standard deduction.

LO 6 27. What is the amount of the tax liability for a married couple with taxable income of $135,500?

    a. $19,490.

    b. $26,250.

    c. $37,940.

    d. $33,875.

LO 7 28. What is the percentage of interest the IRS was charging on assessment during March 2009? You might want to do this research by going to the IRS Web site (www.irs.gov).

    a. 6%.

    b. 5%.

    c. 7%.

    d. 8%.

LO 7 29. When there is negligence on a return, the IRS charges a penalty of _____ of the tax due.

    a. 25%.

    b. 20%.

    c. 18%.

    d. 10%.

LO 7 30. When there is fraud on a return, the IRS charges a penalty of _____ on any portion of understatement of tax that is attributable to the fraud.

    a. 20%.

    b. 25%.

    c. 75%.

    d. 100%.

Problems **LO 1** 31. The benefits of many deductions, credits, or other benefits are limited to taxpayers with Adjusted Gross Income below certain limits.

    a. Explain how the limitation (phaseout) process works.

    b. Give two examples of deductions, credits, or other benefits that are limited.

    c. Why would Congress wish to limit the benefits of these items?

LO 2 32. List the five types of filing status and briefly explain the requirements for the use of each one.

LO 2   33. In which of the following cases may the taxpayer claim head of household filing status?

    a. The taxpayer is single and maintains a household that is the principal place of abode of her infant son.

    b. The taxpayer is single, maintains a household for herself, and maintains a separate household that is the principal place of abode of her dependent widowed mother.

    c. The taxpayer was married from January to October and lived with his spouse from January to May. From June 1 to December 31, the taxpayer maintained a household that was the principal place of abode of his married son and daughter-in-law, whom the taxpayer can claim as dependents.

    d. Same as (c) except the taxpayer lived with his ex-spouse until August and maintained the household from September 1 to the end of the year.

LO 3   34. How many personal exemptions can a taxpayer claim on his or her tax return? Explain your answer.

LO 4   35. Roberta is widowed and lives in an apartment complex. She receives $8,000 of social security income that she uses to pay for rent and other household expenses. The remainder of her living expenses is paid by relatives and neighbors. The total amount of support paid by Roberta and the others totals $22,000. Amounts paid for support during the year are as follows:

Roberta	$8,000
Ed (neighbor)	4,000
Bill (son)	5,000
Jose (neighbor)	2,000
Alicia (niece)	3,000

    a. Which of these persons is entitled to claim Roberta as a dependent absent a multiple support agreement?

    b. Under a multiple support agreement, which of these persons is entitled to claim Roberta as a dependent? Explain your answer.

    c. If Roberta saved all of her social security income and the other persons paid for the shortfall in the same proportions as shown, which of these persons would be entitled to claim Roberta as a dependent under a multiple support agreement? Explain your answer.

LO 4   36. Shelly is a U.S. citizen and is the 67-year-old widowed mother of Janet. After retirement, Shelly decided to fulfill a lifelong dream and move to Paris. Shelly receives $1,000 of interest income, but all of her other living expenses (including rent on her Paris apartment

with spectacular views of the Eiffel Tower) are paid by Janet. Janet resides in Chicago. Is Janet entitled to a dependency exemption for Shelly? Explain your answer.

_____

_____

_____

LO 5 37. Peter is a 21-year-old full-time college student. During 2009 he earned $2,100 from a part-time job and $1,100 in interest income. If Peter is a dependent of his parents, what is his standard deduction amount? If Peter supports himself and is not a dependent of someone else, what is his standard deduction amount?

_____

_____

LO 5 38. Julio and Martina are engaged and are planning to travel to Las Vegas during the 2009 Christmas season and get married around the end of the year. In 2009 Julio expects to earn $45,000 and Martina expects to earn $15,000. Their employers have deducted the appropriate amount of withholding from their paychecks throughout the year. Neither Julio nor Martina has any itemized deductions. They are trying to decide whether they should get married on December 31, 2009, or on January 1, 2010. What do you recommend? Explain your answer (disregard the making work pay credit).

_____

_____

_____

_____

_____

LO 5 39. Determine the amount of the standard deduction for each of the following taxpayers for tax year 2009:

   a. Ann, who is single.

   _____

   b. Adrian and Caroline, who are filing a joint return. Their son is blind.

   _____

   c. Peter and Elizabeth, who are married and file separate tax returns. Elizabeth will itemize her deductions.

   _____

   d. Patricia, who earned $1,100 working a part-time job. She can be claimed as a dependent by her parents.

   _____

   e. Rodolfo, who is over 65 and is single.

   _____

   f. Bernard, who is a nonresident alien with U.S. income.

   _____

   g. Manuel, who is 70, and Esther, who is 62 and blind, will file a joint return.

   _____

   h. Herman, who is 76 and a qualifying widower with a dependent child.

   _____

LO 6 40. Using the appropriate tax tables or tax rate schedules, determine the amount of tax liability in each of the following instances:

    a. A married couple filing jointly with taxable income of $32,991.

    b. A married couple filing jointly with taxable income of $192,257.

    c. A married couple filing separately, one spouse with taxable income of $43,885 and the other with $56,218.

    d. A single person with taxable income of $79,436.

    e. A single person with taxable income of $297,784.

    f. A head of household with taxable income of $96,592.

    g. A qualifying widow with taxable income of $14,019.

    h. A married couple filing jointly with taxable income of $11,216.

LO 6 41. Determine the average tax rate and the marginal tax rate for each instance in question 40.

    a. Average = _____ Marginal = _____
    b. Average = _____ Marginal = _____
    c. Average = _____ Marginal = _____
    d. Average = _____ Marginal = _____
    e. Average = _____ Marginal = _____
    f. Average = _____ Marginal = _____
    g. Average = _____ Marginal = _____
    h. Average = _____ Marginal = _____

LO 6 42. Using the appropriate tax tables or tax rate schedules, determine the tax liability for tax year 2009 in each of the following instances. In each case, assume the taxpayer can take only the standard deduction.

    a. A single taxpayer with AGI of $23,493 and one dependent.

    b. A single taxpayer with AGI of $169,783 and no dependents.

    c. A married couple filing jointly with AGI of $39,945 and two dependents.

    d. A married couple filing jointly with AGI of $162,288 and three dependents.

    e. A married couple filing jointly with AGI of $389,947 and one dependent.

    f. A taxpayer filing married filing separately with AGI of $68,996 and one dependent.

    g. A qualifying widow, age 66, with AGI of $49,240 with one dependent.

    h. A head of household with AGI of $14,392 with two dependents.

_____

    i. A head of household with AGI of $59,226 with one dependent.

_____

LO 7 43. Victoria's 2009 tax return was due on April 15, 2010, but she did not file it until June 12, 2010. Victoria did not file an extension. The tax due on the tax return when filed was $8,500. In 2009, Victoria paid in $12,000 through withholding. Her 2008 tax liability was $11,500. Victoria's AGI for 2009 is less than $150,000. How much penalty will Victoria have to pay (disregard interest)?

_____

_____

_____

_____

_____

LO 7 44. Paul has the following information:

AGI for 2009	$155,000
Withholding for 2009	20,000
Total tax for 2008	29,000
Total tax for 2009	31,250

    a. How much must Paul pay in estimated taxes to avoid a penalty (disregard the making work pay credit)?

_____

_____

    b. If Paul paid $1,000 per quarter, would he have avoided the estimated tax penalty?

_____

_____

LO 7 45. Charles and Joan Thompson file a joint return. In 2008 they had taxable income of $92,370 and paid tax of $15,781. Charles is an advertising executive, and Joan is a college professor. During the fall 2009 semester, Joan is planning to take a leave of absence without pay. The Thompsons expect their taxable income to drop to $70,000 in 2009. They expect their 2009 tax liability will be $9,881, which will be the approximate amount of their withholding. Joan anticipates that she will work on academic research during the fall semester.

    During September, Joan decides to perform consulting services for some local businesses. Charles and Joan had not anticipated this development. Joan is paid a total of $35,000 during October, November, and December for her work.

    What estimated tax payments are Charles and Joan required to make, if any, for tax year 2009? Do you anticipate that the Thompsons will be required to pay an underpayment penalty when they file their 2009 tax return? Explain your answer (disregard the making work pay credit).

_____

_____

_____

_____

_____

Tax Return Problems

Use your tax software to complete the following problems. If you are manually preparing the tax returns, you will need to use a Form 1040 or Form 1040A, depending on the complexity of the problem.

Tax Return Problem 1

Jose and Dora Hernandez are married filing jointly. They are 50 and 45 years old, respectively. Their address is 32010 Lake Street, Atlanta, GA 30300. Additional information about Mr. and Mrs. Hernandez is as follows:

Social security numbers: Jose, 222-11-0000. Dora, 222-11-0001.

W-2 for Jose shows these amounts:

- Wages (box 1) = $45,800.
- Federal W/H (box 2) = $ 9,160.
- Social security wages (box 3) = $45,800.
- Social security W/H (box 4) = $ 2,839.60
- Medicare wages (box 5) = $45,800.
- Medicare W/H (box 6) = $ 664.10.

W-2 for Dora shows these amounts:

- Wages (box 1) = $31,000.
- Federal W/H (box 2) = $ 4,650.
- Social security wages (box 3) = $31,000.
- Social security W/H (box 4) = $ 1,922.
- Medicare wages (box 5) = $31,000.
- Medicare W/H (box 6) = $ 449.50.

Form 1099-INT for Jose and Dora shows this amount:
Box 1 = $300 from City Bank.
Dependent: Daughter Adela is 5 years old. Her social security number is 222-11-0035.
Jose is a store manager, and Dora is a receptionist.
Prepare the tax return for Mr. and Mrs. Hernandez using the appropriate form. They do want to contribute to the presidential election campaign.

Tax Return Problem 2

Marie Lincoln is a head of household. She is 37 years old and her address is 4110 N.E. 13 Street, Miami, FL 33000. Additional information about Ms. Lincoln is as follows:

Social security number: 212-10-0000.

W-2 for Marie shows these amounts:

- Wages (box 1) = $ 43,600.
- Federal W/H (box 2) = $ 6,540.
- Social security wages (box 3) = $ 43,600.
- Social security W/H (box 4) = $ 2,703.20.
- Medicare wages (box 5) = $ 43,600.
- Medicare W/H (box 6) = $ 632.20.

Form 1099-INT for Marie shows this amount:
Box 1 = $500 from A & D Bank.

Dependent: Son Steven is 10 years old. His social security number is 212-10-0155.
Marie is an administrative assistant.
Prepare the tax return for Ms. Lincoln using the appropriate form. She wants to contribute to the presidential election campaign.

Tax Return Problem 3

Margaret O'Hara has been divorced for about two years. She is 28 years old and her address is 979 S. E. 32 Street, Jacksonville, FL 33111. Additional information about Ms. O'Hara is as follows:

Social security number: 212-11-0000.

Alimony received = $24,000.

W-2 for Margaret shows these amounts:

Wages (box 1) = $38,000.

Federal W/H (box 2) = $ 9,500.

Social security wages (box 3) = $38,000.

Social security W/H (box 4) = $ 2,356.

Medicare wages (box 5) = $38,000.

Medicare W/H (box 6) = $ 551.

Margaret is a research assistant.

Prepare the tax return for Ms. O'Hara using the appropriate form. She does not want to contribute to the presidential election campaign.

We have provided selected filled-in source documents on our Web site at www.mhhe.com/cruz2010.

Chapter Three

Gross Income: Inclusions and Exclusions

We now explore the details associated with a tax return. This chapter covers many of the items that compose *gross income.* These items are reported on lines 7 to 14 on Form 1040A or lines 7 to 21 on Form 1040.

Learning Objectives

When you have completed this chapter, you should understand the following learning objectives (LO):

LO 1. Describe when and how to record income for tax purposes.

LO 2. Apply the cash method of accounting to income taxes.

LO 3. Explain the taxability of components of gross income, including interest, dividends, tax refunds, and social security benefits.

LO 4. Apply the rules concerning items excluded from gross income.

LO 5. Apply the rules associated with tax accounting for savings bond interest used for education expenses, below-market interest loans, gift loans, and original issue discount debt (appendix).

INTRODUCTION

This chapter encompasses major components of total income (line 15 on Form 1040A or line 22 on Form 1040) and many types of nontaxable income. Total income is composed of gross income (excluding nontaxable income) minus permitted deductions.

You will recall that gross income is ". . . all income from whatever source derived . . ."[1] Obviously gross income is an extremely broad, all-encompassing concept. Much of this book is devoted to the discussion of various components of gross income and taxable income.

Not all income is subject to tax. In practice, all income is gross income unless the Internal Revenue Code (IRC) specifically excludes it from taxation. In this chapter, you will learn about many gross income exclusions.

WHEN AND HOW TO RECORD INCOME
LO 1

Accountants record (recognize) income for financial statement purposes when it is both realized and earned (the *accrual method of accounting*). *Realization* is the process of converting a noncash resource into cash or a right to cash. Conversion occurs when a company or person

[1] IRC § 61(a).

exchanges a noncash asset or resource for cash or a receivable in a transaction with a third party. Although the most commonly used example is selling inventory for cash or an account receivable, the realization concept applies to professional services (exchanging knowledge for cash), asset sales (exchanging a building for cash or a right to cash), licensing a patent (exchanging an idea for cash or a right to cash), or wages (exchanging time, knowledge, and effort for cash).

Income has been earned when companies or persons have performed all actions necessary to complete the transaction. When a grocery store sells you a can of beans, it has earned the income because it has done everything it needs to do to complete the transaction. The store does not need to open the can, heat the contents, and serve you at the dinner table.

For tax purposes, income recognition follows similar rules with a few twists. In general, an individual must recognize income on his or her tax return if a transaction meets *all* of the following three conditions:

- There must be an economic benefit. If a person is economically better off because of a transaction, the person must normally record income. If someone works for an employer and receives cash for that work, the person has income. If a person sells his or her car to a friend for a note receivable, the person has income.[2] It is important to note that the benefit may be indirect. If an accountant performs some tax work for a client and the client agrees to pay a $500 debt the accountant owes to a local bank, the accountant has $500 of income because he or she has received an economic benefit (less debt) even if the $500 cash was never in the possession of the accountant.

- A transaction must actually have reached a conclusion. Two factors are at work here. First, a transaction must occur. Simply owning an asset that has increased in value does not create income (even though there may be an economic benefit). If an individual owns 100 shares of IBM common stock and the stock increases in price by $1 per share, no income will result because no transaction has occurred. The second factor is that the transaction process must be complete. Often a time gap occurs between the agreement to enter into a transaction and the completion of the transaction. In general, the completion date is the date when income is recognized.

EXAMPLE 3-1	On December 29, 2008, Raul agreed to repair a damaged roof and started to work on that date. On January 6, 2009, he completed the job and received payment. Raul would record income in 2009, not 2008.

- Finally, the income cannot be tax-exempt. Certain income is statutorily excluded from taxation and will not be included in gross income even if the preceding two conditions are met.

CONCEPT CHECK 3-1—LO 1	1. An individual must recognize income on his or her tax return if the transaction meets three conditions. Name the three conditions: _____, _____, _____.
	2. An individual can exclude certain income from taxation even though a transaction that has economic benefits has occurred. True or false?

---

[2] Taxpayers likely have a "cost" or "basis" that can be subtracted from the proceeds to arrive at the net amount of income that must be reported.

CASH METHOD OF ACCOUNTING
LO 2

Almost all individuals use the cash receipts and disbursements method of accounting.[3] Unincorporated businesses without inventories often use the cash method as well. Under the *cash method,* a taxpayer reports income in the year he or she receives or constructively receives the income rather than the year in which the taxpayer earns the income. *Constructive receipt* means that the income is available to or in the control of the taxpayer regardless of whether the taxpayer chooses to utilize the income. Thus interest credited to a taxpayer's savings account on December 31 is income in the year credited, not the year withdrawn.

Income can be "realized in any form, whether in money, property, or services."[4] Note that even cash basis taxpayers do not actually have to receive cash before they record income (although that is quite often the case). Receipt of property or services triggers income recognition. Furthermore, taxpayers recognize income even if they receive it indirectly.

EXAMPLE 3-2	If a lawyer agrees to give legal advice to a neighbor in exchange for the neighbor agreeing to paint the lawyer's house, both parties will have income equal to the fair market value of the services received by them.

EXAMPLE 3-3	Heather owns an unincorporated cash basis architectural firm. She performs architectural services for a client during December 2008. She completed the work in 2008 (so the income was earned), but she did not receive payment by the end of the year. Heather received payment for her services on January 23, 2009, and recognizes income in 2009.

EXAMPLE 3-4	Antonio provided golf lessons worth $300 to Arturo in December 2008. Antonio owed Millie $300, and he asked Arturo to pay the $300 to Millie. In January 2009 Arturo paid Millie $300. Antonio recognizes income of $300 in 2009.

In some instances, a cash basis taxpayer can report income as though he or she were an accrual basis taxpayer. For instance, in the case of interest income on Series EE and Series I U.S. savings bonds, taxpayers can defer the income until the maturity of the bond or can elect to report the interest annually.[5] Special rules also apply to farmers and ranchers, who can elect to average their income over a three-year period and can elect to defer certain insurance proceeds and federal disaster payments.[6]

CONCEPT CHECK 3-2—LO 2	1. Income may be realized in any form, whether in money, property, or services. True or false?
	2. If you provide consulting services to your friend and, in exchange, he fixes your car, you and your friend must report on both tax returns the fair market value of the services provided. True or false?

---

[3] The method of accounting (cash or accrual) used for an individual taxpayer's first tax return effectively establishes that person's accounting method. See Reg. § 1.446-1(c)(1)(i). Thus, although it is possible that an individual can use the accrual method of accounting, it is unlikely that he or she uses the accrual method for the first return.

[4] Reg. § 1.61-1(a).

[5] IRC § 454.

[6] IRC § 1301 and IRC § 451(d).

TAXABILITY OF COMPONENTS OF GROSS INCOME
LO 3

This section discusses the taxability of various types of gross income, including interest, dividends, tax refunds, and social security benefits.

Interest Income (Forms 1040A and 1040, line 8)

Recall that interest is compensation for the use of money with respect to a bona fide debt or obligation imposed by law. For most individuals, interest income comes from interest-earning deposits at financial institutions—banks, savings and loans, or credit unions. These institutions report interest income to taxpayers on Form 1099-INT. Taxpayers can also earn interest income in other ways not reported on an IRS form. An example is a creditor–debtor arrangement between two individuals in which taxpayer A lends some money to taxpayer B and taxpayer A receives $50 in interest. In this instance, taxpayer A would earn interest income, but no IRS document would be required to record the interest income.

Some tax issues pertaining to interest income are complex and less common. These include below-market interest rate loans, gifts, shareholder and similar loans, and interest from original issue discount (OID). The appendix of this chapter provides further details about these subjects. Next we discuss common types of interest income.

Interest on U.S. Savings Bonds

Individuals purchase Series EE and Series E (before July 1980) U.S. savings bonds at a discount from face value. The owners of the bonds do not receive a periodic cash interest payment. Instead the face value of the bond increases over the period to maturity, and that increase represents the amount of interest earned. The owner of such bonds can defer reporting any interest (that is, the increase in bond value) until the bonds mature, are redeemed, or are otherwise disposed of, whichever comes first. Alternatively, the owner can elect to report the annual increase in face value as interest income on each year's income tax return (on an accrual basis).[7] Such election applies to all bonds owned at the time of the election and to any bonds subsequently acquired.

EXAMPLE 3-5

Donna purchased a $1,000 face value Series EE U.S. savings bond for $500 on January 1, 2009. The bond earned interest at a rate of 6% throughout 2009 so that at year-end, the bond had a face value of $530. If Donna does nothing, she does not need to report the $30 interest income for 2009 until she cashes the bond upon maturity. Alternatively, Donna can elect to report the $30 as interest income in 2009. If she does, she must report all future interest income on the bond in the same manner.

The U.S. Treasury sold until August 2004 Series HH bonds at face value. Interest on these bonds is paid by check semiannually and is included in income in the year received.

Tax-Exempt Interest

Certain interest income is exempt from taxation. Taxpayers can exclude from gross income any interest earned on bonds issued by any state, any possession of the United States, any political subdivision of either of the foregoing, or the District of Columbia (such as municipal bonds).[8] However, interest is taxable if received from state or local bonds issued for private activities such as convention centers, industrial parks, or stadiums.[9]

---

[7] IRC § 454(a).
[8] IRC § 103(a), IRC § 103(c).
[9] IRC § 103(b)(1).

From Shoebox to Software   Interest Income

Taxable interest income is on line 8a of Form 1040A and Form 1040. Tax-exempt interest is on line 8b. If any of the following is true, the taxpayer must complete and file Schedule B (Forms 1040A and 1040):

- Had more than $1,500 of interest income.
- Received seller-financed mortgage interest.
- Received tax-exempt interest in any amount.
- Received interest as a nominee.
- Claimed an exclusion for interest on Series EE U.S. savings bonds issued after 1989 or Series I bonds.
- Reported any adjustments for accrued interest, amortizable bond premium, or original issue discount (see the appendix at the end of this chapter).
- Had a foreign account; received a distribution from or was the grantor of or a transferor to a foreign trust.

Schedule B is in Exhibit 3-1. The total from line 4 of the applicable schedule is reported on line 8a of Form 1040A or Form 1040, as appropriate.

Information concerning interest income comes from a number of sources:

- If interest is received from a financial institution, corporation, or branch of government, the taxpayer will receive Form 1099-INT that will indicate, in box 1, the amount of interest received or credited to the taxpayer's account during the year. Form 1099-INT is in Exhibit 3-2.
- Taxpayers who are partners of a partnership or who are shareholders of a Subchapter S corporation will receive Schedule K-1 that will reflect the taxpayer's proportionate share of interest income. We discuss

partnerships and Subchapter S corporations in Chapters 14 and 15, respectively.

- If the taxpayer owns bonds that were purchased at a discount (see the chapter appendix), the taxpayer should receive Form 1099-OID showing, in box 1, the amount of original issue discount that must be reported as income in the current year. A Form 1099-OID is in Exhibit 3-3.
- Taxpayers who receive interest from other sources will need to calculate the appropriate amount of interest to include on Schedule B. Other sources of interest income include
  - Payments received from seller-financed mortgages.
  - Receipts from installment sale receivables or other receivables received over time.
  - Imputed interest on loans made at a below-market interest rate (see the chapter appendix).
  - Interest on bonds sold between interest dates.

When using the tax software, you record the information from all Forms 1099 received onto the appropriate input form in the Documents Received section.

Taxpayers who are eligible to exclude U.S. savings bond interest because they paid qualified higher education expenses (see the chapter appendix) must complete Form 8815 and attach it to their tax return. With the tax software, you enter the required information directly on Form 8815.

Self-employed individuals who receive interest income as a part of their business report the amounts on Schedule C (see Chapter 6).

CONCEPT CHECK 3-3—LO 3

1. All interest received from state or local bonds is not taxable. True or false?
2. Schedule B (Forms 1040A and 1040) is required if an individual receives $1,500 of interest for the tax year. True or false?

Dividends (Form 1040 and Form 1040A, line 9)

Dividends are distributions of property by a corporation to its shareholders. Dividends are generally taxed at capital gains rates to the extent they are made from either a corporation's current earnings and profits or its accumulated earnings and profits.[10] Distributions in excess of

---

[10] IRC § 316(a). Earnings and profits are similar, but not identical, to retained earnings for financial statement purposes. Earnings and profits are beyond the scope of this book.

EXHIBIT 3-1

SCHEDULE B	**Interest and Ordinary Dividends**	OMB No. 1545-0074
(Form 1040A or 1040)		**2009**
Department of the Treasury Internal Revenue Service (99)	►Attach to Form 1040A or 1040. ►See instructions on back.	Attachment Sequence No. **08**

Name(s) shown on return | Your social security number

Part I
Interest

(See instructions on back and the instructions for Form 1040A, or Form 1040, line 8a.)

Note. If you received a Form 1099-INT, Form 1099-OID, or substitute statement from a brokerage firm, list the firm's name as the payer and enter the total interest shown on that form.

		Amount
1	List name of payer. If any interest is from a seller-financed mortgage and the buyer used the property as a personal residence, see instructions on back and list this interest first. Also, show that buyer's social security number and address ►	**1**
2	Add the amounts on line 1	**2**
3	Excludable interest on series EE and I U.S. savings bonds issued after 1989. Attach Form 8815	**3**
4	Subtract line 3 from line 2. Enter the result here and on Form 1040A, or Form 1040, line 8a . . . . ►	**4**

Note. If line 4 is over $1,500, you must complete Part III.

Part II
Ordinary Dividends

(See instructions on back and the instructions for Form 1040A, or Form 1040, line 9a.)

Note. If you received a Form 1099-DIV or substitute statement from a brokerage firm, list the firm's name as the payer and enter the ordinary dividends shown on that form.

		Amount
5	List name of payer ►	**5**
6	Add the amounts on line 5. Enter the total here and on Form 1040A, or Form 1040, line 9a . . . . ►	**6**

Note. If line 6 is over $1,500, you must complete Part III.

Part III
Foreign Accounts and Trusts

(See instructions on back)

You must complete this part if you **(a)** had over $1,500 of taxable interest or ordinary dividends; **(b)** had a foreign account; or **(c)** received a distribution from, or were a grantor of, or a transferor to, a foreign trust.

		Yes	No
7a	At any time during 2009, did you have an interest in or a signature or other authority over a financial account in a foreign country, such as a bank account, securities account, or other financial account? See instructions on back for exceptions and filing requirements for Form TD F 90-22.1		
b	If "Yes," enter the name of the foreign country ►		
8	During 2009, did you receive a distribution from, or were you the grantor of, or transferor to, a foreign trust? If "Yes," you may have to file Form 3520. See instructions on back		

For Paperwork Reduction Act Notice, see Form 1040A or 1040 instructions.   Cat. No. 17146N   Schedule B (Form 1040A or 1040) 2009

EXHIBIT 3-2

☐ CORRECTED (if checked)		

PAYER'S name, street address, city, state, ZIP code, and telephone no.	Payer's RTN (optional)	OMB No. 1545-0112	
	1 Interest income $	**2009** Form **1099-INT**	**Interest Income**
	2 Early withdrawal penalty $		
PAYER'S federal identification number	RECIPIENT'S identification number	**3** Interest on U.S. Savings Bonds and Treas. obligations $	**Copy B** **For Recipient**
RECIPIENT'S name		**4** Federal income tax withheld $	**5** Investment expenses $	This is important tax information and is being furnished to the Internal Revenue Service. If you are required to file a return, a negligence penalty or other sanction may be imposed on you if this income is taxable and the IRS determines that it has not been reported.
Street address (including apt. no.)		**6** Foreign tax paid $	**7** Foreign country or U.S. possession	
City, state, and ZIP code		**8** Tax-exempt interest	**9** Specified private activity bond interest	
Account number (see instructions)		$	$	

Form **1099-INT**   (keep for your records)   Department of the Treasury - Internal Revenue Service

EXHIBIT 3-3

☐ CORRECTED (if checked)		

PAYER'S name, street address, city, state, ZIP code, and telephone no.	**1** Original issue discount for 2009* $	OMB No. 1545-0117 **2009** Form **1099-OID**	**Original Issue Discount**
	2 Other periodic interest $		
PAYER'S federal identification number	RECIPIENT'S identification number	**3** Early withdrawal penalty $	**4** Federal income tax withheld $	**Copy B** **For Recipient**
RECIPIENT'S name		**5** Description	This is important tax information and is being furnished to the Internal Revenue Service. If you are required to file a return, a negligence penalty or other sanction may be imposed on you if this income is taxable and the IRS determines that it has not been reported.
Street address (including apt. no.)		**6** Original issue discount on U.S. Treasury obligations* $	
City, state, and ZIP code		**7** Investment expenses $	
Account number (see instructions)		* This may not be the correct figure to report on your income tax return. See instructions on the back.	

Form **1099-OID**   (keep for your records)   Department of the Treasury - Internal Revenue Service

earnings and profits represent a nontaxable return of capital that reduces the taxpayer's cost basis in the stock. If the distribution is greater than the basis of the stock, the excess is a capital gain.[11]

Corporations normally pay dividends in the form of cash, but they may pay them in property or anything of economic value. The basis of the property received as a dividend in the hands of the shareholder is the property's fair market value at the date of distribution.[12]

A *stock dividend* is a distribution of shares of the corporation's own stock to shareholders. Stock dividends (and stock splits) are generally not taxable to a shareholder.[13] Shareholders

[11] IRC § 301(c).
[12] IRC § 301(d).
[13] IRC § 305(a).

allocate the basis of the stock originally held between the old and the new stock in proportion to the fair market value of each on the date of the distribution. Certain stock dividends are taxable, including these:

- Stock dividends in which a shareholder has the option to receive stock or cash or other property.
- Disproportionate dividends in which some shareholders receive property and other shareholders receive an increase in their stock interest in the corporation.
- Distributions of preferred stock to some common shareholders and common stock to other common shareholders.
- Distributions made on preferred stock.[14]

Mutual funds (known as *regulated investment companies*) are entities that pool the financial resources of thousands of individuals to purchase stocks or bonds. Mutual funds are required to distribute the income they receive, whether in the form of dividends from holding stocks or capital gains and losses from sales of a portion of the portfolio. Real estate investment trusts make similar distributions.

Taxation of Dividends

To this point in the text, all income is the same for purposes of determining the amount of tax. However, certain types of income are taxed at different rates.

Prior to passage of the 2003 Jobs and Growth Act (the "2003 Act") in June 2003, dividends and ordinary income were taxed at the same rate. The 2003 Act states that qualified dividends received in 2003 or later may receive preferential treatment.[15] Specifically, when an individual's marginal ordinary income tax rate is 25% or more, the taxation rate on qualified dividends is 15%. When the marginal rate is less than 25%, the tax rate on qualified dividends is 0% for years beginning after 2007.

Qualified dividends (1) are made from the earnings and profits of the payer corporation and (2) are from domestic corporations or qualified foreign corporations.[16]

EXAMPLE 3-6

Refer to the tax rate schedules inside the front cover of the text. A single individual who has taxable income of $110,000 before dividends will be in the 28% marginal tax bracket. If that individual then receives a qualified dividend of $1,000, the tax rate applied to the dividend would be 15%. The tax liability of the individual would be determined as follows:

Taxable income (before dividend)	$110,000
Less lower bracket amount	82,250
Income taxed at 28%	27,750
Tax rate	× 28%
Tax at highest bracket	7,770
Plus tax on first $82,250	16,750
Tax before dividend	24,520
Tax on dividend ($1,000 × 15%)	150
Total tax liability	$ 24,670

The example also illustrates that taxpayers add the dividend income "at the end" no matter when in the tax year they earned the dividend. In other words, tax is computed first on the nondividend income and then on the dividend income.

[14] IRC § 1.305-5(a).
[15] IRC § 1(h)(11)(A).
[16] IRC § 1(h)(11)(B)(i).

From Shoebox to Software Dividends

Dividends are reported on line 9 of Form 1040A or Form 1040. A taxpayer who receives more than $1,500 of dividend income must complete and file Schedule B (Forms 1040A and 1040). Refer to Exhibit 3-1 for Schedule B. Note that Schedule B contains information about both interest and dividends. The total from line 6 of Schedule B is reported on line 9 of Forms 1040A or 1040.

Corporate and mutual fund payers are required to provide shareholders a Form 1099-DIV (see Exhibit 3-4) that indicates the amount of dividends in box 1a. Note that the amount in box 1b represents how much of

box 1a is *qualified* dividends. If all dividends received by an individual are qualified dividends, the amount in box 1a will be the same as the amount in box 1b. The total amount of qualified dividends is reported on line 9b of Form 1040A or 1040.

Most taxpayers will have no other sources of dividend income other than that reported on Form 1099-DIV.

As was the case with interest payments reported on Form 1099-INT, any dividend income from Form 1099-DIV should be recorded on the tax software using the appropriate supporting form located in the Documents Received section of the software.

CONCEPT CHECK 3-4—LO 3

1. Qualified dividends arise from the earnings and profits of the payer corporation. True or false?
2. A corporation can pay only cash dividends to its shareholders. True or false?

EXHIBIT 3-4

☐ CORRECTED (if checked)			
PAYER'S name, street address, city, state, ZIP code, and telephone no.	**1a** Total ordinary dividends $	OMB No. 1545-0110 20**09** Form **1099-DIV**	**Dividends and Distributions**
	1b Qualified dividends $		
	2a Total capital gain distr. $	**2b** Unrecap. Sec. 1250 gain $	**Copy B** **For Recipient**
PAYER'S federal identification number	RECIPIENT'S identification number		
RECIPIENT'S name	**2c** Section 1202 gain $	**2d** Collectibles (28%) gain $	This is important tax information and is being furnished to the Internal Revenue Service. If you are required to file a return, a negligence penalty or other sanction may be imposed on you if this income is taxable and the IRS determines that it has not been reported.
	3 Nondividend distributions $	**4** Federal income tax withheld $	
Street address (including apt. no.)		**5** Investment expenses $	
City, state, and ZIP code	**6** Foreign tax paid $	**7** Foreign country or U.S. possession	
Account number (see instructions)	**8** Cash liquidation distributions $	**9** Noncash liquidation distributions $	

Form **1099-DIV**   (keep for your records)   Department of the Treasury - Internal Revenue Service

State and Local Tax Refunds (Form 1040, line 10)

Taxpayers may receive a refund of state or local taxes paid in a prior year. If a taxpayer deducted state or local taxes as an itemized deduction on Schedule A (see Chapter 5) in the prior year, the taxpayer must report the refund as income in the year in which it was received. The taxable amount is the lesser of (a) the amount received, (b) the amount deducted on Schedule A, or (c) the amount by which the itemized deductions exceed the standard deduction. If the taxpayer did not itemize deductions in the prior year (that is, the taxpayer took the standard deduction), no amount of the refund is taxable.[17]

EXAMPLE 3-7	Rose, who is single, reported itemized deductions of $9,900 on her 2008 tax return. Her itemized deductions included $1,150 of state taxes paid. In 2009 she received a $120 refund of state taxes paid in 2008. She must include the entire $120 in income in 2009.

EXAMPLE 3-8	Assume that Rose reported itemized deductions of $5,490 in 2008. Only $40 of her $120 tax refund would be taxable in 2009 because her itemized deductions exceeded her standard deduction by only $40 (in 2008, the standard deduction for single individuals was $5,450).

State and local tax refunds are reported to taxpayers on Form 1099-G, box 2 (see Exhibit 3-5). The applicable amount of the refund is reported on line 10 of Form 1040.

TAX YOUR BRAIN 	Steve received a state tax refund of $200 from the state of California and, at the end of the year, received a Form 1099-G showing the payment in box 2. Must Steve report the refund on his Form 1040? **ANSWER** Not necessarily. Just because Steve received a 1099-G does not mean that the amount indicated in box 2 is actually taxable to him. Steve must determine whether he itemized deductions in the prior year and, if so, how much of the $200 is taxable based on how much tax benefit he received in the prior year, if any.

Unemployment Compensation (Form 1040A, line 13, or Form 1040, line 19)

Federal and state unemployment compensation benefits are taxable, except that you can exclude from gross income $2,400 of unemployment compensation received during the year for tax years beginning in 2009.[18] The rationale behind taxing these payments is that they are a substitute for taxable wages. Unemployment benefits are reported to recipients on Form 1099-G in box 1 (see Exhibit 3-5).

A taxpayer who repays some or all of the unemployment compensation received subtracts the repayment from the amount otherwise received. The repayment is reported by indicating, on line 13 (Form 1040A) or line 19 (Form 1040), the net amount of unemployment compensation received (amount received minus amount repaid) and, on the dotted line, writing *repaid* followed by the amount repaid.

---

[17] IRC § 111(a).
[18] IRC § 85(a), (b).

EXHIBIT 3-5

☐ CORRECTED (if checked)			
PAYER'S name, street address, city, state, ZIP code, and telephone no.	**1** Unemployment compensation $	OMB No. 1545-0120 20**09** Form **1099-G**	**Certain Government Payments**
	2 State or local income tax refunds, credits, or offsets $		
PAYER'S federal identification number RECIPIENT'S identification number	**3** Box 2 amount is for tax year	**4** Federal income tax withheld $	**Copy B** **For Recipient**
RECIPIENT'S name	**5** ATAA payments $	**6** Taxable grants $	This is important tax information and is being furnished to the Internal Revenue Service. If you are required to file a return, a negligence penalty or other sanction may be imposed on you if this income is taxable and the IRS determines that it has not been reported.
Street address (including apt. no.)	**7** Agriculture payments $	**8** Box 2 is trade or business income ▶ ☐	
City, state, and ZIP code	**9** Market gain $		
Account number (see instructions)			
Form **1099-G**	(keep for your records)		Department of the Treasury - Internal Revenue Service

Social Security Benefits (Form 1040, line 20, or Form 1040A, line 14)

The taxability of social security benefits depends on the provisional income and filing status of the taxpayer.[19] The effect of the rules is to exclude social security benefits from taxation for lower-income individuals but tax up to 85% of benefits for taxpayers with higher income. You can find additional information concerning the tax treatment of social security benefits in IRS Publication 915.

Provisional income (also called *modified adjusted gross income*) is calculated as follows:[20]

Adjusted Gross Income (before social security benefits)

Plus: Interest on U.S. savings bonds excluded for educational purposes[21]

Most tax-exempt interest[22]

Employer-provided adoption benefits[23]

Excluded foreign income[24]

Deducted interest on educational loans[25]

Deducted tuition and fees (Tax Extenders Act of 2008)

50% of social security benefits

If provisional income exceeds certain thresholds, 50% of social security benefits are taxable. As provisional income increases, the proportion of benefits included in taxable income

---

[19] Social security benefits refer to the monthly retirement and disability benefits payable under social security and to tier-one railroad retirement benefits. They do not include tier-two railroad benefits or supplementary Medicare benefits that cover medical expenses.

[20] IRC § 86(b)(2).

[21] Interest excluded under IRC § 135.

[22] Exclusion under IRC § 103.

[23] IRC § 137.

[24] Under IRC § 911, 931, or 933.

[25] Interest deductible under IRC § 221.

increases to as much as 85%. The thresholds and taxability are shown in the following chart:

	Married, Filing Jointly	**Single, Head of Household, or Qualifying Widow(er)**
Lower limit of provisional income	$32,000	$25,000
Upper limit of provisional income	$44,000	$34,000
Taxable portion of benefits if provisional income is between the two limits	Lesser of 50% of benefits or 50% of the excess of provisional income over $32,000	Lesser of 50% of benefits or 50% of the excess of provisional income over $25,000
Taxable portion of benefits if provisional income is above the upper limit	Lesser of (a) 85% of benefits or (b) 85% of the excess of provisional income over $44,000 PLUS the lesser of (1) $6,000 or (2) 50% of benefits	Lesser of (a) 85% of benefits or (b) 85% of the excess of provisional income over $34,000 PLUS the lesser of (1) $4,500 or (2) 50% of benefits

Taxpayers use the single column if they are married filing separately and have lived apart from their spouse for the entire year. If such persons lived with their spouse at any time during the year, the lower and upper limits are zero. Thus for these persons, social security benefits are taxable to the extent of the lesser of 85% of social security benefits or 85% of provisional income.

EXAMPLE 3-9

Robert and Cindy file a joint return. Their AGI before social security was $15,000, and they received $8,000 in benefits. They had no items to add back to AGI. Their provisional income is $19,000 ($15,000 + $4,000). No social security benefits are taxable.

EXAMPLE 3-10

Karen files a return as a qualifying widow. She received $7,000 of social security benefits, $19,000 of interest income, and $5,000 of nontaxable municipal bond interest. Her provisional income is $27,500 ($3,500 + $19,000 + $5,000). Karen will report taxable social security benefits equal to the lesser of 50% of social security benefits ($3,500) or 50% of the excess of provisional income over $25,000 ($1,250). Thus her taxable benefits total $1,250. (See Exhibit 3-7.)

EXAMPLE 3-11

Ferdinand and Maureen file a joint return showing interest and dividend income of $46,000, self-employment income for Ferdinand of $31,000, and nontaxable municipal bond interest of $10,000. They excluded $1,000 of interest on educational loans. They received social security benefits of $9,000. Their provisional income is $92,500 ($46,000 + $31,000 + $10,000 + $1,000 + $4,500). They will report taxable social security benefits equal to the lesser of 85% of social security benefits ($7,650) or 85% of the excess of provisional income over $44,000 (which is $41,225) plus the lesser of $6,000 or $4,500 (50% of social security benefits). Thus their taxable benefits total $7,650.

From Shoebox to Software   Social Security Benefits

Taxpayers will receive Form SSA-1099 or RRB-1099 showing the amount of social security benefits or railroad retirement benefits received, respectively. See Exhibit 3-7 for Form SSA-1099.

The amount of benefits to use in taxability calculations is in box 5. As with other 1099 forms, you record the information on the appropriate form within the tax software. Specifically, you record both social security and railroad retirement benefits on the "Social Security Benefits Worksheet" in the "worksheet" section of the tax software.

CONCEPT CHECK 3-5—LO 3

1. Linda and Tom file a joint return. Their AGI before social security was $22,000, social security benefits received were $9,000, and tax-exempt interest was $1,250. What is the amount of their provisional income? _____

EXHIBIT 3-6

The 2009 Form SSA-1099 was not issued at presstime. When issued, it will be essentially the same as the form below. Go to the IRS Web site for the most recent document.

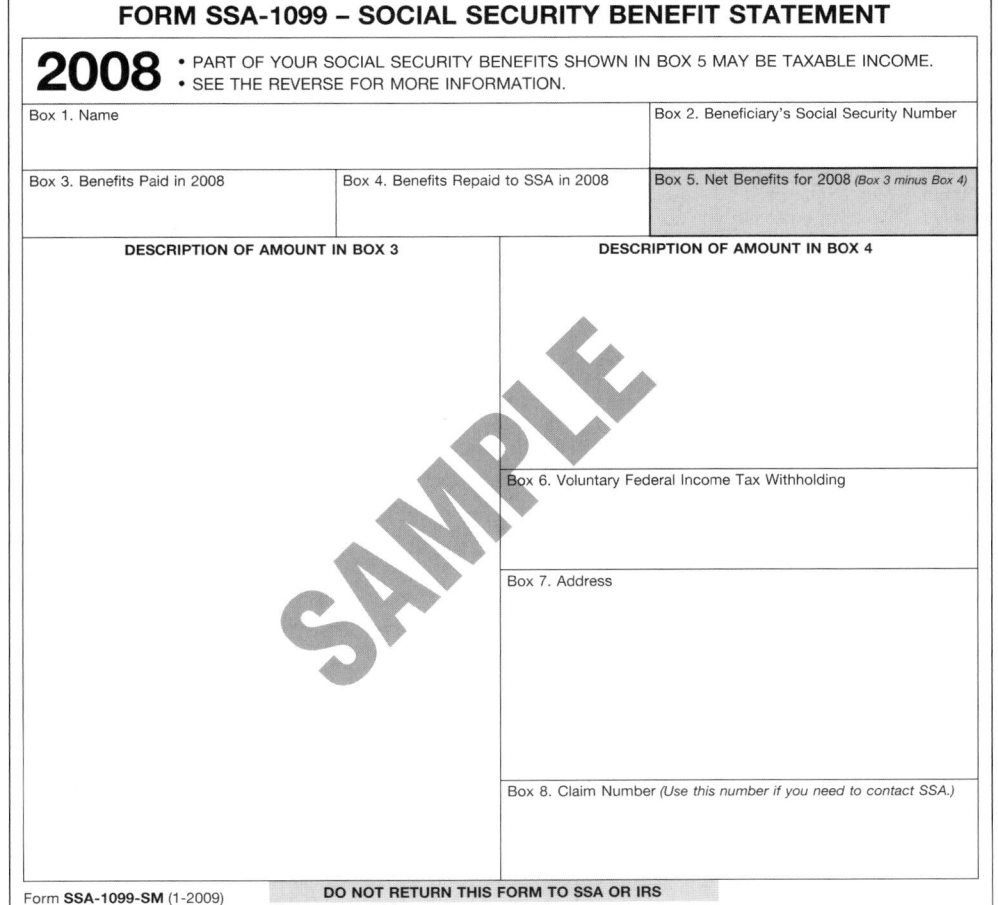

EXHIBIT 3-7

1. Enter the total amount from box 5 of ALL your Forms SSA-1099 and RRB-1099. Also enter this amount on Form 1040, line 20a, or Form 1040A, line 14a	1.	7,000
2. Enter one-half of line 1	2.	3,500
3. Enter the total of the amounts from: **Form 1040:** Lines 7, 8a, 9a, 10 through 14, 15b, 16b, 17 through 19, and 21 **Form 1040A:** Lines 7, 8a, 9a, 10, 11b, 12b, and 13	3.	24,000
4. Enter the amount, if any, from Form 1040 or 1040A, line 8b	4.	

5. **Form 1040 filers:** Enter the total of any exclusions/adjustments for:
    • Qualified U.S. savings bond interest (Form 8815, line 14)
    • Adoption benefits (Form 8839, line 30)
    • Foreign earned income or housing (Form 2555, lines 45 and 50, or Form 2555-EZ, line 18), and
    • Certain income of bona fide residents of American Samoa (Form 4563, line 15) or Puerto Rico
    Form 1040A filers: Enter the total of any exclusions for:
    • Qualified U.S. savings bond interest (Form 8815, line 14)
    • Adoption benefits (Form 8839, line 30) . . . .
	5.	

6. Add lines 2, 3, 4, and 5	6.	27,500
7. **Form 1040 filers:** Enter the amounts from Form 1040, lines 23 through 32, and any write-in adjustments you entered on the dotted line next to line 36. **Form 1040A filers:** Enter the amounts from Form 1040A, lines 16 and 17	7.	0

8. Is the amount on line 7 less than the amount on line 6?
  No. (STOP) None of your social security benefits are taxable. Enter -0- on Form 1040, line 20b, or Form 1040A, line 14b.
  Yes. Subtract line 7 from line 6 . . . .
	8.	27,500

9. If you are:
    • Married filing jointly, enter $32,000
    • Single, head of household, qualifying widow(er), or married filing separately and you **lived apart** from your spouse for all of 2009, enter $25,000 . . . .
  Note. If you are married filing separately and you lived with your spouse at any time in 2009, skip lines 9 through 16; multiply line 8 by 85% (.85) and enter the result on line 17. Then go to line 18.
	9.	25,000

10. Is the amount on line 9 less than the amount on line 8?
  No. (STOP) None of your benefits are taxable. Enter -0- on Form 1040, line 20b, or on Form 1040A, line 14b. If you are married filing separately and you **lived apart** from your spouse for all of 2009, be sure you entered "D" to the right of the word "benefits" on Form 1040, line 20a, or on Form 1040A, line 14a.
  Yes. Subtract line 9 from line 8 . . . .
	10.	2,500

11. Enter $12,000 if married filing jointly; $9,000 if single, head of household, qualifying widow(er), or married filing separately and you **lived apart** from your spouse for all of 2009	11.	9,000
12. Subtract line 11 from line 10. If zero or less, enter -0-	12.	0
13. Enter the **smaller** of line 10 or line 11	13.	2,500
14. Enter one-half of line 13	14.	1,250
15. Enter the **smaller** of line 2 or line 14	15.	1,250
16. Multiply line 12 by 85% (.85). If line 12 is zero, enter -0-	16.	0
17. Add lines 15 and 16	17.	1,250
18. Multiply line 1 by 85% (.85)	18.	5,950
19. **Taxable benefits.** Enter the **smaller** of line 17 or line 18. Also enter this amount on Form 1040, line 20b, or Form 1040A, line 14b	19.	1,250

Other Income (Form 1040, line 21)

Gross income includes ". . . all income from whatever source derived. . . ." The concept is broad, and taxpayers often receive income that does not neatly fit into lines 7 though 20 of Form 1040. Line 21 is where taxpayers report other taxable gross income. A taxpayer who has any other taxable income reportable on line 21 can use only Form 1040. Items that taxpayers must report on line 21 include these:

• **Jury duty pay**: Individuals who serve jury duty receive a small amount of pay for each day served. This pay is included in other income. If the individual is required to remit the payment to his or her employer, the payment is deductible, the net effect of which is that the taxpayer reports zero.[26]

• **Prizes and awards**: If an employee receives a prize or award from his or her employer, the award is included in W-2 income. Prizes and awards received from other sources are taxable as other income unless specifically excluded (such as a scholarship award).

[26] IRC § 62(a)(13).

- **Forgiveness of debt**: If a taxpayer borrows money, it is not taxable income because the taxpayer must repay the loan (that is, the taxpayer does not have a complete, unfettered right to the money). If a lender fully or partially forgives a loan, the taxpayer has income to the extent of the forgiveness.[27] However, a borrower does not report income if payment of the debt would have given rise to a deduction.[28] For example, a lender forgives some interest otherwise due on a loan to a self-employed cash basis taxpayer. A taxpayer who had paid the interest would have recorded a business deduction for the interest paid. Thus the taxpayer reports no income. Other exceptions to the general forgiveness of debt rule (such as forgiveness during bankruptcy proceedings or when the taxpayer is insolvent) are beyond the scope of this text.[29]

- **Certain insurance proceeds**: Taxpayers receiving insurance proceeds in excess of the adjusted basis of the property insured must report taxable income equal to the excess. This category does not include life insurance or health insurance proceeds.

CONCEPT CHECK 3-6—LO 3	1. Name a type of income item that is listed on line 21 of Form 1040.

ITEMS EXCLUDED FROM GROSS INCOME
LO 4

Congress has exempted certain income from tax by statute. These exemptions include the following items.

Nontaxable Employee Fringe Benefits

The general rule is that employee compensation, in whatever form, is taxable to the employee. However, certain types of fringe benefits are tax-free to the employee, and the employer can deduct the cost of providing the benefits.[30] Most benefits are subject to nondiscrimination rules.[31]

The following fringe benefits provided by an employer are not taxable to the employee:

- **No-additional-cost services** provided to an employee, his or her spouse, or dependent children:[32] The employer must ordinarily offer the services for sale to outside customers, and the employer must incur no substantial additional cost (including forgone revenue) to provide the service. Examples include unsold hotel rooms or airline seats (but not if the benefit bumps a paying customer).

- **Discounts** provided employees for products or services normally sold by the business:[33] Examples are reduced price meals in restaurants, discounts on clothing at a retail store, and reduced interest rate loans from a financial institution. In the case of products, the discount cannot exceed the gross profit percentage, and in the case of services, the maximum discount is 20% of the normal selling price.

---

[27] IRC § 61(a)(12).

[28] IRC § 108(e)(2).

[29] These exceptions are found in IRC § 108 and the regulations thereunder.

[30] Employer deductibility is not a focus of this text.

[31] Generally, nondiscrimination rules prohibit or limit the nontaxability of certain benefits if highly compensated employees disproportionately receive the benefits at the expense of lower-paid employees. For example, if discounts (see the text) are given only to employees with salaries over $500,000, it is likely that the nondiscrimination rules would apply and make the discount amount a taxable benefit rather than a tax-free benefit.

[32] IRC § 132(b).

[33] IRC § 132(c).

- **Working condition fringe benefits**: These are services or properties provided to an employee that would have been deductible as a trade or business expense or as depreciation expense had the employee paid for them.[34] Working condition fringes include professional organization dues paid by an employer or the use of an employer-provided vehicle for business purposes.

- **Qualified transportation fringe benefits**: These benefits include transit passes, parking near the employer's business or near a mass transit location, and use of an employer-provided vanpool that holds six or more persons and is used 80% or more for commuting.[35] In 2009, parking benefits cannot exceed $230 per month, and transit passes and vanpool benefits cannot exceed $230 per month. Employees may exclude up to $460 per month in parking and transit benefits.

- **Moving expense reimbursements**: In certain circumstances, an employee can exclude from income any moving reimbursements paid by his or her employer to the extent that the employee does not deduct moving expenses.

- *De minimis* **benefits**: (holiday turkeys, company picnics, flowers or fruit sent when an employee is sick, etc.): A *de minimis* benefit is one whose value is so small that keeping track of which employees received the benefit is administratively impractical.[36]

Employees can exclude from income additional employer-provided benefits. Commonly used benefits follow:

- Employers often provide reduced-cost or fully paid accident and health insurance to employees. The value of the premium paid by the employer is not taxable to the employee.[37] Reimbursement for medical care paid by the insurance policy (or paid directly by the employer if no policy exists or if the policy does not cover the cost) is not taxable income to the employee unless the reimbursement exceeds the cost of the care.

- Employers can pay (or reimburse employees) for up to $5,250 per year of educational assistance, whether or not it is job-related.[38] Expenses include, but are not limited to, tuition, fees, books, and supplies.

- Employer-paid premiums on group term life insurance are not taxable to employees.[39] Tax-free coverage is limited to $50,000 per person. Coverage in excess of the $50,000 limit is taxable to the employee based on the cost of the excess.[40]

- The costs of employer-paid meals and lodging are tax-exempt if the meals and lodging are furnished for the convenience of the employer and are furnished on the business premises (in the case of meals), or the employee is required to accept the lodging as a condition of employment.[41] Examples meeting these criteria would be lodging for employees on an oil rig, at a lumber camp, or on a ship at sea, or meals provided employees who work at a business location far from eating places.

- Payments under written dependent care assistance plans are tax-free.[42] The exclusion cannot exceed $5,000 ($2,500 for married filing separately) and cannot exceed earned income (earned income of the lesser earning spouse for married filing jointly). Dependent care expenses are those that are considered to be employment-related expenses for purposes of the child care credit rules.

- Flexible benefit plans (often referred to as *cafeteria plans* or *flexible spending accounts*) are written plans that permit employees to choose their own benefits (which may include cash

---

[34] IRC § 132(d).

[35] IRC § 132(f).

[36] IRC § 132(e).

[37] IRC § 106(a).

[38] IRC § 127(a).

[39] IRC § 79(a).

[40] To determine the cost of the excess, see Reg. § 1.79-3(d)(2).

[41] IRC § 119(a).

[42] IRC § 129(a).

payments).[43] Normally the law provides that if a person has an opportunity to receive cash but elects to defer the payment or take payment in a noncash asset, income is still recognized. In the case of cafeteria plans (which by their very nature permit employees to choose), the value of the *benefits* received is not taxed to the employee. However, if employees elect to receive cash, the cash is taxable. The menu of options from which employees can choose often includes many of the fringe benefits discussed earlier (health care insurance, group life insurance, educational expenses, transportation fringe benefits, and the like). Under a cafeteria plan, the employee gets to choose the components that he or she finds the most beneficial.

Other Nontaxable Income

Taxpayers can receive certain nontaxable income not directly related to employment. This nontaxable income includes the following items.

Scholarships and Fellowships

In general, scholarships and fellowships are tax-free.[44] The individual must be a degree-seeking student at an educational institution and must use the proceeds for qualified tuition and related expenses (tuition, fees, books, supplies, and equipment). If the scholarship or fellowship payment exceeds permitted expenses, the excess is taxable income. Benefits under tuition reduction plans provided to employees of educational institutions are not taxable. If a student must perform certain services for the educational institution (such as graduate assistantships), the amount paid for the services is not a scholarship or fellowship but is a taxable wage.

EXAMPLE 3-12   Hilda is a graduate student at State University. In 2009, she received a scholarship of $7,000 ($4,000 toward tuition and fees and $3,000 to pay for campus housing) and a graduate assistantship that paid $5,000. Tuition, fees, and books cost $6,000 during the year. Hilda can exclude $4,000 from income. She will be required to report wage income of $5,000 from the graduate assistantship and $3,000 of other income for the housing benefit.

Qualified Tuition Program Withdrawals

A *Qualified Tuition Program* (QTP) is a state program that, in effect, is a tax-free savings account when used exclusively for educational expenses. Individuals make cash contributions to the QTP, and the state invests the contributions. If the contributor makes withdrawals from the QTP and uses the money to pay for qualified higher education expenses at an eligible educational institution, the withdrawal is tax-free. For tax years 2009 and 2010, the definition of qualified higher education expenses includes the purchase of computer equipment or Internet access that will be used by the beneficiary while the beneficiary is enrolled at an eligible educational institution.[45] For tax years 2009 and 2010, the definition of qualified higher education expenses includes the purchase of computer equipment or Internet access that will be used by the beneficiary while the beneficiary is enrolled at an eligible educational institution. These programs are also called *529 plans* (from the IRC section that created them).

Life Insurance Proceeds

Life insurance proceeds, payable because of the death of the insured, are fully excludable from the gross income of the recipient.[46] If proceeds are paid over time (rather than as a lump sum), payments are tax-free except to the extent that the payments exceed the amount payable at the time of death (for example, if there are earnings on the proceeds). The proportion of each payment that is tax-free is the excludable amount divided by the expected number of payments.[47]

[43] IRC § 125(a).
[44] IRC § 117(a), (b).
[45] IRC § 529.
[46] IRC § 101(a)(1).
[47] IRC § 101(d)(1). If payments are made over the life of the recipient, the denominator is determined by reference to appropriate life expectancy tables. Changes are not made to the calculations even if the recipient exceeds the life expectancy.

EXAMPLE 3-13   Joe is entitled to receive $50,000 of life insurance payable because of his wife's death. Instead of receiving a lump sum, he agreed to take five annual payments of $12,000 each. The excluded amount is $50,000/5 = $10,000 per payment. Thus the remaining $2,000 of each payment is interest income.[48]

Accelerated death benefits are amounts received under a life insurance policy on the life of an individual who is terminally ill or chronically ill. Taxpayers can exclude such payments from gross income.[49] A person is *terminally ill* if a physician certifies that he or she is likely to die within 24 months. A *chronically ill* person has a disability requiring long-term care or substantial supervision.[50]

Gifts and Inheritances

Gifts and inheritances are tax-free to the recipient.[51] *Gifts* are transfers made during the lifetime of the giver; *inheritances* are transfers of property at or after death. An individual can classify a transfer as a tax-free gift only if the giver was motivated by kindness, generosity, affection, or similar emotions.

TAX YOUR BRAIN    Norma was the 100,000th customer at her local grocery store. Because of that, the store gave Norma a free trip to Australia as a gift. Is the trip taxable or tax-free?

ANSWER

The trip to Australia is taxable. The owners did not give Norma the trip because they were motivated by kindness or generosity; they gave it to her for promotional reasons. The fair value of the trip is taxable to Norma.

Gifts may be subject to a gift tax that is the responsibility of the giver. Rules concerning gift taxes are beyond the scope of this text.

Compensation for Sickness or Injury

The following items are exempt from income under the umbrella of compensation for injuries or sickness:[52]

- Payments received under workers' compensation acts.
- Damages (other than punitive damages) received as a result of personal physical injuries or sickness.
- Pensions or annuities received for personal injuries or sickness from active service in the armed forces, Coast Guard, public health service, or foreign service.
- Disability income resulting from a terrorist attack while in the employ of the United States engaged in official duties outside the United States.

Other

Other nontaxable income includes

- Child support (nontaxable to the recipient and not deductible by the payer).[53]
- Public assistance payments (such as welfare).
- Employer-provided adoption assistance up to $12,150 per child.

---

[48] Generally the taxpayer will receive a form 1099-INT from the insurance company disclosing the amount of interest income.
[49] IRC § 101(g)(1).
[50] IRC § 101(g)(4).
[51] IRC § 102(a).
[52] IRC § 104(a).
[53] IRC § 71(c)(1).

From Shoebox to Software   Two Comprehensive Examples

We now introduce two new taxpayers.

YIMING CHOW

The first taxpayer is Yiming Chow, who is single and lives at 456 Maple Avenue, Somewhere, OH 45678. His SSN is 111-11-1111. During 2009 Mr. Chow received a W-2 from his employer, a 1099-INT from the local financial institution, and a 1099-DIV associated with a mutual fund investment. He also received a 1099-G from the state of Ohio for a $57 tax refund pertaining to tax year 2008. Mr. Chow did not itemize his deductions in 2008. All these documents are shown in Exhibit 3-8.

Open the tax software. Go to the File pull-down menu and click on New Return. Go through the process to start a new return, and then click on the Forms icon to bring up the list of available forms. Open a Form 1040 to input the basic name, address, and social security number information for Mr. Chow. He is eligible to file Form 1040A, and we will use that form after you enter his personal information.

Now enter the information from the various tax forms into the tax software using the applicable forms in the Documents Received section. Note that you do not need to enter any information concerning the tax refund. Mr. Chow did not itemize deductions in 2008, so you do not need to report his tax refund as income.

Once you have entered the appropriate information, click on Form 1040A. Line 15 should be $41,688. Line 27, taxable income, should be $32,338. Mr. Chow's tax liability on line 28 is $4,416. Because Mr. Chow has wage income and dividend income, you may find it instructive to calculate the tax liability by hand to see if you get the same answer. Because Mr. Chow had $4,670 withheld from his wages, his refund is $654, as shown on lines 45 and 46a.

Make sure you save Mr. Chow's return for use in later chapters.

MR. AND MRS. RAMIREZ

The second taxpayer is the married couple Jose and Maria Ramirez. They live at 1234 West Street, Mytown, GA 33333. They have three children, Arturo, Benito, and Carmen, born in 1996, 1998, and 2000, respectively. The children lived in the household during the entire year. The SSNs are as follows:

Jose 222-22-2222, Maria 333-33-3333

Arturo 222-22-0001, Benito 333-33-0001, Carmen 444-44-0001

Mr. Ramirez received a W-2 from his employer, a 1099-INT from the financial institution, and a 1099-DIV from his stockbroker. He also received a 1099-G from the state of Georgia for a $645 tax refund. The taxpayer itemized deductions last year, and you have determined that the entire refund is taxable.

All of the Ramirezes' documents are shown in Exhibit 3-9.

Open the tax software. Go to the File pull-down menu and click on New Return. Go through the process to start a new return, and then click on the Forms icon to bring up the list of available forms. Open a blank Form 1040 to input the basic name, address, and social security number information for Mr. and Mrs. Ramirez. Use the Dependent Worksheet in the Worksheet section to enter information for the children.

The Ramirezes must file Form 1040 because of the state tax refund. For now we will assume that the couple will take the standard deduction.

Now enter the information from the various tax forms into the tax software using the applicable forms in the Documents Received section.

Because you do not have tax return information for tax year 2008, you need to provide information concerning the tax refund. Enter in the system that the full amount of the refund is taxable.

Once you have entered the appropriate information, the total income and the AGI of the taxpayer should be $106,962. After subtracting a standard deduction of $11,400 and personal exemptions of $18,250 ($3,650 per individual), taxable income should be $77,312.

The tax on line 44 should be $11,662. The tax software automatically calculated a $3,000 child tax credit on line 51. We will discuss credits later in the text. The credit reduces the Ramirezes' tax liability to $8,662. Because the taxpayer had withholding of $9,418, the Ramirezes' return should show a refund of $1,556 on lines 72 and 73a.

Make sure you save the Ramirezes' tax return for use in later chapters. These will be running demonstration problems throughout the text.

CONCEPT CHECK 3-7—LO 4

1. Holiday turkeys given to employees are included in gross income. True or False?
2. In general, scholarships are not taxable if the use of the money is to pay tuition, fees, books, supplies, and equipment. True or false?

EXHIBIT 3-8

☐ CORRECTED (if checked)

PAYER'S name, street address, city, state, ZIP code, and telephone no.		**1a** Total ordinary dividends $ 96.71	OMB No. 1545-0110	**Dividends and Distributions**
Jones Brokerage P.O. Box 500 Somewhere, OH 45678		**1b** Qualified dividends $ 96.71	**2009** Form **1099-DIV**	
		2a Total capital gain distr. $	**2b** Unrecap. Sec. 1250 gain $	**Copy B** **For Recipient**
PAYER'S federal identification number	RECIPIENT'S identification number 111-11-1111			
RECIPIENT'S name Yiming Chow		**2c** Section 1202 gain $	**2d** Collectibles (28%) gain $	This is important tax information and is being furnished to the Internal Revenue Service. If you are required to file a return, a negligence penalty or other sanction may be imposed on you if this income is taxable and the IRS determines that it has not been reported.
		3 Nondividend distributions $	**4** Federal income tax withheld $	
Street address (including apt. no.) 456 Maple Avenue			**5** Investment expenses $	
City, state, and ZIP code Somewhere, OH 45678		**6** Foreign tax paid $	**7** Foreign country or U.S. possession	
Account number (see instructions)		**8** Cash liquidation distributions $	**9** Noncash liquidation distributions $	

Form **1099-DIV**   (keep for your records)   Department of the Treasury - Internal Revenue Service

	a Employee's social security number 111-11-1111	OMB No. 1545-0008	**Safe, accurate, FAST! Use** IRS *e-file*	Visit the IRS website at *www.irs.gov/efile*.
b Employer identification number (EIN)			**1** Wages, tips, other compensation 41,321.34	**2** Federal income tax withheld 4,670.00
c Employer's name, address, and ZIP code Acme Company 900 Oak Street Somewhere, OH 45678			**3** Social security wages 41,321.34	**4** Social security tax withheld 2,561.92
			5 Medicare wages and tips 41,321.34	**6** Medicare tax withheld 599.16
			7 Social security tips	**8** Allocated tips
d Control number			**9** Advance EIC payment	**10** Dependent care benefits
e Employee's first name and initial Last name Suff. Yiming Chow 456 Maple Street Somewhere, OH 45678			**11** Nonqualified plans	**12a** See instructions for box 12
			13 ☐ Statutory employee ☐ Retirement plan ☐ Third-party sick pay	**12b**
			14 Other	**12c**
				12d
f Employee's address and ZIP code				

15 State Employer's state ID number	**16** State wages, tips, etc.	**17** State income tax	**18** Local wages, tips, etc.	**19** Local income tax	**20** Locality name
OH	41,321.34	1,239.63			

Form **W-2** **Wage and Tax Statement**   **2009**   Department of the Treasury—Internal Revenue Service

Copy B—To Be Filed With Employee's FEDERAL Tax Return.
This information is being furnished to the Internal Revenue Service.

EXHIBIT 3-8   *(concluded)*

☐ CORRECTED (if checked)

PAYER'S name, street address, city, state, ZIP code, and telephone no.

State of Ohio
P.O. Box 500
Columbus, OH 45555

1 Unemployment compensation
$

2 State or local income tax refunds, credits, or offsets
$ 57.00

OMB No. 1545-0120
2009
Form **1099-G**

Certain Government Payments

PAYER'S federal identification number	RECIPIENT'S identification number 111-11-1111	**3 Box 2 amount is for tax year** 2008	**4 Federal income tax withheld** $

RECIPIENT'S name

Yiming Chow

5 ATAA payments
$

6 Taxable grants
$

Street address (including apt. no.)
456 Maple Avenue

7 Agriculture payments
$

8 Box 2 is trade or business income ► ☐

City, state, and ZIP code
Somewhere, OH 45678

9 Market gain
$

Account number (see instructions)

Copy B
For Recipient

This is important tax information and is being furnished to the Internal Revenue Service. If you are required to file a return, a negligence penalty or other sanction may be imposed on you if this income is taxable and the IRS determines that it has not been reported.

Form **1099-G**   (keep for your records)   Department of the Treasury - Internal Revenue Service

---

☐ CORRECTED (if checked)

PAYER'S name, street address, city, state, ZIP code, and telephone no.

First National Bank
125 Main Street
Somewhere, OH   45678

Payer's RTN (optional)

1 Interest income
$ 270.12

2 Early withdrawal penalty
$

OMB No. 1545-0112
2009
Form **1099-INT**

Interest Income

PAYER'S federal identification number	RECIPIENT'S identification number 111-11-1111	**3 Interest on U.S. Savings Bonds and Treas. obligations** $

RECIPIENT'S name

Yiming Chow

4 Federal income tax withheld
$

5 Investment expenses
$

Street address (including apt. no.)
456 Maple Avenue

6 Foreign tax paid
$

7 Foreign country or U.S. possession

City, state, and ZIP code
Somewhere, OH 45678

8 Tax-exempt interest
$

9 Specified private activity bond interest
$

Account number (see instructions)

Copy B
For Recipient

This is important tax information and is being furnished to the Internal Revenue Service. If you are required to file a return, a negligence penalty or other sanction may be imposed on you if this income is taxable and the IRS determines that it has not been reported.

Form **1099-INT**   (keep for your records)   Department of the Treasury - Internal Revenue Service

---

EXHIBIT 3-9

☐ CORRECTED (if checked)

PAYER'S name, street address, city, state, ZIP code, and telephone no.

First National Bank
1000 Main Street
Mytown, GA 33333

Payer's RTN (optional)

1 Interest income
$ 851.19

2 Early withdrawal penalty
$

OMB No. 1545-0112
2009
Form **1099-INT**

Interest Income

PAYER'S federal identification number	RECIPIENT'S identification number 222-22-2222	**3 Interest on U.S. Savings Bonds and Treas. obligations** $

RECIPIENT'S name

Jose Ramirez

4 Federal income tax withheld
$

5 Investment expenses
$

Street address (including apt. no.)
1234 West Street

6 Foreign tax paid
$

7 Foreign country or U.S. possession

City, state, and ZIP code
Mytown, GA 33333

8 Tax-exempt interest
$

9 Specified private activity bond interest
$

Account number (see instructions)

Copy B
For Recipient

This is important tax information and is being furnished to the Internal Revenue Service. If you are required to file a return, a negligence penalty or other sanction may be imposed on you if this income is taxable and the IRS determines that it has not been reported.

Form **1099-INT**   (keep for your records)   Department of the Treasury - Internal Revenue Service

EXHIBIT 3-9 *(continued)*

☐ CORRECTED (if checked)

PAYER'S name, street address, city, state, ZIP code, and telephone no.	1a Total ordinary dividends $ 329.40	OMB No. 1545-0110	

1a Total ordinary dividends $ 329.40

Smith Brokerage
P.O. Box 100
Mytown, GA 33333

1b Qualified dividends $ 329.40

2009

Form **1099-DIV**

Dividends and Distributions

2a Total capital gain distr. $

2b Unrecap. Sec. 1250 gain $

Copy B
For Recipient

PAYER'S federal identification number

RECIPIENT'S identification number 222-22-2222

2c Section 1202 gain $

2d Collectibles (28%) gain $

RECIPIENT'S name

Jose Ramirez

3 Nondividend distributions $

4 Federal income tax withheld $

Street address (including apt. no.)

1234 West Street

5 Investment expenses $

City, state, and ZIP code
Mytown, GA 33333

6 Foreign tax paid $

7 Foreign country or U.S. possession

Account number (see instructions)

8 Cash liquidation distributions $

9 Noncash liquidation distributions $

This is important tax information and is being furnished to the Internal Revenue Service. If you are required to file a return, a negligence penalty or other sanction may be imposed on you if this income is taxable and the IRS determines that it has not been reported.

Form **1099-DIV** (keep for your records) Department of the Treasury - Internal Revenue Service

---

a Employee's social security number 222-22-2222	OMB No. 1545-0008	Safe, accurate, FAST! Use IRS e~file	Visit the IRS website at www.irs.gov/efile.

b Employer identification number (EIN)

1 Wages, tips, other compensation 105,137.10 | **2 Federal income tax withheld** 9,418.32

c Employer's name, address, and ZIP code

Beta Tech
500 East Street
Mytown, GA 33333

3 Social security wages 105,137.10 | **4 Social security tax withheld** 6,518.50
5 Medicare wages and tips 105,137.10 | **6 Medicare tax withheld** 1,524.49
7 Social security tips | **8 Allocated tips**

d Control number

9 Advance EIC payment | **10 Dependent care benefits**

e Employee's first name and initial   Last name   Suff.

Jose Ramirez
1234 West Street
Mytown, GA 33333

11 Nonqualified plans | **12a** See instructions for box 12
13 Statutory employee ☐ Retirement plan ☐ Third-party sick pay ☐ | **12b**
14 Other | **12c**
| **12d**

f Employee's address and ZIP code

15 State Employer's state ID number GA	16 State wages, tips, etc. 105,137.10	17 State income tax 3,469.52	18 Local wages, tips, etc.	19 Local income tax	20 Locality name

Form **W-2** **Wage and Tax Statement** 2009

Department of the Treasury—Internal Revenue Service

Copy B—To Be Filed With Employee's FEDERAL Tax Return.
This information is being furnished to the Internal Revenue Service.

EXHIBIT 3-9   *(concluded)*

☐ CORRECTED (if checked)		

PAYER'S name, street address, city, state, ZIP code, and telephone no.	1 Unemployment compensation	OMB No. 1545-0120	**Certain Government Payments**
State of Georgia P.O. Box 500 Atlanta, GA 33333	$	2009	
	2 State or local income tax refunds, credits, or offsets		
	$ 645.00	Form **1099-G**	

PAYER'S federal identification number	RECIPIENT'S identification number 222-22-2222	3 Box 2 amount is for tax year 2008	4 Federal income tax withheld $	**Copy B** **For Recipient**
RECIPIENT'S name Jose Ramirez		5 ATAA payments $	6 Taxable grants $	This is important tax information and is being furnished to the Internal Revenue Service. If you are required to file a return, a negligence penalty or other sanction may be imposed on you if this income is taxable and the IRS determines that it has not been reported.
Street address (including apt. no.) 1234 West Street		7 Agriculture payments $	8 Box 2 is trade or business income ▶ ☐	
City, state, and ZIP code Mytown, GA 33333		9 Market gain $		
Account number (see instructions)				

Form **1099-G**	(keep for your records)	Department of the Treasury - Internal Revenue Service

Appendix

TAX ACCOUNTING FOR SAVINGS BOND INTEREST USED FOR EDUCATION EXPENSES, BELOW-MARKET INTEREST LOANS, GIFT LOANS, AND ORIGINAL ISSUE DISCOUNT DEBT
LO 5

This appendix covers topics pertaining to interest that are important but less common.

Savings Bond Interest Exclusion

Interest on Series EE or Series I savings bonds is not taxable if the taxpayer uses the bond proceeds to pay qualified higher education expenses for the taxpayer, his or her spouse, or their dependent(s).[54] The bonds must have been purchased (not received by gift) after 1989 by an individual, at least 24 years old at the time of purchase, who is the sole owner of the bonds (or joint owner with his or her spouse). Qualified higher education expenses are tuition and fees at a qualified educational institution.[55] However, the taxpayer must reduce qualified expenses by tax-exempt scholarships, certain educational assistance allowances, certain benefits under a qualified state tuition program, and expenses used in determining Hope and lifetime learning credits or a Coverdell Education Savings Account distribution exclusion.[56] Married persons living together must file a joint return in the year of exclusion.

Taxpayers can exclude the full amount of interest only if the amount of qualified higher education expense paid in a year exceeds the redemption proceeds (principal plus interest) for the year. If proceeds exceed expenses, the amount of interest that is excludable is limited to the interest multiplied by a fraction calculated as qualified expenses paid during the year divided by aggregate redemption proceeds.

[54] IRC § 135(a).

[55] IRC § 529(e)(5)

[56] IRC § 135(c)(2) and IRC § 135(d).

EXAMPLE 3-14	In 2009, Angeline and Daryl redeemed $4,000 (principal of $3,000 and interest of $1,000) of Series I savings bonds to pay qualified higher education expenses. Qualified expenses for the year totaled $3,500. Angeline and Daryl may exclude interest of $875 from income in 2009 [$1,000 × ($3,500/$4,000)]. The remaining $125 is taxable interest income.

The amount of savings bond interest exempt from tax is further limited if modified AGI of the taxpayer for tax year 2009 exceeds $104,900 on a joint return or $69,950 on other returns.[57] If modified AGI exceeds those limits, the amount of the reduction is equal to

$$\text{Amount otherwise excludable} \times \frac{\text{Modified AGI} - \text{Limitation amount}}{\$30,000\ (\$15,000\ \text{for single filers})}$$

When modified AGI reaches $134,900 for joint returns and $84,950 for other returns, the amount of exempt interest phases out. Taxpayers calculate the modified AGI limitation after all other limitations.

EXAMPLE 3-15	Al, a single taxpayer, has determined that his excludable savings bond interest is $1,400 prior to any modified AGI limitation. His modified AGI is $70,850. Al will be able to exclude $1,316 of savings bond interest on his 2009 tax return, calculated as follows: $1,400 × [($70,850 − $69,950)/$15,000] = reduction amount of $84. Thus the excludable savings bond interest will be $1,400 − $84 = $1,316. Al must report savings bond interest of $84 on his 2009 tax return.

Modified AGI is AGI adjusted as follows:

Adjusted Gross Income
Plus: Deduction for student loan interest[58]
　　　Deduction for tuition and fees (Tax Extenders Act of 2008)
　　　The savings bond interest exclusion itself[59]
　　　Excluded foreign income and allowances[60]
　　　Excluded adoption assistance from an employer[61]

EXAMPLE 3-16	Veronica has AGI of $41,000 that includes a student loan interest deduction of $800. Her modified AGI for purposes of the savings bond interest exclusion is $41,800.

Below-Market Interest Rate Loans

Most interest-bearing instruments carry an interest rate that approximates the market rate of interest for instruments of similar maturity, credit risk, and collateral. For example, if two persons of equal loan-paying ability and credit rating obtain a loan at a financial institution to finance the purchase of a Ford F-150 on a four-year repayment schedule, the interest rates on the two loans should be approximately equal.

[57] These amounts are subject to annual adjustment for inflation.
[58] Under IRC § 221.
[59] Under IRC § 135.
[60] Under IRC § 911, 931, and 933.
[61] Under § 137.

In some circumstances, one party in a transaction wishes to charge a low rate of interest rather than a market rate.[62] Assume that an individual is selling a parcel of land for $100,000 and will accept $10,000 down with annual interest-only payments on the balance at an interest rate of 10%, with principal due at the end of five years. Total payments would be $100,000 in principal and $45,000 of interest. Because interest income is taxable at a rate up to 35% and capital gains are generally taxed at no more than 15%, it would be beneficial to the seller if the price were raised to, say, $130,000 while lowering the interest rate to 2.5%. Total payments will still be $145,000 ($130,000 principal and $15,000 interest), but the seller will have, in effect, converted $30,000 of interest income into capital gain income, thereby saving almost $6,000 in tax.[63]

The law limits the ability of taxpayers to create debt instruments with interest rates that materially vary from market rates on the date the instrument is created.[64] Taxpayers are required to "impute interest" on a deferred payment contract for which no interest, or a low rate of interest, is stated. Imputing interest reallocates payments so that more of each payment is interest and less is principal. The imputed interest rules apply to installment transactions that are due more than six months after the date of the sale or exchange of property.

An installment obligation arises when a taxpayer sells property and does not receive the entire sales price at the time of sale. The imputed interest rules apply when the gross payments due under an installment contract are greater than the present value of the payments due under the contract, discounted at the applicable federal rate (AFR).[65] In effect, installment contracts with stated interest rates below the AFR will result in the imposition of the imputed interest rules. The AFR is determined monthly, varies with the term of the loan (short-, mid-, or long-term), and is based on the rate paid by the federal government on borrowed funds.

EXAMPLE 3-17

In 2009 Lloyd sells land for $40,000, payable with $5,000 down and the balance in five equal annual installments of $7,642, which include interest at 3%. Lloyd's basis in the land is $30,000. The AFR at the time of sale is 8%. The present value (PV) of the five annual payments discounted at 8% is $30,512. Thus the sales price is $35,512 (the PV of the payments plus the down payment), and Lloyd's capital gain is $5,512.

Here is the amortization schedule:

Year	Payment	Principal	Interest	Balance
				$30,512
2009	$7,642	$5,201	$2,441	25,311
2010	7,642	5,617	2,025	19,694
2011	7,642	6,067	1,575	13,627
2012	7,642	6,552	1,090	7,075
2013	7,642	7,075	567	-0-

The preceding calculations illustrate that Lloyd will have a capital gain of $5,512 and interest income of $7,698 rather than a capital gain of $10,000 and $3,210 of interest income.

---

[62] Charging above-market rates is also possible but less likely.

[63] The $30,000 difference is taxed at 15% rather than 35%, so the taxpayer will save 20% or $6,000.

[64] IRC § 483 and § 1274.

[65] The imputed interest rules in question are at IRC § 483(b). The AFR is determined under IRC § 1274(d).

The imputed interest rules do not apply to the following:[66]

- Debt subject to the original issue discount rules (see the following).
- Sales of property for $3,000 or less.
- Certain carrying charges.[67]
- Sales in which all payments are due in six months or less.
- In the case of sales of patents, any portion of the sales price that is contingent on the productivity, use, or disposition of the patent.

Taxpayers use the accrual basis to calculate imputed interest (even if the taxpayer reports on the cash basis) except in the following instances, when cash basis reporting is permitted:[68]

- Sale of a personal residence.
- Sales of farms for $1 million or less.
- Sales in which total payments are $250,000 or less.
- Certain land transfers between related parties.[69]
- Debt in which the stated principal is $2 million or less and the lender and borrower elect to use the cash method (not applicable to accrual method lenders or dealers).

Gift, Shareholder, and Similar Loans

The concepts associated with imputed interest rules also apply to certain low-interest or interest-free loans involving related parties.[70] Imputed interest rules apply to term loans or demand loans in which the interest rate is less than the AFR and that occur in the following situations:

- Gift loans over $13,000 in which interest forgone is in the form of a gift. An example of a gift loan is a loan from a parent to a child in which no interest rate is stated. The $13,000 limit does not apply if the loan is for acquisition of income-producing assets.[71] However, imputed interest is limited to net investment income if the loan amount is $100,000 or less. No interest imputation is necessary if net investment income is less than $1,000.
- Compensation-related loans over $10,000 between an employee and employer or between an independent contractor and the corporation for which he or she works or any shareholder thereof.
- Loans over $10,000 between a corporation and any shareholder.
- Other loans in which a principal purpose is to avoid tax.
- Other loans in which the below-market or interest-free loan would have a significant effect on the tax liability of the borrower or lender.

EXAMPLE 3-18	Marty made interest-free loans to his three brothers, Pete, Bob, and Bill, of $8,000, $30,000, and $150,000, respectively. Pete used his $8,000 to buy a boat; Bob purchased IBM bonds with his $30,000 and earned $1,500 of investment income; and Bill bought a personal residence with his $150,000. The imputed interest rules would not apply to Pete because the loan is less than $10,000. The loans to Bob and Bill fall under the imputed interest rules because Bob purchased income-producing property (the interest expense would be limited to the $1,500 of net investment income) and Bill's loan was over $100,000.

---

[66] IRC § 483(d).

[67] Covered in IRC § 163(b).

[68] IRC § 1274(c)(3) and IRC § 1274A(c).

[69] Described in IRC § 483(e).

[70] IRC § 7872.

[71] In the case of gift loans between individuals that total $100,000 or less, the amount of imputed interest is limited to the borrower's net investment income.

Imputed interest is determined in a manner similar to that outlined earlier. The lender is deemed to give the borrower the amount of the calculated imputed interest, which the borrower then repays to the lender. Thus the transaction results in taxable interest income to the lender and interest expense to the borrower (which may or may not be deductible). For loans between an employer and employee, the deemed payment from the lender to the borrower creates compensation income to the employee. Similarly, deemed payments on loans between a corporation and a shareholder create dividend income to the shareholder.

Original Issue Discount

If someone purchases a debt instrument (such as a bond) from an issuer for an amount less than par, the transaction creates original issue discount (OID). The initial OID is equal to the difference between the acquisition price and the maturity value.[72]

EXAMPLE 3-19	On January 1, 2009, Leonardo purchased $200,000 of Meno Corporation's newly issued bonds for $176,100, to yield 11%. The bonds carry an interest rate of 9% and mature in 10 years. The initial OID on these bonds is $23,900 (the $200,000 face amount less the $176,100 payment).

OID is deemed to be zero if it is less than .25% of the maturity value, multiplied by the number of complete years to maturity.[73] In Example 3-19, this *de minimis* threshold is $5,000 (.0025 × 10 years × $200,000). Thus if Leonardo purchased the bonds for any amount more than $195,000, no OID is recognized.

If OID exists, the holder must include part of the OID in interest income every year, regardless of the holder's method of accounting (that is, the holder accounts for the income under the accrual method).[74] The taxpayer calculates the imputed interest using the constant interest rate method (sometimes referred to as the *effective interest method* that you probably learned in your financial accounting class). In this method, total interest income is equal to the carrying amount (basis) of the bond multiplied by the effective interest rate (the yield to maturity on the date of purchase). The amount of OID is the difference between interest income so calculated and the amount of cash received. The carrying amount of the bond increases by the amount of OID.

EXAMPLE 3-20

Using the information from Example 3-19, the effective interest calculations for the first four bond payments are as follows (remember that bond interest is paid semiannually):

Payment Date	(1) Interest Income	(2) Cash Received	(3) OID	(4) Carrying Amount
				$176,100
June 30, 09	$9,686	$9,000	$686	176,786
Dec. 31, 09	9,723	9,000	723	177,509
June 30, 10	9,763	9,000	763	178,272
Dec. 31, 10	9,805	9,000	805	179,077

Column (1) is the prior balance in Column (4) times 11% divided by 2.
Column (2) is the $200,000 face amount multiplied by the 9% face rate divided by 2.
Column (3) is Column (1) minus Column (2).
Column (4) is the prior balance in Column (4) plus the OID amount in Column (3).

In 2009 Leonardo would report interest income of $19,409 ($9,686 + $9,723). Leonardo's interest income in 2010 would be $19,568.

[72] IRC § 1273(a)(1).

[73] IRC § 1273(a)(3).

[74] IRC § 1272(a)(1).

OID rules apply to all debt instruments with OID except for[75]

- Tax-exempt debt.
- U.S. savings bonds.
- Debt with a maturity of one year or less on the date of issue.
- Any obligation issued by a natural person before March 2, 1984.
- Nonbusiness loans of $10,000 or less between natural persons.

An individual who sells a debt instrument with OID prior to maturity calculates OID on a daily basis until the date of sale.

The OID rules stated earlier apply to the original purchaser only. The Revenue Reconciliation Act of 1993 extended many of the provisions of the OID rules to market discount bonds,[76] which are bonds purchased in the bond market at a discount. The market discount is the difference between the redemption price (normally par) and the basis (cost) of the bond immediately after purchase.[77] The *de minimis* rule for OID also applies to market discount bonds.

With OID instruments, taxpayers report a portion of the OID as interest income annually. Such is not the case with market discount bonds. Rather, the gain on disposition of the bond, if any, is ordinary income to the extent of the accrued market discount (determined ratably on a straight-line method computed on a daily basis). If a person holds the bond to maturity, the entire market discount amount is ordinary income.

EXAMPLE 3-21	Yvonne purchased $100,000 of the seven-year bonds of Ruby Company on July 1, 2009, for $90,000. The bonds were originally issued on January 1, 2007 (so at the time of purchase they had a remaining maturity of 4½ years). One year later, Yvonne sold the bonds for $96,000. Without the market discount bond rules, Yvonne would recognize a capital gain of $6,000. However, her capital gain is reduced (and her ordinary income is increased) by a portion of the market discount. Yvonne spreads the $10,000 discount over the maturity period (as of the date of purchase) on a straight-line basis, resulting in an allocation of $2,222 per year ($10,000/4.5). Thus Yvonne will recognize a capital gain of $3,778 and ordinary income of $2,222.

CONCEPT CHECK 3-8—LO 5	1. An individual is required to impute interest on a deferred payment contract where no interest, or a low rate of interest, is stated. True or false?
	2. If someone purchases a debt instrument (such as a bond) from an issuer for an amount less than par value, the transaction creates original issue discount (OID). True or false?

Summary

LO 1: Describe when and how to record income for tax purposes.	• Recognition of income for accounting takes place when the income has been realized and earned. • Recognition of income for tax purposes is similar to the recognition of income for accounting, but three additional conditions must be met: economic benefit of the transaction, conclusion of the transaction, and the income derived from the transaction must not be tax-exempt income.

[75] IRC § 1272(a)(2).

[76] IRC § 1278.

[77] IRC § 1278(a)(2)(A).

LO 2: Apply the cash method of accounting to income taxes.

- Almost all individuals use the cash receipts and disbursements method of accounting for taxes.
- An individual reports income in the year he or she receives or constructively receives the income rather than the year in which he or she earns the income.
- Receipt of property or services will trigger income recognition.
- Special situations exist in which a cash basis taxpayer can report income as though he or she were an accrual basis taxpayer.

LO 3: Explain the taxability of components of gross income, including interest, dividends, tax refunds, and social security benefits.

- If the amount of interest is over $1,500, use Schedule 1 for Form 1040A or Schedule B for Form 1040.
- Interest from banks, savings and loans, or credit unions is reported on Form 1099-INT and is taxable.
- Interest earned on Series E, EE, and I U.S. savings bonds can be reported gradually on an annual basis or fully at maturity.
- Some interest received is tax-exempt if the debt is issued by a U.S. state, possession, or subdivision thereof (such as municipal bonds).
- Other sources of interest that must be reported: payments received from seller-financed mortgages, receipts from installment sale receivables, imputed interest on loans made with below-market interest rates, and interest on bonds sold between interest dates.
- If the amount of dividends is over $1,500, use Schedule 1 for Form 1040A or Schedule B for Forms 1040A and 1040.
- Dividends are distributions to shareholders.
- Dividends are taxed at capital gain rates if they are qualified dividends.
- Stock dividends and stock splits are generally not taxable.
- State and local tax refunds are taxable if, in the prior tax year, the tax was deducted as an itemized deduction.
- Unemployment compensation is taxable.
- Part of social security benefits may be taxable. Provisional income must be calculated and compared to the information on the chart (see the text) showing the thresholds and taxability.
- Other income to be reported on the tax return: jury duty pay, prizes and awards, forgiveness of debt, and insurance proceeds in excess of the adjusted basis of the property.

LO 4: Apply the rules concerning items excluded from gross income.

- Congress has exempted certain income from tax by statute.
- Fringe benefits must be subject to nondiscrimination rules by the employer to qualify.
- Examples of fringe benefits not taxable in most circumstances: no-additional-cost services provided to an employee, discounts provided to employees for products or services normally sold by the business, a working condition fringe benefit, qualified transportation, moving expense reimbursements, and *de minimis* benefits.
- Nontaxable fringe benefits with certain limitations: life insurance, educational assistance, dependent care assistance, and cafeteria plans offered to employees.
- Other nontaxable income includes scholarships and fellowships, qualified tuition program (QTP) withdrawals, life insurance proceeds, gifts and inheritances, compensation for sickness or injury, child support, welfare, and employer-provided adoption assistance.

LO 5: Apply the rules associated with tax accounting for savings bond interest used for education expenses, below-market interest loans, gift loans, and original issue discount debt (appendix).

- Savings bond interest exclusion can be taken for the full amount if the amount of qualified higher education expense paid in a year exceeds the redemption proceeds (principal plus interest).
- Limitation applies if modified AGI exceeds $104,900 on a joint return or $69,950 on other returns.
- Taxpayers are required to impute interest on a deferred payment contract if no interest, or a low rate of interest, is stated. Certain exceptions apply.
- Original issue discount (OID) is equal to the difference between the acquisition price and the maturity value.
- If OID exists, the holder must report part of the OID as income every year.

Discussion Questions

LO 2   1. Explain how income is recognized under the cash method of accounting.

_____

_____

_____

_____

LO 2   2. Are there circumstances in which income is recognized even when a cash basis taxpayer does not receive cash? Explain.

_____

_____

_____

_____

LO 2   3. What is meant by the concept of *constructive receipt*?

_____

_____

_____

_____

LO 2   4. Refer to Example 3-4 in the chapter. Explain why Antonio is required to report income even though he did not receive an asset (either cash or property).

_____

_____

_____

_____

LO 3   5. Your friend John files his own tax returns. He received a computer as a dividend from a closely held corporation. He says that he does not need to report the computer as dividend income because the dividend was not paid in cash. Is he right? Why?

_____

_____

_____

_____

LO 3   6. Interest on corporate bonds is taxable to the recipient whereas interest on municipal bonds is tax-free. Would you expect that the interest rate on a corporate bond would be higher or lower than the rate on a municipal bond of comparable quality and term? Why?

_____

_____

_____

_____

LO 3   7. What is a dividend?

_____

_____

_____

_____

LO 3   8. How are dividends taxed?

_____

_____

_____

_____

LO 3   9. Leo owns all of the stock in a newly formed corporation. During 2009, the first year of operation, the corporation realized current earnings and profits of $10,000. Leo received a $12,000 distribution from the corporation. How much, if any, of the distribution is taxable to Leo? Why?

_____

_____

_____

_____

LO 3   10. Under what circumstances is a dividend nontaxable to a shareholder recipient?

_____

_____

_____

_____

LO 3   11. How do dividends and earnings and profits relate to each other?

_____

_____

_____

_____

LO 3   12. Under what circumstances is a state or local income tax refund included in the taxable income of a taxpayer?

_____

_____

_____

_____

LO 3 13. Under what circumstances are social security benefits taxable to a single taxpayer?

_____

_____

_____

_____

LO 3 14. When determining the taxability of social security benefits, the IRC uses the concept of *provisional income.* How is provisional income calculated?

_____

_____

_____

_____

LO 4 15. Congress has chosen to exempt certain income from taxation, such as scholarships, gifts, life insurance proceeds, municipal bond interest, and employee fringe benefits. Given that one of the primary purposes of the IRC is to raise revenue for the government, why do you think Congress would provide these and other exemptions?

_____

_____

_____

_____

LO 4 16. What is an employer-provided fringe benefit?

_____

_____

_____

_____

LO 4 17. Define and give examples of a *de minimis* employee fringe benefit.

_____

_____

_____

_____

LO 4 18. Explain the requirements necessary for a scholarship to be tax-free to the recipient.

_____

_____

_____

_____

Multiple-Choice Questions

LO 1 19. Accountants recognize revenue when it is both realized and
  a. Accumulated.
  b. Recorded.
  c. Collected.
  d. Earned.

LO 1   20. For tax purposes, one of the requirements to recognize income is that
    a. The income must be tax-exempt.
    b. There must be an economic benefit.
    c. The transaction must occur but completion of the transaction is not necessary.
    d. There must be a cash transaction.

LO 2   21. Income may be realized in the form of
    a. Money or services.
    b. Only money.
    c. Money, services, or property.
    d. None of the above.

LO 2   22. When filing their tax returns, almost all individuals use
    a. The cash receipts and disbursements method.
    b. The accrual method.
    c. The recognition method.
    d. The hybrid method.

LO 3   23. An individual must complete Schedule B (Forms 1040A or 1040) if the following situation occurs:
    a. Receive interest income of $1,450.
    b. Receive interest income over $1,500.
    c. Receive qualified dividends of $1,000.
    d. Receive child support payments of $1,600.

LO 3   24. The basis of the property received as a dividend by a shareholder of a corporation is
    a. The book value at the date of distribution.
    b. The original cost at the date of purchase.
    c. The accounting value at the date of distribution.
    d. The fair market value at the date of distribution.

LO 3   25. When an individual's marginal ordinary income tax rate is 25%, the tax rate on qualified dividends is
    a. 5%.
    b. 0%.
    c. 25%.
    d. 15%.

LO 3   26. Gabriela, who is single, reported itemized deductions of $5,550 on her 2008 tax return. Her itemized deductions included $200 of state taxes paid. In 2009 she received a $150 refund of state taxes paid in 2008. What is the amount that Gabriela needs to report on her 2009 tax return? Use the Internet (www.irs.gov) to find out how much the standard deduction was for 2008.
    a. $200.
    b. $100.
    c. $0.
    d. She needs to amend her 2008 tax return.

LO 3 27. Provisional income is calculated by starting with Adjusted Gross Income (AGI) before social security benefits and adding back specific items. One of these items is

    a. Wages earned.

    b. Taxable interest income.

    c. Employer-provided adoption benefits.

    d. Qualified dividends.

LO 3 28. Frank, who is single, received $7,000 of social security benefits. His AGI before the social security benefits was $15,000. He also had $100 of tax-exempt interest. What is the amount of taxable social security benefits?

    a. $0.

    b. $3,500.

    c. $7,000.

    d. $18,600.

LO 3 29. Items that must be reported on line 21 (other income) of Form 1040 include

    a. Interest income.

    b. Jury duty pay.

    c. Dividend income.

    d. Capital gains.

LO 4 30. Which of the following fringe benefits provided by the employer is *not* taxable to the employee?

    a. Sick pay.

    b. Vacation pay.

    c. Bonus.

    d. 10% discount on products sold by the business; the gross profit percentage for the business is 20%.

LO 4 31. Payments to employees under written dependent care assistance plans are tax-free. The exclusion cannot exceed earned income of the lesser earning spouse and cannot exceed _____ for an individual filing as married filing jointly:

    a. $2,500.

    b. $5,000.

    c. $5,150.

    d. $5,250.

LO 4 32. Employers can pay (or reimburse) employees for up to _____ per year of educational assistance, whether or not the education is job-related.

    a. $5,250.

    b. $5,150.

    c. $5,000.

    d. $2,500.

LO 4 33. An example of nontaxable income is

    a. Wages.

    b. Alimony payment.

    c. Child support payment.

    d. Dividend income.

Problems **LO 1** 34. In 2004 Marie borrowed $10,000. In 2009 the debt was forgiven. Marie does not believe she should report the forgiveness of debt as income because she received nothing at the time the debt was forgiven in 2009. Do you agree or disagree? Support your position.

_____

_____

_____

_____

LO 2 35. Determine the amount of taxable income that should be reported by a cash basis taxpayer in 2009 in each of the following independent cases:

a. A taxpayer completes $500 of accounting services in December 2009 for a client who pays for the accounting work in January 2010.

_____

b. A taxpayer is in the business of renting computers on a short-term basis. On December 1, 2009, she rents a computer for a $200 rental fee and receives a $500 deposit. The customer returns the computer and is refunded the deposit on December 20, 2009.

_____

c. Same facts as (b) except that the computer is returned on January 5, 2010.

_____

d. On December 18, 2009, a landlord rents an apartment for $700 per month and collects the first and last months' rent up front. It is customary that tenants apply the security deposit to their last month's rent upon moving out.

_____

e. An accountant agrees to perform $500 of tax services for an auto mechanic who has agreed to perform repairs on the car of the wife of the accountant. The mechanic repairs the car in December 2009 and the accountant starts and completes the tax work in March 2010.

_____

LO 2 36. A taxpayer who purchases a Series EE U.S. savings bond must report the interest income (i.e., increase in value) on the bond on the date the bond is redeemed, or the taxpayer can elect to report the interest currently in income. Under what circumstances should a taxpayer report income at maturity? Under what circumstances is it more advantageous to report income currently?

_____

_____

_____

_____

LO 3 37. Lynn, who is 59 years old, is the beneficiary of a $200,000 life insurance policy. What amount of the insurance proceeds is taxable under each of the following scenarios?

a. She receives the $200,000 proceeds as a lump-sum payment.

_____

b. She receives the proceeds at the rate of $4,000 a month for five years.

_____

c. She receives the proceeds in monthly payments of $1,300 over her remaining life expectancy (assume she will live 25 years).

_____

d. Use the information from (c). If Lynn lives beyond her 25-year life expectancy, what amount of each monthly payment will be taxable in the 26th year?

_____

LO 3 38. Determine the amount of tax liability in the following situations. In all cases, the taxpayer is using the filing status of married filing jointly,

a. Taxable income of $62,449 that includes dividend income of $560.

b. Taxable income of $12,932 that includes dividend income of $322.

c. Taxable income of $144,290 that includes dividend income of $4,384.

d. Taxable income of $43,297 that includes dividend income of $971.

e. Taxable income of $262,403 that includes dividend income of $12,396.

LO 3 39. Each of the following taxpayers received a state income tax refund in 2009. In all cases, the taxpayer has a filing status of married filing jointly. What amount of the refund is properly included in 2009 income?

a. Refund of $729; taxpayer did not itemize deductions in 2008.

b. Refund of $591; taxpayer had $13,220 of itemized deductions in 2008.

c. Refund of $927; taxpayer had itemized deductions of $11,100 in 2008.

LO 3 40. A married couple received $10,000 of social security benefits. Calculate the taxable amount of those benefits if the couple's provisional income is (a) $20,000, (b) $41,000, and (c) $63,000.

LO 3 41. Alberto and Kim file a joint return. Kim earned a salary of $38,000 and received dividends of $3,000, taxable interest income of $2,000, and nontaxable interest of $1,000. Alberto received $9,000 of social security benefits and a gift of $6,000 from his brother. What amount of social security benefits is taxable to Alberto and Kim?

LO 3 42. Sean, who is single, received social security benefits of $8,000, dividend income of $13,000, and interest income of $2,000. Except as noted, those income items are reasonably consistent from year to year. At the end of 2009, Sean is considering selling stock that would result in an immediate gain of $10,000, a reduction in future dividends of $1,000, and an increase in future interest income of $1,500. He has asked you for advice. What course of action do you recommend?

LO 4 43. Burger Store is located near many large office buildings, so at lunch it is extremely busy. Burger Store management previously permitted lunchtime employees a half-hour off-premises lunch break. However, employees could not easily return in a timely manner. Thus, a new policy was instituted to allow employees a 20-minute break for free lunch (only on the Burger Store premises). The company's accountant believes that the cost of these meals must be allocated to employees as additional compensation because the meals do not qualify as a nontaxable fringe benefit for employee discounts. In your opinion, should the cost of these meals be taxable or tax-free to employees? Support your answer.

Discussion Questions Pertaining to the Appendix (LO 5)

LO 5 44. Explain the rules governing the exemption of interest on U.S. savings bonds from taxation if it is used for educational purposes.

LO 5 45. Define *imputed interest.*

LO 5 46. Why were the interest imputation rules created?

LO 5 47. Briefly explain the application of the imputed interest rules.

LO 5 48. The interest imputation rules indirectly use a market rate of interest. What is meant by a *market rate of interest?*

LO 5 49. Define *original issue discount* (OID). Under what circumstances are the OID rules applied?

LO 5 50. Concerning the exemption for U.S. savings bond interest used for education expenses, what are the lower and upper income limitations for married taxpayers, and how is the exemption determined when taxpayer income falls between the limitation amounts?

_____

_____

_____

_____

LO 5 51. On July 1, 2009, Rene, a cash basis taxpayer, purchased $500,000 of the newly issued bonds of Acce Corporation for $452,260. The 10-year bonds carry an interest rate of 8% and were sold to yield 9.5%. What amount of interest income must Rene report in 2009, 2010, and 2011?

_____

_____

_____

_____

LO 5 52. In 2009 Carl and Pat Jefferson redeemed $8,000 of Series EE U.S. savings bonds (principal of $5,500 and interest of $2,500), the proceeds from which were used to pay for qualified higher education expenses of their dependent daughter who is attend-. ing a qualified educational institution. For the year, tuition and fees were $8,000 and room and board cost $7,000. The daughter received a $2,000 tax-exempt scholarship during the year that was used to pay tuition and fees. The Jeffersons' modified AGI was $96,000 in 2009. They do not participate in any other higher education–related programs. Calculate the amount of savings bond interest that the Jeffersons can exclude from gross income in 2009.

_____

_____

_____

_____

LO 5 53. David and Alexis, both 28, are interested in saving for the college education of their twin daughters Alie and Amber. They decide to purchase some Series EE U.S. savings bonds because they know that the interest on the bonds is tax-free in certain circumstances. To easily keep track of the savings for each child, they purchase half of the bonds in the names of David and Alie and the other half in the names of David and Amber. Assuming that current tax law does not change, under what circumstances will David and Alexis be permitted to exclude interest on redemption of these bonds?

_____

_____

_____

_____

LO 5 54. A person is selling some property and wishes to obtain payment partially in cash with the remainder in the form of a carryback note receivable.

    a. Why might the seller wish to increase the sales price and reduce the interest rate on the carryback note? Assume that the cash down payment and the total amount of payments will not change.

_____

b. Would the buyer likely agree to the increased price and decreased interest rate? Why or why not?

_____

_____

_____

Multiple-Choice Questions Pertaining to Appendix (LO 5)

LO 5 55. The amount of savings bond interest exempt from tax is limited when an individual is single and his or her AGI reaches

    a. $134,900.

    b. $69,950.

    c. $67,100.

    d. $84,950.

LO 5 56. Original issue discount (OID) is deemed to be zero if it is less than _____ of the maturity value, multiplied by the number of complete years to maturity.

    a. 0.25%.

    b. 5%.

    c. 25%.

    d. 15%.

LO 5 57. An individual with an OID instrument must annually report a portion of the OID as

    a. Dividend income.

    b. Interest income.

    c. Capital gain income.

    d. Pension income.

Tax Return Problems

Use your tax software to complete the following problems. If you are manually preparing the tax returns, you will need to use a Form 1040 or Form 1040A, depending on the complexity of the problem.

Tax Return Problem 1

John and Martha Holloway are married, filing jointly. They are 35 and 31 years old, respectively. Their address is 10010 Dove Street, Atlanta, GA 30301. Additional information about Mr. and Mrs. Holloway is as follows:

Social security numbers—

John: 111-12-0000.

Martha: 111-12-0001.

W-2 for John shows these amounts:

    Wages (box 1) = $35,500.

    Federal W/H (box 2) = $ 7,100.

    Social security wages (box 3) = $35,500.

    Social security W/H (box 4) = $ 2,201.

    Medicare wages (box 5) = $35,500.

    Medicare W/H (box 6) = $ 514.75

W-2 for Martha shows these amounts:

    Wages (box 1) = $22,000.

    Federal W/H (box 2) = $ 3,300.

    Social security wages (box 3) = $22,000.

    Social security W/H (box 4) = $ 1,364.

    Medicare wages (box 5) = $22,000.

    Medicare W/H (box 6) = $ 319.

Form 1099-DIV for John shows this amount:

Box 1a and box 1b = $345 from MAR Brokerage.

Form 1099-INT for John shows these amounts:

Box 1 = $450 from ABC Bank.

Box 4 = $35.

John is a construction worker, and Martha is a secretary.

Prepare the tax return for Mr. and Mrs. Holloway using the appropriate form. They do want to contribute to the presidential election campaign.

Tax Return Problem 2

Carl and Elizabeth Williams are married filing jointly. They are 45 and 40 years old, respectively. Their address is 19010 N.W. 135 Street, Miami, FL 33022. Additional information about Mr. and Mrs. Williams is as follows:

Social security numbers—
Carl: 112-10-0000.   Elizabeth: 113-10-0001.

W-2 for Carl shows these amounts: W-2 for Elizabeth shows these amounts:
Wages (box 1) = $75,000.   Wages (box 1) = $31,000.
Federal W/H (box 2) = $22,500.   Federal W/H (box 2) = $ 7,750.
Social security wages (box 3) = $75,000.   Social security wages (box 3) = $31,000.
Social security W/H (box 4) = $ 4,650.   Social security W/H (box 4) = $ 1,922.
Medicare wages (box 5) = $75,000.   Medicare wages (box 5) = $31,000.
Medicare W/H (box 6) = $ 1,087.50   Medicare W/H (box 6) = $ 449.50

Form 1099-INT for Carl and Elizabeth shows this amount:
Box 1 = $2,450 from Global Bank.

They also received tax-exempt interest of $500, as well as $45 for jury duty pay when Carl went to court to serve for a few days.

Carl received two weeks of workers' compensation pay for a total of $3,100.

Dependent: Son, Carl Jr., who is seven years old. His social security number is 116-10-0005.

Carl is a sales manager, and Elizabeth is an office clerk.

Prepare the tax return for Mr. and Mrs. Williams using the appropriate form. They do not want to contribute to the presidential election campaign.

Tax Return Problem 3

Robert and Vilma Greene are married filing jointly. They are 68 and 66 years old, respectively. Their address is 1001 N.W. 93 Street, Miami, FL 33022. Additional information about Mr. and Mrs. Greene, who are retired, is as follows:

Social security numbers—
Robert: 100-00-2000.   Vilma: 100-00-2001.

SSA-1099 for Robert shows this amount: SSA-1099 for Vilma shows this amount:
(box 5) = $21,600.   (box 5) = $15,600.

Form 1099-INT for Robert shows this amount: Form 1099-INT for Vilma shows this amount:
(box 1) = $9,100 from CD Bank.   (box 1) = $7,500 from CD Bank.

Prepare the tax return for Mr. and Mrs. Greene using the appropriate form. They do want to contribute to the presidential election campaign.

We have provided selected filled-in source documents on our Web site at www.mhhe.com/cruz2010.

Chapter Four

Adjustments *for* Adjusted Gross Income

Taxpayers can deduct certain items from total income for purposes of computing Adjusted Gross Income (AGI). In this chapter, we introduce you to most of these *for* AGI deductions. This is a key step in determining the actual tax liability of the individual.

Learning Objectives

When you have completed this chapter, you should understand the following learning objectives (LO):

LO 1. Describe the tax rules for student loan interest.

LO 2. Be able to calculate the Health Savings Account deduction.

LO 3. Determine the deduction for moving expenses.

LO 4. Explain the deduction for half of self-employment taxes.

LO 5. Discuss the self-employed health insurance deduction.

LO 6. Explain the penalty on early withdrawal of savings.

LO 7. Be able to calculate the deduction for alimony paid.

LO 8. Determine the deduction for educator expenses.

LO 9. Be able to calculate the deduction for eligible tuition and fees.

INTRODUCTION

In previous chapters, we primarily discussed tax rules and the presentation of many components of total income (line 22 on Form 1040). Taxpayers can also deduct certain items from total income to arrive at Adjusted Gross Income (AGI). These deductible items are *for* AGI deductions, commonly referred to as *above-the-line* deductions (AGI is considered to be "the line"). AGI is critically important to the calculation of other key items on the tax return. *For* AGI deductions are on Form 1040, lines 23 to 35, or Form 1040A, lines 16 to 19.[1] See Exhibit 4-1 for the AGI portion of Form 1040.

You may recall that certain deductions are also subtracted from AGI to arrive at taxable income. These *from* AGI deductions, or *below-the-line* deductions, are standard or itemized deductions and personal exemptions. In effect, gross income minus *for* AGI (above-the-line) deductions equals AGI. If you then subtract *from* AGI (below-the-line) deductions, you will get taxable income.

---

[1] We do not discuss all *for* AGI deductions in this chapter. Taxpayers may also take *for* AGI deductions for contributions to Individual Retirement Accounts (Form 1040, line 32) and to retirement plans for self-employed individuals (Form 1040, line 28). We discuss these deductions in Chapter 11.

EXHIBIT 4-1

Adjusted Gross Income	23	Educator expenses (see page 29)	**23**			
	24	Certain business expenses of reservists, performing artists, and fee-basis government officials. Attach Form 2106 or 2106-EZ	**24**			
	25	Health savings account deduction. Attach Form 8889 .	**25**			
	26	Moving expenses. Attach Form 3903	**26**			
	27	One-half of self-employment tax. Attach Schedule SE .	**27**			
	28	Self-employed SEP, SIMPLE, and qualified plans . .	**28**			
	29	Self-employed health insurance deduction (see page 30)	**29**			
	30	Penalty on early withdrawal of savings	**30**			
	31a	Alimony paid **b** Recipient's SSN ▶ _____	**31a**			
	32	IRA deduction (see page 31)	**32**			
	33	Student loan interest deduction (see page 34) . . .	**33**			
	34	Tuition and fees deduction. Attach Form 8917 . . .	**34**			
	35	Domestic production activities deduction. Attach Form 8903	**35**			
	36	Add lines 23 through 31a and 32 through 35			**36**	
	37	Subtract line 36 from line 22. This is your **adjusted gross income** . . . . . . ▶			**37**	

STUDENT LOAN INTEREST (FORM 1040, LINE 33 OR FORM 1040A, LINE 18)
LO 1

Tax law provides numerous tax benefits for expenses associated with obtaining education beyond high school. These benefits are available for individuals saving for higher education (Coverdell Education Savings Accounts, state tuition programs, and qualified U.S. savings bonds), for many expenses incurred while attending a qualified educational institution (Hope and lifetime learning credits), and for interest paid on loans incurred for higher education expenses.[2]

Paying higher education expenses often requires students or their parents or guardians to borrow money from lending institutions such as banks or from federal or state student loan programs. An individual can take a deduction for "an amount equal to the interest paid by the taxpayer during the taxable year on any qualified education loan."[3] Only the person legally obligated to make the interest payments can take the deduction.[4] *A person who is claimed as a dependent on another person's return cannot claim the deduction,[5] nor can persons whose filing status is married filing separately.[6]*

EXAMPLE 4-1

In 2005 Paula borrowed $5,000 for higher education expenses on a qualified education loan. In 2009, when she began making payments on the loan, she was still living at home and her parents appropriately claimed her as a dependent. Paula cannot claim the student interest deduction. Although she was the person legally obligated to repay the loan, she was claimed on the return of another person.

The amount of this deduction is limited to $2,500 per year.[7] The deduction may be further limited based on the modified Adjusted Gross Income of the taxpayer.

[2] Coverdell Education Savings Accounts and the Hope and lifetime learning credits are discussed in Chapters 11 and 9 respectively.

[3] IRC § 221(a).

[4] Reg. § 1.221-1(b).

[5] IRC § 221(c).

[6] IRC § 221(f)(2).

[7] IRC § 221(b)(1).

Qualified Education Loan

A *qualified education loan* is one incurred by the taxpayer solely to pay qualified education expenses on behalf of the taxpayer, taxpayer's spouse, or any dependent of the taxpayer at the time the loan was incurred.[8] Note that the loan must be *solely* to pay for educational expenses. Thus home equity loans or revolving lines of credit often do not qualify. Qualified education expenses must be paid or incurred within a reasonable period before or after the loan date.[9] Expenses meet this test if the proceeds of the loan are disbursed within 90 days of the start or 90 days after the end of the academic period. Federal education loan programs meet this criterion. The expenses also must occur during the period the recipient was carrying at least half the normal full-time workload for the intended course of study.[10] The course of study can be at the undergraduate or graduate level.

Qualified Education Expenses

Qualified education expenses are the costs of attending an eligible educational institution.[11] These costs include tuition, fees, books, supplies, equipment, room, board, transportation, and other necessary expenses of attendance. However, taxpayers must reduce qualified expenses by the amount of income excluded from gross income in each of the following cases. In each instance, because the income is not included, the item does *not* create a deduction.

- An employer-paid educational assistance program.[12]
- Redemption of U.S. savings bonds used to pay higher education tuition and fees.[13]
- Funds withdrawn from a Coverdell Education Savings Account.[14]
- Qualified tax-free scholarships and fellowships.[15]
- Armed forces' or veterans' educational assistance allowances.[16]
- Any other educational assistance excludable from gross income (not including gifts, bequests, devises, or inheritances).[17] This category includes a state-qualified tuition plan.

EXAMPLE 4-2	In September Ashley spent $3,000 on qualified educational expenses. She received a loan for $2,800 in the same month as she paid the expenses. During the semester, she received a scholarship of $500 that she properly excluded from income. Ashley's qualified educational expenses are $2,500 ($3,000 − $500). As a result, interest on $2,500 of the $2,800 loan will be eligible for student loan interest treatment, while interest on the remaining $300 is nondeductible personal interest.

Other Provisions and Limitations

As noted earlier, deductible education expenses must occur in conjunction with attendance at an eligible educational institution. An *eligible institution* is generally a postsecondary educational institution that meets the requirements to participate in the federal student loan program.[18]

[8] IRC § 221(e)(1)(A).
[9] IRC § 221(e)(1)(B), Reg. § 1.221-1(e)(3)(ii).
[10] IRC § 221(e)(3), IRC § 25A(b)(3).
[11] IRC § 221(e)(2).
[12] IRC § 127.
[13] IRC § 135.
[14] IRC § 530.
[15] IRC § 117.
[16] IRC § 25A(g)(2)(B).
[17] IRC § 25A(g)(2)(C).
[18] IRC § 221(e)(2), IRC § 25A(f)(2).

This includes almost all four-year colleges and universities, two-year community colleges, and many trade and technical schools. The classification also incorporates institutions with an internship or residency program leading to a degree or certificate awarded by an institute of higher education, a hospital, or a health care facility that offers postgraduate training.[19] Qualified expenses must be for an academic period during which the student was enrolled at least half-time in one of these qualifying programs.

The deduction for interest on qualified education loans, may be limited based on the modified Adjusted Gross Income of the taxpayer.[20] *Modified AGI* is equal to AGI on the taxpayer's tax return plus (a) any deduction for student loan interest, (b) any foreign, U.S. possession, or Puerto Rican income excluded from taxable income, (c) any deduction taken for tuition and fees, and (d) any deduction taken with regard to domestic activities production.[21]

The deductible amount of student loan interest is reduced when modified AGI reaches $120,000 on a joint return ($60,000 for a single return) and is totally eliminated when modified AGI reaches $150,000 ($75,000 for single returns).[22] The following formula is used:

$$\text{Preliminary deduction} \times \text{Fraction (see below)} = \text{Disallowed interest}$$

For married taxpayers, the fraction is (Modified AGI – $120,000)/$30,000.

For single taxpayers, the fraction is (Modified AGI – $60,000)/$15,000.

The denominator in these fractions represents the difference between the beginning and the end of the phaseout range (that is, for married filing jointly, the $30,000 denominator is the difference between $120,000 and $150,000). These fractions represent the disallowed proportion of the preliminary deduction.

Note that the preliminary deduction amount cannot exceed the $2,500 maximum allowed deduction.

EXAMPLE 4-3

Al and Marian borrowed $30,000 on a qualified educational loan to pay for qualified higher education expenses for their two children. During 2009 they paid $1,800 interest on the loan. Al and Marian's modified AGI on their joint return was $140,000. They are entitled to deduct $600 as follows:

$$\$1,800 \times \frac{\$140,000 - \$120,000}{\$30,000} = \$1,200 \text{ disallowed}$$

Permitted deduction = $1,800 – $1,200 = $600.

TAX YOUR BRAIN

If Al and Marian paid $3,200 interest on the loan in 2009, what is the allowed deduction for student loan interest?

ANSWER

Because the interest deduction is limited to a total of $2,500 before the AGI limitation, the couple would be entitled to an $833 deduction as follows:

$$\$2,500 \times \frac{\$140,000 - \$120,000}{\$30,000} = \$1,667 \text{ disallowed}$$

Permitted deduction = $2,500 – $1,667 = $833.

---

[19] IRC § 221(e)(2).

[20] IRC § 221(b)(2).

[21] IRC § 221(b)(2)(C)(i).

[22] These limitation amounts are adjusted for inflation under IRC § 221(g).

From Shoebox to Software

There are generally four critical issues concerning student loan interest:

- Whether the loan was taken out solely for education expenses.
- Whether loan funds were used for education expenses.
- The amount of the interest payment for the year.
- Limitation of the deduction based on AGI phaseouts.

Identifying applicable loans and maintaining (or in some cases obtaining) proper documentation is more difficult because a number of years usually transpire between the date that the loan is created, the date that the expenses are paid, and the date the interest deduction is sought. On many student loans, the student can elect to defer payments while enrolled in college and even after that point for certain economic hardship reasons. Be careful, however; deferral does not prevent interest from accruing.

Loans made through the federal student loan program usually meet the first two critical issues because the U.S. government intends that these loans cover education expenses not paid by student earnings or parental contributions. The federal government provides an annual report to the taxpayer (often a substitute Form 1099-INT) that provides the amount of interest paid during the year.

Loans from financial institutions require a higher level of documentation. The taxpayer should review loan documents and canceled checks to determine whether the loan and the expenditures qualify for favored treatment. Lenders normally provide Form 1098-E (see Exhibit 4-2) indicating the amount of interest paid by the taxpayer in a year.

In both cases, when preparing a return using tax software, you enter applicable information on a Student Loan Interest Deduction worksheet.

EXHIBIT 4-2

☐ CORRECTED (if checked)			

RECIPIENT'S/LENDER'S name, address, and telephone number		OMB No. 1545-1576 20**09** Form **1098-E**	**Student Loan Interest Statement**
RECIPIENT'S federal identification no.	BORROWER'S social security number	**1** Student loan interest received by lender $	**Copy B** **For Borrower**
BORROWER'S name Street address (including apt. no.) City, state, and ZIP code			This is important tax information and is being furnished to the Internal Revenue Service. If you are required to file a return, a negligence penalty or other sanction may be imposed on you if the IRS determines that an underpayment of tax results because you overstated a deduction for student loan interest.
Account number (see instructions)		**2** If checked, box 1 does **not** include loan origination fees and/or capitalized interest for loans made before September 1, 2004 . . . . ☐	

Form **1098-E**   (keep for your records)   Department of the Treasury - Internal Revenue Service

---

CONCEPT CHECK 4-1—LO 1

1. For the interest on a student loan to qualify for the deduction, the student must be enrolled at least _____.
2. Under the student loan program, qualified educational expenses include _____ and _____.
3. The deductible amount of student loan interest is reduced when modified AGI for those filing married jointly reaches _____.

HEALTH SAVINGS ACCOUNT DEDUCTION (FORM 1040, LINE 25)
LO 2

A Health Savings Account (HSA) is a tax-exempt savings account used for qualified medical expenses for the account holder, his or her spouse, and dependents. In general, qualified taxpayers can take a *for* AGI deduction for contributions to the HSA.[23] Contributions grow tax-free, and distributions are not taxable if used for qualified medical expenses.

To be eligible to fund an HSA, a taxpayer, under the age of 65, must be self-employed; an employee (or spouse) of an employer who maintains a high-deductible health plan (HDHP); or an employee of a company that has no health coverage, and the employee has purchased a high-deductible policy on his or her own. In addition, the individual cannot have other health insurance except for coverage for accidents, disability, dental care, vision care, long-term care, or workers' compensation.[24] In addition, the taxpayer cannot be enrolled in Medicare and cannot be claimed as a dependent on someone else's return.

An HDHP is a health plan with specified minimum deductible amounts and a maximum annual deductible and out-of-pocket expense limitation.[25] *Out-of-pocket expense* represents the amount the health plan requires the policyholder to pay for covered benefits (other than the premium). For calendar year 2009, these amounts are as follows:

	Minimum Deductible	Maximum Deductible and Annual Out-of-Pocket
Individual coverage	$1,150	$ 5,800
Family coverage	$2,300	$11,600

The employee or employer contributes to the HSA. For individual coverage maximum, the aggregate contribution an individual under age 55 can make to an HSA is $3,000. For family coverage, with a contributor under age 55, the maximum aggregate annual contribution is $5,950.[26]

If the taxpayer is 55 or older, he or she may contribute an additional $1,000 in 2009. Individuals are now allowed to make a one-time contribution to an HSA of an amount distributed from their IRA. The contribution must be made in a direct trustee-to-trustee transfer. Amounts distributed from the IRA are not includible in the individual's income to the extent that the distribution would otherwise be includible in income. Such distributions are not subject to the 10% additional tax on early distributions. An individual who becomes covered by a high-deductible plan during the year can make a contribution to an HSA as if he or she was eligible for the entire year.

Contributions made by a qualified individual are a *for* AGI deduction, assuming that the limitations are met. If an employer contributes, the amount is not deductible (because the employee paid nothing), but the payment is not counted as income to the employee.

Distributions from HSAs are tax-free if they are used to pay for qualified medical expenses.[27] Part I of Form 8889, Health Savings Accounts, is used to report the amount of the deduction that is reported on line 25. Form 8889 must be attached to the taxpayer's return. The form is also used to report the taxable and nontaxable amounts of a distribution from an HSA. You can find additional information on HSAs in IRS Publication 969.

[23] IRC § 223(a).
[24] IRC § 223(c)(1)(B).
[25] IRC § 223(c)(2).
[26] IRC § 223(b).
[27] IRC § 223(d)(2).

From Shoebox to Software

Taxpayers who contribute to or withdraw from an HSA during the year must file a Form 8889 and attach it to their Form 1040. Form 8889 is shown in Exhibit 4-3.

EXHIBIT 4-3

Form **8889**	**Health Savings Accounts (HSAs)**	OMB No. 1545-0074
Department of the Treasury Internal Revenue Service	▶ **Attach to Form 1040 or Form 1040NR.** ▶ **See separate instructions.**	**20**09 Attachment Sequence No. **53**

Name(s) shown on Form 1040 or Form 1040NR	Social security number of HSA beneficiary. If both spouses have HSAs, see page 2 of the instructions ▶

Before you begin: Complete Form 8853, Archer MSAs and Long-Term Care Insurance Contracts, if required.

Part I   **HSA Contributions and Deduction.** See page 3 of the instructions before completing this part. If you are filing jointly and both you and your spouse each have separate HSAs, complete a separate Part I for each spouse.

1	Check the box to indicate your coverage under a high-deductible health plan (HDHP) during 2009 (see page 4 of the instructions) . . . . ▶	☐ Self-only ☐ Family	
2	HSA contributions you made for 2009 (or those made on your behalf), including those made from January 1, 2010, through April 15, 2010, that were for 2009. **Do not** include employer contributions, contributions through a cafeteria plan, or rollovers (see page 4 of the instructions)	**2**	
3	If you were under age 55 at the end of 2009, and on the first day of **every** month during 2009, you were, or were considered, an eligible individual with the **same** coverage, enter $3,000 ($5,950 for family coverage). All others, see page 4 of the instructions for the amount to enter .	**3**	
4	Enter the amount you and your employer contributed to your Archer MSAs for 2009 from Form 8853, lines 3 and 4. If you or your spouse had family coverage under an HDHP at any time during 2009, also include any amount contributed to your spouse's Archer MSAs	**4**	
5	Subtract line 4 from line 3. If zero or less, enter -0-	**5**	
6	Enter the amount from line 5. But if you and your spouse each have separate HSAs and had family coverage under an HDHP at any time during 2009, see the instructions on page 4 for the amount to enter	**6**	
7	If you were age 55 or older at the end of 2009, married, and you or your spouse had family coverage under an HDHP at any time during 2009, enter your additional contribution amount (see page 5 of the instructions)	**7**	
8	Add lines 6 and 7	**8**	
9	Employer contributions made to your HSAs for 2009	**9**	
10	Qualified HSA funding distributions	**10**	
11	Add lines 9 and 10	**11**	
12	Subtract line 11 from line 8. If zero or less, enter -0-	**12**	
13	**HSA deduction.** Enter the **smaller** of line 2 or line 12 here and on Form 1040, line 25, or Form 1040NR, line 25	**13**	
	Caution: *If line 2 is more than line 13, you may have to pay an additional tax (see page 5 of the instructions).*		

Part II   **HSA Distributions.** If you are filing jointly and both you and your spouse each have separate HSAs, complete a separate Part II for each spouse.

14a	Total distributions you received in 2009 from all HSAs (see page 6 of the instructions) . . .	**14a**	
b	Distributions included on line 14a that you rolled over to another HSA. Also include any excess contributions (and the earnings on those excess contributions) included on line 14a that were withdrawn by the due date of your return (see page 6 of the instructions)	**14b**	
c	Subtract line 14b from line 14a	**14c**	
15	Unreimbursed qualified medical expenses (see page 6 of the instructions)	**15**	
16	**Taxable HSA distributions.** Subtract line 15 from line 14c. If zero or less, enter -0-. Also, include this amount in the total on Form 1040, line 21, or Form 1040NR, line 21. On the dotted line next to line 21, enter "HSA" and the amount	**16**	
17a	If any of the distributions included on line 16 meet any of the **Exceptions to the Additional 10% Tax** (see page 6 of the instructions), check here . . . . ▶ ☐		
b	**Additional 10% tax** (see page 6 of the instructions). Enter 10% (.10) of the distributions included on line 16 that are subject to the additional 10% tax. Also include this amount in the total on Form 1040, line 60, or Form 1040NR, line 57. On the dotted line next to Form 1040, line 60, or Form 1040NR, line 57, enter "HSA" and the amount	**17b**	

For Paperwork Reduction Act Notice, see page 5 of the instructions.	Cat. No. 37621P	Form **8889** (2009)

A trustee, normally a bank or insurance company, administers the HSA. Trustees are required to provide HSA holders contribution and distribution information. Contributions are reported on Form 5498-SA (see Exhibit 4-4). Taxpayers use contribution information to prepare Part I of Form 8889.

Distributions are reported by the trustee on Form 1099-SA, shown in Exhibit 4-5. The distributions are reported on Part II of Form 8889 (see Exhibit 4-3).

EXHIBIT 4-4

☐ CORRECTED (if checked)

TRUSTEE'S name, street address, city, state, and ZIP code	**1** Employee or self-employed person's Archer MSA contributions made in 2009 and 2010 for 2009 $	OMB No. 1545-1518 **2009** Form **5498-SA**	**HSA, Archer MSA, or Medicare Advantage MSA Information**
	2 Total contributions made in 2009 $		
TRUSTEE'S federal identification number / PARTICIPANT'S social security number	**3** Total HSA or Archer MSA contributions made in 2010 for 2009 $		**Copy B**
PARTICIPANT'S name	**4** Rollover contributions $	**5** Fair market value of HSA, Archer MSA, or MA MSA $	**For Participant**
Street address (including apt. no.) City, state, and ZIP code	**6** HSA ☐ Archer MSA ☐ MA MSA ☐		The information in boxes 1 through 6 is being furnished to the Internal Revenue Service.
Account number (see instructions)			

Form **5498-SA**   (keep for your records)   Department of the Treasury - Internal Revenue Service

EXHIBIT 4-5

☐ CORRECTED (if checked)

TRUSTEE'S/PAYER'S name, street address, city, state, and ZIP code		OMB No. 1545-1517 **2009** Form **1099-SA**	**Distributions From an HSA, Archer MSA, or Medicare Advantage MSA**
PAYER'S federal identification number / RECIPIENT'S identification number	**1** Gross distribution $	**2** Earnings on excess cont. $	**Copy B For Recipient**
RECIPIENT'S name	**3** Distribution code	**4** FMV on date of death $	
Street address (including apt. no.) City, state, and ZIP code	**5** HSA ☐ Archer MSA ☐ MA MSA ☐		This information is being furnished to the Internal Revenue Service.
Account number (see instructions)			

Form **1099-SA**   (keep for your records)   Department of the Treasury - Internal Revenue Service

---

CONCEPT CHECK 4-2—LO 2

1. To be eligible to fund an HSA, a taxpayer must be _____, an employee (or spouse) of an employer who maintains a high-deductible health plan, or an uninsured employee who has purchased a high-deductible policy on his or her own.

2. If they are used to pay for qualified medical expenses, distributions from HSAs are _____.

3. If taxpayers make contributions to or withdrawals from an HSA during the year, they must file a Form _____ and attach it to their Form _____.

MOVING EXPENSES (FORM 1040, LINE 26)
LO 3

An employee or self-employed individual who moves his or her principal residence because of a change in employment may deduct certain moving expenses.[28] *Moving expenses* are reasonable expenses for the following:

- Moving household goods and personal effects from the old residence to the new residence.
- Traveling from the old residence to the new residence (including lodging but excluding meals).[29]

Additionally, moving expenses include storage of household goods within a consecutive 30-day period after items are moved from the former home and actual expenses or mileage for driving a personal auto at a rate of 24 cents for 2009. Nonqualified moving expenses generally include house-hunting costs before the move, costs incurred in buying and selling a home, and temporary living expense and costs of meals incurred while moving.

Moving expenses of persons other than the taxpayer are permitted if the other persons are members of the taxpayer's household and both the old and new residences are the persons' principal place of abode.[30] This situation most often occurs in the case of family members or other dependents who also move with the taxpayer. Travel is limited to one trip per person.

Tests for Moving Expense Deductibility

To qualify for a moving expense deduction, taxpayers must meet three tests.

Change in Employment

For the first test, the move must be the result of a change in the taxpayer's principal place of work.[31] If there is no change of job location, the taxpayer cannot take the moving expense deduction. However, a taxpayer starting work for the first time qualifies provided he or she meets the distance test outlined next.

Distance Test

The second test is the distance test. The new job location must be at least 50 miles farther from the taxpayer's old residence than was the old job location.[32] For example, if the old residence was 15 miles from the old job, the new job must be at least 65 miles away from the old residence. If the taxpayer had no old job (that is, the taxpayer was unemployed), the new job must be more than 50 miles away from his or her old residence.[33] A diagram illustrating the application of the distance test is shown in Exhibit 4-6.

EXHIBIT 4-6
Distance Test Diagram

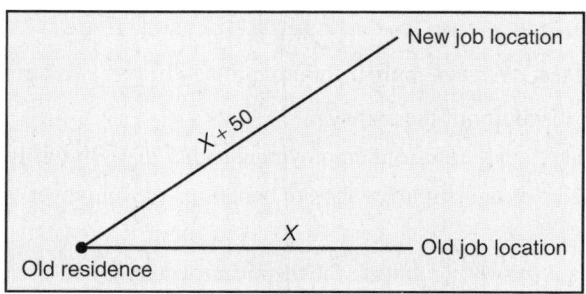

[28] IRC § 217(a).
[29] IRC § 217(b)(1).
[30] IRC § 217(b)(2).
[31] IRC § 217(a).
[32] IRC § 217(c)(1).
[33] IRC § 217(c)(1)(B).

So if the distance between the old residence and the old job is defined as X miles, the new job must be at least $X + 50$ miles from the old residence.

Time Test

The third test is the time test. To meet this test, a taxpayer must meet either of the following:

- Be a full-time employee for a period of 39 weeks during the 12 months immediately following arrival in the new area.
- Be self-employed for at least 78 weeks during the 24 months immediately following arrival in the new area. At least 39 of the 78 weeks must be during the first 12-month period.[34]

To meet the time test, the taxpayer need not remain employed in the new job for the entire 39- or 78-week period; but the full-time employment (or self-employment) must be in the same general location as the new job for which the taxpayer moved.[35] Therefore, a taxpayer who gets a job in a new city, moves there, works for the new employer for 2 months, and then obtains a different full-time job in the same area for the next 10 months meets the time test.

For a married couple, if both obtain new jobs in a new area, the taxpayers can deduct moving expenses if either spouse satisfies the time test.[36] However, spouses must separately account for their weeks worked (weeks worked by one spouse cannot be added to weeks worked by the other spouse).

Moving expenses are deductible only in the year incurred. Often taxpayers do not meet the time test by the due date of the tax return for the appropriate tax year. If the taxpayer expects to be able to comply with the time test, the taxpayer can choose either to deduct the moving expenses in the year incurred or to wait until he or she meets the test and then file an amended return claiming the deduction.[37] If the taxpayer elects to deduct the moving expenses prior to satisfying the time test and later does not meet the test, the moving expenses are disallowed, and the taxpayer must include the previously deducted expenses in income in the subsequent year or file an amended return for the year in which the expenses were deducted.[38]

EXAMPLE 4-4

Greg moved from Atlanta to Chicago in October 2009 because of a new job and incurred moving expenses of $4,000. He filed his 2009 return in March 2010. As of that date, the time test was not satisfied. Greg was employed full-time in Chicago from October 2009 to March 2010; thus it was still possible that the time test could be satisfied. Greg elected to deduct the $4,000 moving expenses on his 2009 tax return. If, by the end of 2010, he satisfied the time test, Greg would take no further action. However, if he did not satisfy the time test by the end of 2010, he must include $4,000 in his 2010 gross income or file an amended return for 2009.

The time test does not apply if failure to meet the test was a result of any of the following:

- Death or disability of the taxpayer.
- Involuntary separation from employment (other than for willful misconduct).
- A retransfer of the employee for the benefit of the employer (that was not initiated by the employee).[39]

In each of the last two exceptions, the taxpayer must have had a reasonable expectation to meet the time test, absent the noted cause.

[34] IRC § 217(c)(2).
[35] Reg. § 1.217-2(c)(4)(iii).
[36] Reg. § 1.217-2(c)(4)(v).
[37] IRC § 217(d)(2) and Reg. § 1.217-2(d)(2).
[38] Reg. § 1.217-2(d)(3).
[39] IRC § 217(d)(1).

Neither the distance nor time test applies to moves made by members of the U.S. armed forces who are on active duty and who have moved pursuant to a military order including a permanent change of station.[40]

Employer Moving Expense Reimbursements

Employers may reimburse employees for some or all of their moving expenses. If the taxpayer would have been able to deduct the reimbursed expenses had the taxpayer paid them directly, the taxpayer can exclude the reimbursement from income.[41] In such a case, the taxpayer cannot deduct the reimbursed moving expenses.[42] If the employer reimburses less than the amount of deductible expenses, the taxpayer can deduct the excess expenses. If the reimbursement is more than the amount of deductible expenses (for example, if the employer reimburses the employee for meals), the excess reimbursement is gross income.

CONCEPT CHECK 4-3—LO 3	1. Moving expenses can be deducted either as a *for* AGI deduction or as an itemized deduction on Schedule A. True or false?
	2. A taxpayer who meets the time test does not have to be concerned about the distance test. True or false?
	3. If an employer reimburses an employee for moving costs, the employee cannot deduct those expenses on the tax return. True or false?

DEDUCTION FOR HALF OF SELF-EMPLOYMENT TAX (FORM 1040, LINE 27)
LO 4

Self-employed individuals must pay self-employment tax equal to 15.3% of their net earnings from self-employment.[43] The self-employment tax is the FICA tax for social security and Medicare that W-2 employees have deducted from their paychecks at a rate of 7.65% and that employers must match at the same rate. Self-employed individuals are responsible for both halves of the tax, and the tax is calculated on the net earnings of the business. Self-employed persons are allowed a *for* AGI deduction equal to one-half of the self-employment tax imposed.[44] The tax software will automatically calculate the appropriate amount for line 27. Self-employment tax is calculated on Form SE; it is covered in more detail in Chapter 6.

CONCEPT CHECK 4-4—LO 4	1. Self-employment tax is calculated on the _____ earnings of the business.
	2. For W-2 employees, the FICA tax is calculated at a rate of _____ of their gross earnings.

---

[40] IRC § 217(g).

[41] IRC § 132(a)(6) and IRC § 132(g).

[42] See Reg. § 1.217-2(a)(2) for guidance when the reimbursement and moving expenses occur in different tax years.

[43] IRC § 1401.

[44] IRC § 164(f).

From Shoebox to Software

When using tax software to report moving expenses, there are multiple sources of tax-related information and two different forms used by taxpayers. Open the tax software using any of the clients we have used in the book so you can look at the worksheets and forms used for moving expenses.

To determine whether a taxpayer can take the moving expense deduction, the first task is to provide information concerning the time and distance tests. This information is usually provided on the Form 3903—Distance and Time Tests worksheet section. On this worksheet, you enter information concerning the two tests. If the taxpayer does not meet one or both of the tests, it is not necessary to continue because no moving expense deduction is permitted.

If a taxpayer meets the tests, you must then provide information concerning the amount of moving expenses and associated reimbursement, if any. Form 3903 is used for this purpose (see Exhibit 4-7).

Note that lines 1 and 2 of Form 3903 are shown in green in the tax software. This means that you input the data for these lines directly on Form 3903. The amount on line 1 pertains to the cost of moving and storing the household goods, and line 2 is for reporting the travel and lodging expenses for the individuals being moved.

Employers report reimbursements (if any) to the employee on Form W-2. The reimbursement amount is in box 12 and will have a code of P. When you enter the W-2 data, any code P amount will automatically be shown on line 4 of Form 3903. If expenses exceed reimbursements, the software will show the excess on Form 1040, line 26. Similarly, the software will report reimbursements in excess of expenses on Form 1040, line 21, as other income.

Sources of information for moving expenses include canceled checks and credit card statements (accompanied by supporting documentation) and miscellaneous cash receipts. If the taxpayer obtains reimbursement from his or her employer, the documentation provided to the employer is often an excellent source document.

EXHIBIT 4-7

Form **3903**	**Moving Expenses**	OMB No. 1545-0074
Department of the Treasury Internal Revenue Service (99)	▶ Attach to Form 1040 or Form 1040NR.	20**09** Attachment Sequence No. **62**

Name(s) shown on return		**Your social security number**

Before you begin: ✓ See the **Distance Test** and **Time Test** in the instructions to find out if you can deduct your moving expenses.

                ✓ See **Members of the Armed Forces** on the back, if applicable.

1 Transportation and storage of household goods and personal effects (see instructions) . . .   **1**

2 Travel (including lodging) from your old home to your new home (see instructions). **Do not** include the cost of meals **2**

3 Add lines 1 and 2 . . . .   **3**

4 Enter the total amount your employer paid you for the expenses listed on lines 1 and 2 that is **not** included in box 1 of your Form W-2 (wages). This amount should be shown in box 12 of your Form W-2 with code **P** **4**

5 Is line 3 **more than** line 4?

    ☐ **No.** You **cannot** deduct your moving expenses. If line 3 is less than line 4, subtract line 3 from line 4 and include the result on Form 1040, line 7, or Form 1040NR, line 8.

    ☐ **Yes.** Subtract line 4 from line 3. Enter the result here and on Form 1040, line 26, or Form 1040NR, line 26. This is your **moving expense deduction** **5**

SELF-EMPLOYED HEALTH INSURANCE DEDUCTION (FORM 1040, LINE 29)
LO 5

Payments for health insurance for self-employed individuals, their spouse, and their dependents are not deductible as a business expense on Schedule C.[45] However, applicable taxpayers can deduct, as a *for* AGI deduction, 100% of self-employed health insurance premiums.[46]

The amount of the deduction may be limited in two respects. First, taxpayers cannot take a deduction for any amount in excess of net earnings from self-employment from the trade or business under which coverage is provided.[47]

EXAMPLE 4-5	Alice had net earnings of $2,800 from self-employment. She paid $160 per month for health insurance ($1,920 per year). Alice is entitled to a *for* AGI deduction of $1,920 for health insurance. If Alice's net earnings from self-employment were $1,500, her deduction would have been limited to $1,500.

The second limitation pertains to availability of other health insurance coverage. If the taxpayer is entitled to participate in any subsidized health plan maintained by any employer of the taxpayer or of the taxpayer's spouse, a deduction is not allowed.[48] Eligibility for alternative coverage is determined on a monthly basis. A *subsidized health plan* is one in which someone other than the employee pays for part or all of the cost of the plan.

EXAMPLE 4-6	Wendy is self-employed and had net earnings from self-employment of $17,000 for the year. She has an individual-only health insurance policy through her business for which she pays $145 per month. An unrelated local business employs Taylor, her husband. Taylor's employer provides health insurance coverage for all employees and pays $100 toward the monthly premium of each employee. Taylor can cover Wendy under his policy, but the couple has chosen not to do so because the cost would be higher than Wendy's current policy. In this case, Wendy cannot deduct any of her health insurance premiums because she is entitled to participate under a subsidized plan. The fact that she chooses not to be covered does not matter.

TAX YOUR BRAIN 	Using the information from Example 4-6, assume that Taylor did not begin work at the local business until April 1, 2009. Prior to that time, he was an employee of Wendy's business, and both he and Wendy were covered under a group policy that cost $300 per month. On April 1 Wendy changed to an individual policy at $145 per month. How much can Wendy deduct for self-employed health insurance in 2009? **ANSWER** $900. Wendy is entitled to deduct the health insurance costs for herself and her spouse for the first three months of the year ($300 × 3 months). After that time, she is eligible under Taylor's policy, so she cannot take any additional deductions.

The alternative coverage rule is applied separately to plans that provide long-term care services or are qualified long-term care insurance contracts and to plans that do not provide such services.[49]

---

[45] IRC § 164(l)(4). Chapter 6 covers the taxation of self-employed individuals.

[46] IRC § 164(l)(1)(B).

[47] Generally, net earnings from self-employment are defined in IRC § 1402(a). For purposes of the health insurance deduction, that definition is modified by IRC § 401(c)(2).

[48] IRC § 164(l)(2)(B).

[49] IRC § 164(l)(2)(B).

EXAMPLE 4-7	Patrick is self-employed and is entitled to participate in a subsidized qualified long-term care insurance plan through his wife Jennifer's employer. The general health care plan offered by Jennifer's employer is not subsidized. Patrick is entitled to participate in both health plans. He chooses to obtain general health care and qualified long-term care insurance through his own business. Patrick will be able to deduct the cost of the general health care plan (subject to the income limitation), but he cannot deduct the cost of the long-term care insurance. The general rule is that if someone else is willing to pay for insurance coverage, fully or partially, the premiums are not deductible.

The self-employed health insurance deduction is also available to a partner in a partnership and to a shareholder in a Subchapter S corporation who owns more than 2% of the stock in the corporation.[50] In the case of a Subchapter S shareholder, wages from the corporation are included in self-employed income for purposes of determining the deduction limitation based on net earnings from self-employment.

CONCEPT CHECK 4-5—LO 5	1. Self-employed individuals are allowed to take a *for* AGI deduction for up to 80% of the cost of their self-employed health insurance premiums. True or false? 2. One limitation on this deduction is that taxpayers cannot deduct the premium cost that exceeds gross earnings from self-employment. True or false? 3. Another limitation on this deduction is that eligible participation in a health plan subsidized by the employer of either the taxpayer or the taxpayer's spouse will prohibit the deduction. True or false?

PENALTY ON EARLY WITHDRAWAL OF SAVINGS (FORM 1040, LINE 30)
LO 6

Certificates of deposit (CDs) and time savings accounts normally require holding an investment for a fixed period ranging from three months to five years. Often the rules associated with these financial instruments state that the depositor who withdraws the funds prior to the end of the fixed term will forfeit a certain amount of interest to which he or she would otherwise be entitled. For example, a two-year CD might state that the depositor will forfeit three months of interest on the CD in the event the depositor withdraws the money before the end of the two-year period. If such a premature withdrawal occurs, the taxpayer will be credited with the entire amount of interest (and that amount must be reported as interest income), but the financial institution will deduct three months of interest as a penalty.

If a taxpayer incurs an early withdrawal of savings penalty, the taxpayer is entitled to report the penalty as a *for* AGI deduction on line 30 of Form 1040.[51]

EXAMPLE 4-8	On February 1, 2009, Ricardo and Marie deposited $10,000 into a one-year CD earning 2% interest at State Bank and Trust. If the couple withdrew their money prior to the end of the term, they would forfeit one month's interest as a penalty. On October 1, 2009, they withdrew their money. Ricardo and Marie would report $133 interest income on Schedule B ($10,000 × 2% × 8/12). They would also report a *for* AGI deduction of $17 ($10,000 × 2% × 1/12) as a penalty on early withdrawal of savings.

[50] IRC § 164(l)(5) and IRC § 1372(a).
[51] IRC § 62(a)(9).

From Shoebox to Software

Financial institutions report early withdrawal penalties in box 2 of Form 1099-INT (see Exhibit 4-8). When you record the Form 1099-INT, the software automatically carries forward the box 2 amount onto line 30 of Form 1040.

EXHIBIT 4-8

☐ CORRECTED (if checked)

PAYER'S name, street address, city, state, ZIP code, and telephone no.			Payer's RTN (optional)	OMB No. 1545-0112	
			1 Interest income $	20**09** Form **1099-INT**	**Interest Income**
			2 Early withdrawal penalty $		
PAYER'S federal identification number	RECIPIENT'S identification number		**3** Interest on U.S. Savings Bonds and Treas. obligations $		**Copy B** **For Recipient**
RECIPIENT'S name			**4** Federal income tax withheld $	**5** Investment expenses $	This is important tax information and is being furnished to the Internal Revenue Service. If you are required to file a return, a negligence penalty or other sanction may be imposed on you if this income is taxable and the IRS determines that it has not been reported.
Street address (including apt. no.)			**6** Foreign tax paid $	**7** Foreign country or U.S. possession	
City, state, and ZIP code			**8** Tax-exempt interest	**9** Specified private activity bond interest	
Account number (see instructions)			$	$	

Form **1099-INT**   (keep for your records)   Department of the Treasury - Internal Revenue Service

---

CONCEPT CHECK 4-6—LO 6

1. The early withdrawal penalty is reported on Form 1040 as a(n) _____ deduction.
2. The amount of the penalty is reported to the taxpayer by the financial institution on Form _____.

ALIMONY PAID (FORM 1040, LINE 31A)
LO 7

In a divorce or legal separation, certain payments may flow from one party to the other. These payments are (a) alimony, (b) child support, or (c) a property settlement. Of the three, only alimony has a tax consequence, and it is important to be able to distinguish it from the other two types of payments.

Child support is a fixed payment (in terms of dollars or a proportion of the payment) that is payable for the support of children of the payer spouse.[52] A *property settlement* is a division of property of the marital community incident to a divorce.[53] For tax purposes, child support payments and property settlement payments do not result in income to either spouse; nor does either spouse receive a tax deduction.

[52] IRC § 71(c)(1).
[53] IRC § 1041.

From Shoebox to Software

Alimony received is reported on line 11 of Form 1040. Alimony paid is reported on line 31a. Persons making alimony payments must report the taxpayer identification number of the recipient on line 31b.

In the tax software, you report information concerning alimony received or paid on a worksheet (Alimony Income or Alimony Paid Adjustment as the case may be). The tax software carries the information forward to the appropriate line on the Form 1040.

Canceled checks or other forms of payment provide information about the amount of alimony payments. Whether the payments constitute alimony is determined by reference to the divorce decree or separation agreement. In particularly complex cases, the taxpayer should obtain the advice of an attorney.

The payment of alimony, however, has tax ramifications.[54] Alimony received is taxable to the payee (receiving) spouse in the year received.[55] It is income on line 11 of Form 1040. Alimony payments are deductible by the payer spouse in the year paid as a *for* AGI deduction.[56]

To qualify as *alimony*, a payment must be cash and must be required under the provisions of a decree of divorce or separate maintenance or the provisions of a written separation agreement or other decree requiring one spouse to make payments to support the other spouse.[57] All payments must occur after the decree or after the execution of the agreement. Any payments made prior to this time would be neither deductible by the payer spouse nor included in the income of the payee spouse.

All payments must end at the payee spouse's death. There can be no provisions to make payments to the estate of the spouse or in any other manner after the death of the spouse. If this rule is not satisfied, then none of the payments are alimony, even those made during the life of the spouse.[58]

Alimony includes payments made to third parties on behalf of the payee spouse under the terms of the divorce decree or separate maintenance agreement.[59] Such payments might include paying the spouse's rent, mortgage, car payment, or property taxes. Payments made to maintain property owned by the payer spouse but used by the payee spouse do not qualify as alimony.[60]

EXAMPLE 4-9	Joe and Taylor entered into a separation agreement on July 20, 2009. The agreement required Joe to make payments of $300 per month to Taylor beginning on July 20, 2009. Their divorce decree was final on December 12, 2009, and Joe moved into a different residence on January 5, 2010. Under terms of the divorce, Joe transferred title on the couple's house to Taylor's name. The house was worth $100,000 at the time of the transfer. The divorce decree also mandated that, beginning in December 2009, Joe make payments on the 12th of each month of (a) $200 to Taylor for maintenance of the couple's only child, (b) $400 per month to Taylor, and (c) mortgage payments of $800 to the bank on behalf of Taylor. Payments for the child will continue until she reaches age 18; payments to or on behalf of Taylor will cease upon her death. They will file separate returns for 2009. How much can Joe deduct in 2009 and 2010 for alimony?
	In 2009, Joe may deduct the $300 payments required under the separate maintenance agreement for July through November, one $400 payment to Taylor, and one $800 payment to the bank. The alimony payments total $2,700 for 2009. The value of the house is a property settlement, and the monthly $200 for their child is child support. Neither of these items has any tax effect for either party. For 2010, Joe will be able to deduct $1,200 per month ($400 + $800), or $14,400 for the year. Note also that the amount of alimony income that Taylor must report is the same as the amount of alimony deduction calculated by Joe.

[54] The IRC refers to payments for "alimony or separate maintenance." In general, *separate maintenance* refers to payments made by one spouse to another while separated but still married, whereas *alimony* payments are those made after the divorce becomes final. For purposes of this section, we will refer to these payments simply as *alimony*.

[55] IRC § 71.

[56] IRC § 62(a)(10) and IRC § 215(a).

[57] IRC § 71(b)(2).

[58] IRC § 71(b)(1)(D) and Reg. § 1.71-1T(b), Q&A-10.

[59] IRC § 71(b)(1).

[60] Reg. § 1.71-1T(b), Q&A-6.

Payments are not alimony if the spouses file a joint return or if they live in the same household when payments occur.[61] However, if a payment is made when the spouses are living together and one spouse is preparing to leave the household and does so within one month after the payment, such payment will be considered alimony. Furthermore, if the spouses are not yet legally separated under a decree of divorce and a payment is made under a written separation agreement, such payment will count as alimony even if the spouses are members of the same household when the payment is made.[62]

Finally, if the divorce decree or separate maintenance agreement states that certain payments are not alimony, the agreement will control.[63]

TAX YOUR BRAIN

Would the answer to Example 4-9 change if Joe did not move out until January 30, 2010?

ANSWER

Yes. The payments Joe made on December 12 are not alimony because both he and Taylor were members of the same household on the date of the payment, and Joe did not move out within one month thereafter. Deductible payments for 2010 would not change.

Alimony Recapture Rules

If alimony payments decrease sharply in the second or third year of payment, the payments may be subject to a recapture provision.[64] This relates to the concept of "substance over form"; the payments may be called alimony but are, in substance, a property settlement. Note that these recapture rules do not apply after the third year of payment.

The recapture rules effectively reclassify payments from alimony to a property settlement. If recapture is required, the recipient (who previously recorded income) treats the recapture amount as a deduction, and the payer (who previously recorded a deduction) must count the recapture as income. The recapture occurs in the third postseparation year.[65]

TAX YOUR BRAIN

Why would the IRS care about the timing and magnitude of alimony payments?

ANSWER

Alimony payments create income for one taxpayer and a deduction for another, whereas property settlements have no tax effect on either party. In practice, it is likely that the tax rates of the spouses will differ after the divorce, perhaps significantly. For example, one spouse could be in the 35% bracket while the other one is in the 15% bracket. Taxpayers may try, in effect, to shift income from the high-tax spouse to the low-tax spouse.

CONCEPT CHECK 4-7—LO 7

1. Alimony may be paid in either cash or property, as long as the payments are made on a regular basis to a non-live-in ex-spouse. True or false?
2. For payments to qualify as alimony, the couple must be legally divorced at the time payments are made. True or false?
3. The goal of the alimony recapture rules is to properly define the substance of payments made to a former spouse to ensure proper tax treatment. True or false?

---

[61] IRC § 71(e) and IRC § 71(b)(1)(C).
[62] Reg. § 1.71-T(b), Q&A-9.
[63] IRC § 71(b)(1)(B).
[64] IRC § 71(f).
[65] IRC § 71(f)(6).

EDUCATOR EXPENSES (FORM 1040, LINE 23)
LO 8

Eligible educators can deduct up to $250 of qualified education expenses as an above-the-line AGI deduction.[66] The deduction is taken on Form 1040. If the taxpayer's filing status is married filing jointly and both individuals are eligible educators, the maximum deduction is $500, but neither spouse can deduct more than $250 of his or her expenses. Taxpayers must reduce otherwise permitted qualified expenses by any reimbursements received pertaining to the expenses.

An eligible educator is a teacher, instructor, counselor, principal, or aide in a kindergarten through 12th grade school who devotes at least 900 hours in the school year to that job.[67] Qualification under the 900-hour test is measured within the academic year, while the $250 deduction applies to expenses paid for during the calendar year.

Qualified education expenses are those for books, supplies, equipment (including computers and software), and other materials used in the classroom. The expense must also be ordinary (common and accepted in the educational field) and necessary (helpful and appropriate in the taxpayer's educational profession). Expenses for home schooling or for nonathletic supplies for health or physical education courses do not qualify.

Expenses exceeding $250 and nonclassroom supplies may be deducted as an employment-related miscellaneous deduction subject to the 2% floor by eligible taxpayers who itemize. (See Chapter 5.)

EXAMPLE 4-10	Lenroy and Lakeisha are married and will file a joint tax return. Both are eligible educators. Lenroy spent $420 on eligible expenses for his 4th grade class, and he received a $190 reimbursement from his school. Lakeisha spent $360 pertaining to her 11th grade science class and received no reimbursement. In total, the couple spent $780 and received reimbursement of $190, for a net expense of $590. However, Lenroy's deduction is limited to his net expenses of $230 ($420 − $190), and Lakeisha's is limited to a maximum of $250. Thus the total deduction on their joint tax return is $480.

CONCEPT CHECK 4-8—LO 8	Please fill in the blanks with the best answer(s). 1. To be eligible for the deduction, an educator must work at least _____ hours in the job. 2. The maximum deduction for a couple who are both eligible educators and filing MFJ is _____. 3. Expenses for _____ and _____ do not qualify for this deduction.

TUITION AND FEES DEDUCTION (FORM 1040, LINE 34)
LO 9

Taxpayers can take a deduction for qualified tuition and related expenses paid during the year for the taxpayer, taxpayer's spouse, or a dependent.[68] The deduction is a maximum of $4,000 but can be smaller if the modified AGI of the taxpayer exceeds certain limits.[69] For 2009 the $4,000 above-the-line deduction is available to single taxpayers with Adjusted Gross Incomes (AGI) of $65,000 or less ($130,000 for joint filers). A $2,000 above-the-line deduction is available to single taxpayers with AGI up to $80,000 ($160,000 for joint filers). The deduction is zero above those amounts. Payments must be to a qualified educational institution (see the definition in the "Student Loan Interest" section) and must be for a student

[66] IRC § 62(a) (2) (D).
[67] IRC § 62(d)(1).
[68] IRC § 222(a).
[69] IRC § 222(b).

taking one or more courses at that institution. Taxpayers cannot claim a deduction for tuition paid for elementary and secondary school education. Taxpayers must attach Form 8917 when claiming this deduction.

Only tuition and related expenses qualify.[70] Related expenses are student activity fees and fees for course-related books, supplies, and equipment but only if the school requires the payment as a condition of enrollment or attendance. For instance, some schools include books as part of the tuition fees.

EXAMPLE 4-11	Sal enrolls in an art class at a qualified educational institution. In addition to applicable tuition, the school charges $50 to pay for supplies used in the class. The $50 fee would qualify as a related expense.

EXAMPLE 4-12	The school in Example 4-11 requires art students either to provide their own supplies or to pay the $50 fee. Sal decides to pay the $50 fee directly to the school. The fee would not be a qualified expense because the school does not require payment of the fee as a condition of enrollment or attendance.

Permitted related expenses do not include amounts spent for insurance, medical expenses (including student health fees), room and board, transportation, and other personal living expenses even if the educational institution requires these payments.

The deduction is not available to an individual whose filing status is married filing separately or who can be claimed as a dependent on someone else's return.

EXAMPLE 4-13	In 2009 Sharon paid $1,500 for tuition at State University. She lives at home, and her parents can claim her as a dependent. Sharon cannot claim a deduction for tuition and fees (her parents can claim her as a dependent), nor can her parents (they did not pay the tuition).

Taxpayers cannot take the deduction if they claim a Hope or lifetime learning credit using the same expenses.[71] In effect, taxpayers can use tuition and related expenses only once—if expenses are used to claim one of the credits, the expenses cannot be used again to claim the tuition and fees deduction. However, a parent who pays the education expenses of several children who are claimed as dependents could potentially use this deduction for one child and a Hope or lifetime credit for another. It is important to note that the education deduction has a higher phaseout than the credits, making it the only education tax break available to many taxpayers.

Taxpayers must reduce amounts paid for tuition and related expenses by tax-free educational assistance such as scholarships, Pell grants, employer-provided educational assistance, and veterans' educational assistance. Note that loans, including student loans, personal savings, gifts, inheritances, and student earnings, do not reduce expenses.

CONCEPT CHECK 4-9—LO 9	1. The maximum amount of the tuition and fees deduction that an eligible taxpayer can take is $4,000. True or false?
	2. Normally, expenses for books purchased for school can qualify for the tuition and fees deduction. True or false?

[70] IRC § 25A(f).
[71] These credits are covered in Chapter 9.

From Shoebox to Software   Comprehensive Examples

In this section, we will add information to the tax returns of two taxpayers introduced in Chapter 3.

YIMING CHOW

Open the tax return file of Yiming Chow that you saved from Chapter 3. You are now going to add some information pertaining to two *for* AGI deductions.

Moving Expense

Mr. Chow moved from Somewhere, Colorado, to Mytown, Georgia, on February 3, 2009, as a direct result of changing jobs. The distance between those two towns is 1,844 miles, and the distance from his old house to his old workplace was 27 miles. Beta Tech has continuously employed him in Mytown since his move. He paid the moving company $1,106 to move his belonging including his auto and spent another $219 in air travel and lodging expenses and $71 in meals pertaining to his move. His employer reimbursed him $742 for the move.

To properly report Mr. Chow's moving expense deduction, you need to perform the following steps:

Modify the W-2 information previously entered for Mr. Chow to reflect the newly created employer re-imbursement. To do this, open his W-2. Go to box 12. Click on the code area of box 12 and highlight the P code. Then enter $742 in the amount box.

Go to the worksheets area and open the federal Form 3903 Distance and Time worksheet. You might first want to enter the information in the distance worksheet at the bottom of the form and then, if applicable, continue entering the remainder of the information.

Student Loan Interest Deduction

Mr. Chow also incurred $422 of interest expense pertaining to a federal student loan incurred while he was a student at State University in Colorado.

You must perform the following steps to report the student loan interest.

Open Mr. Chow's Form 1040.

Click on line 33. Then click on the yellow folder to open the supporting form. Alternatively, you could have opened the Student Loan Interest Deduction worksheet in the worksheet section.

On line 1 enter the $422 interest payment beside Mr. Chow's name.

Line 16 of the worksheet should now read $422. If you reopen Mr. Chow's Form 1040, the $422 deduction should be reflected on line 33.

After you have entered the moving expense and student loan interest data, Mr. Chow's AGI is $40,683 and his taxable income is $31,333. His total tax liability is $4,267. Because his total tax withholdings were $5,070, he should now receive a refund of $803 (rather than having a refund of $654 as determined in Chapter 3).

As mentioned, Mr. Chow now reports on Form 1040 rather than the 1040A that he was able to use in Chapter 3. This is so because Form 1040A does not accommodate a moving expense deduction. The tax software automatically chose the proper reporting form.

When you have finished, remember to save Mr. Chow's tax return for use in later chapters.

JOSE AND MARIA RAMIREZ

Open the tax return file of Mr. and Mrs. Ramirez that you saved from Chapter 3. You will now add some information pertaining to alimony.

Mr. Ramirez pays alimony of $500 per month to his former wife (her SSN is 333-33-3333). He paid 12 payments during the year.

To record the alimony payments in the tax software, perform the following steps:

Open the Ramirezes' tax return and then open their Form 1040.

Go to the form's worksheet tab and bring up the Alimony Paid Adjustment worksheet.

On the worksheet, enter $6,000 as the amount of alimony paid by Jose and enter his ex-wife's SSN.

Open the Ramirezes' Form 1040. The $6,000 alimony payment is on line 31a and the ex-wife's SSN is on the adjacent dotted line.

After you have entered the alimony information, the AGI of the Ramirezes is $100,962. Their taxable income is $71,312, and their total tax liability is $10,168. After the child tax credit of $3,000, and income tax with held of $9,418 and the making work pay credit of $800, they will receive a refund of $3,050.

When you have finished, make sure you save the Ramirezes' tax return for use in later chapters.

Summary

LO 1: Describe the tax rules for student loan interest.	• Only interest on a *qualified* student loan is potentially deductible. • A *qualified* loan is one used solely to pay for qualified education expenses. • The deduction for student loan expense may be limited based on the modified AGI of the taxpayer.
LO 2: Be able to calculate the Health Savings Account deduction.	• A Health Savings Account (HSA) is a tax-exempt savings account used to pay for qualified medical expenses. • To be eligible for an HSA, the taxpayer must be self-employed, an employee (or spouse) of an employer with a high-deductible health plan, or an uninsured employee who has purchased a high-deductible policy on his or her own. • Distributions from an HSA are tax-free as long as they are used to pay for qualified medical expenses.
LO 3: Determine the deduction for moving expenses.	• If a taxpayer moves due to a change in employment location, certain expenses related to moving may be deducted. • The costs of moving goods and people from the old residence to the new residence are considered suitable expenses. • The deductibility of moving expenses is subject to *both* time and distance tests.
LO 4: Explain the deduction for half of self-employment taxes.	• Self-employed individuals pay both halves of the FICA tax and therefore pay self-employment tax of 15.3%. • Half of this amount is a *for* AGI (above-the-line) deduction. • The tax is based on the *net* earnings from self-employment.

LO 5: Discuss the self-employed health insurance deduction.	• Self-employed individuals may be able to deduct 100% of self-employed health insurance premiums.
	• The amount of the deduction may be limited by two factors:
	  1. Self-employed individuals cannot take a deduction in excess of the *net* earnings from self-employment.
	  2. The amount is a function of the availability of other health insurance coverage.

LO 6: Explain the penalty on early withdrawal of savings.	• A taxpayer who withdraws funds early from a time deposit account may be subject to an early withdrawal penalty. • The amount of the penalty is reported on a Form 1099-INT issued by the financial institution.
LO 7: Be able to calculate the deduction for alimony paid.	• Alimony is one of three potential payments that can exist in a divorce or legal separation. • Of the three, only alimony has a tax consequence. • If payments properly qualify as alimony, they are deductible by the payer as a *for* AGI (above-the-line) deduction. • The recipient (the payee) of the payments must include these payments as income on his or her tax return. • When dealing with the character of payments in a divorce, it is important to use the "substance over form" rule.

LO 8: Determine the deduction for educator expenses.

- Educators can deduct up to $250 of qualified out-of-pocket expenses paid in 2009.
- If both spouses are eligible educators and file a joint return, each may deduct up to $250.
- Qualified educators who work at least 900 hours during the school year are eligible to take the deduction.
- Qualifying expenditures include classroom supplies such as paper, pens, glue, scissors, books, and computers.

LO 9: Be able to calculate the deduction for eligible tuition and fees.

- An above-the-line education tuition deduction is available for both single and joint filers.
- It is a two-tiered deduction ($4,000 or $2,000) that is tied to AGI thresholds.
- Only higher education tuition and qualifying fees are eligible for the deduction.
- Taxpayers must attach Form 8917 when claiming this deduction.
- Taxpayers taking this above-the-line deduction cannot also claim the Hope or lifetime learning credit for the same student.

Discussion Questions

LO 1

1. What is a qualified education loan for purposes of the student loan interest deduction?

_____

_____

_____

LO 1

2. What are qualified education expenses for purposes of the student loan interest deduction?

_____

_____

_____

LO 1

3. For purposes of the student loan interest deduction, what is modified AGI, and how is it determined?

_____

_____

_____

LO 1

4. For purposes of the student loan interest deduction, what is an eligible educational institution?

_____

_____

_____

LO 1

5. Explain the limitations associated with the deductibility of student loan interest.

_____

_____

_____

LO 1

6. In 2005 Mary incurred a loan to pay for qualified higher education expenses for her 20-year-old daughter, who was a dependent. In 2009 her daughter graduated from college, moved away to start a new job, and ceased to be a dependent on Mary's tax return. Mary started making payments on the loan in 2009. Without regard to any modified Adjusted Gross Income limitations, is Mary permitted to deduct interest on the loan?

_____

_____

_____

LO 1   7. Charles borrowed money to pay for a portion of the qualified higher education expenses of his dependent nephew, who was living with him. After graduation, the nephew moved away in search of a job and ceased to be a dependent. Can Charles deduct interest on the loan as student loan interest? Why or why not?

_____

_____

_____

LO 2   8. Explain the purpose of a Health Savings Account (HSA).

_____

_____

_____

LO 2   9. What are the qualifications to be eligible for a Health Savings Account deduction?

_____

_____

_____

LO 3   10. Explain the three tests associated with deductibility of moving expenses.

_____

_____

_____

LO 3   11. Describe the types of moving expenses that can be deducted.

_____

_____

_____

LO 3   12. A taxpayer incurs moving expenses in conjunction with a job-related move that meets the distance test. At the end of the year, the taxpayer has not yet met the time test. Under what circumstances can the taxpayer deduct the moving expenses?

_____

_____

_____

LO 3   13. Nathan quit his job in Los Angeles and moved to Seattle, incurring $1,500 of moving expenses. Upon arriving in Seattle, he sought employment and found a position three weeks later. Without regard to the time test, what amount, if any, of his moving expenses can Nathan deduct?

_____

_____

_____

LO 3   14. In January 2009 Jeff incurred $1,200 of moving expenses when he moved from Des Moines to Detroit. When he moved, he had no job but found one a week after moving. He stayed on that job for two months, changed to another job for four months, and changed again to a long-term position that he held for the remainder of the year. What is the amount of moving expense deduction Jeff can report in 2009, if any?

_____

_____

_____

LO 4 15. Explain why self-employed taxpayers pay double the amount of FICA taxes that regular wage earners do.

LO 4 16. Refer to Question 15. How does the tax code attempt to remedy this seeming inequity?

LO 5 17. Explain the two limitations associated with the deduction for health insurance by self-employed individuals.

LO 6 18. What is meant by a *penalty on early withdrawal of savings*, and under what circumstances is it deductible?

LO 7 19. Define *alimony, child support,* and *property settlement.*

LO 7 20. Why is it important to distinguish between a property settlement and alimony?

LO 8 21. Who is eligible to take an above-the-line AGI deduction for educator expenses, and what is the maximum amount of the permitted deduction?

22. What expenses qualify as deductible educator expenses?

LO 8 23. In the case of a joint return, what is the treatment of educator expenses?

LO 9   24. Briefly explain the tax rules associated with the tuition and fees deduction.

_____

_____

_____

LO 9   25. Mr. and Mrs. Lopez paid tuition of $1,400 and required fees of $650 for their 25-year-old daughter, who is attending State University, living on her own, and working 30 hours per week as a restaurant hostess. Their AGI is $50,000. The daughter paid for all her other school and living expenses, which amounted to more than 50% of her total living expenses. What is the permitted amount of tuition and fees deduction for the Lopezes? Why?

_____

_____

_____

Multiple-Choice Questions

26. (Introduction) *For* AGI, or above-the-line, deductions
    a. Are determined by the taxpayer.
    b. Are set by statute.
    c. Increase tax liability.
    d. Are reported in Schedule A.

27. (Introduction) *For* AGI, or above-the-line, deductions
    a. Increase AGI.
    b. Reduce tax credits.
    c. Are available only for MFJ.
    d. Can reduce overall tax liability.

LO 1   28. Student loan interest is reported on Form
    a. 1098-SA.
    b. 1098-E.
    c. 1099-S.
    d. 1098-GA.

LO 1   29. Taxpayers eligible to take the student loan interest deduction do *not* include
    a. A student who is claimed as a dependent on another's return.
    b. A self-supporting student.
    c. The parents of a dependent student who took out the loan on their child's behalf.
    d. A married student filing jointly.

LO 1   30. In 2005 through 2008, Korey borrowed a total of $25,000 for higher education expenses on qualified education loans. In 2009, while still living at home and being claimed by his parents as a dependent, he began making payments on the loan. The first year's interest on the loan was reported as $550. The amount that Korey can claim on his tax return is
    a. $0.
    b. $225.
    c. $340.
    d. $550.

LO 2   31. For 2009 the maximum aggregate annual contribution that a taxpayer, under age 55, can make to a Health Savings Account (HSA) for family coverage is
    a. $1,150.
    b. $3,000.

      c. $5,800.

      d. $11,600.

LO 2 32. To be eligible to fund a Health Savings Account (HSA), a taxpayer must be

      a. An employee (or spouse) who works for an employer with a high-deductible health plan.

      b. An uninsured employee who has purchased a high-deductible health plan on his or her own.

      c. A self-employed individual.

      d. All of the above.

LO 3 33. To be eligible to deduct moving expenses, a taxpayer

      a. Must meet the time test.

      b. Must meet the distance test.

      c. Must meet either the time or distance test.

      d. Must meet both the time and distance tests.

LO 3 34. Deductible expenses for moving do not include

      a. The cost of transporting household goods.

      b. Hotel costs while moving to the new location.

      c. Meals incurred during the move.

      d. Storage of household goods for a limited time upon arrival at the new location.

LO 3 35. To meet the distance test, the new job location must be

      a. 100 miles from the old job location.

      b. At least 50 miles farther than the old residence was from the old job location.

      c. At least 50 miles farther than the new residence from the old job location.

      d. 100 miles from the old residence.

LO 4 36. The deduction for half of the self-employment tax is

      a. Based on a total of 7.65% of FICA taxes.

      b. Based on the gross earnings of the business.

      c. Based on filing status.

      d. Based on the net earnings of the business.

LO 5 37. As a *for* AGI deduction, self-employed health insurance premiums are deductible at

      a. 50%.

      b. 70%.

      c. 80%.

      d. 100%.

LO 5 38. Rick is a self-employed carpenter who had net earnings from self-employment of $3,500. He paid $325 per month for health insurance over the last year. Rick is entitled to a *for* AGI deduction for health insurance of

      a. $0.

      b. $325.

      c. $3,500.

      d. $3,900.

LO 6   39. Penalties for the early withdrawal on savings are reported by the financial institution on
   a. Box 2 of Form 1099-INT.
   b. Form EWIP.
   c. A letter of notification.
   d. None of the above.

LO 7   40. Roger is required under a 2007 divorce decree to pay $600 of alimony and $300 of child support per month for 12 years. In addition, Roger makes a voluntary payment of $100 per month. How much of the total monthly payments can Roger deduct?
   a. $100.
   b. $300.
   c. $600.
   d. $700.

LO 7   41. The Hamiltons were granted a decree of divorce in 2008. In accordance with the decree, Rick Hamilton is to pay his ex-wife $24,000 a year until their only child, Evelyn, now 10, turns 18, and then the payments will decrease to $14,000 per year. For 2009, how much can Rick deduct as alimony?
   a. $10,000.
   b. $14,000.
   c. $24,000.
   d. None of the above.

LO 7   42. At the beginning of June of this year, John left his wife and is currently living in an apartment. The couple has no children. At the end of the current year, no formal proceedings have occurred in relation to the separation or potential divorce. John has been making a $2,000 a month maintenance payment since moving out. How much can John deduct as alimony for 2009?
   a. 0.
   b. $2,000.
   c. $6,000.
   d. $12,000.

Problems   **LO 1**   43. What are some of the limitations concerning deductibility of student loan interest? Be specific and comprehensive.

_____

_____

_____

LO 1   44. Discuss the characteristics of an *eligible educational institution* as it relates to the deductibility of student loan interest.

_____

_____

_____

LO 1   45. Barbara attended State University during 2004–2008. She lived at home and was claimed by her parents as a deduction during her entire education. She incurred education expenses of $10,000 during college of which $2,000 was paid for by scholarships. To finance her education, she borrowed $7,000 through a federal student loan program and borrowed

another $3,000 from a local lending institution for educational purposes. After graduation, she married and moved with her husband to a distant city. In 2009 she incurred $700 of interest on the federal loans and $300 on the lending institution loan. She filed a joint return with her husband showing modified AGI of $122,000. What amount of student loan interest can Barbara and her husband deduct in 2009, if any?

_____

_____

_____

LO 2   46. If an employer contributes to an HSA on behalf of an employee,

      a. Is the contribution deductible by the employee?

      _____

      _____

      b. Is the payment considered income to the employee?

      _____

      _____

LO 3   47. Jose, an engineer, was employed and resided in New Hampshire. On July 1, 2009, his company transferred him to Florida. Jose worked full-time for the entire year. During 2009 he incurred and paid the following expenses related to the move:

Premove house-hunting costs	$1,500
Lodging and travel expenses while moving	1,800
Cost of moving furniture and personal belongings	2,700

He did not receive reimbursement for any of these expenses from his employer; his AGI for the year was $85,500. What amount can Jose deduct as moving expenses on his 2009 return?

_____

_____

_____

LO 3   48. In May 2009 Maria graduated from the University of San Diego with a degree in accounting and moved to Denver to look for work. Shortly after arriving in Denver, she obtained work as a staff accountant in a local CPA firm. In her move to Denver, Maria incurred the following costs:

    $450 in gasoline.

    $250 for renting a truck from UPAYME rentals.

    $100 for a tow trailer for her car.

    $85 in food.

    $35 in double lattes from Starbucks.

    $300 for motel lodging on the way to Denver.

    $350 for a previous plane trip to Denver to look for an apartment.

    $175 in temporary storage costs for her collection of antique bassoons.

How much, if any, may Maria take as a moving expense deduction on her 2009 tax return? Is that deduction subject to any conditions that could change its deductibility in the future?

_____

_____

_____

LO 3   49. Are the moving expenses of other people besides the taxpayer deductible? If so, what are the requirements for deductibility?

_____

_____

_____

LO 4, 5   50. Juan, who is single, is a self-employed carpenter as well as an employee of Frame It, Inc. His self-employment net income is $35,000, and he received a W-2 from Frame It for wages of $25,000. He is covered by his employer's pension plan, but his employer does not offer a health plan in which he could participate.

     a. Up to how much of his self-employed health insurance premiums could he deduct for this year, if any? Why?

_____

_____

_____

     b. How much of Juan's self-employment taxes would be deductible?

_____

_____

_____

LO 6   51. Sheniqua has received a 1099-INT from her financial institution showing $90 in box 2 of the form. How should she handle this on her 2009 tax return and why?

_____

_____

_____

LO 7   52. Three types of payments are associated with a decree of separation or a divorce.

     a. What are those three payments?

_____

_____

     b. Which one has a tax consequence?

_____

_____

     c. What is the timing rule regarding the recapture period of those payments?

_____

_____

LO 7   53. Under the terms of a divorce decree executed May 1, 2009, Rob transferred a house worth $650,000 to his ex-wife, Linda, and was to make alimony payments of $3,000 per month. The property has a tax basis to Rob of $300,000.

     a. How much of this must be reported on Linda's tax return?

_____

_____

     b. Of that amount, how much is taxable gain or loss that Linda must recognize related to the transfer of the house?

_____

_____

LO 7   54. Under the alimony recapture rules, what amounts are designated for recapture reclassification, and what are the tax consequences?

_____

_____

LO 1–7   55. Indicate whether each of the following items is considered a *for* AGI (above-the-line) deduction for the 2009 tax year:

   a. Student loan interest.

   b. Gambling losses.

   c. Early withdrawal penalty.

   d. Child support payments.

   e. Charitable contributions.

   f. One-half of self-employment taxes.

   g. Alimony.

   h. Scholarships for tuition and books.

   i. Moving expenses.

   j. Property taxes.

   k. Self-employed health insurance premiums.

_____

_____

_____

Tax Return Problems

Use your tax software to complete the following problems. If you are manually preparing the tax returns, you will need a Form 1040 for each problem.

Tax Return Problem 1

Brenda Carlyle attended Kansas State University during 2005–2009. She incurred education expenses of $10,000. To finance her education, she borrowed $7,000 through a federal student loan program and borrowed another $3,000 from Kansas State Credit Union for educational purposes. After graduation, she accepted a position with the Houston Deloitte & Touche office and moved there in June 2009. She lives at 4560 Apple Blossom Lane with her cat, Misty. Her social security number is 555-55-5555.

   Her W-2 contained the following information:

Wages (box 1) = $61,533.05

Federal W/H (box 2) = $ 8,829.95

Social security wages (box 3) = $61,533.05

Social security W/H (box 4) = $ 3,815.05

Medicare wages (box 5) = $61,533.05

Medicare W/H (box 6) = $ 892.23

In moving to Houston, she incurred the following moving expenses:

$475 in gasoline.

$295 for renting a truck from IGOTYA rentals.

$75 in food.

$410 for motel lodging on the way to Houston.

She also received two Forms 1098-E. One was from the federal student loan program, which showed $850 of student loan interest; the other was from Kansas State Credit Union and

showed $450.75 of student loan interest.

Prepare a Form 1040 for Brenda using the appropriate worksheets.

Tax Return Problem 2

In February 2009 Phillip and Barbara Jones and their two dependent children, who are both over 17, moved from Chicago to Albuquerque, a distance of 1,327 miles, which they drove. The children's names are Roger and Gwen. The move was a result of a job transfer for Phillip. The distance from their old home to Phillip's old office was 30 miles. Barbara quit her job in Chicago and decided to perform volunteer work for a year before seeking further employment. Phillip and Barbara incurred expenses of $4,550 to the moving company (which included $320 for furniture storage), hotel charges of $550, and meals of $712 en route from Chicago to Albuquerque. Their new home is located at 7432 Desert Springs Way. Phillip, but not Barbara, was employed in the new location throughout the year. Phillip's social security number is 555-66-5555, Barbara's is 555-55-4444, Roger's is 666-11-2222, and Gwen's is 666-22-3333.

Phillip is an attorney for a national law firm; his W-2 contained the following information:

Wages (box 1) = $124,220.45
Federal W/H (box 2) = $ 29,765.12
Social security wages (box 3) = $106,800.00
Social security W/H (box 4) = $ 6,621.60
Medicare wages (box 5) = $124,220.45
Medicare W/H (box 6) = $ 1,801.20

Employer moving expense reimbursement
(box 12, Code P) = $ 5,000.00

In addition, both he and Barbara received Forms 1098-E from the federal student loan program. Phillip had student loan interest of $1,050, and Barbara had student loan interest of $750.

Prepare a Form 1040 for Phillip and Barbara as well as Form 3903 and a student loan worksheet.

Tax Return Problem 3

Karen and Carl Sanders obtained a divorce effective May 1, 2009. In accordance with the divorce decree, Carl was required to pay Karen $4,000 per month until their only child turns 18; then the payments would be reduced to $2,000 per month. Furthermore, he was to transfer title of their house, which had a cost of $150,000 and a fair value of $200,000 on the date of transfer, to Karen and was to continue making the monthly mortgage payments of $1,500 on behalf of Karen. Carl works for a large oil distributor in Santa Fe, New Mexico, and after the divorce lives at 1132 Northgate Avenue in Santa Fe. Karen's social security number is 555-73-9897, and Carl's number is 555-29-1035.

His W-2 contained the following information:

Wages (box 1) = $113,100.25
Federal W/H (box 2) = $ 28,275.12
Social security wages (box 3) = $106,800.00
Social security W/H (box 4) = $ 6,621.60
Medicare wages (box 5) = $113,100.25
Medicare W/H (box 6) = $ 1,639.95

He also received a Form 1099-INT from First New Mexico Bank with $336 of interest income in box 1 and a 1099-MISC from Oil Research Quarterly Magazine for other income of $490 for an article that he wrote.

Prepare a Form 1040 for Carl.

We have provided selected filled-in source documents on our Web site at www.mhhe.com/cruz2010.

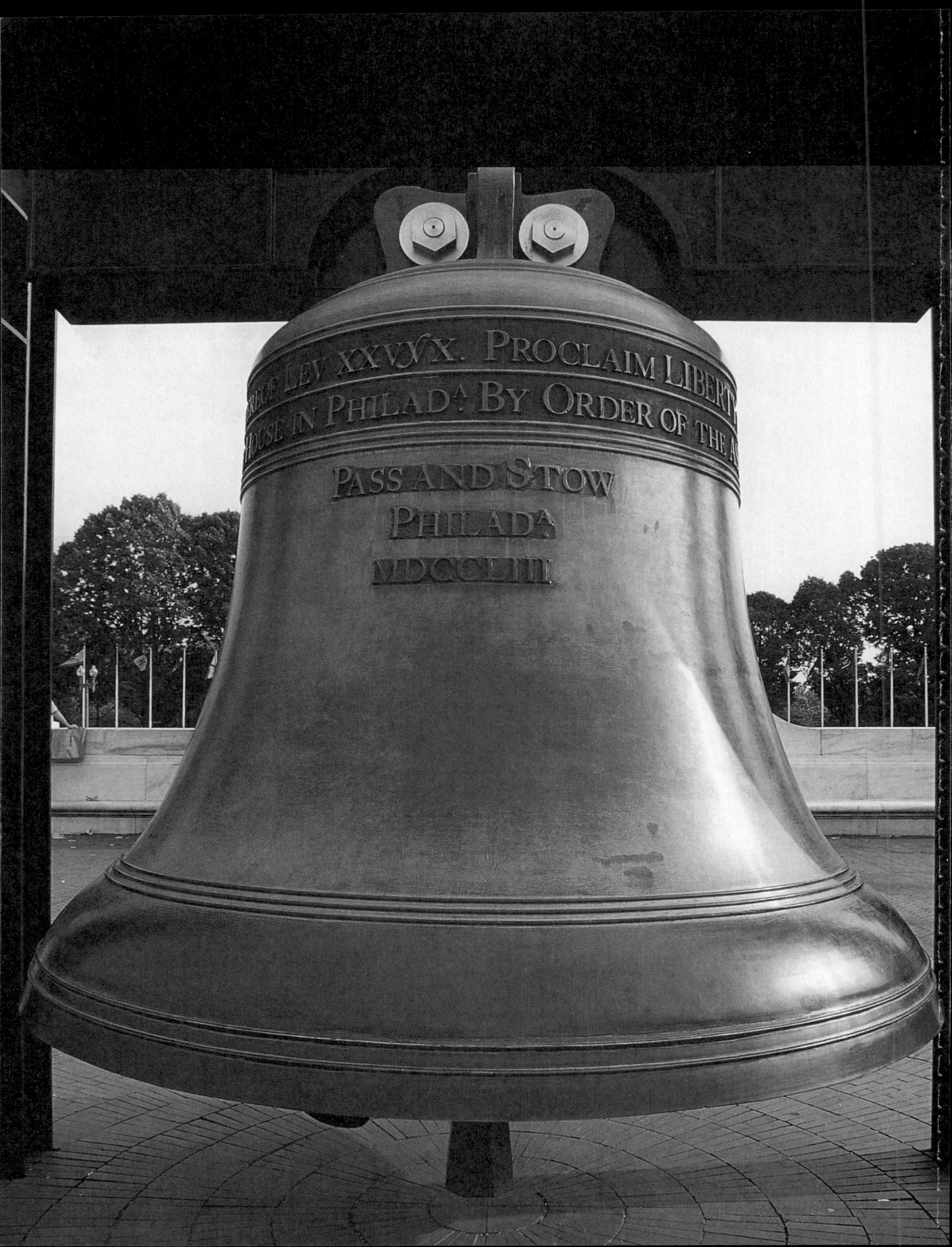
PROCLAIM
BY ORDER OF THE
PASS AND STOW
PHILADA
MDCCLIII

Chapter Five

Itemized Deductions

This chapter provides a detailed investigation of Schedule A and itemized deductions. Specifically, we present the laws, rules, and complete tax authority encompassing the six basic categories of the primarily personal expenditures allowed as tax deductions. In addition to the law and rules for deductibility, we present the practical application of the law on Schedule A and related forms.

Learning Objectives

When you have completed this chapter, you should understand the following learning objectives (LO):

LO 1. Describe the deductibility and reporting of medical expenses.

LO 2. Be able to explain the state and local tax deductions.

LO 3. Apply the tax rules associated with the interest deduction.

LO 4. Explain the deductibility and reporting of charitable contributions.

LO 5. Discuss the casualty loss deduction.

LO 6. Know how to report miscellaneous expenditures.

LO 7. Apply the tax rules for limitations on total itemized deductions for high-income taxpayers.

INTRODUCTION

The Internal Revenue Code allows taxpayers to deduct certain items from gross income when determining taxable income. One type of permitted deduction is a *for* (or *above-the-line*) AGI deduction such as moving expenses, student loan interest, and health savings accounts. We discussed these *for* AGI deductions in Chapter 4.

The other type of permitted deduction is a *from* (*below-the-line*) AGI deduction. You are already familiar with one *from* AGI deduction—the standard deduction, discussed in Chapter 2. We now introduce you to another *from* AGI deduction—the itemized deduction.

Itemized deductions are reported on Schedule A (see Exhibit 5-1). If you review Schedule A, you will see that itemized deductions are organized into six major categories:

1. Medical.

2. State and local taxes.

3. Interest.

4. Charitable gifts.

5. Casualty losses.

6. Miscellaneous deductions, including unreimbursed employee expenses.

The first six learning objectives of this chapter are tied to these six categories of itemized deductions.

EXHIBIT 5-1

SCHEDULE A **(Form 1040)** Department of the Treasury Internal Revenue Service (99)	**Itemized Deductions** ▶ **Attach to Form 1040.**　　▶ **See Instructions for Schedule A (Form 1040).**	OMB No. 1545-0074 **2009** Attachment Sequence No. **07**

Name(s) shown on Form 1040　　　　　　　　　　　　　　　　　　　　　　　**Your social security number**

Medical and Dental Expenses

Caution. Do not include expenses reimbursed or paid by others.

1	Medical and dental expenses (see page A-1)	1
2	Enter amount from Form 1040, line 38 ⟨2⟩	
3	Multiply line 2 by 7.5% (.075)	3
4	Subtract line 3 from line 1. If line 3 is more than line 1, enter -0-	4

Taxes You Paid

(See page A-2.)

5	State and local **(check only one box):** 　a ☐ Income taxes, **or** 　b ☐ General sales taxes	5
6	Real estate taxes (see page A-5)	6
7	New motor vehicle taxes from line 11 of the worksheet on back. Skip this line if you checked box 5b	7
8	Other taxes. List type and amount ▶	8
9	Add lines 5 through 8	9

Interest You Paid

(See page A-5.)

Note. Personal interest is not deductible.

10	Home mortgage interest and points reported to you on Form 1098	10
11	Home mortgage interest not reported to you on Form 1098. If paid to the person from whom you bought the home, see page A-6 and show that person's name, identifying no., and address ▶	11
12	Points not reported to you on Form 1098. See page A-6 for special rules	12
13	Qualified mortgage insurance premiums (see page A-6)	13
14	Investment interest. Attach Form 4952 if required. (See page A-6.)	14
15	Add lines 10 through 14	15

Gifts to Charity

If you made a gift and got a benefit for it, see page A-7.

16	Gifts by cash or check. If you made any gift of $250 or more, see page A-7	16
17	Other than by cash or check. If any gift of $250 or more, see page A-8. You **must** attach Form 8283 if over $500	17
18	Carryover from prior year	18
19	Add lines 16 through 18	19

Casualty and Theft Losses

20	Casualty or theft loss(es). Attach Form 4684. (See page A-8.)	20

Job Expenses and Certain Miscellaneous Deductions

(See page A-9.)

21	Unreimbursed employee expenses—job travel, union dues, job education, etc. Attach Form 2106 or 2106-EZ if required. (See page A-9.) ▶	21
22	Tax preparation fees	22
23	Other expenses—investment, safe deposit box, etc. List type and amount ▶	23
24	Add lines 21 through 23	24
25	Enter amount from Form 1040, line 38 ⟨25⟩	
26	Multiply line 25 by 2% (.02)	26
27	Subtract line 26 from line 24. If line 26 is more than line 24, enter -0-	27

Other Miscellaneous Deductions

28	Other—from list on page A-10. List type and amount ▶	28

Total Itemized Deductions

29	Is Form 1040, line 38, over $166,800 (over $83,400 if married filing separately)? ☐ **No.** Your deduction is not limited. Add the amounts in the far right column for lines 4 through 28. Also, enter this amount on Form 1040, line 40a. ☐ **Yes.** Your deduction may be limited. See page A-10 for the amount to enter.　▶　29
30	If you elect to itemize deductions even though they are less than your standard deduction, check here ▶ ☐

For Paperwork Reduction Act Notice, see Form 1040 instructions.　　　Cat. No. 17145C　　　**Schedule A (Form 1040) 2009**

Most itemized deductions are, in effect, personal living expenses: medical expenses, interest expenses, payments for taxes, and the like. Permitted personal living expenses can be deducted only if they are expressly permitted.

Itemized deductions also include two other types of expenses: unreimbursed employee business expenses (part of miscellaneous deductions) and investment-related expenses (part of the interest category as well as miscellaneous deductions).

In practice, taxpayers determine their (1) standard deduction and (2) total itemized deductions and use the higher number. In other words, a taxpayer cannot take *both* the standard deduction *and* the itemized deduction but only the higher of the two. Recall, for example, that the standard deduction is $11,400 for a married couple.[1] Thus a married couple who has itemized deductions of $8,000 should claim the standard deduction, but if the itemized deductions total $12,000, the couple should choose to itemize the deductions.

DEDUCTIBLE MEDICAL EXPENSES (SCHEDULE A, LINE 4)
LO 1

Taxpayers can deduct an itemized deduction for medical expenses (net of insurance proceeds) for themselves, their spouse, and dependent(s). The qualifying relationship must exist at the date the taxpayer incurs or pays the expenses. Only the amount in excess of 7.5% of AGI is deductible.[2] Because the threshold is so high, medical expenditures usually must be substantial for the taxpayer(s) to benefit from a medical deduction. A formula for calculating the amount of deductible medical expense is shown in Table 5-1.

TABLE 5-1 **Medical Expense** **Deduction Formula**	**Calculation of Deductible Medical Expenses**
	Allowable medical expenses minus (Insurance reimbursements)
	Allowable net paid medical expenses minus (7.5% of adjusted gross income)
	Deductible medical expenses

EXAMPLE 5-1 Alice and Bob are married taxpayers with adjusted gross income (AGI) of $100,000 in tax year 2009. To benefit from an itemized deduction for medical expenses, Alice and Bob must have medical costs in excess of $7,500 ($100,000 × 7.5% floor).

Two special rules apply for determining whether an individual qualifies as a dependent for purposes of the medical expense deduction:

1. The dependent child of divorced parents is treated as a dependent of both parents. The parent who pays the child's medical expenses may deduct the expenses even if the parent is not permitted to claim the child's dependency exemption.

2. The gross income and the joint return tests for the dependency exemption are waived. A taxpayer who pays the medical expenses of an individual who satisfies the relationship,

---

[1] The standard deduction for a qualifying widow(er) is $11,400, for head of household is $8,350, and for a single person as well as married filing separately is $5,700.

[2] IRC § 213.

citizenship, and support tests for the dependency exemption may deduct the medical expenses paid for that person.[3]

A deduction may be claimed only for medical expenses actually paid during the taxable year regardless of when the care was provided and regardless of the taxpayer's method of accounting.[4] A medical expense charged to a credit card is considered paid.

The taxpayer may deduct costs for medical care, which includes the following:

1. The diagnosis, cure, mitigation, treatment, or prevention of disease, or for the purpose of affecting any structure or function of the body.
2. Transportation primarily for and essential to medical care.
3. Qualified long-term care services.
4. Insurance for medical care or qualified long-term care services.

In most instances, medical expenses are relatively straightforward and include all costs for licensed medical treatment. Ambiguity occurs when expenditures for personal, living, and family purposes (generally not deductible) are incidental to medical care (generally deductible).

TAX YOUR BRAIN

A physician prescribes a special diet consisting of low-fat, high-fiber foods to lower cholesterol. The physician's bill is definitely deductible. However, is the cost of the food a deductible medical expense?

ANSWER

The mere fact that a physician prescribes or recommends a course of action does not automatically qualify the expenditure as a deduction.[5] If an expense item is ordinarily for personal purposes, the excess of the cost of the special items (excess over the ordinary-use goods) qualifies as a medical deduction. For example, the extra cost of a specially designed auto (above the normal cost of the auto) for a taxpayer confined to a wheelchair would qualify as a medical deduction.[6] Therefore, the special food would be deductible only to the extent the food costs exceeded normal food costs. This would be difficult to substantiate. Thus, it is unlikely that the food would qualify as a deductible medical expense.

Taxpayers may *not* deduct expenditures that are merely for the benefit of the general health of an individual.[7] For example, expenditures for cosmetic surgery are normally not deductible. Clearly, any payments made for operations or treatments for any part of the body or function of the body are deductible if they serve a distinct medical need. Plastic surgery to repair a birth defect would be a deductible expense. This includes payments to virtually all health care providers, such as doctors, dentists, ophthalmologists, nurses, and physical therapists as well as many unconventional medical treatments, from acupuncture to treatments by Christian Science practitioners.[8]

---

[3] Reg. § 1.213-1(a)(3)(i).

[4] IRC § 213(a).

[5] *Atkinson, H.* (1965) 44 TC 39, acq. 1965-2 CB 4.

[6] Rev. Rul. 76-80, 1976-1 CB 71.

[7] See Reg. § 1.213-1(e)(1).

[8] Rev. Rul. 72-593, 1972-2 CB 180; Rev. Rul. 55-261, 1955-1 CB 307. Payments to the following medical providers are specifically included as deductible charges: psychologists, physicians, surgeons, specialists or other medical practitioners, chiropractors, dentists, optometrists, osteopaths, psychiatrists, and Christian Science practitioners.

TAX YOUR BRAIN

Can a capital expenditure such as an addition of a swimming pool to a house qualify as a deductible medical expense?

ANSWER

If the capital expenditure for the swimming pool is for the primary medical care of the taxpayer, his or her spouse, or his or her dependent(s), it may qualify for a deduction.[9] This area has been highly litigated by the IRS. To ensure the deduction for the pool, a physician must prescribe swimming and there can be no recreational element (such as a diving board or slide) to the pool. Other factors used in determining the deductibility of a swimming pool include the availability of other types of exercise and access to a community pool.[10]

For medical capital expenditures that improve the taxpayer's property, the deduction is available only to the extent that the medical expenditure exceeds the increase in the fair market value (FMV) of the residence. Thus if the cost of a swimming pool for medical purposes was $30,000 and the increase in FMV to the residence was $20,000, the medical deduction would be limited to $10,000 (the excess cost over the FMV increase).

EXAMPLE 5-2

Jose suffers from a severe knee condition and is unable to climb steps. Consequently, he installed an elevator in his home at a cost of $7,000. An appraiser indicates that the elevator increased the value of the home by $2,000. The cost of the elevator, $7,000, is a medical expense to the extent that it exceeds the increase in the value of the property, $2,000. Thus $5,000 of the cost of the elevator is included in the calculation of Jose's medical expense deduction.

Generally, deductible medical costs do not include cosmetic surgery unless the surgery is necessary to correct a deformity arising from a congenital abnormality, personal injury, or disfiguring disease.[11]

EXAMPLE 5-3

Tommy was riding his all-terrain vehicle and lost control. His head and face hit a cement culvert, severely disfiguring the right side of his face. The cost of the cosmetic surgery to repair the damage, the hospital stay, and all physician fees would qualify as a medical deduction.

Medical expenses are *not* deductible if they have been "compensated for by insurance or otherwise."[12] As a result, any insurance reimbursements or partial reimbursements reduce the deductible medical expenses subject to the 7.5% AGI limitation.

Medicine and Drugs

For the cost of a drug to be deductible, a physician must first prescribe it.[13] This would include payments for birth control pills or drugs to alleviate nicotine withdrawal as long as a prescription was required.[14] It is worth noting that certain nonprescription medications are now eligible for reimbursement from qualified medical reimbursement plans, even though not deductible on the tax return.[15]

One other limitation to the deductibility of medicine or drug costs is that the taxpayer must obtain the drug legally. Thus even if a physician prescribes an otherwise illegal drug for medicinal purposes, the cost of acquiring the drug is illegal and not deductible.

[9] Reg. § 1.213-1(e)(1)(iii).
[10] Rev. Rul. 83-33 (1983-1 CB 70) specially addresses the swimming pool issue.
[11] IRC § 213(d)(9).
[12] IRC § 213(a).
[13] IRC § 213(b).
[14] Rev. Rul. 73-200, 1973-1 CB 140; Rev. Rul. 99-28, 1999-25 IRB 6.
[15] Rev. Rul. 2003-102, 2003-2 C.B. 559.

Prescription drugs obtained from sources outside the United States, such as Canada, are deductible if they are prescribed by a physician for the treatment of a medical condition and the FDA has approved that they can be legally imported.

TAX YOUR BRAIN

A physician prescribes marijuana for pain control purposes for a terminally ill cancer patient. The use of marijuana for medicinal purposes is legal under state law. Can a taxpayer deduct the cost of marijuana?

ANSWER

Because marijuana cannot be legally procured, its cost is not deductible.[16]

Travel and Transportation for Medical Purposes

Transportation costs for medical purposes could include such items as cab, bus, or train fares, as well as expenses for a personal auto. The cost of the transportation must be primarily for, and essential to, deductible medical care.[17]

EXAMPLE 5-4

Jake Avery, who currently lives in New Orleans, must fly to Memphis to see a specialist concerning an inner ear condition. Mrs. Avery, a big Elvis fan, decides to go along to visit Graceland. The travel costs for Jake, but not Mrs. Avery, are deductible as a medical expense. If, on the other hand, Mrs. Avery accompanied Jake because her assistance was required due to problems stemming from the ear condition, her costs would also be deductible.[18]

There are two ways to calculate the deduction for the use of a personal auto for medical transportation: (1) the *actual cost* of operating the car for medical purposes or (2) the *standard mileage allowance*.[19]

When using the actual costs, the taxpayer must keep documentation for items such as gasoline, oil, repairs, and so on that are directly associated with transportation to and from medical care. However, the taxpayer gets no deduction for general repairs, maintenance, or insurance. The simpler approach for deducting personal auto expense is to use the standard mileage allowance, which in 2009 is 24 cents per mile. The taxpayer can deduct other supplemental costs such as parking and tolls in addition to the 24 cents per mile.

EXAMPLE 5-5

Maria has an inoperable brain tumor that requires treatment at Johns Hopkins Medical Center twice a month. It is a 400-mile round trip. She pays a total of $10 in tolls, $20 in parking, and gasoline of $60 for each round trip. Assuming that Maria made the trip six times in the current tax year, what is the maximum transportation expense deduction for medical purposes (disregarding the 7.5% AGI floor)?

ANSWER

Actual costs follow:

Gasoline ($60 × 6)	$360
Tolls ($10 × 6)	60
Parking ($20 × 6)	120
Total deduction	$540

(continued)

[16] Reg. § 1.213-1(e)(2); Rev. Rul. 97-9, 1997-1 CB 77.
[17] IRC § 213(d)(1)(B).
[18] *Kelly, Daniel*, TC Memo 1969-231 reversed on another issue (1971, CA-7), 440 F2d 307.
[19] Rev. Proc. 80-32, 1980-2 CB 767.

EXAMPLE 5-5
(concluded)

Use of the standard mileage rate in effect for the year gives this deduction:

Mileage (400 miles × $.24/mile × 6)	$576
Tolls ($10 × 6)	60
Parking ($20 × 6)	120
Total deduction	$756

Maria would choose the standard mileage rate in this situation because it produces a higher deduction. This is not always the case, however. In reality, the convenience and the lack of receipt substantiation make the standard mileage rate more popular even though the deduction of actual costs could be higher.

In addition to the mileage, meals and lodging from the taxpayer's home to the medical facility are deductible.[20] Lodging near the related medical facility is deductible as long as no significant element of personal pleasure, recreation, or vacation is involved. The lodging expenditures are limited to $50 for each night for each individual and meals are not deductible.[21]

Long-Term Care

As the population ages, more funds will be spent providing long-term care for senior citizens. *Qualified long-term care services* are medical, maintenance, and personal care services provided to a chronically ill individual pursuant to a plan of care prescribed by a licensed health care practitioner.

The general rule concerning the deductibility of nursing home or other long-term care institution costs provides that amounts spent are deductible if the principal reason for the individual's stay is medical care as opposed to enjoyment or convenience. The entire cost of the long-term institution is deductible as a medical expense. If full-time medical care is not required, only the fee allocable to actual medical care is deductible, and costs for food and lodging are nondeductible.[22]

Determining medical expenses is usually quite easy for the individual or client who keeps good records. Generally, medical care providers supply the necessary receipts to document the medical charges incurred in a hospital or doctor's office. Other source documents for medical charges include checkbook registers, bank records, and credit card statements. Be careful, however, in taking a medical deduction for a check made out to a local drugstore that sells items in addition to prescription drugs. The IRS may require an itemized receipt for the prescription drugs. Pharmacy departments usually provide this information. Another major item, which is easy to misclassify, is the payment of health insurance premiums. These are deductible only if the taxpayer pays the premiums with after-tax funds (not in an employer pretax plan).

Insurance for Medical Care or Long-Term Care

Premiums for medical insurance, such as major medical, hospitalization, dental, and vision insurance, are deductible. This includes Medicare B premiums for voluntary supplemental coverage, but it does not include Medicare A insurance withheld from the taxpayer's paycheck. For 2009 the amount of deductible Medicare Part B premiums is $1,156.80. Premiums for long-term care policies are deductible, subject to dollar limitations. Deductible amounts for 2009[23] follow:

---

[20] *Montgomery, Morris v. Comm.* (1970, CA6), 428 F2d 243 affg (1968) 51 TC 410.
[21] IRC § 213(d)(2)2(A)1(B)(B).
[22] Reg. § 1.213-1(e)(1)(v).
[23] IRC § 213(d)(10).

Age at Close of Taxable Year	2009 Amount
40 and under	$ 320
More than 40, but not more than 50	600
More than 50, but not more than 60	1,190
More than 60, but not more than 70	3,180
Age 71 and over	3,980

TAX YOUR BRAIN

Vincent is an elderly man who does not require any medical or nursing care. However, he has recently become legally blind and needs help with normal living activities such as cooking, cleaning, and bathing. Vincent enters an assisted living facility where he feels he will be happier and less of a burden to his children. Does the cost of the facility qualify as a medical deduction?

ANSWER

Because medical care is not the principal reason for the stay at the facility, there is no medical deduction.[24] Of course any actual medical costs are still deductible.

From Shoebox to Software

EXAMPLE 5-6

We will return to Maria and Jose Ramirez in terms of Example 5-5. In Chapter 4, you created and saved a tax file on the Ramirezes. They had an AGI of $100,962. For this chapter, you will add the following medical costs.

Maria's hospital charges	$13,000
Maria's physician charges	8,000
Maria's prescription drugs	3,000
Jose's high blood pressure drugs	300
Jose's eye surgery	750
Regular dental visits (4 total)	280
Jose's regular physician charges	400
Transportation (from Example 5-5)	756
Lodging for trips to Johns Hopkins (for both Jose & Maria—Maria could not drive because the treatments affected her vision—6 nights @ $127/night)	762
High-fiber health food recommended for Jose	450

Assuming that Jose and Maria do not have health insurance, how much is their medical deduction, and how is it presented on Form 1040, Schedule A?

Tax software: Retrieve the Ramirezes' file saved from Chapter 4. Because of the numerous types of medical expenses allowed, it is easier to go directly to Schedule A to enter the medical deductions.

To complete the form, you must understand tax law. All of the expenses qualify for a deduction with the exception of the high-fiber health food. Additionally, the lodging is limited to $50 per person per night. In this case, because Jose was required to drive Maria, expenses for both of them qualify, and lodging would be limited to $100 per night ($50 for Jose, $50 for Maria) for six nights. Thus the total medical deduction before the 7.5% AGI limitation is $27,086.

The $27,086 deduction could be placed on line 1 of Schedule A; or if you wished to list all of the deductions, you could right-click on line 1 and then list the expenses on the "add line item detail" provided. The taxpayer's AGI ($100,962) would automatically transfer to line 2, and the 7.5% limitation ($7,572) would be calculated. Any changes to other areas of the tax return would automatically update AGI and thus change the allowable medical deduction.

The medical expense presentation on Schedule A (Exhibit 5-2) is as follows:

(continued)

---

[24] *Robinson, John v. Comm.* (1968) 51 TC 520, affirmed, vacated, and remanded by (1970, CA9) 422 F2d 873.

EXHIBIT 5-2

Medical and Dental Expenses	Caution. Do not include expenses reimbursed or paid by others.				
	1 Medical and dental expenses (see page A-1)	**1**	27,086		
	2 Enter amount from Form 1040, line 38 **2** 100,962				
	3 Multiply line 2 by 7.5% (.075)	**3**	7,572		
	4 Subtract line 3 from line 1. If line 3 is more than line 1, enter -0-			**4**	19,514

The net medical expense deduction would be $19,514. If Jose and Maria had health insurance and received benefits of $18,000, the amount shown on line 1 would be $9,086 ($27,086 – $18,000). You could either directly enter $9,086 on line 1 or show the insurance benefits as a negative on the line item detail. The result would be a deduction of only $1,514 (see Exhibit 5-3). Save the file showing $1,514 in net medical expenses for use later in the text.

EXHIBIT 5-3

Medical and Dental Expenses	Caution. Do not include expenses reimbursed or paid by others.				
	1 Medical and dental expenses (see page A-1)	**1**	9,086		
	2 Enter amount from Form 1040, line 38 **2** 100,962				
	3 Multiply line 2 by 7.5% (.075)	**3**	7,572		
	4 Subtract line 3 from line 1. If line 3 is more than line 1, enter -0-			**4**	1,514

Example 5-6 assumes that Maria and Jose received an $18,000 insurance reimbursement in the year in which they paid the medical expenses. What happens if Maria and Jose receive the insurance benefits in the subsequent year? In this case, the insurance reimbursement would be included in income in the year received to the extent of the tax benefit received in the prior year.

EXAMPLE 5-7

Use the same facts as in Example 5-6. If Jose and Maria received the $18,000 medical insurance benefits in the subsequent year, they must include the benefit amount in income to the extent of the tax benefit received. Their medical expense deduction would have been $19,514, so they would have received a tax benefit equal to the entire $18,000. In this case, they would report the $18,000 in income in the tax year received on line 21, Other Income, on Form 1040.

One common misconception is that the entire amount will always be included in income. If the insurance reimbursement caused the itemized deductions to be lower than the standard deduction, only a limited amount of the reimbursement would be included in income. The taxpayer would have to compare the taxable income in the deduction year tax return as it was reported to the taxable income that would have been reported had the insurance reimbursement been received in that year. The difference is the amount of income reported.

CONCEPT CHECK 5-1—LO 1

1. Medical expenses are deductible only to the extent that they exceed _____ of AGI.
2. Medical expenses can be deducted only in the year the expenses are _____.
3. The deductible amount of medical expense is reduced by _____ for those expenses.
4. The cost of long-term care insurance premiums is deductible, but the extent of the deduction depends on the taxpayer's _____.

DEDUCTIBLE STATE AND LOCAL TAXES (SCHEDULE A, LINE 9)
LO 2

Taxes are deductible in various places on a tax return. In this section, we discuss taxes that are personal; that is, they are not paid in connection with a trade or business or any other activity relating to the production of income. For example, if an individual taxpayer owns rental

property, the property taxes relating to the rental property are a *for* AGI deduction and are deducted on Schedule E (see Chapter 8). Likewise, if an individual taxpayer operates a business as a sole proprietorship, any payroll or property taxes paid relating to the business are deductible on Schedule C (see Chapter 6) and thus reduce AGI (*for* AGI deductions).

There are four major categories of deductible taxes on individual returns:

1. Personal property taxes.
2. Local real estate taxes.
3. Other state and local taxes, including sales taxes.
4. Foreign taxes.

The taxes that most individual taxpayers deduct on Schedule A are state and local income taxes and property taxes on real estate and personal property.[25] For cash method taxpayers, deductible taxes are generally deductible in the year paid. For accrual method taxpayers, taxes are generally deductible in the year in which the taxes are accrued. One important note is that federal taxes generally are not deductible on the federal tax return.

Personal Property Taxes

Personal property taxes paid on personal use assets, such as the family car, are deductible on Schedule A. Personal property taxes paid on rental property are deducted on Schedule E. Personal property taxes paid on assets used in a proprietor's business are deducted on Schedule C.

State or local property taxes must meet three tests to be deductible:

- The tax must be levied on personal property.
- The tax must be an *ad valorem tax*; that is, it must be based on the value of the property.
- The tax must be imposed, at a minimum, on an annual basis with respect to personal property.

TAX YOUR BRAIN  David lives in Johnson County and his brother Joseph lives in Lee County. Johnson County imposes a property tax of 2% of the value of personal vehicles. Lee County, on the other hand, imposes a flat fee of $250 per personal auto. Both counties impose the tax on an annual basis. How should David and Joseph treat these taxes?

ANSWER

David may deduct the tax he pays because it is an annual tax based on the value of personal property. Joseph, on the other hand, cannot deduct the property tax because it is a flat fee that is not based on value.

Many counties and states have different names for the taxes they levy. For example, some counties levy vehicle registration fees, which are deductible if they meet the preceding three tests. Usually the primary determinant is whether the fee is based on the value of the vehicle. If it is, the fee is deductible (assuming that it passes the other two tests).

Property taxes on real estate must meet the three tests as well. Taxes on real property usually are much higher than personal property taxes and may create additional controversy. Problems may develop in the following situations:

1. Jointly owned real property.
2. Sale of property during the tax year.

Property Taxes on Property Owned Jointly

In most states and counties, joint owners of property are jointly and severally liable for property taxes. In other words, if an individual is a part owner of a parcel of real estate and the

[25] IRC § 164.

other owner does not pay the property taxes, that individual is liable for the full payment. In this situation, the owner who pays the tax may deduct the tax amount.[26]

EXAMPLE 5-8

Two brothers, Jake and Stan, own a parcel of real estate with ownership interests of 30% to Jake and 70% to Stan. Jake pays the entire $2,300 county real estate tax. If Jake and Stan live in a state where all joint owners are jointly and severally liable for the tax, then Jake can deduct the entire $2,300 on Schedule A.[27]

If local law mandates that co-owners of property do not have joint and several liability for a tax, then only the proportionate share of the taxes can be deducted.

EXAMPLE 5-9

Assume the same facts as in Example 5-8. However, Jake and Stan live in a state that does not have joint and several liability for the tax. In this case, Jake's deduction is $690 ($2,300 × 30%) even though he paid the entire amount.[28]

Property Taxes on Property Sold during the Year

When property is sold during the year, both the buyer and the seller receive a deduction for a portion of the real estate tax paid according to the number of days each owner held the property.[29]

EXAMPLE 5-10

On March 1, David sold some land to Marsha. The real estate tax of $3,300 was not due until August, and Marsha properly paid it. How much, if anything, can David and Marsha deduct? In this case, the buyer and seller prorate the real estate tax on a daily basis. Therefore, David would deduct $533 ($3,300 × 59/365), and Marsha would deduct the remainder of $2,767 ($3,300 × 306/365). Note that the day of sale is not included in David's holding period.

The previous example could raise a question. If Marsha paid the tax, how can David get a deduction? At the time of transfer of ownership, a closing agent (often an attorney) prepares a *closing agreement* that prorates, or divides, the taxes (and other items) between the seller and the buyer. The taxes owed by the seller are withheld from the amount otherwise due to the seller. In effect, David paid the tax at the time of sale instead of at the due date.

Real Estate Taxes

Real estate taxes are deductible in the calculation of federal taxable income. If the tax is paid on personal-use real estate, such as the taxpayer's principal residence, it is an itemized deduction on Schedule A. If it is paid on rental real estate, it is deducted on Schedule E in the calculation of the taxpayer's net income or loss from the rental property. If it is paid on business real estate, such as an office building that the taxpayer owned and used as a proprietor, it is deducted on Schedule C in the calculation of net profit or loss from self-employment.

Many individuals make monthly mortgage payments that include real estate taxes as well as mortgage principal and interest. Each month, the real estate tax payment is deposited into an escrow account that the mortgage company uses to pay the property taxes when they are due. In this case, the taxpayer deducts the actual amount of property taxes ultimately paid to the local taxing authority from the escrow account, not the amount paid to the mortgage holder. The mortgage company notifies the individual of the amount of the taxes paid on a year-end statement, normally a Form 1098.

[26] Rev. Rul. 72-79, 1972-1 CB 51.
[27] This assumes the real estate is not business or "for the production of income" property. If the property were business use property, the taxes would be *for* AGI deductions and deducted on Schedule C (business), Schedule E (rental property), or Schedule F (farming property). See Chapters 6 and 8.
[28] *James, Joseph J.* (1995) TC Memo 1995-562.
[29] IRC § 164(d)(1).

EXAMPLE 5-11	Miriam's monthly mortgage payment for her principal residence is $1,500, of which $1,250 is mortgage principal and interest and $250 is for real estate taxes. Every month the mortgage company deposits the $250 tax payment into an escrow account. In November 2009 the mortgage company paid the actual tax bill of $2,800 from the escrow account. Miriam can deduct $2,800 of real estate taxes on her 2009 Schedule A.

State and Local Taxes

The deduction for state income taxes is one of the largest itemized deductions for many taxpayers. Only seven states in the United States do not have some form of a state income tax.[30]

EXAMPLE 5-12	Kelly lives in North Carolina and has state taxable income of $120,000. Her state income tax is $7,200. She gets a deduction on Schedule A for that amount in the year the tax is paid.

In any year, an individual taxpayer can deduct the amount of state income taxes paid, whether through withholding, estimated taxes, or filing the prior year's state tax return. However, if the state tax payments that were deducted result in the taxpayer receiving a refund in the following year, the state tax refund must be included as taxable income in the year of receipt. This is the *tax benefit rule.* That rule states that if a taxpayer receives a federal tax benefit from an expense when the expense is paid, that taxpayer is taxed on a refund of that expense when the refund is received. If the taxpayer does not receive a tax benefit from the expense when it is paid, he or she is not taxed on a refund of that expense when it is received.

EXAMPLE 5-13	In 2008 Richard had $4,700 in state income tax withheld from his paycheck. When he filed his 2008 federal tax return in April 2009 he was eligible to itemize and thus deducted the $4,700 in state income taxes paid, thus reducing his 2008 taxable income and federal tax liability. When he filed his 2008 state tax return (also in April 2009), he found that he had overpaid his state taxes and was due a refund of $800. He received the $800 state refund in June 2009. The $800 refund must be included in federal taxable income for the tax year 2009. The reasoning behind the inclusion is that Richard received a tax benefit for the entire $4,700 even though, in the end, he paid only $3,900 ($4,700 tax paid less the $800 refund). The inclusion of the $800 in income in the subsequent year corrects the excess deduction. The $800 is included on Form 1040, line 10, Taxable refunds, credits, or offsets of state and local taxes.

Taxpayers who do not itemize deductions (but claim the standard deduction) cannot deduct state income tax. Thus, if they get a refund, it is nontaxable income on their federal return because they received no tax benefit from a nondeductible expense. A refund of that expense is therefore not subject to tax. The same rules apply to taxpayers who are required to pay city or other local income taxes.

Employers may be required to withhold *state disability insurance* (SDI) from the paycheck of their employees in the state of California. California SDI is treated as state income tax for purposes of calculating federal taxable income.

For 2009 taxpayers can elect to take an itemized deduction for the amount of either (1) state and local income taxes or (2) state and local general sales taxes paid during the tax year.[31] Taxpayers generally cannot deduct both; however, for 2009 there is a special exception related to new vehicle purchases, which is noted next. In general, taxpayers in states with an income tax will take the income tax deduction, whereas taxpayers in states with no income tax will take the sales tax deduction. In states with both a state income tax and a state sales tax, the taxpayer will take the one with the greater benefit.

The amount of the sales tax deduction is determined by calculating actual sales taxes paid during the year. From a practical perspective, most taxpayers would find it difficult to

---

[30] Currently the only states that do *not* have some form of income tax are Alaska, Florida, Nevada, South Dakota, Texas, Washington, and Wyoming.

[31] IRC § 164(b)(5).

determine and document actual sales tax payments. Thus a deduction is permitted using sales tax tables provided by the IRS in Publication 600.

When using the sales tax tables, taxpayers determine their sales tax deduction based on their income and number of exemptions. Income is defined as AGI plus any nontaxable items such as tax-exempt interest, workers' compensation, nontaxable social security or retirement income, and similar items. The number of exemptions is equal to the exemptions claimed on Form 1040, line 6d.

EXAMPLE 5-14	Lester and Charmaine live in Florida with their two dependent children. Florida does not have a state income tax. The couple had AGI of $79,337 and interest income from a tax-exempt municipal bond of $2,190. Using the state and local sales tax tables for income between $80,000 and $90,000 with four exemptions, you can calculate the itemized general sales tax deduction available to Lester and Charmaine.

The American Recovery and Reinvestment Act of 2009 added a new provision to this area. Effective February 17, 2009, the law allows both itemizers and nonitemizers a deduction for sales and excise taxes incurred on the purchase of a new motor vehicle, motorcycle, or motor home during 2009.

Taxpayers who itemize are allowed to deduct the state or local sales or excise taxes imposed on the vehicle, even if they *do not elect* to deduct all state and local sales taxes incurred throughout the year in lieu of deducting state or local income taxes. In this case, the taxpayer enters the amount calculated on the worksheet on line 7 of Schedule A. Taxpayers who instead deduct all state and local sales tax incurred during the year, including the sales taxes on a new vehicle purchase, would skip this step and simply put the total amount of deductible sales taxes on line 5 of Schedule A. [32]

If the taxpayer is a nonitemizer, the deduction for the new vehicle sales or excise tax is added to the standard deduction. On page 2 of Form 1040, the taxpayer will check the box on line 40b and put the amount calculated on Schedule L on line 40b. The taxpayer must also attach Schedule L to the return.

There are some restrictions to this deduction. First, the amount of the tax that can be deducted is limited to the tax on the first $49,500 of the purchase price. If the state or local sales tax were 10% and the taxpayer purchased a new vehicle for $40,000, then $4,000 would be the potential tax deduction. Second, in the case of a car, truck, SUV, or motorcycle, the gross weight vehicle rating must not exceed 8,500 pounds. Lastly, the deduction is phased out for taxpayers with modified adjusted gross income between $125,000 and $135,000 and between $250,000 and $260,000 for a joint return.

Both domestic and foreign vehicles qualify for this treatment. However, sales tax paid on lease agreements does not qualify for this deduction. Note once again that this treatment applies only to the purchase of a new vehicle.

If taxpayers purchase an aircraft, boat, or in most cases a home or addition to a home, the taxpayer can add the amount of sales tax paid on those items to the amount of sales tax determined with reference to the IRS tables.[33]

EXAMPLE 5-15	Use the information from Example 5-14. Lester and Charmaine paid sales tax of $600 on the purchase of a car during 2009. Their itemized deduction for general sales tax will include an additional $600. However, if Lester and Charmaine took the standard deduction, they would fill out Schedule L and add the $600 to their standard deduction on line 40b on page 2 of Form 1040.

Taxpayers claim the general sales tax deduction on Schedule A, line 5, box b. IRS Publication 600 contains a worksheet for calculating the state and local sales tax deduction. The IRS also offers an online calculator on its Web site at http://apps.irs.gov/app/stdc/.

[32] IRC § 164(b)(6).
[33] IRC § 164(b)(5)(H)(i) and IRS Publication 600.

Foreign Taxes

Foreign taxes paid are deductible.[34] The taxpayer has the option of taking a credit (discussed in Chapter 9) for foreign taxes paid or deducting them on Schedule A. Individual taxpayers are usually better off utilizing the credit rather than the deduction because the credit is a dollar-for-dollar reduction in taxes, but the deduction reduces only taxable income, and the net tax effect depends on the taxpayer's tax rate.

EXAMPLE 5-16	Daniel, a U.S. citizen and resident, has several investments in Canada. The investments produced substantial income, and he had to pay $3,500 in Canadian income taxes. Assume that Daniel's effective U.S. federal tax rate is 35%. He has a choice: File Form 1116 and take a $3,500 credit for the Canadian tax or deduct the taxes on Schedule A as an itemized deduction. The credit will reduce Daniel's net U.S. tax by $3,500. If he takes the deduction option, his net tax savings is only $1,225 ($3,500 × 35%). Clearly the better tax option is to file Form 1116 and take the credit.

A taxpayer cannot take both the credit and the deduction for the same foreign taxes paid. In most instances, the credit produces the better tax effect. However, if a taxpayer pays taxes to a country with which the United States has severed diplomatic relations or to a country that supports international terrorism, the credit is not allowed.[35] In this case, the deduction of the tax on Schedule A is the only option.

Documentation for State and Local Taxes

Generally the source document for property taxes (both personal and real property) is the receipt from the county or city tax collector. Other sources for property taxes are canceled checks. Many lending institutions escrow the property taxes along with the mortgage payment. If this is the case, the amount of property taxes is listed on the year-end mortgage interest statement (Form 1098) the lending institution supplies. When real property is sold during the year, the allocation of the property taxes is usually shown on the closing statements signed when title changes hands.

For state income taxes, there are normally three source documents. For the majority of clients, the largest portion of state income taxes paid comes from the taxpayer's W-2 wage statement as state income tax withholding. Taxpayers who are self-employed or have considerable investment income could also pay quarterly estimated payments during the year. Usually, canceled checks to the state's department of revenue or other tax authority suffice as documentation. The third source document is the prior year's state tax return. Reviewing the prior year return is crucial because it will show any tax paid with the prior year's return. If there was a refund, the tax preparer will know to include the refund in income for the current year (assuming the taxpayer itemized his or her return and deducted state taxes in the previous year).

Foreign taxes are sometimes more difficult to locate. The traditional source documents to locate foreign taxes paid include these:

1. The prior year's tax return from the foreign country.
2. Mutual fund or stock brokerage statements.
3. Canceled checks.

Some mutual funds or brokerage offices are required to withhold or pay foreign taxes at the sale of stock within the mutual fund. These taxes, in turn, pass through to investors. In addition, if a taxpayer invests in foreign stocks, taxes are often withheld from foreign dividends received. These withholdings are reported to the taxpayer on Form 1099-B.

---

[34] IRC § 164(a)(3).

[35] IRC § 901(j)(2).

From Shoebox to Software

Determining the amount of the total interest deduction usually is not difficult. In most cases, a financial institution sends the taxpayer Form 1098 reporting the interest expense. See Exhibit 5-5 for an example of a common Form 1098 from a financial institution.[45]

EXAMPLE 5-23

Assume that the Form 1098 in Exhibit 5-5 was for Jose and Maria Ramirez and had $7,300 on line 1. To enter the $7,300 on line 10 of Schedule A, you must enter the amount on a Form 1098. Enter the $7,300 on line 1, and it will automatically be transferred to Schedule A. Save the Ramirezes' return for future use.

Difficulty can arise when a taxpayer has numerous loans outstanding. Typically the lending institution labels the interest as related to the principal residence (either acquisition indebtedness or home equity indebtedness). However, if the taxpayer has several loans, some of which are personal loans (like a car loan) and others are investment loans, the tax preparer must question the client to discover which loans are for what activities.

EXHIBIT 5-5

☐ CORRECTED (if checked)

RECIPIENT'S/LENDER'S name, address, and telephone number		* **Caution:** *The amount shown may not be fully deductible by you. Limits based on the loan amount and the cost and value of the secured property may apply. Also, you may only deduct interest to the extent it was incurred by you, actually paid by you, and not reimbursed by another person.*	OMB No. 1545-0901 20**09** Form **1098**	**Mortgage Interest Statement**
RECIPIENT'S federal identification no.	PAYER'S social security number	**1** Mortgage interest received from payer(s)/borrower(s)* $		**Copy B For Payer**
PAYER'S/BORROWER'S name		**2** Points paid on purchase of principal residence $		The information in boxes 1, 2, 3, and 4 is important tax information and is being furnished to the Internal Revenue Service. If you are required to file a return, a negligence penalty or other sanction may be imposed on you if the IRS determines that an underpayment of tax results because you overstated a deduction for this mortgage interest or for these points or because you did not report this refund of interest on your return.
Street address (including apt. no.)		**3** Refund of overpaid interest $		
City, state, and ZIP code		**4** Mortgage insurance premiums $		
Account number (see instructions)		**5**		

Form **1098**   (keep for your records)   Department of the Treasury - Internal Revenue Service

2. The taxpayer has no other deductible investment expenses.
3. The taxpayer has no disallowed investment interest expense from 2008.

CONCEPT CHECK 5-3—LO 3

1. Acquisition indebtedness means any debt incurred to _____, _____, or _____ any qualified residence.
2. The aggregate amount treated as acquisition indebtedness for any period cannot exceed $ _____ for married filing jointly.
3. The deduction of investment interest expense is limited to the _____ income for the year.
4. Each point paid to acquire a home loan equals _____ of the loan principal.

---

[45] Many financial institutions develop their own Form 1098 (labeled Form 1098 Substitute). Therefore, the form may differ somewhat depending on the institution. The form, however, reports the same information.

DEDUCTIBLE GIFTS TO CHARITY (SCHEDULE A, LINE 19)
LO 4

The government encourages the private sector to support charitable organizations by granting individual taxpayers a charitable contribution deduction, which may be claimed as an itemized deduction on Schedule A. Contributions must be to one of the following five types of organizations:[46]

1. Any governmental unit or subdivision of the United States or its possession as long as the gift is for exclusively public purposes.
2. Any nonprofit organization that is organized and operated exclusively for religious, charitable, scientific, literary, or educational purposes or to foster international amateur sports competition and is not disqualified from tax-exempt status under IRC §501(c)(3).
3. A post or organization of war veterans for which no part of the net earnings benefit any private shareholder or individual.
4. A domestic fraternal society or association that uses the contribution only for religious, charitable, scientific, or educational purposes.
5. A cemetery company owned and operated exclusively for the benefit of its members.

If you are uncertain whether an organization is a qualified donee organization, check IRS Publication 78, *Cumulative List of Organizations*.

The amount of the deduction depends on the type of donated property and is subject to AGI limitations. To be deductible, the donation must be cash or other property of value. The government imposes strict documentation requirements for both types of contributions.

A taxpayer receives no deduction for services rendered to a charitable organization.[47] The services do not give rise to taxable income to the taxpayer, so no deduction is permitted.

EXAMPLE 5-24

Kathy, a local CPA, is an ardent supporter of the Boys Club in Hickory Hills, AL. Each year she compiles monthly financial statements and prepares the Form 990 tax return for the club. Kathy estimates that she spends 20 hours per year working for the Boys Club. Her normal rate is $100 per hour. Because Kathy's donation is her services and she has recorded no income for those services, she receives no charitable contribution deduction.

Kathy is able to deduct any out-of-pocket expenses she paid in connection with her service to the Boys Club. Actual expenditures are deductible for automotive travel, or the taxpayer has the option to deduct 14 cents per mile as a standard rate for charitable contributions.

A taxpayer who travels away from home overnight to attend a convention as a representative of a charitable organization may deduct related transportation and travel expenses, including meals and lodging. If the taxpayer incurs travel expenses as a volunteer for a qualified charity, the expenses are deductible if he or she has significant duties throughout the course of the trip and no significant amount of personal recreation is attached to the trip.

Property Donations: Capital versus Ordinary Income Property

Not all donations to charity are in the form of cash. In fact, many large donations are made with capital gain property (such as stocks, bonds, land, and other investments). Still other donations are made with ordinary income property (inventory and accounts receivable). Generally, if capital gain property is donated to a public charity, the deductible donation amount is the property's FMV.

Charitable Contribution of Personal Tangible Property Clarification

A key exception to this general rule concerns the contribution of tangible personal property. If the donated property is put to a use that is unrelated to the purpose or function of the charity's

[46] IRC § 170(c).
[47] Reg. § 1.170A-1(g).

tax-exempt status, the contribution must be reduced by the amount of any long-term capital gain that would have been realized if the property had been sold at its fair market value at the time of the contribution. For example, if a sculpture is donated to a museum and is put on display for the public, that would be a related purpose. If, however, the museum had simply sold the sculpture without displaying it and used the funds for museum operations, that would be an unrelated purpose and would require this exception. A second exception occurs if the investment property is short-term property (held one year or less). In this case, the deduction is limited to the tax basis of the asset (its cost). The donation of investment/capital gain property is also subject to additional limitations depending on the type of the recipient organization (see the following section on limitations).

EXAMPLE 5-25	Kimberly donated her old computer to Helping Hands Industries. She had purchased the computer for personal use several years ago at a cost of $1,500. The computer's FMV at the date of donation was $500. The computer is a capital asset held for more than one year, so Kimberly may deduct the $500 FMV as a charitable contribution.

Generally, when ordinary income property (such as inventory and accounts receivable) is donated to charity, the deduction amount is limited to the tax basis of the property donated. The deduction does not depend on the type of recipient organization.

Percentage Limitations of Charitable Donations

There are three limitations concerning charitable contributions by individual taxpayers: 50%, 30%, and 20% limitations. The general limitation is the 50% limitation. All charitable contributions to public charities are limited to 50% of the individual taxpayer's AGI.[48] A contribution in excess of the limitation is carried forward for the next five tax years, subject to the overall 50% limitation in those years. For each category of contributions, the taxpayer must deduct carryover contributions only after deducting all allowable contributions in that same category for the current year. The deduction of amounts from previous years is done on a first-in, first-out, basis.

EXAMPLE 5-26	Doris is a wealthy widow and has $200,000 in AGI from various investments. If she makes a $150,000 cash donation to State University, her charitable deduction is limited to $100,000. The remaining $50,000 is carried forward for up to five years.

The 30% limitation applies to contributions of capital gain property. When capital gain property is contributed to a public charity, the taxpayer can take a deduction for the asset's FMV. However, the deduction is limited to 30% of the taxpayer's AGI.[49] Again, any excess is carried forward for five years.

EXAMPLE 5-27	Assume the same facts as in Example 5-26. However, instead of giving cash of $150,000, Doris contributed a vacation cottage that she has owned for many years. The cottage, which is in a marshland and could be used for research purposes, has a FMV of $150,000. The university promptly sold the cottage. In this case, Doris's deduction is limited to $60,000 ($200,000 AGI × 30% limitation). The excess $90,000 is carried forward for the next five years.

There is one exception to this rule: If the taxpayer elects to reduce the fair market value of the contributed property by the amount of long-term capital gain that would have been recognized if the property had been sold at its fair market value at the time of the contribution, the 50% limitation would apply to the contribution.[50]

---

[48] IRC § 170(b)(1)(A).

[49] IRC § 170(b)(1)(C).

[50] IRC § 170(b)(1)(C)(iii).

EXAMPLE 5-28	Assume the same facts as in Example 5-27. However, Doris elects to reduce the fair market value of the cottage by the amount of long-term capital gain she would have recognized if she had sold the cottage. Her adjusted basis in the cottage is $60,000. Her charitable contribution would therefore be $60,000 because 50% of her AGI of $200,000 would be a $100,000 limitation on charitable contributions.

The 30% limitation also applies to any contribution (cash or property) to charities that are not 50% limitation charities such as war veterans' organizations, fraternal orders, cemetery companies, and certain nonoperating private foundations.

The 20% limitation refers to the donation of capital gain property to a private foundation. The deduction for cash given to a private foundation is limited to 30% of AGI, whereas capital gain property given to the same organization is limited to 20% of AGI.[51]

One final limitation involves a charitable contribution to an educational institution that gives the taxpayer the right or benefit to preferential treatment at athletic events. The most common example is preferential seating rights at football and basketball games. If an otherwise deductible contribution to a university or college allows the taxpayer to get preferential seating, that donation is limited to 80% of the payment.[52] Any portion of the payment that is for tickets is nondeductible, and the excess is limited to 80%.

EXAMPLE 5-29	Jack, a wealthy business owner, gave the following amounts to State University: $4,500 for 30 season football tickets and $10,000 donation to the athletic foundation for preferential seating location and parking. The $4,500 is not deductible at all because the taxpayer is buying a product; the $10,000 donation is limited to $8,000 (80% of $10,000).

Required Documentation of Charitable Gifts

Recently the substantiation requirements for charitable contributions have become more stringent. The nonprofit organizations themselves bear most of the increased requirements. They are now required to provide summary receipts to donors. From the taxpayer's perspective, when a gift to a charitable organization is less than $250 in cash, the contributor is required to keep a canceled check, a receipt from the organization, or other written records to substantiate the deduction.[53] If the donation is more than $250, the taxpayer must have written acknowledgment from the recipient organization stating (1) the date and amount of the contribution, (2) whether the taxpayer received any goods or services from the charity as a result of the contribution, and (3) a description and good faith estimate of the value of any goods and services that the taxpayer received. A canceled check does not meet the substantiation requirements for donations of more than $250.

EXAMPLE 5-30	John goes to a church function organized to raise funds for a new youth group building. He pays $500 for a painting that has a $100 FMV. John's charitable contribution to the church is $400. To substantiate the deduction, he must get a receipt from the church and keep his canceled check.

Taxpayers are not required to aggregate multiple contributions they make to a charity during the year for purposes of the $250 limit. The required documentation is based on the amount of each separate contribution.

EXAMPLE 5-31	Every week, Suki donates $50 to her temple. In October 2009 she made an additional $500 contribution to the temple building fund. Suki may document each weekly contribution with a canceled check. To take the $500 contribution as a deduction, she must receive a written acknowledgment from the temple. It must state the date and amount of the contribution and the fact that Suki received no goods or services from the temple as a result of her donation.

[51] IRC § 170(b)(1)(D).
[52] IRC § 170(l)(2).
[53] Reg. § 1.170A-13(a)(1)(i)–(iii).

From Shoebox to Software

EXAMPLE 5-32   Jose and Maria Ramirez gave the following items to their church: (1) cash $1,000, (2) a painting with a FMV of $750, basis $500, and (3) three large bags of used clothing. The Ramirezes' charitable contribution would be calculated and placed on Schedule A and Form 8283 as follows:

Cash	$1,000
Painting	750
Clothes (thrift value)[54]	200
Total	$1,950

Open their tax return. Enter the cash contributions directly on line 16 of Schedule A. Form 8283 is required for noncash gifts in excess of $500. Double-click on line 17 or open a Form 8283. Enter the required information as shown on Form 8283 in Exhibit 5-6. Make sure you save your file when you have finished.

EXHIBIT 5-6

Gifts to Charity				
	16 Gifts by cash or check. If you made any gift of $250 or more, see page A-7	**16**	1,000	
If you made a gift and got a benefit for it, see page A-7.	**17** Other than by cash or check. If any gift of $250 or more, see page A-8. You **must** attach Form 8283 if over $500 . . .	**17**	950	
	18 Carryover from prior year	**18**		
	19 Add lines 16 through 18 . . .	**19**	1,950	

The substantiation requirements are the same for noncash gifts. A taxpayer who donates noncash property valued at less than $250 should obtain a receipt or letter from the charity showing the name of the charity, the date and location of the contribution, and a description of the donated property. The charity is not required to value the donated property, but the taxpayer should keep a record of the property's FMV at the date of the donation and how that FMV was determined.

However, if noncash gifts are worth more than $500, the taxpayer must file Form 8283 on which he or she must list the organization's name, a description of the property, the date acquired, the acquisition method of the property, the cost or basis, and the FMV. If the value of the donated property is more than $5,000, an appraisal is required within 60 days prior to the date of contribution.

CONCEPT CHECK 5-4—LO 4

1. Depending on the type and amount of a charitable donation, it can be claimed either as a *for AGI* deduction or as an itemized deduction on Schedule A. True or false?
2. The overall limitation on the deductibility of charitable contributions is 30% of AGI. True or false?
3. If noncash gifts are worth more than $500, the taxpayer must file Form 8283. True or false?

DEDUCTIBLE CASUALTY AND THEFT LOSSES (SCHEDULE A, LINE 20)
LO 5

The Internal Revenue Code notes three instances in which an individual taxpayer can deduct a loss of property.[55] The first two deal with business or "production of income" property. Such losse are *for* AGI deductions[56] and are treated differently than losses to personal-use property. Losses discussed in this section pertain to losses of personal-use property (such as a personal residence, personal auto, or vacation home).

---

[54] Thrift value is the value for which the clothes could be sold. In most cases, thrift value is a very subjective value.

[55] IRC § 165(c).

[56] Casualty losses of business property are discussed in Chapter 6 and Chapter 8.

EXHIBIT 5-6   *(concluded)*

Form **8283** (Rev. December 2006) Department of the Treasury Internal Revenue Service	**Noncash Charitable Contributions** ▶ **Attach to your tax return if you claimed a total deduction of over $500 for all contributed property.** ▶ **See separate instructions.**	OMB No. 1545-0908 Attachment Sequence No. **155**

Name(s) shown on your income tax return	Identifying number

Note. Figure the amount of your contribution deduction before completing this form. See your tax return instructions.

Section A. Donated Property of $5,000 or Less and Certain Publicly Traded Securities—List in this section **only** items (or groups of similar items) for which you claimed a deduction of $5,000 or less. Also, list certain publicly traded securities even if the deduction is more than $5,000 (see instructions).

Part I   **Information on Donated Property**—If you need more space, attach a statement.

1	**(a)** Name and address of the donee organization	**(b)** Description of donated property (For a donated vehicle, enter the year, make, model, condition, and mileage, and attach Form 1098-C if required.)
A		
B		
C		
D		
E		

Note. If the amount you claimed as a deduction for an item is $500 or less, you do not have to complete columns (d), (e), and (f).

	(c) Date of the contribution	**(d)** Date acquired by donor (mo., yr.)	**(e)** How acquired by donor	**(f)** Donor's cost or adjusted basis	**(g)** Fair market value (see instructions)	**(h)** Method used to determine the fair market value
A						
B						
C						
D						
E						

Part II   **Partial Interests and Restricted Use Property**—Complete lines 2a through 2e if you gave less than an entire interest in a property listed in Part I. Complete lines 3a through 3c if conditions were placed on a contribution listed in Part I; also attach the required statement (see instructions).

2a Enter the letter from Part I that identifies the property for which you gave less than an entire interest ▶_____ .
If Part II applies to more than one property, attach a separate statement.

 b Total amount claimed as a deduction for the property listed in Part I: **(1)** For this tax year ▶_____ .
(2) For any prior tax years ▶_____ .

 c Name and address of each organization to which any such contribution was made in a prior year (complete only if different from the donee organization above):

Name of charitable organization (donee)
_____

Address (number, street, and room or suite no.)
_____

City or town, state, and ZIP code
_____

 d For tangible property, enter the place where the property is located or kept ▶ _____

 e Name of any person, other than the donee organization, having actual possession of the property ▶ _____

		Yes	No
3a	Is there a restriction, either temporary or permanent, on the donee's right to use or dispose of the donated property?		
b	Did you give to anyone (other than the donee organization or another organization participating with the donee organization in cooperative fundraising) the right to the income from the donated property or to the possession of the property, including the right to vote donated securities, to acquire the property by purchase or otherwise, or to designate the person having such income, possession, or right to acquire?		
c	Is there a restriction limiting the donated property for a particular use?		

For Paperwork Reduction Act Notice, see separate instructions.   Cat. No. 62299J   Form **8283** (Rev. 12-2006)

What Is a Casualty?

Over the years, court cases and IRS administrative rulings have developed a generally accepted definition of *casualty:* an identifiable event of a sudden, unexpected, or unusual nature.[57] *Sudden* means the event is not gradual or progressive. If a loss is due to progressive deterioration, such as termite damage, it is not deductible as a casualty. A casualty is also an unusual event caused by external forces. Common household accidents, such as accidentally breaking furniture or damage caused by a pet, are not casualties. To claim a deduction, the taxpayer must own the damaged property.

EXAMPLE 5-33	Damage to walls and flooring from the progressive deterioration of a roof is a nondeductible casualty loss because the event was not sudden but gradual and progressive.[58] Likewise, when a patio porch collapses as a result of excessive dry rot, the casualty loss is disallowed.[59]

Unexpected refers to an event that is unanticipated and occurs without the intent of the taxpayer. An *unusual* event is one that is extraordinary and nonrecurring.[60]

TAX YOUR BRAIN 	Since 1995, the North Carolina coast has been hit by seven hurricanes, each of which caused substantial casualty losses. If a hurricane strikes the North Carolina coast in 2009, is the event still a casualty? **ANSWER** With a strict reading of the tax authority concerning casualty losses, the hurricane probably would not qualify as a casualty. The hurricane is not unexpected or unusual in recent history. However, the IRS is very unlikely to challenge a natural disaster if for no other reason than the negative public opinion that would result. A hurricane could provide a sudden loss even if it were not unusual. The Tax Court has held that even if an event is foreseeable, it does not preclude a casualty loss deduction.[61]

The magnitude of the casualty is not the primary factor in deciding whether the event is a casualty. Thus a minor event could qualify as a casualty. A formula that can be used to determine the amount of deductible casualty loss is shown in Table 5-2.

TABLE 5-2
Personal Casualty Expense Deduction Formula

Calculation of Deductible Casualty Loss

Determine:

FMV immediately before the casualty
minus (FMV immediately after the casualty)
- -
Amount A: Decline in FMV

Amount B: Adjusted basis of the property

Select the smaller of Amount A or Amount B
minus (Insurance recovery)
- -
Allowable loss
minus ($500 per event)
- -
Eligible loss
minus (10% of Adjusted Gross Income)
- -
Deductible casualty loss

[57] Rev. Rul. 76-134,1976-1 CB 54.
[58] *Whiting, Laurin* (1975) 34 TCM 241.
[59] *Chipman* (1981) 41 TCM 1318.
[60] Rev. Rul. 72-592, 1972-2 CB 101
[61] *Heyn, Harry* (1966) 46 TC 302, acq 1967-2 CB 2.

The Amount of a Casualty Loss and the Year Deductible

The taxpayer may deduct uninsured loss or out-of-pocket loss subject to certain limits detailed here. The taxpayer's uninsured loss is calculated as follows:

Uninsured loss = Loss due to casualty or theft − Insurance recovery

In general, the casualty loss is the lower of the following:

1. The FMV immediately before the casualty reduced by the FMV immediately after the casualty.
2. The amount of the adjusted basis for determining the loss from the sale or other disposition of the property involved.[62]

The taxpayer is required to provide proof of the adjusted basis and FMV. *Adjusted basis* is the original cost or basis of the asset minus any depreciation or amortization and plus the cost of any capital improvements. The FMV is normally determined by an appraised value before and after the casualty event. Repair costs can also play an important role in determining the casualty loss. If the property is only partially destroyed, the casualty loss is its decline in value.

EXAMPLE 5-34	Joel and Susan purchased their personal residence in 1981 for $75,000. In March 2009, when the appraised value of the house was $180,000, it and most of their belongings in it were destroyed by fire. The amount of the casualty for the house is $75,000 (the lower of the adjusted basis of $75,000 or the decrease in FMV of $180,000). Susan and Joel received no insurance reimbursement for the damage. Losses for the personal belongings would be calculated on an item-by-item basis (from an inventory list of everything in the house).

EXAMPLE 5-35	In 2006 Lee purchased an automobile (used for nonbusiness purposes) for $17,000. In April 2009 he had an accident with another automobile. Lee's auto had a FMV of $14,500 when the accident occurred. The FMV after the accident is difficult to determine. However, the cost to repair the auto to its precasualty condition was $5,000. The $5,000 would be a reasonable amount to deduct as a casualty loss. If Lee receives any insurance proceeds, he would reduce his loss accordingly.

Typically a taxpayer reports a casualty loss on the tax return in the tax year it took place. However, in three instances, casualty losses may be deducted in different tax years:

1. Theft losses.
2. Reimbursement by insurance or otherwise (such as from a negligence claim against an individual or company that caused the loss).
3. Disaster area losses.

Theft losses are deducted in the tax year in which the theft was discovered rather than the year of theft, if different.

EXAMPLE 5-36	As a hobby, John collects rare coins. He had his collection appraised by an expert in October 2008. In January 2009 when John was reviewing his collection, he noted that two extremely rare coins had been replaced with forgeries. John would deduct the loss in 2009.[63]

In all cases, taxpayers must subtract any insurance reimbursement in determining their loss. Even when the insurance reimbursement has not yet been received, if a reasonable prospect of recovery exists with respect to a claim of insurance, the casualty loss should be adjusted for

---

[62] Reg § 1.167-7(b)(1).

[63] This loss may be difficult to prove if John did not have adequate documentation noting that he owned the rare coins prior to the theft.

the anticipated recovery.[64] Should the loss be deducted and recovery occur in the subsequent tax year, the taxpayer must include the reimbursement in income in the year of reimbursement to the extent a tax benefit was gained from the casualty loss.

Individuals are required to file an insurance claim for insured personal casualty and theft losses to claim a deduction. If no insurance claim is filed, no deduction is permitted.

If the casualty loss occurred as the result of a major event (usually a natural disaster), and the president of the United States declares the area a national disaster area, the taxpayer can elect to deduct the casualty loss against the preceding year's taxable income. Congress added this provision to allow taxpayers suffering major disasters to get immediate assistance from a tax refund. The taxpayer files an amended return (Form 1040X) for the previous tax year including the casualty loss in the calculation. If the preceding year tax return had not been filed at the time of the casualty, the loss can be deducted on the original return.

Limitation on Personal Casualty Losses

The tax law places two general limitations on personal casualty deductions. First for 2009, each separate casualty is reduced by $500. It is important to note that this is $500 per *casualty,* not $500 per *item of property.*[65] For example, a taxpayer may lose his home, car, and other personal belongings in a tornado. This is one casualty and only one $500 reduction is necessary. If the events are closely related, they are considered a single casualty. If the taxpayer had a theft loss early in the year and the tornado occurred later in the year, each loss would be reduced by $500.

The second and more substantial limitation is the 10% of AGI limitation. For the taxpayer to obtain any benefit from a casualty loss, the total losses for the year after the $500 per casualty deduction must exceed 10% of AGI. Because of the 10% limitation, most taxpayers do not benefit from casualty losses unless the loss was substantial.

In late 2008 Congress passed the National Disaster Relief Act as part of the Emergency Economic Stabilization Act. The new rules under this act apply primarily to losses of personal-use property attributable to a federally declared disaster area (formerly termed presidential declared disaster area), but there are some provisions that apply to all personal casualty losses. Key provisions of this act include these:

- An expansion of the availability of the casualty loss deduction to include not only individual taxpayers who itemize, but also those who claim the standard deduction. Taxpayers would complete Form 4684 and enter the net disaster loss on line 6 of the standard deduction worksheet, line 40, in the Form 1040 instructions.
- A waiver of the requirement that the net casualty be allowed only if the casualty loss exceeds 10 percent of the taxpayer's adjusted gross income.
- The creation of a special five-year net operating loss carryback for qualified disaster losses.
- And for all taxpayers beginning in 2009, an increase in the amount by which all individual taxpayers must reduce their personal casualty losses from each casualty from $100 to $500 (the $100 floor is scheduled at this point to return for tax years after 2009).

Certain provisions of the National Disaster Relief Act do not apply to the Midwestern disaster area—specifically disasters that were declared from May 20, 2008, through July 31, 2008. These areas are covered under other legislation. For more information, refer to IRS Publication 547, Casualties, Disasters, and Thefts.

EXAMPLE 5-37	Debra is a single taxpayer with an AGI of $75,000. For her to receive any tax benefit, a casualty loss must exceed $8,000 ($500 per casualty plus 10% of AGI). Recall that the $8,000 is net of any insurance recovery.

[64] Reg. § 1.165-1(d)(2)(i).
[65] IRC § 165(h).

Shoebox to Software

EXAMPLE 5-38   Jose and Maria Ramirez (see the saved file) had the following casualties from a large storm during the tax year 2009. Recall that they had AGI of $100,962 in 2009. The area has not yet been declared a federal disaster area.

Asset	Cost or Basis	Decrease in FMV	Date Destroyed or Damaged	Insurance Proceeds
Furniture	$ 3,000	$ 3,000	04/12/2009	$ –0–
Auto	15,500	9,500	04/12/2009	–0–
Personal residence damaged by storm	225,000	55,000	04/12/2009	50,000

Casualty loss	
Residence (lower of cost or decrease in value)	$ 55,000
Insurance proceeds	(50,000)
Furniture	3,000
Auto (lower of cost or decrease in value)	9,500
Casualty before limitations	$ 17,500
$500 per event	(500)
10% AGI floor	(10,096)
Net casualty loss	$ 6,904

Jose and Maria would have a $6,904 casualty loss deduction for the year. If the area of the damage were declared a national disaster area, they could elect to take the deduction against their 2008 taxable income and waive the 10% of AGI threshold.

Open the tax return file you previously saved for the Ramirezes. Report the casualty losses on line 20 of Schedule A. The taxpayers first report the losses on Form 4684. Double-click on line 20 of Schedule A to go to Form 4684 or open Form 4684 directly. Personal casualties are reported on lines 1 through 12. Click on open supporting form and enter the data here. If you open Schedule A, you will see the net casualty loss of $7,304 on line 20.

The completed Form 4684 (Exhibit 5-7) follows.

TAX YOUR BRAIN

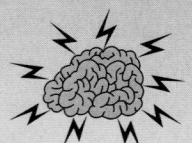

Dan suffered a $40,000 casualty loss in a nationally declared disaster in September 2009. Assuming that he had AGI of $200,000 in 2008 and $110,000 in 2009 (the disaster also affected his business), what is the best way to treat the casualty loss?

ANSWER

Dan can elect to amend his 2008 tax return and get an immediate refund against his 2008 taxes, or he can wait until April 2010 and deduct the loss on his 2009 return.

An amendment to the 2008 return is as follows:

Disaster loss	$40,000
$500 per casualty	(500)
Casualty loss deduction	$39,500

(continued)

(concluded)

If he files on his 2009 return, the deduction is as follows:

Disaster loss	$40,000
$500 per casualty	(500)
Casualty loss deduction	$39,500

Because of the waiver of the 10% AGI threshold for federally declared disaster areas, Dan receives the same amount in both scenarios. The advantage to filing an amended return for 2008 is that he will receive the funds more quickly.

The taxpayer must be able to prove both the fact of the casualty or theft and the amount of the loss. Newspaper articles, photographs, and police reports are commonly used to document the fact of a casualty or theft. When a casualty results from a sudden, unexpected, or unusual event, the amount of the loss is not always easy to determine. In many instances, an appraisal of the property is required to calculate the loss. Casualty losses are first reported on Form 4684, and the net loss is carried to the appropriate form (Schedule A for personal casualties). If the insurance or other reimbursement is more than the basis in the property damaged or destroyed, the reimbursement is a gain. The gain is generally taxable if the taxpayer does not use the reimbursement proceeds to purchase replacement property that is related in service or use. However, there are several circumstances where the gain may be postponed; and in the instance of gain realized on homes in declared disaster areas, the gain may escape taxation.

The IRS has recently issued guidance concerning the tax treatment of investment scam losses, similar to the Madoff scandal, and the safe harbor options for deducting such losses.[66] In a situation where a taxpayer unknowingly invested in a brokerage activity that was in fact fraudulent, and the taxpayer experienced a loss as a result of the fraudulent activities, the loss is considered a theft loss, not a capital loss. However, the loss is not subject to the general deductibility limitations just outlined. It is entered on Form 4864 and carried to line 28 of the Schedule A as a miscellaneous itemized deduction, not subject to the 2% of AGI limitation.

**CONCEPT CHECK
5-5—LO 5**

✓

1. A casualty is an identifiable event of a _____, _____, or _____ nature.
2. Casualty losses are first reported on Form _____.
3. Generally, the tax law places _____ limitations on personal casualty deductions. First, each separate casualty is reduced by _____.
4. To obtain any benefit from non-federally declared disaster area casualty loss, the loss must be in excess of _____ of AGI.

MISCELLANEOUS ITEMIZED DEDUCTIONS (SCHEDULE A, LINE 27)
LO 6

The final category of itemized deduction is the catch-all of miscellaneous itemized deductions. Typically miscellaneous itemized deductions are subject, in aggregate, to a 2% AGI floor. In other words, the sum of all miscellaneous deductions must exceed 2% of the taxpayer's

[66] Rev, Rul. 2009-9.

EXHIBIT 5-7

Form **4684**	**Casualties and Thefts**	OMB No. 1545-0177
Department of theTreasury Internal Revenue Service	▶ See separate instructions. ▶ Attach to your tax return. ▶ Use a separate Form 4684 for each casualty or theft.	**20**09 Attachment Sequence No. **26**

Name(s) shown on tax return Jose and Maria Ramirez

Identifying number

SECTION A—Personal Use Property (Use this section to report casualties and thefts of property **not** used in a trade or business or for income-producing purposes.)

1 Description of properties (show type, location, and date acquired for each property). Use a separate line for each property lost or damaged from the same casualty or theft.

Property **A** Furniture

Property **B** Automobile

Property **C** Personal Residence

Property **D**

			Properties		
		A	**B**	**C**	**D**
2 Cost or other basis of each property	**2**	3,000	15,500	225,000	
3 Insurance or other reimbursement (whether or not you filed a claim) (see instructions)	**3**			50,000	
Note: If line 2 is **more** than line 3, skip line 4.					
4 Gain from casualty or theft. If line 3 is **more** than line 2, enter the difference here and skip lines 5 through 9 for that column. See instructions if line 3 includes insurance or other reimbursement you did not claim, or you received payment for your loss in a later tax year	**4**				
5 Fair market value **before** casualty or theft	**5**	3,000	15,500	225,000	
6 Fair market value **after** casualty or theft	**6**	0	6,000	170,000	
7 Subtract line 6 from line 5	**7**	3,000	9,500	55,000	
8 Enter the **smaller** of line 2 or line 7	**8**	3,000	9,500	55,000	
9 Subtract line 3 from line 8. If zero or less, enter -0-	**9**	3,000	9,500	5,000	

10 Casualty or theft loss. Add the amounts on line 9 in columns A through D	**10**	17,500
11 Enter the **smaller** of line 10 or $500	**11**	500
12 Subtract line 11 from line 10	**12**	17,000
Caution: Use only one Form 4684 for lines 13 through 24.		
13 Add the amounts on line 12 of all Forms 4684	**13**	17,000
14 Add the amounts on line 4 of all Forms 4684	**14**	0
15 ● If line 14 is **more** than line 13, enter the difference here and on Schedule D. **Do not** complete the rest of this section (see instructions). ● If line 14 is **less** than line 13, enter -0- here and go to line 16. ● If line 14 is **equal** to line 13, enter -0- here. **Do not** complete the rest of this section.	**15**	0
16 If line 14 is **less** than line 13, enter the difference	**16**	17,000
17 Add the amounts on line 12 of all Forms 4684 on which you entered a disaster loss (see instructions)	**17**	0
18 Is line 17 more than line 14? ☐ **Yes.** Enter the difference. If you are filing Schedule A (Form 1040), go to line 19. Otherwise, enter this amount on line 6 of Schedule L (Form 1040A or 1040). Do not complete the rest of Section A. Form 1040NR filers, see instructions. ☒ **No.** Enter -0-. If you claim the standard deduction, do not complete the rest of Section A.	**18**	0
19 Subtract line 18 from line 16	**19**	17,000
20 Enter 10% of your adjusted gross income from Form 1040, line 38, or Form 1040NR, line 36. Estates and trusts, see instructions	**20**	10,096
21 Subtract line 20 from line 19. If zero or less, enter -0-	**21**	6,904
22 Add lines 18 and 21. Also enter the result on Schedule A (Form 1040), line 20, or Form 1040NR, Schedule A, line 8. Estates and trusts, enter the result on the "Other deductions" line of your tax return	**22**	6,904

For Paperwork Reduction Act Notice, see page 5 of the instructions.   Cat. No. 12997O   Form **4684** (2009)

AGI before any benefit is received. The most common miscellaneous deductions are for the following:

1. Unreimbursed employee business expenses.
2. Union or professional dues and subscriptions.
3. Expenses related to investment income or property.
4. Investment counsel and advisory fees.
5. Tax return preparation fees.
6. Safe deposit box fees.
7. Gambling losses to the extent of gambling income.[67]

Unreimbursed employee business expenses are usually the largest and are most likely to cause the total miscellaneous deduction to exceed the 2% floor. These expenses are costs incurred by the taxpayer as a part of his or her employment (as opposed to being self-employed) but not reimbursed. If any travel, transportation, meals, or entertainment expenses were incurred or some expenses were reimbursed, the taxpayer must complete Form 2106. Examples of unreimbursed employee business expenses include these:

1. Safety equipment needed on the taxpayer's job.
2. Uniforms required for employment that the taxpayer would not usually wear away from work.
3. Protective clothing such as hard hats, safety shoes or boots, and glasses.
4. Business dues and subscriptions.
5. Certain business use of the taxpayer's home.
6. Certain education expenses that do not qualify the taxpayer for a new job.[68]
7. Vehicle mileage not reimbursed by the employer.

EXAMPLE 5-39 Jane's AGI is $43,000. During the year, she had unreimbursed business expenses for supplies, a computer, and travel of $5,200. Jane's deduction would be limited to $4,340 ($5,200 − $860 [$43,000 × 0.02]).

If an employee is required as a condition of employment to wear special clothing that is not suitable for general street wear, the cost of the clothing and its upkeep (such as laundry) is generally a tax-deductible expense. The determination of whether clothing is suitable for general street wear is based on "general objective standards," not personal taste. Examples include uniforms worn by safety, transportation, and health care personnel and protective clothing such as hard hats, safety goggles, and steel-tipped shoes.

A taxpayer who is looking for a new job in the same business or profession in which he or she is already employed may deduct the costs of the job search, such as the cost of preparing and printing résumés, postage, employment agency fees, and long-distance telephone calls to prospective employers. The costs of looking for a new job are deductible whether or not the taxpayer accepts a new position. However, if the taxpayer is looking for a first job or for a job in a new field, his or her job-hunting expenses are generally nondeductible. This is so because to deduct the expense, it must be related to the current occupation. If a taxpayer has no occupation or is changing occupations, the expense is not related to current employment.

[67] Gambling losses are one miscellaneous deduction that is not subject to the 2% floor; instead they are limited to gambling income and are reported on line 28 of Schedule A.
[68] The deduction for education expenses is explained in detail in Chapter 6 (relating to a trade or business).

Many individuals purchase portfolio investments, such as stocks, bonds, and mutual funds. Expenses to manage, conserve, or maintain these income-producing investments are deductible on Schedule A. Examples include safety deposit box rental to store stock and bond certificates, investment advisory fees, subscriptions to investment publications, software to track investment portfolios, and depreciation on a home computer used to monitor personal investments. One element of these deductions that taxpayers often miss is investment advice. If a taxpayer has a large portfolio of stock or investments, the advisory cost can be substantial. Investment fees, however, are not deductible if they are added to the cost basis of the investment. Examples include brokerage commissions or items paid with tax-deferred funds.[69]

EXAMPLE 5-40	Jason has a $1 million investment portfolio and pays a flat fee of 2% of the FMV of the portfolio. The 2% fee would be deductible if Jason paid it directly. If the portfolio were a tax-deferred account or if the fee were paid on a commission basis that increased the basis of the investment, the investment fee would not be deductible.

If any of these expenses were related to a trade or business or rental property, the taxpayer would receive a higher tax benefit by taking the deduction as a *for* AGI deduction on Schedule C or Schedule E (discussed in Chapters 6 and 8, respectively).

CONCEPT CHECK 5-6—LO 6	1. The sum of all miscellaneous deductions must exceed 3.5% of the taxpayer's AGI before receiving any benefit. True or false?
	2. If a taxpayer as part of his or her employment incurs any travel, transportation, meals, and entertainment expenses or the employer reimburses him or her for some of the expenses, the taxpayer must complete Form 2106. True or false?
	3. An example of deductible unreimbursed employee business expenses would include the blue suit needed by an accountant for his job. True or false?

LIMITATION OF TOTAL ITEMIZED DEDUCTIONS (SCHEDULE A, LINE 29)
LO 7

Individuals who are high-income taxpayers forfeit part of their itemized deductions. This effectively increases the tax rate of high-income individuals by denying deductions rather than increasing rates. For 2009 a high-income taxpayer has an AGI exceeding $166,800 ($83,400 for married filing separately). The AGI threshold amounts are indexed annually for inflation.

In general, high-income taxpayers' itemized deductions are reduced by the lesser of the following:

1. 3% of the excess of AGI over the applicable amount.
2. 80% of the itemized deductions otherwise allowable for the tax year.[70]

The 3%/80% rule does not apply to medical expenses, investment interest, casualty or theft losses, or gambling losses.

---

[69] For example, a 1% fee (on the outstanding value) paid to a custodian of an IRA that is paid from the IRA funds would not qualify as a miscellaneous itemized deduction.
[70] IRC § 68(a).

These items would be computed and subtracted from the total deductions in computing the limitation. The high-income limitation on itemized deductions is being phased out from 2006 through 2009. For the tax years 2008 and 2009, the limit will be reduced by two-thirds. So for 2009, after the regular limitation is determined, the taxpayer must take this amount and multiply it by one-third. This effectively reduces the 3% limitation to 1%. The IRS instructions for Schedule A include a worksheet for determining the limitation, if any, on itemized deductions.

EXAMPLE 5-41

Rob, who is married and files jointly, has AGI of $248,000 and a total of $43,000 of itemized deductions: state taxes, $13,000; property taxes, $2,500; mortgage interest, $15,500; and charitable contributions, $12,000. Rob calculates his allowable itemized deductions as follows:

AGI	$248,000
Applicable amount	166,800
	$ 81,200
	×0.03
a. 3% potential limit	$ 2,436
b. 80% of total ($43,000 × 0.80)	$ 34,400
1/3 of the lesser of *a* or *b*	$ 812

Rob's itemized deductions would be reduced to $42,188 ($43,000 − $812). If his AGI had been $2,400,000, his itemized deductions would be reduced by $11,467 to $31,533 ($43,000 − $11,467).

EXAMPLE 5-42

Assume the same facts as in Example 5-41 except that Rob had the following itemized deductions: medical expenses after 7.5% AGI limit of $13,000, investment interest of $15,500, and a casualty loss after 10% AGI limit of $12,000 (plus the property taxes of $2,500).

AGI	$248,000
Applicable amount	166,800
	$ 81,200
	×0.03
a. 3% potential limit	$ 2,436
b. 80% of total ($2,500 × 0.80)	$ 2,000
1/3 of the lesser of *a* or *b*	$ 667

Medical, investment interest, and casualty losses are not subject to the limit. Therefore, Rob's itemized deductions would be $42,333 ($43,000 − $667 reduction).

CONCEPT CHECK
5-7—LO 7

1. For 2009 in regard to the limitations of itemized deductions, taxpayers filing jointly are high-income taxpayers if their AGI exceeds _____.
2. The threshold amount for reducing the deduction of itemized deductions is _____ for inflation.

From Shoebox to Software   Comprehensive Example

In this example, you will create a new return for a high-income taxpayer. Open the tax software and create a new return.

Alan (SSN 444-44-444) and Cherie (SSN 555-55-5555) Masters are married filing a joint return and reside at 1483 Tax Street, Highland, MO 12345. They have two children under the age of 17:

Scotty (SSN 666-77-7777), born 2000.

Brittney (SSN 666-88-8888), born 2002.

The couple had the following 2009 income items that you need to enter in the tax software:

Alan's W-2	
Wages	$161,398
Federal withholding	33,437
Social security wages	106,800
Social security withholding	6,622
Medicare withholding	2,340
State withholding	6,456
Cherie's W-2	
Wages	$100,000
Federal withholding	23,394
Social security wages	100,000
Social security withholding	6,200
Medicare withholding	1,450
State withholding	4,123
Taxable amount on 1099-G from Missouri state tax refund ($12,000 deducted on 2008 return)	897
1099-INT, New Bank	2,300
1099-DIV, Shake Co, Inc. (qualified)	3,100

They also had the following itemized deductions:

Medical expenses	$6,400
Personal property taxes	2,000
Real estate taxes	4,532
Mortgage interest from line 1 of Form 1098	16,300
Charitable contributions (cash)	9,300
Unreimbursed employee business expenses (travel)	6,000
Tax preparation fee	800
Safety deposit box	75

See Exhibit 5-8, the completed Schedule A for Alan and Cherie.

Notice the following in the tax software:

1. The medical expenses are entered directly on line 1. In Alan and Cherie's case, they get no benefit from their medical expenditures due to the 7.5% AGI floor.

2. Note that the state income tax paid flows through to line 5 when the amounts are entered on the W-2 input form.

3. The real estate taxes and personal property taxes are entered directly on lines 6 and 7, respectively.

4. The mortgage interest is entered through the documents received section. To enter it, click on Form 1098 and enter $16,300 on line 1. The interest transfers to line 10 of Schedule A.

5. The charitable contributions are entered directly on line 16 of Schedule A.

6. The miscellaneous deductions are also limited. The 2% AGI floor calculations are shown on Schedule A itself. Recall that a Form 2106 must be filed for employee business expenses if any portion of the expenses is reimbursed or if job-related vehicle, travel, transportation, meals, or entertainment expenses are involved. Because travel was involved in Alan and Cherie's case, Form 2106 is required to be filed (Form 2106 is not shown). To access Form 2106 through the tax software, double-click line 21 on Schedule A. Enter the unreimbursed business expenses on the appropriate lines of Form 2106, and the amount flows through to Schedule A. In this case, $6,000 is entered on line 3 of Form 2106.

The final limitation involves the phaseout of itemized deductions for high-income taxpayers. The 2009 tax year phaseout starts at $166,800. The itemized deductions are reduced by the lower of 3% of the excess of AGI over the applicable amount or 80% of the otherwise allowable deductions, multiplied by one-third. Note that the tax software does this calculation automatically. The reduction is calculated as follows:

AGI	$267,695
Applicable amount for 2009	166,800
Excess	$100,895
	×0.03
a. 3% limitations	$ 3,027
b. Total $44,232 × 0.80	$ 35,386
1/3 of the lesser of a or b	$ 1,009

Because the reduction is the lower of the two numbers, multiplied by one-third, the total itemized deductions are reduced by $1,009 to a total of $43,223 (total deductions of $44,232 − $1,009). Note that on the bottom of Schedule A, a box is checked indicating that the total deductions were limited.

Make sure you save the return for the Masters.

EXHIBIT 5-8

SCHEDULE A (Form 1040) Department of the Treasury Internal Revenue Service (99)	**Itemized Deductions** ▶ **Attach to Form 1040.**　　▶ **See Instructions for Schedule A (Form 1040).**	OMB No. 1545-0074 **20**09 Attachment Sequence No. **07**

Name(s) shown on Form 1040	Your social security number
Alan and Cherie Masters	444-44-4444

Draft as of 08/11/2009

Medical and Dental Expenses					
	Caution. Do not include expenses reimbursed or paid by others.				
	1 Medical and dental expenses (see page A-1)	**1**	6,400		
	2 Enter amount from Form 1040, line 38	**2**	267,695		
	3 Multiply line 2 by 7.5% (.075)	**3**	20,077		
	4 Subtract line 3 from line 1. If line 3 is more than line 1, enter -0-			**4**	0

Taxes You Paid (See page A-2.)					
	5 State and local **(check only one box):**				
	a ☒ Income taxes, **or**	**5**	10,579		
	b ☐ General sales taxes				
	6 Real estate taxes (see page A-5)	**6**	4,532		
	7 New motor vehicle taxes from line 11 of the worksheet on back. Skip this line if you checked box 5b	**7**			
	8 Other taxes. List type and amount ▶ personal property taxes	**8**	2,000		
	9 Add lines 5 through 8			**9**	17,111

Interest You Paid (See page A-5.) **Note.** Personal interest is not deductible.					
	10 Home mortgage interest and points reported to you on Form 1098	**10**	16,300		
	11 Home mortgage interest not reported to you on Form 1098. If paid to the person from whom you bought the home, see page A-6 and show that person's name, identifying no., and address ▶	**11**			
	12 Points not reported to you on Form 1098. See page A-6 for special rules	**12**			
	13 Qualified mortgage insurance premiums (see page A-6) .	**13**			
	14 Investment interest. Attach Form 4952 if required. (See page A-6.)	**14**			
	15 Add lines 10 through 14			**15**	16,300

Gifts to Charity If you made a gift and got a benefit for it, see page A-7.					
	16 Gifts by cash or check. If you made any gift of $250 or more, see page A-7 . . .	**16**	9,300		
	17 Other than by cash or check. If any gift of $250 or more, see page A-8. You **must** attach Form 8283 if over $500 . . .	**17**			
	18 Carryover from prior year	**18**			
	19 Add lines 16 through 18			**19**	9,300

Casualty and Theft Losses					
	20 Casualty or theft loss(es). Attach Form 4684. (See page A-8.).			**20**	

Job Expenses and Certain Miscellaneous Deductions (See page A-9.)					
	21 Unreimbursed employee expenses—job travel, union dues, job education, etc. Attach Form 2106 or 2106-EZ if required. (See page A-9.) ▶	**21**	6,000		
	22 Tax preparation fees	**22**	800		
	23 Other expenses—investment, safe deposit box, etc. List type and amount ▶ safe deposit box	**23**	75		
	24 Add lines 21 through 23	**24**	6,875		
	25 Enter amount from Form 1040, line 38 **25** 267,695				
	26 Multiply line 25 by 2% (.02)	**26**	5,354		
	27 Subtract line 26 from line 24. If line 26 is more than line 24, enter -0-			**27**	1,521

Other Miscellaneous Deductions					
	28 Other—from list on page A-10. List type and amount ▶			**28**	

Total Itemized Deductions					
	29 Is Form 1040, line 38, over $166,800 (over $83,400 if married filing separately)?				
	☐ **No.** Your deduction is not limited. Add the amounts in the far right column for lines 4 through 28. Also, enter this amount on Form 1040, line 40a.	} ▶	**29**	43,223	
	☒ **Yes.** Your deduction may be limited. See page A-10 for the amount to enter.				
	30 If you elect to itemize deductions even though they are less than your standard deduction, check here . . . . ▶ ☐				

For Paperwork Reduction Act Notice, see Form 1040 instructions.   Cat. No. 17145C   Schedule A (Form 1040) 2009

Summary

LO 1: Describe the deductibility and reporting of medical expenses.

- Itemized, or below-the-line, deductions are taken in lieu of the standard deduction. They are reported on Schedule A.
- Medical expenses are deductible to the extent that they exceed 7.5% of AGI.
- Taxpayers may deduct just about all medical expenses that are doctor prescribed. Expenses related to the maintenance of general health are usually not deductible.
- Medical capital expenditures are deductible only to the extent that the expenditures exceed the increase in FMV of the property.
- Premiums for long-term care insurance are deductible, but the extent to which they are depends on the taxpayer's age.

LO 2: Be able to explain the state and local tax deductions.

- The four major categories of deductible taxes on individual returns are personal property taxes, local real estate taxes, other state and local taxes, and foreign taxes.
- For a property tax to be deductible, it must be based on the value of the property.
- An individual taxpayer can deduct the amount of state income taxes actually paid or has the option of deducting state and local sales taxes paid. For 2009 the taxpayer may deduct the sales or excise tax imposed on a new vehicle purchase, while still taking the option of deducting state and local income taxes.
- Taxpayers have the option of taking a credit for foreign taxes or deducting the taxes as an itemized deduction on Schedule A.

LO 3: Apply the tax rules associated with the interest deduction.

- Interest paid on an acquisition loan or a home equity loan secured by a qualified residence is deductible up to certain limits.
- For acquisition indebtedness, the interest is deductible only on principal amounts up to $1,000,000.
- For home equity indebtedness, the interest is deductible only on principal amounts up to $100,000.
- Points are amounts paid by borrowers to obtain a mortgage. Typically taxpayers deduct points ratably over the term of the loan; however, there are some exceptions.

LO 4: Explain the deductibility and reporting of charitable contributions.

- All charitable contributions to public charities are limited to an overall 50% of the individual taxpayer's AGI.
- Depending on the nature of the item contributed, there are three deduction limitations for charitable contributions by individual taxpayers: 50%, 30%, and 20%.
- The substantiation requirements for charitable contributions have become more stringent, and the taxpayer is subject to more stringent reporting requirements.
- Contributions above the limitation amounts can be carried forward five years.

LO 5: Discuss the casualty loss deduction.

- *Casualty* is defined as an identifiable event of a sudden, unexpected, or unusual nature. *Sudden* means the event is not gradual or progressive.

- The taxpayer's uninsured loss is calculated as Uninsured loss = Loss due to casualty or theft − Insurance recovery.
- Typically a taxpayer reports a casualty on the tax return in the tax year the casualty took place; however, there are exceptions.
- The deductible amount is generally limited. First, each separate casualty is reduced by $500. Second, the loss must be in excess of 10% of AGI.
- For those personal casualty losses occurring in federally declared disaster areas, the 10% of AGI threshold is waived.

LO 6: Know how to report miscellaneous expenditures.

- The sum of all miscellaneous deductions must exceed 2% of the taxpayer's AGI before the taxpayer receives any benefit.
- Unreimbursed employee business expenses are usually the largest and are most likely to cause the total miscellaneous deduction to exceed the 2% floor.
- One deduction often missed by taxpayers is investment advice. If a taxpayer has a large portfolio of stock or investments, the advisory cost can be substantial.

LO 7: Apply the tax rules for limitations on total itemized deductions for high-income taxpayers.

- High-income taxpayers' total itemized deductions are limited.
- For 2009 a high-income taxpayer is a person whose AGI exceeds $166,800 ($83,400 for married filing separately).
- A high-income taxpayer's itemized deductions are reduced by the lower of
  - 3% of the excess of AGI over the applicable amount or
  - 80% of the itemized deductions otherwise allowable for the tax year
  which is then multiplied by one-third for the reduction.

Discussion Questions

1. (Introduction) What is the difference between deductions *from* AGI and deductions *for* AGI?

_____

_____

_____

2. (Introduction) What are the six types of personal expenses that can be classified as itemized deductions on Schedule A, Form 1040?

_____

_____

_____

LO 1   3. Describe the concept of a 7.5% floor for medical deductions.

_____

_____

_____

LO 1   4. Can an individual take a medical deduction for a capital improvement to his or her personal residence? If so, how is it calculated?

_____

_____

_____

LO 1   5. What are the general requirements for a medical expense to be considered deductible?

_____

_____

_____

LO 1   6. When are travel costs deductible as medical costs? How are medical travel costs calculated?

_____

_____

_____

LO 1   7. What is the proper tax treatment for prescription drugs obtained outside the United States, such as from Canada?

_____

_____

_____

LO 1   8. Can a taxpayer take a deduction for premiums paid for health insurance? How do reimbursements from health insurance policies affect the amount of the medical deduction? What happens if an insurance reimbursement for medical expenses is received in a subsequent tax year?

_____

_____

_____

LO 2   9. What are the four major categories of deductible taxes on individual returns?

_____

_____

_____

LO 2   10. For a tax to be deductible as an itemized deduction, what three tests are required?

_____

_____

_____

LO 2   11. If state or local income taxes are deducted on the current year's tax return, what is required if the taxpayer receives a refund in the next year?

_____

_____

_____

LO 2   12. For 2009, how is the amount of the sales tax deduction determined?

_____

_____

_____

LO 2   13. For 2009, what are the taxpayer's options in regard to sales or excise tax on a new vehicle purchase?

_____

_____

_____

LO 2   14. What options does a taxpayer who paid foreign taxes have when considering his or her tax treatment? Which option is usually more tax beneficial?

_____

_____

_____

LO 3 15. What is qualified residence interest? Are there any limits to the deductibility of acquisition loan interest?

_____
_____
_____

LO 3 16. What is a home equity loan? Is the interest tax-deductible? Are there any limits to the deductibility of home equity loan interest?

_____
_____
_____

LO 3 17. What is investment interest? What are the limits to the deductibility of investment interest?

_____
_____
_____

LO 4 18. Donations to what types of organizations are tax-deductible?

_____
_____
_____

LO 4 19. Distinguish between the tax treatment for donations to charitable organizations of cash, ordinary income property, and capital gain property.

_____
_____
_____

LO 4 20. What happens to a charitable contribution that is in excess of the AGI limits?

_____
_____
_____

LO 5 21. Define *personal casualty loss.* Include in your discussion the concepts of sudden, unexpected, and unusual.

_____
_____
_____

LO 5 22. How is a personal casualty loss calculated? Include in your discussion how the determination of the loss is made and limits or floors placed on personal casualties, and any exceptions to those limits.

_____
_____
_____

LO 6 23. Give three examples of miscellaneous itemized deductions. Why are miscellaneous itemized deductions often limited?

_____
_____
_____

LO 6 24. What is usually the largest miscellaneous deduction for individual taxpayers? Are any special reporting issues associated with it?

_____

_____

_____

LO 7 25. Explain the 3%/80% and one-third limitations for high-income taxpayers.

_____

_____

_____

Multiple-Choice Questions

26. (Introduction) Itemized deductions are taken when
    a. The taxpayer wants to.
    b. They are less than the standard deduction.
    c. They are greater than the standard deduction.
    d. The standard deducton is limited by high AGI.

27. (Introduction) The majority of itemized deductions are
    a. Business expenses.
    b. Tax credits.
    c. Personal living expenses.
    d. None of the above.

LO 1 28. Generally, a taxpayer may deduct the cost of medical expenses for which of the following?
    a. Marriage counseling.
    b. Health club dues.
    c. Doctor-prescribed birth control pills.
    d. Trips for general health improvement.

LO 1 29. The threshold amount for the deductibility of allowable medical expenses is
    a. 2.5% of AGI.
    b. 7.5% of AGI.
    c. 10% of taxable income.
    d. 15% of taxable income.

LO 1 30. During 2009 Sheniqua incurred and paid the following expenses:

Prescription drugs	$ 470
Vitamins and over-the-counter cold remedies	130
Doctors and dentist visits	700
Health club fee	250
Cosmetic surgery	2,400

What is the total amount of medical expenses (before considering the limitation based on AGI) that would enter into the calculation of itemized deductions for Sheniqua's 2009 income tax return?
    a. $1,170.
    b. $1,300.
    c. $1,550.
    d. $3,950.

LO 1   31. Prescription drugs obtained from sources outside the United States, such as Canada, are

    a. Always deductible no matter how they were obtained.

    b. Deductible only for citizens of Canada living in the United States.

    c. Deductible if prescribed by a physician and approved by the FDA for legal importation.

    d. Never deductible.

LO 1   32. For 2009 Miguel, who is single and 45 years of age, had AGI of $40,000. During the year, he incurred and paid the following medical costs:

Doctor and dentist fess	$2,350
Prescription medicines	325
Medical care insurance premiums	380
Long-term care insurance premiums	600
Hearing aid	150

What amount can Miguel take as a medical expense deduction (after the AGI limitation) for his 2009 tax return?

    a. $3,805.

    b. $3,785.

    c. $805.

    d. $785.

LO 2   33. For 2009 the amount of the sales tax deduction is calculated by

    a. Determining the actual sales tax paid during the year.

    b. Adding the calculated sales tax to the assessed state income tax.

    c. Using the sales tax tables provided by the IRS in Publication 600.

    d. Either (*a*) or (*c*).

LO 2   34. Daryl, who has significant itemized deductions, purchased a new vehicle in 2009 for $27,000 with a state sales tax of 5%. Daryl also paid state income taxes of $4,100, which exceeds his allowable deduction for other incurred state sales taxes. Daryl's best option to maximize his tax savings would be to

    a. Deduct his total amount of allowable state sales tax deduction on Schedule A.

    b. Simply take the standard deduction with the additional amount for the new car purchase sales tax.

    c. Take the deduction for the state income taxes paid, as well as the sales tax paid on the new car purchase, on Schedule A.

    d. Take only the deduction for state income taxes paid on the Schedule A.

LO 2   35. During 2009 Yvonne paid the following taxes related to her home:

Property taxes on residence (paid from escrow account)	$1,800
State personal property tax on her automobile (based on value)	600
Property taxes on land held for long-term appreciation	300

What amount can Yvonne deduct as property taxes in calculating itemized deductions for 2009?

    a. $2,100.

    b. $2,700.

    c. $3,100.

    d. $3,700.

LO 3 36. What is the maximum amount of personal residence acquisition debt on which interest is fully deductible?

    a. $1,000,000.

    b. $500,000.

    c. $250,000.

    d. $0.

LO 3 37. For 2009 the deduction by a taxpayer for investment interest is

    a. Not limited.

    b. Limited to the taxpayer's net investment income for 2009.

    c. Limited to the investment interest paid in 2009.

    d. Limited to the taxpayer's gross investment income for 2009.

LO 3 38. For 2009 Elizabeth, a single mother, reported the following amounts relating to her investments:

Investment income from interest	$7,000
Interest expense on a loan to purchase stocks	2,000
Interest expense on funds borrowed in 2008 to purchase land for investment	6,000

What is the maximum amount that Elizabeth can deduct in 2009 as investment interest expense?

    a. $1,000.

    b. $2,000.

    c. $6,000.

    d. $7,000.

LO 3 39. Referring to the previous question, what is the treatment for the interest expense that Elizabeth could not deduct in 2009?

    a. It is lost.

    b. It cannot be used except as a carryback to previous years.

    c. It can be carried forward and deducted in succeeding years.

    d. None of the above.

LO 4 40. Which of the following organizations qualifies for deductible charitable contributions?

    a. A nonprofit educational institution.

    b. The Salvation Army.

    c. Churches.

    d. All of the above.

LO 4 41. Which of the following statements is *not* true regarding documentation requirements for charitable contributions?

    a. If the total deduction for all noncash contributions for the year is more than $500, Section A of Form 8283, Noncash Charitable Contributions, must be completed.

    b. A noncash contribution of less than $250 must be supported by a receipt or other written acknowledgment from the charitable organization.

    c. A contribution charged to a credit card is a noncash contribution for purposes of documentation requirements.

    d. A deduction of more than $5,000 for one property item generally requires that a written appraisal be obtained and attached to the return.

LO 5 42. In 2009 the president declared a federal disaster due to brush fires in the Southwest. Lisa lives in that area and lost her home in the fires. What choice does she have regarding when she can claim the loss on her tax return?

    a. It may be claimed in 2008 or 2009.

    b. It must be claimed in 2008 if the loss is greater than the modified adjusted gross income.

    c. It may be claimed in 2010 if an election is filed with the 2009 return.

    d. It must be claimed in 2008 if the return has not been filed by the date of the loss.

LO 5 43. In 2009 the Bells' vacation cottage was severely damaged by an earthquake. The area has been declared a federal disaster area. They had an AGI of $110,000 in 2009, and following is information related to the cottage:

Cost basis	$ 95,000
FMV before casualty	135,000
FMV after casualty	25,000

    The Bells had insurance and received an $80,000 insurance settlement. What is the amount of allowable casualty loss deduction for the Bells in 2009?

    a. $3,500.

    b. $14,500.

    c. $25,500.

    d. $30,000.

LO 6 44. Which expense, incurred and paid in 2009, can be claimed as an itemized deduction subject to the 2% of AGI floor?

    a. Self-employed health insurance.

    b. Unreimbursed moving expenses.

    c. Employee's unreimbursed business car expense.

    d. Self-employment taxes.

LO 6 45. Raquel, who works in medical sales, drives her own vehicle to various locations for client sales meetings. Her employer reimburses her $400 each month for various business expenses and does not expect Raquel to provide proof of her expenses. Her employer included this $4,800 reimbursement in Raquel's 2009 W-2 as part of her wages. In 2009 Raquel incurred $3,000 in transportation expense, $1,000 in parking and tolls expense, $1,800 in car repair expense, and $600 for expenses while attending a professional association convention. Assume that Raquel uses the vehicle for business purposes only and that she maintains adequate documentation to support all of these expenditures. What amount is Raquel entitled to deduct on her Schedule A for miscellaneous itemized deductions?

    a. $6,400 of expenses subject to the 2% of AGI limitation.

    b. $4,800 because her employer follows a nonaccountable plan.

    c. $1,600, the difference between her expenditures and her reimbursement.

    d. $0 because her employer follows a nonaccountable plan.

LO 7 46. Individuals who are high-income forfeit part of their itemized deductions. This effectively

    a. Reduces their overall tax rate.

    b. Does not affect their overall tax rate.

    c. Increases their overall tax rate.

    d. None of the above.

LO 7   47. The high-income limitation on itemized deductions is being phased out from 2006 through 2009. For 2009, after the regular limitation is determined, the taxpayer must multiply this amount by

  a. 3/4.

  b. 2/3.

  c. 1/2.

  d. 1/3.

Problems **LO 1**   48. Mickey is a 12-year-old dialysis patient. Three times a week he and his mother Sue drive 20 miles one way to Mickey's dialysis clinic. On the way home they go 10 miles out of their way to stop at Mickey's favorite restaurant. Their total round trip is 50 miles per day. How many of those miles, if any, can Sue use to calculate an itemized deduction for transportation? Use the mileage rate in effect for 2009. Explain your answer.

_____

_____

_____

LO 1   49. Tom had AGI of $32,000 in 2009. During the year, he paid the following medical expenses:

Drugs (prescribed by physicians)	$ 200
Marijuana (prescribed by physicians)	1,400
Health insurance premiums—after taxes	850
Doctors' fees	1,250
Eyeglasses	375
Over-the-counter drugs	200

Tom received $500 in 2009 for a portion of the doctors' fees from his insurance. What is Tom's medical expense deduction?

_____

_____

_____

LO 1   50. Joe and Flo are married and have a combined AGI of $45,000 in year 2009. Due to certain medical problems, Joe has been prescribed Viagra® by a physician. For year 2009, Joe spent a total of $3,100 on the medication and $750 on doctor's bills. Can Joe deduct the medical costs as an itemized deduction? Explain your answer.

_____

_____

_____

LO 2   51. Leslie and Jason paid the following expenses during 2009:

Interest on a car loan	$ 100
Interest on lending institution loan (used to purchase municipal bonds)	3,000
Interest on home mortgage	2,100

What is the maximum amount that they can use in calculating itemized deductions for 2009?

_____

_____

_____

LO 2   52. On April 1, 2009, Paul sold a house to Amy. The property tax on the house, which is based on a calendar year, was due September 1, 2009. Amy paid the full amount of property tax of $2,500. Calculate both Paul's and Amy's allowable deductions for the property tax.

_____

_____

_____

LO 2   53. In 2008 Sherri, a single taxpayer, had $3,600 in state tax withheld from her paycheck. She properly deducted that amount on her 2008 tax return as an itemized deduction, that she qualified for thus reducing her tax liability. After filing her 2008 tax return, Sherri discovered that she had overpaid her state tax by $316. She received her refund in July 2009. What must Sherri do with the $316 refund? Explain your answer.

_____

_____

_____

LO 2   54. Steve purchased a personal residence from Adam. To sell the residence, Adam agreed to pay $4,500 in points related to Steve's mortgage. Discuss the tax consequences from the perspective of both Steve and Adam.

_____

_____

_____

LO 3   55. Shelby has investment interest income of $18,450 and other income of $76,000. She paid investment interest expense of $19,000. What is Shelby's deduction for investment interest expense? Explain your answer.

_____

_____

_____

LO 3   56. Tyrone and Akira incurred and paid the following amounts of interest during 2009:

Acquisition debt interest	$15,000
Credit card interest	5,000
Home equity loan interest	6,500
Investment interest expense	10,000

With 2009 investment interest income of $2,000, calculate the amount of their allowable deduction for investment interest and their total deduction for allowable interest.

_____

_____

_____

LO 4   57. Marlene purchased a ticket to a concert to raise money for the local university. The ticket cost $350, but the normal cost of a ticket to this concert is $100. How much is deductible as a charitable contribution?

_____

_____

_____

LO 4 58. Tom made charitable contributions to his church in the current year. He donated common stock valued at $33,000 (acquired as an investment in 1997 for $14,000). Tom's AGI in the current year is $75,000. What is his allowable charitable contribution deduction? How are any excess amounts treated?

_____

_____

_____

LO 4 59. Adrian contributed an antique vase she had owned for 25 years to a museum. At the time of the donation, the vase had a value of $35,000. The museum displayed this vase in the art gallery.

   a. Assume that Adrian's AGI is $80,000, and her basis in the vase is $15,000. How much may Adrian deduct?

   b. Assume that Adrian's AGI is $80,000, and her basis in the vase is $40,000. How much may Adrian deduct?

   c. How would your answer change if the museum sold the vase to an antique dealer?

_____

_____

_____

LO 5 60. In 2009 Arturo's pleasure boat that he purchased in 2007 for $40,000 was destroyed by a hurricane. His insurance policy had lapsed at the time of the storm. On what form(s) will Arturo report this loss?

_____

_____

_____

LO 5 61. Reynaldo and Sonya, a married couple, had flood damage in their home due to a faulty water heater during 2009 that ruined the furniture in their garage. The following items were completely destroyed and not salvageable:

Damaged Items	Fair Market Value Just Prior to Damage	Original Item Cost
Antique poster	$6,000	$ 5,000
Pool table	7,000	11,000
Large-screen TV	700	2,500

Their homeowner's insurance policy had a $10,000 deductible for the personal property, which was deducted from their insurance reimbursement of $12,700, resulting in a net payment of $2,800. Their AGI for 2009 was $30,000. What is the amount of casualty loss that Reynaldo and Sonya can claim on their joint return for 2009?

_____

_____

_____

LO 6 62. During the year 2009, Ricki, who is not self-employed and does not receive employer reimbursement for business expenses, drove her car 5,000 miles to visit clients, 10,000 miles to get to her office, and 500 miles to attend business-related seminars. She spent $300 for airfare to another business seminar and $200 for parking at her office.

Using the car expense rate of 55 cents per mile, what is her deductible transportation expense?

_____

_____

_____

LO 6 63. Louis is employed as an accountant for a large firm in San Diego. During 2009 he paid the following miscellaneous expenses:

Unreimbursed employee business expenses	$520
Union dues	400
Tax return preparation fee	175
Job-hunting expenses within the same profession	200

Louis plans to itemize his deductions in 2009; what amount could he claim as miscellaneous itemized deductions before applying the 3%/80% limit?

_____

_____

_____

Tax Return Problems

Use your tax software to complete the following problems. If you are manually preparing the tax returns, you will need a Form 1040 and Schedule A for each problem and a Form 8283 for the third problem.

Tax Return Problem 1

Jonathan Michaels is single, has no dependents, has $55,000 in wages, and lives at 55855 Ridge Dr. in Santa Fe, New Mexico. His social security number is 333-33-3333, and he has federal withholding of $11,000. He has gambling winnings of $500 and the following expenses:

State income taxes	$2,200
Property taxes	1,000
Medical expenses	500
Charitable cash contributions	450
Mortgage interest expense	9,500
Gambling losses	650
Job-hunting expenses within the same profession (he did not get a new position)	275

Prepare a Form 1040 and a Schedule A for Jonathan using the appropriate worksheets and forms.

Tax Return Problem 2

In 2009 John and Shannon O'Banion, who live at 3222 Pinon Drive, Mesa, Colorado, and file as married filing jointly, had wages of $85,000. John's social security number is 555-77-6666, and Shannon's is 555-66-5555. The federal withholding on John's wages was $12,750. Shannon did not work for the year due to her medical condition. In the same year, they had the following medical costs:

Shannon's prescribed diabetes medication	$3,150
John's hospital charges	2,500
Shannon's regular physician visits	700
Shannon's eye doctor	75
Shannon's diabetes blood testing supplies	65
Insurance reimbursements	1,000

In addition, they had the following other expenses:

State income taxes	$2,200
Personal property taxes	1,000
Car loan interest	500
Cash charitable contributions	450
Mortgage interest expense	4,500
Union dues for John	685

Prepare a Form 1040 and Schedule A for the O'Banions using the appropriate worksheets and forms.

Tax Return Problem 3 Keisha Sanders, a single taxpayer, lives at 9551 Oak Leaf Lane in Pine Cove, AZ. Her social security number is 666-88-7777. She reports wages of $83,400 with federal withholding of $12,510, and provides the following information for Schedule A, itemized deductions:

Interest expense

Home mortgage (qualified residence interest)	$8,100
MasterCard (used exclusively for personal expenses and purchases)	425
Car loan	600

Taxes paid

State income tax withheld	2,950
State income tax deficiency (for 2008)	350
Real estate taxes—principal residence	1,700
Personal property taxes—car	150
Registration fee—car	50

Medical expenses

Doctors' fees	500
Prescription drugs	200
Vitamins and over-the-counter drugs	250
Dental implant to correct a bite problem	1,600
Health club fee	400

**Charitable contributions
(all required documentation is maintained)**

Cash:	
Church	3,100
United Way	100
PBS annual campaign	200
Property:	
Goodwill—used clothing and household items	
Thrift shop value at date of donation	350
Adjusted tax basis at date of donation	1,300

Other

Investment publications	150
Tax return preparation fee	275
Business dues and subscriptions	350
Safe deposit box	75

Prepare a Form 1040 and Schedule A for Keisha using the appropriate worksheets and forms.

We have provided selected filled-in source documents on our Web site at www.mhhe.com/cruz2010.

Chapter Six

Self-Employed Business Income (Line 12 of Form 1040 and Schedule C)

Many taxpayers in the United States attribute a large portion of their taxable income to self-employment trade or businesses. Self-employment status automatically increases the complexity of a taxpayer's tax return. It also increases the importance of understanding applicable tax law to minimize a taxpayer's tax liability. In this chapter, we present and discuss the tax rules for recognizing income and maximizing expenses on Schedule C for self-employed businesses.

Learning Objectives

When you have completed this chapter, you should understand the following learning objectives (LO):

LO 1. Describe how income and expenses for a self-employed individual are recognized and reported.

LO 2. Explain the concept of ordinary and necessary business expenses.

LO 3. Explain the calculation of depreciation for trade or business assets.

LO 4. Describe travel and entertainment expenses and discuss their deductibility.

LO 5. Apply the rules for deducting the business portion of a residence and business bad debts.

LO 6. Explain the hobby loss rules and the limits on education expense deductibility.

LO 7. Describe the calculation of self-employment taxes.

INTRODUCTION

This chapter discusses the taxation of self-employed trade or businesses (sole proprietors). In Chapter 4, the concept of a *for* Adjusted Gross Income (AGI) deduction was presented. Chapter 4 discussed several income components of AGI in detail. However, this is the first chapter in which income items and *for* AGI deductions are aggregated to determine the effect on AGI. Simply put, the income from a sole proprietorship is netted with related ordinary and necessary business expenses to determine the increase (or decrease if a net loss results) in AGI. A sole proprietor reports trade or business income or loss on Schedule C of Form 1040. Taxpayers must use Schedule C when the trade or business is neither incorporated nor conducting business as some other entity form (such as a partnership or limited liability company). Schedule C is shown in Exhibit 6-1.

EXHIBIT 6-1

SCHEDULE C (Form 1040) Department of the Treasury Internal Revenue Service (99)	**Profit or Loss From Business** (Sole Proprietorship) ▶ **Partnerships, joint ventures, etc., generally must file Form 1065 or 1065-B.** ▶ **Attach to Form 1040, 1040NR, or 1041.** ▶ See Instructions for Schedule C (Form 1040).	OMB No. 1545-0074 **2009** Attachment Sequence No. **09**

Name of proprietor		Social security number (SSN)

A Principal business or profession, including product or service (see page C-3 of the instructions)   **B** Enter code from pages C-9, 10, & 11 ▶

C Business name. If no separate business name, leave blank.   **D** Employer ID number (EIN), if any

E Business address (including suite or room no.) ▶
City, town or post office, state, and ZIP code

F Accounting method: **(1)** ☐ Cash **(2)** ☐ Accrual **(3)** ☐ Other (specify) ▶

G Did you "materially participate" in the operation of this business during 2009? If "No," see page C-4 for limit on losses   ☐ Yes   ☐ No

H If you started or acquired this business during 2009, check here . . . . ▶ ☐

Part I   Income

1	Gross receipts or sales. **Caution.** See page C-4 and check the box if:
	  • This income was reported to you on Form W-2 and the "Statutory employee" box on that form was checked, or
	  • You are a member of a qualified joint venture reporting only rental real estate income not subject to self-employment tax. Also see page C-4 for limit on losses. ▶ ☐
		1	

2	Returns and allowances	2	
3	Subtract line 2 from line 1	3	
4	Cost of goods sold (from line 42 on page 2)	4	
5	**Gross profit.** Subtract line 4 from line 3	5	
6	Other income, including federal and state gasoline or fuel tax credit or refund (see page C-4)	6	
7	**Gross income.** Add lines 5 and 6 . . . . ▶	7	

Part II   Expenses. Enter expenses for business use of your home **only** on line 30.

8	Advertising	8		18	Office expense	18	
9	Car and truck expenses (see page C-5)	9		19	Pension and profit-sharing plans .	19	
10	Commissions and fees .	10		20	Rent or lease (see page C-6):		
11	Contract labor (see page C-5)	11		a	Vehicles, machinery, and equipment	20a	
12	Depletion	12		b	Other business property . . .	20b	
13	Depreciation and section 179 expense deduction (not included in Part III) (see page C-5)	13		21	Repairs and maintenance . . .	21	
				22	Supplies (not included in Part III) .	22	
				23	Taxes and licenses	23	
				24	Travel, meals, and entertainment:		
				a	Travel	24a	
14	Employee benefit programs (other than on line 19) . .	14		b	Deductible meals and entertainment (see page C-7) . .	24b	
15	Insurance (other than health)	15		25	Utilities	25	
16	Interest:			26	Wages (less employment credits) .	26	
a	Mortgage (paid to banks, etc.)	16a		27	Other expenses (from line 48 on page 2)	27	
b	Other	16b					
17	Legal and professional services	17					

28	**Total expenses** before expenses for business use of home. Add lines 8 through 27 . . . . ▶	28	
29	Tentative profit or (loss). Subtract line 28 from line 7	29	
30	Expenses for business use of your home. Attach **Form 8829**	30	

31	**Net profit or (loss).** Subtract line 30 from line 29.
	  • If a profit, enter on both **Form 1040, line 12,** and **Schedule SE, line 2,** or on **Form 1040NR, line 13** (if you checked the box on line 1, see page C-7). Estates and trusts, enter on **Form 1041, line 3.**
	  • If a loss, you **must** go to line 32.
		31	

32	If you have a loss, check the box that describes your investment in this activity (see page C-8).
	  • If you checked 32a, enter the loss on both **Form 1040, line 12,** and **Schedule SE, line 2,** or on **Form 1040NR, line 13** (if you checked the box on line 1, see the line 31 instructions on page C-7). Estates and trusts, enter on **Form 1041, line 3.**
	  • If you checked 32b, you **must** attach **Form 6198.** Your loss may be limited.
		32a ☐ All investment is at risk.
		32b ☐ Some investment is not at risk.

For Paperwork Reduction Act Notice, see page C-9 of the instructions.	Cat. No. 11334P	Schedule C (Form 1040) 2009

EXHIBIT 6-1 *(concluded)*

Schedule C (Form 1040) 2009   Page **2**

Part III   **Cost of Goods Sold** (see page C-8)

33 Method(s) used to value closing inventory: **a** ☐ Cost   **b** ☐ Lower of cost or market   **c** ☐ Other (attach explanation)

34 Was there any change in determining quantities, costs, or valuations between opening and closing inventory? If "Yes," attach explanation . . . . ☐ Yes   ☐ No

35 Inventory at beginning of year. If different from last year's closing inventory, attach explanation . . . **35**

36 Purchases less cost of items withdrawn for personal use **36**

37 Cost of labor. Do not include any amounts paid to yourself **37**

38 Materials and supplies **38**

39 Other costs **39**

40 Add lines 35 through 39 . . . . **40**

41 Inventory at end of year **41**

42 **Cost of goods sold.** Subtract line 41 from line 40. Enter the result here and on page 1, line 4 . . . **42**

Part IV   **Information on Your Vehicle.** Complete this part **only** if you are claiming car or truck expenses on line 9 and are not required to file Form 4562 for this business. See the instructions for line 13 on page C-5 to find out if you must file Form 4562.

43 When did you place your vehicle in service for business purposes? (month, day, year) ▶ ____/____/____

44 Of the total number of miles you drove your vehicle during 2009, enter the number of miles you used your vehicle for:

a Business _____   **b** Commuting (see instructions) _____   **c** Other _____

45 Was your vehicle available for personal use during off-duty hours? . . . . ☐ Yes   ☐ No

46 Do you (or your spouse) have another vehicle available for personal use?. . . . . ☐ Yes   ☐ No

47a Do you have evidence to support your deduction? . . . . ☐ Yes   ☐ No

  b If "Yes," is the evidence written? . . . . ☐ Yes   ☐ No

Part V   **Other Expenses.** List below business expenses not included on lines 8–26 or line 30.

_____

_____

_____

_____

_____

_____

_____

_____

48 **Total other expenses.** Enter here and on page 1, line 27 . . . . **48**

Schedule C (Form 1040) 2009

Neither the tax law nor the regulations directly define the term *trade* or *business*. However, the term is used quite frequently in various code sections, particularly when addressing the deductibility of expenses. The general consensus of the relevant tax authority (mainly Tax Court cases, IRS Publication 334, and the IRS instructions accompanying Schedule C) is that a "trade or business" is any activity that is engaged in for profit.[1] The profit motive is necessary, and the activity should be engaged in with continuity and regularity. Thus, sporadic activity or hobby activities are not considered trade or business activity.

If an activity produces a profit, there is usually no problem with the trade or business classification. However, when substantial losses result from an activity, a profit motive may be questioned. To combat losses from hobbylike activities, Congress developed hobby loss rules.[2] Once the taxpayer can establish that an activity is a trade or business, income and expenses from the activity are reported on Schedule C.[3]

Schedule C

A review of Schedule C shows that the form is fundamentally an income statement for the trade or business. The first section is primarily information related. The proprietor's name and social security number, business address, business code, and accounting method are required for each business. A separate business name must be listed if it exists. An employer identification number is required only if the business has a Keogh retirement plan or is required to file various other tax returns.[4]

A business code for each business is required in box B.[5] The taxpayer elects the accounting method used in the first year of business.[6] However, because nearly all individual taxpayers are cash method taxpayers, the cash receipts and disbursements method is the norm for sole proprietorships. If inventory is a material income-producing factor, the accrual method of accounting is required for reporting sales, purchases, and cost of goods sold. In practice, if inventory is material, most Schedule C businesses use a hybrid method of accounting. That is, they use the accrual method for sales, inventory, and cost of goods sold, but they use the cash method to report other income and expense items.

Question G in the top section of Schedule C refers to "material participation." If the taxpayer does not materially participate in the business, the income or loss is classified as *passive*. With passive activities, losses can be taken only to the extent of passive income. We discuss the concepts of material participation and passive activities in detail in Chapter 13.

INCOME FOR A SCHEDULE C TRADE OR BUSINESS
LO 1

Taxpayers report the gross receipts from the trade or business on line 1 of Schedule C. Gross receipts include direct sales to customers, work performed for other businesses as an independent contractor,[7] and amounts reported to the taxpayer on a Form W-2 as a "statutory employee."

---

[1] *Doggett v. Burnet* (1933 CA Dist Col) 65 F2d 191; *Coffey, R. v. Comm.* (1944, CA5) 141 F2d 204; *Black Dome Corp.*, (1946) 5 TCM 455.

[2] IRC § 183 and Chapter 1 of IRS Publication 535. The hobby loss rules are discussed in detail later in this chapter.

[3] If the business has expenses of $5,000 or less, the taxpayer may be able to file Schedule C-EZ.

[4] The ID number is required if the business must file an employment, excise, estate, trust, or alcohol, tobacco, and firearms tax return. If an ID number is required, the social security number of the owner should not be listed. An ID number can be acquired by filing Form SS-4 with the IRS.

[5] The business codes are located in the instructions for Form 1040, Schedule C. The codes are also usually included with the tax software. To review the business codes in your tax software, you generally open a Schedule C and double-click on box B.

[6] IRC § 446.

[7] *Independent contractor* is a term that is used synonymously with self-employed. An individual is an independent contractor when he or she is not considered an employee of the person or business making the payment for a service.

EXAMPLE 6-1

Jason owns a drywall business. He contracts with various general contractors to complete drywall work during the construction of numerous personal residences. He is paid directly by the contractors but is not an employee of any one contractor. Jason would report the proceeds from his work on Schedule C (assuming his business is not incorporated). If Jason worked for only one contractor, he would likely be considered an employee and a Schedule C would not be required.

Amounts received by an independent contractor are usually reported to the taxpayer on Form 1099-MISC. Businesses that pay a nonemployee for services rendered are required to send a Form 1099-MISC to the independent contractor and to the IRS. A Form 1099-MISC (see Exhibit 6-2) is typically required when more than $600 is paid to an independent contractor in a given tax year.

EXAMPLE 6-2

Jake is an accounting systems professor at State University. He also has a consulting business through which he performs accounting systems analysis for local industries. In 2009, Jake consulted with five different corporations and received five Forms 1099-MISC of $2,500 each (in addition to a W-2 from State University). Jake is required to report $12,500 in income on Schedule C, line 1. He reports his wages from State University on line 7 of Form 1040. He does not combine the wages with the gross receipts of his trade or business on Schedule C.

EXHIBIT 6-2

CORRECTED (if checked)		
PAYER'S name, street address, city, state, ZIP code, and telephone no.	**1** Rents $	OMB No. 1545-0115
	2 Royalties $	20**09** Form **1099-MISC** — **Miscellaneous Income**
	3 Other income $	**4** Federal income tax withheld $ — **Copy B For Recipient**
PAYER'S federal identification number / **RECIPIENT'S identification number**	**5** Fishing boat proceeds $	**6** Medical and health care payments $
RECIPIENT'S name	**7** Nonemployee compensation $	**8** Substitute payments in lieu of dividends or interest $
Street address (including apt. no.)	**9** Payer made direct sales of $5,000 or more of consumer products to a buyer (recipient) for resale ▶ ☐	**10** Crop insurance proceeds $
City, state, and ZIP code	**11**	**12**
Account number (see instructions)	**13** Excess golden parachute payments $	**14** Gross proceeds paid to an attorney $
15a Section 409A deferrals $ / **15b** Section 409A income $	**16** State tax withheld $ .... $	**17** State/Payer's state no.	**18** State income $ .... $

This is important tax information and is being furnished to the Internal Revenue Service. If you are required to file a return, a negligence penalty or other sanction may be imposed on you if this income is taxable and the IRS determines that it has not been reported.

Form **1099-MISC**   (keep for your records)   Department of the Treasury - Internal Revenue Service

TAX YOUR BRAIN

Does the amount reported on line 1 of Schedule C always match the Forms 1099-MISC received by the taxpayer?

ANSWER

No; recall that a 1099-MISC is not required if the payment is below $600 or if the payments were received from individuals (businesses are required to report payments to the IRS via the 1099-MISC). Thus if one or more of the consulting jobs in Example 6-2 was for less than $600, the company involved is not required to send a 1099-MISC to Jake. However, he must still report the income on line 1 of Schedule C. If for some reason the amount reported on line 1 is less than the total from the Forms 1099-MISC, the taxpayer is required to attach a statement explaining the difference.

The final amount reported on line 1 of Schedule C is proceeds to "statutory employees." Statutory employees receive a W-2 from their employer, but box 13 (on the W-2) is checked indicating that the employee is to be treated as a statutory employee. Statutory employees include full-time life insurance agents, certain agents or commission drivers, traveling sales-persons, and certain at-home workers. These taxpayers are employees, but their statutory status allows them to reduce their income with *for* AGI expenses.[8]

Cost of Goods Sold

Recall that if inventory is a material income-producing factor, taxpayers must use the accrual method of accounting (at least for sales, cost of goods sold, and inventory). Likewise, inventory must be accounted for at the beginning and the end of each tax year. The inventory can be valued at cost or the lower of cost or market.[9] If the taxpayer's annual gross receipts in each of the three prior tax years exceed $10 million, the taxpayer must also capitalize certain indirect costs in inventory (allocate these costs between cost of goods sold and inventory) under the Uniform Capitalization Rules.[10] These indirect costs consist of costs associated with the production or resale of inventory such as equipment repairs, utilities, rent, supervisory wages, and depreciation.[11] You report cost of goods sold for a Schedule C business on page 2 (Part III). The calculation is similar to the traditional financial accounting calculation:

> Beginning inventory
> + Purchases
> + Cost of labor
> − Ending inventory
> = Cost of goods sold

CONCEPT CHECK 6-1—LO 1

1. Schedule C is used only when an individual is an employee of a company. True or false?
2. The income reported on a Schedule C will always match the amount the individual receives on one or more Forms 1099-MISC. True or false?
3. If inventory is a material income-producing factor, the accrual method of accounting must be used to account for inventory. True or false?

[8] Employers withhold social security and Medicare tax from the earnings of statutory employees. Thus statutory employees do not owe self-employment tax on these earnings. We discuss the specifics of the self-employment tax later in the chapter.

[9] If the taxpayer uses LIFO valuation, lower of cost or market cannot be used [Reg. § 1.472-2(b)].

[10] IRC § 263A.

[11] See Reg. § 1.263A-1T for a more comprehensive list of costs to be capitalized in inventory under the Uniform Capitalization Rules.

ORDINARY AND NECESSARY TRADE OR BUSINESS EXPENSES
LO 2

For an expense to be deductible, it must be "ordinary" and "necessary." For an expense to be *ordinary*, it must be customary or usual in the taxpayer's particular business. The *necessary* criterion refers to an expense that is appropriate and helpful rather than one that is essential to the taxpayer's business.[12] The courts have added a third standard: "reasonableness."[13] The courts have held that a trade or business expense must not only be ordinary and necessary but also reasonable in amount and reasonable in relation to its purpose. In most situations, making payments to related parties that are larger than normally required when the payee is an unrelated third party violates the reasonableness standard.

EXAMPLE 6-3

Martin owns a successful landscaping business and is in the 35% marginal tax bracket. He employs his 17-year-old son, Brian, as a laborer. To reduce his taxable income and provide money to Brian for college in the fall, Martin pays Brian $25 per hour. An unrelated laborer for the business is normally paid $8 to $10 per hour. The extra $15 per hour would be disallowed because it is unreasonable.

TAX YOUR BRAIN

The wages will be taxable to Brian, so why would the IRS contest Martin paying his son an unreasonable wage?

ANSWER

Brian would most likely pay a lower percentage of income tax on his wages than his father (probably 15%). Assuming an excess of $10,000 was paid to Brian, the tax savings for the family would be $2,000 ($10,000 × [35% − 15%]).

In addition to the three criteria of ordinary, necessary, and reasonable, certain other expenditures are expressly forbidden as deductibles. The most common forbidden expenses are

1. Illegal bribes, kickbacks, and other payments.
2. Payments for certain lobbying and political expenses.
3. Payments for fines and penalties.[14]

A taxpayer cannot deduct these expenses even if the preceding payments are ordinary, necessary, and reasonable in the taxpayer's trade or business.

EXAMPLE 6-4

Shane owns a hazardous waste management company. To transport the waste from the refining plant to the approved disposal area, he must cross a public highway with the waste. The state permit for transporting waste on state roads is $2,500 a year. However, the fine for not having the permit is only $50 per offense. Because Shane must cross the road only once every two weeks, he decides to forgo the permit and pay the penalty if he gets a ticket. Even though he can make an argument that the fines are ordinary, necessary, and reasonable business expenses (and make economic sense), the fine charges are not tax-deductible.

[12] *Welch, T.* (1933, S. Ct., 290 US 111).
[13] *Lincoln Electric Co. v. Com.* (1949, CA6, cert den 1950, S Ct), 176 F2d 815; *Haskel Engineering & Supply Co. v. Com.* (1967, CA9) 380 F2d 786.
[14] IRC § 162(c)(e)(f).

On Schedule C, the IRS provides a sample of possible expenses. Many are self-explanatory, but the listed expenses are not exhaustive. If the criteria of ordinary, necessary, and reasonable are met, an expense is deductible. However, many expenses have additional conditions and limits to their deductibility. The remainder of this chapter focuses on these conditions and limits.

CONCEPT CHECK 6-2—LO 2	1. For an expense to be deductible on Schedule C, the expense must be _____, _____, and _____. 2. Certain types of expenditures are expressly forbidden from being deductible from income on Schedule C. What are two examples of forbidden expenses? _____ and _____

DEPRECIATION
LO 3

The depreciation allowance (commonly called cost recovery) is the expense allowed for the wear or loss of usefulness of a business asset. Understanding the concept of depreciation is extremely important to comprehending the overall tax system. Why? Depreciation is a material noncash expense on the tax return that provides a large cash flow savings in terms of a tax reduction. Depreciation is allowed for every tangible asset (except land) used in a trade or business or for the production of income.[15] For each activity that uses depreciable assets, a taxpayer must complete Form 4562 to report depreciation.

Components of Depreciation

For depreciation to be allowed, the property must be used in a business or held for the production of income (such as rental property) and not be inventory or investment property. For property placed in service on or after January 1, 1987, depreciation is calculated under the Modified Accelerated Cost Recovery System (MACRS). For tax purposes, the depreciation calculation has four principal factors:

1. Basis (usually the cost of the asset).
2. Depreciation periods (asset class lives).
3. Depreciation convention (half-year, mid-quarter, or mid-month).
4. Depreciation method (200% or 150% declining balance or straight-line).

Depreciable Basis

Basis is a concept similar to book value on a financial accounting balance sheet. Typically, the depreciable basis of property is its initial cost. Cost is equal to the cash paid for the asset plus liabilities created or assumed plus expenses associated with the purchase.

The depreciable basis can differ depending on how the property was acquired. For example, if the property is inherited, the basis is generally fair market value (FMV) at the date of death of the decedent. If the property was converted from personal use property to business use property, the depreciable cost basis is the lower of the FMV or the cost at the date of conversion. Basis can also differ from cost if the property is acquired in a nontaxable exchange (trade-in). Typically the depreciable basis of an asset received after a trade-in is the cost of

---

[15] Thus, depreciation is calculated for Schedule C (trades or businesses—discussed in this chapter), Schedule E (rents and royalties—Chapter 8), and Form 2106 (unreimbursed employee business expenses—Chapter 5).

TABLE 6-1
Depreciable Basis

How Business Asset Was Acquired	Depreciable Basis
Purchase	Cost of asset
Converted from personal to business use	Lower of cost or FMV at the conversion date
Nontaxable exchange	Typically asset's cost less the deferred gain on the old asset
Inherited	Typically the FMV at the decedent's death

the new asset less any deferred gain on the old asset.[16] Table 6-1 summarizes how basis is determined for various acquisition methods. Often the primary tax authorities refer to adjusted basis, which is the cost basis less any accumulated depreciation.

EXAMPLE 6-5

Ashley purchased a computer for $2,500 to use in her sole proprietorship business. She also inherited land and a building from her father. The land had a basis of $10,000 and a FMV of $18,000 at the death of her father. The building had a $150,000 adjusted basis and a $300,000 FMV at his death. Ashley now uses both the land and building for her office. In this case, the computer has a $2,500 depreciable basis (cost). The building's depreciable basis is $300,000 because it was inherited and its basis is "stepped up" to its FMV. The land's basis would also be the FMV of $18,000 but is not depreciable.

EXAMPLE 6-6

Ashley also converted to business use an old van (basis $13,000; FMV $6,000 on the date of conversion) that she had held for personal use. She now plans to use the van 100% for business. The van's depreciable basis is $6,000 (the lower of the adjusted basis or the FMV at conversion). Had the van been used less than 100% for business, its $6,000 basis would be multiplied by the business use percentage to determine the depreciable basis.

TAX YOUR BRAIN

If a taxpayer buys an eight-year-old piece of equipment to use in a business for $4,000, can the taxpayer depreciate the $4,000 cost even though the equipment is used and was most likely fully depreciated by the prior owner?

ANSWER

Yes, the taxpayer depreciates the $4,000 basis as if it were new. The theory in this case is that the equipment has some useful productive life; otherwise, it would not have been purchased. Depreciation is based on the taxpayer's cost; it does not matter if the asset is new or used.

CONCEPT CHECK 6-3—LO 3

1. Shelly purchased a laptop computer for her personal use last year for $2,200. This year, she started her own business and transferred the computer to business use. The value of the computer at transfer was $1,300. What is Shelly's depreciable basis in her computer? _____
2. Jackson purchased a van for $22,000 and used it 100% for business. In the current year, he deducted $4,400 in depreciation related to the van. What is Jackson's adjusted basis in the van at the end of the current year? _____

[16] Nontaxable exchanges are discussed in greater detail in Chapter 12. For nontaxable exchanges, the basis is determined under IRC § 1031(d).

Depreciation Periods (Class Lives of Assets)

The IRS has established class lives and MACRS recovery classes for various types of assets.[17] The MACRS system makes a distinction between personal property and real property. *Personal property* includes equipment, furniture, and fixtures or anything else that is not classified as real property. *Real property* consists of land and buildings as well as any other structural components attached to land. Personal properties usually have shorter useful lives, and thus have recovery periods of 3, 5, and 7 years. Real properties have recovery periods of 27.5 years and 39 years. The other recovery classes (10, 15, and 20 years) could apply to either real or personal property. A summary of recovery periods for various types of assets is provided in Table 6-2.

Depreciation Conventions

Depreciation expense for tax purposes differs from depreciation for financial accounting calculations. With financial accounting, the depreciation calculation depends on the number of months the property was used in a given year. For the tax calculation, certain conventions (assumptions) are established:[18]

1. **Half-year convention:** The half-year convention treats all property placed in service during any taxable year as being placed in service at the midpoint of that taxable year.[19]

2. **Mid-quarter convention:** The mid-quarter convention treats all property placed in service during any quarter of a taxable year as being placed in service at the midpoint of that quarter.[20]

3. **Mid-month convention:** The mid-month convention treats all property placed in service during any month as being placed in service at the midpoint of that month.[21]

These conventions are built into the depreciation tables issued by the IRS and are shown in the appendix of this chapter. It is important to determine the convention to use when calculating depreciation expense.

TABLE 6-2
Summary of Recovery Period and Asset Types Placed in Service on or after January 1, 1987

Source: IRS Publication 946.

MACRS Recovery Period	Typical Assets Included in Recovery Period
3-year	Racehorses less than 2 years old and certain specialized industry tools
5-year	Autos and light trucks; computers and peripheral equipment
7-year	Furniture, fixtures, and equipment
10-year	Vessels, barges, tugs, and fruit- or nut-bearing plants
15-year	Wastewater treatment plants and telephone distribution plants
20-year	Farm buildings
27.5-year	Residential real property (e.g., apartments)
31.5-year	Nonresidential property acquired between January 1, 1987, and May 13, 1993
39-year	Nonresidential property acquired after May 13, 1993

[17] See IRS Publication 946, *How to Depreciate Property*. Also, Rev. Proc. 87-56, 1987-2 CB 674 contains the class lives for most assets. This Rev. Proc. is essential for tax preparers to have on hand as a quick depreciation reference source.
[18] IRC § 168(d)(4).
[19] IRC § 168(d)(4)(A).
[20] IRC § 168(d)(4)(C).
[21] IRC § 168(d)(4)(B).

CONCEPT CHECK 6-4—LO 3

1. An auto used in a trade or business would be depreciated over what period of time for MACRS tax purposes?
   a. 3 years.
   b. 5 years.
   c. 7 years.
   d. 10 years.

2. An apartment complex would be depreciated over what period of time for MACRS tax purposes?
   a. 10 years.
   b. 20 years.
   c. 27.5 years.
   d. 39 years.

3. A warehouse would be depreciated over what period of time for MACRS tax purposes?
   a. 10 years.
   b. 20 years.
   c. 27.5 years.
   d. 39 years.

Half-Year Convention

The convention used most often is the half-year convention. With the half-year convention, one-half year of depreciation is taken no matter when the asset is purchased during the year. A taxpayer uses the half-year convention for all personal property unless required to use the mid-quarter convention (discussed next).[22]

EXAMPLE 6-7

Cal purchased the following assets during the tax year for his sole proprietorship:

January 6	Equipment	$ 7,400
May 4	Truck	20,000
December 1	Equipment	2,000

Even though he purchased the assets at different times, he takes one-half year of depreciation on each asset. The equipment (both the January and the December purchases) would be 7-year MACRS property; the truck would be 5-year MACRS property.

Mid-Quarter Convention

Taxpayers must use the mid-quarter convention when they place more than 40% of their personal property in service during the last three months of the tax year or if the tax year consists of three months or less.[23] The 40% threshold is measured in terms of aggregate bases of the property placed in service and does not include the basis of real property acquired.[24]

TAX YOUR BRAIN

Mid-quarter convention is mandated when more than 40% of the asset purchases are made in the fourth quarter. How are assets purchased in the first quarter treated when the mid-quarter convention is required?

ANSWER

The first quarter property is treated as being placed in service at the midpoint of the first quarter. The IRS depreciation tables published in Rev. Proc. 87-57 account for the different quarters by having separate tables for assets placed in service in the first, second, third, and fourth quarters.

[22] IRC § 168(d)(1).
[23] IRC § 168(d)(3).
[24] IRC § 168(d)(3).

EXAMPLE 6-8	Assume the same facts as Example 6-7, but Cal purchased the truck on November 5 instead of May 4. Because he purchased 75% of the assets ($22,000/$29,400) in the fourth quarter, he must use the mid-quarter convention. The January equipment is treated as being placed in service at the midpoint of the first quarter, and the other two assets are treated as being placed in service at the midpoint of the fourth quarter.

Mid-Month Convention

The final convention is mid-month, which applies only to real property (27.5-year, 31.5-year, and 39-year property). Under the mid-month convention, the property is treated as being placed in service at the midpoint of the month acquired. Thus, real property acquired on March 3 is treated as acquired halfway through the month (9.5 months of depreciation would be taken in the first year).

Convention for Year of Disposal

Regardless of the convention required for a given asset (half-year, mid-quarter, or mid-month), the property is subject to the same convention in the year of disposal. For example, if a 7-year MACRS asset is disposed of in Year 3, a half-year of depreciation is taken on the asset regardless of whether the date of disposal was in January or December. Likewise, mid-quarter assets receive half a quarter of depreciation, and mid-month assets receive half a month of depreciation in the month of disposition.

TAX YOUR BRAIN 	Can the IRS build the percentages for the year of disposal into the depreciation tables?
	ANSWER
	No, the IRS can build the first-year depreciation percentages into the tables because they are known (for example, half a year of depreciation is taken in the first year). However, the IRS does not know in which year every taxpayer will dispose of the property. Thus, in the year of disposal, taxpayers must divide the table percentage by 2 for the half-year convention and by the appropriate months for the mid-quarter and mid-month conventions.

EXAMPLE 6-9	Jessica purchased a business computer system on November 3, 2007, for $3,000. The computer was subject to the mid-quarter convention because more than 40% of Jessica's total asset purchases occurred in the fourth quarter. Jessica sold the computer on March 5, 2009. Thus, in the 2009 tax year, Jessica would take 1.5 months of depreciation on the computer (one-half of the first quarter, or 1.5/12). If she sold the computer in December 2009, Jessica would depreciate the computer for 10.5 months (one-half of the final quarter plus the first three quarters, or 10.5/12).

CONCEPT CHECK 6-5—LO 3	1. A taxpayer can choose any depreciation convention as long as she or he is consistent in doing so. True or false? 2. A taxpayer must use the mid-quarter convention for personal property if more than 40% of the property is purchased in the fourth quarter. True or false? 3. The half-year convention is the most often-used convention for personal property. True or false? 4. To depreciate an apartment complex, a taxpayer should use the half-year convention. True or false? 5. The taxpayer must use the same depreciation convention in the year of disposal as the convention used in the year of acquisition. True or false?

Depreciation Methods

Only three depreciation methods are allowed for MACRS property purchased on or after January 1, 1987:

1. 200% declining balance switching to straight-line.

2. 150% declining balance switching to straight-line.

3. Straight-line.[25]

The 200% declining balance method is required for all 3-, 5-, 7-, or 10-year MACRS property (personal property). For 15-year and 20-year property, 150% declining balance is used. In both cases, the depreciation switches to straight-line in the tax year in which straight-line yields a higher depreciation allowance. Straight-line is required for all depreciable real property. In all cases, salvage value is ignored for tax purposes. The taxpayer can make an irrevocable election to use straight-line for any of the classes.[26]

Showing the Calculation

To correctly calculate depreciation, the taxpayer or tax preparer must know only the type of property, the recovery period, and the depreciable basis.

EXAMPLE 6-10

In May 2009, Samantha purchased equipment for $8,000, a work truck for $19,000, and an office building for $120,000. The depreciation calculation for each asset follows (numbers may be rounded in the final year):

Property Type	Recovery Period	Conventions	Depreciation Expense
Equipment	7-year property	Half-year	$ 8,000 basis
2009	Table 6A-1*	($8,000 × 14.29%)	1,143
2010		($8,000 × 24.49%)	1,959
2011		($8,000 × 17.49%)	1,399
2012		($8,000 × 12.49%)	999
2013		($8,000 × 8.93%)	714
2014		($8,000 × 8.92%)	714
2015		($8,000 × 8.93%)	714
2016		($8,000 × 4.46%)	358
Truck	5-year property	Half-year	$ 19,000 basis
2009	Table 6A-1*	($19,000 × 20.00%)	3,800
2010		($19,000 × 32.00%)	6,080
2011		($19,000 × 19.20%)	3,648
2012		($19,000 × 11.52%)	2,189
2013		($19,000 × 11.52%)	2,189
2014		($19,000 × 5.76%)	1,094
Building	39-year property	Mid-month	$120,000 basis
2009 App.	Table 6A-8*	($120,000 × 1.605%)	1,926
2010–2047		($120,000 × 2.564%)	3,077
2048		($120,000 × 0.963%)	1,148

* In the appendix to this chapter.

In Example 6-10, if both the equipment and the truck had been purchased in the fourth quarter and exceeded 40% of the aggregate basis of acquired personal property, the mid-quarter convention would be required. In this case, the appropriate table for the two personal property assets would be Table 6A-5 in the appendix to this chapter. The first-year percentage would be 3.57% for the equipment and 5.00% for the truck.

[25] Depreciation for alternative minimum tax (AMT) purposes is calculated separately for each asset using either 150% declining balance or straight-line. We provide a detailed presentation of AMT depreciation calculations in Chapter 13.

[26] IRC § 168(b)(5).

TABLE 6-3
Summary of MACRS Depreciation

Source: IRS Publication 946.

Asset Type	Convention	Method	Depr. Table†
Personal property			
3 yr.—racehorses	Half-year/mid-quarter*	200% double declining balance to straight-line	6A-1†
5 yr.—cars, trucks, computers	Half-year/mid-quarter*	200% double declining balance to straight-line	6A-1
7 yr.—furniture and equipment	Half-year/mid-quarter*	200% double declining balance to straight-line	6A-1
Real property			
27.5 residential	Mid-month	Straight-line	6A-6
31.5 nonresidential: 12/31/86–5/13/93	Mid-month	Straight-line	6A-7
39 nonresidential: 5/14/93 to present	Mid-month	Straight-line	6A-8

* For mid-quarter conventions, use Table 6A-2, 6A-3, 6A-4, or 6A-5 (in the appendix to this chapter), depending on which quarter the asset was placed in service.
† Refers to the tables in the appendix to this chapter.

Table 6-3 summarizes depreciation conventions and methods for various asset types. Table 6-3 also indicates the appropriate depreciation table (located in the appendix to this chapter) to use for calculations.

CONCEPT CHECK 6-6—LO 3

1. Shu purchased a piece of business equipment for $12,000 on May 3, 2009. This equipment is the only business asset Shu purchased during the year. What is Shu's depreciation expense related to the equipment? _____
2. If Shu sold the equipment on January 5, 2011, what would the depreciation expense be for 2010? _____
3. Davis purchased an apartment complex on March 5, 2009, for $330,000. What is Davis's depreciation expense related to the complex? _____

IRC §179 Expense Election

Instead of MACRS depreciation, the taxpayer can elect to expense a certain portion of personal property purchased during the year (real property is excluded). See Table 6-4 for the maximum IRC §179 amounts.

The §179 deduction is designed to benefit small businesses by permitting them to expense the cost of the assets in the year of purchase rather than over time. The expense is allowed in full only if the total of personal property purchases is less than $800,000 in 2009 in aggregate cost. The expense election is phased out dollar-for-dollar for purchases in excess of $800,000. Thus, the expense election is completely eliminated when asset purchases reach $1,050,000 ($800,000 + $250,000). Several other limitations apply to the §179 expense election:

1. The property must be used in an active trade or business. Purchased property associated with investment or rental property is not eligible for the expense election.
2. The §179 expense cannot create a net operating loss. However, the total amount of wages, salaries, tips, or other pay earned as an employee is included as income derived from a trade or business. Thus, a taxpayer who is an employee and has an active business on the side can have a loss in the side business caused by the §179 expense as long as his or her salary exceeds the loss. Any §179 expense disallowed by the lack of business income can be carried over indefinitely.

TABLE 6-4
Applicable Maximum
§179 Expense

2006	108,000
2007	125,000
2008	250,000
2009	250,000

3. The property cannot be acquired from a related party or by gift or inheritance.
4. If the property is acquired with a trade-in, the §179 expense is limited to the cash paid for the property.

EXAMPLE 6-11

ABC Co. purchased $285,000 of personal property in 2009. The company can elect to expense $250,000 under §179. The remaining $35,000 is depreciated using regular MACRS rates.

A taxpayer who purchases several assets during the year can pick the asset(s) he or she wishes to expense under §179 (up to the yearly limit).

CONCEPT CHECK 6-7—LO 3

1. Assume the same asset purchase as Concept Check 6-6. Shu purchased a piece of business equipment for $12,000 on May 3, 2009. This equipment was the only business asset purchased during the year, and the business has substantial income. What is Shu's deduction for the equipment, assuming §179 expense is elected? Would there be any additional MACRS regular depreciation? §179 expense $_____ Additional MACRS _____
2. What if the equipment Shu purchased had cost $275,000? What would the total expense deduction be if §179 were elected? §179 expense $_____ Additional MACRS _____

50% Bonus Depreciation: Property Placed in Service from 01/01/08 through 12/31/09

The Economic Stimulus Act of 2008, which was signed into law on February 13, 2008, created an accelerated depreciation deduction equal to 50% of the basis of certain property if the year of acquisition is 2008 or 2009. This provision was extended through December 31, 2009, by the American Recovery and Reinvestment Act of 2009. Eligible property includes

1. Property with a MACRS recovery period of less than 20 years.
2. Property acquired and placed in service on or after January 1, 2008, and before December 31, 2009.

Regular depreciation rules apply to the additional basis. Any allowable §179 expense reduces the basis before the new 50% allowance is taken.

EXAMPLE 6-12

Jack purchases a piece of new equipment (7-year MACRS) for $270,000 for his business on March 1, 2009. Jack is allowed the following depreciation deductions for the equipment:

$270,000 × 50%	=	$135,000 (50% bonus)
$135,000 × 14.29%	=	19,292 (remaining basis at first year % − 7 year)
Depreciation		$154,292

The remaining $135,000 in basis would be depreciated as normal 7-year MACRS property.

EXAMPLE 6-13

Same facts as Example 6-12 except that Jack also is eligible for $250,000 (the maximum in 2009) in §179 expense.

§179	$250,000
50% allowance ($20,000 × 50%)	10,000
7-yr. MACRS ($270,000 − $250,000 − $10,000) × 14.29%	1,429
Total cost recovery in 2009	$261,429

Listed Property

Because of the fear of loss of revenue from the use of accelerated depreciation methods on assets that have both business and personal use components to them, Congress established limitations and restrictions on "listed property." Listed property consists of the following:

- Any passenger automobile.
- Any other property used as a means of transportation (not included are vehicles that constitute a trade or business, such as taxis).
- Any property of a type generally used for entertainment, recreation, or amusement (such as a boat).
- Any computer or peripheral equipment.
- Any cellular telephone or other telecommunications equipment.[27]

Listed property does not include the above items that are used exclusively for business at a regular business establishment.

For the normal MACRS rules discussed earlier to apply, listed property must be used predominantly for business, which means that it is used more than 50% for business. If a taxpayer is an employee (not self-employed), the use of the asset is not business use unless it is both used for the employer's convenience and required as a condition of employment.

EXAMPLE 6-14

Linda is a public relations officer for her local city government. She purchased a computer to complete work on press releases and to return e-mail from home at night. Her computer use is 70% business related, but her employer does not require the computer as a condition of employment, nor is its use for the employer's convenience. Because Linda is an employee and the computer does not meet the business use test, no depreciation is allowed.

If the listed property does not meet the predominantly business use test, the taxpayer cannot claim an IRC §179 expense deduction for the property and must use straight-line depreciation (usually over a 5-year recovery period).[28]

EXAMPLE 6-15

Jack purchased a computer for $2,500 for use in his home office (he is self-employed). The computer is used 70% for business and 30% by his children to play computer games. Because the computer is predominantly used for business and is 5-year property, the MACRS depreciation for the first year would be $350 ($2,500 × 70% business use × 20% [Table 6A-1]). If the business use were only 30%, straight-line depreciation would be required and the depreciation deduction in the first year would be $75 ($2,500 × 30% × 10%).[29]

If in the first year of the asset's life the 50% test is met, but in subsequent years the business use falls below the 50% threshold, the depreciation must be calculated using the straight-line method. Additionally, depreciation must be recalculated for all years for which MACRS

---

[27] IRC § 280F(d)(4).

[28] Chapter 5 of IRS Publication 946 discusses the treatment of listed property.

[29] The 10% is calculated by taking the straight-line rate of 20% (1/5) and applying the half-year convention (1/2).

depreciation was used, and the excess MACRS depreciation (or IRC §179 expense) must be included in the taxpayer's gross income (recaptured) in the year the business use test is *not* met.[30]

EXAMPLE 6-16	Assume the same facts as Example 6-15 but the business use was 70% in year 1 and 30% in year 2. The depreciation and recapture amounts would be calculated as follows:

	MACRS	**Straight-Line**	**Difference**
Year 1	$350	$175	$175
Year 2	—	150	

The depreciation deduction would be $150 (full-year at 1/5 straight-line) in year 2, and the excess depreciation taken in year 1 ($175) would be included (recaptured) in gross income. The straight-line method would be required for future years even if the business use percentage subsequently increased above 50%.

Luxury Automobile Limitations

In addition to the business use limitation, the amount of depreciation allowed for luxury automobiles is limited. Passenger autos are defined as four-wheeled vehicles made primarily for use on public streets, roads, and highways with a gross vehicle weight of less than 6,000 pounds.[31] Light trucks or vans that are 6,000 pounds or less have a slightly higher limit.[32] The depreciation expense limits for luxury autos and light trucks placed in service in tax year 2009 follow:

	Auto Limit	**Light Truck/Van Limit**[33]
Year 1 (2009)	$10,960	$11,060
Year 2 (2010)	4,800	4,900
Year 3 (2011)	2,850	2,950
Year 4 (2012) and succeeding	1,775	1,775

These limits apply to both §179 and regular MACRS depreciation. They are reduced further if the business use of the auto is less than 100%.

EXAMPLE 6-17	Allison purchased in 2009 a Toyota Camry for $22,000 to be used exclusively for business. Regular MACRS depreciation plus the 50% bonus would equal $13,200 ($22,000 × 50%) + (11,000 × 20% for 5-year MACRS). Because the maximum depreciation for 2009 is $10,960, the depreciation allowance is limited to $10,960.

EXAMPLE 6-18	Jackson purchased a new car for $19,000 on July 7, 2009, and used it 75% for business during 2009. The maximum amount of expense for the car in the first year is $8,220 ($10,960 limit × 75%).

Prior to 2005, many taxpayers circumvented the luxury auto rules by purchasing vehicles with a gross weight of more than 6,000 lbs. Thus if a taxpayer purchased a large SUV, the taxpayer could use §179 to expense the entire purchase amount up to the §179 limit. For purchases after October 22, 2004, the §179 deduction is limited to $25,000 on these large SUVs. However, the regular MACRS depreciation is still unaffected by the luxury ceiling amounts, thus keeping the purchase of these vehicles attractive in terms of depreciation.

---

[30] IRC § 280F(b)(2).

[31] IRC § 280F(d)(5).

[32] Other information concerning the auto limitation can be found in Rev. Proc. 2009-24.

[33] The increased limit is for vehicles eligible for the 50% bonus depreciation. If the auto/truck is not eligible for the 50% bonus, the limits are decreased to $2,960 for autos and $3,060 for trucks.

EXAMPLE 6-19	Javier purchased a new GMC Yukon for $46,000 on May 3, 2009, to be used 100% for business. During 2009, he could deduct a maximum of $25,000 in §179 expense, $10,500 in 50% bonus, and $2,100 in MACRS depreciation ([$46,000 − $25,000] × 50% + ($46,000 − $25,000 − $10,500) × 20% − 5-year/half-year convention).

CONCEPT CHECK 6-8—LO 3	1. Zachary purchased a Ford Expedition (more than 6,000 lbs.) for $39,000 in March 2009. What is the maximum depreciation expense allowed, assuming that Zachary is eligible for the IRC §179 expense election?
	a. $7,800.
	b. $25,000.
	c. $3,260.
	d. $33,400.
	2. Assume the same facts as in Question 1. However, the Expedition was used only 80% for business. What is the maximum depreciation expense allowed, assuming that Zachary is eligible for the IRC §179 expense election?
	a. $7,800.
	b. $26,720.
	c. $2,608.
	d. $20,000.

Leased Vehicles

To circumvent the luxury auto depreciation limitations, leasing business vehicles became popular. However, the IRS limited the lease deduction for vehicles by requiring taxpayers to include a certain amount in income to offset the lease deduction. The "lease inclusion amount" is based on the vehicle's FMV and the tax year in which the lease began. The full lease payment is deducted (unless the business use is less than 100%), and the income inclusion reduces the net deduction. The IRS annually provides current lease inclusion amounts in a Revenue Procedure.[34]

Adequate Records

Taxpayers must have adequate records to document the business use and the time or mileage accumulated. IRS Publication 946 (see Chapter 5) notes that "an account book, diary, log, statement of expense, trip sheet, or similar record . . ." is sufficient to establish an expenditure or use. Adequate records for a portion of the year (which is then annualized) are acceptable if the taxpayer can show that the records represent the use throughout the year.

TRANSPORTATION AND TRAVEL
LO 4

Ordinary and necessary travel expenses are deductible by a trade or business.[35] A distinction is made between transportation and travel. *Transportation,* in a tax sense, traditionally means the expense of getting from one workplace to another workplace within the taxpayer's home area. *Travel,* on the other hand, generally refers to business travel away from the home area that requires an overnight stay.

[34] The 2009 inclusion amounts are published in Rev. Proc. 2009–24, 2009–17 IRB 885.
[35] IRC § 162(a)(2).

From Shoebox to Software

After completing several tax returns, depreciation calculations become routine. However, for new tax preparers, depreciation calculations and proper placement on the tax return can cause a great deal of stress. In practice, tax software performs most of the calculations. However, the old computer adage "garbage in, garbage out" also holds true for tax software. All current year software calculations should be checked because the type of property, recovery class, and §179 expense election must be input into the software. In this section, we calculate the depreciation for a new client in the insurance business. We also show the correct presentation of the depreciation information on Form 4562.

EXAMPLE 6-20

Alan Masters, a taxpayer from Chapter 5, started his own insurance agency on July 1, 2009. Later in the chapter, we incorporate business income and other nondepreciation expenses, but now we focus on depreciation. For the tax year 2009, Alan's business acquired the following assets:

Asset	Date Purchased	Percentage of Business Use	Cost	Class and Depreciation Method
Computer	07/12/09	100%	$ 2,500	5-yr DDB*
Phone system	07/12/09	100	2,300	5-yr DDB
Auto	07/15/09	90	22,000	5-yr DDB
Furniture	07/12/09	100	23,000	7-yr DDB
Office building	07/01/09	100	120,000	39-yr S/L†

* DDB = double declining balance method.
† S/L = straight-line method.

Assume that Alan took no IRC §179 deduction. Because less than 40% of the aggregate basis was purchased in the fourth quarter, the mid-quarter convention is not required. The half-year convention is used for these assets. The 50% bonus would be allowed for the 2009 tax year.

Current Year Depreciation

Computer ($2,500 × 50% bonus) + ($1,250 × 20%)	$ 1,500
Phone system ($2,300 × 50% bonus) + ($1,150 × 20%)	1,380
Auto ($22,000 x 90% x 50% bonus) + ($9,900 × 20%)	9,864*
Furniture ($23,000 × 50% bonus) + ($11,500 × 14.29%)	13,143
Office building ($120,000 × 1.177%)	1,412
Total depreciation expense	$27,299

* The auto is limited to the luxury limit times the business percentage ($10,960 × 90%).

Open the tax return file of Alan and Cherie Masters and then open Schedule C. Answer the questions at the top of Schedule C. Alan uses the cash method of accounting and does "materially participate" in the business. Most tax software programs have a Form 4562 Asset Depreciation and Vehicle Expenses worksheet. Enter the information for each asset on a separate worksheet. You need to enter the business and personal mileage for the auto to determine the business percentage. In this case, use 9,000 business miles and 1,000 personal miles.

Exhibit 6-3 shows the presentation on Form 4562. Note that the listed property is individually entered on page 2 of Form 4562. The total depreciation deduction is $27,299 under the assumption that no IRC §179 expense election was made.

If the IRC §179 election were made, the entire amount of personal property (everything but the building) purchased could be expensed. Because the §179 expense limit is now $250,000, most small businesses will be able to expense all of their non–real property purchases assuming that doing so does not produce a net operating loss. If §179 expense were taken, which in all likelihood it would be, all of the assets would be listed in Part I of Form 4562 and the total expense shown.

EXHIBIT 6-3

Form **4562**	**Depreciation and Amortization** (Including Information on Listed Property)	OMB No. 1545-0172
Department of the Treasury Internal Revenue Service (99)	► See separate instructions. ► Attach to your tax return.	20**09** Attachment Sequence No. **67**

Name(s) shown on return	Business or activity to which this form relates	Identifying number
Alan Masters	Insurance	444-44-4444

Part I **Election To Expense Certain Property Under Section 179**

Note: *If you have any listed property, complete Part V before you complete Part I.*

1	Maximum amount. See the instructions for a higher limit for certain businesses	**1**	$250,000
2	Total cost of section 179 property placed in service (see instructions)	**2**	
3	Threshold cost of section 179 property before reduction in limitation (see instructions)	**3**	$800,000
4	Reduction in limitation. Subtract line 3 from line 2. If zero or less, enter -0-	**4**	
5	Dollar limitation for tax year. Subtract line 4 from line 1. If zero or less, enter -0-. If married filing separately, see instructions	**5**	

6	**(a)** Description of property	**(b)** Cost (business use only)	**(c)** Elected cost	

7	Listed property. Enter the amount from line 29 . . . . **7**		
8	Total elected cost of section 179 property. Add amounts in column (c), lines 6 and 7	**8**	
9	Tentative deduction. Enter the **smaller** of line 5 or line 8	**9**	
10	Carryover of disallowed deduction from line 13 of your 2008 Form 4562	**10**	
11	Business income limitation. Enter the smaller of business income (not less than zero) or line 5 (see instructions)	**11**	
12	Section 179 expense deduction. Add lines 9 and 10, but do not enter more than line 11	**12**	
13	Carryover of disallowed deduction to 2010. Add lines 9 and 10, less line 12 ► **13**		

Note: *Do not use Part II or Part III below for listed property. Instead, use Part V.*

Part II **Special Depreciation Allowance and Other Depreciation (Do not** include listed property.**)** (See instructions.)

14	Special depreciation allowance for qualified property (other than listed property) placed in service during the tax year (see instructions)	**14**	13,900
15	Property subject to section 168(f)(1) election	**15**	
16	Other depreciation (including ACRS)	**16**	

Part III **MACRS Depreciation (Do not** include listed property.**)** (See instructions.)

Section A

17	MACRS deductions for assets placed in service in tax years beginning before 2009	**17**	
18	If you are electing to group any assets placed in service during the tax year into one or more general asset accounts, check here ► ☐		

Section B—Assets Placed in Service During 2009 Tax Year Using the General Depreciation System

(a) Classification of property	**(b)** Month and year placed in service	**(c)** Basis for depreciation (business/investment use only—see instructions)	**(d)** Recovery period	**(e)** Convention	**(f)** Method	**(g)** Depreciation deduction
19a 3-year property						
b 5-year property		2,400	5 yrs	HY	DDB	480
c 7-year property		11,500	7 yrs	HY	DDB	1,643
d 10-year property						
e 15-year property						
f 20-year property						
g 25-year property			25 yrs.		S/L	
h Residential rental property			27.5 yrs.	MM	S/L	
			27.5 yrs.	MM	S/L	
i Nonresidential real property	07/09	120,000	39 yrs.	MM	S/L	1,412
				MM	S/L	

Section C—Assets Placed in Service During 2009 Tax Year Using the Alternative Depreciation System

20a Class life					S/L	
b 12-year			12 yrs.		S/L	
c 40-year			40 yrs.	MM	S/L	

Part IV **Summary** (See instructions.)

21	Listed property. Enter amount from line 28	**21**	9,864
22	**Total.** Add amounts from line 12, lines 14 through 17, lines 19 and 20 in column (g), and line 21. Enter here and on the appropriate lines of your return. Partnerships and S corporations—see instructions	**22**	27,299
23	For assets shown above and placed in service during the current year, enter the portion of the basis attributable to section 263A costs **23**		

For Paperwork Reduction Act Notice, see separate instructions.	Cat. No. 12906N	Form **4562** (2009)

EXHIBIT 6-3   *(concluded)*

Form 4562 (2009)   Page **2**

Part V   **Listed Property** (Include automobiles, certain other vehicles, cellular telephones, certain computers, and property used for entertainment, recreation, or amusement.)

Note: *For any vehicle for which you are using the standard mileage rate or deducting lease expense, complete **only** 24a, 24b, columns (a) through (c) of Section A, all of Section B, and Section C if applicable.*

Section A—Depreciation and Other Information (Caution: *See the instructions for limits for passenger automobiles.*)

24a Do you have evidence to support the business/investment use claimed? ☒ Yes ☐ No   **24b** If "Yes," is the evidence written? ☒ Yes ☐ No

(a) Type of property (list vehicles first)	(b) Date placed in service	(c) Business/investment use percentage	(d) Cost or other basis	(e) Basis for depreciation (business/investment use only)	(f) Recovery period	(g) Method/Convention	(h) Depreciation deduction	(i) Elected section 179 cost
25 Special depreciation allowance for qualified listed property placed in service during the tax year and used more than 50% in a qualified business use (see instructions) **25**							9,864	
26 Property used more than 50% in a qualified business use:								
Auto	7/15/09	90 %	22,000	9,936	5 yr	DDB		
		%						
		%						
27 Property used 50% or less in a qualified business use:								
		%			S/L –			
		%			S/L –			
		%			S/L –			

28 Add amounts in column (h), lines 25 through 27. Enter here and on line 21, page 1 . . .   **28**   9,864
29 Add amounts in column (i), line 26. Enter here and on line 7, page 1 . . . .   **29**

Section B—Information on Use of Vehicles

Complete this section for vehicles used by a sole proprietor, partner, or other "more than 5% owner," or related person. If you provided vehicles to your employees, first answer the questions in Section C to see if you meet an exception to completing this section for those vehicles.

		(a) Vehicle 1		(b) Vehicle 2		(c) Vehicle 3		(d) Vehicle 4		(e) Vehicle 5		(f) Vehicle 6	
30	Total business/investment miles driven during the year (**do not** include commuting miles) . . .	9,000											
31	Total commuting miles driven during the year	0											
32	Total other personal (noncommuting) miles driven	1,000											
33	Total miles driven during the year. Add lines 30 through 32	10,000											
34	Was the vehicle available for personal use during off-duty hours?	Yes	No	Yes	No	Yes	No	Yes	No	Yes	No	Yes	No
		X											
35	Was the vehicle used primarily by a more than 5% owner or related person?	X											
36	Is another vehicle available for personal use?	X											

Section C—Questions for Employers Who Provide Vehicles for Use by Their Employees

Answer these questions to determine if you meet an exception to completing Section B for vehicles used by employees who **are not** more than 5% owners or related persons (see instructions).

		Yes	No
37	Do you maintain a written policy statement that prohibits all personal use of vehicles, including commuting, by your employees?		
38	Do you maintain a written policy statement that prohibits personal use of vehicles, except commuting, by your employees? See the instructions for vehicles used by corporate officers, directors, or 1% or more owners . . .		
39	Do you treat all use of vehicles by employees as personal use?		
40	Do you provide more than five vehicles to your employees, obtain information from your employees about the use of the vehicles, and retain the information received?		
41	Do you meet the requirements concerning qualified automobile demonstration use? (See instructions.) . .		

Note: *If your answer to 37, 38, 39, 40, or 41 is "Yes," do not complete Section B for the covered vehicles.*

Part VI   **Amortization**

(a) Description of costs	(b) Date amortization begins	(c) Amortizable amount	(d) Code section	(e) Amortization period or percentage	(f) Amortization for this year
42 Amortization of costs that begins during your 2009 tax year (see instructions):					

43 Amortization of costs that began before your 2009 tax year **43**
44 **Total.** Add amounts in column (f). See the instructions for where to report **44**

Form **4562** (2009)

Local Transportation Expenses

Taxpayers may take a deduction for business transportation expenses from one place of work to another as long as the expense is not for commuting (from home to workplace). These costs could include travel by air, rail, bus, taxi, or car. To differentiate between commuting costs and business transportation expenses, a taxpayer must first determine his or her *tax home*, which is the taxpayer's regular place of business, regardless of where the taxpayer actually lives. Exhibit 6-4 is an excerpt from IRS Publication 463 that summarizes when transportation costs can be deducted.

Local transportation costs are deductible in the following situations:

- Getting from one workplace to another in the course of conducting a business or profession when traveling within the city or general area of the taxpayer's tax home.

- Visiting clients or customers.

- Going to a business meeting away from the taxpayer's regular workplace.

EXHIBIT 6-4

Source: IRS Publication 463.

When Are Transportation Expenses Deductible?
Most employees and self-employed persons can use this chart.
(Do not use this chart if your home is your principal place of business.
See *Office in the home.*)

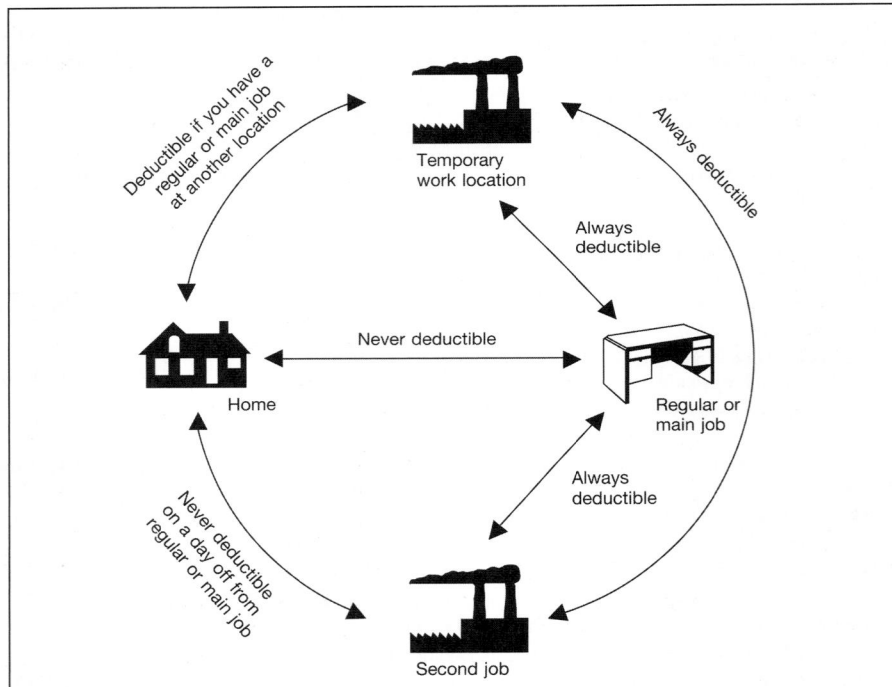

Home: The place where you reside. Transportation expenses between your home and your main or regular place of work are personal commuting expenses.

Regular or main job: Your principal place of business. If you have more than one job, you must determine which one is your regular or main job. Consider the time you spend at each, the activity you have at each, and the income you earn at each.

Temporary work location: A place where your work assignment is realistically expected to last (and does in fact last) one year or less. Unless you have a regular place of business, you can only deduct your transportation expenses to a temporary work location <u>outside</u> your metropolitan area.

Second job: If you regularly work at two or more places in one day, whether or not for the same employer, you can deduct your transportation expenses of getting from one workplace to another. You cannot deduct your transportation costs between your home and a second job on a day off from your main job.

- Getting from home to a temporary workplace when the taxpayer has one or more regular places of work. These temporary workplaces can be either inside or outside the taxpayer's tax home.[36]

EXAMPLE 6-21	Karen is a self-employed computer analyst in downtown Atlanta. She maintains an office at the downtown location but lives 30 miles out of town. She is currently performing a job that will last approximately a week that is 45 miles on the other side of Atlanta (75-mile one-way trip from her home). Because this is a temporary work location, Karen can deduct the cost of her transportation from her home to the temporary location.

EXAMPLE 6-22	Assume the same facts as Example 6-21. However, every morning Karen goes to the office for two hours. In this case, only the cost of her trip from her office to the temporary workplace is deductible. The cost of the trip from home to the office is commuting.

If the taxpayer's principal residence is his or her principal place of business, the cost of transportation between the residence and either a temporary location or a client/customer is deductible.[37]

Automobile Expenses: Standard Mileage Rate

If an automobile is used as transportation in a trade or business activity, a deduction is allowed for the cost of the auto's use. Taxpayers calculate the auto deduction in one of two ways: Use either the standard mileage rate or the actual expenses of business operation.[38] A taxpayer can use the standard mileage rate if

- The taxpayer owns the vehicle and uses the standard mileage rate for the first year it was placed in service.
- The taxpayer leases the auto and uses the standard mileage rate for the entire lease period.

The standard mileage rate *cannot* be used in the following instances:

- The auto is for hire (taxis).
- The taxpayer operates five or more cars *simultaneously* in business operations.
- Any depreciation or §179 expense deduction was claimed on the auto in an earlier tax year.
- The taxpayer used actual car expenses after 1997 for a leased vehicle.

For tax year 2009, the standard mileage rate is 55 cents per business mile driven: If the standard mileage rate is used, the taxpayer cannot deduct any actual car expenses. The mileage rate encompasses depreciation or lease payments, maintenance and repairs, gasoline, oil, insurance, and vehicle registration fees. The taxpayer simply takes the business miles driven and multiplies them by the standard rate to determine the deduction.

Certain vehicle information is required concerning the auto (date placed in service and miles driven). If Form 4562 is not required (for depreciation of other business assets), this auto information is placed in Part IV of Schedule C. Otherwise this information is shown on Form 4562.

[36] IRS Publication 463, p. 14.

[37] Rev. Rul. 99-7, 1999-1 CB 361; IRS Publication 463, p. 15.

[38] The standard mileage rate is available to employees (as opposed to self-employed taxpayers) for the unreimbursed portion of business miles. These costs are deducted as miscellaneous itemized deductions on Schedule A. See Chapter 5 for more information about miscellaneous itemized deductions.

EXAMPLE 6-23	Marta is a self-employed baker who makes wedding cakes and other pastries for parties. She owns a car for going to meetings with clients and a van that she uses for delivering cakes and pastries. Marta can use the standard mileage rate for both the car and the van.

A self-employed taxpayer can still deduct the business portion of any interest paid in acquiring a vehicle even if the standard mileage rate is used for the vehicle. Other permitted deductions include parking fees, tolls, and property taxes on the vehicle. If the vehicle is used less than 100% for business, the business portion of the property taxes should be reported on Schedule C, and the personal portion of the property taxes should be reported on Schedule A as an itemized deduction.

EXAMPLE 6-24	Ed purchased a vehicle for business and personal use. In 2009 he used the vehicle 60% for business (14,000 miles) and used the standard mileage rate to calculate his vehicle expenses. He also paid $1,600 in interest and $180 in county property tax on the car. The total business deductions related to Ed's car are calculated as follows:

Standard mileage rate (14,000 miles × 55 cents/mile)	$7,700
Interest ($1,600 × 60%)	960
Property taxes ($180 × 60%)	108
Total auto deduction on Schedule C	$8,768

The 40% personal interest is disallowed, and the remaining $72 of personal property tax is deducted on Schedule A as an itemized deduction.

Automobile Expenses: Actual Car Expenses

The second option for deducting business auto expenses is to use actual car expenses. Actual car expenses include the following:

- Depreciation or lease payments.
- Gas, oil, tires, repairs.
- Insurance, licenses, registration fees.[39]

The expenses must be divided between business and personal use (an allocation based on mileage can be used). Once depreciation on a vehicle has been taken, the taxpayer cannot use the standard mileage rate in future years on that vehicle. A taxpayer who has used the standard mileage rate in the past and decides to switch to the actual expense method must use straight-line depreciation and must reduce the depreciable basis by 21 cents per mile driven in 2008 and 2009.[40]

The actual expense method usually results in a larger deduction but also requires receipts for actual expenses as well as a mileage log to determine business use versus personal use. With the standard mileage rate, only mileage documentation is required. Taxpayers can use the standard mileage rate for one vehicle and actual expenses for another vehicle.

Travel Expenses

Travel expenses are different from transportation expenses because travel involves an overnight stay for business purposes. The basic travel requirement is that the trip requires sleep or rest.[41] The significance of meeting the "travel away from home" standard is that it allows the

[39] IRS Publication No. 463, p. 16.

[40] The rate is 19 cents for 2007 and 17 cents for tax years 2005 and 2006. The amount is 16 cents per mile for miles driven in 2003 and 2004. Rev Proc. 2008-72, 2008-50 IRB 1286.

[41] *U.S. v. Correll, H.* (1967, S Ct), 389 US 299.

deduction of meals, lodging, and other incidental expenses such as dry cleaning. All travel expenses can be deducted if the trip was entirely business-related.

EXAMPLE 6-25	Debra is self-employed and has her primary business in New York City. Debra flew to Washington, D.C., in the morning for a business meeting and then flew to Boston for an afternoon meeting with a client. She then took a late flight home that evening. The trip would not qualify as travel because Debra did not require sleep. Thus only the transportation cost is deductible.

If a temporary work assignment can be expected to last less than one year, travel from the taxpayer's tax home to the work assignment and temporary living costs at the remote location are deductible. If the work assignment is expected to last longer than one year, the position is considered permanent, and meals and lodging are considered nondeductible personal living expenses.[42] Limitations exist if the trip is partly personal or if lavish or extravagant expenditures for meals or lodging are incurred.

Limits on Travel Cost: Personal and Luxury

Tax challenges occur when a trip consists of both personal and business activity. If the trip is primarily a vacation but some business is transacted on the trip, transportation costs are not deductible. Any expenses directly related to business activities, however, are deductible. If the trip was primarily business-related even if some personal vacation was involved, the taxpayer can deduct the transportation expenses.

EXAMPLE 6-26	Timothy is currently self-employed in Raleigh, North Carolina, as a personal financial adviser. He flies to New York to visit his parents for seven days. While in New York, Timothy rents a car to meet with a business client one afternoon. The rental car and other costs associated with the business meeting are deductible, but the cost of the flight is not. The trip was primarily personal.

EXAMPLE 6-27	Assume the same facts as in Example 6-26. However, in this case, Timothy spends five days in New York conducting business and then drives to his parents' house for the weekend (two days). Because the trip is primarily business, the transportation expenses are deductible in addition to meals and lodging while on business. Expenses incurred while visiting his parents for two days are not deductible.

Additional limitations are placed on foreign business travel.[43] For foreign travel, a trip is considered entirely for business if it meets one of the following four criteria:

- The taxpayer does not have substantial control over arranging the trip.
- The taxpayer is outside the United States no more than seven consecutive days (do not count the days on which the taxpayer leaves or returns).
- The taxpayer spends less than 25% of his or her time on personal activities (the days on which the trip began and ended are counted).
- Vacation is not a major consideration for the taxpayer.

If one or more of the conditions are met and the trip to the foreign country is considered primarily business, the taxpayer still must allocate travel time between business days and nonbusiness days. To calculate the deductible amount of the round-trip travel expenses, the

[42] Rev. Rul. 93-86, 1993-2 CB 71.
[43] IRC § 274 and related regulations.

taxpayer multiplies total trip costs by the fraction of the number of business days to the total number of travel days outside of the United States. Weekends and holidays that intervene the business days are considered business days.[44] If a vacation is taken beyond the place of business activities, the travel deduction is limited to those expenses to and from the business location.[45]

Deductibility of Meals and Entertainment

In general, any business meals and entertainment expenditures are limited to 50% of the amount incurred. The 50% limit pertains to any expense for food or beverage and any expense with respect to an activity that is generally considered to constitute entertainment, amusement, or recreation. To qualify for any deduction, meals and entertainment expenses must be both ordinary and necessary business expenses as well as be either "directly related" to or "associated with 'business.'" *Directly related* or *associated with business* primarily means that the activity took place in a business setting or the entertainment directly preceded or followed business discussions. Club dues and membership fees are expressly denied as deductions.[46]

The taxpayer's meals while away from home on business may be deducted if the taxpayer either keeps track of the actual cost of meals or uses the federal per diem rates. The federal meal and incidental per diem rates vary and depend on the location of the meals and lodging.[47] For the tax year 2009, the continental standard per diem rate (CONUS rate) is $39 for meals and incidentals and $70 per day for lodging. These standard amounts are increased for business travel in IRS-designated high-cost areas. Using a per diem rate eliminates the need for detailed recordkeeping.

The 50% limit does not apply to self-employed individuals in certain circumstances.[48] Self-employed taxpayers who meet the following three requirements can deduct 100% of meals and entertainment expenses:

1. The taxpayer incurs these expenses as an independent contractor.
2. The customer or client reimburses the taxpayer or gives the taxpayer allowances for these expenses in connection with the services performed.
3. The taxpayer provides adequate records of these expenses to the customer or client.

TAX YOUR BRAIN

Why does the IRS allow self-employed taxpayers who meet the three requirements to deduct 100% of meals and entertainment expenses?

ANSWER

If the taxpayer is an independent contractor and the client reimburses him or her for meals and entertainment, the reimbursement would be included in the taxpayer's 1099-MISC from the client and thus be required to be reported in full as income. If the taxpayer is then allowed only a 50% deduction, the extra 50% would remain in taxable income (100% included in income but only 50% deductible) when, in fact, those amounts are expense reimbursements, not income.

Table 6-5 provides a summary of deductible meals and entertainment expenses.

[44] Reg. § 1.274-4(d)(2)(v).

[45] There are additional limitations concerning luxury water travel. See IRS Publication 463 for more information.

[46] IRC § 274(a)(3).

[47] These limits are subject to adjustment and depend on the location within the continental United States. Go to www.gsa.gov and click on per diems for the most recent figures.

[48] IRS Publication 463, pp. 11-12. The 50% rule also does not apply if the expenses for meals and entertainment were for advertising or if the meals and entertainment are actually sold or provided by the business (e.g., a nightclub).

TABLE 6-5 **Summary of** **Deductible Meals and** **Entertainment**	General rule	Entertainment is deductible for clients, customers, or employees if the "directly related" business test or "associated" business test is met. Meals are deductible if the business trip is overnight or business is conducted with clients, customers, or employees.

	Tests to be met	Directly related test:
		    Activity took place in a clear business setting.
		    Main purpose was the active conduct of business.
		Associated test:
		    Activity was associated with the trade or business.
		    Entertainment directly preceded or followed a substantial business discussion.

	Limits	Expenses cannot be lavish or extravagant under the circumstances. Generally, meals and entertainment are limited to 50% of expenses.

Source: IRS Publication 436, p. 11.

CONCEPT CHECK 6-9—LO 4

1. A taxpayer can take depreciation on a business auto and use the standard mileage rate in the same year. True or false?
2. Transportation costs are allowed only when the taxpayer visits a client. True or false?
3. A deduction is allowed for meals, lodging, and incidental expenses when a taxpayer travels away from home requiring sleep. True or false?
4. A taxpayer can deduct $39/day for meals and incidentals and $70/day for lodging without keeping receipts on a business trip (subject to the 50% limitation). True or false?
5. Taking five clients to a major league baseball game immediately following a substantial business discussion is deductible up to 50% of costs. True or false?

BUSINESS USE OF THE HOME AND BUSINESS BAD DEBTS
LO 5

Typically no deduction is allowed with respect to a taxpayer's residence (except for itemized deductions for mortgage interest, taxes, and casualty losses concerning the primary residence). Difficulties arise when a taxpayer uses the primary residence or a portion of it for business purposes.

A self-employed taxpayer can deduct expenses for the business use of the home if the business use is exclusive, regular, and for the taxpayer's trade or business.[49] The home must be the principal place of business or a place where the taxpayer meets patients, clients, or customers. The exclusive use test is satisfied if a specific area of the home is used *only* for the trade or business (such as a separate room). To meet the regular use test, a taxpayer must use the home office on a continuing basis, not just occasionally or incidentally.[50]

To determine whether the taxpayer's home is the principal place of business, several factors must be considered. First, what is the relative importance of the activities performed at each business location? Second, what amount of time is spent at each business location? Business home use also includes administration or management activities if there is no other fixed location to conduct such business.

EXAMPLE 6-28   Rob is a self-employed independent insurance agent who works exclusively from two rooms in his home. He rarely meets clients at his home because most of his client contact occurs over the phone or at the client's home or office. Even though most of Rob's client contact is not in his home, all of the administrative work is completed in the home office. The two rooms qualify as a home office if they are used exclusively for business.

The preceding rules also apply both to employees and to self-employed individuals. The standards for an employee are higher because the employee must meet the exclusive use test (for business) and the home office must be *for the convenience of his employer.* The employee

[49] IRC § 280A(c)(1).
[50] IRS Publication No. 587, p. 3.

cannot rent all or part of the residence to the employer and use the rented portion to perform services as an employee. Employee home office expenses are reported on Schedule A as miscellaneous itemized deductions (see Chapter 5).

Home Office Deduction for Self-Employed Taxpayers

The home office deduction for self-employed individuals is reported on Form 8829 and transferred to Schedule C, line 30. The first objective in determining the home office deduction is to calculate the area (in square footage) used regularly and exclusively for business.

EXAMPLE 6-29	The five-room home that Rob owns (see Example 6-28) has 3,000 square feet. According to the floor plan of the house, the two rooms used exclusively for business are 750 square feet each. Thus one-half (1,500/3,000) of Rob's house is used exclusively for business.

The next objective in calculating the home office deduction for self-employed individuals is to separate the home expenses into direct and indirect expenses. *Direct expenses* are those that are only for the business part of the home. For example, repairs and painting expenses for the business portion are direct expenses. Direct expenses are deducted in full in column (a) of Form 8829. Indirect expenses are expenses of running the entire household (insurance, utilities, taxes, interest, and so on). The indirect expenses are multiplied by the business percentage calculated in Part I of Form 8829 to derive the deductible portion.

Deduction Limit

Home office expenses that are not otherwise deductible (such as insurance, utilities, and depreciation) are limited to the gross income from the business use of the home. *Gross income* is first reduced by the amount of regular trade or business expenses (non–home related) and home office expenses that would be deductible in any event (mortgage interest and property taxes). If any positive income remains, the business use portions of insurance, utilities, and depreciation (note that depreciation is last) can be deducted.

EXAMPLE 6-30	Assume the same facts as in Example 6-29. Rob had $19,000 of gross income from his home trade or business and the following expenses:

Trade or business expenses	$12,000
Mortgage interest	9,800
Real estate taxes	1,200
Utilities	1,500
Insurance	1,700
Repairs	2,000
Depreciation (for business started in January: house basis $200,000 [$200,000 × 50% business × 2.461%])	2,461

Expenses allowed are calculated as follows:

Gross income	$19,000
Trade or business expenses	(12,000)
Interest ($9,800 × 50%)	(4,900)
Taxes ($1,200 × 50%)	(600)
Deduction limit	$ 1,500

Even though one-half of the utilities, insurance, repairs, and depreciation are for the exclusive use of the home office, they are limited to $1,500. The excess is indefinitely carried over (assuming continued home office use) to the following tax year and deducted, subject to the limit in that year. Exhibit 6-5 shows the presentation of the preceding example on Form 8829.

EXHIBIT 6-5

Form **8829**	**Expenses for Business Use of Your Home**	OMB No. 1545-0074
Department of the Treasury Internal Revenue Service (99)	► File only with Schedule C (Form 1040). Use a separate Form 8829 for each home you used for business during the year. ► See separate instructions.	20**09** Attachment Sequence No. **66**

Name(s) of proprietor(s)	Your social security number
Rob Taxpayer	123-45-6789

Part I Part of Your Home Used for Business

1	Area used regularly and exclusively for business, regularly for daycare, or for storage of inventory or product samples (see instructions)	**1**	1,500
2	Total area of home	**2**	3,000
3	Divide line 1 by line 2. Enter the result as a percentage	**3**	50 %

For daycare facilities not used exclusively for business, go to line 4. All others go to line 7.

4	Multiply days used for daycare during year by hours used per day	**4**		hr.
5	Total hours available for use during the year (365 days x 24 hours) (see instructions)	**5**	8,760	hr.
6	Divide line 4 by line 5. Enter the result as a decimal amount . . .	**6**		
7	Business percentage. For daycare facilities not used exclusively for business, multiply line 6 by line 3 (enter the result as a percentage). All others, enter the amount from line 3 . . . . . ►	**7**	50 %	

Part II Figure Your Allowable Deduction

		(a) Direct expenses	(b) Indirect expenses		
8	Enter the amount from Schedule C, line 29, **plus** any net gain or (loss) derived from the business use of your home and shown on Schedule D or Form 4797. If more than one place of business, see instructions			**8**	7,000
	See instructions for columns **(a)** and **(b)** before completing lines 9–21.				
9	Casualty losses (see instructions) . . .	**9**			
10	Deductible mortgage interest (see instructions)	**10**	9,800		
11	Real estate taxes (see instructions) . .	**11**	1,200		
12	Add lines 9, 10, and 11	**12**	11,000		
13	Multiply line 12, column (b) by line 7	**13** 5,500			
14	Add line 12, column (a) and line 13 . . .			**14**	5,500
15	Subtract line 14 from line 8. If zero or less, enter -0-			**15**	1,500
16	Excess mortgage interest (see instructions) .	**16**			
17	Insurance	**17**	1,700		
18	Rent	**18**			
19	Repairs and maintenance	**19**	2,000		
20	Utilities	**20**	1,500		
21	Other expenses (see instructions) . . .	**21**			
22	Add lines 16 through 21	**22**	5,200		
23	Multiply line 22, column (b) by line 7	**23** 2,600			
24	Carryover of operating expenses from 2008 Form 8829, line 42 . .	**24** 0			
25	Add line 22 column (a), line 23, and line 24			**25**	2,600
26	Allowable operating expenses. Enter the **smaller** of line 15 or line 25			**26**	1,500
27	Limit on excess casualty losses and depreciation. Subtract line 26 from line 15			**27**	
28	Excess casualty losses (see instructions)	**28**			
29	Depreciation of your home from line 41 below	**29** 2,461			
30	Carryover of excess casualty losses and depreciation from 2008 Form 8829, line 43	**30**			
31	Add lines 28 through 30			**31**	2,461
32	Allowable excess casualty losses and depreciation. Enter the **smaller** of line 27 or line 31 . .			**32**	
33	Add lines 14, 26, and 32			**33**	7,000
34	Casualty loss portion, if any, from lines 14 and 32. Carry amount to **Form 4684** (see instructions)			**34**	
35	**Allowable expenses for business use of your home.** Subtract line 34 from line 33. Enter here and on Schedule C, line 30. If your home was used for more than one business, see instructions ►			**35**	7,000

Part III Depreciation of Your Home

36	Enter the **smaller** of your home's adjusted basis or its fair market value (see instructions) . .	**36**	200,000
37	Value of land included on line 36	**37**	
38	Basis of building. Subtract line 37 from line 36	**38**	200,000
39	Business basis of building. Multiply line 38 by line 7	**39**	100,000
40	Depreciation percentage (see instructions)	**40**	2.461 %
41	Depreciation allowable (see instructions). Multiply line 39 by line 40. Enter here and on line 29 above	**41**	2,461

Part IV Carryover of Unallowed Expenses to 2010

42	Operating expenses. Subtract line 26 from line 25. If less than zero, enter -0-	**42**	1,100
43	Excess casualty losses and depreciation. Subtract line 32 from line 31. If less than zero, enter -0-	**43**	2,461

For Paperwork Reduction Act Notice, see page 4 of separate instructions. Cat. No. 13232M Form **8829** (2009)

Business Bad Debts and Business Casualty Losses

Certain bad debt losses can be deducted as ordinary deductions if incurred in a trade or business.[51] Generally, the same rules for deducting trade or business expenses also apply to bad debts. In other words, if a debt is considered a bona fide business bad debt, it must have been ordinary, necessary, and reasonable in the trade or business. The distinction between a business bad debt and a nonbusiness bad debt is extremely important. A *nonbusiness bad debt* is treated as a short-term capital loss and can be deducted only when it becomes completely worthless.[52] *Business bad debts,* on the other hand, can be deducted when either partially worthless or completely worthless and are treated as an ordinary deduction.

Bona Fide Business Bad Debt

To be a business bad debt, a debt must be a *bona fide debt,* which consists of debt that arises from a debtor–creditor relationship based on a valid and enforceable obligation to pay a fixed sum of money.[53] Additionally, for a note or account receivable to be considered a debt, the receivable must have been previously included in income. Thus, a cash basis taxpayer cannot write off, as a bad debt, any account receivable that is not collected. Because the receivable has not been included in income on Schedule C, it therefore has no basis, and no deduction is allowed.

EXAMPLE 6-31	Mike, a cash basis sole proprietor (consultant), gave advice to a corporate client that he billed $700. Subsequently the corporate client went out of business and filed for bankruptcy. Because the $700 receivable was never included in income, Mike cannot take a bad debt deduction.

EXAMPLE 6-32	In addition to the $700 bill for the consulting services, Mike lent the corporate client $5,000 (evidenced by a valid note) to help the client pay bills and avoid bankruptcy. The business purpose for the loan was that the corporate officers were a source of many client referrals for Mike's firm. When the corporate client later went bankrupt, Mike could take an ordinary deduction for the $5,000.

If a bad debt is deducted, any recoveries of the bad debt in subsequent years must be included in gross income.[54]

Business Casualty Losses

An individual taxpayer reports a loss from a business casualty on page 2 of Form 4684.[55] When business property is lost in a fire, storm, shipwreck, theft, or other casualty, the taxpayer normally receives an ordinary loss deduction for the basis of the property unless the property

---

[51] IRC § 165(c).

[52] Reg. § 1.166(d).

[53] Reg. § 1.166-1(c).

[54] Reg. § 1.166-1(f).

[55] More details on casualty losses are provided in Chapter 5. The limits for casualties of personal use (nonbusiness use) property are discussed at that time.

TAX YOUR BRAIN

Can a taxpayer have a casualty gain?

ANSWER

Yes. As an example, a business building purchased in 1983 for $55,000 is now worth $200,000. The building is likely to be insured for its replacement cost and to be fully depreciated ($0 adjusted basis). If the building were completely destroyed by fire and the insurance proceeds were $200,000, the taxpayer could have a gain of $200,000 ($200,000 proceeds less the $0 adjusted basis).

EXAMPLE 6-33

On September 17, 2009, Duane's office building was destroyed by a tornado. Duane had purchased the building in 1983 for $90,000 but had recently made improvements to it. The adjusted basis and FMV at the time of the tornado were $80,000 and $110,000, respectively. Duane had not updated his insurance policy in several years, and thus received only $70,000 from the insurance company. Because the building was totally destroyed, the business casualty is $10,000 (the adjusted basis of $80,000 less the $70,000 insurance reimbursement). See Exhibit 6-6 for the proper reporting. The $10,000 is transferred from Form 4684, page 2, to Form 4797 and eventually to Form 1040, page 1. Note that although the loss relates to Schedule C, it does not appear on Schedule C but goes directly to Form 1040 as a *for* AGI deduction.

CONCEPT CHECK 6-10—LO 5

1. Jose uses 20% of his home exclusively for business. He had the entire exterior of the house painted and the interior of one room that he uses for an office painted for $3,000 and $500, respectively. What is the total deduction Jose can take as a home office expense for the painting?
   a. $500.
   b. $3,500.
   c. $700.
   d. $1,100.

2. Which of the following comments is true regarding the home office deduction?
   a. The taxpayer must see clients at home to be allowed a home office deduction.
   b. The home office deduction is limited to income from the Schedule C business.
   c. The taxpayer is allowed to take a §179 expense election on the business portion of the home itself.
   d. Depreciation on the home is never allowed as a home office deduction.

3. When business property is partially destroyed by a casualty, the loss is calculated using which of the following?
   a. The decrease in the FMV of the property.
   b. The adjusted basis of the property.
   c. The lower of the FMV or the adjusted basis of the property.
   d. The adjusted basis of the property less 10% of AGI.

is only partially destroyed. With partial losses, the loss is the lower of the decrease in FMV before and after the casualty or the adjusted basis. All losses are reduced by insurance proceeds.[56]

[56] The gain can be avoided by the replacement of similar property. Deferrals of gains from involuntary conversions are discussed in Chapter 12.

EXHIBIT 6-6

Version A, Cycle 2

Form 4684 (2009) | Attachment Sequence No. **26** | Page **2**

Name(s) shown on tax return. Do not enter name and identifying number if shown on other side.
Duane Taxpayer

Identifying number
123-45-6789

SECTION B—Business and Income-Producing Property

Part I Casualty or Theft Gain or Loss (Use a separate Part I for each casualty or theft.)

23 Description of properties (show type, location, and date acquired for each property). Use a separate line for each property lost or damaged from the same casualty or theft.

Property **A** Office Building, 123 Ally Drive, Anywhere, USA
Property **B**
Property **C**
Property **D**

			Properties		
		A	B	C	D
24	Cost or adjusted basis of each property	80,000			
25	Insurance or other reimbursement (whether or not you filed a claim). See the instructions for line 3	70,000			
	Note: *If line 24 is **more** than line 25, skip line 26.*				
26	Gain from casualty or theft. If line 25 is **more** than line 24, enter the difference here and on line 33 or line 38, column (c), except as provided in the instructions for line 37. Also, skip lines 27 through 31 for that column. See the instructions for line 4 if line 25 includes insurance or other reimbursement you did not claim, or you received payment for your loss in a later tax year.				
27	Fair market value **before** casualty or theft	110,000			
28	Fair market value **after** casualty or theft	0			
29	Subtract line 28 from line 27	110,000			
30	Enter the **smaller** of line 24 or line 29	80,000			
	Note: *If the property was totally destroyed by casualty or lost from theft, enter on line 30 the amount from line 24.*				
31	Subtract line 25 from line 30. If zero or less, enter -0-	10,000			
32	Casualty or theft loss. Add the amounts on line 31. Enter the total here and on line 33 or line 38 (see instructions) 32	10,000			

Part II   Summary of Gains and Losses (from separate Parts I)

(a) Identify casualty or theft	(b) Losses from casualties or thefts		(c) Gains from casualties or thefts includible in income
	(i) Trade, business, rental or royalty property	(ii) Income-producing and employee property	

Casualty or Theft of Property Held One Year or Less

33	(	)(	)	
	(	)(	)	
34	Totals. Add the amounts on line 33 34 (	)(	)	

35 Combine line 34, columns (b)(i) and (c). Enter the net gain or (loss) here and on Form 4797, line 14. If Form 4797 is not otherwise required, see instructions **35**

36 Enter the amount from line 34, column (b)(ii) here. Individuals, enter the amount from income-producing property on Schedule A (Form 1040), line 28, or Form 1040NR, Schedule A, line 16, and enter the amount from property used as an employee on Schedule A (Form 1040), line 23, or Form 1040NR, Schedule A, line 11. Estates and trusts, partnerships, and S corporations, see instructions **36**

Casualty or Theft of Property Held More Than One Year

37	Casualty or theft gains from Form 4797, line 32			**37**	
38	Tornado Damage	(10,000)(	)		
		( )(	)		
39	Total losses. Add amounts on line 38, columns (b)(i) and (b)(ii) 39	(10,000)(	)		
40	Total gains. Add lines 37 and 38, column (c)			**40**	
41	Add amounts on line 39, columns (b)(i) and (b)(ii)			**41**	(10,000)

42 If the loss on line 41 is **more** than the gain on line 40:
  a Combine line 39, column (b)(i) and line 40, and enter the net gain or (loss) here. Partnerships (except electing large partnerships) and S corporations, see the note below. All others, enter this amount on Form 4797, line 14. If Form 4797 is not otherwise required, see instructions **42a** (10,000)
  b Enter the amount from line 39, column (b)(ii) here. Individuals, enter the amount from income-producing property on Schedule A (Form 1040), line 28, or Form 1040NR, Schedule A, line 16, and enter the amount from property used as an employee on Schedule A (Form 1040), line 23, or Form 1040NR, Schedule A, line 11. Estates and trusts, enter on the "Other deductions" line of your tax return. Partnerships (except electing large partnerships) and S corporations, see the note below. Electing large partnerships, enter on Form 1065-B, Part II, line 11. **42b**

43 If the loss on line 41 is **less** than or **equal** to the gain on line 40, combine lines 40 and 41 and enter here. Partnerships (except electing large partnerships), see the note below. All others, enter this amount on Form 4797, line 3 **43**

Note: *Partnerships, enter the amount from line 42a, 42b, or line 43 on Form 1065, Schedule K, line 11. S corporations, enter the amount from line 42a or 42b on Form 1120S, Schedule K, line 10.*

Form **4684** (2009)

HOBBY LOSS RULES AND EDUCATION EXPENSES
LO 6

To limit deductible losses from activities that are primarily for personal pleasure instead of a trade or business, Congress established the hobby loss rules.[57] If an activity is characterized as a hobby (rather than a trade or business), the tax treatment is different. Instead of reporting all income and expenses on Schedule C, the income is reported on Form 1040, line 21, as other income, and the expenses are treated as miscellaneous itemized deductions.[58] The deductible expenses are limited to the income from the activity.

EXAMPLE 6-34	Alex is a successful CPA who enjoys decorative woodworking. He makes decorative rocking chairs, tables, and other handcrafted furniture. He spends 10 to 15 hours a week (considerably less time during tax season) making the furniture and had gross sales of $3,000. His expenses for the year were $10,000. If this activity is treated as a trade or business, Alex would have a $7,000 loss to deduct against other income. If the woodworking is treated as a hobby, the deductible expenses would be limited to the $3,000 of income.

What is the deciding factor in determining whether an activity is a hobby or business? Nine factors are used in the hobby determination:

1. Manner in which the taxpayer carries on the activity.
2. Expertise of the taxpayer or his or her advisers.
3. Time and effort expended by the taxpayer in carrying on the activity.
4. Expectations that assets used in the activity can appreciate in value.
5. Success of the taxpayer in carrying on other similar or dissimilar activities.
6. Taxpayer's history of income or losses with respect to the activity.
7. Amount of occasional profits, if any, that are earned.
8. Taxpayer's financial status.
9. Elements of personal pleasure or recreation.[59]

The regulations note that taxpayers are to take *all* of the facts and circumstances into account and that no one factor is controlling in the hobby determination.[60] If the IRS asserts that an activity is a hobby, the burden to prove that the activity is a trade or business rests with the taxpayer. However, if the taxpayer has shown a profit for three out of five consecutive tax years (two out of seven for horseracing), the burden of proof shifts to the IRS.[61]

After the activity is characterized as a hobby, expenses are allowed only to the extent of income and only in the following order:

1. Expenses that would be allowed to reduce taxable income regardless of the presence of the hobby (such as mortgage interest or property taxes).
2. Expenses pertaining to the hobby that do not reduce the basis of property (utilities, supplies).
3. Expenses pertaining to the hobby that reduce the basis of property (depreciation).[62]

---

[57] IRC § 183.

[58] See Chapter 5 for the treatment of miscellaneous itemized deductions.

[59] Reg § 1.183-2(b).

[60] Reg. § 1.183-2(b).

[61] IRC § 183(d).

[62] Reg. § 1.183-1(b)(1)(i)(ii)(iii).

Education Expenses

A major expense for many self-employed individuals is the cost incurred for education. However, with education expenses, it is sometimes difficult to distinguish whether the education is an ordinary and necessary business expense (deductible) or qualifies the taxpayer for a new profession (not deductible). This ambiguity has led to considerable litigation between taxpayers and the IRS. Education expenses are deductible if the education meets either of these criteria:

- Maintains or improves skills required by the individual in his or her employment or other trade or business.
- Meets the express requirements of the individual's employer or the requirements of applicable law or regulation.[63]

However, even if one of the two preceding requirements is met, the education expenses are not deductible if the education is required to meet minimum educational requirements for employment or if the education qualifies the taxpayer for a new trade or business. The definition of what constitutes a new trade or business has been the source of much confusion.

TAX YOUR BRAIN

Assume that Leon is a CPA who has been practicing for 10 years in audit. He decides that he would like to start a tax practice. He begins taking classes in a masters of taxation program. Are the expenses for the classes deductible?

ANSWER

Yes, they are because the education does not qualify Leon for a new profession. The education only improves his skills in the CPA profession for which he already qualifies.

Eligible education expenses include not only tuition but also books, supplies, fees, and travel.

CONCEPT CHECK 6-11—LO 6

1. If a taxpayer has shown a net profit for the last three years, the activity is not considered a hobby. True or false?
2. A taxpayer can never take a net loss on an activity considered a hobby. True or false?
3. Expenses that can be deducted elsewhere on the tax return must be the first expenses deducted from hobby income. True or false?
4. Education expenses that help qualify a taxpayer for a new trade or business (or profession) are deductible. True or false?

SELF-EMPLOYMENT TAX
LO 7

One of the major disadvantages to being self-employed is the requirement to pay self-employment tax. *Self-employment (SE) tax* consists of two parts: (1) the social security tax and (2) the Medicare tax.[64] Self-employed taxpayers are not discriminated against because

---

[63] Reg. § 1.162-5.

[64] The social security tax is the old age, survivors, and disability insurance tax (OASDI), and the Medicare tax is a hospital insurance tax.

every U.S. citizen or resident (with few exceptions) must pay these taxes. However, because most taxpayers are employees, the employer is required to pay half of these taxes, and the employee pays the other half. The employee's one-half share is commonly reported as FICA on most paychecks. Self-employed taxpayers must pay *both* the employer's and the employee's shares.[65] Any self-employed taxpayer with $400 or more in self-employment income must pay self-employment taxes. Income from Schedule C and as a partner in a partnership are sources of SE income.

The tax base for the social security tax is limited. In tax year 2009, the first 106,800 of wages and self-employment income is subject to the social security tax. The tax base for the Medicare tax, on the other hand, is not limited. The social security tax and Medicare rates are:

	Rate (Percent)	Income Limit
Social security	12.40%	$106,800
Medicare	2.90	Unlimited
Total SE	15.30%[66]	

The total SE rate is multiplied by 92.35% of SE income. The self-employed taxpayer receives a *for* AGI deduction for one-half of the SE tax paid (see Chapter 4).

EXAMPLE 6-35

In 2009 Linda is employed at a local bank and has wages of $110,000. She also has a Schedule C business of selling jewelry at night and on the weekends. Linda has net income from the Schedule C of $15,000. In this case, Linda owes zero additional social security tax because she is over the $106,800 limit for 2009. She would have to pay the Medicare tax on her Schedule C income:

$$\$15,000 \times .9235 \times 2.9\% = \$402$$

Linda paid social security tax and Medicare tax on the first $106,800 through withholding from her paycheck at the bank.

EXAMPLE 6-36

Suppose Linda's wages from the bank (see Example 6-35) were only $79,200. Linda would have to pay SE tax (both parts) on the additional $15,000 from her Schedule C business:

Social security $15,000 × 0.9235 × 12.40% =	$1,718
Medicare $15,000 × 0.9235 × 2.90%	=	402
Total SE tax		$2,120

The SE tax is reported on Schedule SE, which must accompany any Schedule C the taxpayer files. If a taxpayer has more than one Schedule C, only one Schedule SE is required. However, if the tax return is a joint return, each spouse is individually subject to the $106,800 limit and must file his or her own Schedule SE. Exhibit 6-7 illustrates a completed Schedule SE for Linda in Example 6-36.

[65] IRC § 1401.

[66] An employee pays only 7.65% because the employer pays the other half.

EXHIBIT 6-7

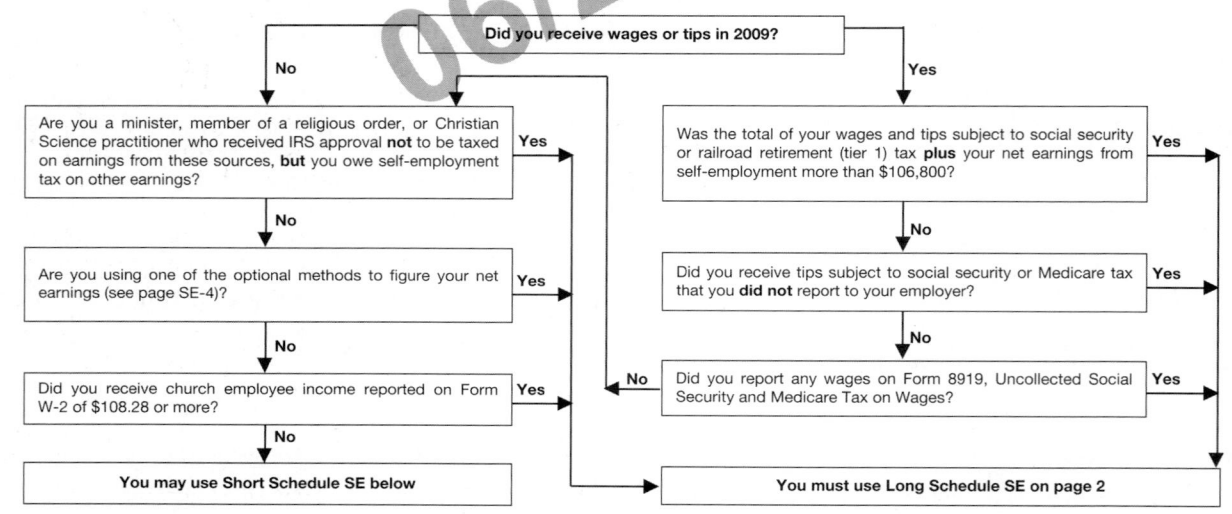

SCHEDULE SE (Form 1040)	Self-Employment Tax	OMB No. 1545-0074
Department of the Treasury Internal Revenue Service (99)	▶ Attach to Form 1040. ▶ See Instructions for Schedule SE (Form 1040).	20**09** Attachment Sequence No. **17**

Name of person with **self-employment** income (as shown on Form 1040) Linda Taxpayer	Social security number of person with **self-employment** income ▶ 123-45-6789

Who Must File Schedule SE

You must file Schedule SE if:

- You had net earnings from self-employment from **other than** church employee income (line 4 of Short Schedule SE or line 4c of Long Schedule SE) of $400 or more, **or**
- You had church employee income of $108.28 or more. Income from services you performed as a minister or a member of a religious order **is not** church employee income (see page SE-1).

Note. Even if you had a loss or a small amount of income from self-employment, it may be to your benefit to file Schedule SE and use either "optional method" in Part II of Long Schedule SE (see page SE-4).

Exception. If your only self-employment income was from earnings as a minister, member of a religious order, or Christian Science practitioner **and** you filed Form 4361 and received IRS approval not to be taxed on those earnings, **do not** file Schedule SE. Instead, write "Exempt—Form 4361" on Form 1040, line 56.

May I Use Short Schedule SE or Must I Use Long Schedule SE?

Note. Use this flowchart **only if** you must file Schedule SE. If unsure, see *Who Must File Schedule SE,* above.

Section A—Short Schedule SE. Caution. Read above to see if you can use Short Schedule SE.

1a	Net farm profit or (loss) from Schedule F, line 36, and farm partnerships, Schedule K-1 (Form 1065), box 14, code A	**1a**	
b	If you received social security retirement or disability benefits, enter the amount of Conservation Reserve Program payments included on Schedule F, line 6b, or listed on Schedule K-1 (Form 1065), box 20, code X	**1b** (	)
2	Net profit or (loss) from Schedule C, line 31; Schedule C-EZ, line 3; Schedule K-1 (Form 1065), box 14, code A (other than farming); and Schedule K-1 (Form 1065-B), box 9, code J1. Ministers and members of religious orders, see page SE-1 for types of income to report on this line. See page SE-3 for other income to report	**2**	15,000
3	Combine lines 1a, 1b, and 2	**3**	15,000
4	**Net earnings from self-employment.** Multiply line 3 by 92.35% (.9235). If less than $400, **do not** file this schedule; you do not owe self-employment tax . . . . ▶	**4**	13,853
5	**Self-employment tax.** If the amount on line 4 is: • $106,800 or less, multiply line 4 by 15.3% (.153). Enter the result here and on **Form 1040, line 56.** • More than $106,800, multiply line 4 by 2.9% (.029). Then, add $13,243.20 to the result. Enter the total here and on **Form 1040, line 56.**	**5**	2,120
6	**Deduction for one-half of self-employment tax.** Multiply line 5 by 50% (.50). Enter the result here and on **Form 1040, line 27** **6** | 1,060		

For Paperwork Reduction Act Notice, see Form 1040 instructions.   Cat. No. 11358Z   Schedule SE (Form 1040) 2009

From Shoebox to Software

Schedule C Business Comprehensive Example

Alan Masters (see Example 6-20) left his job and opened his own independent insurance agency on July 1, 2009. His business produces the following income and expenses during the year:

Gross Receipts from Three Insurance Companies

1099-MISC received:	
XYZ Insurance	$22,000
All Country Insurance	21,550
State Wide Insurance	14,830
Total revenue	58,380
Advertising	(1,250)
Postage	(1,500)
Wages	(7,000)
Payroll taxes	(535)
License fee	(125)
Supplies	(2,300)
Continuing professional education (registration)	(975)
Travel to CPE course	
Plane	385
Taxi	25
Lodging $89/night × 2 nights	178
Meals per diem $39 × 2 days	78
Business asset depreciation (see Example 6-20)	(27,299)
Cell phone	(588)
Internet service	(780)

Alan does not elect to use §179 expenses but does use the 50% bonus.

Go to the Schedule C for Alan Masters created earlier.

Open a Form 1099-MISC and enter the amounts from the three Forms 1099-MISC. The total income should equal $58,380.

Enter the expenses directly on Schedule C. If there is not a listed line item, enter the expenses on the Other Expenses section on page 2 of Schedule C.

When you combine numbers on a line, include information about the items combined on the "line item detail" using tax software (for example, combine the payroll tax and license fee on line 23).

Exhibit 6-8, Exhibit 6-9, and Exhibit 6-10 show the completed Schedule C, Form 4562, and Schedule SE, respectively. Form 4562 is the same as shown with Example 6-20. Note that travel expenses are on Schedule C as the total of the plane, taxi, and lodging. Also note that Alan had wages greater than the SE tax limit of $106,800 in 2009 (see Chapter 5). The taxes and licenses amount on line 23 is the total of the payroll tax and the license fee. It is good practice to clearly note in your working papers when you combine two or more numbers. If you do that, not only will your working papers tie directly to the tax return, but you will also be able to see what you did when you work on the tax return in a subsequent year.

TAX YOUR BRAIN

Why would employers prefer not to treat individuals working for them as employees?

ANSWER

If an individual is not an employee, the *payer* does not have to pay the *employer's* share of FICA taxes or withhold income taxes. In essence, the worker is treated as self-employed and must pay SE tax (both shares). Many less-than-ethical employers treat part-time employees as self-employed. The part-time employee enjoys the classification at first because the paycheck is larger (no income tax or FICA is withheld). However, when the employee files his or her tax return the following spring, he or she must pay income tax and SE tax. Sometimes the money is not available then. The individual could also be subject to underpayment penalties.

CONCEPT CHECK 6-12—LO 7

1. Kia had $43,000 of income from a self-employed consulting practice and had no other income during the year. What is Kia's total self-employment tax?

2. Assume the same facts as in Question 1. In addition to her $43,000 in self-employment income, Kia received a W-2 from her employer (different from her self-employed business) with $107,000 in wages. What is Kia's self-employment tax in this situation?

3. Assume the same facts as in Question 2. In addition to her $43,000 in self-employment income, Kia received a W-2 from her employer (different from her self-employed business) with $85,000 in W-2 wages. What is Kia's self-employment tax in this situation?

EXHIBIT 6-8

SCHEDULE C (Form 1040) Department of the Treasury Internal Revenue Service (99)	**Profit or Loss From Business** (Sole Proprietorship) ▶ **Partnerships, joint ventures, etc., generally must file Form 1065 or 1065-B.** ▶ **Attach to Form 1040, 1040NR, or 1041.** ▶ **See Instructions for Schedule C (Form 1040).**	OMB No. 1545-0074 2009 Attachment Sequence No. 09

Name of proprietor Alan Masters		Social security number (SSN) 444-44-4444

A	Principal business or profession, including product or service (see page C-3 of the instructions) Insurance		**B** Enter code from pages C-9, 10, & 11 ▶ 5 2 4 2 1 0
C	Business name. If no separate business name, leave blank.		**D** Employer ID number (EIN), if any
E	Business address (including suite or room no.) ▶ City, town or post office, state, and ZIP code		
F	Accounting method: (1) ☒ Cash (2) ☐ Accrual (3) ☐ Other (specify) ▶		
G	Did you "materially participate" in the operation of this business during 2009? If "No," see page C-4 for limit on losses		☒ Yes ☐ No
H	If you started or acquired this business during 2009, check here . . . . ▶		☒

Part I **Income**

1	Gross receipts or sales. **Caution.** See page C-4 and check the box if: • This income was reported to you on Form W-2 and the "Statutory employee" box on that form was checked, or • You are a member of a qualified joint venture reporting only rental real estate income not subject to self-employment tax. Also see page C-4 for limit on losses. ▶ ☐	**1**	58,380
2	Returns and allowances	**2**	0
3	Subtract line 2 from line 1	**3**	58,380
4	Cost of goods sold (from line 42 on page 2)	**4**	0
5	**Gross profit.** Subtract line 4 from line 3	**5**	58,380
6	Other income, including federal and state gasoline or fuel tax credit or refund (see page C-4) . . .	**6**	0
7	**Gross income.** Add lines 5 and 6 . . . . ▶	**7**	58,380

Part II **Expenses.** Enter expenses for business use of your home **only** on line 30.

8	Advertising	**8**	1,250	18	Office expense	**18**		
9	Car and truck expenses (see page C-5)	**9**		19	Pension and profit-sharing plans .	**19**		
10	Commissions and fees .	**10**		20	Rent or lease (see page C-6):			
11	Contract labor (see page C-5)	**11**		a	Vehicles, machinery, and equipment	**20a**		
12	Depletion	**12**		b	Other business property . . .	**20b**		
13	Depreciation and section 179 expense deduction (not included in Part III) (see page C-5)	**13**	27,299	21	Repairs and maintenance . . .	**21**		
				22	Supplies (not included in Part III) .	**22**	2,300	
				23	Taxes and licenses	**23**	660	
				24	Travel, meals, and entertainment:			
				a	Travel	**24a**	588	
14	Employee benefit programs (other than on line 19) . .	**14**		b	Deductible meals and entertainment (see page C-7) . .	**24b**	39	
15	Insurance (other than health)	**15**		25	Utilities	**25**		
16	Interest:			26	Wages (less employment credits) .	**26**	7,000	
a	Mortgage (paid to banks, etc.)	**16a**		27	Other expenses (from line 48 on page 2)	**27**	2,343	
b	Other	**16b**						
17	Legal and professional services	**17**						

28	**Total expenses** before expenses for business use of home. Add lines 8 through 27 . . . . . ▶	**28**	42,979
29	Tentative profit or (loss). Subtract line 28 from line 7	**29**	15,401
30	Expenses for business use of your home. Attach **Form 8829**	**30**	
31	**Net profit or (loss).** Subtract line 30 from line 29. • If a profit, enter on both **Form 1040, line 12,** and **Schedule SE, line 2,** or on **Form 1040NR, line 13** (if you checked the box on line 1, see page C-7). Estates and trusts, enter on **Form 1041, line 3.** • If a loss, you **must** go to line 32.	**31**	15,401
32	If you have a loss, check the box that describes your investment in this activity (see page C-8). • If you checked 32a, enter the loss on both **Form 1040, line 12,** and **Schedule SE, line 2,** or on **Form 1040NR, line 13** (if you checked the box on line 1, see the line 31 instructions on page C-7). Estates and trusts, enter on **Form 1041, line 3.** • If you checked 32b, you **must** attach **Form 6198.** Your loss may be limited.	**32a** ☒ All investment is at risk. **32b** ☐ Some investment is not at risk.	

For Paperwork Reduction Act Notice, see page C-9 of the instructions.	Cat. No. 11334P	Schedule C (Form 1040) 2009

EXHIBIT 6-8   *(concluded)*

Schedule C (Form 1040) 2009   Page **2**

Part III   **Cost of Goods Sold** (see page C-8)

33   Method(s) used to
value closing inventory: **a** ☐ Cost   **b** ☐ Lower of cost or market   **c** ☐ Other (attach explanation)

34   Was there any change in determining quantities, costs, or valuations between opening and closing inventory?
If "Yes," attach explanation . . . .   ☐ **Yes**   ☐ **No**

35 Inventory at beginning of year. If different from last year's closing inventory, attach explanation . . .	**35**	
36 Purchases less cost of items withdrawn for personal use	**36**	
37 Cost of labor. Do not include any amounts paid to yourself	**37**	
38 Materials and supplies	**38**	
39 Other costs	**39**	
40 Add lines 35 through 39	**40**	
41 Inventory at end of year	**41**	
42 **Cost of goods sold.** Subtract line 41 from line 40. Enter the result here and on page 1, line 4 . . .	**42**	

Part IV   **Information on Your Vehicle.** Complete this part **only** if you are claiming car or truck expenses on line 9 and are not required to file Form 4562 for this business. See the instructions for line 13 on page C-5 to find out if you must file Form 4562.

43   When did you place your vehicle in service for business purposes? (month, day, year)   ▶ _____/_____/_____

44   Of the total number of miles you drove your vehicle during 2009, enter the number of miles you used your vehicle for:

a Business _____   **b** Commuting (see instructions) _____   **c** Other _____

45   Was your vehicle available for personal use during off-duty hours? . . . .   ☐ **Yes**   ☐ **No**

46   Do you (or your spouse) have another vehicle available for personal use?. . . . .   ☐ **Yes**   ☐ **No**

47a Do you have evidence to support your deduction? . . . .   ☐ **Yes**   ☐ **No**

b   If "Yes," is the evidence written? . . . .   ☐ **Yes**   ☐ **No**

Part V   **Other Expenses.** List below business expenses not included on lines 8–26 or line 30.

Continuing Education	975
Cell Phone	588
Internet	780
48 **Total other expenses.** Enter here and on page 1, line 27 . . . . **48**	2,343

Schedule C (Form 1040) 2009

EXHIBIT 6-9

Form 4562

Department of the Treasury
Internal Revenue Service (99)

Depreciation and Amortization
(Including Information on Listed Property)

▶ See separate instructions.   ▶ Attach to your tax return.

OMB No. 1545-0172

2009

Attachment Sequence No. **67**

Name(s) shown on return: Alan Masters

Business or activity to which this form relates: Insurance

Identifying number: 444-44-4444

Part I   Election To Expense Certain Property Under Section 179
Note: *If you have any listed property, complete Part V before you complete Part I.*

1	Maximum amount. See the instructions for a higher limit for certain businesses	**1** $250,000
2	Total cost of section 179 property placed in service (see instructions)	**2**
3	Threshold cost of section 179 property before reduction in limitation (see instructions)	**3** $800,000
4	Reduction in limitation. Subtract line 3 from line 2. If zero or less, enter -0-	**4**
5	Dollar limitation for tax year. Subtract line 4 from line 1. If zero or less, enter -0-. If married filing separately, see instructions	**5**

6	(a) Description of property	(b) Cost (business use only)	(c) Elected cost

7	Listed property. Enter the amount from line 29 **7**	
8	Total elected cost of section 179 property. Add amounts in column (c), lines 6 and 7	**8**
9	Tentative deduction. Enter the **smaller** of line 5 or line 8	**9**
10	Carryover of disallowed deduction from line 13 of your 2008 Form 4562	**10**
11	Business income limitation. Enter the smaller of business income (not less than zero) or line 5 (see instructions)	**11**
12	Section 179 expense deduction. Add lines 9 and 10, but do not enter more than line 11	**12**
13	Carryover of disallowed deduction to 2010. Add lines 9 and 10, less line 12 ▶ **13**	

Note: *Do not use Part II or Part III below for listed property. Instead, use Part V.*

Part II   Special Depreciation Allowance and Other Depreciation (Do not include listed property.) (See instructions.)

14	Special depreciation allowance for qualified property (other than listed property) placed in service during the tax year (see instructions)	**14** 13,900
15	Property subject to section 168(f)(1) election	**15**
16	Other depreciation (including ACRS)	**16**

Part III   MACRS Depreciation (Do not include listed property.) (See instructions.)

Section A

17	MACRS deductions for assets placed in service in tax years beginning before 2009	**17**
18	If you are electing to group any assets placed in service during the tax year into one or more general asset accounts, check here ▶ ☐	

Section B—Assets Placed in Service During 2009 Tax Year Using the General Depreciation System

(a) Classification of property	(b) Month and year placed in service	(c) Basis for depreciation (business/investment use only—see instructions)	(d) Recovery period	(e) Convention	(f) Method	(g) Depreciation deduction
19a 3-year property						
b 5-year property		2,400	5 yrs	HY	DDB	480
c 7-year property		11,500	7 yrs	HY	DDB	1,643
d 10-year property						
e 15-year property						
f 20-year property						
g 25-year property			25 yrs.		S/L	
h Residential rental property			27.5 yrs.	MM	S/L	
			27.5 yrs.	MM	S/L	
i Nonresidential real property	07/09	120,000	39 yrs.	MM	S/L	1,412
				MM	S/L	

Section C—Assets Placed in Service During 2009 Tax Year Using the Alternative Depreciation System

20a Class life					S/L	
b 12-year			12 yrs.		S/L	
c 40-year			40 yrs.	MM	S/L	

Part IV   Summary (See instructions.)

21	Listed property. Enter amount from line 28	**21** 9,864
22	**Total.** Add amounts from line 12, lines 14 through 17, lines 19 and 20 in column (g), and line 21. Enter here and on the appropriate lines of your return. Partnerships and S corporations—see instructions	**22** 27,299
23	For assets shown above and placed in service during the current year, enter the portion of the basis attributable to section 263A costs **23**	

For Paperwork Reduction Act Notice, see separate instructions.   Cat. No. 12906N   Form **4562** (2009)

EXHIBIT 6-9   *(concluded)*

Form 4562 (2009)   Page **2**

Part V   **Listed Property**   (Include automobiles, certain other vehicles, cellular telephones, certain computers, and property used for entertainment, recreation, or amusement.)

Note: *For any vehicle for which you are using the standard mileage rate or deducting lease expense, complete only 24a, 24b, columns (a) through (c) of Section A, all of Section B, and Section C if applicable.*

Section A—Depreciation and Other Information (Caution: *See the instructions for limits for passenger automobiles.***)**

24a Do you have evidence to support the business/investment use claimed? ☒ **Yes** ☐ **No** **24b** If "Yes," is the evidence written? ☒ **Yes** ☐ **No**

(a) Type of property (list vehicles first)	(b) Date placed in service	(c) Business/ investment use percentage	(d) Cost or other basis	(e) Basis for depreciation (business/investment use only)	(f) Recovery period	(g) Method/ Convention	(h) Depreciation deduction	(i) Elected section 179 cost
25 Special depreciation allowance for qualified listed property placed in service during the tax year and used more than 50% in a qualified business use (see instructions) . . .					**25**		9,864	
26 Property used more than 50% in a qualified business use:								
Auto	7/15/09	90 %	22,000	9,936	5 yr	DDB		
		%						
		%						
27 Property used 50% or less in a qualified business use:								
		%				S/L –		
		%				S/L –		
		%				S/L –		

28 Add amounts in column (h), lines 25 through 27. Enter here and on line 21, page 1 . . . **28** 9,864

29 Add amounts in column (i), line 26. Enter here and on line 7, page 1 . . . . **29**

Section B—Information on Use of Vehicles

Complete this section for vehicles used by a sole proprietor, partner, or other "more than 5% owner," or related person. If you provided vehicles to your employees, first answer the questions in Section C to see if you meet an exception to completing this section for those vehicles.

		(a) Vehicle 1		(b) Vehicle 2		(c) Vehicle 3		(d) Vehicle 4		(e) Vehicle 5		(f) Vehicle 6	
30	Total business/investment miles driven during the year (**do not** include commuting miles)	9,000											
31	Total commuting miles driven during the year	0											
32	Total other personal (noncommuting) miles driven	1,000											
33	Total miles driven during the year. Add lines 30 through 32	10,000											
34	Was the vehicle available for personal use during off-duty hours?	Yes	No	Yes	No	Yes	No	Yes	No	Yes	No	Yes	No
		X											
35	Was the vehicle used primarily by a more than 5% owner or related person?	X											
36	Is another vehicle available for personal use?	X											

Section C—Questions for Employers Who Provide Vehicles for Use by Their Employees

Answer these questions to determine if you meet an exception to completing Section B for vehicles used by employees who **are not** more than 5% owners or related persons (see instructions).

		Yes	No
37	Do you maintain a written policy statement that prohibits all personal use of vehicles, including commuting, by your employees?		
38	Do you maintain a written policy statement that prohibits personal use of vehicles, except commuting, by your employees? See the instructions for vehicles used by corporate officers, directors, or 1% or more owners . . .		
39	Do you treat all use of vehicles by employees as personal use?		
40	Do you provide more than five vehicles to your employees, obtain information from your employees about the use of the vehicles, and retain the information received?		
41	Do you meet the requirements concerning qualified automobile demonstration use? (See instructions.) . .		

Note: *If your answer to 37, 38, 39, 40, or 41 is "Yes," do not complete Section B for the covered vehicles.*

Part VI   **Amortization**

(a) Description of costs	(b) Date amortization begins	(c) Amortizable amount	(d) Code section	(e) Amortization period or percentage	(f) Amortization for this year
42 Amortization of costs that begins during your 2009 tax year (see instructions):					

43 Amortization of costs that began before your 2009 tax year **43**

44 Total. Add amounts in column (f). See the instructions for where to report **44**

Form **4562** (2009)

EXHIBIT 6-10

Schedule SE (Form 1040) 2009   Attachment Sequence No. **17**   Page **2**

Name of person with **self-employment** income (as shown on Form 1040) Alan Masters	Social security number of person with **self-employment** income ▶ 444-44-4444

Section B—Long Schedule SE

Part I   Self-Employment Tax

Note. If your only income subject to self-employment tax is **church employee income,** skip lines 1 through 4b. Enter -0- on line 4c and go to line 5a. Income from services you performed as a minister or a member of a religious order **is not** church employee income. See page SE-1.

A   If you are a minister, member of a religious order, or Christian Science practitioner **and** you filed Form 4361, but you had $400 or more of **other** net earnings from self-employment, check here and continue with Part I . . . . ▶ ☐

1a	Net farm profit or (loss) from Schedule F, line 36, and farm partnerships, Schedule K-1 (Form 1065), box 14, code A. **Note.** Skip lines 1a and 1b if you use the farm optional method (see page SE-4)	**1a**		
b	If you received social security retirement or disability benefits, enter the amount of Conservation Reserve Program payments included on Schedule F, line 6b, or listed on Schedule K-1 (Form 1065), box 20, code X	**1b**		
2	Net profit or (loss) from Schedule C, line 31; Schedule C-EZ, line 3; Schedule K-1 (Form 1065), box 14, code A (other than farming); and Schedule K-1 (Form 1065-B), box 9, code J1. Ministers and members of religious orders, see page SE-1 for types of income to report on this line. See page SE-3 for other income to report. **Note.** Skip this line if you use the nonfarm optional method (see page SE-4)	**2**	15,401	
3	Combine lines 1a, 1b, and 2	**3**	15,401	
4a	If line 3 is more than zero, multiply line 3 by 92.35% (.9235). Otherwise, enter amount from line 3	**4a**	14,223	
b	If you elect one or both of the optional methods, enter the total of lines 15 and 17 here . .	**4b**		
c	Combine lines 4a and 4b. If less than $400, **stop**; you do not owe self-employment tax. **Exception.** If less than $400 and you had **church employee income,** enter -0- and continue ▶	**4c**	14,223	
5a	Enter your **church employee income** from Form W-2. See page SE-1 for definition of church employee income . . . . . [**5a**]			
b	Multiply line 5a by 92.35% (.9235). If less than $100, enter -0-	**5b**	0	
6	**Net earnings from self-employment.** Add lines 4c and 5b	**6**	14,223	
7	Maximum amount of combined wages and self-employment earnings subject to social security tax or the 6.2% portion of the 7.65% railroad retirement (tier 1) tax for 2009	**7**	*106,800*	*00*
8a	Total social security wages and tips (total of boxes 3 and 7 on Form(s) W-2) and railroad retirement (tier 1) compensation. If $106,800 or more, skip lines 8b through 10, and go to line 11 [**8a** 106,800]			
b	Unreported tips subject to social security tax (from Form 4137, line 10) [**8b**]			
c	Wages subject to social security tax (from Form 8919, line 10) [**8c**]			
d	Add lines 8a, 8b, and 8c	**8d**	106,800	
9	Subtract line 8d from line 7. If zero or less, enter -0- here and on line 10 and go to line 11 ▶	**9**	0	
10	Multiply the **smaller** of line 6 or line 9 by 12.4% (.124)	**10**	0	
11	Multiply line 6 by 2.9% (.029)	**11**	412	
12	**Self-employment tax.** Add lines 10 and 11. Enter here and on **Form 1040, line 56.** . . .	**12**	412	
13	**Deduction for one-half of self-employment tax.** Multiply line 12 by 50% (.50). Enter the result here and on **Form 1040, line 27** . [**13**]			

Part II   Optional Methods To Figure Net Earnings   (see page SE-4)

Farm Optional Method. You may use this method **only** if (a) your gross farm income[1] was not more than $6,540, **or** (b) your net farm profits[2] were less than $4,721.

14	Maximum income for optional methods	**14**	*4,360*	*00*
15	Enter the **smaller** of: two-thirds (2/3) of gross farm income[1] (not less than zero) **or** $4,360. Also include this amount on line 4b above	**15**		

Nonfarm Optional Method. You may use this method **only** if (a) your net nonfarm profits[3] were less than $4,721 and also less than 72.189% of your gross nonfarm income,[4] **and** (b) you had net earnings from self-employment of at least $400 in 2 of the prior 3 years. **Caution.** You may use this method no more than five times.

16	Subtract line 15 from line 14	**16**		
17	Enter the **smaller** of: two-thirds (2/3) of gross nonfarm income[4] (not less than zero) **or** the amount on line 16. Also include this amount on line 4b above	**17**		

[1] From Sch. F, line 11, and Sch. K-1 (Form 1065), box 14, code B.

[2] From Sch. F, line 36, and Sch. K-1 (Form 1065), box 14, code A—minus the amount you would have entered on line 1b had you not used the optional method.

[3] From Sch. C, line 31; Sch. C-EZ, line 3; Sch. K-1 (Form 1065), box 14, code A; and Sch. K-1 (Form 1065-B), box 9, code J1.

[4] From Sch. C, line 7; Sch. C-EZ, line 1; Sch. K-1 (Form 1065), box 14, code C; and Sch. K-1 (Form 1065-B), box 9, code J2.

Schedule SE (Form 1040) 2009

Summary

LO 1: Describe how income and expenses from a self-employed individual are recognized and reported.	<ul><li>Reported on Schedule C.</li><li>Usually reported on 1099-MISC.</li><li>Usually reported on the cash basis except for inventory, which is reported on the accrual basis.</li></ul>
LO 2: Explain the concept of ordinary and necessary business expenses.	<ul><li>Expenses must be ordinary, necessary, and reasonable.<ul><li>Ordinary—customary or usual.</li><li>Necessary—appropriate and helpful.</li><li>Reasonable—amount and relation to business.</li></ul></li><li>Illegal payments, lobbying, or payments for fines and penalties not allowed.</li></ul>
LO 3: Explain the calculation of depreciation for trade or business assets.	<ul><li>Basis—typically the cost of the asset.</li><li>Periods—3, 5, 7 years for personal property; 27.5 and 39 years for real property.</li><li>Conventions—half-year, mid-quarter, mid-month conventions.</li><li>Methods—200% declining balance (DB), 150% DB, and straight line.</li><li>§179 expense up to $250,000 in 2009.</li><li>Luxury autos limited to $10,960 in 2009.</li></ul>
LO 4: Describe travel and entertainment expenses and discuss their deductibility.	<ul><li>Transportation deductible unless for commuting.</li><li>Standard mileage rate 55 cents per mile for 2009.</li><li>Travel—overnight stay for business purposes, meals included.</li><li>Meals and entertainment limited to 50%.</li></ul>
LO 5: Apply the rules for deducting the business portion of a residence and business bad debts.	<ul><li>Portion of the home must be used exclusively and regularly in the trade or business.</li><li>Direct expenses 100% deductible.</li><li>Indirect expenses deductible in relation to business ratio.</li><li>Deductions limited to the gross income from the business.</li><li>Business bad debts create an ordinary deduction.</li></ul>
LO 6: Explain the hobby loss rules and the limits on education expense deductibility.	<ul><li>Hobby—primarily for personal pleasure.</li><li>Not a hobby if a profit is shown for 3 of the last 5 years.</li><li>No net loss allowed from the hobby.</li><li>Education expenses deductible if the education maintains or improves skills.</li></ul>
LO 7: Describe the calculation of self-employment taxes.	<ul><li>Reported on Schedule SE.</li><li>Social security 12.40%.</li><li>Medicare 2.9%.</li><li>Social security limit $106,800 in 2009.</li></ul>

Appendix

General Depreciation System

TABLE 6A-1
General Depreciation
System 200% or 150%
Declining Balance
Switching to Straight-
Line*

Recovery Year	Half-Year Convention					
	3-Year	5-Year	7-Year	10-Year	15-Year	20-Year
1	33.33	20.00	14.29	10.00	5.00	3.750
2	44.45	32.00	24.49	18.00	9.50	7.219
3	14.81	19.20	17.49	14.40	8.55	6.677
4	7.41	11.52	12.49	11.52	7.70	6.177
5		11.52	8.93	9.22	6.93	5.713
6		5.76	8.92	7.37	6.23	5.285
7			8.93	6.55	5.90	4.888
8			4.46	6.55	5.90	4.522
9				6.56	5.91	4.462
10				6.55	5.90	4.461
11				3.28	5.91	4.462
12					5.90	4.461
13					5.91	4.462
14					5.90	4.461
15					5.91	4.462
16					2.95	4.461
17						4.462
18						4.461
19						4.462
20						4.461
21						2.231

* May not be used for farm business property generally placed in service after 1988. See Table 14, Rev. Proc. 87-57.

TABLE 6A-2
General Depreciation
System 200% or 150%
Declining Balance
Switching to Straight-
Line*

Recovery Year	Mid-Quarter Convention (Property Placed in Service in 1st Quarter)					
	3-Year	5-Year	7-Year	10-Year	15-Year	20-Year
1	58.33	35.00	25.00	19.50	8.75	6.563
2	27.78	26.00	21.43	16.50	9.13	7.000
3	12.35	15.60	15.31	13.20	8.21	6.482
4	1.54	11.01	10.93	10.56	7.39	5.996
5		11.01	8.75	8.45	6.65	5.546
6		1.38	8.74	6.76	5.99	5.130
7			8.75	6.55	5.90	4.746
8			1.09	6.55	5.91	4.459
9				6.56	5.90	4.459
10				6.55	5.91	4.459
11				0.82	5.90	4.459
12					5.91	4.460
13					5.90	4.459
14					5.91	4.460
15					5.90	4.459
16					0.74	4.460
17						4.459
18						4.460
19						4.459
20						4.460
21						0.557

* May not be used for farm business property generally placed in service after 1988. See Table 15, Rev. Proc. 87-57.

TABLE 6A-3
General Depreciation
System 200% or 150%
Declining Balance
Switching to Straight-
Line*

Mid-Quarter Convention (Property Placed in Service in 2nd Quarter)						
Recovery Year	3-Year	5-Year	7-Year	10-Year	15-Year	20-Year
1	41.67	25.00	17.85	12.50	6.25	4.688
2	38.89	30.00	23.47	17.50	9.38	7.148
3	14.14	18.00	16.76	14.00	8.44	6.612
4	5.30	11.37	11.97	11.20	7.59	6.116
5		11.37	8.87	8.96	6.83	5.658
6		4.26	8.87	7.17	6.15	5.233
7			8.87	6.55	5.91	4.841
8			3.33	6.55	5.90	4.478
9				6.56	5.91	4.463
10				6.55	5.90	4.463
11				2.46	5.91	4.463
12					5.90	4.463
13					5.91	4.463
14					5.90	4.463
15					5.91	4.462
16					2.21	4.463
17						4.462
18						4.463
19						4.462
20						4.463
21						1.673

* May not be used for farm business property generally placed in service after 1988. See Table 16, Rev. Proc. 87-57.

TABLE 6A-4
General Depreciation
System 200% or 150%
Declining Balance
Switching to Straight-
Line*

Mid-Quarter Convention (Property Placed in Service in 3rd Quarter)						
Recovery Year	3-Year	5-Year	7-Year	10-Year	15-Year	20-Year
1	25.00	15.00	10.71	7.50	3.75	2.813
2	50.00	34.00	25.51	18.50	9.63	7.289
3	16.67	20.40	18.22	14.80	8.66	6.742
4	16.67	12.24	13.02	11.84	7.80	6.237
5	8.33	11.30	9.30	9.47	7.02	5.769
6		7.06	8.85	7.58	6.31	5.336
7			8.86	6.55	5.90	4.936
8			5.53	6.55	5.90	4.566
9				6.56	5.91	4.460
10				6.55	5.90	4.460
11				4.10	5.91	4.460
12					5.90	4.460
13					5.91	4.461
14					5.90	4.460
15					5.91	4.461
16					3.69	4.460
17						4.461
18						4.460
19						4.461
20						4.460
21						2.788

* May not be used for farm business property generally placed in service after 1988. See Table 17, Rev. Proc. 8.

TABLE 6A-5
General Depreciation
System 200% or 150%
Declining Balance
Switching to Straight-
Line*

	Mid-Quarter Convention (Property Placed in Service in 4th Quarter)					
Recovery Year	3-Year	5-Year	7-Year	10-Year	15-Year	20-Year
1	8.33	5.00	3.57	2.50	1.25	0.938
2	61.11	38.00	27.55	19.50	9.88	7.430
3	20.37	22.80	19.68	15.60	8.89	6.872
4	10.19	13.68	14.06	12.48	8.00	6.357
5		10.94	10.04	9.98	7.20	5.880
6		9.58	8.73	7.99	6.48	5.439
7			8.73	6.55	5.90	5.031
8			7.64	6.55	5.90	4.654
9				6.56	5.90	4.458
10				6.55	5.91	4.458
11				5.74	5.90	4.458
12					5.91	4.458
13					5.90	4.458
14					5.91	4.458
15					5.90	4.458
16					5.17	4.458
17						4.458
18						4.459
19						4.458
20						4.459
21						3.901

* May not be used for farm business property generally placed in service after 1988. See Table 18, Rev. Proc. 87-57.

TABLE 6A-6   General Depreciation System Straight-Line Applicable Recovery Period: 27.5 Years Mid-Month Convention

Recovery Year	Month in the First Recovery Year the Property Is Placed in Service											
	1	**2**	**3**	**4**	**5**	**6**	**7**	**8**	**9**	**10**	**11**	**12**
1	3.485	3.182	2.879	2.576	2.273	1.970	1.667	1.364	1.061	0.758	0.450	0.152
2	3.636	3.636	3.636	3.636	3.636	3.636	3.636	3.636	3.636	3.636	3.630	3.636
3	3.636	3.636	3.636	3.636	3.636	3.636	3.636	3.636	3.636	3.636	3.630	3.636
4	3.636	3.636	3.636	3.636	3.636	3.636	3.636	3.636	3.636	3.636	3.630	3.636
5	3.636	3.636	3.636	3.636	3.636	3.636	3.636	3.636	3.636	3.636	3.630	3.636
6	3.636	3.636	3.636	3.636	3.636	3.636	3.636	3.636	3.636	3.636	3.630	3.636
7	3.636	3.636	3.636	3.636	3.636	3.636	3.636	3.636	3.636	3.636	3.630	3.636
8	3.636	3.636	3.636	3.636	3.636	3.636	3.636	3.636	3.636	3.636	3.630	3.636
9	3.636	3.636	3.636	3.636	3.636	3.636	3.636	3.636	3.636	3.636	3.630	3.636
10	3.637	3.637	3.637	3.637	3.637	3.637	3.636	3.636	3.636	3.636	3.630	3.636
11	3.636	3.636	3.636	3.636	3.636	3.636	3.637	3.637	3.637	3.637	3.630	3.637
12	3.637	3.637	3.637	3.637	3.637	3.637	3.636	3.636	3.636	3.636	3.630	3.636
13	3.636	3.636	3.636	3.636	3.636	3.636	3.637	3.637	3.637	3.637	3.630	3.637
14	3.637	3.637	3.637	3.637	3.637	3.637	3.636	3.636	3.636	3.636	3.630	3.636
15	3.636	3.636	3.636	3.636	3.636	3.636	3.637	3.637	3.637	3.637	3.630	3.637
16	3.637	3.637	3.637	3.637	3.637	3.637	3.636	3.636	3.636	3.636	3.630	3.636
17	3.636	3.636	3.636	3.636	3.636	3.636	3.637	3.637	3.637	3.637	3.630	3.637
18	3.637	3.637	3.637	3.637	3.637	3.637	3.636	3.636	3.636	3.636	3.630	3.636
19	3.636	3.636	3.636	3.636	3.636	3.636	3.637	3.637	3.637	3.637	3.630	3.637
20	3.637	3.637	3.637	3.637	3.637	3.637	3.636	3.636	3.636	3.636	3.630	3.636
21	3.636	3.636	3.636	3.636	3.636	3.636	3.637	3.637	3.637	3.637	3.630	3.637
22	3.637	3.637	3.637	3.637	3.637	3.637	3.636	3.636	3.636	3.636	3.630	3.636
23	3.636	3.636	3.636	3.636	3.636	3.636	3.637	3.637	3.637	3.637	3.630	3.637
24	3.637	3.637	3.637	3.637	3.637	3.637	3.636	3.636	3.636	3.636	3.630	3.636
25	3.636	3.636	3.636	3.636	3.636	3.636	3.637	3.637	3.637	3.637	3.630	3.637
26	3.637	3.637	3.637	3.637	3.637	3.637	3.636	3.636	3.636	3.636	3.630	3.636
27	3.636	3.636	3.636	3.636	3.636	3.636	3.637	3.637	3.637	3.637	3.630	3.637
28	1.970	2.273	2.576	2.879	3.182	3.485	3.636	3.636	3.636	3.636	3.630	3.636
29	0.000	0.000	0.000	0.000	0.000	0.000	0.152	0.455	0.758	1.061	1.360	1.667

TABLE 6A-7 General Depreciation System Straight-Line Applicable Recovery Period: 31.5 Years Mid-Month Convention

Recovery Year	Month in the First Recovery Year the Property Is Placed in Service											
	1	2	3	4	5	6	7	8	9	10	11	12
1	3.042	2.778	2.513	2.249	1.984	1.720	1.455	1.190	0.926	0.661	0.390	0.132
2	3.175	3.175	3.175	3.175	3.175	3.175	3.175	3.175	3.175	3.175	3.170	3.175
3	3.175	3.175	3.175	3.175	3.175	3.175	3.175	3.175	3.175	3.175	3.170	3.175
4	3.175	3.175	3.175	3.175	3.175	3.175	3.175	3.175	3.175	3.175	3.170	3.175
5	3.175	3.175	3.175	3.175	3.175	3.175	3.175	3.175	3.175	3.175	3.170	3.175
6	3.175	3.175	3.175	3.175	3.175	3.175	3.175	3.175	3.175	3.175	3.170	3.175
7	3.175	3.175	3.175	3.175	3.175	3.175	3.175	3.175	3.175	3.175	3.170	3.175
8	3.175	3.174	3.175	3.174	3.175	3.174	3.175	3.175	3.175	3.175	3.170	3.175
9	3.174	3.175	3.174	3.175	3.174	3.175	3.174	3.175	3.174	3.175	3.170	3.175
10	3.175	3.174	3.175	3.174	3.175	3.174	3.175	3.174	3.175	3.174	3.170	3.174
11	3.174	3.175	3.174	3.175	3.174	3.175	3.174	3.175	3.174	3.175	3.170	3.175
12	3.175	3.174	3.175	3.174	3.175	3.174	3.175	3.174	3.175	3.174	3.170	3.174
13	3.174	3.175	3.174	3.175	3.174	3.175	3.174	3.175	3.174	3.175	3.170	3.175
14	3.175	3.174	3.175	3.174	3.175	3.174	3.175	3.174	3.175	3.174	3.170	3.174
15	3.174	3.175	3.174	3.175	3.174	3.175	3.174	3.175	3.174	3.175	3.170	3.175
16	3.175	3.174	3.175	3.174	3.175	3.174	3.175	3.174	3.175	3.174	3.170	3.174
17	3.174	3.175	3.174	3.175	3.174	3.175	3.174	3.175	3.174	3.175	3.170	3.175
18	3.175	3.174	3.175	3.174	3.175	3.174	3.175	3.174	3.175	3.174	3.170	3.174
19	3.174	3.175	3.174	3.175	3.174	3.175	3.174	3.175	3.174	3.175	3.170	3.175
20	3.175	3.174	3.175	3.174	3.175	3.174	3.175	3.174	3.175	3.174	3.170	3.174
21	3.174	3.175	3.174	3.175	3.174	3.175	3.174	3.175	3.174	3.175	3.170	3.175
22	3.175	3.174	3.175	3.174	3.175	3.174	3.175	3.174	3.175	3.174	3.170	3.174
23	3.174	3.175	3.174	3.175	3.174	3.175	3.174	3.175	3.174	3.175	3.170	3.175
24	3.175	3.174	3.175	3.174	3.175	3.174	3.175	3.174	3.175	3.174	3.170	3.174
25	3.174	3.175	3.174	3.175	3.174	3.175	3.174	3.175	3.174	3.175	3.170	3.175
26	3.175	3.174	3.175	3.174	3.175	3.174	3.175	3.174	3.175	3.174	3.170	3.174
27	3.174	3.175	3.174	3.175	3.174	3.175	3.174	3.175	3.174	3.175	3.170	3.175
28	3.175	3.174	3.175	3.174	3.175	3.174	3.175	3.174	3.175	3.174	3.170	3.174
29	3.174	3.175	3.174	3.175	3.174	3.175	3.174	3.175	3.174	3.175	3.170	3.175
30	3.175	3.174	3.175	3.174	3.175	3.174	3.175	3.174	3.175	3.174	3.170	3.174
31	3.174	3.175	3.174	3.175	3.174	3.175	3.174	3.175	3.174	3.175	3.170	3.175
32	1.720	1.984	2.249	2.513	2.778	3.042	3.175	3.174	3.175	3.174	3.170	3.174
33	0.000	0.000	0.000	0.000	0.000	0.000	0.132	0.397	0.661	0.926	1.190	1.455

TABLE 6A-8 General Depreciation System Straight-Line Applicable Recovery Period: 39 Years Mid-Month Convention

Recovery Year	Month in the First Recovery Year the Property Is Placed in Service											
	1	2	3	4	5	6	7	8	9	10	11	12
1	2.461	2.247	2.033	1.819	1.605	1.391	1.177	.963	.749	.535	.32	.107
2–39	2.564	2.564	2.564	2.564	2.564	2.564	2.564	2.564	2.564	2.564	2.564	2.564
40	0.107	0.321	0.535	0.749	0.963	1.177	1.391	1.605	1.819	2.033	2.24	2.461

Discussion Questions

LO 1   1. Discuss the definition of *trade* or *business.* Why does it matter whether a taxpayer is classified as an employee or as self-employed?

_____

_____

_____

LO 2   2. Discuss the concepts of *ordinary, necessary,* and *reasonable* in relation to trade or business expenses.

_____

_____

_____

LO 3   3. On what form is depreciation reported, and how does it relate to other forms such as Schedules C, E, F, and Form 2106?

_____

_____

_____

LO 3   4. On what type of property is depreciation allowed?

_____

_____

_____

LO 3   5. Discuss the word *basis* in relation to the financial accounting term *book value.* What is meant by the term *adjusted basis*?

_____

_____

_____

LO 3   6. Discuss the difference between personal property and real property. Give examples of each.

_____

_____

_____

LO 3   7. What is a *depreciation convention?* What conventions are available under MACRS?

_____

_____

_____

LO 3   8. When calculating depreciation for personal property (assuming the half-year convention) using the IRS depreciation tables, does the taxpayer need to multiply the first year table depreciation percentage by one-half? What about in the year of disposal, assuming the property is disposed of prior to the end of its recovery period?

_____

_____

_____

LO 3   9. Discuss the concept of electing §179 expense. Does the election allow a larger expense deduction in the year of asset acquisition?

_____
_____
_____

LO 3 10. Discuss the concept of *listed property.*

_____
_____
_____

LO 4 11. Distinguish between travel and transportation expenses.

_____
_____
_____

LO 4 12. When can a taxpayer use the standard mileage rate? Is the standard mileage rate better than the actual auto costs?

_____
_____
_____

LO 4 13. Discuss the limits on meals and entertainment. Are meals and entertainment expenses always limited to 50%?

_____
_____
_____

LO 5 14. Discuss the limits on home office expense deductibility.

_____
_____
_____

LO 6 15. Why were the hobby loss rules established? What factors determine whether an activity is a trade or business or a hobby? Is any one factor controlling?

_____
_____
_____

LO 7 16. What are the two components of the self-employment tax? Is either component limited?

_____
_____
_____

Multiple-Choice Questions

LO 1 17. Trade or business expenses are treated as
a. A deduction *for* AGI.
b. An itemized deduction if not reimbursed.
c. A deduction *from* AGI.
d. A deduction *from* AGI limited to the amount in excess of 2% of AGI.

LO 1   18. Which of the following is *not* a "trade or business" expense?

      a. Interest on investment indebtedness.

      b. Property taxes on business equipment.

      c. Depreciation on business property.

      d. Cost of goods sold.

LO 1   19. Atlas, a financial consultant, had the following income and expenses in his business:

Fee income	$235,000
Expenses:	
Rent expense	18,000
Penalties assessed by the SEC	2,500
Office expenses	6,000
Supplies	6,000
Interest paid on note used to acquire office equipment	2,700
Speeding tickets going to see clients	650

How much net income must Atlas report from this business?

      a. $199,150.

      b. $202,300.

      c. $202,950.

      d. $205,450.

LO 2   20. Mandy, a CPA, flew from Raleigh to Seattle to attend an accounting conference that lasted four days. Then she took three days of vacation to go sightseeing. Mandy's expenses for the trip are as follows:

Airfare	$ 625
Lodging (7 days × $145)	1,015
Meals (7 days × $75)	525
Taxi from airport to hotel and back	70

Mandy's travel expense deduction is

      a. $1,425.

      b. $1,575.

      c. $1,973.

      d. $2,235.

LO 3   21. On May 5, 2004, Jill purchased equipment for $40,000 to be used in her business. She did not elect to expense the equipment under Section 179 or bonus depreciation. On January 1, 2009, she sells the equipment to a scrap metal dealer. What is the cost recovery deduction for 2008?

      a. $892.

      b. $1,784.

      c. $3,568.

      d. No deduction allowed.

LO 3   22. On April 15, 2007, Andy purchased some furniture and fixtures (7-year property) for $10,000 to be used in his business. He did not elect to expense the equipment under §179

or bonus depreciation. On June 30, 2009, he sells the equipment. What is the cost recovery deduction for 2009?

   a. $0.

   b. $875.

   c. $1,429.

   d. $1,749.

LO 3 23. Lawrence purchased an apartment building on February 10, 2009, for $330,000, $30,000 of which was for the land. What is the cost recovery deduction for 2009?

   a. $0.

   b. $6,741.

   c. $9,546.

   d. $10,660.

LO 3 24. Roy purchased an office building on March 30, 2006, for $250,000, $25,000 of which was for the land. On July 30, 2009, he sold the office building. What is the cost recovery deduction for 2009?

   a. $0.

   b. $3,125.

   c. $5,769.

   d. $6,410.

LO 3 25. On June 30, 2009, Ken purchased an apartment building for $500,000. Determine the cost recovery deduction for 2009:

   a. $4,925.

   b. $5,335.

   c. $6,955.

   d. $9,850.

LO 3 26. During the year, Cory purchased a log skidder (7-year property) for $55,000 for his business. Assume that he has income from his business of $30,000, and he and his wife have combined salaries and wages income of $40,000. What is the maximum deduction he can take for his business in relation to the log skidder purchase?

   a. $7,860.

   b. $30,000.

   c. $31,429.

   d. $55,000.

LO 3 27. Section 179 expense is available for all of the following business assets except

   a. Office building.

   b. Office furniture.

   c. Computer.

   d. Delivery truck.

LO 4 28. Jordan has two jobs. She works as a night auditor at the Moonlight Motel. When her shift at the motel is over, she works as a short-order cook at the Greasy Spoon Restaurant. On a typical day, she drives the following number of miles:

Home to Moonlight Motel	4
Moonlight Motel to Greasy Spoon Restaurant	7
Greasy Spoon Restaurant to home	12

How many miles would qualify as transportation expenses for tax purposes?

a. 4.

b. 7.

c. 11.

d. 12.

LO 4   29. Which of the following is false with respect to the standard mileage rate?

a. It can be used if the taxpayer owns the vehicle and uses the standard mileage rate for the first year it was placed in service.

b. It includes parking fees, tolls, and property taxes on the vehicle.

c. It encompasses depreciation or lease payments, maintenance and repairs, gasoline, oil, insurance, and vehicle registration fees.

d. It does not include interest expense on acquisition of the automobile.

LO 4   30. Frank purchased a vehicle for business and personal use. In 2009, he used the vehicle 70% for business (11,000 miles) and calculated his vehicle expenses using the standard mileage rate. Frank also paid $1,800 in interest and $480 in county property tax on the car. What is the total business deduction related to business use of the car?

a. $4,235.

b. $6,050.

c. $7,646.

d. $8,330.

LO 1, 4   31. Jimmy took a business trip from Dallas to Brazil. He was there for a total of seven days, of which two were weekend. Over the weekend, he spent his time sightseeing and relaxing. His expenses were as follows:

Airfare	$1,400
Lodging (7 days × $300)	2,100
Meals (7 days × $85)	595
Taxi fares ($600 to and from business meetings)	800

How much is Jimmy allowed to deduct?

a. $3,404.

b. $3,496.

c. $4,598.

d. $4,895.

LO 5   32. Jake runs a business out of his home. He uses 600 square feet of his home exclusively for the business. His home is 2,400 square feet in total. Jake had $27,000 of business revenue and $22,000 of business expenses from his home-based business. The following expenses relate to his home:

Mortgage interest	$10,800
Real estate taxes	1,600
Utilities	2,400
Insurance	600
Repairs	2,400
Depreciation (on business use portion of home)	1,200

What is Jake's net income from his business? What amount of expenses is carried over to the following year, if any?

a. ($14,000) and $0 carryover.

b. ($650) and $0 carryover.

c. $0 and $650 carryover.

d. $550 and $0 carryover.

LO 6 33. Which of the following is *not* a relevant factor to be considered in deciding whether an activity is profit seeking or a hobby?

a. Manner in which the taxpayer carries on the activity.

b. Expertise of the taxpayer or his or her advisers.

c. Time and effort expended by the taxpayer in carrying on the activity.

d. All of the above are relevant factors.

LO 6 34. Which of the following individuals can deduct education expenses?

a. A real estate broker who attends college to get an accounting degree.

b. A CPA who attends a review course to obtain his building contractor's license.

c. A corporate executive attending an executive MBA program.

d. An accounting bookkeeper taking a CPA review course to pass the CPA exam and become a CPA.

LO 7 35. Annie is self-employed and has $58,000 in income from her business. She also has investments that generated dividends of $3,000 and interest of $2,500. What is Annie's self-employment tax for the year?

a. $8,195.

b. $8,548.

c. $8,619.

d. $8,874.

LO 7 36. The maximum tax bases and percentages for 2008 for the two portions of the self-employment tax are which of the following?

	Social Security	Medicare
a.	$106,800; 12.4%	Unlimited; 2.9%.
b.	$106,800; 15.3%	Unlimited; 15.3%.
c.	$102,000; 12.4%	Unlimited; 2.9%.
d.	$102,000; 15.3%	Unlimited; 15.3%.

Problems **LO 1** 37. Kelly is a self-employed tax attorney whose practice primarily involves tax planning. During the year, she attended a three-day seminar regarding new changes to the tax law. She incurred the following expenses:

Lodging	$400
Meals	95
Course registration	350
Transportation	150

a. How much can Kelly deduct? _____

b. Kelly believes that obtaining a CPA license would improve her skills as a tax attorney. She enrolls as a part-time student at a local college to take CPA review courses. During

the current year, she spends $1,500 for tuition and $300 for books. How much of these expenses can Kelly deduct? Why?

_____

_____

_____

LO 1, 2, 4   38. Jackie owns a temporary employment agency that hires personnel to perform accounting services for clients. During the year, her entertainment expenses for her clients include the following:

Cab fare to and from restaurants	$ 350
Gratuity at restaurants	300
Meals	4,000
Cover charges	250

Jackie also held a holiday party for her employees, which cost $1,500. All expenses are reasonable.

a. Can Jackie deduct any of these expenses? If so, how much? _____

b. How is the deduction classified? _____

LO 1, 2   39. David is a college professor who does some consulting work on the side. He uses 25% of his home exclusively for the consulting practice. He is single and 63 years old. His AGI (without consideration of consulting income) is $45,000. Other information follows:

Income from consulting business	$4,000
Consulting expenses other than home office	1,500
Total costs relating to home:	
Interest and taxes	6,500
Utilities	1,500
Maintenance and repairs	450
Depreciation (business part only)	1,500

Calculate David's AGI. _____

LO 1, 2   40. In 2007 Gerald loaned Main Street Bakery $55,000. In 2008 he learned that he would probably receive only $6,400 of the loan. In 2009 Gerald received $3,000 in final settlement of the loan. Calculate Gerald's possible deductions with respect to the loan for 2007, 2008, and 2009.

2007: _____

2008: _____

2009: _____

LO 1, 2   41. Charles, a self-employed real estate agent, attended a conference on the impact of some new building codes on real estate investments. His unreimbursed expenses were as follows:

Airfare	$480
Lodging	290
Meals	100
Tuition and fees	650

How much can Charles deduct on his return? _____

LO 3   42. Betsy acquired a new network system on June 5, 2009 (5-year class property), for $75,000. She expects taxable income from the business will always be about $175,000 without regard to the §179 election. Betsy will elect §179 expensing immediately. She also acquired 7-year property in July 2009 for $350,000. Determine Betsy's maximum cost recovery deduction with respect to her purchases in 2009: _____

LO 3   43. Janet purchased her personal residence in 2000 for $250,000. In January 2009 she converted it to rental property. The fair market value at the time of conversion was $210,000.

    a. Determine the amount of cost recovery that can be taken in 2009: _____

    b. Determine the amount of cost recovery that could be taken in 2009 if the fair market value of the property were $350,000: _____

LO 3   44. On February 4, 2009, Jackie purchased and placed in service a car she purchased for $21,500. The car was used exclusively for her business. Compute Jackie's cost recovery deduction in 2009 assuming no §179 expense was taken: _____

LO 3   45. Rueben acquires a warehouse on September 1, 2009, for $3 million. On March 1, 2013, he sells the warehouse. Determine Rueben's cost recovery for 2009–2013:

_____

LO 3   46. Michael is the sole proprietor of a small business. In June 2009 his business income is $12,000 before consideration of any §179 deduction. He spends $245,000 on furniture and equipment in 2009. If Michael elects to take the §179 deduction on a conference table that cost $25,000 (included in the $245,000 total), determine the cost recovery for 2009 with respect to the conference table: _____

LO 3   47. On June 10, 2009, Huron purchased equipment (7-year class property) for $75,000. Determine Huron's cost recovery deduction for computing 2009 taxable income. Assume Huron does not make the §179 election or take the 50% bonus. _____

LO 3   48. Brittany purchased a building for $500,000 on January 1, 2001. The purchase price does not include land. Calculate the cost recovery for 2001 and 2009 if the real property is

    a. Residential real property: _____

    b. A warehouse: _____

LO 3   49. Walt purchased a computer for $5,000. He could use the computer exclusively for his business, or he could allow his family to use the computer 60% of the time and 40% would be for business use. Determine the tax deduction for the year of acquisition under both alternatives. What is the overall tax savings between the two alternatives? Assume that Walt would not elect §179 expensing or the 50% bonus and that he is in the 25% tax bracket.

_____

LO 3, 4   50. In 2007 Jessica bought a new truck for $45,000 to use 80% for her sole proprietorship. Total miles driven include 12,000 in 2007, 14,500 in 2008, and 13,000 in 2009.

    a. If Jessica uses the standard mileage method, how much may she deduct on her 2009 tax return (miles were incurred ratably throughout the year)? _____

    b. What is the deduction for 2009 assuming the actual method was used from the beginning? Calculate depreciation only; the truck is not limited by the luxury auto rules. Also assume §179 was not elected in the year of purchase. _____

LO 3, 4   51. Jose purchased a vehicle for business and personal use. In 2009 he used the vehicle 18,000 miles (80%) for business and calculated his vehicle expenses using the standard mileage rate. He paid $1,400 in interest and $150 in property taxes on the car. Calculate the total business deduction related to the car:

LO 4   52. Jordan took a business trip from New York to Denver. She spent two days in travel, conducted business for nine days, and visited friends for five days. She incurred the following expenses:

Airfare	$ 550
Lodging	3,000
Meals	900
Entertainment of clients	750

How much of these expenses can Jordan deduct?

LO 5   53. Derrick owns a farm in eastern North Carolina. A hurricane hit the area and destroyed a farm building and some farm equipment and damaged a barn.

Item	Adjusted Basis	FMV before Damage	FMV after Damage	Insurance Proceeds
Building	$85,000	$115,000	$ 0	$55,000
Equipment	68,000	49,000	0	15,000
Barn	95,000	145,000	95,000	35,000

Due to the extensive damage throughout the area, the president of the United States declared all areas affected by the hurricane as a disaster area. Derrick, who files a joint return with his wife, had $45,000 of taxable income last year. Their taxable income for the current year is $150,000, excluding the loss from the hurricane. Calculate the amount of the loss by Derrick and his wife and the years in which they should deduct the loss. (*Hint:* Chapter 5 provides information concerning nationally declared disaster areas.)

LO 6   54. Rebecca is a doctor with an AGI of $125,000 before consideration of income or loss from her dog breeding business. Her home is on 15 acres, 10 of which she uses to house the animals and provide them with ample space to play and exercise. Her records show the following related income and expenses for the current year:

Income from fees and sales	$2,500
Expenses:	
Dog food	$4,000
Veterinary bills	3,500
Supplies	1,200
Publications and dues	350

a. How must Rebecca treat the income and expenses of the operation if the dog breeding business is held to be a hobby? _____

_____

b. How would your answer differ if the operation were held to be a business? _____

_____

LO 6 55. Eric, who is single, participates in an activity that is appropriately classified as a hobby. The activity produces the following revenue and expenses:

Revenue	$12,000
Property taxes	2,000
Materials and supplies	4,000
Utilities	1,500
Advertising	1,900
Insurance	775
Depreciation	5,000

Without regard to this activity, Eric's AGI is $55,000. Determine how much income Eric must report, the amount of the expenses he is permitted to deduct, and his AGI:

_____

LO 7 56. In 2009 Landon has self-employment earnings of $205,000. Compute Landon's self-employment tax liability and the allowable income tax deduction of the self-employment tax paid. SE tax: _____ SE deduction: _____

LO 3 57. (Comprehensive) Casper used the following assets in his Schedule C trade or business in the tax year 2009:

Asset	Date Purchased	Date Sold	Business Use (percentage)	Cost
Computer 1	03/12/06		100%	$ 3,000
Computer 2	05/05/06	05/15/09	100	2,500
Printer	08/25/09		100	2,200
Computer 3	05/25/09		100	2,800
Equipment	03/20/07		100	2,700
Auto	05/01/09		90%	20,000
Furniture 1	02/12/07	08/25/09	100	22,000
Furniture 2	08/15/07		100	3,600
Office building	04/01/09		100	330,000

Casper is a new client and unfortunately does not have a copy of his prior year tax return. He recalls that all of the assets purchased in prior years used MACRS depreciation (no §179 expense or 50% bonus was taken). Casper does not wish to take a §179 deduction this year because he feels he will be more profitable in the future and would like the depreciation deduction at that time. He will take the 50% bonus this year. Calculate the current year depreciation allowance for Casper's business. Correctly report the amounts on Form 4562.

Tax Return Problems

Use your tax software to complete the following problems. If you are manually preparing the tax returns, the problem indicates the forms or schedules you will need.

Tax Return Problem 1

Cassi has a home cleaning business she runs as a sole proprietorship. The following are the results from business operations for the tax year 2009:

Gross receipts	$203,000
Business mileage: 27,000 (miles incurred ratably throughout the year)	
35,000 miles total during the year 2009	
Van (over 6,000 lbs) placed in service 11/01/09, cost 27,000	
Postage	(500)
Wages	(26,000)
Payroll taxes	(1,950)
Supplies	(12,500)
Phone	(1,250)
Internet service	(600)
Rent	(2,400)
Insurance	(2,800)
Van expenses	(4,500)

Business Assets	Date Purchased	Cost
Computer 1	5/18/09	$2,200
Computer 2	6/01/09	2,700
Printer	3/01/08	900
Copier	3/02/08	2,100
Furniture	3/01/08	6,000

Determine Cassi's self-employment income and prepare Schedule C and Schedule SE. §179 expense is elected on all eligible assets (§179 was not taken on assets purchased last year). The 50% was elected on all 2008 and 2009 assets.

Tax Return Problem 2

During 2009, Cassandra Albright, who is single, worked part-time at a doctor's office and received a W-2. She also had a consulting practice that had the following income and expenses:

Revenue	$48,000
Laptop computer purchased 4/23/09 (§179 elected)	2,300
Travel 2,500 miles for business, 13,000 personal	
Supplies	500
Cell phone charge	540

Cassandra (SSN 333-33-3333) resides at 1400 Medical Street, Apt. 3A, Lowland, CA 12345. Her W-2 shows the following:

Wages	$45,300
Federal withholding	4,983
Social security wages	45,300
Social security withholding	2,809
Medicare withholding	657
State withholding	2,265
Other income:	
1099-INT Old Bank	2,300
1099-DIV Bake Co., Inc. -Ordinary dividends	3,100
Qualified dividends	3,100

Cassandra had the following itemized deductions:

State income tax withholding	$ 2,265
State income tax paid with the 2007 return	350
Real estate tax	3,450
Mortgage interest	12,300

Cassandra made two federal estimated payments of $7,000 each on June 15 and September 15. Prepare Form 1040 for Cassandra for 2009. You will need Form 1040, Schedule A, Schedule B, Schedule C, Form 4562, and Schedule SE.

Tax Return Problem 3

During 2009, Jason and Vicki Hurting, who are married with two children, had the following tax information. Jason owns a landscaping business, and Vicki works as an executive assistant at a university.

Jason (SSN 333-44-4444) and Vicki (SSN 444-33-3333) reside at 123 Bate Street, Bright, AL 54321. Both children are under the age of 17:

Jason Jr. (455-55-5555) born 2002
Catlin (466-66-6666) born 2006
Vicki's W-2 information is as follows:

Wages	$45,800
Federal withholding	6,870
Social security wages	45,800
Social security withholding	2,840
Medicare withholding	664
State withholding	2,290
Other income:	
1099-G Alabama state tax refund is taxable because $2,500 was deducted on last year's return	$ 897
1099-INT First Bank of Alabama	225
1099-DIV IBM, Inc. -Ordinary dividends	125
Qualified dividends	125

The following information is for Jason's landscaping business:

Revenue	$153,000		
Wages	41,600		
Payroll tax	3,182		
Cell phone charge	425		
Assets (§179 elected)			

Item	Date Purchased	Business Use Amount	Percentage
Truck (100% business)	2/05/09	$28,000	100%
Mower 1	3/08/09	12,000	100
Mower 2	3/08/09	3,400	100
Equipment	6/25/09	1,595	100

TABLE 7-1

Basis	The amount of investment in property for tax purposes. Basis is the starting point in determining gain or loss on the sale or disposition of investment property.
Cost Basis	The cost of the property bought in cash, debt obligations, other property or services.
Other Cost Basis	Property acquired other than through a purchase: • Gift. • Inheritance. • Divorce. • Exchanges.
Adjusted Basis	Increases and/or decreases to the original cost basis of an asset. • Examples of increases: a room addition to a home, replacing an entire roof, the cost of defending and perfecting a title to property or a patent, commission fees for purchasing stock, and stock dividends received through dividend reinvestment plans. • Examples of decreases: Section 179 deductions, deductions previously allowed such as depreciation or amortization, nontaxable stock dividends or stock splits, or postponed gain from the sale of a home (discussed in Chapter 12).
Fair Market Value	The price at which the property would change hands between a buyer and a seller, neither being forced to buy or sell and both having reasonable knowledge of all the relevant facts. Sales of similar property, around the same date, are typically used in figuring fair market value.

that the taxpayer is receiving. The difference between the amount realized and the adjusted basis determines if there is a gain or loss on the sale. The following chart summarizes this process:

Amount realized < Adjusted basis	Loss
Amount realized > Adjusted basis	Gain

The last term to discuss is the amount of gain or loss that will be recognized for tax purposes. The *amount recognized* from a sale or trade of property is the amount that will be recorded on the tax return as a gain or loss. Gains and losses can be realized and recognized, or they can be realized and not recognized, such as in a nontaxable exchange, or a loss on the disposition of property that is held for personal use, or a gain that is excluded as with the sale of a residence (see Chapter 12).

For example, if the adjusted basis of the property sold is $8,000 and the amount realized is $10,000, there is a gain of $2,000. This $2,000 gain is recognized for tax purposes because it is not from a nontaxable exchange. If the adjusted basis of the property sold is $8,000 and the amount realized is $7,000, there is a loss of $1,000. If the loss is from the disposition of personal-use property, the $1,000 is not recognized for tax purposes. If the loss is *not* from the disposition of personal-use property, it is recognized as a loss for tax purposes.

It is possible that, when a sale occurs, the sales proceeds (amount the seller realizes) include not only cash but also the fair market value (FMV) of other property received as well as any assumption of liabilities by the buyer, as illustrated in Examples 7-1 and 7-2.[6]

EXAMPLE 7-1   Debra sold a parcel of land for $55,000 cash. The buyer also assumed a $15,000 note attached to the land. Debra originally purchased the land for $34,000, so she reports a gain on the land of $36,000 ($55,000 cash + $15,000 release of liability less the $34,000 basis).

EXAMPLE 7-2   Larry needed cash and sold a parcel of land for $55,000. The buyer also assumed a $15,000 note attached to the land. Larry originally purchased the land for $72,000, so he reports a loss on the land of $2,000 ($55,000 cash + $15,000 release of liability less the $72,000 basis).

[6] Reg. § 1.1001-2(a)(1),

The nature of the tax reporting for gains and losses on the sale of property depends primarily on the use of the asset rather than on its form. After the appropriate asset use has been determined, the taxpayer will possibly record the taxable event on different tax forms. Examples 7-1 and 7-2 involved the sale of land. If the land were used in a trade or business, the gain or loss would be reported on Form 4797. If the land were an investment held in a trade or business, the gain or loss would be reported on Schedule D. Exhibit 7-1 is a sample of Form 4797, and Exhibit 7-2 is a sample of Schedule D.

CONCEPT CHECK 7-1—LO 1	1. A gain or loss on a sale is the difference between the cash received and the original cost of the asset. True or false?
	2. The gain or loss on the sale of an asset used for investment or in a trade or business appears on Form 4797. True or false?
	3. When the buyer assumes the seller's liability, the seller includes this amount in computing the amount realized from the sale. True or false?

CLASSIFICATION OF ASSETS
LO 2

All assets can be classified into one of three categories. The classification of the asset determines how gains and losses on the sale are reported for tax purposes. The three asset categories follow:

1. Ordinary income property.
2. § 1221 property (capital assets).
3. § 1231 trade or business property.

The following sections discuss the rules associated with classifying assets into each of the categories. (Refer to Table 7-2 for a summary of asset classifications.)

Ordinary Income Property

The tax code does not directly define *ordinary income property* except to state that it is any asset that is "not a capital asset." The two most common ordinary assets are inventory and accounts or notes receivable, defined in Chapter 2 of IRS Publication 544 as follows:

- Inventory: property held mainly for sale to customers or property that will physically become part of merchandise for sale to customers.

- Receivables: accounts or notes receivable acquired in the ordinary course of business or from the sale of any inventory properties.

Typically the sale of inventory appears on the income statement of a business as a cost of goods sold. Gross profit (sales – cost of goods sold) is ordinary income subject to tax and is entered on Schedule C for a sole proprietorship.[7] The collection of an account or note receivable is ordinary income to a cash basis taxpayer when the cash is collected. Neither selling inventory nor collecting accounts or notes receivable requires reporting on Form 4797 or Schedule D. Other assets such as copyrights and literary, musical, and artistic compositions are also ordinary assets in the hands of the creator or artist.

§1221 Capital Property (Capital Assets)

In general, a *capital asset* is any asset used for personal purposes or investment.[8] A common example of a capital asset is an investment in stocks or bonds. Other capital assets include these:

- A home owned and occupied by the taxpayer and the taxpayer's family.

- Timber grown on home property or investment property, even if the taxpayer makes only casual sales of the timber.

[7] The sale, related cost of goods sold, and gross profit are reported directly on Schedule C.
[8] Publication 544, Chapter 2.

TABLE 7-2
Asset Classification Summary

Ordinary Income Asset	§1221—Capital Asset	§1231—Trade or Business
Short-term asset used in a trade or business	Any asset held for investment	Long-term depreciable trade or business property
Inventory	Personal-use property	Long-term land used in the trade or business
Accounts receivable	Not inventory	Not short-term trade or business property
Notes receivable	Not depreciable trade or business property	Not inventory
	Not a copyright*	Not a copyright
	Not accounts receivable	
	Not notes receivable	

* Refer to new election provision for musical compositions and copyrights in musical works.

- Household furnishings.
- A car used for pleasure or commuting.
- Coin or stamp collections, gems, and jewelry.
- Gold, silver, and other metals.[9]

The Internal Revenue Code (IRC) actually defines a capital asset not by what it *is* but by what it is *not*. Capital assets include all assets held by the taxpayer except[10]

1. Those held mainly for sale to customers, including stock in trade, inventory, and other property held mainly for sale to customers in a trade or business.
2. Property used in a trade or business subject to depreciation.
3. A copyright; a literary, musical, or artistic composition; a letter or memorandum; or similar property, held by a taxpayer whose personal efforts created the property or, in the case of a letter or memo, for which the letter was prepared.
4. Accounts or notes receivable acquired in the ordinary course of business.
5. Real property used in the taxpayer's trade or business.
6. Any commodities derivative financial instrument held by a dealer.
7. Certain hedging transactions entered in the normal course of a trade or business.
8. Supplies used or consumed by the taxpayer in the ordinary course of a trade or business of the taxpayer.

TAX YOUR BRAIN

Is land a capital asset?

ANSWER

The answer is the typical tax answer—it depends. Land held for investment is a capital asset. However, land used in a trade or business is not a capital asset but a §1231 asset (discussed in the next section). Additionally, land held for resale by a real estate developer is inventory (an ordinary asset).

[9] Publication 544, page 18.
[10] IRC § 1221.

Musical compositions and copyrights in musical works are generally not capital assets. However, there is an election available to treat these types of property as capital assets if they are sold or exchanged in the years beginning after May 17, 2006, and

- The taxpayer's personal efforts created the property, or
- The taxpayer under certain circumstances (such as by gift) is entitled to the basis of the person who created the property or for whom it was prepared or produced.

By definition, artistic works are specifically not capital assets of the taxpayer who created the property (the artist), but any artistic work purchased is a capital asset in the hands of the purchaser. In all instances of artistic works, copyrights, letters, or publications of the U.S. government, if the taxpayer's basis is determined by reference to the basis of the property in the hands of the creator of the property (such as by gift from the creator), then the property is not a capital asset.[11]

EXAMPLE 7-3	Jacque, a world-renowned artist, painted a lovely new work. He then gave the painting to his current girlfriend as a gift. Because the property is a gift, the girlfriend's basis is the same as the basis to Jacque. Consequently, the painting is not a capital asset to the girlfriend and would be treated as ordinary income property.

Trade or Business Property (§1231 Asset)

IRC §1231 property is depreciable or nondepreciable property (such as land) used in a trade or business and held for more than one year.[12] Land purchased and held for investment (even if purchased through the business) is a capital asset under §1221.

Timber, coal, domestic iron ore, and certain livestock held for breeding, dairy, or sporting purposes are also considered §1231 property.[13] The most typical examples of §1231 assets are machinery and equipment used in a business, business buildings, and business land. If a business asset is disposed of within one year of acquisition, it is treated as a short-term asset, and the amount received for it is considered ordinary income. Furthermore, §1231 assets do not include property that is considered inventory or artistic works.

EXAMPLE 7-4	Jake, a sole proprietor, purchased a three-acre lot for $55,000. He constructed a building for his business on a portion of the land and used the rest of the land for customer parking. The land, building, and pavement for the parking lot are considered §1231 property.

CONCEPT CHECK 7-2—LO 2	1. Inventory sold by a company is an ordinary income asset that appears on Form 4797—Sale of Business Assets. True or false?
	2. A capital asset includes all of the following except
	   a. A taxpayer's vacation home.
	   b. Inherited property.
	   c. Property used in a trade or business.
	   d. A stock portfolio.
	3. An ordinary income asset is any short-term or long-term asset used in a business. True or false?
	4. A §1221 asset is any asset held for investment. True or false?
	5. A §1231 asset is any depreciable or nondepreciable property used in a trade or business and not considered an ordinary income asset. True or false?

---

[11] IRC § 1221(a)(3)(A), IRC § 1221(a)(5)(B). When property is received by gift, the new basis is determined by the basis (old basis) to the person giving the gift (donor).

[12] IRC § 1231(b)(1).

[13] IRC § 1231(b)(3).

From Shoebox to Software

To report ordinary income or loss from the sale of an ordinary asset, use Form 4797, Part II. The description of the property sold, the date acquired, the date sold, the gross sales price, the depreciation allowed, the cost basis, and the gain or loss are shown on Form 4797. Exhibit 7-1 illustrates the reporting of Examples 7-5 and 7-6. Note that the gains are combined (netted if a loss had occurred) on line 18. If any ordinary gains or losses had resulted from the sale of §1231 property (discussed later), they would also be included in the final figure on line 18. For an individual taxpayer, the $12,869 ordinary income is reported on line 14 of Form 1040.

TAX PREPARATION SOFTWARE

The sale of a receivable is a unique transaction (it does not happen often in practice). To enter this type of sale in tax preparation software, enter the information directly on Part II of Form 4797. For an asset that has already been entered on Form 4562, Asset Depreciation Worksheet (see Chapter 6), simply go to the asset depreciation worksheet and enter the date sold. Then click the Asset Disposed of link and enter the sales price. The depreciation should recalculate, and the gain or loss will appear in the appropriate section of Form 4797.[14]

SALES OF ORDINARY ASSETS

LO 3

When an asset is sold (or otherwise disposed of), the gain or loss produced is considered either "ordinary" or "capital." For example, when an ordinary asset is sold, the gain or loss is termed "an ordinary gain or loss." When a capital asset (§1221 asset) is sold, the gain or loss is a "capital gain or loss." When a §1231 asset is sold, the gain can be either ordinary or capital.

Why is the distinction between ordinary and capital so important? The primary reason is that capital gains are taxed at lower capital gains tax rates compared to ordinary gains that are taxed at ordinary rates. Capital losses are also limited in their deductibility.[15] The specifics of ordinary gains and losses, capital gains and losses, and §1231 gains and losses are described in detail in the following sections.

Recognized Gain or Loss from Ordinary Assets

Recall that the primary ordinary income assets are inventory and accounts receivable. Inventory sold in the normal course of a trade or business generates sales revenue. The cost of the inventory is a deduction (cost of goods sold). The type of transaction discussed in this chapter is the sale of an ordinary asset outside the normal course of business. Typically, ordinary gains or losses produced outside (not part of) the normal course of business relate to the sale of business property held less than one year or the sale of accounts receivable.[16]

EXAMPLE 7-5

Jason is a sole proprietor who needs cash. He decides to sell his outstanding accounts receivable. They have a $10,000 FMV and a zero basis. He is able to sell the receivables on July 1, 2009, for $8,500. Jason recognizes an $8,500 ordinary gain ($8,500 received less $0 basis).

EXAMPLE 7-6

Jason sold some equipment for $22,000 on October 7, 2009, that he had originally purchased for $24,000 on November 8, 2008. The equipment was subject to depreciation of $6,369 for 2008 and 2009. The adjusted basis is $17,631 ($24,000 cost – $6,369 depreciation). Jason recognizes a $4,369 ordinary gain ($22,000 amount realized – $17,631 adjusted basis).

---

[14] Remember from Chapter 6 that only a half-year of depreciation is allowed in the year of disposal for half-year convention assets. Depreciation for midquarter and midmonth convention assets also changes in the year of disposal.

[15] Capital gains and losses are treated differently for corporate taxpayers. The discussion in this chapter pertains exclusively to noncorporate taxpayers.

[16] The sale of § 1231 property where the gain is a result of depreciation taken also produces an ordinary gain. These gains are discussed later in the chapter.

EXHIBIT 7-1   Examples 7-5 and 7-6

Form **4797**		**Sales of Business Property** (Also Involuntary Conversions and Recapture Amounts Under Sections 179 and 280F(b)(2)) ▶ Attach to your tax return. ▶ See separate instructions.				OMB No. 1545-0184 **20**09 Attachment Sequence No. **27**

Department of the Treasury
Internal Revenue Service   (99)

Name(s) shown on return	Identifying number
Jason Taxpayer	123-45-6789

1 Enter the gross proceeds from sales or exchanges reported to you for 2009 on Form(s) 1099-B or 1099-S (or substitute statement) that you are including on line 2, 10, or 20 (see instructions) **1**

Part I   Sales or Exchanges of Property Used in a Trade or Business and Involuntary Conversions From Other Than Casualty or Theft—Most Property Held More Than 1 Year   (see instructions)

2	(a) Description of property	(b) Date acquired (mo., day, yr.)	(c) Date sold (mo., day, yr.)	(d) Gross sales price	(e) Depreciation allowed or allowable since acquisition	(f) Cost or other basis, plus improvements and expense of sale	(g) Gain or (loss) Subtract (f) from the sum of (d) and (e)

3 Gain, if any, from Form 4684, line 43 . . . . **3**

4 Section 1231 gain from installment sales from Form 6252, line 26 or 37 . . . . **4**

5 Section 1231 gain or (loss) from like-kind exchanges from Form 8824 . . . . **5**

6 Gain, if any, from line 32, from other than casualty or theft **6**

7 Combine lines 2 through 6. Enter the gain or (loss) here and on the appropriate line as follows: **7**

Partnerships (except electing large partnerships) and S corporations. Report the gain or (loss) following the instructions for Form 1065, Schedule K, line 10, or Form 1120S, Schedule K, line 9. Skip lines 8, 9, 11, and 12 below.

Individuals, partners, S corporation shareholders, and all others. If line 7 is zero or a loss, enter the amount from line 7 on line 11 below and skip lines 8 and 9. If line 7 is a gain and you did not have any prior year section 1231 losses, or they were recaptured in an earlier year, enter the gain from line 7 as a long-term capital gain on the Schedule D filed with your return and skip lines 8, 9, 11, and 12 below.

8 Nonrecaptured net section 1231 losses from prior years (see instructions) **8**

9 Subtract line 8 from line 7. If zero or less, enter -0-. If line 9 is zero, enter the gain from line 7 on line 12 below. If line 9 is more than zero, enter the amount from line 8 on line 12 below and enter the gain from line 9 as a long-term capital gain on the Schedule D filed with your return (see instructions) **9**

Part II   Ordinary Gains and Losses   (see instructions)

10 Ordinary gains and losses not included on lines 11 through 16 (include property held 1 year or less):

Accounts Receivable	various	07/01/09	8,500	0	0	8,500
Equipment	11/08/08	10/07/09	22,000	6,369	24,000	4,369

11 Loss, if any, from line 7 . . . . **11** ( )

12 Gain, if any, from line 7 or amount from line 8, if applicable **12**

13 Gain, if any, from line 31 . . . . **13**

14 Net gain or (loss) from Form 4684, lines 35 and 42a **14**

15 Ordinary gain from installment sales from Form 6252, line 25 or 36 . . . . **15**

16 Ordinary gain or (loss) from like-kind exchanges from Form 8824 . . . . **16**

17 Combine lines 10 through 16 . . . . **17** 12,869

18 For all except individual returns, enter the amount from line 17 on the appropriate line of your return and skip lines a and b below. For individual returns, complete lines a and b below:

a If the loss on line 11 includes a loss from Form 4684, line 39, column (b)(ii), enter that part of the loss here. Enter the part of the loss from income-producing property on Schedule A (Form 1040), line 28, and the part of the loss from property used as an employee on Schedule A (Form 1040), line 23. Identify as from "Form 4797, line 18a." See instructions . . **18a**

b Redetermine the gain or (loss) on line 17 excluding the loss, if any, on line 18a. Enter here and on Form 1040, line 14 **18b** 12,869

For Paperwork Reduction Act Notice, see separate instructions.   Cat. No. 13086I   Form **4797** (2009)

CONCEPT CHECK 7-3—LO 3

1. When an ordinary asset is sold, the gain or loss is subject to capital gain or loss tax treatment. True or false?
2. Why is the distinction between "ordinary" and "capital" so important?
3. Ordinary gains or losses produced outside the normal course of business relate to the sale of business property held for less than one year or the sale of receivables. True or false?

TABLE 7-3
Summary of the
Different Holding
Periods for Capital
Assets

Type of Acquisition	When the Holding Period Starts
Stock or bond purchased on a securities market	The day after the trading day the taxpayer purchased the security.
Nontaxable exchanges	The day after the taxpayer acquired the old property.
Gift	If the taxpayer's basis is the donor's basis, the holding period includes the donor's holding period. If the taxpayer's basis is the FMV, the holding period starts the day after the date of the gift.
Inherited property	The property is considered to be held longer than one year regardless of how long the property was actually held.
Real property purchase	The day after the date the taxpayer received title to the property.
Real property repossessed	The date the taxpayer originally received title to the property, but not including the time between the original sale and the date of repossession.

Source: IRS Publication 544.

SALES OF CAPITAL ASSETS
LO 4

Recall that a capital asset is any personal-use asset or any asset held for investment that is not one of the exclusions listed earlier. The tax treatment of a capital gain or loss varies depending on several factors:

- The period of time the capital asset is held.
- Whether the sale of the asset produced a gain or loss.
- The type of capital asset sold (for example, collectibles are treated differently).
- The taxpayer's tax bracket.
- The combination (or netting) of all capital gains and losses to derive a net capital gain or a net capital loss.
- Whether a capital asset sold is stock of a qualified small business.

Holding Period of a Capital Asset

Only long-term capital gains receive preferential tax treatment. A *long-term capital asset* is any capital asset held for more than one year.[17] A *short-term capital asset* is any capital asset held for one year or less, and any gain or loss on its sale is taxed using ordinary tax rates. Typically the holding period starts the day after the taxpayer acquired the property and includes the day the property is sold. Table 7-3 summarizes the determination of holding periods for capital assets.

EXAMPLE 7-7   Jackie purchased 100 shares of IBM stock on January 6, 2008. The stock is a long-term asset on January 7, 2009. If the stock is sold prior to January 7, 2009, the gain or loss is short-term and no preferential treatment is applicable on any gain.

Capital assets are typically acquired through a purchase. However, what if an asset is received by gift, nontaxable exchange, or inheritance?[18] Generally, if the property received has the same basis as the basis in the hands of the transferor (the person giving the property),

[17] IRC § 1222(3).

[18] Often when one asset is traded for another asset, no gain or loss is recognized. These are nontaxable exchanges covered in Chapter 12.

TABLE 7-4
Summary of Capital Gain Tax Rates

Source of Net Capital Gain	Post May 5, 2003, Sales—the Maximum Capital Gain Rate
Collectibles gain	28%
§1202 gain	28
Unrecaptured §1250 gain	25
Other capital gains when in the 25% or higher tax bracket	15
Other capital gains when the tax bracket is less than 25%	0*

*Beginning in 2008.

the holding period includes the transferor's holding period. The exception to this rule is for property received by inheritance. Inherited property is *always* long-term property regardless of how long the asset belonged to the decedent or beneficiary.[19]

EXAMPLE 7-8

Matthew gave a gift of 500 shares of GM stock to his son, Jim, on November 12, 2008, when the stock was worth $50 per share. Matthew had purchased the stock for $30 per share in 1990. Because the basis to Jim, the son, would be the same as in the hands of Matthew, the father, the holding period for Jim includes Matthew's holding period. Thus Jim's holding period is more than one year, and the stock is considered a long-term capital asset. When Jim sells the stock, any gain will be taxed using capital gain rates.

Capital Gain Rates

The taxes on net long-term capital gains are calculated using 15%, 25%, and 28% rates. Prior to 2008, there was a 5% rate for taxpayers in the 10% or 15% tax bracket. For tax years after 2007, the 5% maximum tax rate on qualified dividends and net capital gain is reduced to 0%. The 15% tax rate remains for taxpayers in the 25%, 28%, 33%, or 35% regular tax brackets. In 2009, this 15% gain rate starts when taxable income is over $33,950 for single taxpayers and $67,900 for married taxpayers filing a joint return. The lower rates of 0% and 15% are called *maximum capital gain rates*. Table 7-4 summarizes the capital gain tax rates in effect for 2009.

EXAMPLE 7-9

Bill is a married taxpayer who files a joint return. In tax year 2009, his taxable income is $115,000. He sold stock in April 2009 that he had held for four years. The gain on the sale was $30,000. Bill is in the 25% tax bracket, so his $30,000 capital gain is taxed using a 15% tax rate.

The 25% bracket is a special rate that relates to capital gains generated from depreciable real property (buildings) used in a trade or business. The Internal Revenue Code has special tax rules for depreciable real property (buildings) used in a trade or business, called *§1250 property*. In general, when depreciable real property is sold for a gain, the taxpayer has to bring back (recapture) as income that part of the gain due to the difference between MACRS depreciation and straight-line depreciation. As of 1987, all §1250 property is depreciated using the straight-line method; therefore, there is no recapture of depreciation. However, the IRS implemented a special provision for this nonrecaptured depreciation of real property; it is called *unrecaptured §1250 gain*. Instead of the entire gain from §1250 real property being taxed at preferential capital gain rates, the gain attributable to any depreciation allowable is

[19] IRC § 1223(11).

taxed at a special 25% rate, and any gain in excess of this amount is given preferential capital gains tax treatment. To avoid the possibility that a taxpayer might get around this special tax provision by not claiming depreciation, the IRS included depreciation recapture in the tax law so the taxpayer must include depreciation deductions whether or not the taxpayer actually took depreciation deductions on the real property. §1250 property is covered in greater detail under LO5 (Sales of Business Property) later in this chapter.

EXAMPLE 7-10	David purchased a business building in 1995 for $200,000 and took $51,000 of straight-line depreciation on the building, so the adjusted basis is $149,000. If David sold the building for $190,000 in 2009, the $41,000 gain ($190,000 amount realized − $149,000 adjusted basis) would be a long-term capital gain subject to the 25% rate because the gain is attributable to the depreciation recapture requirement.

EXAMPLE 7-11	If David sold the building for $220,000, the total gain would be $71,000 ($220,000 amount realized − $149,000 adjusted basis). Of that gain, $51,000 would be subject to the 25% rate (the unrecaptured depreciation) and $20,000 would be a §1231 gain subject to a potential 0% or 15% rate.

The 28% capital gain rate applies to collectibles gains. A *collectibles gain or loss* is a gain or loss from the sale or exchange of a work of art, rug, antique, metal, gem, stamp, coin, or alcoholic beverage held longer than one year.[20]

The 28% rate also applies to §1202 gains. IRC §1202 has a provision to limit the taxation on a gain from the sale of *qualified small business (QSB) stock,* which is stock from any domestic corporation whose aggregate gross assets at all times after August 10, 1993, up to the date of issue, have been less than $50,000,000.[21] In the case of a taxpayer other than a corporation, gross income excludes 50% of any gain from the sale or exchange of qualified small business stock held for more than five years.[22] Any remaining gain is taxed at a 28% rate.

EXAMPLE 7-12	Richard invested in a midsize local corporation with gross assets of $15,000,000. He purchased 500 shares for $25,000 in 1997. On April 6, 2009, he sold the stock for $45,000, realizing a gain of $20,000. One-half of the $20,000 gain is excluded from gross income under §1202. The remaining $10,000 gain is recognized and taxed at a rate of 28%.

Netting Capital Gains and Capital Losses

After all long- and short-term capital gains and losses have been calculated, they need to be combined in a certain manner before applying special tax rate provisions. First, combine all short-term capital gains and short-term capital losses to obtain a *net* short-term gain or loss. Next, combine all long-term capital gains and losses to obtain a *net* long-term capital gain or loss. Finally, combine the net short-term gain or loss with the net long-term gain or loss. If netting results in a net short term capital gain and a net long term capital gain or a net short term capital loss and a net long term capital loss, the netting process ends. In this final phase, taxpayers must take care to separate the gains that are taxed at 28% (collectibles and §1202 gains). If an overall net loss results, IRC §1211 permits the taxpayer to deduct up to a maximum of $3,000

[20] IRC § 408(m)(2).
[21] IRC § 1202(d)(1).
[22] IRC § 1202(a). *NOTE:* For stock acquired after February 17, 2009, and before January 1, 2011, this exclusion increases to 75%.

From Shoebox to Software

When capital gains or losses occur, the taxpayer must file Schedule D to report the gain or loss. Schedule D is the document on which the netting process for long-term and short-term gains and losses occurs. The following examples illustrate the preparation of Schedule D.

Taxpayers receive Form 1099-B from corporations and brokerage firms. These forms report information concerning the sale of stock by the taxpayer (see Exhibit 7-7). Often brokerage firms send a "substitute" 1099-B form to report multiple sales transactions occurring throughout the year.

Exhibit 7-2 illustrates the reporting of the gains from Example 7-14 on Schedule D. A taxpayer who has 28% capital gains also uses the 28% Rate Gain Worksheet shown. The taxpayer uses the rates from the tax rate schedules to calculate the tax on the ordinary income and calculates the tax on qualified dividends using a 0%, 5% or 15% rate.

TAX PREPARATION SOFTWARE

Open the tax return for the Masters and go to the forms. Open Schedule D and double-click on the first sales price cell. This will open the Form 1099-B box. The taxpayer receives a sales confirmation after a sale throughout the year and a 1099-B (Brokerage Sales) at year-end from the brokerage company.

Open a new copy for each 1099-B received. Enter the name of the stock, the sales price, the dates purchased, and the dates sold. For the collectibles, make sure you check the box on the bottom of the input form that indicates that the asset sold is a collectible. Tax preparation software will classify the gains as short- or long-term and enter them on the correct section of Schedule D. The tax is automatically calculated on the Schedule D Qualified Dividends and Capital Gain Tax Worksheet (not shown).

---

against other income.[23] IRC §1212 allows any net loss exceeding $3,000 to be carried over to future years (indefinitely) to offset other capital gains.[24]

The netting process can result in the following outcomes:

- **Net short-term gain and net long-term gain:** Short-term gains are taxed at regular tax rates, and net long-term gains are taxed at the appropriate capital gain rate of 0%, 15%, 25%, or 28%.

- **Net short-term gain and net long-term loss:** A long-term loss is offset against a short-term gain. If a net short-term gain results, the short-term gain is taxed using regular tax rates. If a long-term loss results, the loss, up to $3,000, reduces other income, and any excess carries forward indefinitely.

- **Net short-term loss and net long-term gain:** In this case, separate the long-term gains into 28%, 25%, and 15% or 0% groups. Any net short-term loss is first offset against the 28% group, then the 25% group, and if any loss remains, the 15% or 0% group.[25]

- **Net short-term loss and net long-term loss:** In this case, only $3,000 of the loss is deductible against other income in any one year. First, the short-term losses are deducted against other income, and if any of the $3,000 maximum remains, deduct the long-term loss up to the maximum $3,000 annual loss limit.

Excess losses are carried forward to the next year and retain their original character. A short-term loss carries over as a short-term loss and a long-term loss carries over as a long-term loss.

EXAMPLE 7-13   Mary and John Garcia sold property in 2009. The sale resulted in a long-term loss of $8,000. They had no other capital transactions and filed a joint return for 2009. They had taxable income of $50,000. The Garcias deduct $3,000 of the loss in 2009. The unused $5,000 of the loss ($8,000 – $3,000) carries over to 2010 as a long-term loss. If their loss had been less than $3,000, there would be no carryover to 2010.

---

[23] IRC § 1211(b)—only a $1,500 loss is allowed for married taxpayers filing a separate return.

[24] IRC § 1212(b).

[25] IRS Notice 97-59, 1997-2 CB 309.

EXAMPLE 7-14   Alan Masters, the taxpayer from previous chapters, had the following capital transactions:

	Purchased	**Sold**	**Sales Price**	**Basis**	**Gain/Loss**
Stock 1 (held 9 months)	12/01/08	09/01/09	$15,000	$ 9,000	$6,000
Stock 2 (held 4 months)	12/01/08	04/01/09	17,000	25,000	(8,000)
Stock 3 (held 30 months)	06/05/07	12/05/09	38,000	20,000	18,000
Collectibles	07/01/08	08/01/09	20,000	14,000	6,000

The results follow:

Net short-term capital loss ($8,000 − $6,000)	$ (2,000)
Net long-term capital gain	18,000
28% collectibles capital gain	6,000

The net short-term loss of $2,000 first offsets the 28% gain on the collectibles. The result is a long-term capital gain of $18,000 and a $4,000, 28% gain. The appropriate rates are applied:

$$\$18,000 \times 15\% = \$2,700$$
$$\$ 4,000 \times 28\% = 1,120$$
$$\overline{\$3,820} \text{ increase in tax due to capital gains}$$

Schedule D and the 28% gains worksheet are illustrated in Exhibit 7-2.

EXAMPLE 7-15   Assume similar facts from Example 7-14, except that stock 3 was sold for $20,000 with a basis of $38,000, producing a loss of $18,000.

	Purchased	**Sold**	**Sales Price**	**Basis**	**Gain/Loss**
Stock 1 (held 9 months)	12/01/08	09/01/09	$15,000	$ 9,000	$ 6,000
Stock 2 (held 4 months)	12/01/08	04/01/09	17,000	25,000	(8,000)
Stock 3 (held 30 months)	06/05/07	12/05/09	20,000	38,000	(18,000)
Collectibles	07/01/08	08/01/09	20,000	14,000	6,000

The results follow:

Net short-term capital loss ($8,000 − $6,000)	$ (2,000)
Net long-term loss against collectibles gain ($18,000) − $6,000	(12,000)

Only $3,000 of the $14,000 loss can be taken this year. The net short-term loss of $2,000 is allowed   plus $1,000 of the long-term loss. The $11,000 remaining loss is carried forward indefinitely.

Schedule D and the Capital Loss Carryover Worksheet created from Example 7-15 are shown in Exhibit 7-3. For purposes of this example, assume AGI is $75,000.

EXHIBIT 7-2 **Schedule D for Example 7-14**

SCHEDULE D (Form 1040)	Capital Gains and Losses	OMB No. 1545-0074
Department of the Treasury Internal Revenue Service (99)	▶ Attach to Form 1040 or Form 1040NR. ▶ See Instructions for Schedule D (Form 1040). ▶ Use Schedule D-1 to list additional transactions for lines 1 and 8.	20**09** Attachment Sequence No. **12**

Name(s) shown on return	Your social security number
Alan and Cherie Masters	444-44-4444

Part I Short-Term Capital Gains and Losses—Assets Held One Year or Less

(a) Description of property (Example: 100 sh. XYZ Co.)	(b) Date acquired (Mo., day, yr.)	(c) Date sold (Mo., day, yr.)	(d) Sales price (see page D-7 of the instructions)	(e) Cost or other basis (see page D-7 of the instructions)	(f) Gain or (loss) Subtract (e) from (d)
1 Stock 1	12/01/08	09/01/09	15,000	9,000	6,000
Stock 2	12/01/08	04/01/09	17,000	25,000	(8,000)

2 Enter your short-term totals, if any, from Schedule D-1, line 2	**2**			
3 **Total short-term sales price amounts.** Add lines 1 and 2 in column (d)	**3**	32,000		
4 Short-term gain from Form 6252 and short-term gain or (loss) from Forms 4684, 6781, and 8824	**4**			
5 Net short-term gain or (loss) from partnerships, S corporations, estates, and trusts from Schedule(s) K-1	**5**			
6 Short-term capital loss carryover. Enter the amount, if any, from line 10 of your **Capital Loss Carryover Worksheet** on page D-7 of the instructions	**6**	( )		
7 **Net short-term capital gain or (loss).** Combine lines 1 through 6 in column (f)	**7**	(2,000)		

Part II Long-Term Capital Gains and Losses—Assets Held More Than One Year

(a) Description of property (Example: 100 sh. XYZ Co.)	(b) Date acquired (Mo., day, yr.)	(c) Date sold (Mo., day, yr.)	(d) Sales price (see page D-7 of the instructions)	(e) Cost or other basis (see page D-7 of the instructions)	(f) Gain or (loss) Subtract (e) from (d)
8 Stock 3	06/05/07	12/05/09	38,000	20,000	18,000
Collectibles	07/01/08	08/01/09	20,000	14,000	6,000

9 Enter your long-term totals, if any, from Schedule D-1, line 9	**9**			
10 **Total long-term sales price amounts.** Add lines 8 and 9 in column (d)	**10**	58,000		
11 Gain from Form 4797, Part I; long-term gain from Forms 2439 and 6252; and long-term gain or (loss) from Forms 4684, 6781, and 8824	**11**			
12 Net long-term gain or (loss) from partnerships, S corporations, estates, and trusts from Schedule(s) K-1	**12**			
13 Capital gain distributions. See page D-2 of the instructions	**13**			
14 Long-term capital loss carryover. Enter the amount, if any, from line 15 of your **Capital Loss Carryover Worksheet** on page D-7 of the instructions	**14**	( )		
15 **Net long-term capital gain or (loss).** Combine lines 8 through 14 in column (f). Then go to Part III on the back	**15**	24,000		

For Paperwork Reduction Act Notice, see Form 1040 or Form 1040NR instructions.   Cat. No. 11338H   Schedule D (Form 1040) 2009

EXHIBIT 7-2   *(concluded)*

Schedule D (Form 1040) 2009   Page **2**

Part III   **Summary**

16 Combine lines 7 and 15 and enter the result	**16**	22,000

If line 16 is:
- A **gain**, enter the amount from line 16 on Form 1040, line 13, or Form 1040NR, line 14. Then go to line 17 below.
- A **loss**, skip lines 17 through 20 below. Then go to line 21. Also be sure to complete line 22.
- **Zero**, skip lines 17 through 21 below and enter -0- on Form 1040, line 13, or Form 1040NR, line 14. Then go to line 22.

17 Are lines 15 and 16 **both** gains?
    ☐ **Yes.** Go to line 18.
    ☐ **No.** Skip lines 18 through 21, and go to line 22.

18 Enter the amount, if any, from line 7 of the **28% Rate Gain Worksheet** on page D-8 of the instructions . . . . ▶	**18**	4,000
19 Enter the amount, if any, from line 18 of the **Unrecaptured Section 1250 Gain Worksheet** on page D-9 of the instructions . . . . ▶	**19**	

20 Are lines 18 and 19 **both** zero or blank?
    ☐ **Yes.** Complete Form 1040 through line 43, or Form 1040NR through line 40. Then complete the **Qualified Dividends and Capital Gain Tax Worksheet** on page 38 of the Instructions for Form 1040 (or in the Instructions for Form 1040NR). **Do not** complete lines 21 and 22 below.
    ☐ **No.** Complete Form 1040 through line 43, or Form 1040NR through line 40. Then complete the **Schedule D Tax Worksheet** on page D-10 of the instructions. **Do not** complete lines 21 and 22 below.

21 If line 16 is a loss, enter here and on Form 1040, line 13, or Form 1040NR, line 14, the **smaller** of:

- The loss on line 16 or
- ($3,000), or if married filing separately, ($1,500)

}   . . . .   **21** (   )

  Note. When figuring which amount is smaller, treat both amounts as positive numbers.

22 Do you have qualified dividends on Form 1040, line 9b, or Form 1040NR, line 10b?

    ☐ **Yes.** Complete Form 1040 through line 43, or Form 1040NR through line 40. Then complete the **Qualified Dividends and Capital Gain Tax Worksheet** on page 38 of the Instructions for Form 1040 (or in the Instructions for Form 1040NR).
    ☐ **No.** Complete the rest of Form 1040 or Form 1040NR.

                                                        Schedule D (Form 1040) 2009

28% Rate Gain Worksheet—Line 18   *Keep for Your Records*

1. Enter the total of all collectibles gain or (loss) from items you reported on line 8, column (f), of Schedules D and D-1	**1.**	6.000
2. Enter as a positive number the amount of any section 1202 exclusion you reported on line 8, column (f), of Schedules D and D-1, for which you excluded 50% of the gain, plus ⅔ of any section 1202 exclusion you reported on line 8, column (f), of Schedules D and D-1, for which you excluded 60% of the gain	**2.**	0
3. Enter the total of all collectibles gain or (loss) from Form 4684, line 4 (but only if Form 4684, line 15, is more than zero); Form 6252; Form 6781, Part II; and Form 8824	**3.**	0
4. Enter the total of any collectibles gain reported to you on: • Form 1099-DIV, box 2d; • Form 2439, box 1d; and • Schedule K-1 from a partnership, S corporation, estate, or trust. }	**4.**	0
5. Enter your long-term capital loss carryovers from Schedule D, line 14, and Schedule K-1 (Form 1041), box 11, code C	**5.** (	0)
6. If Schedule D, line 7, is a (loss), enter that (loss) here. Otherwise, enter -0-	**6.** (	2.000)
7. Combine lines 1 through 6. If zero or less, enter -0-. If more than zero, also enter this amount on Schedule D, line 18	**7.**	4.000

EXHIBIT 7-3 Schedule D and Capital Loss Carryover Worksheet for Example 7-15

SCHEDULE D (Form 1040)	**Capital Gains and Losses**	OMB No. 1545-0074
Department of the Treasury Internal Revenue Service (99)	► Attach to Form 1040 or Form 1040NR. ► See Instructions for Schedule D (Form 1040). ► Use Schedule D-1 to list additional transactions for lines 1 and 8.	**2009** Attachment Sequence No. **12**

Name(s) shown on return: Alan and Cherie Masters   Your social security number: 444-44-4444

Part I Short-Term Capital Gains and Losses—Assets Held One Year or Less

(a) Description of property (Example: 100 sh. XYZ Co.)	(b) Date acquired (Mo., day, yr.)	(c) Date sold (Mo., day, yr.)	(d) Sales price (see page D-7 of the instructions)	(e) Cost or other basis (see page D-7 of the instructions)	(f) Gain or (loss) Subtract (e) from (d)
1 Stock 1	12/01/08	09/01/09	15,000	9,000	6,000
Stock 2	12/01/08	04/01/09	17,000	25,000	(8,000)

2 Enter your short-term totals, if any, from Schedule D-1, line 2 . . . . **2**

3 **Total short-term sales price amounts.** Add lines 1 and 2 in column (d) **3** 32,000

4 Short-term gain from Form 6252 and short-term gain or (loss) from Forms 4684, 6781, and 8824   **4**

5 Net short-term gain or (loss) from partnerships, S corporations, estates, and trusts from Schedule(s) K-1 . . . . . . **5**

6 Short-term capital loss carryover. Enter the amount, if any, from line 10 of your **Capital Loss Carryover Worksheet** on page D-7 of the instructions . . . . **6** ( )

7 **Net short-term capital gain or (loss).** Combine lines 1 through 6 in column (f) **7** (2,000)

Part II Long-Term Capital Gains and Losses—Assets Held More Than One Year

(a) Description of property (Example: 100 sh. XYZ Co.)	(b) Date acquired (Mo., day, yr.)	(c) Date sold (Mo., day, yr.)	(d) Sales price (see page D-7 of the instructions)	(e) Cost or other basis (see page D-7 of the instructions)	(f) Gain or (loss) Subtract (e) from (d)
8 Stock 3	06/05/07	12/05/09	20,000	38,000	(18,000)
Collectibles	07/01/08	08/01/09	20,000	14,000	6,000

9 Enter your long-term totals, if any, from Schedule D-1, line 9 . . . . **9**

10 **Total long-term sales price amounts.** Add lines 8 and 9 in column (d) **10** 40,000

11 Gain from Form 4797, Part I; long-term gain from Forms 2439 and 6252; and long-term gain or (loss) from Forms 4684, 6781, and 8824 . . . . **11**

12 Net long-term gain or (loss) from partnerships, S corporations, estates, and trusts from Schedule(s) K-1 . . . . **12**

13 Capital gain distributions. See page D-2 of the instructions **13**

14 Long-term capital loss carryover. Enter the amount, if any, from line 15 of your **Capital Loss Carryover Worksheet** on page D-7 of the instructions . . . . **14** ( )

15 **Net long-term capital gain or (loss).** Combine lines 8 through 14 in column (f). Then go to Part III on the back **15** (12,000)

For Paperwork Reduction Act Notice, see Form 1040 or Form 1040NR instructions.   Cat. No. 11338H   Schedule D (Form 1040) 2009

EXHIBIT 7-3   *(concluded)*

Schedule D (Form 1040) 2009   Page **2**

Part III   **Summary**

16 Combine lines 7 and 15 and enter the result . . . . **16** | (14,000)

If line 16 is:
- A **gain**, enter the amount from line 16 on Form 1040, line 13, or Form 1040NR, line 14. Then go to line 17 below.
- A **loss**, skip lines 17 through 20 below. Then go to line 21. Also be sure to complete line 22.
- **Zero**, skip lines 17 through 21 below and enter -0- on Form 1040, line 13, or Form 1040NR, line 14. Then go to line 22.

17 Are lines 15 and 16 **both** gains?
☐ **Yes.** Go to line 18.
☒ **No.** Skip lines 18 through 21, and go to line 22.

18 Enter the amount, if any, from line 7 of the **28% Rate Gain Worksheet** on page D-8 of the instructions . . . . ▶ **18**

19 Enter the amount, if any, from line 18 of the **Unrecaptured Section 1250 Gain Worksheet** on page D-9 of the instructions . . . . ▶ **19**

20 Are lines 18 and 19 **both** zero or blank?
☐ **Yes.** Complete Form 1040 through line 43, or Form 1040NR through line 40. Then complete the **Qualified Dividends and Capital Gain Tax Worksheet** on page 38 of the Instructions for Form 1040 (or in the Instructions for Form 1040NR). **Do not** complete lines 21 and 22 below.
☐ **No.** Complete Form 1040 through line 43, or Form 1040NR through line 40. Then complete the **Schedule D Tax Worksheet** on page D-10 of the instructions. **Do not** complete lines 21 and 22 below.

21 If line 16 is a loss, enter here and on Form 1040, line 13, or Form 1040NR, line 14, the **smaller** of:
- The loss on line 16 or
- ($3,000), or if married filing separately, ($1,500)

. . . . **21** (3,000)

Note. When figuring which amount is smaller, treat both amounts as positive numbers.

22 Do you have qualified dividends on Form 1040, line 9b, or Form 1040NR, line 10b?

☐ **Yes.** Complete Form 1040 through line 43, or Form 1040NR through line 40. Then complete the **Qualified Dividends and Capital Gain Tax Worksheet** on page 38 of the Instructions for Form 1040 (or in the Instructions for Form 1040NR).
☐ **No.** Complete the rest of Form 1040 or Form 1040NR.

Schedule D (Form 1040) 2009

Capital Loss Carryover Worksheet—Lines 6 and 14   *Keep for Your Records*

Use this worksheet to figure your capital loss carryovers from 2008 to 2009 if your 2008 Schedule D, line 21, is a loss and **(a)** that loss is a smaller loss than the loss on your 2008 Schedule D, line 16, **or (b)** the amount on your 2008 Form 1040, line 41 (or your 2008 Form 1040NR, line 38, if applicable), reduced by any amount on your 2008 Form 8914, line 2, is less than zero. Otherwise, you do not have any carryovers.

1. Enter the amount from your 2008 Form 1040, line 41, or your 2008 Form 1040NR, line 38. If a loss, enclose the amount in parentheses **1.** 75,000
2. Did you file Form 8914 (to claim an exemption amount for housing a Midwestern displaced individual) for 2008?
☒ **No.** Enter -0-.
☐ **Yes.** Enter the amount from your 2008 Form 8914, line 2 . . . . . . **2.** 0
3. Subtract line 2 from line 1. If the result is less than zero, enclose it in parentheses **3.** 75,000
4. Enter the loss from your 2008 Schedule D, line 21, as a positive amount **4.** 3,000
5. Combine lines 3 and 4. If zero or less, enter -0- **5.** 78,000
6. Enter the **smaller** of line 4 or line 5 . . . . **6.** 3,000
   If line 7 of your 2008 Schedule D is a loss, go to line 7; otherwise, enter -0- on line 7 and go to line 11.
7. Enter the loss from your 2008 Schedule D, line 7, as a positive amount **7.** 2,000
8. Enter any gain from your 2008 Schedule D, line 15. If a loss, enter -0- **8.** 0
9. Add lines 6 and 8 . . . . **9.** 3,000
10. **Short-term capital loss carryover for 2009.** Subtract line 9 from line 7. If zero or less, enter -0-. If more than zero, also enter this amount on Schedule D, line 6 . . . . **10.** 0
   If line 15 of your 2008 Schedule D is a loss, go to line 11; otherwise, skip lines 11 through 15.
11. Enter the loss from your 2008 Schedule D, line 15, as a positive amount **11.** 12,000
12. Enter any gain from your 2008 Schedule D, line 7. If a loss, enter -0- **12.** 0
13. Subtract line 7 from line 6. If zero or less, enter -0- **13.** 1,000
14. Add lines 12 and 13 . . . . **14.** 1,000
15. **Long-term capital loss carryover for 2009.** Subtract line 14 from line 11. If zero or less, enter -0-. If more than zero, also enter this amount on Schedule D, line 14 . . . . **15.** 11,000

CONCEPT CHECK 7-4—LO 4

1. The tax treatment of a capital gain or loss varies depending on all of the following except
   a. The holding period.
   b. The basis of the asset sold.
   c. The taxpayer's tax bracket.
   d. The netting of all gains and losses.

2. If property received has the same basis as the basis in the hands of the transferor, the holding period includes the holding period of the transferor. True or false?

3. The holding period of inherited property can be either short-term or long-term to the beneficiary. True or false?

4. Which of the following are termed "maximum gain rates"?
   a. 15% and 28%.
   b. 5% and 25%.
   c. 0% and 15%.
   d. 10% and 15%.

5. For sales after May 5, 2003, what are the maximum capital gain rates on the following?
   a. Collectibles gains.
   b. §1202 gains.
   c. Unrecaptured §1250 gains.
   d. Taxpayer's regular tax rate ≥ 25%.
   e. Taxpayer's regular tax rate < 25%.

SALES OF BUSINESS PROPERTY
LO 5

§1231 assets are assets used in a trade or business that are held longer than one year. The sales treatment of a §1231 asset varies depending on three factors:

1. Whether the asset was sold at a gain or loss.
2. If a gain, whether the asset had been depreciated.
3. Whether the asset was depreciable real property (like a building) or depreciable personal property (such as equipment).

As with capital assets, gains and losses from the sale of §1231 assets must be netted. If a net §1231 gain results, the net gain is taxed as a long-term capital gain subject to the depreciation recapture provisions discussed in the next section.[26] Thus net §1231 gains receive preferential tax rate treatment. If a net §1231 loss results, the loss is treated as an ordinary loss. Ordinary loss treatment allows an unlimited loss deduction rather than the $3,000 limit placed on capital losses. The sale of §1231 assets (both gains and losses) is initially reported on Form 4797.

EXAMPLE 7-16

Josh sold land used in his trade or business for $15,000 in 2009. He had purchased the land in 1990 for $7,000. The $8,000 gain is a §1231 gain and goes on Form 4797, Part I. The $8,000 gain would be netted with other §1231 transactions, and if a net §1231 gain results, the gain is transferred to Schedule D as long-term capital gain. If the netted transactions result in a net §1231 loss, the loss from Form 4797 is transferred to Form 1040, page 1, as an ordinary loss.

[26] IRC §1231(a)(1).

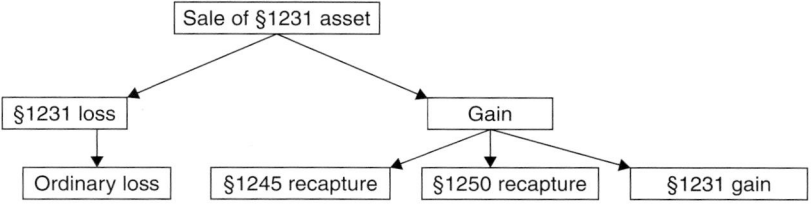

Recapture Provisions

The term *depreciation recapture* can be a difficult concept to understand. Recall from Chapter 6 that depreciation is an income tax deduction that permits the taxpayer to recover the cost or other basis of an asset used in a trade or business. The longer the taxpayer owns and uses the property, the more cost is "recovered"; therefore, the adjusted basis is reduced. The lower the adjusted basis, the greater the gain to be included in the taxpayer's taxable income. When the taxpayer sells §1231 property for a gain, this gain can qualify for capital gain tax preference. The position of the IRS is that if a taxpayer was allowed to reduce taxable income by taking a depreciation deduction and paid less in taxes, when the property is sold some of that gain attributable to depreciation deductions should be taxed at regular rates; this is depreciation recapture. The theory is to transform (recapture), as ordinary income, the portion of a gain that was created by taking a deduction for depreciation. For personal property (§1245 property) used in a business, this gain attributable to depreciation is taxed as ordinary income, while the gain attributable to depreciation for real property (§1250 property) is taxed at a special rate of 25%. Note that when a §1231 asset is sold at a loss, the loss is always treated as an ordinary loss provided there are no §1231 gains to offset the loss. The accompanying chart illustrates the treatment of gains or losses on depreciable §1231 assets. Recall that the only §1231 asset that is not depreciated is land.

§1245 Recapture

§1245 property is personal trade or business property subject to depreciation. This definition encompasses most assets used in a trade or business with the exception of real property. Land, buildings, and building structural components (with the exception to be noted) are *not* included as §1245 property. Although the most common example of §1245 property is machinery and equipment used in a business, the §1245 definition also includes such assets as autos, livestock, and certain buildings placed in service between 1981 and 1986.[27] The general rule concerning §1245 recapture is that any gain recognized on the sale of §1245 property is "ordinary" to the extent of depreciation taken.

For example, in 2007 a taxpayer purchased a truck to be used 100% in a trade or business (5-year property) for $10,000. Using MACRS and the half-year convention, $6,160 of depreciation was taken. In May 2009 the truck was sold for $7,000. Here is how the gain on the sale is calculated and taxed:

Truck cost basis	$ 10,000
Less depreciation	6,160
Adjusted basis	$ 3,840
Selling price	$ 7,000
Less adjusted basis	3,840
Realized gain	$ 3,160

[27] IRC § 1245(a)(3). The only buildings considered §1245 property are buildings placed in service from 1981 through 1986 and depreciated under the 15-, 18-, or 19-year ACRS rules.

From Shoebox to Software

Tax preparation software makes most of the calculations for you. When a §1245 asset is sold, simply go to the asset's Form 4562 Asset Depreciation Worksheet and double-click on the "asset disposed of" icon. Enter the date sold and the proceeds from the sale. The gain and recapture amounts will automatically be calculated and placed in the appropriate section of Form 4797. This transaction cannot be done for existing clients Alan and Cherie Masters because none of Alan's business assets have been held longer than one year. Thus do not enter this transaction on the Masters' tax return file.

The gain treated as ordinary income is the lesser of the depreciation taken ($6,160) or the realized gain ($3,160); in this example that would be $3,160. In practice, however, a §1231 gain (in excess of depreciation) on §1245 property is unusual because equipment rarely appreciates, and any gain is usually caused by the depreciation taken.

EXAMPLE 7-17

On May 1, 2007, Jason purchased equipment costing $10,000 for his business. Depreciation deducted on the equipment from 2007 to 2009 was $4,753; the adjusted basis of the equipment is $5,247. Using the following independent situations, calculate the amount of any gain or loss assuming the equipment was sold on July 8, 2009, for the following amounts:

Situation	Amount Realized	Adjusted Basis ($10,000 – $4,753)	Gain (Loss)	§ 1245 Recapture	§ 1231 Gain/Loss
1	$11,000	$5,247	$5,753	$4,753	$1,000
2	$ 8,000	$5,247	$2,753	$2,753	-0-
3	$5,000	$5,247	$ (247)	-0-	$(247) Ordinary loss/no recapture

Exhibit 7-4 shows the reporting of the first sale situation in Example 7-17 on Form 4797. The sale and total gain appear on Part III, lines 19–24. Lines 25a and 25b separate the recapture amount. The ordinary income of $4,753 is transferred to Part II on page 1 of Form 4797, and the §1231 gain of $1,000 is transferred to Part I on page 1 of Form 4797. Business property sales that occur during the year are netted, and these netted gains and losses are reported on page 1 of Form 4797.

§1250 Recapture

The phrase "§1250 recapture" refers to the portion of the capital gain from §1250 property representing the tax benefit of a depreciation deduction previously taken. §1250 property includes depreciable real property used in a trade or business that has never been considered §1245 property. Thus §1250 property includes all buildings, residential and nonresidential, used in a business or for the production of income.[28] The general rule for §1250 recapture is that any gain on §1250 property is considered ordinary to the extent the depreciation taken exceeds straight-line depreciation. Any other gain is considered §1231 gain.

---

[28] One exception is buildings placed in service from 1981 through 1986, as noted in footnote 27.

EXHIBIT 7-4   Example of §1245 Recapture on Form 4797 from Example 7-17, Situation 1

Form **4797**	**Sales of Business Property**	OMB No. 1545-0184
Department of the Treasury Internal Revenue Service (99)	(Also Involuntary Conversions and Recapture Amounts Under Sections 179 and 280F(b)(2)) ► Attach to your tax return. ► See separate instructions.	**2009** Attachment Sequence No. **27**

Name(s) shown on return: Jason Taxpayer   Identifying number:

1 Enter the gross proceeds from sales or exchanges reported to you for 2009 on Form(s) 1099-B or 1099-S (or substitute statement) that you are including on line 2, 10, or 20 (see instructions) **1**

Part I   Sales or Exchanges of Property Used in a Trade or Business and Involuntary Conversions From Other Than Casualty or Theft—Most Property Held More Than 1 Year (see instructions)

2	(a) Description of property	(b) Date acquired (mo., day, yr.)	(c) Date sold (mo., day, yr.)	(d) Gross sales price	(e) Depreciation allowed or allowable since acquisition	(f) Cost or other basis, plus improvements and expense of sale	(g) Gain or (loss) Subtract (f) from the sum of (d) and (e)

3 Gain, if any, from Form 4684, line 43	**3**	
4 Section 1231 gain from installment sales from Form 6252, line 26 or 37	**4**	
5 Section 1231 gain or (loss) from like-kind exchanges from Form 8824	**5**	
6 Gain, if any, from line 32, from other than casualty or theft	**6**	1,000
7 Combine lines 2 through 6. Enter the gain or (loss) here and on the appropriate line as follows:	**7**	1,000

Partnerships (except electing large partnerships) and S corporations. Report the gain or (loss) following the instructions for Form 1065, Schedule K, line 10, or Form 1120S, Schedule K, line 9. Skip lines 8, 9, 11, and 12 below.

Individuals, partners, S corporation shareholders, and all others. If line 7 is zero or a loss, enter the amount from line 7 on line 11 below and skip lines 8 and 9. If line 7 is a gain and you did not have any prior year section 1231 losses, or they were recaptured in an earlier year, enter the gain from line 7 as a long-term capital gain on the Schedule D filed with your return and skip lines 8, 9, 11, and 12 below.

8 Nonrecaptured net section 1231 losses from prior years (see instructions)	**8**	
9 Subtract line 8 from line 7. If zero or less, enter -0-. If line 9 is zero, enter the gain from line 7 on line 12 below. If line 9 is more than zero, enter the amount from line 8 on line 12 below and enter the gain from line 9 as a long-term capital gain on the Schedule D filed with your return (see instructions)	**9**	

Part II   Ordinary Gains and Losses (see instructions)

10 Ordinary gains and losses not included on lines 11 through 16 (include property held 1 year or less):

11 Loss, if any, from line 7	**11**	( )
12 Gain, if any, from line 7 or amount from line 8, if applicable	**12**	
13 Gain, if any, from line 31	**13**	4,753
14 Net gain or (loss) from Form 4684, lines 35 and 42a	**14**	
15 Ordinary gain from installment sales from Form 6252, line 25 or 36	**15**	
16 Ordinary gain or (loss) from like-kind exchanges from Form 8824.	**16**	
17 Combine lines 10 through 16	**17**	4,753

18 For all except individual returns, enter the amount from line 17 on the appropriate line of your return and skip lines a and b below. For individual returns, complete lines a and b below:

a If the loss on line 11 includes a loss from Form 4684, line 39, column (b)(ii), enter that part of the loss here. Enter the part of the loss from income-producing property on Schedule A (Form 1040), line 28, and the part of the loss from property used as an employee on Schedule A (Form 1040), line 23. Identify as from "Form 4797, line 18a." See instructions . . **18a**

b Redetermine the gain or (loss) on line 17 excluding the loss, if any, on line 18a. Enter here and on Form 1040, line 14 | **18b** | 4,753

For Paperwork Reduction Act Notice, see separate instructions.	Cat. No. 13086I	Form **4797** (2009)

(continued)

EXHIBIT 7-4 *(concluded)*

Version A, Cycle 1

Form 4797 (2009)   Page **2**

Part III **Gain From Disposition of Property Under Sections 1245, 1250, 1252, 1254, and 1255** (see instructions)

19	(a) Description of section 1245, 1250, 1252, 1254, or 1255 property:	(b) Date acquired (mo., day, yr.)	(c) Date sold (mo., day, yr.)
A	Equipment	05/01/07	07/08/09
B			
C			
D			

	These columns relate to the properties on lines 19A through 19D. ▶		Property A	Property B	Property C	Property D
20	Gross sales price (**Note:** *See line 1 before completing.*)	20	11,000			
21	Cost or other basis plus expense of sale	21	10,000			
22	Depreciation (or depletion) allowed or allowable	22	4,753			
23	Adjusted basis. Subtract line 22 from line 21	23	5,247			
24	Total gain. Subtract line 23 from line 20	24	5,753			
25	**If section 1245 property:**					
a	Depreciation allowed or allowable from line 22	25a	4,753			
b	Enter the **smaller** of line 24 or 25a	25b	4,753			
26	**If section 1250 property:** If straight line depreciation was used, enter -0- on line 26g, except for a corporation subject to section 291.					
a	Additional depreciation after 1975 (see instructions)	26a				
b	Applicable percentage multiplied by the **smaller** of line 24 or line 26a (see instructions)	26b				
c	Subtract line 26a from line 24. If residential rental property or line 24 is not more than line 26a, skip lines 26d and 26e	26c				
d	Additional depreciation after 1969 and before 1976	26d				
e	Enter the **smaller** of line 26c or 26d	26e				
f	Section 291 amount (corporations only)	26f				
g	Add lines 26b, 26e, and 26f	26g				
27	**If section 1252 property:** Skip this section if you did not dispose of farmland or if this form is being completed for a partnership (other than an electing large partnership).					
a	Soil, water, and land clearing expenses	27a				
b	Line 27a multiplied by applicable percentage (see instructions)	27b				
c	Enter the **smaller** of line 24 or 27b	27c				
28	**If section 1254 property:**					
a	Intangible drilling and development costs, expenditures for development of mines and other natural deposits, mining exploration costs, and depletion (see instructions)	28a				
b	Enter the **smaller** of line 24 or 28a	28b				
29	**If section 1255 property:**					
a	Applicable percentage of payments excluded from income under section 126 (see instructions)	29a				
b	Enter the **smaller** of line 24 or 29a (see instructions)	29b				

Summary of Part III Gains. Complete property columns A through D through line 29b before going to line 30.

30	Total gains for all properties. Add property columns A through D, line 24	30	5,753
31	Add property columns A through D, lines 25b, 26g, 27c, 28b, and 29b. Enter here and on line 13	31	4,753
32	Subtract line 31 from line 30. Enter the portion from casualty or theft on Form 4684, line 37. Enter the portion from other than casualty or theft on Form 4797, line 6	32	1,000

Part IV **Recapture Amounts Under Sections 179 and 280F(b)(2) When Business Use Drops to 50% or Less** (see instructions)

			(a) Section 179	(b) Section 280F(b)(2)
33	Section 179 expense deduction or depreciation allowable in prior years	33		
34	Recomputed depreciation (see instructions)	34		
35	Recapture amount. Subtract line 34 from line 33. See the instructions for where to report	35		

Form **4797** (2009)

TAX YOUR BRAIN

Why are fewer building sales resulting in ordinary gains for taxpayers?

ANSWER

The main reason is that any depreciable real property purchased after 1986 must be depreciated using the straight-line method.[29] If the required depreciation is straight-line, there cannot be any depreciation in *excess* of straight-line.

In recent years, few §1250 sales have been subject to the §1250 recapture provisions. Most real property placed in service from 1981 through 1986 used accelerated depreciation methods over periods of 15, 18, or 19 years. Although it is likely that the same taxpayers still own many of these buildings, recall that these properties are considered §1245 property. Most other buildings placed in service prior to 1981 are likely to be fully depreciated under either straight-line or some other method.[30] Thus the depreciation taken would be the same under all methods.

The more important aspect of §1250 property in recent years is the capital gain rate applied to the gain. The term *unrecaptured* refers to the amount of capital gain attributable to depreciation previously taken and is taxed at a 25% capital gain rate rather than the 0% or 15% rate. For example, in February 2000 a taxpayer purchased for $200,000 a building to be used 100% in a trade or business (31.5-year property) and took $56,356 in total depreciation deductions. In 2009 the taxpayer sold the building for $275,000. Assume the taxpayer is in the 33% tax bracket. Here is how the gain on the sale is calculated and taxed:

Building cost basis	$200,000
Less depreciation	56,356
Adjusted basis	$143,644
Selling price	$275,000
Less adjusted basis	143,644
Realized gain	$131,356
Realized gain	$131,356
Less §1250 provision	56,356
Gain on §1231 asset	$ 75,000

The gain treated as income subject to the 25% tax is the lesser of the depreciation taken ($56,356) or the realized gain ($131,356); in this example that would be $56,356 taxed at a rate of 25%, resulting in $14,089 tax. If this was the only sale of a §1231 asset, the remaining $75,000 gain due to the appreciation in value (selling price $275,000 − cost basis $200,000) would qualify for the 15% rate, resulting in $11,250 additional tax. Given this example, the total tax liability on the sale of the building would be $25,339. If there were no recapture provisions, the entire $131,356 gain would have been taxed at the 15% rate, generating only $19,704 in tax liability.

The portion of the gain that is attributable to depreciation is taxed at 25%; any gain in excess of the depreciation taken is considered a normal §1231 gain and is potentially taxed at the preferential rate of 0% or 15%.

[29] Recall from Chapter 6 that the required MACRS depreciation for nonresidential real property is 39-year straight-line, and the required method for residential real property is 27.5 year straight-line.

[30] If the §1250 property purchased before 1981 is not fully depreciated, it will be late in its depreciation life. Because most accelerated methods for tax purposes switch to straight-line late in the asset's life or the depreciation allowed goes below straight-line, any possible recapture would be limited.

EXAMPLE 7-18

Joe used a building in his trade or business that he purchased in June 2005 for $165,000. He sold the building in June 2009. Assume straight-line depreciation was taken in the amount of $16,222. The adjusted basis is $148,778 ($165,000 − $16,222). Using the following independent situations, calculate the amount of any gain or loss, assuming the building sells in 2009 for the following amounts. Assume the maximum gain rate of 15%

Situation	Amount Realized	Adjusted Basis	Gain/ (Loss)	§1250 Amount	§1231 Gain/Loss
1	$172,000	$148,778	$23,222	$16,222 × 25% $4,056	$7,000 × 15% $ 1,050
2	160,000	148,778	11,222	$11,222 × 25% $2,806	-0-
3	140,000	148,778	(8,778)	0	(8,778) ordinary loss

From Shoebox to Software

Any sale of §1250 property is originally reported on page 2 of Form 4797, and the gain is transferred to Schedule D. Exhibit 7-5 illustrates the reporting on Form 4797 for situation 1 in Example 7-18. Note that the entire gain appears on page 1 of Form 4797. Because the gain is all capital, the gain transfers to Schedule D.

On page 2 of Schedule D, separate the 25% gain and the 15% gain, and then calculate the tax. The tax preparation software will calculate the §1250 gain. The unrecaptured §1250 gain worksheet shows the tax effect of this transaction.

CONCEPT CHECK 7-5—LO 5

1. Under §1231, gains receive preferential tax rate treatment but losses are limited to $3,000 per year. True or false?
2. The only pure §1231 asset is land used in a trade or business. True or false?
3. What is meant by the term *depreciation recapture?*
4. What is the difference between a §1245 asset and a §1250 asset?
5. What is the difference between recaptured and unrecaptured gain provisions?

TAX ISSUES FOR SPECIAL TYPES OF SALES
LO 6

Sales of Block Stock, Mutual Fund Capital Gain Distributions, and Sales of Shares from Mutual Funds

When shares of stock are purchased on different dates or for different prices, the shares are termed purchases of *blocks* of stock. Each block of stock may differ in basis and holding period (short-term or long-term). The taxpayer can specify which block is being sold (specific identification), or if the blocks are not specified, they are treated as coming from the earliest purchases (first-in, first-out).

A *mutual fund* is an investment vehicle that pools the resources of numerous taxpayers and purchases shares of stock in a portfolio. Tax treatment of a mutual fund investment can be difficult. For example, a mutual fund buys and sells individual stocks throughout the year, generating capital gains and losses from these sales. At year-end, the individual investors are

EXHIBIT 7-5   Sale of §1250 Property on Form 4797 and Schedule D from Example 7-18, Situation 1

Form **4797** Department of the Treasury Internal Revenue Service (99)	**Sales of Business Property** **(Also Involuntary Conversions and Recapture Amounts** **Under Sections 179 and 280F(b)(2))** ► **Attach to your tax return.** ► **See separate instructions.**	OMB No. 1545-0184 **2009** Attachment Sequence No. **27**

Name(s) shown on return

Joe Taxpayer

Identifying number

1 Enter the gross proceeds from sales or exchanges reported to you for 2009 on Form(s) 1099-B or 1099-S (or substitute statement) that you are including on line 2, 10, or 20 (see instructions) . . . . | **1** |

Part I   Sales or Exchanges of Property Used in a Trade or Business and Involuntary Conversions From Other Than Casualty or Theft—Most Property Held More Than 1 Year (see instructions)

2	**(a)** Description of property	**(b)** Date acquired (mo., day, yr.)	**(c)** Date sold (mo., day, yr.)	**(d)** Gross sales price	**(e)** Depreciation allowed or allowable since acquisition	**(f)** Cost or other basis, plus improvements and expense of sale	**(g)** Gain or (loss) Subtract (f) from the sum of (d) and (e)

3 Gain, if any, from Form 4684, line 43	**3**	
4 Section 1231 gain from installment sales from Form 6252, line 26 or 37	**4**	
5 Section 1231 gain or (loss) from like-kind exchanges from Form 8824	**5**	
6 Gain, if any, from line 32, from other than casualty or theft	**6**	23,222
7 Combine lines 2 through 6. Enter the gain or (loss) here and on the appropriate line as follows:	**7**	23,222

Partnerships (except electing large partnerships) and S corporations. Report the gain or (loss) following the instructions for Form 1065, Schedule K, line 10, or Form 1120S, Schedule K, line 9. Skip lines 8, 9, 11, and 12 below.

Individuals, partners, S corporation shareholders, and all others. If line 7 is zero or a loss, enter the amount from line 7 on line 11 below and skip lines 8 and 9. If line 7 is a gain and you did not have any prior year section 1231 losses, or they were recaptured in an earlier year, enter the gain from line 7 as a long-term capital gain on the Schedule D filed with your return and skip lines 8, 9, 11, and 12 below.

8 Nonrecaptured net section 1231 losses from prior years (see instructions)	**8**	
9 Subtract line 8 from line 7. If zero or less, enter -0-. If line 9 is zero, enter the gain from line 7 on line 12 below. If line 9 is more than zero, enter the amount from line 8 on line 12 below and enter the gain from line 9 as a long-term capital gain on the Schedule D filed with your return (see instructions)	**9**	

Part II   Ordinary Gains and Losses (see instructions)

10 Ordinary gains and losses not included on lines 11 through 16 (include property held 1 year or less):

11 Loss, if any, from line 7	**11** (	)
12 Gain, if any, from line 7 or amount from line 8, if applicable	**12**	
13 Gain, if any, from line 31	**13**	
14 Net gain or (loss) from Form 4684, lines 35 and 42a	**14**	
15 Ordinary gain from installment sales from Form 6252, line 25 or 36	**15**	
16 Ordinary gain or (loss) from like-kind exchanges from Form 8824	**16**	
17 Combine lines 10 through 16	**17**	

18 For all except individual returns, enter the amount from line 17 on the appropriate line of your return and skip lines a and b below. For individual returns, complete lines a and b below:

a If the loss on line 11 includes a loss from Form 4684, line 39, column (b)(ii), enter that part of the loss here. Enter the part of the loss from income-producing property on Schedule A (Form 1040), line 28, and the part of the loss from property used as an employee on Schedule A (Form 1040), line 23. Identify as from "Form 4797, line 18a." See instructions . . | **18a** |

b Redetermine the gain or (loss) on line 17 excluding the loss, if any, on line 18a. Enter here and on Form 1040, line 14 | **18b** |

For Paperwork Reduction Act Notice, see separate instructions.   Cat. No. 13086I   Form **4797** (2009)

(continued)

EXHIBIT 7-5 *(continued)*

Form 4797 (2009)   Page **2**

Part III   Gain From Disposition of Property Under Sections 1245, 1250, 1252, 1254, and 1255 (see instructions)

19	(a) Description of section 1245, 1250, 1252, 1254, or 1255 property:		(b) Date acquired (mo., day, yr.)	(c) Date sold (mo., day, yr.)
A	Building		06/01/05	06/01/09
B				
C				
D				

	These columns relate to the properties on lines 19A through 19D. ▶		Property A	Property B	Property C	Property D
20	Gross sales price (**Note:** See line 1 before completing.)	20	172,000			
21	Cost or other basis plus expense of sale	21	165,000			
22	Depreciation (or depletion) allowed or allowable	22	16,222			
23	Adjusted basis. Subtract line 22 from line 21	23	148,778			
24	Total gain. Subtract line 23 from line 20	24	23,222			
25	**If section 1245 property:**					
a	Depreciation allowed or allowable from line 22	25a				
b	Enter the **smaller** of line 24 or 25a	25b				
26	**If section 1250 property:** If straight line depreciation was used, enter -0- on line 26g, except for a corporation subject to section 291.					
a	Additional depreciation after 1975 (see instructions)	26a				
b	Applicable percentage multiplied by the **smaller** of line 24 or line 26a (see instructions)	26b				
c	Subtract line 26a from line 24. If residential rental property **or** line 24 is not more than line 26a, skip lines 26d and 26e	26c				
d	Additional depreciation after 1969 and before 1976	26d				
e	Enter the **smaller** of line 26c or 26d	26e				
f	Section 291 amount (corporations only)	26f				
g	Add lines 26b, 26e, and 26f	26g	0			
27	**If section 1252 property:** Skip this section if you did not dispose of farmland or if this form is being completed for a partnership (other than an electing large partnership).					
a	Soil, water, and land clearing expenses	27a				
b	Line 27a multiplied by applicable percentage (see instructions)	27b				
c	Enter the **smaller** of line 24 or 27b	27c				
28	**If section 1254 property:**					
a	Intangible drilling and development costs, expenditures for development of mines and other natural deposits, mining exploration costs, and depletion (see instructions)	28a				
b	Enter the **smaller** of line 24 or 28a	28b				
29	**If section 1255 property:**					
a	Applicable percentage of payments excluded from income under section 126 (see instructions)	29a				
b	Enter the **smaller** of line 24 or 29a (see instructions)	29b				

Summary of Part III Gains. Complete property columns A through D through line 29b before going to line 30.

30	Total gains for all properties. Add property columns A through D, line 24	30	23,222
31	Add property columns A through D, lines 25b, 26g, 27c, 28b, and 29b. Enter here and on line 13	31	0
32	Subtract line 31 from line 30. Enter the portion from casualty or theft on Form 4684, line 37. Enter the portion from other than casualty or theft on Form 4797, line 6	32	23,222

Part IV   Recapture Amounts Under Sections 179 and 280F(b)(2) When Business Use Drops to 50% or Less (see instructions)

			(a) Section 179	(b) Section 280F(b)(2)
33	Section 179 expense deduction or depreciation allowable in prior years	33		
34	Recomputed depreciation (see instructions)	34		
35	Recapture amount. Subtract line 34 from line 33. See the instructions for where to report	35		

Form **4797** (2009)

EXHIBIT 7-5 *(continued)*

SCHEDULE D (Form 1040) Department of the Treasury Internal Revenue Service (99)	**Capital Gains and Losses** ► **Attach to Form 1040 or Form 1040NR.** ► **See Instructions for Schedule D (Form 1040).** ► **Use Schedule D-1 to list additional transactions for lines 1 and 8.**	OMB No. 1545-0074 20**09** Attachment Sequence No. **12**

Name(s) shown on return	Your social security number
Joe Taxpayer

Part I   Short-Term Capital Gains and Losses—Assets Held One Year or Less

(a) Description of property (Example: 100 sh. XYZ Co.)	(b) Date acquired (Mo., day, yr.)	(c) Date sold (Mo., day, yr.)	(d) Sales price (see page D-7 of the instructions)	(e) Cost or other basis (see page D-7 of the instructions)	(f) Gain or (loss) Subtract (e) from (d)
1					

2 Enter your short-term totals, if any, from Schedule D-1, line 2 . . . . **2**

3 **Total short-term sales price amounts.** Add lines 1 and 2 in column (d) **3**

4 Short-term gain from Form 6252 and short-term gain or (loss) from Forms 4684, 6781, and 8824 **4**

5 Net short-term gain or (loss) from partnerships, S corporations, estates, and trusts from Schedule(s) K-1 . . . . **5**

6 Short-term capital loss carryover. Enter the amount, if any, from line 10 of your **Capital Loss Carryover Worksheet** on page D-7 of the instructions . . . . **6** ( )

7 **Net short-term capital gain or (loss).** Combine lines 1 through 6 in column (f) **7**

Part II   Long-Term Capital Gains and Losses—Assets Held More Than One Year

(a) Description of property (Example: 100 sh. XYZ Co.)	(b) Date acquired (Mo., day, yr.)	(c) Date sold (Mo., day, yr.)	(d) Sales price (see page D-7 of the instructions)	(e) Cost or other basis (see page D-7 of the instructions)	(f) Gain or (loss) Subtract (e) from (d)
8					

9 Enter your long-term totals, if any, from Schedule D-1, line 9 . . . . **9**

10 **Total long-term sales price amounts.** Add lines 8 and 9 in column (d) **10**

11 Gain from Form 4797, Part I; long-term gain from Forms 2439 and 6252; and long-term gain or (loss) from Forms 4684, 6781, and 8824 . . . . **11** | 23,222

12 Net long-term gain or (loss) from partnerships, S corporations, estates, and trusts from Schedule(s) K-1 . . . . **12**

13 Capital gain distributions. See page D-2 of the instructions **13**

14 Long-term capital loss carryover. Enter the amount, if any, from line 15 of your **Capital Loss Carryover Worksheet** on page D-7 of the instructions . . . . . . **14** ( )

15 **Net long-term capital gain or (loss).** Combine lines 8 through 14 in column (f). Then go to Part III on the back . . . . **15** | 23,222

For Paperwork Reduction Act Notice, see Form 1040 or Form 1040NR instructions.	Cat. No. 11338H	Schedule D (Form 1040) 2009

(continued)

EXHIBIT 7-5
(concluded)

Schedule D (Form 1040) 2009   Page **2**

Part III   Summary

16 Combine lines 7 and 15 and enter the result **16**   23,222

If line 16 is:
- A **gain**, enter the amount from line 16 on Form 1040, line 13, or Form 1040NR, line 14. Then go to line 17 below.
- A **loss**, skip lines 17 through 20 below. Then go to line 21. Also be sure to complete line 22.
- **Zero**, skip lines 17 through 21 below and enter -0- on Form 1040, line 13, or Form 1040NR, line 14. Then go to line 22.

17 Are lines 15 and 16 **both** gains?
- ☐ **Yes.** Go to line 18.
- ☐ **No.** Skip lines 18 through 21, and go to line 22.

18 Enter the amount, if any, from line 7 of the **28% Rate Gain Worksheet** on page D-8 of the instructions . . . . ▶ **18**   0

19 Enter the amount, if any, from line 18 of the **Unrecaptured Section 1250 Gain Worksheet** on page D-9 of the instructions . . . . ▶ **19**   16,222

20 Are lines 18 and 19 **both** zero or blank?
- ☐ **Yes.** Complete Form 1040 through line 43, or Form 1040NR through line 40. Then complete the **Qualified Dividends and Capital Gain Tax Worksheet** on page 38 of the Instructions for Form 1040 (or in the Instructions for Form 1040NR). **Do not** complete lines 21 and 22 below.
- ☒ **No.** Complete Form 1040 through line 43, or Form 1040NR through line 40. Then complete the **Schedule D Tax Worksheet** on page D-10 of the instructions. **Do not** complete lines 21 and 22 below.

21 If line 16 is a loss, enter here and on Form 1040, line 13, or Form 1040NR, line 14, the **smaller** of:
- The loss on line 16 or
- ($3,000), or if married filing separately, ($1,500)

     . . . . **21** (   )

Note. When figuring which amount is smaller, treat both amounts as positive numbers.

22 Do you have qualified dividends on Form 1040, line 9b, or Form 1040NR, line 10b?
- ☐ **Yes.** Complete Form 1040 through line 43, or Form 1040NR through line 40. Then complete the **Qualified Dividends and Capital Gain Tax Worksheet** on page 38 of the Instructions for Form 1040 (or in the Instructions for Form 1040NR).
- ☐ **No.** Complete the rest of Form 1040 or Form 1040NR.

Schedule D (Form 1040) 2009

Unrecaptured Section 1250 Gain Worksheet—Line 19   *Keep for Your Records*

If you are not reporting a gain on Form 4797, line 7, skip lines 1 through 9 and go to line 10.

1. If you have a section 1250 property in Part III of Form 4797 for which you made an entry in Part I of Form 4797 (but not on Form 6252), enter the **smaller** of line 22 or line 24 of Form 4797 for that property. If you did not have any such property, go to line 4. If you had more than one such property, see instructions . . . . **1.**	16,222
2. Enter the amount from Form 4797, line 26g, for the property for which you made an entry on line 1 . . . . **2.**	0
3. Subtract line 2 from line 1 . . . . **3.**	16,222
4. Enter the total unrecaptured section 1250 gain included on line 26 or line 37 of Form(s) 6252 from installment sales of trade or business property held more than 1 year (see instructions) . . . . **4.**	0
5. Enter the total of any amounts reported to you on a Schedule K-1 from a partnership or an S corporation as "unrecaptured section 1250 gain" . . . . **5.**	0
6. Add lines 3 through 5 . . . . **6.**	16,222
7. Enter the **smaller** of line 6 or the gain from Form 4797, line 7 . . . . **7.** 16,222	
8. Enter the amount, if any, from Form 4797, line 8 . . . . **8.** 0	
9. Subtract line 8 from line 7. If zero or less, enter -0- . . . . **9.**	16,222
10. Enter the amount of any gain from the sale or exchange of an interest in a partnership attributable to unrecaptured section 1250 gain (see instructions) . . . . **10.**	0
11. Enter the total of any amounts reported to you on a Schedule K-1, Form 1099-DIV, or Form 2439 as "unrecaptured section 1250 gain" from an estate, trust, real estate investment trust, or mutual fund (or other regulated investment company) . . . . **11.**	0
12. Enter the total of any unrecaptured section 1250 gain from sales (including installment sales) or other dispositions of section 1250 property held more than 1 year for which you did not make an entry in Part I of Form 4797 for the year of sale (see instructions) . . . . **12.**	0
13. Add lines 9 through 12 . . . . **13.**	16,222
14. If you had any section 1202 gain or collectibles gain or (loss), enter the total of lines 1 through 4 of the **28% Rate Gain Worksheet** on page D-8. Otherwise, enter -0- **14.** 0	
15. Enter the (loss), if any, from Schedule D, line 7. If Schedule D, line 7, is zero or a gain, enter -0- **15.** (0)	
16. Enter your long-term capital loss carryovers from Schedule D, line 14, and Schedule K-1 (Form 1041), box 11, code C **16.** (0)	
17. Combine lines 14 through 16. If the result is a (loss), enter it as a positive amount. If the result is zero or a gain, enter -0- . . . . **17.**	0
18. **Unrecaptured section 1250 gain.** Subtract line 17 from line 13. If zero or less, enter -0-. If more than zero, enter the result here and on Schedule D, line 19 . . . . **18.**	16,222

EXAMPLE 7-19

Mashun purchased the following blocks of stock:

Date	Shares	Price
February 5, 2007	100	$10
August 15, 2007	50	9
December 9, 2008	150	8

Mashun sold 200 shares of stock on July 26, 2009, for $8.50 per share for a total of $1,700.

Using the specific identification method:

The shares sold were identified as being 100 shares from the February 5, 2007, and 100 shares from the December 9, 2008, purchases. The basis for each block is calculated as follows:

February 5, 2007, purchase	100 shares x $10	= $1,000
July 26, 2009, sale	100 shares x $8.50	= 850
Loss on sale		$ (150) long-term

December 9, 2008, purchase	100 shares x $8	= $ 800
July 26, 2009, sale	100 shares x $8.50	= 850
Gain on sale		$50 short-term

Using the first-in, first-out method:

February 5, 2007, purchase	100 shares x $10	= $1,000
August 15, 2007, purchase	50 shares x $9	= 450
Basis		$1,450
July 26, 2009, sale	150 shares x $8.50	= $1,275
Loss on the sale		$(175) long-term

December 9, 2008, purchase	50 shares x $8	= $400
July 26, 2009, sale	50 shares x $8.50	= 425
Gain on sale		$25 short-term

responsible for paying taxes on their share of these gains and losses, which are considered to be long-term regardless of how long they are held by shareholders. These capital gains, known as *capital gain distributions,* are reported to the taxpayer (investor) on Form 1099-DIV.[31] The taxpayer reports the capital gain distribution on line 13 of Schedule D (any gains subject to a rate of 28% appear on the annual mutual fund statement and are reported by the taxpayer on Schedule D). If there are no other capital gains or losses, the amounts on Form 1099-DIV, line 2a, can go directly on Form 1040, line 13, or Form 1040 A, line 10 (see Exhibit 7-6).

Remember that ordinary dividends are a distribution from the earnings and profits of the corporation, are ordinary income, and include short-term capital gains.[32] Ordinary dividends are reported to taxpayers on Form 1099-DIV, and sales of stock are reported on Form 1099-B. Many mutual funds and stock brokerages use a substitute Form 1099-DIV or 1099-B to record multiple events under the taxpayer's account. The form does not typically include the cost of the shares of stock sold.

Many brokerage firms provide the taxpayer with an annual statement on which all activity for the year is reported. Many firms, but not all, automatically calculate the average cost of the shares for the taxpayer's convenience.

[31] The mutual fund may also pass through dividends to the investors.
[32] Publication 550, Chapter 1—Dividends and Other Corporate Distributions.

EXHIBIT 7-6

Excerpt from Form 1040

			12		
12	Business income or (loss). Attach Schedule C or C-EZ		13		
13	Capital gain or (loss). Attach Schedule D if required. If not required, check here ▶ ☐		14		
14	Other gains or (losses). Attach Form 4797				

Excerpt from Schedule D

12	Net long-term gain or (loss) from partnerships, S corporations, estates, and trusts from Schedule(s) K-1	12		
13	Capital gain distributions. See page D-2 of the instructions	13		
14	Long-term capital loss carryover. Enter the amount, if any, from line 15 of your **Capital Loss Carryover Worksheet** on page D-7 of the instructions	14	(	)

A tax challenge occurs in determining the basis of units or shares of the mutual funds sold. Often mutual fund stock purchases can occur at different times with regular purchases, dividend reinvestment programs, or automatic monthly investments. The simplest case is the sale of *all* shares. The gain or loss is the difference between the sales price and the total cost basis of the shares. However, if a taxpayer who has invested in a mutual fund for 10 years at $200 per month with all of the capital gains and dividends reinvested sells *some* (not all) of those shares, the taxpayer will have a challenge in establishing a cost basis from which to calculate gain or loss. For example, suppose the taxpayer has 1,000 mutual fund shares acquired at many different times over decades. This taxpayer then sells 56.125 units of the mutual fund for $5,000. The challenge is in establishing a cost of these shares that had different purchase prices to calculate the gain or loss on the sale. To simplify this challenge, the taxpayer can use one of three methods in determining the basis of the units in the mutual fund:[33]

- **First-in, first-out:** The first shares purchased are assumed to be the first shares sold. This usually results in the largest gain when the value of the mutual fund units appreciates.
- **Specific identification:** The taxpayer specifies exactly which units are sold from the fund.
- **Average basis:** The taxpayer takes the total cost basis and divides by the total number of units to get an average cost per unit (single-category method). The taxpayer can also use a double-category method by calculating an arithmetic average for the short-term basis and short-term units and an arithmetic average for the long-term basis and long-term units.

After the basis has been determined, any gain or loss is reported on Schedule D as for other stock sales. Using the information in Example 7-20, the gain on the sale of the stock held in this mutual fund will be $3,500 using the first-in, first-out method, $1,500 using the specific identification method, $2,000 using the single-category average basis method, and $500 short-term loss and $1,800 long-term gain using the double-category average basis. Using the information from Example 7-20, Exhibits 7-7 and 7-8 illustrate the recording of mutual fund dividends and sales on Schedule D and the Qualified Dividends and Capital Gain Tax Worksheet.

[33] Reg. §1.1012-1(e).

EXHIBIT 7-8 *(concluded)*

Form 1040—Line 44

Qualified Dividends and Capital Gain Tax Worksheet—Line 44

Keep for Your Records

Before you begin: ✓ See the instructions for line 44 that begin on page 37 to see if you can use this worksheet to figure your tax.

✓ If you do not have to file Schedule D and you received capital gain distributions, be sure you checked the box on line 13 of Form 1040.

1.	Enter the amount from Form 1040, line 43. However, if you are filing Form 2555 or 2555-EZ (relating to foreign earned income), enter the amount from line 3 of the worksheet on page 38 . . . . **1.**	34,750
2.	Enter the amount from Form 1040, line 9b* . . . . **2.**	300
3.	Are you filing Schedule D?* ☒ **Yes.** Enter the **smaller** of line 15 or 16 of Schedule D. If either line 15 or line 16 is a loss, enter -0- ☐ **No.** Enter the amount from Form 1040, line 13 } **3.**	3,000
4.	Add lines 2 and 3 . . . . **4.**	3,300
5.	If you are claiming investment interest expense on Form 4952, enter the amount from line 4g of that form. Otherwise, enter -0- . . . . **5.**	0
6.	Subtract line 5 from line 4. If zero or less, enter -0- . . . . **6.**	3,300
7.	Subtract line 6 from line 1. If zero or less, enter -0- . . . . **7.**	31,450
8.	Enter the **smaller** of: • The amount on line 1, or • $33,950 if single or married filing separately, $67,900 if married filing jointly or qualifying widow(er), $45,500 if head of household. } . . . . **8.**	33,950
9.	Is the amount on line 7 equal to or more than the amount on line 8? ☐ **Yes.** Skip lines 9 and 10; go to line 11 and check the "No" box. ☒ **No.** Enter the amount from line 7 . . . . **9.**	31,450
10.	Subtract line 9 from line 8 . . . . **10.**	2,500
11.	Are the amounts on lines 6 and 10 the same? ☐ **Yes.** Skip lines 11 through 14; go to line 15. ☒ **No.** Enter the **smaller** of line 1 or line 6 . . . . **11.**	3,300
12.	Enter the amount from line 10 (if line 10 is blank, enter -0-) . . . . **12.**	2,500
13.	Subtract line 12 from line 11 . . . . **13.**	800
14.	Multiply line 13 by 15% (.15) . . . . **14.**	120
15.	Figure the tax on the amount on line 7. Use the Tax Table or Tax Computation Worksheet, whichever applies . . . . **15.**	4,304
16.	Add lines 14 and 15 . . . . **16.**	4,424
17.	Figure the tax on the amount on line 1. Use the Tax Table or Tax Computation Worksheet, whichever applies . . . . **17.**	4,881
18.	**Tax on all taxable income.** Enter the **smaller** of line 16 or line 17. Also include this amount on Form 1040, line 44. If you are filing Form 2555 or 2555-EZ, do not enter this amount on Form 1040, line 44. Instead, enter it on line 4 of the worksheet on page 38 . . . . **18.**	4,424

If you are filing Form 2555 or 2555-EZ, see the footnote in the worksheet on page 38 before completing this line.

capital loss limitation rules for deductibility. If a security becomes worthless during the year, the taxpayer reports a loss from a sale or exchange of a capital asset on the last day of the taxable year.[34] The mere fact that a company declares bankruptcy is not sufficient to indicate worthlessness. It is often difficult to pinpoint exactly when a security became worthless and hence determine a sale date for long-term versus short-term treatment. Thus, for these purposes, a loss on a worthless security is assumed to occur on the last day of the taxable year.[35]

[34] IRC §165(g).
[35] IRC §165(g).

EXAMPLE 7-21	Diane purchased 500 shares in Bad News, Inc., for $10,000 on December 12, 2008. The company promptly went bankrupt in February 2009 with no hope of recovery for the shareholders. Accordingly, the date the stock is deemed to be worthless occurs on December 31, 2009; Diane would have a long-term capital loss of $10,000 in tax year 2009.

Sales of Inherited Property

Remember that in this situation the basis to the beneficiaries is the FMV at the date of death or alternate valuation date (if the estate qualifies for and elects to use the alternate date) and that the holding period is always considered long-term. If no federal estate tax return is filed, use the FMV at the date of death. For example, Taylor inherits property from a relative with a FMV of $5,000 on June 13, 2009. On November 21, 2009, Taylor sells the property for $7,000 for a $2,000 gain. Even though Taylor held the property for less than one year, the gain is taxed as a long-term capital gain.

Sales of Property Received as a Gift

To figure the gain or loss from the sale of property received as a gift, the person who received the gift must know the adjusted basis of the property to the donor and the FMV when the gift was given. If the FMV is less than the donor's adjusted basis at the time of the gift, the basis for figuring the gain is the donor's basis and the FMV is the basis for figuring a loss. If the FMV is equal to or more than the donor's adjusted basis, the basis for any gain or loss on a sale is the donor's adjusted basis.[36]

EXAMPLE 7-22	Juan receives property as a gift. At the time of the gift, the property had a FMV of $7,000. The donor's basis was $9,000. Using the following situations, calculate Juan's gain or loss on the sale of the gifted property:

Situation	Sell Price	Donor Basis	FMV at Date of Gift	Gain/Loss
1	$11,000	$9,000	$7,000	$2,000 gain (use donor basis)
2	6,000	9,000	7,000	$(1,000) loss (use FMV at date of gift)
3	8,000	9,000	7,000	No gain or loss; sale price in between basis and FMV

Note: If the FMV of the gift was $10,000 at the date of the gift, the donor's basis of $9,000 would be used to calculate any gains or losses on a subsequent sale.

CONCEPT CHECK 7-6—LO 6	1. Explain the three types of methods used to determine the basis of the units in a mutual fund.
	2. It is often difficult to pinpoint exactly when a security becomes worthless, so the loss on a worthless security is treated as occurring on the last day of the taxable year. True or false?
	3. The basis for property given as a gift is always the fair market value of the property at the time of the gift. True or false?
	4. The tax treatment of a gain on the sale of inherited property depends on the holding period of the deceased taxpayer. True or false?

Table 7-5 is a summary table for the sale of all assets. These assets include ordinary assets, §1221 capital assets, §1231 assets, §1245 assets, and §1250 assets.

[36] See Chapter 4 in Publication 550 for more detailed information about sales of property received as a gift subject to gift tax.

TABLE 7-5 Summary of Asset Sales

			Asset Type		
	Ordinary Asset	**§1221 Capital Asset**	**§1231 Asset**	**§1245 Asset**	**§1250 Asset**
	1. Short-term business assets 2. Short-term gains or losses 3. Inventory 4. Accounts receivable or notes receivable	1. Not inventory 2. Not depreciable business assets 3. Not copyrights* 4. Not accounts receivable or notes receivable	1. Depreciable or nondepreciable business assets held ≧ 1 year 2. Long-term depreciable or nondepreciable real property 3. Not inventory 4. Not copyrights 5. Not short-term business assets	1. Subset of §1231 2. Depreciable personal property	1. Subset of §1231 2. Depreciable real property
Gain (Loss) Treatment	Ordinary income/loss	**Gains** Net short-term capital gains held ≦ 1 year Net long-term capital gains held > 1 year 0% or 15% rate† Collectibles 28% §1202 investments **Losses** Net short-term capital losses held ≦ 1 year Net long-term capital losses held > 1 year	**Gains** Net long-term taxed at long-term capital gains preferential rates **Losses** Net capital losses deducted as an ordinary loss	**Gains** Ordinary to the extent of depreciation taken; excess is true §1231 capital gain **Losses** §1231 loss—ordinary loss	**Gains** Ordinary to the extent depreciation taken exceeds straight-line; subject to 25% rate to the extent of depreciation taken; excess is true §1231 capital gain **Losses** §1231 loss—ordinary loss
Form Reported	Form 4797 Part II	Schedule D	Form 4797 Part I	Form 4797 Part III	Form 4797 Part III
Asset Example	Inventory or account receivable	Stocks and securities	Business land	Business equipment	Business building

*Refer to new election provisions for musical works.

†5% or 15% for post–May 6, 2003, sales until 12/31/07.

Summary

LO 1: Define the terms and identify the tax forms used in sales of property transactions.

- The amount realized (or sales proceeds) and the adjusted basis of the asset must be determined before a gain or loss on the sale of the asset can be determined.
- *A gain or loss on the sale of property* is the difference between the amount realized from the sale and the asset's adjusted basis.
- The nature of tax reporting for gains and losses on the sale of property depends primarily on the use of the asset.
- Schedule D and Form 4797 are used to record sales of property

LO 2: Classify assets sold as ordinary assets, §1221 capital assets, or §1231 business assets.

- Ordinary income property is any asset that is "not a capital asset."
- In general, any asset used for personal purposes or investment is a *capital asset*, but there are eight basic exceptions to this definition.
- §1231 property is property used in a trade or business that is depreciable or real and held for more than one year.
- Any business asset that is disposed of within one year of acquisition is an ordinary income asset.

LO 3: Explain and apply the tax rules for recognizing gains or losses on the sale of ordinary assets.

- Inventory and accounts receivable are not ordinary income assets unless they are outside (not part of) the normal course of business.
- Inventory sold is a part of the cost of goods sold, whereas accounts receivable are generated from sales of the inventory.
- Gains are taxed at the taxpayer's regular tax rate; there is no preferential tax treatment.

LO 4: Explain and apply the tax rules for recognizing short-term and long-term gains or losses on the sale of capital assets (§1221).

- Tax treatment for a capital gain or loss depends on the holding period of the asset. Assets must be held for more than one year for preferential treatment.
- Generally, the property received through a gift or nontaxable exchange has the same basis as the basis in the hands of the transferor.
- The exception to this rule is property received through inheritance, in which case the asset is always long-term property.
- Tax rates differ depending on the holding period; short-term assets are taxed at regular taxpayer rates, whereas long-term assets are taxed at preferential rates.
- The 0% and 15% rates are for long-term gains on capital assets.
- The 25% rate is applied to that portion of the gain attributable to the depreciation on real property used in a trade or business.
- The 28% rate applies to "collectibles" gains and gains on §1202 property (qualified small business stock).
- All short-term gains and losses are netted, as are all long-term gains and losses. The resultant gain or loss determines the deductibility of a loss and the tax rate used for gains.

LO 5: Calculate the recognized gain or loss on the sale of §1231 business assets, including gain recapture provisions of §1245 and §1250 property.

- Gains and losses from the sale of §1231 assets must be netted before tax rates are applied.
- A net §1231 gain is taxed as a long-term capital gain subject to recapture provisions.
- Net §1231 gains receive preferential tax rate treatment.
- Net §1231 losses are treated as ordinary losses and are fully deductible.
- Losses disallowed in the current year can be carried over to future years.
- Depreciation recapture rules are designed to transform some or all of a §1231 gain into an ordinary gain.
- §1245 (personal trade or business property) and §1250 (buildings, residential and nonresidential) are subsets of §1231 property and apply only when there is a gain on the sale of a property that has been depreciated.
- The tax rate for unrecaptured depreciation on §1250 property is 25%.

LO 6: Describe the tax rules for special types of sales, including block stock sales, capital gain distributions, sales of mutual funds, worthless securities, and sales of property received as a gift or through inheritance.

- Block stock sales are shares that are sold at one time but were purchased at different times or prices. Use either specific identification or the first-in, first-out method to calculate share basis.
- A mutual fund pools resources from various sources and purchases shares of stock in a portfolio.
- Capital gain distributions from mutual funds can be reported either on Schedule D or directly on Form 1040 if Schedule D is not being prepared.
- Determining the basis of mutual fund shares can be challenging. Three methods are available for calculating the basis of the shares: first-in, first-out, specific identification, and single- or double-category average basis.
- Worthless securities are treated as losses from a sale or exchange of a capital asset on the last day of the taxable year.
- Property received through an inheritance is always considered to be long-term regardless of the holding period by the beneficiary. The basis to the beneficiary is valued at the FMV at the date of death or alternate valuation date chosen by the personal representative if qualified under estate tax rules.
- The FMV and adjusted basis of the property at the date given by the donor must be known for the donee to properly calculate a gain or loss on the sale of gifted property in the future.

Discussion Questions

LO 1   1. How are the terms *basis, adjusted basis,* and *fair market value* defined as they apply to the calculation of gains and losses?

_____

_____

_____

LO 1   2. What is meant by the terms *realized gain (loss)* and *recognized gain (loss)* as they apply to the sale of assets by a taxpayer?

_____

_____

_____

LO 2   3. How can the gain from the sale of property be characterized? Why is it important to correctly characterize the gain on the sale of property?

_____

_____

_____

LO 2   4. What is a *capital* as*set?* What factors affect the determination of whether an asset is classified as a capital asset?

_____

_____

_____

LO 2   5. What determines whether land is a capital asset? How else can land be classified?

_____

_____

_____

LO 2   6. What is a §1231 asset? How are gains and losses from the sale of §1231 assets treated? On what tax form are gains and losses from the sale of §1231 assets reported?

_____

_____

_____

LO 2   7. When we determine whether an asset is a §1231 asset, does the length of time the asset is held affect the classification? Explain.

_____

_____

_____

LO 2   8. What are the different classifications of capital assets? Define each classification and explain the difference in the preferential tax treatment (the rate at which the gains are taxed).

_____

_____

_____

LO 3   9. Discuss the concept of ordinary income property and give some examples.

_____

_____

_____

LO 4   10. What factors affect the taxability of capital gains and losses?

_____

_____

_____

LO 4   11. Does the length of time a capital asset is held affect the gain or loss on the sale of the asset? Explain.

_____

_____

_____

LO 4   12. How is a net capital loss treated? Include in your answer a discussion of how a net capital loss is treated in relation to other income.

_____

_____

_____

LO 4   13. In what ways can a capital asset be acquired, and how is the holding period determined for each method of acquisition?

_____

_____

_____

LO 4   14. Capital gains can be taxed at several different rates. What determines the rate?

_____

_____

_____

LO 4   15. What is a §1202 gain, and how is it taxed?

LO 4   16. Discuss the netting process of capital gains and losses. What are the possible outcomes of the netting process, and how would each situation be taxed?

LO 5   17. What is a §1245 asset? How is it related to a §1231 asset?

LO 5   18. What is a §1250 asset? How is it related to a §1231 asset?

LO 5   19. Explain the terms *recapture* and *unrecaptured provisions* as they apply to §1250 assets.

LO 6   20. What is a capital gain distribution, and how is it taxed?

LO 6   21. How can a taxpayer determine the basis of units from a mutual fund?

LO 6   22. How are gains (losses) from the sale of property acquired from a decedent taxed?

LO 6   23. Explain how gains (losses) from the sale of property acquired as a gift are taxed.

Multiple-Choice Questions

LO 1   24. Jim sells a parcel of land for $60,000 cash, and the buyer assumes Jim's liability of $8,000 on the land. Jim's basis is $50,000. What is the gain or loss on the sale?
   a. $2,000 gain.
   b. $10,000 gain.
   c. $18,000 gain.
   d. $18,000 loss.

LO 1 25. All of the following statements regarding the definition of basis other than cost are true except

    a. The basis for assets received as a gift depends on whether the FMV is greater than, equal to, or less than the donor's basis at the time of the gift.

    b. The basis of property transferred to a taxpayer from a former spouse pursuant to a divorce decree is valued at the FMV at the date of the decree.

    c. The basis of inherited property is the FMV at the date of death or alternate valuation date that the personal representative is allowed by law to choose.

    d. The basis for property received in exchange for services rendered is the FMV of the property if the FMV of the services is not known beforehand.

LO 1 26. All of the following expenses increase the basis of stock held for investment except

    a. Commission fees on the purchase of the stock.

    b. Stock splits.

    c. Stock dividends from a dividend reinvestment plan.

    d. All of the above increase the basis of stock held for investment.

LO 2 27. In 2002 Matthew purchased land for $97,000 for use in his business. He sold it in 2009 for $103,000. What are the amount and type of gain on this sale before netting of any other gains and/or losses?

    a. $6,000 short-term capital gain.

    b. $6,000 long-term capital gain.

    c. $6,000 ordinary income.

    d. $6,000 §1231 gain.

LO 3 28. On May 20, 2008, Jessica purchased land for $92,000 to use in her business. She sold it on May 21, 2009, for $87,000. What are the amount and type of loss on this sale if Jessica does not have any other sales from a trade or business?

    a. $5,000 deferred loss.

    b. $5,000 long-term capital loss.

    c. $5,000 ordinary loss.

    d. $5,000 §1231 loss.

LO 4 29. What are the maximum capital gain rates?

    a. 33% and 35%.

    b. 15% and 25%.

    c. 25% and 28%.

    d. 0% and 15%.

LO 4 30. In 1999 Sam purchased 2,000 shares of stock for $50,000 in a midsize local company with gross assets of $15,000,000. In 2009, Sam sold the stock for $88,000. How is the gain treated for tax purposes?

    a. $38,000 capital gain and taxed at preferential rates.

    b. $19,000 excluded from gross income under §1202 with the remaining gain recognized and taxed at regular rates.

    c. $19,000 excluded from gross income under §1202 and 9,500 taxed at 28%.

    d. $19,000 excluded from gross income under §1202 and 9,500 taxed at preferential rates.

LO 4 31. Blair sold the following stocks in 2009: 200 shares of Dearborn Investments, purchased May 15, 2008, for $3,050 and sold January 9, 2009 for $4,135 and 40 shares of State

Street Investments, purchased November 7, 2006, for $11,875 and sold March 29, 2009, for $8,675. What are the pre-net amount and nature of the gain (loss) on the sale of these transactions on Blair's 1040 return for 2009?

a. $1,085 short-term gain and $3,000 long-term loss.

b. $1,085 short-term gain and $3,200 long-term loss.

c. $1,915 net long-term loss.

d. $2,115 net long-term loss.

LO 4 32. Which statement is true regarding short-term capital gains?

a. If there are a net short-term gain and a net long-term gain, both gains are taxed at regular rates.

b. A long-term loss offsets a short-term gain, and if a gain results, the gain is taxed at regular rates.

c. A long-term loss offsets a short-term gain, and if a gain results, the gain is taxed at preferential rates.

d. If there are a net short-term gain and a net long-term gain, both gains are taxed at preferential rates.

LO 4 33. Which is true regarding long-term capital gains?

a. A net long-term gain can offset a short-term gain but not a short-term loss.

b. A net long-term gain can be taxed at 28%, 25%, 15%, or 0%, depending on the type of gain generated.

c. A net long-term loss can be offset against a long-term gain, and if there is a resulting long-term gain, it is taxed at regular rates.

d. A long-term loss can offset a long-term gain only if the netting result produces a loss of more than $3,000.

LO 4 34. When there are a net short-term loss and a net long-term loss, which of the following is true?

a. The entire short-term loss is used to reduce other income before the long-term loss can be used to offset other income.

b. A long-term loss is used to reduce other income before the short-term loss.

c. Regardless of the amount of a short-term or long-term loss, the maximum amount of loss that can be taken in any one year is $3,000. Any remaining loss amounts can be carried forward for three years for individual taxpayers.

d. Regardless of the amount of a short-term or long-term loss, the maximum amount of loss that can be taken in any one year is $3,000. Any remaining loss amounts can be carried forward indefinitely for individual taxpayers.

LO 4 35. Alton received a Form 1099-B that shows a net sales price of $1,500 on the sale of 600 shares of FNP Company. He bought the stock on October 21, 2008, and sold it on October 22, 2009. His basis in the stock is $1,325, of which $25 is a commission fee. What are the amount and nature of Alton's gain?

a. $175 short-term gain.

b. $200 short-term gain.

c. $175 long-term gain.

d. $200 long-term gain.

LO 4, 6 36. Amal received a Form 1099-DIV with a capital gain distribution of $170. She also received a Form 1099-B from the sale of 240 shares of AMS stock she purchased for $2,400 plus a $28 commission fee on February 22, 2008. The net proceeds of the stock

sale were $2,200 (the commission fee was $14) and the trade date was February 22, 2009. What are the amount and nature of Amal's gain (loss) on these transactions?

a. $214 short-term loss and $170 long-term gain.

b. $214 long-term loss and $170 short-term gain.

c. $228 long-term loss and $170 short-term gain.

d. $228 short-term loss and $170 long-term gain.

LO 5 37. Shannon bought an apartment building in July 2003 for $360,000 and sold it for $480,000 in 2009. There was $95,000 of accumulated straight-line depreciation on the apartment building. Assuming that Shannon is in the 33% tax bracket, how much of her gain is taxed at 25%?

a. $0.

b. $95,000.

c. $120,000.

d. $215,000.

LO 5 38. Karen, a single taxpayer, has income from her W-2 of $60,000. She also has a short-term capital loss of $8,000, a short-term capital gain of $3,000, and a long-term capital gain of $4,000. What is Karen's AGI for 2009?

a. $59,000.

b. $61,000.

c. $64,000.

d. $67,000.

LO 6 39. In 2009 Ann received 1,000 shares of stock as a gift from her husband, Tim, who purchased them in 2002. At the time of the gift, the FMV of the stock was $20,000 and Tim's basis was $25,000. If Ann sells the stock for $28,000 in 2009, what are the nature and amount of the gain from the sale?

a. $3,000 long-term gain.

b. $8,000 long-term gain.

c. $3,000 short-term gain and $5,000 long-term gain.

d. $3,000 long-term gain and $5,000 short-term gain.

LO 6 40. In 2009 Ann received 1,000 shares of stock as a gift from her husband, Tim, who purchased them in 2002. At the time of the gift, the FMV of the stock was $20,000 and Tim's basis was $25,000. If Ann sells the stock for $18,000 in 2009, what are the nature and amount of the loss from the sale?

a. $2,000 short-term loss.

b. $5,000 long-term loss.

c. $7,000 long-term loss.

d. $2,000 short-term loss and $5,000 long-term loss.

Problems **LO 2** 41. Explain the differences between an ordinary income asset, a § 1221 (capital) asset, and a § 1231 asset and how the gains or losses on the sale of each asset are treated for tax purposes.

_____

_____

_____

_____

LO 3 42. Stanley buys a painting for $500 from a museum for resale in his art gallery. He sold it 18 months later for $1,400. What is the most favorable tax treatment for Stanley?

Would the tax treatment be different if Stanley had purchased the painting for personal enjoyment?

_____

_____

_____

LO 3 43. Lani sold some equipment she used in her business on August 29, 2009, that was originally purchased for $60,000 on November 21, 2008. The equipment was depreciated using the straight-line method over a five-year useful life and the half-year convention for a total of $5,000.

    a. Assume Lani sold the equipment for $50,000:

        (1) What is the gain or loss on the sale of the equipment?

        (2) What is the nature of the gain or loss, on what form(s) will this event be recorded, and how is the gain or loss treated for tax purposes on Lani's 2009 1040 tax return? Assume she has no other sales that will generate gains or losses.

        _____

        _____

        _____

    b. Assume Lani sold the equipment for $60,000:

        (1) What is the gain or loss on the sale of the equipment?

        (2) What is the nature of the gain or loss, on what form(s) will this event be recorded, and how is the gain or loss treated for tax purposes on Lani's 2009 1040 tax return? Assume she has no other sales that will generate gains or losses.

        _____

        _____

        _____

LO 1, 2, 4 44. Alice owns undeveloped land with an adjusted basis of $140,000. She sells the property to George for $185,000.

    a. What is Alice's realized and recognized gain or loss?

    _____

    _____

    b. What is the character of the gain or loss?

    _____

    _____

    c. If the land is used in a trade or business, is the character of the gain or loss different? Explain.

    _____

    _____

    _____

LO 4 45. Gaylord has taxable income of $95,000 without consideration of capital gain or loss transactions. He has a short-term capital gain of $10,000, a long-term capital loss of $2,000, and a short-term capital gain of $4,000. What is the effect of these gains and the loss on taxable income? What are the amount and nature of any carryover? Assuming that none of the gains or losses is from collectibles or unrecaptured §1250 property, at what rate will the gains or losses be taxed to Gaylord, who is in the 25% tax bracket for ordinary income?

_____

_____

_____

_____

_____

_____

_____

LO 5   46. Jake purchased a $200,000 crane for his construction business. He sold the crane for $145,000 after taking $110,000 of depreciation. What are the nature and the amount of gain or loss on the sale? On what tax form would the gain or loss originally be reported?

_____

_____

_____

LO 4   47. Larry owns an automobile for personal use. The adjusted basis is $16,000, and the FMV is $13,500. Assume Larry has owned the automobile for two years.

     a. Calculate the realized and recognized gain or loss if Larry sells the vehicle for $13,500. _____

     b. Calculate the realized and recognized gain or loss if Larry sells the vehicle for $17,000. _____

LO 4   48. Antoine sold the following stock in 2009. ABC, Inc., is a § 1202 qualified small business (QSB).

Asset	Cost	Acquired	Sales Price	Sale Date
ABC, Inc. 200 shares	$148,000	1/10/03	$200,000	4/30/09
DEF, Inc. 100 shares	21,000	11/15/06	14,000	2/28/09
GHI, Inc. 50 shares	18,000	3/31/08	17,000	8/30/09

     a. Determine the amount and the character of the realized and recognized gain or loss from each sale.

_____

_____

_____

     b. How would the gains and losses be netted?

_____

_____

_____

     c. On what form would the gains and losses be reported? Complete page 1 of that form to show the proper reporting of these stock sales.

LO 5   49. Ricardo acquired a warehouse for business purposes on August 30, 1992. The building cost $200,000. He took $133,333 of depreciation on the building and then sold it for $350,000 on July 1, 2009. What are the amount and nature of Ricardo's gain or loss on the sale of the warehouse?

_____

_____

_____

LO 1. 2, 3, 4, 5 50. Davidson Industries, a sole proprietorship, sold the following assets in 2009:

Asset	Cost	Acquired	Depreciation	Sales Price	Sale Date
Warehouse	$150,000	10/10/05	$28,000	$175,000	3/15/09
Truck	18,000	1/15/08	4,500	16,000	1/15/09
Computer	25,000	7/31/08	3,000	21,000	8/31/09

  a. Determine the amount and the character of the realized and recognized gain or loss from the sale of each asset.

  b. Prepare Form 4797 to report the gains and losses.

  c. How would your answer change if the computer were a personal computer used at home?

LO 3, 4, 5 51. In 2009, Juanita sold stock considered short-term for a gain of $875 and stock considered long-term for a loss of $2,400. She also had a $2,000 short-term loss carryover from 2008 and a $240 long-term loss carryover from 2008.

  a. What amount will be shown as a short-term gain (loss) for 2009? _____

  b. What amount will be shown as a long-term gain (loss) for 2009? _____

  c. Will there be a carryover for 2010? If so, what are the nature and amount of the carryover?

  d. Prepare a Schedule D. (Detailed stock information has been omitted; use reasonable assumptions.)

LO 6 52. Lois purchased the following blocks of Westgate stock:

Date	Shares	Price
June 12, 2007	1,000	$4.225
October 21, 2007	2,000	4.775
December 18, 2008	1,500	5.500

Lois sold 1,600 shares of the stock on November 20, 2009, for $5.00 per share for a total of $8,000. Using the first-in, first-out method, calculate the gain or loss on the sale of the Westgate stock.

What if 750 of the shares sold were identified as being from the October 21, 2007, purchase and the remaining 850 shares from the December 18, 2008, purchase? Using the specific identification method, calculate the gain or loss on the sale of the Westgate stock.

53. During 2009 Roberto sold 830 shares of Casual Investor Mutual Fund for $8.875 per share. The shares were purchased on the following dates:

Date	Shares	Price
May 31, 2006	400	$9.375
September 18, 2007	225	8.500
October 21, 2007	425	10.000
January 12, 2008	276	7.125

Required: Calculate the gain (loss) on the sale under the following assumptions (carry your calculations to three places):

a. Basis is calculated using the first-in, first-out method.

b. Basis is calculated using the average cost method (assume all shares are long-term).

LO 3, 4, 5 54. Suzette inherited property from her father on April 19, 2009. The FMV at the date of death was $40,000. The property was worth $35,000 six months later and had a basis to her father of $25,000.

   a. What is the basis of the inherited property to Suzette:

   (1). If the alternate valuation date was not elected? _____

   (2). If this property qualifies for using the alternate valuation date? _____

   _____

   b. Assuming that Suzette sold the property on November 1, 2009, for $47,500, what is the amount and nature of the gain:

   (1). If the alternate valuation date was not elected: _____

   (2). If this property qualifies for using the alternate valuation date? _____

LO 5 55. Using the following independent situations, answer the following questions:

Situation 1

Clara received from her Aunt Sona property with a FMV at the date of the gift of $40,000. Aunt Sona purchased the property five years ago for $35,000. Clara sold the property for $43,000.

   a. What is the basis to Clara? _____

   b. What is Clara's gain on the sale? _____

   c. If Clara is in the 33% tax bracket, what is the tax on the gain (assuming she has no other gains/losses to be netted)? _____

   d. If Clara is in the 15% tax bracket, what is the tax on the gain (assuming she has no other gains/losses to be netted)? _____

Situation 2

Clara received from her Aunt Sona property with a FMV at the date of the gift of $30,000. Aunt Sona purchased the property five years ago for $35,000.

   a. What if Clara sold the property for $43,000, what is her gain or loss on the sale?

   _____

   b. What if Clara sold the property for $33,000, what is her gain or loss on the sale?

   _____

   c. What if Clara sold the property for $28,000, what is her gain or loss on the sale?

   _____

LO 6 56. Ramon received a gift of stock from his uncle. The basis of the stock to his uncle was $20,000, and it had an FMV at the date of the gift of $13,000. The donor held the property for more than one year. Complete the following chart under the independent situations shown:

	Situation 1	Situation 2	Situation 3
Donor's basis	$20,000	$20,000	$20,000
FMV at gift date	13,000	13,000	13,000
Ramon's selling price	25,000	10,000	15,000
Basis to Ramon	—	—	—
Taxable gain (if any)	—	—	—
Deductible loss (if any)	—	—	—

Tax Return Problems

Use your tax software to complete the following problems. If you are manually preparing the tax returns, you will need Form 1040, Schedule A, Schedule B, Schedule D, Schedule D worksheets, and Form 4797, or other forms depending on the problems.

Tax Return Problem 1

Jeffery Norville is a single taxpayer. His SSN is 123-44-7788, and he lives at 5037 Circle Court, Crestview, Illinois. His W-2 for 2009 shows gross wages of $83,000 with $5,146 of social security and $1,203.50 of Medicare taxes withheld. He has $17,747 of federal withholding and $2,490 in state withholding. Jeffery does not itemize. He had the following stock transactions for the year:

Stock Shares	Date Purchased	Date Sold	Sales Price	Cost Basis
5,500	7/8/08	9/12/09	$15,000	$18,000
800	3/12/09	10/21/09	54,000	58,000
2,800	2/13/03	10/21/09	34,000	22,000

He also has interest from a savings account with Local Neighborhood Bank of $168 and a dividend from a Form 1099-DIV of $1,389 in ordinary dividends, of which $1,106 are considered qualified dividends.

Prepare a 2009 Form 1040 for Jeffery and all related schedules and forms.

Tax Return Problem 2

Janis Blakeley is single and lives at 5411 Melbourne Avenue, Chicago, Illinois. Her SSN is 123-45-6789. Using the following information, complete her tax return for 2009:

Kimber Company W-2:

Gross	$80,000
Social security tax	4,960
Medicare tax	1,160
Federal withholding tax	15,378
State withholding tax	2,400

Lee Company W-2:

Gross	$20,000
Social security tax	1,240
Medicare tax	290
Federal withholding tax	2,000
State withholding tax	600

Janis has the following itemized deductions:

Real estate tax	$ 7,633
Mortgage interest	8,445
Charitable contributions	3,000

Janis has the following investments:

1099-INT	$ 2,850
1099-DIV	
Ordinary dividends	$ 2,634
Qualified dividends	891
Capital gain distribution	4,711
2008 short-term loss carryover	($1,000)

Janis received a gift of 2,000 shares of FNP Inc. stock from her Aunt Jane on January 19, 2009. The basis of the shares to Aunt Jane was $3,300, and they had a FMV of $3,600 on the date of the gift. Aunt Jane purchased the stock on December 30, 2008. On June 30, 2009, Janis sold all the shares for $5,000.

Janis is an avid stamp collector and purchased a rare stamp on March 20, 2005, for $4,000. She sold the stamp for $6,000 on April 8, 2009.

Prepare Form 1040 and all related schedules, forms, and worksheets for 2009. Janis does not donate to the presidential election campaign.

Tax Return Problem 3

Tony and Agnes Miller are married and file a joint return in 2009. They live at 12345 Hemenway Avenue, Marlboro, MA. Tony is a self-employed tax preparer and his SSN is 444-55-6666. Agnes is a manager and her SSN is 444-55-7777. They had the following income and expenses for the year:

Agnes' W-2:

Gross wages	$90,000
Social security tax	5,580
Medicare tax	1,305
Federal withholding tax	21,178
State withholding tax	4,800

Tony was the sole proprietor of TM Tax Service. His business is located at 123 Main Street, Marlboro, MA, and his business code is 541213. He had the following revenue and expenses:

Revenue	$80,000
Expenses:	
Advertising	1,200
Insurance	3,200
Telephone	2,400
Office rent	18,000
Utilities	4,800
Office supplies	5,000
Depreciation	6,041 (must be allocated to the §1231 assets listed next)

Expenses paid by the tenant or services provided by the tenant in lieu of rent payments are also components of rental income. If the tenant pays an expense normally paid by the taxpayer, the taxpayer must include that payment in rental income. Likewise, if the tenant performs services in exchange for free rent or reduced rent, the value of those services is included in rental income.[7]

EXAMPLE 8-3	Bill is the owner of a house that rents for $900 per month. During the winter while Bill was on vacation, the furnace failed. The tenants of the house had the furnace repaired and paid $300 in repair costs. On the first of the following month, the tenants reduced the rent payment by $300, paying just $600. Bill is required to include $900 as rental income: the net rental payment plus the repair cost paid by the tenants. Bill can then deduct a repair expense of $300.

EXAMPLE 8-4	Bill owns a second rental house in need of repairs. He allows a new tenant (a carpenter) to live rent-free for three months ($1,800 value); in exchange, the tenant will complete the necessary repairs. Bill must include $1,800 in rental income. He can then take a corresponding deduction for the repairs, assuming that they are not capital improvements.

Rental Expenses

Recall that an ordinary expense is customary or usual for the taxpayer's business or activity (in this case rental property). The "necessary" criterion refers to an expense that is appropriate and helpful rather than one that is essential to the taxpayer's activity. Table 8-1 summarizes expenses that are common to most rental activities.

The information in Table 8-1 is not comprehensive because any expense that meets the ordinary and necessary criteria is deductible. We discussed the rules concerning the deductibility of many of these expenses in Chapter 6. For example, we distinguished between travel and transportation. The same rules apply to rental property. Consequently, travel costs from the taxpayer's home to a rental property are deductible if the travel is for business purposes (such as to conduct repairs or attend a condominium association meeting). Likewise, if a taxpayer

TABLE 8-1
Common Rental Activity Expenses

Expense	Purpose
Advertising	Payments to advertise property for rent.
Travel	Travel to and from property for rental business such as repairs or maintenance.
Repair and maintenance costs	Normal repair and maintenance costs that are not capital improvements.
Insurance	Policy to guard the property against casualty and liability.
Management fees	Fees paid to have someone manage the property and provide services such as security, rental agency, repairs, and maintenance.
Interest	Payments on mortgage to purchase or improve rental property.
Taxes	Payments for property taxes (e.g., county property taxes).
Depreciation	Residential: 27.5-year MACRS straight-line. Nonresidential: 39-year MACRS straight-line.

[7] IRS Publication 527, p. 2.

stays overnight, meals are also deductible. Use caution when deducting meals, however, especially if elements of personal vacation are involved.[8] Typically the standard mileage rate is used to calculate any travel expenses concerning rental property because the rental activity (on Schedule E) is not the taxpayer's trade or business, and thus the taxpayer likely does not drive enough to merit using actual auto costs.

EXAMPLE 8-5	Bryan lives in Birmingham, Alabama, and owns a rental condominium on the beach in Destin, Florida. Twice a year he drives to Destin to perform general maintenance on the condominium. The round-trip mileage from Birmingham to Destin is 602 miles. In tax year 2009, Bryan could deduct $662 in travel costs (602 miles × 2 trips × 55 cents per mile).

General repairs and maintenance are also deductible from gross rental income. However, the taxpayer cannot deduct amounts that are "capital improvements"; allowable repairs are expenditures that neither materially add to the value of the property nor appreciably prolong the property's life.[9] Any repairs in the nature of a replacement are considered *capital improvements* and are, consequently, capitalized and depreciated over the appropriate depreciable life.[10] The distinction is important because a taxpayer receives an immediate expense deduction for repairs, whereas capital improvements require depreciation over 27.5 years (residential) or 39 years (nonresidential). Table 8-2 shows examples of expenditures that are considered capital improvements.[11]

Rental property is also depreciated. We provided a complete review of depreciation in Chapter 6. However, some aspects specifically relating to rental property merit additional discussion. For the rental structure, the depreciable life is 27.5 years for residential structures and 39 years for nonresidential structures. The applicable depreciation method is straight-line. The IRC §179 deduction is not allowed for rental property.

When a furnished rental property is purchased for a lump sum, depreciation may be calculated over 27.5 (or 39) years on the total purchase price of the rental property. However, to accelerate the tax deduction, the taxpayer should allocate the purchase price to the structure separately from the furniture, appliances, carpet, and even shrubbery or fences (because depreciating over 5 or 7 years allows a much faster deduction than over 27.5 or 39 years). The depreciable lives and methods for these asset types follow:

TABLE 8-2

Examples of Capital Improvements

Source: IRS Publication 527.

Additions:	**Heating and air conditioning:**	**Lawn and grounds landscaping:**	**Plumbing:**
Bedroom	Heating system	Driveway	Septic system
Bathroom	Central air	Walkway	Water heater
Deck	conditioning	Fence	Soft water system
Garage	Furnace	Retaining wall	Filtration system
Porch	Ductwork	Sprinkler system	**Miscellaneous:**
Patio	Central humidifier	Swimming pool	Storm windows,
Interior improvements:	Filtration system	**Insulation:**	doors
Built-in appliances		Attic	New roof
Kitchen		Walls, floor	Central vacuum
modernization		Pipes, ductwork	Wiring upgrades
Flooring			Satellite dish
Wall-to-wall			Security system
carpeting			

[8] The rules concerning the deduction of expenses on vacation homes that are also rented are presented in the next section.

[9] Reg. §1.162–4.

[10] Reg. §1.162–4.

[11] IRS Publication 527, p. 3.

EXAMPLE 8-6   Alan and Cherie Masters purchased a furnished beach house in San Clemente, California, for $1,364,000 on June 1, 2009. The land was valued at $700,000; furniture, $15,000; appliances, $3,000; carpet, $4,000; and landscaping, $8,000. The Masters rent the house full-time (no personal use). If the Masters depreciate the house as a single lump sum (as 27.5-year property), their first-year depreciation would be as follows (see Table 6A-6 in Chapter 6):

$$\$664,000 \times 1.970\% = \$13,081$$

On the other hand, if the Masters divided the assets into depreciable components, their first-year depreciation would be as calculated here:

House	$634,000 (27.5 years, straight-line) × 1.970% =	$12,490
Furniture	$15,000 (5 years, 200 declining balance [DB]) × 20.00% =	3,000
Appliances	$3,000 (5 years, 200 DB) × 20.00% =	600
Carpet	$4,000 (5 years, 200 DB) × 20.00% =	800
Landscaping	$8,000 (15 years, 200 DB) × 5.00% =	400
Total depreciation		$17,290

By allocating the purchase price to the structure and to the other assets, the Masters would benefit from an additional depreciation deduction of $4,209 ($17,290 − $13,081) in the first year.

Asset	MACRS Life	MACRS Method
Furniture used in rental*	5 years	200% declining balance
Appliances	5 years	200% declining balance
Carpets	5 years	200% declining balance
Office furniture	7 years	200% declining balance
Shrubbery	15 years	150% declining balance
Fences	15 years	150% declining balance

* In Chapter 6, we depreciated furniture and fixtures for a trade or business over a seven-year period. Furniture used in a rental activity has a five-year depreciation period. IRS Publication 527 makes a distinction between furniture used in a rental (five years) and office furniture and equipment (seven years).

From Shoebox to Software

In this section, we present a comprehensive example of rental income and expenses. The Masters, from Example 8-6, have the following income and expenses in addition to the depreciation deduction calculated earlier. During the tax year, neither the Masters nor their family used the house at any time for personal reasons.

Rental income (12 wks @ $3,500 per week)	$42,000
Rental management company (10% of gross)	4,200
Travel (3 trips for maintenance at 200 miles round-trip: 600 miles × 55 cents per mile)	330
Repairs (leaking roof & plumbing repairs)	2,500
Mortgage interest	1,300
Property taxes	3,800
Depreciation (see Example 8-6)	17,290
Insurance	1,800
Utilities	2,000

Open the Masters' tax return file. Then open Schedule E and enter the type and location of the property (123 Beach Rd., San Clemente, California 92900). Next, enter the income and the expenses. Enter the auto (2009 Yukon, placed in service on March 3, 2009), and enter the Business Use worksheet to fill in the mileage. Then check the box to use the standard mileage rate and answer the questions in step 3 (all "yes" in this case).

The depreciation can be complex. Double-click line 20 on Schedule E and add each individual asset on the asset entry worksheet (as in Chapter 6 and Schedule C). Some tax software programs do not provide an "asset type" for rental furniture, appliances, or carpet.[12] Thus use the Other asset type and enter the five-year life and MACRS method on the life and method input lines. Exhibit 8-1 shows the presentation of the preceding information on Schedule E, and Exhibit 8-2 shows the depreciation reported on Form 4562.

[12] If you choose "office furniture and fixtures" on some programs, seven-year MACRS is used for the depreciation life when a five-year life is allowed.

EXHIBIT 8-1

SCHEDULE E **(Form 1040)** Department of the Treasury Internal Revenue Service (99)	**Supplemental Income and Loss** OMB No. 1545-0074 **20**09 (From rental real estate, royalties, partnerships, S corporations, estates, trusts, REMICs, etc.) Attachment ▶ **Attach to Form 1040, 1040NR, or Form 1041.** ▶ **See Instructions for Schedule E (Form 1040).** Sequence No. **13**

Name(s) shown on return

Alan and Cherie Masters

Your social security number

444-44-4444

Part I   **Income or Loss From Rental Real Estate and Royalties**   **Note.** If you are in the business of renting personal property, use **Schedule C** or **C-EZ** (see page E-3). If you are an individual, report farm rental income or loss from **Form 4835** on page 2, line 40.

1   List the type and address of each **rental real estate property:**

A   123 Beach Road
    San Clemente, CA   92900

B

C

2 For each rental real estate property listed on line 1, did you or your family use it during the tax year for personal purposes for more than the greater of:
- 14 days **or**
- 10% of the total days rented at fair rental value?
(See page E-3)

	Yes	No
A		X
B		
C		

Income:		Properties A	B	C	Totals (Add columns A, B, and C.)
3 Rents received	**3**	42,000			**3** 42,000
4 Royalties received	**4**				**4**
Expenses:					
5 Advertising	**5**				
6 Auto and travel (see page E-4)	**6**	330			
7 Cleaning and maintenance	**7**				
8 Commissions	**8**				
9 Insurance	**9**	1,800			
10 Legal and other professional fees	**10**				
11 Management fees	**11**	4,200			
12 Mortgage interest paid to banks, etc. (see page E-5)	**12**	1,300			**12** 1,300
13 Other interest	**13**				
14 Repairs	**14**	2,500			
15 Supplies	**15**				
16 Taxes	**16**	3,800			
17 Utilities	**17**	2,000			
18 Other (list) ▶ _____	**18**				
19 Add lines 5 through 18	**19**	15,930			**19** 15,930
20 Depreciation expense or depletion (see page E-5)	**20**	17,290			**20** 17,290
21 Total expenses. Add lines 19 and 20	**21**	33,220			
22 Income or (loss) from rental real estate or royalty properties. Subtract line 21 from line 3 (rents) or line 4 (royalties). If the result is a (loss), see page E-5 to find out if you must file **Form 6198**.	**22**				
23 Deductible rental real estate loss. **Caution.** Your rental real estate loss on line 22 may be limited. See page E-5 to find out if you must file **Form 8582**. Real estate professionals **must** complete line 43 on page 2	**23**	(	)(	)(	)
24 Income. Add positive amounts shown on line 22. **Do not** include any losses					**24** 8,780
25 Losses. Add royalty losses from line 22 and rental real estate losses from line 23. Enter total losses here					**25** ( )
26 Total rental real estate and royalty income or (loss). Combine lines 24 and 25. Enter the result here. If Parts II, III, IV, and line 40 on page 2 do not apply to you, also enter this amount on Form 1040, line 17, or Form 1040NR, line 18. Otherwise, include this amount in the total on line 41 on page 2					**26** 8,780

For Paperwork Reduction Act Notice, see page E-8 of the instructions.   Cat. No. 11344L   Schedule E (Form 1040) 2009

EXHIBIT 8-2

Form **4562** Department of the Treasury Internal Revenue Service (99)	**Depreciation and Amortization** **(Including Information on Listed Property)** ▶ See separate instructions. ▶ Attach to your tax return.	OMB No. 1545-0172 **2009** Attachment Sequence No. **67**

Name(s) shown on return Alan and Cherie Masters	Business or activity to which this form relates Rental	Identifying number

Part I **Election To Expense Certain Property Under Section 179**
Note: *If you have any listed property, complete Part V before you complete Part I.*

1	Maximum amount. See the instructions for a higher limit for certain businesses	**1** $250,000
2	Total cost of section 179 property placed in service (see instructions)	**2**
3	Threshold cost of section 179 property before reduction in limitation (see instructions) . . .	**3** $800,000
4	Reduction in limitation. Subtract line 3 from line 2. If zero or less, enter -0-	**4**
5	Dollar limitation for tax year. Subtract line 4 from line 1. If zero or less, enter -0-. If married filing separately, see instructions	**5**

6	**(a)** Description of property	**(b)** Cost (business use only)	**(c)** Elected cost	

7	Listed property. Enter the amount from line 29	**7**
8	Total elected cost of section 179 property. Add amounts in column (c), lines 6 and 7	**8**
9	Tentative deduction. Enter the **smaller** of line 5 or line 8	**9**
10	Carryover of disallowed deduction from line 13 of your 2008 Form 4562	**10**
11	Business income limitation. Enter the smaller of business income (not less than zero) or line 5 (see instructions) . . .	**11**
12	Section 179 expense deduction. Add lines 9 and 10, but do not enter more than line 11	**12**
13	Carryover of disallowed deduction to 2010. Add lines 9 and 10, less line 12 ▶	**13**

Note: *Do not use Part II or Part III below for listed property. Instead, use Part V.*

Part II **Special Depreciation Allowance and Other Depreciation (Do not** include listed property.) (See instructions.)

14	Special depreciation allowance for qualified property (other than listed property) placed in service during the tax year (see instructions)	**14**
15	Property subject to section 168(f)(1) election	**15**
16	Other depreciation (including ACRS)	**16**

Part III **MACRS Depreciation (Do not** include listed property.) (See instructions.)

Section A

17	MACRS deductions for assets placed in service in tax years beginning before 2009	**17**
18	If you are electing to group any assets placed in service during the tax year into one or more general asset accounts, check here . . . . ▶ ☐	

Section B—Assets Placed in Service During 2009 Tax Year Using the General Depreciation System

(a) Classification of property	**(b)** Month and year placed in service	**(c)** Basis for depreciation (business/investment use only—see instructions)	**(d)** Recovery period	**(e)** Convention	**(f)** Method	**(g)** Depreciation deduction
19a 3-year property						
b 5-year property		22,000	5 YR	HY	200 DB	4,400
c 7-year property						
d 10-year property						
e 15-year property		8,000	15 YR	HY	150 DB	400
f 20-year property						
g 25-year property			25 yrs.		S/L	
h Residential rental property	6/1/09	634,000	27.5 yrs.	MM	S/L	12,490
			27.5 yrs.	MM	S/L	
i Nonresidential real property			39 yrs.	MM	S/L	
				MM	S/L	

Section C—Assets Placed in Service During 2009 Tax Year Using the Alternative Depreciation System

20a Class life					S/L	
b 12-year			12 yrs.		S/L	
c 40-year			40 yrs.	MM	S/L	

Part IV **Summary** (See instructions.)

21	Listed property. Enter amount from line 28	**21**
22	**Total.** Add amounts from line 12, lines 14 through 17, lines 19 and 20 in column (g), and line 21. Enter here and on the appropriate lines of your return. Partnerships and S corporations—see instructions	**22** 17,290
23	For assets shown above and placed in service during the current year, enter the portion of the basis attributable to section 263A costs	**23**

For Paperwork Reduction Act Notice, see separate instructions.	Cat. No. 12906N	Form **4562** (2009)

(continued)

EXHIBIT 8-2   *(concluded)*

Form 4562 (2009)
Page **2**

Part V **Listed Property** (Include automobiles, certain other vehicles, cellular telephones, certain computers, and property used for entertainment, recreation, or amusement.)

Note: *For any vehicle for which you are using the standard mileage rate or deducting lease expense, complete only 24a, 24b, columns (a) through (c) of Section A, all of Section B, and Section C if applicable.*

Section A—Depreciation and Other Information (Caution: *See the instructions for limits for passenger automobiles.***)**

24a Do you have evidence to support the business/investment use claimed? ☐ Yes ☐ No   **24b** If "Yes," is the evidence written? ☐ Yes ☐ No

(a) Type of property (list vehicles first)	(b) Date placed in service	(c) Business/investment use percentage	(d) Cost or other basis	(e) Basis for depreciation (business/investment use only)	(f) Recovery period	(g) Method/Convention	(h) Depreciation deduction	(i) Elected section 179 cost
25 Special depreciation allowance for qualified listed property placed in service during the tax year and used more than 50% in a qualified business use (see instructions) . . .					**25**			
26 Property used more than 50% in a qualified business use:								
		%						
		%						
		%						
27 Property used 50% or less in a qualified business use:								
2009 Yukon	3/3/09	3.85 %				S/L –		
		%				S/L –		
		%				S/L –		

28 Add amounts in column (h), lines 25 through 27. Enter here and on line 21, page 1 . . . **28**
29 Add amounts in column (i), line 26. Enter here and on line 7, page 1 . . . . **29**

Section B—Information on Use of Vehicles

Complete this section for vehicles used by a sole proprietor, partner, or other "more than 5% owner," or related person. If you provided vehicles to your employees, first answer the questions in Section C to see if you meet an exception to completing this section for those vehicles.

	(a) Vehicle 1		(b) Vehicle 2		(c) Vehicle 3		(d) Vehicle 4		(e) Vehicle 5		(f) Vehicle 6	
30 Total business/investment miles driven during the year (**do not** include commuting miles)	600											
31 Total commuting miles driven during the year												
32 Total other personal (noncommuting) miles driven	15,000											
33 Total miles driven during the year. Add lines 30 through 32	15,600											
	Yes	No	Yes	No	Yes	No	Yes	No	Yes	No	Yes	No
34 Was the vehicle available for personal use during off-duty hours?	X											
35 Was the vehicle used primarily by a more than 5% owner or related person?	X											
36 Is another vehicle available for personal use?	X											

Section C—Questions for Employers Who Provide Vehicles for Use by Their Employees

Answer these questions to determine if you meet an exception to completing Section B for vehicles used by employees who **are not** more than 5% owners or related persons (see instructions).

		Yes	No
37	Do you maintain a written policy statement that prohibits all personal use of vehicles, including commuting, by your employees?		
38	Do you maintain a written policy statement that prohibits personal use of vehicles, except commuting, by your employees? See the instructions for vehicles used by corporate officers, directors, or 1% or more owners . . .		
39	Do you treat all use of vehicles by employees as personal use?		
40	Do you provide more than five vehicles to your employees, obtain information from your employees about the use of the vehicles, and retain the information received?		
41	Do you meet the requirements concerning qualified automobile demonstration use? (See instructions.) . . .		

Note: *If your answer to 37, 38, 39, 40, or 41 is "Yes," do not complete Section B for the covered vehicles.*

Part VI **Amortization**

(a) Description of costs	(b) Date amortization begins	(c) Amortizable amount	(d) Code section	(e) Amortization period or percentage	(f) Amortization for this year
42 Amortization of costs that begins during your 2009 tax year (see instructions):					

43 Amortization of costs that began before your 2009 tax year **43**
44 **Total.** Add amounts in column (f). See the instructions for where to report **44**

Form **4562** (2009)

One important exception to trade or business depreciation rules is that the IRC §179 deduction *cannot* be claimed for property held to produce rental income.

If a rental property incurs a loss, there are potential limitations on the deductibility of the losses. By definition, rental property is a *passive activity.* The rules concerning passive activity losses are complex and are discussed briefly at the end of this chapter and more fully in Chapter 13.[13]

CONCEPT CHECK 8-1—LO 1

1. Rental income is generally reported on Schedule E. True or false?
2. All expenses related to rental property are deductible in the current year, including capital improvements. True or false?
3. Rental property structures must be depreciated using the straight-line method. True or false?
4. If a taxpayer's rental property is considered a trade or business, he or she reports the income on Schedule E. True or false?
5. If a tenant provides a service in lieu of rent, the taxpayer is not required to report the value of that amount as rental income. True or false?

RENTAL OF VACATION HOMES
LO 2

When a taxpayer uses a property for both personal use (vacation home) and rental property, tax complexities arise. Vacation home rental property falls into one of the following three possible categories: (1) primarily rental use, (2) primarily personal use, and (3) personal/rental use.

The appropriate category is determined by comparing the number of rental use days to the number of personal use days. The category determines how much of the expenses for the property may be deducted. If the property

1. Is not used for more than 14 days (or 10% of the total rental days, if greater) for personal use, and it is rented for 15 days or more, it is primarily rental.
2. Is rented for less than 15 days, it is primarily personal.
3. Is rented for 15 days or more and the personal use of the property is more than the greater of[14]

    a. 14 days or

    b. 10% of the total rental days at the fair rental value

   it is personal/rental property.

EXAMPLE 8-7

John owns a cabin in the mountains. If he rents the cabin for the ski season (four months) and uses the property for personal use for 13 days, the cabin would be classified as primarily rental property. If John used the property for personal use for 21 days, the property would be classified as personal/rental. If John rented the cabin for less than 15 days, the cabin would be classified as primarily personal.

Personal use of a dwelling is any use by

1. The taxpayer, any member of the taxpayer's family, or any other person with an interest in the unit.
2. Any individual who uses the unit under an arrangement that enables the taxpayer to use some other dwelling unit.
3. Any individual unless for such day the dwelling unit is rented for its fair rental value.[15]

---

[13] For a detailed discussion of the passive activity loss rules, and the loss rules of rental property in particular, see Chapter 13.

[14] IRC §280A(d)(1).

[15] IRC §280A(d)(2).

If a taxpayer lets anyone, family or nonfamily, use the rental property free of a rental charge, those days are considered personal use days by the taxpayer. If any family member uses the rental property (even if the family member pays the full rental value), the days are considered personal use days.[16] *Family* is defined as the taxpayer's brothers and sisters (whether whole or half blood), spouse, ancestors, and lineal descendants.[17] Any day spent working substantially full-time repairing and maintaining the property does not count as a personal use day. This is true even if other family members use the property for recreational purposes on the same day.[18]

EXAMPLE 8-8	Nick owns a rental beach house. He and his two daughters drive to the house, where Nick spends two days repairing the deck and the screened porch. During this time, his daughters relax on the beach. The two days are not considered personal use days.

Primarily Rental Use

If rental property is not used for more than 14 days for personal purposes (or 10% of the total rental days if greater) and is rented for 15 days or more, it is primarily rental property. As such, the taxpayer must report all of the income and ordinary and necessary expenses (rental portion). The portion of expenses that are allocated to the personal use are not deductible unless they are normally allowed as itemized deductions (such as mortgage interest and property taxes). If a loss results, it is deductible to the extent allowed by the passive activity loss rules (see the end of this chapter and Chapter 13).

Primarily Personal Use

A property rented for less than 15 days but otherwise used as a personal residence is considered primarily personal property. When property is rented for less than 15 days, *none* of the rental income derived from the short rental period is included in gross income. Likewise, no deduction is allowed for rental expenses.

EXAMPLE 8-9	Kirk and his family live in Augusta, Georgia. Each year during the Masters golf tournament, they rent their house to a major corporation for $10,000 for the entire week. Because Kirk rents his house for only seven days, the property is considered primarily personal, and Kirk reports none of the rental income or expenses.

Personal/Rental Property

When a rental property is used for personal use for more than 14 days, or 10% of the total rental days, and is rented for more than 15 days, the property is considered personal/rental property. In the case of personal/rental property, a taxpayer can deduct expenses only to the extent that there is rental income (that is, no net loss is allowed). A summary of vacation home rental rules is presented in Table 8-3.

EXAMPLE 8-10	**Case 1: Primarily Rental Property:** Frank owns a condominium at the beach that he rents for 90 days during the summer and uses the property for personal use for 13 days. **Case 2: Personal/Rental Property:** Frank rents the condominium for 90 days and uses it for personal use for 16 days. **Case 3: Primarily Personal Property:** Frank rents the property for 10 days, and he uses the condominium for the remainder of the year for personal use.

---

[16] Prop. Reg. §1.280A-1(e)(7), ex. (1).

[17] IRC §267(c)(4).

[18] IRS Publication 527, p. 7.

TABLE 8-3 **Summary of Vacation Home Rental Rules**

	Primarily Personal	Primarily Rental	Personal/Rental
Rental days	Rented less than 15 days.	Rented 15 days or more.	Rented 15 days or more.
Personal days	No limit.	No more than the greater of (a)14 days or (b) 10% of the total rental days.	More than the greater of (a)14 days or (b) 10% of the total rental days.
Income and expense reporting	The income does not have to be reported. (It is not taxable!) Mortgage interest and property taxes are allowed as itemized deductions, as with any personal residence.	All rental income must be reported on Schedule E. The expenses must be allocated between personal and rental days and reported on Schedule E.	All rental income must be reported on Schedule E. The expenses must be allocated between personal and rental days and reported on Schedule E.
Net loss treatment	Not allowed; none of the net income or net loss is reported.	Allowed up to $25,000 (limited by passive activity loss rules).	Not allowed; expenses deducted only to the extent there is rental income (i.e., breakeven).

EXAMPLE 8-11

Susan owns a beach house in Seal Beach, California. Each year she uses her beach house for four months and rents it for three months in the summer. The property is considered personal/rental, and the expenses related to the beach house must be allocated between personal and rental use. Remember, if the rental portion of her expenses is higher than her rental income, the resulting net loss is not allowed.

CONCEPT CHECK 8-2—LO 2

Indicate the correct letter that identifies whether the rental property in the following situations would be classified as (a) primarily rental, (b) primarily personal, or (c) personal/rental:

1. Jamie rented her lake home for $2,000 for 12 days, and she and her family used it for the rest of the year, usually on weekends and holidays.
2. Julie rented her home in Seal Beach for 180 days for $12,000; she used it for 17 days.
3. Darren rented his beach house for 45 days for $9,000 and stayed there on weekends with his family for a total of 16 days. During his stay, he spent 7 of the days rebuilding the deck while his family enjoyed the beach.
4. Alex rented her mountain cabin for 90 days for $13,500, and she and her family used it for 50 days.

Allocation of Rental Expenses

For both primarily rental and personal/rental properties, the expenses related to those properties must be allocated between personal and rental use. The following are the two methods used to allocate expenses between the personal and rental use of a rental property:

1. **The IRS method:** The expenses should be allocated between personal and rental days based on the ratio of the number of rental days to the total number of days used.
2. **The Tax Court method:** The interest and taxes on the rental property should be allocated based on the ratio of the number of rental days to the full number of days in the year (365),[19]

[19] The denominator in the allocation is the number of days owned during the year if the property was purchased or sold during the year.

and the remaining rental expenses should be allocated using the IRS method.[20] The courts' rationale is that interest and taxes occur ratably over the entire year whereas other expenses occur only when the property is used.

Regardless of the allocation method used, certain expenses are not allocated but are deducted in full, subject to sufficient rental income. These are expenses that have no personal element to them such as travel and management fees.

In addition, for personal/rental properties, expenses must be deducted in a certain order. First, expenses that are always deductible (mortgage interest and property taxes) are deducted. Next to be deducted are expenses such as utilities, insurance, and travel. Lastly, if any rental income remains, depreciation is deducted, but only to the extent that there is income.

EXAMPLE 8-12	Assume the same rental property example as illustrated in the "From Shoebox to Software" box for the Masters (page 8-5) except that rental income was $21,600 and the taxpayer used the property for 22 days for personal use and rented it for 84 days. Also assume that the property was held the entire year when using the Tax Court method.

Rent income (12 weeks at $1,800 per week)	$21,600
Rental management (10% of gross rent)	2,160
Travel (3 trips for maintenance at 200 miles round-trip: 600 miles × 55 cents per mile)	330
Repairs (leaking roof and plumbing repairs)	2,500
Mortgage interest	1,300
Property taxes	3,800
Depreciation	17,290
Insurance	1,800
Utilities	2,000

IRS Method

The rental expenses are allocated based on the ratio of the number of rental days (84) to the total days used (106). The remaining expenses are allocated to personal use.

Expense	Total	Rental Ratio	Allocated to Personal	Deductible on Schedule E
Mortgage interest	$ 1,300	84/106	$270*	$ 1,030
Taxes	3,800	84/106	789*	3,011
Travel	330	100%	–0–	330
Insurance	1,800	84/106	374	1,426
Management fees	2,160	100%	–0–	2,160
Repairs	2,500	84/106	519	1,981
Utilities	2,000	84/106	415	1,585
Depreciation	17,290	84/106	–0–	10,077[†]

* These amounts are deducted on Schedule A.
[†] The depreciation is $13,702. However, the deduction is limited to the remaining rental income of $10,077.
Note: Remember that the taxpayer cannot have a net loss on a personal/rental property.

Tax Court Method

Using the Tax Court allocation method, taxpayers allocate interest and taxes by the ratio of rental days (84) to the entire year (365).[21] This yields a smaller percentage of the interest and taxes being

---

[20] *Bolton, Dorance* (1981) 77 TC 104, affd (1982, CA9) 694 F2d 556; *McKinney, Edith* (1983, CA10), 732 F2d 414.

[21] If the property was held for less than the entire year (i.e., purchased or sold during the year), the number of days owned during the year is substituted for 365 days.

allocated to rental income on Schedule E and more allocated to personal use as itemized deductions on Schedule A. The remaining expenses are allocated using the IRS method (84/106).

Expense	Total	Rental Ratio	Allocated to Personal	Deductible on Schedule E
Mortgage interest	$ 1,300	84/365	$1,001*	$ 299
Taxes	3,800	84/365	2,925*	875
Travel	330	100%	–0–	330
Insurance	1,800	84/106	374	1,426
Management fees	2,160	100%	–0–	2,160
Repairs	2,500	84/106	519	1,981
Utilities	2,000	84/106	415	1,585
Depreciation	17,290	84/106	–0–	12,944†

* These amounts are deducted on Schedule A.
† The depreciation is $13,702. However, the deduction is limited to the remaining rental income of $12,944.
Note: Remember that the taxpayer cannot have a net loss on a personal/rental property.

From Shoebox to Software

Tax software allocates rental expenses for you. Check whether your software calculates the expense allocation using the IRS method or the Tax Court method. Usually, if you enter the number of personal days on Schedule E (line 2), a note appears stating that the "vacation home limits will be applied." If you double-click on this note, the vacation home worksheet appears showing the allocation. If you wish to use a method different than your software normally does, you must make the calculations yourself and enter the expense items directly on Schedule E. Exhibits 8-3 and 8-4 illustrate the IRS method and the Tax Court method, respectively, on Schedule E, for the Masters using Example 8-12.

Note that the Tax Court method allocates more interest and taxes to personal use and deducts them on Schedule A as itemized deductions.[22] By allocating a higher percentage of interest and taxes to Schedule A, the taxpayer is able to deduct an additional $2,867 of depreciation expense ($12,944 versus $10,077) and increase the overall deductible expenses. Also note that the travel costs and management fees are 100% deductible. As discussed earlier, these expenses are 100% deductible because if this property was not rented, these expenses would not have occurred.

CONCEPT CHECK 8-3—LO 2

Lynn and Dave Wood own a vacation home in Park City, Utah. During the year, the Woods rented the home for 75 days and used it for personal use for 30 days. The following are income and expenses related to the property:

Rental income	$15,000
Mortgage interest	6,000
Property taxes	1,000
Insurance	1,400
Repairs and maintenance	800
Depreciation	2,000

1. Which of the three categories of rental property would apply to this property and why?
2. Using the IRS method, how much of the expenses can be allocated to the rental property?
3. Using the Tax Court method, how much of the expenses can be allocated to the rental property?
4. Using the IRS method, what is the net income or loss that should be reported for this rental property?

[22] Mortgage interest is deductible on Schedule A for interest on a personal residence and one vacation home; but if the taxpayer has more than one vacation home, the interest may not be deductible on Schedule A (for details on mortgage interest, see Chapter 5).

EXHIBIT 8-3 **Schedule E Using the IRS Method**

SCHEDULE E (Form 1040)	**Supplemental Income and Loss**	OMB No. 1545-0074
Department of the Treasury Internal Revenue Service (99)	(From rental real estate, royalties, partnerships, S corporations, estates, trusts, REMICs, etc.) ▶Attach to Form 1040, 1040NR, or Form 1041. ▶ See Instructions for Schedule E (Form 1040).	**20**09 Attachment Sequence No. **13**

Name(s) shown on return: Alan and Cherie Masters

Your social security number: 444-44-4444

Part I Income or Loss From Rental Real Estate and Royalties Note. If you are in the business of renting personal property, use Schedule C or C-EZ (see page E-3). If you are an individual, report farm rental income or loss from Form 4835 on page 2, line 40.

1 List the type and address of each **rental real estate property**:
A 123 Beach Road San Clemente, CA 92900
B
C

2 For each rental real estate property listed on line 1, did you or your family use it during the tax year for personal purposes for more than the greater of:
• 14 days **or**
• 10% of the total days rented at fair rental value? (See page E-3)

	Yes	No
A	X	
B		
C		

Income:

			Properties A	B	C		Totals (Add columns A, B, and C.)
3	Rents received	3	21,600			3	21,600
4	Royalties received	4				4	

Expenses:

			A	B	C		
5	Advertising	5					
6	Auto and travel (see page E-4)	6	330				
7	Cleaning and maintenance	7					
8	Commissions	8					
9	Insurance	9	1,426				
10	Legal and other professional fees	10					
11	Management fees	11	2,160				
12	Mortgage interest paid to banks, etc. (see page E-5)	12	299			12	299
13	Other interest	13					
14	Repairs	14	1,981				
15	Supplies	15					
16	Taxes	16	875				
17	Utilities	17	1,585				
18	Other (list) ▶	18					
19	Add lines 5 through 18	19	8,656			19	8,656
20	Depreciation expense or depletion (see page E-5)	20	12,944			20	12,944
21	Total expenses. Add lines 19 and 20	21	21,600				
22	Income or (loss) from rental real estate or royalty properties. Subtract line 21 from line 3 (rents) or line 4 (royalties). If the result is a (loss), see page E-5 to find out if you must file **Form 6198**.	22					
23	Deductible rental real estate loss. **Caution.** Your rental real estate loss on line 22 may be limited. See page E-5 to find out if you must file **Form 8582**. Real estate professionals **must** complete line 43 on page 2	23	( )	( )	( )		
24	Income. Add positive amounts shown on line 22. **Do not** include any losses					24	0
25	Losses. Add royalty losses from line 22 and rental real estate losses from line 23. Enter total losses here					25	( )
26	**Total rental real estate and royalty income or (loss).** Combine lines 24 and 25. Enter the result here. If Parts II, III, IV, and line 40 on page 2 do not apply to you, also enter this amount on Form 1040, line 17, or Form 1040NR, line 18. Otherwise, include this amount in the total on line 41 on page 2					26	0

For Paperwork Reduction Act Notice, see page E-8 of the instructions. Cat. No. 11344L Schedule E (Form 1040) 2009

EXHIBIT 8-4 Schedule E Using the Tax Court Method

SCHEDULE E (Form 1040)	Supplemental Income and Loss	OMB No. 1545-0074
Department of the Treasury Internal Revenue Service (99)	(From rental real estate, royalties, partnerships, S corporations, estates, trusts, REMICs, etc.) ▶ Attach to Form 1040, 1040NR, or Form 1041. ▶ See Instructions for Schedule E (Form 1040).	2009 Attachment Sequence No. **13**

Name(s) shown on return: **Alan and Cherie Masters**
Your social security number: **444-44-4444**

Part I Income or Loss From Rental Real Estate and Royalties **Note.** If you are in the business of renting personal property, use **Schedule C** or **C-EZ** (see page E-3). If you are an individual, report farm rental income or loss from **Form 4835** on page 2, line 40.

1 List the type and address of each **rental real estate property:**
A 123 Beach Road San Clemente, CA 92900
B
C

2 For each rental real estate property listed on line 1, did you or your family use it during the tax year for personal purposes for more than the greater of:
● 14 days **or**
● 10% of the total days rented at fair rental value?
(See page E-3)

	Yes	No
A	X	
B		
C		

Income:

			Properties A	B	C		Totals (Add columns A, B, and C.)
3	Rents received	3	21,600			3	21,600
4	Royalties received	4				4	

Expenses:

			A	B	C		
5	Advertising	5					
6	Auto and travel (see page E-4)	6	330				
7	Cleaning and maintenance	7					
8	Commissions	8					
9	Insurance	9	1,426				
10	Legal and other professional fees	10					
11	Management fees	11	2,160				
12	Mortgage interest paid to banks, etc. (see page E-5)	12	1,030			12	1,030
13	Other interest	13					
14	Repairs	14	1,981				
15	Supplies	15					
16	Taxes	16	3,011				
17	Utilities	17	1,585				
18	Other (list) ▶	18					
19	Add lines 5 through 18	19	11,523			19	11,523
20	Depreciation expense or depletion (see page E-5)	20	10,077			20	10,077
21	Total expenses. Add lines 19 and 20	21	21,600				
22	Income or (loss) from rental real estate or royalty properties. Subtract line 21 from line 3 (rents) or line 4 (royalties). If the result is a (loss), see page E-5 to find out if you must file **Form 6198**.	22					
23	Deductible rental real estate loss. **Caution.** Your rental real estate loss on line 22 may be limited. See page E-5 to find out if you must file **Form 8582**. Real estate professionals **must** complete line 43 on page 2	23 (	)(	)(	)		
24	**Income.** Add positive amounts shown on line 22. **Do not** include any losses					24	0
25	**Losses.** Add royalty losses from line 22 and rental real estate losses from line 23. Enter total losses here					25 (	)
26	**Total rental real estate and royalty income or (loss).** Combine lines 24 and 25. Enter the result here. If Parts II, III, IV, and line 40 on page 2 do not apply to you, also enter this amount on Form 1040, line 17, or Form 1040NR, line 18. Otherwise, include this amount in the total on line 41 on page 2					26	0

For Paperwork Reduction Act Notice, see page E-8 of the instructions. Cat. No. 11344L Schedule E (Form 1040) 2009

ROYALTY INCOME
LO 3

A *royalty* is a payment for the right to use intangible property. Royalties are paid for the use of books, stories, plays, copyrights, trademarks, formulas, and patents and from the exploitation of natural resources such as coal, gas, or timber.[23] When royalties are paid, the payer sends the recipient a 1099-MISC noting the amount paid in box 2. The recipient (taxpayer) reports that amount on line 4 of Schedule E. A sample 1099-MISC is shown in Exhibit 8-5.

Royalty payments do not include payments for services even when the services performed relate to a royalty-producing asset. Likewise, payments received for the transfer or sale of a copyright or patent are not royalties but proceeds from the sale of a capital asset.[24] Should royalty income be reported on Schedule E or Schedule C? If the royalty is a result of a trade or business, the taxpayer should report the royalty on Schedule C. If the royalty is from a nontrade or business activity, such as an investment, then the royalty income should be reported on line 4 of Schedule E.

EXAMPLE 8-13	Shea is the author of a best-selling book of poetry for which he receives royalties. He also presents seminars and readings of his book of poetry throughout the country. Shea's payments for the readings and seminars are not royalties. He reports his income from the readings and seminars on Schedule C and the royalties on Schedule E.

EXHIBIT 8-5

[23] Reg. §1.61-8.
[24] Reg. §1.61-8.

TAX YOUR BRAIN 	Would the taxpayer prefer royalty income to be reported on Schedule E or on Schedule C? The royalty is included in income on both forms, so why does it matter? **ANSWER** It is true that the royalty will be included in income on either form. However, if the royalty is reported on Schedule C, the net income is subject to self-employment tax, whereas on Schedule E, it is not.

EXAMPLE 8-14	John is a full-time author of mystery novels. He has an office in his home and has no other source of income. The royalties John receives from his novels are trade or business income and are reported on Schedule C.

EXAMPLE 8-15	Lilly is a business executive with a large import/export company. She also owns some land in south Texas. Recently a small oil reserve was discovered on her land, and she began receiving royalties for the oil produced. Lilly reports these royalties on Schedule E because owning the land is not a trade or a business, but an investment.

Whether royalties are reported on Schedule C or Schedule E, any ordinary and necessary expenses are allowed as deductions.

CONCEPT CHECK 8-4—LO 3	Indicate whether the following items would be reported on Schedule E (E) or Schedule C (C). 1. Royalty income received by Debra, a full-time author, for her mystery novel. 2. Royalty income received by Mark, a professional baseball player, for coal mined on his land in Wyoming. 3. Nathan recently wrote a book about proverbs. He received income for his readings at various bookstores throughout the country. 4. Royalty income that Jane, a full-time professor at the University of San Diego, received for a textbook she wrote.

FLOW-THROUGH ENTITIES
LO 4

Every partnership, limited liability company (LLC), S corporation, and certain types of trusts and estates must file a tax return indicating the amount of income or loss that flows through to the taxpayer (partner, shareholder, or owner). These entities are known as *flow-through entities* because they are not taxed directly. Instead, the income or loss items of these entities "flow through" to the partners (and others) who then report the income or loss on their individual Forms 1040.[25]

The flow-through entity must supply each partner (shareholder or owner) with a Schedule K-1 indicating the partner's distributive share of income, expenses, or losses. The partners (shareholders or owners) report the income and loss from the K-1s in Part II and Part III on Schedule E. Although trusts and estates are technically considered separate taxable entities, any income or property distributed to a beneficiary must also be reported on a Schedule K-1 similar to a flow-through entity. The net amounts are then accumulated on line 17 of Form 1040. Exhibit 8-6 is a sample Schedule K-1 from a partnership Form 1065.

The K-1s from LLCs, S corporations, trusts, and estates are similar in appearance to the partnership K-1 presented in Exhibit 8-6.

---

[25] Of course partners, shareholders, and owners can be entities as well. For example, a corporation can be a partner in a partnership. If this is the case, the corporate partner is taxed on the flow-through income. The focus in this text is the individual partner, shareholder, or owner.

Reporting of Flow-Through Items

Flow-through entities file "informational returns" because the returns do just that: provide tax information to the taxpayer and the IRS regarding the income or loss from the entity. The K-1 provides not only specific income or loss data but also the type of entity (a partnership in this case) and the partner relationship. Typically a partnership is either an active trade or business or a passive activity.[26] A passive activity usually involves an investor relationship whereas, in general, a partner materially participates in an active trade or business.

EXAMPLE 8-16   Dave is a partner in a local CPA firm (partnership) and works there full-time. He is also an investor as a limited partner in several real estate partnerships. The CPA firm partnership is an active trade or business partnership, and the real estate partnerships are passive investments.[27]

In this section, the focus is on a trade or business partnership in which the partner materially participates in the business (an active trade or business). The K-1 in Exhibit 8-6 reports the partner's share of ordinary income (line 1, Schedule K-1) from the partnership and other separately stated items (all other lines). The amounts of separately stated items (such as interest income or capital gains and losses) are not included in the income or expenses of the partnership but are allocated separately to each of the partners.

TAX YOUR BRAIN  Why are the different types of income and expenses that flow through from a partnership (ordinary income, interest, dividends, royalties, capital gains, charitable contributions, §179 expense deductions, etc.) separately stated? Why not just lump them all together and have one income or loss number from the partnership?

ANSWER
Any item that could be treated differently by different partners (individuals, corporations, etc.) is separately stated. For example, one individual partner might have capital gains from other sources to offset capital losses from the partnership, whereas another individual partner might not have any capital gains and be limited in the amount of capital losses allowed. Another example concerns a corporate partner[28] who receives a dividends-received deduction and no deduction for net capital losses. An individual partner in the same partnership would have to include the dividends in income but could deduct up to $3,000 of net capital losses. Additionally, for an individual taxpayer, most charitable deductions are limited to 50% of AGI. The limit occurs at the individual level and could result in a different outcome, depending on the individual partner's particular tax situation.

Separately stated items are items that the partnership does not deduct or include in income, but each partner's share is reported directly to the partner. When dealing with an individual partner, items from the K-1s are placed in various locations on his or her tax return. For example, the income or loss from the partnership (line 1, 2, or 3 of Schedule K-1) is reported on Schedule E, interest and dividends are reported on Schedule B, royalties on Schedule E, and capital gains and losses on Schedule D. Charitable contributions from a partnership are reported on Schedule A, and §179 expense deductions are reported on Schedule E, page 2.

Two other pieces of essential information are reported on Schedule K-1: line 4—Guaranteed payments and line 14—Self-employment earnings (loss). A partner is not an employee of the partnership and thus cannot have a deductible salary (to the partnership). A partner can receive a guaranteed payment, however, for services rendered to the partnership.[29]

[26] All of the various partnership forms file a Form 1065 and issue related Schedule K-1s to partners. A partnership form can be a limited liability company, a limited liability partnership, a limited partnership, or a general partnership.

[27] Chapter 13 focuses, in part, on passive activities.

[28] Corporate partners are taxed differently than individual partners with respect to many items. Thus various items must be separately stated because the tax treatment by the partners may differ.

[29] IRC §707(c).

LO 3: Know how to report royalty income on Schedule E.

- A *royalty* is a payment for the right to use intangible property.
- Royalty income is generally reported on Schedule E.
- If a payment is received while performing a service related to the royalty-producing asset or the royalty is a result of a trade or business, the royalty income is reported on Schedule C.

LO 4: Discuss the different types of flow-through entities reported on Schedule E, such as partnerships, S corporations, LLCs, trusts, and estates.

- Partnerships, LLCs, S corporations, trusts, and estates are known as flow-through entities.
- Flow-through entities file "informational returns" and provide their owners with Schedule K-1s.
- The income and expenses from K-1s are reported on the individual partner's (shareholder or owner) Schedule E.
- Certain limited partnerships and rental activity are considered passive activities and, as such, the amounts of net loss that are deductible against nonpassive income are limited by the passive activity rules (discussed in detail in Chapter 13).

Discussion Questions

LO 1   1. Can an owner of a rental property be treated as conducting a trade or business with respect to the rental property? If so, what must the owner do for it to be considered a trade or business?

_____

_____

_____

LO 1   2. For rental expenses to be deductible, what criteria must be met? For this question, assume no personal use of the rental property.

_____

_____

_____

LO 1   3. What is the difference between a deductible repair expense and a capital expenditure that must be depreciated?

_____

_____

_____

LO 1   4. When depreciation is deducted on a rental property, why is it beneficial for the taxpayer to allocate the cost of the property to other assets (furniture, appliances, etc.) connected with the property, not just the building itself?

_____

_____

_____

LO 2   5. Can travel expenses to and from rental property be deducted? If so, what are the rules concerning the deductibility of travel, and how is the deduction calculated? (*Hint:* You may need to review Chapter 6 to help with this answer.)

_____

_____

_____

LO 2   6. Les's personal residence is in uptown New Orleans. Every year during Mardi Gras, Les rents his house for 10 days to a large corporation that uses it to entertain clients. How does Les treat the rental income? Explain.

_____

_____

_____

LO 2   7. Two methods are used to allocate expenses between personal and rental uses of property. Explain the Tax Court method and the IRS method. Which method is more beneficial to the taxpayer?

_____

_____

_____

LO 2   8. Discuss the three classifications of vacation home rentals. Include in your discussion how personal use of the property affects the reporting of income and losses of vacation homes.

_____

_____

_____

LO 2   9. What is considered personal use of a vacation rental property?

_____

_____

_____

LO 2 10. Jake has a vacation rental house at the beach. During the tax year, he and his immediate family used the house for 12 days for personal vacation. Jake and his son spent two more weekends (4 days) repairing the steps from the property to the beach. The beach house was rented for 100 days. How is the beach house classified this year? Explain your answer.

_____

_____

_____

LO 2 11. Would your answer to Question 10 change if Jake also rented his house (at fair value) to his brother and his family for 7 days?

_____

_____

_____

LO 3 12. What is royalty income, and where is it reported? What determines where the royalties are reported?

_____

_____

_____

LO 1, 2, 3, 4 13. What types of income are reported on Schedule E?

_____

_____

_____

LO 4 14. What is meant by the term *flow-through entity*? Give some examples.

_____

_____

_____

_____

LO 2 36. Alice rented her personal residence for 13 days to summer vacationers for $4,500. She has income from other sources of $105,000. Related expenses for the year include these:

Real property taxes	$ 4,500
Utilities	5,000
Insurance	900
Mortgage interest	7,000
Repairs	800
Depreciation	15,000

Calculate the effect of the rental on Alice's AGI. Explain your rationale, citing tax authority.

_____

_____

_____

_____

_____

_____

LO 2 37. Matt and Marie own a vacation home at the beach. During the year, they rented the house for 42 days (6 weeks) at $890 per week and used it for personal use for 58 days. The total costs of maintaining the home are as follows:

Mortgage interest	$4,200
Property taxes	700
Insurance	1,200
Utilities	3,200
Repairs	1,900
Depreciation	5,500

a. What is the proper tax treatment of this information on their tax return using the Tax Court Method?

b. Are there options for how to allocate the expenses between personal and rental use? Explain.

c. What is the proper tax treatment if Matt and Marie rented the house for only 14 days?

_____

_____

_____

_____

_____

_____

LO 2 38. Janet owns a condominium at the beach. She incurs the following expenses:

Mortgage interest	$1,300
Property taxes	800
Insurance	1,500
Utilities	1,800
Repairs	300
Depreciation	4,000

What is the proper treatment of these expenses as applied to the following situations? Use the Tax Court allocation method, if applicable.

Case	Rental Income	Days Rented	Personal Use Days
A	$ 9,000	45	10
B	12,000	55	25
C	6,000	10	30
D	22,000	365	–0–

_____

_____

_____

_____

_____

_____

LO 2 39. Randolph and Tammy own a qualified second home. They spent 45 days there and rented it for 88 days at $150 per day during the year. The total costs relating to the home include the following:

Mortgage interest	$4,500
Property taxes	1,200
Insurance	1,800
Utilities	2,300
Repairs	1,500
Depreciation	6,500

What is the proper treatment of these items relating to the second home? Would you use the Tax Court allocation or the IRS allocation? Explain.

_____

_____

_____

_____

_____

_____

LO 4 40. Mabel, Loretta, and Margaret are equal partners in a local restaurant. The restaurant reports the following items for the current year:

Revenue	$600,000
Business expenses	310,000
Investment expenses	150,000
Short-term capital gains	157,000
Short-term capital losses	(213,000)

Each partner receives a Schedule K-1 with one-third of the preceding items reported to her. How must each individual report these results on her Form 1040?

_____

_____

_____

_____

_____

_____

Chapter Nine

Tax Credits (Form 1040, Lines 47 through 53 and Lines 63 through 67)

Congress has provided a variety of tax credits designed to reduce the tax liability of specific groups of taxpayers. The intended purpose of these tax credits is to accomplish certain social or economic goals or to encourage participation in certain activities deemed desirable by policymakers. Tax credits are different from tax deductions. A tax credit is subtracted directly from the total amount of tax liability, thus reducing or even eliminating the taxpayer's tax obligation. Tax deductions decrease the taxable income used to calculate tax liability. Thus tax credits provide equal relief to all taxpayers regardless of their marginal tax rate and are more beneficial to the taxpayer than a deduction.

Learning Objectives

When you have completed this chapter, you should understand the following learning objectives (LO):

LO 1. Apply the tax rules and calculate the Credit for Child and Dependent Care Expenses.

LO 2. Apply the tax rules and calculate the Credit for the Elderly or the Disabled.

LO 3. Apply the tax rules and calculate the Education Credits.

LO 4. Apply the tax rules and calculate the Foreign Tax Credit (FTC).

LO 5. Apply the tax rules and calculate the Child Tax Credit.

LO 6. Apply the tax rules and calculate the Retirement Savings Contributions Credit.

LO 7. Apply the tax rules and calculate the Adoption Credit.

LO 8. Apply the tax rules and calculate the Earned Income Credit (EIC).

LO 9. Discuss some of the other types of tax credits available.

INTRODUCTION

Congress has elected to offer a number of tax credits, generally enacted to encourage certain outcomes or to accomplish specified societal goals. Some of these goals include assisting families with children, ensuring additional tax relief for low-income taxpayers, encouraging taxpayers to enhance their education, encouraging adoptions, and providing incentives for taxpayers to work.

Almost all individual income tax credits are nonrefundable. This means that a taxpayer whose credits exceed his or her tax liability will reduce tax owed to zero but will *not* receive a refund for the excess of credits. There are some major exceptions to this rule, such as the

earned income credit and others. In these cases, a taxpayer with credits in excess of the tax liability will receive the excess amount as a refund.

Most tax credits are reported on lines 47 through 53 and lines 63 through 67 of Form 1040. Many of the credits require additional forms or schedules and are discussed under the appropriate learning objectives of this chapter.

CREDIT FOR CHILD AND DEPENDENT CARE EXPENSES (FORM 1040, LINE 48 [FORM 2441], OR FORM 1040A, LINE 29 [SCHEDULE 2])
LO 1

Many taxpayers with dependents incur expenses to care for those dependents while they work. The credit for child and dependent care expenses provides some relief for working taxpayers by providing a credit for a portion of the expenses incurred to care for a qualified dependent.[1] To qualify for the credit, the taxpayer must incur employment-related expenses to care for one or more qualifying individuals.

Qualifying Expenses

All necessary expenses, including those paid for household services and expenses for the care of qualified individuals so that the taxpayer can be gainfully employed,[2] are eligible. Appropriate expenses include those incurred in the home for a babysitter, housekeeper, cook, or nanny. Expenses paid to a family member (such as a grandmother) are eligible as long as the relative is not a child of the taxpayer under the age 19 or can be claimed as a dependent by the taxpayer.[3]

If the expenses are incurred outside the home at a dependent care facility (such as a day care center), the expenses qualify only if the facility provides care for a fee for six or more individuals. The facility must comply with all applicable state and local laws.[4] In addition, out-of-the-home expenses incurred while caring for an older dependent or spouse (who is incapacitated) qualify. However, the qualifying individual(s) must live in the household of the taxpayer for at least eight hours a day. These rules allow credit for expenses incurred for a handicapped older dependent who otherwise would be institutionalized.

Qualifying Individual

A qualifying individual includes (1) a person under age 13 for whom the taxpayer is entitled to a dependency deduction or (2) a dependent or spouse of the taxpayer who is incapable of caring for himself or herself and who lived with the taxpayer for at least half of the year.[5] A child under age 13 meeting the special dependency test of divorced parents is deemed to be a qualifying individual for the custodial parent even if that parent cannot claim the child as a dependent.[6]

Generally married taxpayers must file a joint return to claim the credit (legally separated taxpayers are not considered to be married). A married taxpayer filing a separate return is entitled to claim the credit only if he or she meets *all* the following conditions:

- Lived apart from his or her spouse.
- Furnished more than half of the cost of maintaining a household that a qualified individual lived in for more than half the year.
- Has a spouse who was not a member of the household for the last six months of the year.[7]

Credit Calculation

The credit is calculated as a percentage of employment-related expenses paid during the year. The percentage varies between 20% and 35%, depending on the taxpayer's AGI. The maximum

[1] IRC § 21.
[2] IRC § 21(b)(2)(A).
[3] *Family member* is defined in IRC § 151(c)(3).
[4] IRC § 21(b)(2)(C) and IRC § 21(b)(2)(D).
[5] IRC § 21(b)(1).
[6] IRC § 21(e)(5) and IRC § 152(e).
[7] IRC § 21(e)(4).

amount of qualifying expenses for any year is limited to $3,000 if there is one qualifying individual and to $6,000 for two or more qualifying individuals.[8] These amounts are further limited to the amount of earned income of the taxpayer (or the earned income of the taxpayer's spouse, if smaller).[9] If a taxpayer receives dependent care assistance from an employer that is excluded from gross income, the expense limit is reduced by the amount excluded from income.[10] The amount of the credit is limited to the taxpayer's tax liability.

If the taxpayer's spouse is unable to care for himself or herself or is a full-time student, the spouse is deemed to have earned income for the purpose of the credit calculation. The amount of earned income is $250 per month if the taxpayer cares for one qualifying person and $500 per month if caring for two or more persons.

EXAMPLE 9-1	Bill and Suzie paid $6,400 in qualified employment-related expenses for their three children. Suzie received $2,500 of dependent care assistance that her employer properly excluded from Suzie's gross income. The amount of employment-related expenses Bill and Suzie can use to determine their credit is $3,500 (the maximum amount allowed of $6,000 reduced by $2,500 of excluded dependent care assistance). Note that the taxpayer must apply the dependent care assistance exclusion against the $6,000 limitation, not against the total amount paid of $6,400 (unless the amount paid is less than the limitation amount).

EXAMPLE 9-2	Rick and Vanessa paid $3,800 in qualified employment-related expenses for their dependent daughter. Their AGI was $42,000, which included $40,500 from Vanessa's job and $1,500 of net self-employment income from Rick's business (as reported on Schedule C). Qualified employment-related expenses would be limited to $1,500.

EXAMPLE 9-3	Ethan and Jenny paid $4,200 in qualified employment-related expenses for their dependent son. Ethan's AGI was $42,000; Jenny was a full-time student for nine months of the year. Ethan and Jenny's qualified employment-related expenses would be limited to $2,250 ($250 × 9 months).

The percentage used to determine the credit, which ranges from 20% to 35%, depends on the taxpayer's AGI. The percentage is 35% for taxpayers with AGI of $15,000 or less and is reduced by 1% for each additional $2,000 of AGI (or fraction thereof), with a minimum percentage of 20%. The following chart provides applicable percentages:

Adjusted Gross Income	Applicable Percentage
$15,000 or less	35%
15,001–17,000	34
17,001–19,000	33
19,001–21,000	32
21,001–23,000	31
23,001–25,000	30
25,001–27,000	29
27,001–29,000	28
29,001–31,000	27
31,001–33,000	26
33,001–35,000	25
35,001–37,000	24
37,001–39,000	23
39,001–41,000	22
41,001–43,000	21
43,001 or more	20

[8] IRC § 21(c).

[9] IRC § 21(d).

[10] IRC § 21(c). The income exclusion would be made in accordance with IRC § 129.

From Shoebox to Software

Taxpayers use Form 2441 to calculate the child and dependent care credit (Exhibit 9-1).

Complete identification of the qualifying child is required. Taxpayers must also provide information for the person or entity that provided the care, including taxpayer ID numbers. Most established day care programs provide taxpayers with end-of-year statements listing the amounts paid for day care and the taxpayer ID of the day care establishment.

Within the tax software, you enter most required information directly on Form 2441. Part I is used to report information about the child care provider, including the amount paid. Part II shows data on the qualifying individual(s) and the expenses paid for each one. The tax software automatically determines lines 3 through 11. If the taxpayer received any nontaxable dependent care benefits from his or her employer, the software will then complete Part III (not shown). The amount of tax-free benefit is in box 10 of Form W-2.

The tax software reports the final credit amount (line 13) on line 48 on Form 1040 or line 29 on Form 1040A.

EXAMPLE 9-4

Walt has AGI of $18,744 from his employment, and he spent $1,240 on qualified expenses for his child during the year. He is entitled to a tax credit of $409 ($1,240 × 33%). If Walt's AGI were $15,200, his credit would be $422 ($1,240 × 34%). If Walt's AGI were $25,500, his credit would be $360 ($1,240 × 29%).

EXAMPLE 9-5

Rachel, a single mother, maintains a household for her 4-year-old son, Eric. Rachel, who spent $3,800 to care for her son while she was at work, had AGI of $34,500 from her job during the year. Her child and dependent care tax credit will be $750 ($3,000 × 25%). Rachel is entitled to 25% of qualifying expenses, which are limited to $3,000.

TAX YOUR BRAIN

Why would Congress want to provide a credit for child and dependent care expenses?

ANSWER

Remember that the credit pertains to qualifying expenses paid to enable the taxpayer to be gainfully employed. It is reasonable to expect that the credit will allow more individuals to be employed (or be employed more hours), resulting in higher payroll and other taxes to offset at least some of the cost of providing the credit. In addition, overall employment levels should increase, which is beneficial to the economy in general.

CONCEPT CHECK 9-1—LO 1

1. Jamie is a single mother with one dependent child, Joey, age 7. She has AGI of $75,000, and she paid $4,500 to a qualified day care center for after-school care for Joey. Calculate Jamie's child and dependent care credit.

2. Tom and Katie are married, file a joint return, and have two dependent children: Jack, age 11, and Jill, age 5. Tom has earned income of $41,000; Katie was a full-time student (for nine months) with no income. They paid a qualified day care/after-school care center $6,000. Calculate the amount of qualified employment-related expenses that would be used for the child and dependent care credit for Tom and Katie.

3. Antonio is a widower and cares for his son Elio, age 4. Antonio has AGI of $24,000 and paid qualified child care expenses for Elio of $2,900. In addition, Antonio received $1,000 of dependent care assistance that his employer properly excluded from Antonio's gross income. Calculate Antonio's child and dependent care credit.

EXHIBIT 9-1

Form **2441**

Department of the Treasury
Internal Revenue Service (99)

Child and Dependent Care Expenses

▶ Attach to Form 1040, Form 1040A, or Form 1040NR.
▶ See separate instructions.

1040
1040A
1040NR

2441

OMB No. 1545-0074

20**09**

Attachment
Sequence No. **21**

Name(s) shown on return

Your social security number

Part I Persons or Organizations Who Provided the Care—You **must** complete this part.
(If you have more than two care providers, see the instructions.)

1	**(a)** Care provider's name	**(b)** Address (number, street, apt. no., city, state, and ZIP code)	**(c)** Identifying number (SSN or EIN)	**(d)** Amount paid (see instructions)

Did you receive **dependent care benefits?**

No ▶ Complete only Part II below.
Yes ▶ Complete Part III on the back next.

Caution. If the care was provided in your home, you may owe employment taxes. If you do, you cannot file Form 1040A. For details, see the instructions for Form 1040, line 59, or Form 1040NR, line 56.

Part II Credit for Child and Dependent Care Expenses

2 Information about your **qualifying person(s).** If you have more than two qualifying persons, see the instructions.

(a) Qualifying person's name		**(b)** Qualifying person's social security number	**(c)** **Qualified expenses** you incurred and paid in 2009 for the person listed in column (a)
First	Last		

3 Add the amounts in column (c) of line 2. **Do not** enter more than $3,000 for one qualifying person or $6,000 for two or more persons. If you completed Part III, enter the amount from line 34 . . . . **3**

4 Enter your **earned income.** See instructions **4**

5 If married filing jointly, enter your spouse's earned income (if your spouse was a student or was disabled, see the instructions); **all others,** enter the amount from line 4 . . . . . **5**

6 Enter the **smallest** of line 3, 4, or 5 . . . . **6**

7 Enter the amount from Form 1040, line 38; Form 1040A, line 22; or Form 1040NR, line 36. . . . . **7**

8 Enter on line 8 the decimal amount shown below that applies to the amount on line 7

If line 7 is:				If line 7 is:		
Over	**But not over**	**Decimal amount is**		**Over**	**But not over**	**Decimal amount is**
$0—15,000		.35		$29,000—31,000		.27
15,000—17,000		.34		31,000—33,000		.26
17,000—19,000		.33		33,000—35,000		.25
19,000—21,000		.32		35,000—37,000		.24
21,000—23,000		.31		37,000—39,000		.23
23,000—25,000		.30		39,000—41,000		.22
25,000—27,000		.29		41,000—43,000		.21
27,000—29,000		.28		43,000—No limit		.20

8 X .

9 Multiply line 6 by the decimal amount on line 8. If you paid 2008 expenses in 2009, see the instructions **9**

10 Enter the amount from Form 1040, line 46; Form 1040A, line 28; or Form 1040NR, line 43. . . . . **10**

11 Enter the amount from Form 1040, line 47; or Form 1040NR, line 44. Form 1040A filers, enter -0- . . . **11**

12 Subtract line 11 from line 10. If zero or less, **stop.** You cannot take the credit **12**

13 **Credit for child and dependent care expenses.** Enter the **smaller** of line 9 or line 12 here and on Form 1040, line 48; Form 1040A, line 29; or Form 1040NR, line 45 . . . . **13**

For Paperwork Reduction Act Notice, see page 4 of the instructions.   Cat. No. 11862M   Form **2441** (2009)

CREDIT FOR THE ELDERLY OR THE DISABLED (FORM 1040, LINE 53 [AND SCHEDULE R], OR FORM 1040A, LINE 30)

LO 2

The credit for the elderly or the disabled was originally enacted to provide some tax relief to low-income elderly or disabled individuals.[11] To be eligible, the taxpayer must be over age 65 or have retired on permanent and total disability and be receiving taxable disability income. In addition, certain AGI and nontaxable social security income limits apply.

Credit Calculation

The maximum allowable credit is equal to 15% of the taxpayer's base amount of qualifying income (depending on the filing status) limited to the following:

- $5,000 for single individuals or joint returns when only one spouse qualifies.
- $7,500 for joint returns when both spouses qualify.
- $3,750 for a married person filing a separate return.[12]

This base amount must be reduced by (1) the amount of nontaxable social security (or similar) payments received and (2) one-half of the amount of AGI that exceeds $7,500 for single returns, $10,000 for joint returns, or $5,000 for married filing separately.[13]

EXAMPLE 9-6

Lou and Greta file a joint return. Lou is age 66, and Greta is 63. Note that only Lou is eligible for this credit. They have AGI of $11,500 and received $1,000 of nontaxable social security benefits. They would be entitled to a credit for the elderly or the disabled of $488 calculated as follows:

Base amount	$ 5,000
Less: Nontaxable social security	(1,000)
One-half of AGI over $10,000	(750)
Allowable base amount	$ 3,250
Applicable percentage	× 15%
Tax credit allowed	$ 488*

* Lou and Greta would have had a maximum credit for the elderly or disabled of $750 ($5,000 × 15%). However, that amount is reduced by social security and one-half of the amount of AGI over $10,000 ($750).

In practice, few elderly or disabled taxpayers are eligible for the credit because they generally receive nontaxable social security benefits in excess of the income limitations. In fact, if some social security benefits are taxable, the taxpayer will have exceeded the AGI limits. Furthermore, because the credit is not a refundable credit, the allowed credit is often zero because low-income elderly taxpayers often have no tax liability.

TAX YOUR BRAIN

If a single taxpayer receives no social security benefits, what is the maximum AGI amount he or she would have to earn to become ineligible for the elderly or disabled credit?

ANSWER

The base amount for a single taxpayer is $5,000, reduced by one-half of the amount in excess of AGI of $7,500. Once excess AGI is more than $10,000, the base amount is reduced to zero. Thus, if total AGI exceeds $17,500 ($7,500 + $10,000), a single taxpayer would not be eligible for the credit.

---

[11] IRC § 22.

[12] IRC § 22(c)(2).

[13] IRC § 22(c)(3) and IRC § 22(d).

From Shoebox to Software

Taxpayers use Schedule R to report the credit for the elderly or disabled. (For page 2 of Schedule R, see Exhibit 9-2).

With the exception of checking an appropriate box in Part I denoting the taxpayer's age and filing status, the tax software automatically determines the credit for the person who is elderly or disabled. The amount on line 24 of Schedule R is included on Form 1040, line 53, or Form 1040A, line 30.

CONCEPT CHECK 9-2—LO 2

1. Vincent and Maria are ages 70 and 67, respectively, and file a joint return. They have AGI of $21,000 and received $1,000 in nontaxable social security benefits. Calculate Vincent and Maria's credit for the elderly or the disabled.

EDUCATION CREDITS (FORM 1040, LINE 49 [AND FORM 8863], OR FORM 1040A, LINE 31)
LO 3

There are two education credits available: the Hope scholarship credit (Hope credit) and the lifetime learning credit (see Table 9-1). Both credits are available to taxpayers for qualified higher education expenses paid for themselves, their spouses, or a dependent.[14] As a result of recent federal tax law changes, the Hope credit has been modified considerably and is sometimes referred to as the American opportunity tax credit. Qualifying expenses are amounts paid for tuition, fees, and other related expenses paid to an eligible educational institution while taxpayers (or their spouses and dependents) are pursuing undergraduate, graduate, or vocational degrees.[15] The recent tax changes redefined "qualified tuition and related expenses" to also include amounts paid for course materials such as books and supplies. These expenses were previously excluded from the credit calculation. The expenses must be for an academic period that begins in the same tax year as the year of the payment or that begins in the first three months of the following year.

TABLE 9-1
Comparison of Hope and Lifetime Learning Credits

Source: IRS Publication 17, Chapter 35.

Hope Credit	Lifetime Learning Credit
Up to $2,500 credit per **eligible student.**	Up to $2,000 credit per **return.**
Available for the first four years of postsecondary education.	Available for all years of postsecondary education and for courses to acquire or improve job skills.
Student must be pursuing an undergraduate degree or other recognized education credential.	Student does not need to be pursuing a degree or other recognized education credential.
Student must be enrolled at least half-time for at least one academic period beginning during the year.	Available for one or more courses.
No felony drug conviction on student's record.	Felony drug conviction rule does not apply.

[14] IRC § 25A.
[15] IRC § 25A(f)(1).

EXHIBIT 9-2

Schedule R (Form 1040A or 1040) 2009   Page **2**

Part III	**Figure Your Credit**	

10   **If you checked (in Part I):**   **Enter:**

Box 1, 2, 4, or 7 . . . .$5,000
Box 3, 5, or 6 . . . .$7,500 } **10**
Box 8 or 9 . . . .$3,750

Did you check box 2, 4, 5, 6, or 9 in Part I?	→	Yes ——————▶	You **must** complete line 11.
		No ——————▶	Enter the amount from line 10 on line 12 and go to line 13.

11   **If you checked (in Part I):**

● Box 6, add $5,000 to the taxable disability income of the spouse who was under age 65. Enter the total.
● Box 2, 4, or 9, enter your taxable disability income. } **11**
● Box 5, add your taxable disability income to your spouse's taxable disability income. Enter the total.

(TIP)   For more details on what to include on line 11, see page R-3.

12   If you completed line 11, enter the **smaller** of line 10 or line 11. **All others,** enter the amount from line 10 . . . . **12**

13   Enter the following pensions, annuities, or disability income that you (and your spouse if filing jointly) received in 2009.

   a   Nontaxable part of social security benefits and nontaxable part of railroad retirement benefits treated as social security (see page R-3) **13a**

   b   Nontaxable veterans' pensions and any other pension, annuity, or disability benefit that is excluded from income under any other provision of law (see page R-3) **13b**

   c   Add lines 13a and 13b. (Even though these income items are not taxable, they **must** be included here to figure your credit.) If you did not receive any of the types of nontaxable income listed on line 13a or 13b, enter -0- on line 13c **13c**

14   Enter the amount from Form 1040A, line 22, or Form 1040, line 38 . . . . . | **14**

15   **If you checked (in Part I):**   **Enter:**
   Box 1 or 2 . . . . . . $7,500
   Box 3, 4, 5, 6, or 7 . . . $10,000 } **15**
   Box 8 or 9 . . . . . . $5,000

16   Subtract line 15 from line 14. If zero or less, enter -0- . . . . | **16**

17   Enter one-half of line 16 . . . . **17**

18   Add lines 13c and 17 . . . . **18**

19   Subtract line 18 from line 12. If zero or less, **stop;** you **cannot** take the credit. Otherwise, go to line 20 . . . . **19**

20   Multiply line 19 by 15% (.15). **20**

21   Enter the amount from Form 1040A, line 28, or Form 1040, line 46 . . . . | **21**

22   Enter the total of any amounts from Form 1040A, line 29, or Form 1040, lines 47 and 48 . . . . | **22**

23   Subtract line 22 from line 21. If zero or less, **stop;** you **cannot** take the credit **23**

24   **Credit for the elderly or the disabled.** Enter the **smaller** of line 20 or line 23. Also enter this amount on Form 1040A, line 30, or include on Form 1040, line 53 (check box **c** and enter "Sch R" in the space next to that box) **24**

Schedule R (Form 1040A or 1040) 2009

An eligible educational institution is a postsecondary educational institution (college, university, vocational school, or the like.) that is eligible to participate in a student aid program administered by the U.S. Department of Education. Almost all postsecondary institutions qualify.

EXAMPLE 9-7	In December 2009, Fred pays his son's college tuition for spring semester 2010. The semester starts in February 2010. Fred can deduct the expenses in tax year 2009.

Payments made using borrowed funds (such as student loans) are qualifying expenses. If a student receives a scholarship or other income that is excludable from gross income (such as Pell grants or employer-provided educational assistance), the excludable income reduces qualifying expenses.[16] If a dependent pays for qualified expenses, the expenses are deemed paid by the taxpayer. Similarly, if someone other than the taxpayer, spouse, or dependent pays the expenses directly to the educational institution on behalf of the student, the expenses are deemed paid by the student.

EXAMPLE 9-8	Uncle George pays the college tuition for his nephew, Franklin. For purposes of the education credits, the expenses are deemed paid by Franklin. If Franklin is a dependent of his parents, his parents can take the credit.

Hope Scholarship Credit (American Opportunity Tax Credit)

The Hope credit is equal to 100% of the first $2,000 and 25% of the next $2,000 paid for qualified tuition and related expenses,[17] for a maximum of $2,500 per year.

To be eligible, a student must be carrying at least *half* of the normal full-time course load applicable to his or her course of study for at least one academic period (semester or quarter) during the year.[18] The student must be enrolled in a program leading to a degree or other educational credential. The Hope credit is available for a student's first four years of postsecondary education, measured as of the beginning of the year.

Generally, up to 40% of the Hope credit (that is, $1,000) may be a refundable credit. This means that a taxpayer may receive a refund even if he or she owes no taxes. However, none of the credit is refundable if the taxpayer claiming the credit is (a) a child under age 18 (or a student who is at least 18 and under 24) whose earned income is less than one-half of his or her own support, (b) who has at least one living parent, and (c) who does not file a joint return.

EXAMPLE 9-9	Ed and Lauren paid $1,600 of qualified tuition and related expenses for their son who is in his fourth year of college. These expenses included $450 for books and supplies. Without regard to AGI limitations or other credits, they can take a Hope credit of $1,600 ($1,600 × 100%).

Lifetime Learning Credit

The lifetime learning credit is equal to 20% of up to $10,000 of qualified tuition and related expenses paid during the year.[19] The credit is determined per taxpayer, not per student. Thus the maximum credit allowed for a taxpayer is $2,000 per year.

[16] IRC § 25A(g)(2). Gifts, bequests, or inheritances are not excluded.

[17] These amounts are indexed for inflation.

[18] IRC § 25A(b)(2) and (3).

[19] IRC § 25A(c).

EXAMPLE 9-10	During the year, Emmit and Francine paid qualified higher education expenses of $3,000 for their daughter and $4,000 for their son. Without regard to AGI limitations or other credits, they can take a lifetime learning credit of $1,400 ($7,000 × 20%).

A student can qualify for the lifetime learning credit regardless of whether he or she enrolls in a degree program or the number of courses taken in a semester. Qualified expenses for courses taken to acquire or improve job skills are eligible as well as expenses for any postsecondary education, including graduate school.

Phaseout of the Education Credits

The Hope credit and the lifetime learning credit are intended to defray the cost of higher education for low- to middle-income taxpayers. As such, the credit is phased out when modified AGI (MAGI) exceeds certain limits. MAGI is equal to AGI plus income earned abroad or in certain U.S. territories or possessions.[20]

The Hope credit begins to phase out at $80,000 of MAGI for single taxpayers and $160,000 for joint filers. The lifetime learning credit phases out when MAGI exceeds $50,000 and $100,000 for single and joint taxpayers, respectively.[21] You cannot claim a Hope credit if your MAGI is $90,000 or more ($180,000 or more if you are filing jointly). Similarly, you cannot claim a lifetime learning credit if your MAGI exceeds $60,000 ($120,000 if you are filing jointly).

When MAGI is within the phaseout range, the amount of the credit is reduced by multiplying the amount by a fraction, calculated as follows:

Hope Credit	
For Married Taxpayers	**For Single Taxpayers**
$\dfrac{\$180,000 - \text{MAGI}}{\$20,000}$	$\dfrac{\$90,000 - \text{MAGI}}{\$10,000}$

Lifetime Learning Credit	
For Married Taxpayers	**For Single Taxpayers**
$\dfrac{\$120,000 - \text{MAGI}}{\$20,000}$	$\dfrac{\$60,000 - \text{MAGI}}{\$10,000}$

EXAMPLE 9-11	Chuck and Becky have modified AGI of $103,000 and a pre-limitation lifetime learning credit of $1,200. Due to their MAGI, their lifetime learning credit is limited to $1,020 ([$120,000 − $103,000]/$20,000 × $1,200). If they had MAGI of $100,000 or less, they would have received the entire $1,200 as credit. If they had MAGI of $120,000 or more, they would be entitled to no credit.

Coordination with Other Education-Related Benefits

Taxpayers can use qualifying expenses for the Hope credit or lifetime learning credit but not both. Similarly, if a tuition and fees deduction is taken (as discussed in Chapter 4), the taxpayer cannot claim the education credits for the same student. A taxpayer who is an eligible student, or has dependents that are eligible students, should take the credit or deduction (or a combination thereof) that yields, the greatest tax savings for his or her individual tax situation.

[20] IRC § 25A(d).

[21] These income limitation amounts are indexed for inflation.

From Shoebox to Software

Taxpayers report education credits on Form 8863 (Exhibit 9-3).

Hope credits are in Part I, lifetime learning credits in Part II, and limitations are determined in Part III. With the tax software, you initially enter information concerning qualified expenses on a Federal Information for Higher Education worksheet located in the worksheet section. The software will automatically take the credit or deduction that is most advantageous. Alternatively, you can force the software to take the deduction or credit of your choice by placing an x in the appropriate box on the worksheet.

The data for the worksheet generally come from Form 1098-T (Exhibit 9-4). Schools and universities provide this form to report the amount of qualifying tuition and related expenses paid. You must reduce the amount in box 1 by any amount shown in box 4 prior to entering the information on the tax worksheet.

The information on the worksheet carries forward to Form 8863, and the entire form is automatically calculated. Note that on line 18 of Form 8863, allowed credits may be limited to tax liability minus various other credits.

EXAMPLE 9-12

Art and Arlene paid $3,200 of qualified expenses for their dependent son, Albert, who is a freshman. Their MAGI is $73,000. The couple could choose to take either a Hope credit of $2,300 ($2,000 plus 25% of the next $1,200) or a lifetime learning credit of $640 ($3,200 × 20%) but not both.

TAX YOUR BRAIN

Using the information from Example 9-12, assume that Art and Arlene also have a dependent daughter, Chris, who is a sophomore, and they paid $6,000 of qualified expenses for her. What are the credit options for Art and Arlene? Which option would they choose?

ANSWER

Art and Arlene could take (1) two Hope credits of $2,300 and $2,500 (for a total of $4,800) or (2) a Hope credit of $2,300 for Albert and a lifetime learning credit of $1,200 for Chris or (3) a lifetime learning credit of $640 for Albert and a Hope credit of $2,500 for Chris or (4) a single lifetime learning credit of $1,840. In this case, they would obviously choose option 1.

A taxpayer can claim a Hope credit or lifetime learning credit in the same year he or she takes a tax-free distribution from a Coverdell Education Savings Account, as long as the taxpayer does not use the same expenses for both benefits.

For individuals attending eligible education institutions located in the Midwestern disaster area in 2009, both the Hope credit and lifetime learning credit maximums may be increased in some cases. For more details, refer to IRS Pulication 970.

CONCEPT CHECK 9-3—LO 3

1. Jewels is a single taxpayer and paid $2,900 in qualifying expenses for her daughter, who attended the University of Arizona full-time as a freshman. How much is Jewels's lifetime learning credit without regard to modified AGI limitations or other credits?
2. Assume the same facts as in Question 1. Jewels has modified AGI of $85,000 and wants to claim the Hope credit. What is her allowable Hope credit after the credit phaseout based on AGI is taken into account?
3. Assume the same facts as in Question 1. Jewels has modified AGI of $98,000 and wants to claim the Hope credit. What is her Hope credit after the credit phaseout based on AGI is taken into account?
4. Vern and Whitney paid $1,600 and $2,100 in qualifying expenses for their twin daughters Kimberly and Janet, respectively, to attend the nursing program at the community college. Without regard to modified AGI limitations or other credits, how much is their lifetime learning credit?

EXHIBIT 9-3

Form **8863**	**Education Credits (American Opportunity, Hope, and Lifetime Learning Credits)**	OMB No. 1545-0074
Department of the Treasury Internal Revenue Service (99)	▶ See separate Instructions to find out if you are eligible to take the credits. ▶ Attach to Form 1040 or Form 1040A.	**20**09 Attachment Sequence No. **50**

Name(s) shown on return	**Your social security number**

Caution: *You **cannot** take both an education credit and the tuition and fees deduction (see Form 8917) for the **same student** for the same year.*

Part I   American Opportunity Credit

Use Part II if you are claiming the Hope credit for a student attending school in a Midwestern disaster area and elect to waive the computation method in this part for all students.

Caution: *You **cannot** take the American opportunity credit for more than **4 tax years** for the **same student**.*

1	**(a)** Student's name (as shown on page 1 of your tax return) First name / Last name	**(b)** Student's social security number (as shown on page 1 of your tax return)	**(c)** Qualified expenses (see instructions). **Do not** enter more than $4,000 for each student.	**(d)** Subtract $2,000 from the amount in column (c). If zero or less, enter -0-.	**(e)** Multiply the amount in column (d) by 25% (.25)	**(f)** If column (d) is zero, enter the amount from column (c). Otherwise, add $2,000 to the amount in column (e).

| 2 | **Tentative American opportunity credit.** Add the amounts on line 1, column (f). Skip Part II if line 2 is more than zero. If you are taking the lifetime learning credit for a different student, go to Part III; otherwise, go to Part IV . . . . ▶ | **2** | |

Part II   Hope Credit

Use this part if you are claiming the Hope credit for a student attending school in a Midwestern disaster area and elect to waive the computation method in Part I for all students.

Caution: *You **cannot** take the Hope credit for more than **2 tax years** for the **same student**.*

3	**(a)** Student's name (as shown on page 1 of your tax return) First name / Last name	**(b)** Student's social security number (as shown on page 1 of your tax return)	**(c)** Qualified expenses (see instructions). **Do not** enter more than $2,400* for each student.	**(d)** Enter the **smaller** of the amount in column (c) or $1,200**	**(e)** Add column (c) and column (d)	**(f)** Enter one-half of the amount in column (e)

*For each student who attended an eligible educational institution in a Midwestern disaster area, **do not** enter more than $4,800.

For each student who attended an eligible educational institution in a Midwestern disaster area, enter the **smaller of the amount in column (c) or $2,400.

| 4 | **Tentative Hope credit.** Add the amounts on line 3, column (f). If you are taking the lifetime learning credit for another student, go to Part III; otherwise, go to Part V . . . . ▶ | **4** | |

Part III   Lifetime Learning Credit. Caution: *You **cannot** take the American opportunity credit or the Hope credit and the lifetime learning credit for the **same student** in the same year.*

5	**(a)** Student's name (as shown on page 1 of your tax return) First name Last name	**(b)** Student's social security number (as shown on page 1 of your tax return)	**(c)** Qualified expenses (see instructions)

6	Add the amounts on line 5, column (c), and enter the total	**6**	
7a	Enter the **smaller** of line 6 or $10,000	**7a**	
b	For students who attended an eligible educational institution in a Midwestern disaster area, enter the **smaller** of $10,000 or their qualified expenses included on line 6 (see special rules on page 3 of the instructions) .	**7b**	
c	Subtract line 7b from line 7a	**7c**	
8a	Multiply line 7b by 40% (.40)	**8a**	
b	Multiply line 7c by 20% (.20)	**8b**	
c	**Tentative lifetime learning credit.** Add lines 8a and 8b. If you have an entry on line 2, go to Part IV; otherwise go to Part V	**8c**	

For Paperwork Reduction Act Notice, see page 4 of separate instructions.   Cat. No. 25379M   Form **8863** (2009)

EXHIBIT 9-4

☐ CORRECTED		

FILER'S name, street address, city, state, ZIP code, and telephone number	**1** Payments received for qualified tuition and related expenses $	OMB No. 1545-1574
	2 Amounts billed for qualified tuition and related expenses $	② ⓪ **09** Form **1098-T**

Tuition Statement

FILER'S federal identification no.	STUDENT'S social security number	**3** If this box is checked, your educational institution has changed its reporting method for 2009 ☐	**Copy B For Student**

STUDENT'S name	**4** Adjustments made for a prior year $	**5** Scholarships or grants $

This is important tax information and is being furnished to the Internal Revenue Service.

Street address (including apt. no.)	**6** Adjustments to scholarships or grants for a prior year $	**7** Checked if the amount in box 1 or 2 includes amounts for an academic period beginning January - March 2010 ► ☐
City, state, and ZIP code		

Service Provider/Acct. No. (see instr.)	**8** Checked if at least half-time student ☐	**9** Checked if a graduate student ☐	**10** Ins. contract reimb./refund $

Form **1098-T**   (keep for your records)   Department of the Treasury - Internal Revenue Service

FOREIGN TAX CREDIT (FTC) (FORM 1040, LINE 47, AND FORM 1116)
LO 4

U.S. citizens and residents are subject to taxation on income earned worldwide. Although most U.S. taxpayers earn income solely from U.S. sources, taxpayers with income from foreign sources may be subject to double taxation (the same income is taxed both in the United States and in the foreign country). Most often this foreign-source income is investment income such as interest or dividends, although other types are possible.[22] To mitigate double taxation, the Internal Revenue Code (IRC) provides a foreign tax credit for income taxes paid or accrued to a foreign country or U.S. possession.[23]

The foreign tax credit is available for taxes levied on income such as wages, interest, dividends, and royalties. The amount of the credit is equal to the amount paid or accrued, but the credit cannot exceed that portion of U.S. income tax attributable to the foreign income.[24] The limitation is determined as follows:[25]

$$\frac{\text{Foreign-source taxable income}}{\text{Worldwide taxable income}} \times \begin{array}{c} \text{U.S. income} \\ \text{tax liability} \\ \text{before FTC} \end{array} = \begin{array}{c} \text{Foreign tax} \\ \text{credit} \\ \text{limitation} \end{array}$$

EXAMPLE 9-13

Kim reported total taxable income of $84,010 that included $1,000 of foreign-source interest. Her U.S. tax liability was $18,273. She paid foreign taxes of $250 on the foreign income. Kim is entitled to a foreign tax credit of $218. Although she paid $250 in foreign tax, her credit is limited to $218 calculated as follows: ($1,000/$84,010) × $18,273 = $218. If Kim's foreign tax were $218 or less, she would be entitled to a credit equal to the amount of foreign tax paid.

---

[22] This section does not discuss foreign-source income earned by U.S. citizens living abroad. Law concerning the taxation and credits associated with such income is found in IRC § 911. Taxation of foreign-source wages is complex and is not discussed in this text.

[23] IRC § 901.

[24] IRC § 904(a).

[25] In practice, the limitation is calculated separately for certain categories of income as indicated in IRC § 904 (d) and as shown on the top of Form 1116. This text focuses only on the passive income category because the other categories seldom apply to individual taxpayers.

From Shoebox to Software

The majority of taxpayers who earn foreign-source income do so through mutual funds that invest in foreign stocks or bonds. These taxpayers will receive a Form 1099-INT or 1099-DIV from their mutual fund company. The statements report the amount of income and the corresponding foreign tax paid. Some taxpayers may own foreign stocks or bonds directly. If the investment is through a brokerage firm, the taxpayer will receive an appropriate Form 1099. If the taxpayer owns foreign investments outside of a brokerage account, the taxpayer often needs to gather the income and taxation information separately.

Taxpayers report the foreign tax credit on Form 1116 (Exhibit 9-5). A taxpayer may elect to claim the credit without filing a Form 1116 if he or she meets *all* of the following:[26]

- All of the foreign-source income is passive income.
- All of the income and foreign taxes paid are reported to the taxpayer on appropriate Forms 1099.
- Total foreign taxes paid were less than $300 ($600 if married filing a joint return).

- The taxpayer is not subject to the foreign tax limitation rules.

A taxpayer who meets all of these rules reports the foreign tax credit directly on Form 1040, line 47. No Form 1116 is required.

You enter the appropriate information directly onto Form 1116 when using the tax software. Most taxpayers enter information concerning the gross income that was taxed by the foreign country on line 1, columns (A) through (C), and enter the appropriate amount of foreign taxes paid in Part II, columns (k) through (s). In most situations, the tax software completes the remainder of the form and shows the total credit on line 29.

A taxpayer who earns passive income through investment in a mutual fund often provides the foreign country name in Parts I and II as "various" because there is seldom one country from which the income is earned. If the passive income were from a direct investment in one country, the taxpayer would enter that country's name.

Cash basis taxpayers take the foreign tax credit in the year paid. However, cash basis taxpayers can make a binding election to take the credit for all foreign taxes in the year they accrue.[27]

Taxpayers may choose to deduct foreign taxes as an itemized deduction rather than as a credit. From a practical standpoint, it is seldom advantageous to use a deduction instead of a credit. However, there are at least two instances for which a deduction is preferred. One is when a taxpayer has income from one country (on which tax was paid) and an equal loss from another country. The net foreign taxable income would be zero, and taxpayers would receive no credit. In such a case, the benefit for the taxes paid in the positive income country would be lost unless the taxpayer took the foreign taxes as an itemized deduction. Another instance relates to foreign taxes not based on income (e.g., property taxes). Taxpayers can take these foreign taxes as a deduction because the foreign tax credit is only available for foreign taxes paid based on income.[28]

CONCEPT CHECK 9-4—LO 4

1. Joy has $63,000 worldwide taxable income, which includes $8,000 of taxable income from New Zealand. She paid $2,500 in foreign income taxes, and her U.S. tax liability is $17,640. Calculate Joy's foreign tax credit.

---

[26] IRS instructions for Form 1116.

[27] IRC § 905(a).

[28] Reg. § 1.901-2(a)(1).

EXHIBIT 9-5

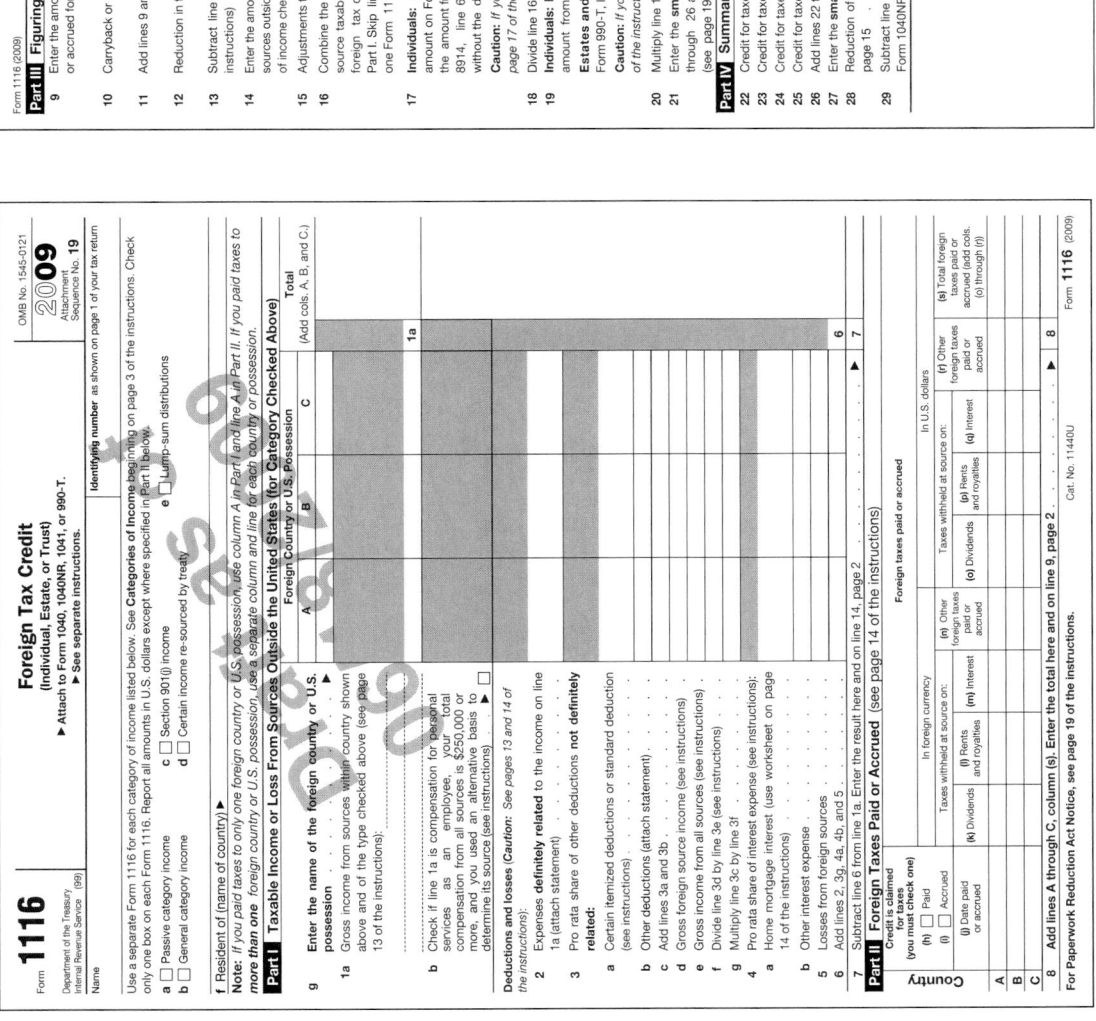

From Shoebox to Software

Taxpayers calculate the child tax credit using a worksheet found in the instructions to Form 1040. In the tax software, this document is in the worksheet section. When you examine the worksheet, you will see that the software automatically creates virtually all of it.

When we entered the tax information for Jose and Maria Ramirez in Chapter 3, we noted that they had a $3,000 child tax credit shown on line 51. This amount is $1,000 for each child. If you open the Ramirezes' tax return, click on line 51, and then click on the yellow folder, you will see the child tax credit worksheet. You will note that the amount of the preliminary credit on line 1 is not limited.

If you open the tax return of Alan and Cherie Masters, you will see that there is no child tax credit listed on line 51 even though they have two children under the age of 17. If you click on line 51 and then click on the yellow folder to get to the worksheet, you will see that the preliminary credit of $2,000 is zero on line 8 of the worksheet because of the AGI limitation. Recall that the credit is limited once modified AGI reaches $110,000 for a married couple and that the credit is zero when modified AGI exceeds $150,000 (for two children). The Masters have modified AGI far in excess of $150,000, so they receive no child tax credit.

The credit is reported on Form 1040, line 51, or Form 1040A, line 33.

CHILD TAX CREDIT (FORM 1040, LINE 51, OR FORM 1040A, LINE 33)
LO 5

Taxpayers receive a $1,000 tax credit for each qualifying child.[29] A *qualifying child* is a son or daughter, or a descendant of either, a stepson or stepdaughter, or a descendant of either, or a foster child whom the taxpayer can claim as a dependent. The qualifying child must also be under age 17 as of the end of the tax year and must be a U.S. citizen or resident.[30]

The credit is reduced by $50 for each $1,000, or fraction thereof, of modified AGI in excess of $110,000 for taxpayers who are married filing jointly, $75,000 for single filers, and $55,000 for married filing separately.[31] *Modified AGI* is AGI plus income earned abroad or in certain U.S. territories or possessions.

EXAMPLE 9-14	Fred and Paula have two qualifying children. Their modified AGI was $116,322. Their child tax credit will be $1,650 calculated as [($116,322 − $110,000) = $6,322/$1,000 ≈ 7 and, therefore, $2,000 − (7 × $50)].

Additional Child Tax Credit

In most cases, the child tax credit is nonrefundable (that is, the credit cannot exceed the tax liability). In certain cases, however, if a taxpayer qualifies, a taxpayer may receive a child tax credit refund in excess of the tax liability. The additional child tax credit allows the taxpayer to receive up to 15% of earned income above $3,000. To claim this as a refundable credit, the taxpayer must attach and report the amount on Form 8812, and on line 65 of Form 1040 (or line 42 on Form 1040A).

CONCEPT CHECK 9-5—LO 5	1. Pat and Lisa have two qualifying children, ages 11 and 8. Their AGI is $112,000. What amount of child tax credit can they claim after their AGI limitation is considered?

[29] IRC § 24(a).
[30] IRC § 24(c).
[31] IRC § 24(b).

RETIREMENT SAVINGS CONTRIBUTIONS CREDIT (FORM 1040, LINE 50 [AND FORM 8880], OR FORM 1040A, LINE 32)

LO 6

Eligible individuals can take a tax credit based on contributions toward a retirement savings account, multiplied by an applicable percentage ranging from 0% to 50%.[32] The percentage is based on the taxpayer's modified adjusted gross income and filing status. Subject to the maximum, the credit is determined using Table 9-2.

Contributions can be made to Individual Retirement Accounts (traditional or Roth), 401(k), 403(b), or 457 plans, a SIMPLE or SEP plan, or other qualified retirement plans.[33] Distributions from the noted retirement accounts will reduce the allowed contribution. Modified AGI is equal to AGI plus income earned abroad or in certain U.S. territories or possessions. The maximum contribution amount for the credit is $2,000 per person, and on a joint return, $2,000 is taken into account for each spouse.

TABLE 9-2
Rates for Retirement Savings Contributions Credit

Modified Adjusted Gross Income						Applicable Percentage
Joint Return		Head of Household		All Other Filing Status		
Over	Not Over	Over	Not Over	Over	Not Over	
$ –0–	$33,000	$ –0–	$24,750	$ –0–	$16,500	50%
33,000	36,000	24,750	27,000	16,500	18,000	20
36,000	55,500	27,000	41,625	18,000	27,750	10
55,500		41,625		27,750		–0–

EXAMPLE 9-15

Hector is a single filer with modified AGI of $25,000. He makes a $1,000 contribution to an IRA. His retirement savings contributions credit is $100 ($1,000 × 10%). If Hector's modified AGI was $17,000, his credit would be $200 ($1,000 × 20%).

EXAMPLE 9-16

Bo and Rachelle are married filing jointly with modified AGI of $30,000. Bo makes a $2,000 contribution to a qualified retirement plan. Their credit is $1,000 ($2,000 × 50%).

CONCEPT CHECK 9-6—LO 6

1. Enrique and Lupe have AGI of $40,000, are married filing jointly, and contributed $1,500 during the year to a qualified retirement plan for Enrique. How much is their retirement savings contributions credit?

2. Roger is a head of household taxpayer with AGI of $36,000. He made a $2,200 contribution to a qualified retirement plan. How much is his retirement savings contributions credit?

---

[32] IRC § 25B(a).

[33] These plans are discussed in more detail in Chapter 11.

EXHIBIT 9-6

Form **8880**	**Credit for Qualified Retirement Savings Contributions**	OMB No. 1545-0074
Department of the Treasury Internal Revenue Service	▶ **Attach to Form 1040, Form 1040A, or Form 1040NR.** ▶ **See instructions on back.**	20**09** Attachment Sequence No. **54**

Name(s) shown on return | Your social security number

 CAUTION You **cannot** take this credit if **either** of the following applies.

- The amount on Form 1040, line 38; Form 1040A, line 22; or Form 1040NR, line 36 is more than $27,750 ($41,625 if head of household; $55,500 if married filing jointly).
- The person(s) who made the qualified contribution or elective deferral **(a)** was born after January 1, 1992, **(b)** is claimed as a dependent on someone else's 2009 tax return, or **(c)** was a **student** (see instructions).

Before you begin: Figure the amount of any credit for the elderly or the disabled you are claiming on Form 1040, line 53.

(Draft as of 06/18/2009)

		(a) You	**(b) Your spouse**
1	Traditional and Roth IRA contributions for 2009. **Do not** include rollover contributions **1**		
2	Elective deferrals to a 401(k) or other qualified employer plan, voluntary employee contributions, and 501(c)(18)(D) plan contributions for 2009 (see instructions) **2**		
3	Add lines 1 and 2 . . . . **3**		
4	Certain distributions received **after** 2006 and **before** the due date (including extensions) of your 2009 tax return (see instructions). If married filing jointly, include **both** spouses' amounts in **both** columns. See instructions for an exception **4**		
5	Subtract line 4 from line 3. If zero or less, enter -0- **5**		
6	In each column, enter the **smaller** of line 5 or $2,000 . . . . . . **6**		
7	Add the amounts on line 6. If zero, **stop**; you cannot take this credit **7**		
8	Enter the amount from Form 1040, line 38*; Form 1040A, line 22; or Form 1040NR, line 36 . . . . **8**		
9	Enter the applicable decimal amount shown below:		

If line 8 is—		**And your filing status is—**		
Over—	But not over—	Married filing jointly	Head of household	Single, Married filing separately, or Qualifying widow(er)
		Enter on line 9—		
---	$16,500	.5	.5	.5
$16,500	$18,000	.5	.5	.2
$18,000	$24,750	.5	.5	.1
$24,750	$27,000	.5	.2	.1
$27,000	$27,750	.5	.1	.1
$27,750	$33,000	.5	.1	.0
$33,000	$36,000	.2	.1	.0
$36,000	$41,625	.1	.1	.0
$41,625	$55,500	.1	.0	.0
$55,500	---	.0	.0	.0

(line 9 column): **9** | X .

Note: *If line 9 is zero,* **stop**; *you cannot take this credit.*

10	Multiply line 7 by line 9 . . . . **10**	
11	Enter the amount from Form 1040, line 46; Form 1040A, line 28; or Form 1040NR, line 43 . . . . **11**	
12	**1040 filers:** Enter the total of your credits from lines 47 through 49, and Schedule R, line 24. **1040A filers:** Enter the total of your credits from lines 29 through 31. **1040NR filers:** Enter the total of your credits from lines 44 and 45.	**12**
13	Subtract line 12 from line 11. If zero, **stop**; you cannot take this credit **13**	
14	**Credit for qualified retirement savings contributions.** Enter the **smaller** of line 10 or line 13 here and on Form 1040, line 50; Form 1040A, line 32; or Form 1040NR, line 46 . . . . **14**	

*See Pub. 590 for the amount to enter if you are filing Form 2555, 2555-EZ, or 4563 or you are excluding income from Puerto Rico.

For Paperwork Reduction Act Notice, see back of form.   Cat. No. 33394D   Form **8880** (2009)

From Shoebox to Software

Taxpayers claim the retirement savings credit on Form 8880 (Exhibit 9-6).

The information shown on line 1 comes from an IRA Contribution Summary in the worksheet section. You must enter any retirement account distributions on line 4. The software will calculate the remainder of the form and will report the appropriate credit on Form 1040, line 50, or Form 1040A, line 32. Distributions are generally reported to taxpayers on Form 1099-R.

ADOPTION CREDIT (FORM 1040, LINE 52, AND FORM 8839)
LO 7

Taxpayers can claim an adoption credit of 100% of qualified adoption expenses paid or incurred, up to a maximum of $12,150 per adopted child.[34] Married taxpayers generally must file jointly to take the credit.

Qualified adoption expenses include reasonable and necessary expenses such as adoption fees, court costs, attorney fees, and similar expenses directly related to and the principal purpose of which is the legal adoption of an eligible child.[35] Qualified expenses do not include reimbursements under an employer program. An eligible child is one who is under age 18 or is incapable of caring for himself or herself but does not include a child of an individual's spouse.

Adoption proceedings are often protracted. Taxpayers often incur expenses in a tax year other than the year in which the adoption becomes final. In the case of expenses paid in a year before the adoption becomes final, taxpayers take the credit in the year immediately after it is paid or incurred. For expenses paid or incurred in the year of legal adoption or after, taxpayers take the credit in the year paid or incurred.[36] The total amount of qualified adoption expenses over all years cannot exceed $12,150 per child.

EXAMPLE 9-17	Warren and Lois legally adopted a child in 2009. They incurred and paid qualified adoption expenses of $6,000 in 2008, $3,200 in 2009, and $3,700 in 2010. Without any limitations, Warren and Lois would be entitled to an adoption credit of $9,200 ($6,000 + $3,200) in 2009 and an additional $2,950 credit in 2010. Expenses over $12,150 are disallowed.

If a taxpayer adopts a child who is not a citizen or resident of the United States (a foreign adoption), the credit is allowed only in the year in which the adoption becomes final or in a later year if the expenses were paid or incurred in a later year.

Additional rules apply to a special-needs child. This is a child who has a special factor or condition that a state agency determines prevents the child from being placed with adoptive parents without providing adoption assistance. Such a child must also be a U.S. citizen or resident.[37] In the case of adoption of a special-needs child, taxpayers can take a $12,150 credit regardless of whether the taxpayer incurred any qualifying expenses.[38] Taxpayers take the credit in the year the adoption becomes final.

[34] IRC § 23(a) and (b).

[35] IRC § 23(d)(1).

[36] IRC § 23(a)(2).

[37] IRC § 23(d)(3).

[38] IRC § 23(a)(3).

Phaseout of Adoption Credit

The adoption credit is subject to phaseout when modified AGI exceeds certain limits. Modified AGI is equal to AGI plus income earned abroad or in certain U.S. territories or possessions. The phaseout begins when modified AGI exceeds $182,180, and the credit is completely phased out when modified AGI reaches $222,180.

When modified AGI is within the phaseout range, the allowable credit is equal to the tentative credit multiplied by the following fraction:

$$\frac{\$222,180 \ - \ \text{Modified AGI}}{\$40,000}$$

EXAMPLE 9-18	Nicholas and Elaine spent $18,000 in qualified adoption expenses. Their modified AGI is $189,000. Their adoption credit is $10,078 ([($222,180 – $189,000)/$40,000] × $12,150). Note that they multiply the fraction by the $12,150 maximum amount allowed, not the total spent of $18,000.

If a taxpayer receives employer-provided adoption benefits, the amount of qualified adoption expenses for purposes of the adoption credit is limited to the amount paid or incurred in excess of the employer-provided assistance, if any. If the assistance exceeds the expenses, the excess is taxable income. The credit is limited to the amount of tax liability. Taxpayers can carry forward any unused credit for up to five years.

CONCEPT CHECK 9-7—LO 7	1. Adam and Michelle incurred the following expenses in the adoption of their infant daughter, which was finalized in 2009. 2008 $10,500 2009 3,950 If they did not claim any credits for adoption expenses in 2008 and their 2009 modified AGI is $120,000, how much can they claim in 2009? 2. Zhang and Umiko spent $16,000 in qualified adoption expenses in 2009 in the adoption of their son, which was finalized in 2009. Their modified AGI is $205,000. How much is their adoption credit for 2009?

EARNED INCOME CREDIT (EIC) (FORM 1040, LINE 64a, OR FORM 1040A, LINE 41a)
LO 8

The earned income credit (EIC) is designed to help workers who are economically disadvantaged and to alleviate the burden of certain additional taxes such as gasoline and social security taxes.[39] Unlike most of the other personal credits, the EIC is a refundable tax credit, which means that the EIC amount is treated like payments made and may result in a tax refund even if a taxpayer has no tax liability. To claim the credit, the taxpayer must meet certain requirements and file a tax return. Taxpayers with or without a qualifying child may claim the EIC, but the amount of the credit will depend on their earned income and whether the taxpayer has no qualifying children, one qualifying child, two qualifying children, or three or more qualifying children.

Earned Income

The EIC is determined by multiplying the taxpayer's earned income by the appropriate percentage. *Earned income* includes wages, salaries, tips, and earnings from self-employment

[39] IRC § 32.

From Shoebox to Software

Taxpayers report the adoption credit on Form 8839 (see Exhibit 9-7).

You enter most of the required information directly onto Form 8839. In Part I, you provide information concerning the adopted child. On line 3, you enter the amount of any adoption credit taken in a prior year for the child. The tax software completes the remainder of the form. It also transfers the total adoption credit shown on line 18 onto Form 1040, line 52, and checks the box "b" for Form 8839.

Part III of Form 8839 (not shown) is used to report and account for employer-provided adoption benefits. Employers report any such benefits on Form W-2, box 12, with a code of "T." The tax software will automatically record the box 12 amount on the proper lines on Part III of Form 8839.

(minus one-half of the self-employment taxes).[40] A taxpayer who has a net loss from self-employment must reduce earned income by the amount of the loss.[41]

Qualifying Child

To be eligible for the credit, a taxpayer must either have a qualifying child or meet certain criteria. A qualifying child is one of the following:

- The taxpayer's son or daughter, grandchildren, or descendants.
- A stepson or stepdaughter, or descendants of either.
- An eligible foster child, defined as someone the taxpayer cares for as his or her own child and who is (1) a brother, sister, stepbrother, or stepsister or (2) a descendant of a person in (1), or (3) a child placed with the taxpayer by an authorized placement agency.
- An adopted child.[42]

In addition, the child must:

- Live with the taxpayer for more than half the year and be under the age 19 (or full-time student under the age 24).
- Be younger than the person claiming the child.
- Not have filed a joint return other than to claim a refund.

If a taxpayer has no qualifying child, *all* of the following criteria must be met:

- Have a principal place of abode in the United States for more than half the tax year.
- Be older than 24 but younger than 65 before the end of the tax year. In the case of married individuals, at least one person must satisfy this requirement.
- Not be claimed as a dependent of another taxpayer.
- Not be a nonresident alien for any part of the tax year.

Calculating the Earned Income Credit

To calculate the EIC, multiply earned income up to a certain amount by a percentage; if earned income exceeds certain levels, the credit could be phased out. The percentage and phaseout amounts vary depending on filing status and the number of qualifying children claimed by the taxpayer. The appropriate percentages and earned income amounts are in Table 9-3.[43]

At first glance, the chart seems intimidating, but its application is straightforward. For example, married taxpayers with two eligible children use the column "Two" (the second column from the right). For earned income up to $12,570, the taxpayer is entitled to a credit of 40% of earned income, or $5,028 ($12,570 × 40%), the maximum for a joint filer with two qualifying children.

[40] IRC § 32(c)(2).
[41] Reg. § 1.32-2(c)(2).
[42] IRC § 32(c)(3).
[43] Derived from IRC § 32(b).

EXHIBIT 9-7

Form **8839**	**Qualified Adoption Expenses**	OMB No. 1545-0074
Department of the Treasury Internal Revenue Service (99)	▶ Attach to Form 1040 or 1040NR. ▶ See separate instructions.	**2009** Attachment Sequence No. **38**

Name(s) shown on return | Your social security number

Before you begin ✓ Figure the amounts of any of the following credits you are claiming: credit for the elderly or the disabled, nonbusiness energy property credit, qualified plug-in electric vehicle credit, alternative motor vehicle credit, and qualified plug-in electric drive motor vehicle credit.
✓ See **Definitions** on page 1 of the instructions.

Part I **Information About Your Eligible Child or Children**—You **must** complete this part. See page 2 of the instructions for details, including what to do if you need more space.

	(a) Child's name		(b) Child's year of birth	(c) born **before** 1992 and disabled	(d) a child with special needs	(e) a foreign child	(f) Child's identifying number
1	First	Last		Check if child was—			
Child 1				☐	☐	☐	
Child 2				☐	☐	☐	

Caution. If the child was a foreign child, see **Special rules** in the instructions for line 1, column (e), that begin on page 2, before you complete Part II or Part III. If you received **employer-provided adoption benefits,** complete Part III on the back next.

Part II **Adoption Credit**

			Child 1	Child 2		
2	Maximum adoption credit per child	2	$12,150 00	$12,150 00		
3	Did you file Form 8839 for a prior year for the same child? ☐ **No.** Enter -0-. ☐ **Yes.** See page 3 of the instructions for the amount to enter.	3				
4	Subtract line 3 from line 2	4				
5	**Qualified adoption expenses** (see page 3 of the instructions)	5				
	Caution. Your qualified adoption expenses may not be equal to the adoption expenses you paid in 2009.					
6	Enter the **smaller** of line 4 or line 5	6				
7	Add the amounts on line 6. If zero, skip lines 8 through 11 and enter -0- on line 12			7		
8	Modified adjusted gross income (see page 3 of the instructions)		8			
9	Is line 8 more than $182,180? ☐ **No.** Skip lines 9 and 10, and enter -0- on line 11. ☐ **Yes.** Subtract $182,180 from line 8		9			
10	Divide line 9 by $40,000. Enter the result as a decimal (rounded to at least three places). Do not enter more than 1.000			10	✕ .	
11	Multiply line 7 by line 10			11		
12	Subtract line 11 from line 7			12		
13	Credit carryforward from prior years (line 23 of your **Credit Carryforward Worksheet** on page 5 of the **2008** Form 8839 instructions)			13		
14	Add lines 12 and 13			14		
15	Enter the amount from Form 1040, line 46, or Form 1040NR, line 43	15				
16	**1040 filers:** Enter the total of any amounts from Form 1040, lines 47 through 50; Form 5695, line 11; and line 12 of the Line 11 Worksheet in Pub. 972 (see page 3 of the instructions); Form 8396, line 11; Form 8834, line 22; Form 8910, line 21; Form 8936, line 14; and Schedule R, line 24.	16				
	1040NR filers: Enter the total of any amounts from Form 1040NR, lines 44 through 46; Form 5695, line 11; and line 12 of the Line 11 Worksheet in Pub. 972 (see page 3 of the instructions); Form 8396, line 11; Form 8834, line 22; Form 8910, line 21; and Form 8936, line 14.					
17	Subtract line 16 from line 15			17		
18	**Adoption credit.** Enter the smaller of line 14 or line 17 here and include on Form 1040, line 52, or Form 1040NR, line 48. Check box **b** on that line. If line 17 is smaller than line 14, you may have a credit carryforward (see page 5 of the instructions)			18		

For Paperwork Reduction Act Notice, see page 6 of the instructions. Cat. No. 22843L Form **8839** (2009)

TABLE 9-3
Earned Income Credit
Tax Year 2009

	Number of Eligible Children			
	None	**One**	**Two**	**Three or more**
EIC percentage	7.65%	34.0%	40.0%	45.0%
For earned income up to	$ 5,970*	$ 8,950*	$12,570*	$12,570*
Maximum EIC available	$ 457	$ 3,043	$ 5,028	$ 5,657
Phaseout percentage	7.65%	15.98%	21.06%	21.06%
For joint filers				
Phaseout starts at earned income of	$12,470	$21,420	$21,420	$21,420
Phaseout ends at earned income of	$18,440	$40,463	$45,295	$48,281
For all other filers				
Phaseout starts at earned income of	$ 7,470	$16,420	$16,420	$16,420
Phaseout ends at earned income of	$13,440	$35,463	$40,295	$43,281

* The dollar amounts in the table are subject to annual adjustments for inflation.

Married joint return filers (with two qualifying children) with earned income between $12,570 and the phaseout starting point of $21,420 are also entitled to the maximum credit (of $5,028). However, once earned income rises above $21,420, the EIC is reduced by 21.06% of the excess (that is, amounts over $21,420) until earned income reaches $45,295. Once earned income reaches $45,295, the EIC is eliminated.

EXAMPLE 9-19

Danny and Wanda have three eligible children and file a joint return. They have earned income of $25,450. Their EIC is $4,808, calculated as follows:

Maximum credit	$ 5,657
Less: ($25,450 − $21,420) × 21.06%	849
Earned income credit	$ 4,808

EXAMPLE 9-20

Saul and Tammy have a 4-year-old daughter, Brenda, who is a dependent. Because of a layoff at work, Saul worked for only a portion of the year and reported wage income of $24,500. Tammy did not work outside the home. The couple had no other income. In this case, the couple qualifies for the EIC with one qualifying child. Their EIC is $2,551, calculated as follows:

Maximum credit	$ 3,043
Less: ($24,500 − $21,420) × 15.98%	492
Earned income credit	$ 2,551

A taxpayer is ineligible to take the credit if he or she has disqualified income in excess of $3,100.[44] *Disqualified income* includes dividends, interest (taxable and nontaxable),

[44] This amount is adjusted annually for inflation.

From Shoebox to Software

Taxpayers use Schedule EIC to claim the EIC credit (Exhibit 9-8). The tax software will automatically calculate the amount of the credit based on the information provided elsewhere in the tax return. Taxpayers claim the credit directly on Form 1040, line 64a, or Form 1040A, line 41a. In practice, the EIC is determined using Worksheet A (Exhibit 9-9) and referencing the EIC table provided by the IRS.[46] The EIC table can be found at the end of the chapter in the appendix.

To obtain the credit, the taxpayer must provide ID numbers of the taxpayer, the taxpayer's spouse (if applicable), and the name, age, and taxpayer ID of any qualifying child (if applicable).

Taxpayers who expect to be eligible for the EIC can file Form W-5 with their employer to receive advance payments of the earned income credit during the year (rather than waiting to claim the credit when they file their tax return).[47] The amount of advance payment is determined from IRS tables. Employers report the advance payments to employees on Form W-2, box 9. The tax software carries forward the box 9 information to Form 1040. In effect, the software subtracts the advance payments from the credit earned.

net rental income, net royalty income, net capital gain income, and net passive income.[45] If certain required forms are filed, a taxpayer with a qualifying child may receive advance payments of the EIC through his or her employer, not to exceed 60% of the total available credit.

CONCEPT CHECK 9-8—LO 8	1. Josh and Danielle both work and have one qualifying child. They had earned income of $29,000. What is their EIC? 2. Tiffany is a head of household taxpayer with two qualifying children. She had earned income of $15,000. (a) If she qualifies for the EIC, how much is her credit? (b) If her tax liability is $800 for the tax year, what is the amount of her tax refund or tax owed?

OTHER CREDITS
LO 9

First-Time Homebuyers Credit

During the summer of 2008, Congress enacted the 2008 Housing Act, which in part added a new refundable tax credit for first-time homebuyers. The amount of the credit for 2009 is equal to 10% of the home's purchase price up to to $80,000 (or a maximum of $8,000). The home must be a principal residence for the taxpayer and purchased between December 31, 2008, and December 1, 2009. The credit is phased out for taxpayers with modified AGI between $75,000 and $95,000 ($150,000 and $170,000 for joint filers). A *first-time home-buyer* is an individual who had no present ownership interest in a principal residence during the three-year period ending on the date of the purchase of the principal residence to which the credit applies. If the individual is married, neither the individual nor his spouse may have had a present ownership interest in a principal residence during that three-year period. Like the EIC and in some cases, the child tax credit and Hope credit, the first-time homebuyer credit is refundable.

Form 5405 must be filed to claim the credit, and the credit must be repaid if the house is sold within three years of the purchase date.

[45] IRC § 32(i).

[46] IRC § 32(f).

[47] IRC § 3507.

EXHIBIT 9-8

SCHEDULE EIC (Form 1040A or 1040) Department of the Treasury Internal Revenue Service (99)	**Earned Income Credit** Qualifying Child Information *Complete and attach to Form 1040A or 1040 only if you have a qualifying child.*	OMB No. 1545-0074 20**09** Attachment Sequence No. **43**

Name(s) shown on return · Your social security number

Before you begin:
- See the instructions for Form 1040A, lines 41a and 41b, or Form 1040, lines 64a and 64b, to make sure that **(a)** you can take the EIC, and **(b)** you have a qualifying child.
- Be sure the child's name on line 1 and social security number (SSN) on line 2 agree with the child's social security card. Otherwise, at the time we process your return, we may reduce or disallow your EIC. If the name or SSN on the child's social security card is not correct, call the Social Security Administration at 1-800-772-1213.

- If you take the EIC even though you are not eligible, you may not be allowed to take the credit for up to 10 years. See back of schedule for details.
- It will take us longer to process your return and issue your refund if you do not fill in all lines that apply for each qualifying child.

Qualifying Child Information

		Child 1		**Child 2**		**Child 3**	
1	**Child's name** If you have more than three qualifying children, you only have to list three to get the maximum credit.	First name	Last name	First name	Last name	First name	Last name
2	**Child's SSN** The child must have an SSN as defined on page 43 of the Form 1040A instructions or page 50 of the Form 1040 instructions unless the child was born and died in 2009. If your child was born and died in 2009 and did not have an SSN, enter "Died" on this line and attach a copy of the child's birth certificate, death certificate, or hospital medical records.						
3	**Child's year of birth**	Year ___ ___ ___ ___ *If born after 1990, skip lines 4a and 4b; go to line 5.*		Year ___ ___ ___ ___ *If born after 1990, skip lines 4a and 4b; go to line 5.*		Year ___ ___ ___ ___ *If born after 1990, skip lines 4a and 4b; go to line 5.*	
4	**If the child was born before 1991—** **a** Was the child under age 24 at the end of 2009 and a student?	☐ **Yes.** *Go to line 5.*	☐ **No.** *Continue.*	☐ **Yes.** *Go to line 5.*	☐ **No.** *Continue.*	☐ **Yes.** *Go to line 5.*	☐ **No.** *Continue.*
	b Was the child permanently and totally disabled during any part of 2009?	☐ **Yes.** *Continue.*	☐ **No.** The child is not a qualifying child.	☐ **Yes.** *Continue.*	☐ **No.** The child is not a qualifying child.	☐ **Yes.** *Continue.*	☐ **No.** The child is not a qualifying child.
5	**Child's relationship to you** (for example, son, daughter, grandchild, niece, nephew, foster child, etc.)						
6	**Number of months child lived with you in the United States during 2009** • If the child lived with you for more than half of 2009 but less than 7 months, enter "7." • If the child was born or died in 2009 and your home was the child's home for the entire time he or she was alive during 2009, enter "12."	_____ months *Do not enter more than 12 months.*		_____ months *Do not enter more than 12 months.*		_____ months *Do not enter more than 12 months.*	

For Paperwork Reduction Act Notice, see Form 1040A or 1040 instructions. Cat. No. 13339M **Schedule EIC (Form 1040A or 1040) 2009**

EXHIBIT 9-9

Worksheet A—Earned Income Credit (EIC)—Lines 64a and 64b

Keep for Your Records

Before you begin: ✓ Be sure you are using the correct worksheet. Use this worksheet only if you answered "No" to Step 5, question 3, on page 50. Otherwise, use Worksheet B that begins on page 53.

Part 1 **All Filers Using Worksheet A**	1. Enter your earned income from Step 5 on page 50.	**1** ____
	2. Look up the amount on line 1 above in the EIC Table on pages 55–71 to find the credit. Be sure you use the correct column for your filing status and the number of children you have. Enter the credit here. If line 2 is zero, **STOP** You cannot take the credit. Enter "No" on the dotted line next to line 64a.	**2** ____
	3. Enter the amount from Form 1040, line 38.	**3** ____
	4. Are the amounts on lines 3 and 1 the same? ☐ **Yes.** Skip line 5; enter the amount from line 2 on line 6. ☐ **No.** Go to line 5.	
Part 2 **Filers Who Answered "No" on Line 4**	5. If you have: ● No qualifying children, is the amount on line 3 less than $7,500 ($12,500 if married filing jointly)? ● 1 or more qualifying children, is the amount on line 3 less than $16,450 ($21,450 if married filing jointly)? ☐ **Yes.** Leave line 5 blank; enter the amount from line 2 on line 6. ☐ **No.** Look up the amount on line 3 in the EIC Table on pages 55–71 to find the credit. Be sure you use the correct column for your filing status and the number of children you have. Enter the credit here. Look at the amounts on lines 5 and 2. Then, enter the **smaller** amount on line 6.	**5** ____
Part 3 **Your Earned Income Credit**	6. **This is your earned income credit.**	**6** ____ Enter this amount on Form 1040, line 64a.
	Reminder— ✓ If you have a qualifying child, complete and attach Schedule EIC.	
	⚠ **CAUTION** *If your EIC for a year after 1996 was reduced or disallowed, see page 51 to find out if you must file Form 8862 to take the credit for 2009.*	

Note: As of October 2008, the IRS did not issue a final EIC worksheet form. The IRS inserted the boxes next to the old line numbers to indicate where amounts should be inserted from the new 1040 draft.

From Shoebox to Software   Comprehensive Example

Using the tax software, open the tax return for Mr. and Mrs. Ramirez.

The Ramirezes already have a $3,000 child tax credit—$1,000 for each of their three children. We will now add some education credits.

Maria Ramirez attended State University, where she is working on an undergraduate degree in accounting. She is taking three classes a semester (a full load is four classes). At the beginning of the year, she was a sophomore. In 2009 she paid the university $9,000 for tuition and fees, the local bookstore $700 for books, and $235 for food at the student union between classes.

Jose is taking a few graduate classes at State University to help him with certain aspects of his job. He is not enrolled in a degree program. During 2009 he spent $1,000 on tuition and fees and $300 for books.

Go to Form 1040 for the Ramirezes. Click on line 49, education credits. Click on the yellow file folder, and then click on the information sheet. Alternatively, you could go to the Documents Received section and click on the Federal Information for Higher Education sheet.

The only expenses that Jose and Maria can use are the tuition and fees and books. The expenses for food are not qualified expenses for purposes of the credits. Enter the $9,700 of expenses for Maria and the $1,300 for Jose. Then click the Qualifies for Hope Credit box beside Maria's name because she is in her first four years of higher education.

Now open the Ramirezes' Form 8863. Part I should show a $2,500 credit for Maria, and Part II should show a $260 credit for Jose. If the Ramirezes have modified AGI in excess of $100,000, their total $2,760 credit will be limited in Part III. Line 19 of Form 8863 and line 49 of Form 1040 should both reflect this limited credit.

Save the Ramirezes' return for future chapters.

Making Work Pay and Government Retiree Credits

Two new credits for 2009 are the making work pay credit and the government retiree credit. Generally, to claim either credit, you would file a Schedule M and include the amount on Form 1040, line 63. You must have a social security number to claim either credit, which does not include an identification number issued by the IRS. Like the EIC and first-time homebuyers credit, both credits are refundable.

The making work pay credit is 6.2% of earned income, not to exceed $400 ($800 if married filing jointly), and reduced by any economic recovery payment received in 2009 or if your modified AGI exceeds $75,000 ($150,000 if married filing jointly). If your modified AGI exceeds $95,000 ($190,000 if married filing jointly), you are ineligible for the credit. You are also ineligible for the credit if you are a nonresident alien or if you can be claimed as a dependent on someone else's return.

You can take the government retiree credit of $250 ($500 if married filing jointly) if you received a pension or annuity payment in 2009 for services performed for the U.S. government or any U.S. state or local government, and you were not covered by social security.

CONCEPT CHECK 9-9—LO 9

1. Crystal and Juan are first-time homebuyers and purchased their home in 2009 for $190,000. (*a*) Calculate their first-time homebuyers credit, and (*b*) What form would they need to fill out?

2. Michael is single and had earned income of $26,000 as a preschool teacher. He did not receive an economic recovery payment in 2009. If his tax liability is $1,000 and he had taxes withheld during the year of $980, (*a*) how much is his making work pay credit, and (*b*) what, if any, is his tax refund in 2009 (assuming he has no other credits or tax liabilities)?

Limitation on Personal Credits and Other

The IRC provides for other credits that are less common. As with the adoption credit, many of these credits are reported on line 52 or line 53 of Form 1040 (most require additional forms to be attached). These credits include, among others, the nonconventional source fuel credit, the residential energy efficient property (REEP) credit, the credit for qualified electric vehicles, and the mortgage interest credit.

Generally, the preceding credits (reported on Form 1040, lines 47–53) are personal, nonrefundable credits. The exceptions are the EIC, the first-time homebuyers credit, the making work pay credit, the government retiree credit, a portion of the Hope credit, and, for certain taxpayers with earned income in excess of $3,000, the child tax credit (discussed earlier). *Nonrefundable credits* simply mean that the credits are limited to the amount of tax liability shown on line 44. In other words, these credits cannot result in a refund, only a reduction of regular tax liability to zero.[49]

Summary

LO 1: Apply the tax rules and calculate the Credit for Child and Dependent Care Expenses.	• The credit is available to working taxpayers with dependent care expenses (of qualifying individuals). • The credit is calculated as a percentage of the qualified expenses incurred to care for dependents. • For qualifying expenses and qualifying individuals, certain criteria must be met. • The percentage (20%–35%) used in the calculation is dependent on AGI. • Certain expense limitations exist.
LO 2: Apply the tax rules and calculate the Credit for the Elderly or the Disabled.	• The credit is available to taxpayers over 65 years of age or permanently and totally disabled. • The credit is equal to 15% of allowable base amounts. • The base amount is reduced by certain amounts of social security benefits and excess AGI.
LO 3: Apply the tax rules and calculate the Education Credits.	• Two credits available are Hope and lifetime learning. • Both allow credit for higher education expenses for the taxpayer, spouse, or dependent. • Recent tax law changes have modified the Hope credit considerably; it is sometimes referred to as the American opportunity tax credit. • The Hope credit has a maximum of $2,500 per student. • The lifetime learning credit has a maximum per taxpayer of $2,000. • Both credits are phased out at certain amounts of AGI. • For the lifetime learning credit, married filing jointly and single filers phase out completely at MAGI amounts of $120,000 and $60,000, respectively. • For the Hope credit, married filing jointly and single filers phase out completely at MAGI amounts of $180,000 and $90,000, respectively.

[48] IRC § 29, IRC § 30, and IRC § 25, respectively.

[49] IRC § 26.

2009 Earned Income Credit (EIC) Table—Continued   (Caution. This is not a tax table.)

If the amount you are looking up from the worksheet is—		And your filing status is—							
		Single, head of household, or qualifying widow(er) and you have—				Married filing jointly and you have—			
At least	But less than	No Children	One Child	Two Children	Three Children	No Children	One Child	Two Children	Three Children
		Your credit is—				Your credit is—			
17,250	17,300	0	2,906	4,848	5,476	89	3,043	5,028	5,657
17,300	17,350	0	2,898	4,837	5,466	85	3,043	5,028	5,657
17,350	17,400	0	2,890	4,827	5,455	81	3,043	5,028	5,657
17,400	17,450	0	2,882	4,816	5,445	78	3,043	5,028	5,657
17,450	17,500	0	2,874	4,806	5,434	74	3,043	5,028	5,657
17,500	17,550	0	2,866	4,795	5,424	70	3,043	5,028	5,657
17,550	17,600	0	2,858	4,785	5,413	66	3,043	5,028	5,657
17,600	17,650	0	2,850	4,774	5,403	62	3,043	5,028	5,657
17,650	17,700	0	2,842	4,764	5,392	59	3,043	5,028	5,657
17,700	17,750	0	2,834	4,753	5,382	55	3,043	5,028	5,657
17,750	17,800	0	2,826	4,743	5,371	51	3,043	5,028	5,657
17,800	17,850	0	2,818	4,732	5,361	47	3,043	5,028	5,657
17,850	17,900	0	2,810	4,722	5,350	43	3,043	5,028	5,657
17,900	17,950	0	2,803	4,711	5,340	39	3,043	5,028	5,657
17,950	18,000	0	2,795	4,701	5,329	36	3,043	5,028	5,657
18,000	18,050	0	2,787	4,690	5,318	32	3,043	5,028	5,657
18,050	18,100	0	2,779	4,679	5,308	28	3,043	5,028	5,657
18,100	18,150	0	2,771	4,669	5,297	24	3,043	5,028	5,657
18,150	18,200	0	2,763	4,658	5,287	20	3,043	5,028	5,657
18,200	18,250	0	2,755	4,648	5,276	16	3,043	5,028	5,657
18,250	18,300	0	2,747	4,637	5,266	13	3,043	5,028	5,657
18,300	18,350	0	2,739	4,627	5,255	9	3,043	5,028	5,657
18,350	18,400	0	2,731	4,616	5,245	5	3,043	5,028	5,657
18,400	18,450	0	2,723	4,606	5,234	*	3,043	5,028	5,657
18,450	18,500	0	2,715	4,595	5,224	0	3,043	5,028	5,657
18,500	18,550	0	2,707	4,585	5,213	0	3,043	5,028	5,657
18,550	18,600	0	2,699	4,574	5,203	0	3,043	5,028	5,657
18,600	18,650	0	2,691	4,564	5,192	0	3,043	5,028	5,657
18,650	18,700	0	2,683	4,553	5,182	0	3,043	5,028	5,657
18,700	18,750	0	2,675	4,543	5,171	0	3,043	5,028	5,657
18,750	18,800	0	2,667	4,532	5,161	0	3,043	5,028	5,657
18,800	18,850	0	2,659	4,522	5,150	0	3,043	5,028	5,657
18,850	18,900	0	2,651	4,511	5,139	0	3,043	5,028	5,657
18,900	18,950	0	2,643	4,500	5,129	0	3,043	5,028	5,657
18,950	19,000	0	2,635	4,490	5,118	0	3,043	5,028	5,657
19,000	19,050	0	2,627	4,479	5,108	0	3,043	5,028	5,657
19,050	19,100	0	2,619	4,469	5,097	0	3,043	5,028	5,657
19,100	19,150	0	2,611	4,458	5,087	0	3,043	5,028	5,657
19,150	19,200	0	2,603	4,448	5,076	0	3,043	5,028	5,657
19,200	19,250	0	2,595	4,437	5,066	0	3,043	5,028	5,657
19,250	19,300	0	2,587	4,427	5,055	0	3,043	5,028	5,657
19,300	19,350	0	2,579	4,416	5,045	0	3,043	5,028	5,657
19,350	19,400	0	2,571	4,406	5,034	0	3,043	5,028	5,657
19,400	19,450	0	2,563	4,395	5,024	0	3,043	5,028	5,657
19,450	19,500	0	2,555	4,385	5,013	0	3,043	5,028	5,657
19,500	19,550	0	2,547	4,374	5,003	0	3,043	5,028	5,657
19,550	19,600	0	2,539	4,364	4,992	0	3,043	5,028	5,657
19,600	19,650	0	2,531	4,353	4,982	0	3,043	5,028	5,657
19,650	19,700	0	2,523	4,342	4,971	0	3,043	5,028	5,657
19,700	19,750	0	2,515	4,332	4,960	0	3,043	5,028	5,657
19,750	19,800	0	2,507	4,321	4,950	0	3,043	5,028	5,657
19,800	19,850	0	2,499	4,311	4,939	0	3,043	5,028	5,657
19,850	19,900	0	2,491	4,300	4,929	0	3,043	5,028	5,657
19,900	19,950	0	2,483	4,290	4,918	0	3,043	5,028	5,657
19,950	20,000	0	2,475	4,279	4,908	0	3,043	5,028	5,657

*If the amount you are looking up from the worksheet is at least $18,400 but less than $18,440, your credit is $2. Otherwise, you cannot take the credit.

2009 Earned Income Credit (EIC) Table—Continued   (Caution. This is not a tax table.)

If the amount you are looking up from the worksheet is—		And your filing status is—							
		Single, head of household, or qualifying widow(er) and you have—				Married filing jointly and you have—			
At least	But less than	No Children	One Child	Two Children	Three Children	No Children	One Child	Two Children	Three Children
		Your credit is—				Your credit is—			
20,000	20,050	0	2,467	4,269	4,897	0	3,043	5,028	5,657
20,050	20,100	0	2,459	4,258	4,887	0	3,043	5,028	5,657
20,100	20,150	0	2,451	4,248	4,876	0	3,043	5,028	5,657
20,150	20,200	0	2,443	4,237	4,866	0	3,043	5,028	5,657
20,200	20,250	0	2,435	4,227	4,855	0	3,043	5,028	5,657
20,250	20,300	0	2,427	4,216	4,845	0	3,043	5,028	5,657
20,300	20,350	0	2,419	4,206	4,834	0	3,043	5,028	5,657
20,350	20,400	0	2,411	4,195	4,824	0	3,043	5,028	5,657
20,400	20,450	0	2,403	4,185	4,813	0	3,043	5,028	5,657
20,450	20,500	0	2,395	4,174	4,803	0	3,043	5,028	5,657
20,500	20,550	0	2,387	4,163	4,792	0	3,043	5,028	5,657
20,550	20,600	0	2,379	4,153	4,781	0	3,043	5,028	5,657
20,600	20,650	0	2,371	4,142	4,771	0	3,043	5,028	5,657
20,650	20,700	0	2,363	4,132	4,760	0	3,043	5,028	5,657
20,700	20,750	0	2,355	4,121	4,750	0	3,043	5,028	5,657
20,750	20,800	0	2,347	4,111	4,739	0	3,043	5,028	5,657
20,800	20,850	0	2,339	4,100	4,729	0	3,043	5,028	5,657
20,850	20,900	0	2,331	4,090	4,718	0	3,043	5,028	5,657
20,900	20,950	0	2,323	4,079	4,708	0	3,043	5,028	5,657
20,950	21,000	0	2,315	4,069	4,697	0	3,043	5,028	5,657
21,000	21,050	0	2,307	4,058	4,687	0	3,043	5,028	5,657
21,050	21,100	0	2,299	4,048	4,676	0	3,043	5,028	5,657
21,100	21,150	0	2,291	4,037	4,666	0	3,043	5,028	5,657
21,150	21,200	0	2,283	4,027	4,655	0	3,043	5,028	5,657
21,200	21,250	0	2,275	4,016	4,645	0	3,043	5,028	5,657
21,250	21,300	0	2,267	4,006	4,634	0	3,043	5,028	5,657
21,300	21,350	0	2,259	3,995	4,624	0	3,043	5,028	5,657
21,350	21,400	0	2,251	3,984	4,613	0	3,043	5,028	5,657
21,400	21,450	0	2,243	3,974	4,602	0	3,043	5,028	5,657
21,450	21,500	0	2,235	3,963	4,592	0	3,034	5,016	5,645
21,500	21,550	0	2,227	3,953	4,581	0	3,026	5,006	5,634
21,550	21,600	0	2,219	3,942	4,571	0	3,018	4,995	5,624
21,600	21,650	0	2,211	3,932	4,560	0	3,010	4,985	5,613
21,650	21,700	0	2,203	3,921	4,550	0	3,002	4,974	5,603
21,700	21,750	0	2,195	3,911	4,539	0	2,994	4,964	5,592
21,750	21,800	0	2,187	3,900	4,529	0	2,986	4,953	5,582
21,800	21,850	0	2,179	3,890	4,518	0	2,978	4,943	5,571
21,850	21,900	0	2,171	3,879	4,508	0	2,970	4,932	5,561
21,900	21,950	0	2,163	3,869	4,497	0	2,962	4,922	5,550
21,950	22,000	0	2,155	3,858	4,487	0	2,954	4,911	5,540
22,000	22,050	0	2,147	3,848	4,476	0	2,946	4,901	5,529
22,050	22,100	0	2,139	3,837	4,466	0	2,938	4,890	5,519
22,100	22,150	0	2,131	3,827	4,455	0	2,930	4,880	5,508
22,150	22,200	0	2,123	3,816	4,444	0	2,922	4,869	5,497
22,200	22,250	0	2,115	3,805	4,434	0	2,914	4,858	5,487
22,250	22,300	0	2,107	3,795	4,423	0	2,906	4,848	5,476
22,300	22,350	0	2,099	3,784	4,413	0	2,898	4,837	5,466
22,350	22,400	0	2,091	3,774	4,402	0	2,890	4,827	5,455
22,400	22,450	0	2,083	3,763	4,392	0	2,882	4,816	5,445
22,450	22,500	0	2,075	3,753	4,381	0	2,874	4,806	5,434
22,500	22,550	0	2,067	3,742	4,371	0	2,866	4,795	5,424
22,550	22,600	0	2,059	3,732	4,360	0	2,858	4,785	5,413
22,600	22,650	0	2,051	3,721	4,350	0	2,850	4,774	5,403
22,650	22,700	0	2,043	3,711	4,339	0	2,842	4,764	5,392
22,700	22,750	0	2,035	3,700	4,329	0	2,834	4,753	5,382
22,750	22,800	0	2,027	3,690	4,318	0	2,826	4,743	5,371
22,800	22,850	0	2,019	3,679	4,308	0	2,818	4,732	5,361
22,850	22,900	0	2,011	3,669	4,297	0	2,810	4,722	5,350
22,900	22,950	0	2,004	3,658	4,287	0	2,803	4,711	5,340
22,950	23,000	0	1,996	3,648	4,276	0	2,795	4,701	5,329

(Continued on page 34)

Discussion Questions

LO 1   1. A taxpayer has $2,000 of qualified employment-related expenses paid on behalf of one qualifying child. Determine the maximum and minimum amounts of child and dependent care tax credit available to the taxpayer and explain the circumstances in which the maximum and minimum credits would be permitted.

_____

_____

_____

LO 1   2. Briefly explain the requirements that must be met to receive a tax credit for child and dependent care expenses.

_____

_____

_____

LO 1   3. For purposes of the tax credit for child and dependent care expenses, explain the limitations concerning the amount of qualified expenses that can be used to calculate the credit.

_____

_____

_____

LO 1   4. A taxpayer maintains a household and is entitled to a dependency exemption for an incapacitated adult child. The child lives during the week at an adult day care center and on the weekends at home with the taxpayer. The taxpayer pays a fee to the center so the taxpayer can be gainfully employed. Does the fee qualify for treatment as a qualifying expense for purposes of the child and dependent care tax credit? Why or why not?

_____

_____

_____

LO 2   5. To determine the amount of credit for people who are elderly or disabled, the appropriate base amount must be adjusted by the effect of two items. What are those two items, and in what way is the base amount adjusted?

_____

_____

_____

LO 3   6. Two kinds of educational tax credits are available. Name them and briefly discuss the criteria necessary to claim the credits.

_____

_____

_____

LO 3   7. Explain what qualifies as educational expenses for the purposes of educational tax credits.

_____

_____

_____

LO 3   8. Jerome is single and cannot be claimed by anyone as a dependent. He is a student at a local university enrolled full-time in an MBA program. His tuition bill was $5,000. He paid the bill by withdrawing $2,000 from his savings account and borrowing the remainder from

a local bank. For purposes of the educational tax credits, what is the amount of Jerome's qualifying expenses?

_____

_____

_____

LO 3 9. Briefly explain when and how each of the two education credits is phased out.

_____

_____

_____

LO 4 10. Explain at least two instances in which taxpayers may choose to deduct foreign taxes as an itemized deduction rather than as a credit.

_____

_____

_____

LO 4 11. Explain how the foreign tax credit limitation works.

_____

_____

_____

LO 5 12. Taxpayers can claim a child tax credit for a qualifying child. Define *qualifying child.*

_____

_____

_____

LO 5 13. Paul and Olivia filed a joint tax return and reported modified AGI of $92,000. They have two qualifying children. What is the amount of their child tax credit? What is the amount of their credit if their modified AGI is $112,000?

_____

_____

_____

LO 6 14. Explain the limitations pertaining to the retirement savings contributions credit.

_____

_____

_____

LO 6 15. Leonardo's filing status is head of household. He has modified adjusted gross income of $26,000, and he made a $3,000 contribution to his IRA. What is the amount of his retirement savings contributions credit? What would the credit be if he had a filing status of single?

_____

_____

_____

LO 7 16. What limitations are associated with the adoption credit, in terms of both dollar amounts and eligibility?

_____

_____

_____

LO 7 17. For purposes of the adoption credit, what is the definition of *special-needs child?* Give some examples (you may find it helpful to refer to the IRC and Regulations to prepare your answer).

_____

_____

_____

LO 7 18. In the case of the adoption credit, what special rules apply when adopting a child who is a citizen of another country?

_____

_____

_____

LO 8 19. What is the definition of *qualifying child* for purposes of the earned income credit?

_____

_____

_____

LO 9 20. Briefly explain what a refundable tax credit is and discuss the three types of credits discussed under other credits (LO9).

_____

_____

_____

Multiple-Choice Questions

LO 1 21. Jamison is a single dad with two dependent children: Zoey, age 7, and Conner, age 3. He has an AGI of $81,000 and paid $6,300 to a qualified day care center for the two children. What amount of credit can Jamison receive for child and dependent care credit?

 a. $600.

 b. $1,200.

 c. $1,260.

 d. $6,300.

LO 1 22. Allie and Buddy are married, file a joint return, and have one son, Zack, age 5. Buddy has earned income of $42,000, and Allie was a full-time student for eight months (with no income). They paid a qualified child care center $3,450. How much is Allie and Buddy's child and dependent care credit for the year?

 a. $0.

 b. $420.

 c. $630.

 d. $725.

LO 2 23. Avril and John are ages 70 and 72, respectively, and file a joint return. They have AGI of $18,000 and received $1,500 in nontaxable social security benefits. How much can Avril and John take as a credit for the elderly or the disabled?

 a. $300.

 b. $1,125.

 c. $1,500.

 d. $2,000.

LO 2   24. Dennis and Vera are ages 69 and 59, respectively, and file a joint return. They have AGI of $28,000 and received $2,000 in nontaxable social security benefits. How much can Dennis and Vera take as a credit for the elderly or the disabled?

    a. $0.

    b. $1,125.

    c. $2,000.

    d. $7,500.

LO 3   25. Nathan paid $2,750 in qualifying expenses for his daughter, who attended a community college. How much is Nathan's lifetime learning credit *without* regard to AGI limitations or other credits?

    a. $250.

    b. $550.

    c. $825.

    d. $1,375.

LO 3   26. DJ and Gwen paid $3,200 in qualifying expenses for their son, Nikko, who is a freshman attending University of Colorado. DJ and Gwen have AGI of $170,000 and file a joint return. What is their allowable Hope credit after the credit phaseout based on AGI is taken into account?

    a. $0.

    b. $1,150.

    c. $2,500.

    d. $3,200.

LO 3   27. Darren paid the following expenses during November 2009 for his son Sean's college expenses for the spring 2010 semester, which begins in January 2010:

Tuition	$12,000
Housing	8,000
Books	1,500

In addition, Sean's uncle paid $500 in fees on behalf of Sean directly to the college. Sean is claimed as Darren's dependent on his tax return. How much of the expenses qualify for the purpose of the education credit deduction for Darren in 2009?

    a. $3,500.

    b. $8,000.

    c. $12,000.

    d. $14,000.

LO 3   28. Which of the following expenses are qualifying expenses for the purposes of the education credits?

    a. Books.

    b. Tuition.

    c. Room and board.

    d. Both *(a)* and *(b)*.

LO 4   29. Which of the following conditions must be met for a taxpayer to be able to claim the foreign tax credit (FTC) *without* filing Form 1116?

a. All of the foreign-source income is passive income.

b. All of the foreign-source income was reported on Form 1099.

c. Total foreign taxes paid were less than $300 (or $600 if married filing jointly).

d. All of the above must be met to claim the FTC without Form 1116.

LO 4   30. Joyce has $83,000 total taxable income, which includes $11,000 of taxable income from China. She paid $2,200 in foreign income taxes, and her U.S. tax liability is $21,610. Joyce's foreign tax credit is

a. $0.

b. $2,200.

c. $2,864.

d. $11,000.

LO 4   31. Michael paid $3,350 in foreign income taxes to Argentina. His total income was $75,000, which included $9,800 of foreign income. His U.S. tax liability is $18,750. How much can Michael claim as foreign tax credit?

a. $2,450.

b. $2,800.

c. $3,350.

d. $9,800.

LO 4   32. Under which of the following situations would a taxpayer take the foreign taxes paid as an itemized deduction rather than as a foreign tax credit?

a. The foreign tax paid was less than 15%.

b. The foreign tax was paid to a European country.

c. The foreign tax paid was a property tax.

d. The foreign tax paid was an income tax.

LO 5   33. Justin and Janet, whose AGI is $156,000, have twin boys, Jake and Jaime, age 5. How much child tax credit can they take?

a. $0.

b. $1,000.

c. $2,000.

d. $2,300.

LO 5   34. Julian is a single father with a son, Alex, who is 8 years old. If Julian's AGI is $87,000, what is his child tax credit for Alex?

a. $0.

b. $400.

c. $600.

d. $1,000.

LO 6   35. Jerry and Ellen are married filing jointly with AGI of $45,000. They made a $1,500 contribution to a qualified retirement plan. How much is their retirement savings contributions credit?

a. $0.

b. $150.

c. $300.

d. $750.

LO 6 36. Marcia is a single filer and has AGI of $25,500. During the year, she contributed $800 to a Roth IRA. What amount of retirement savings contributions credit can Marcia take?

    a. $0.

    b. $80.

    c. $160.

    d. $800.

LO 7 37. After two and one-half years of working with the orphanage and the government, Jake and Nikki adopted a little girl from Korea. The adoption process, which became final in January 2010, incurred the following qualified adoption expenses. For how much and in which year can Jake and Nikki take the adoption credit? (Assume no limitation of the credit due to AGI.)

Year 2008	$4,000
Year 2009	2,000
Year 2010	1,000

    a. $6,000 in 2009 and $1,000 in 2010.

    b. $4,000 in 2008 and $3,000 in 2010.

    c. $7,000 in 2009.

    d. $7,000 in 2010.

LO 7 38. Abel and Loni adopted a boy from Illinois during the current tax year and incurred a total of $14,675 in qualified adoption expenses. Abel and Loni have modified AGI of $198,000. What is the amount of adoption credit they can take?

    a. $0.

    b. $7,345.

    c. $12,150.

    d. $14,675.

LO 8 39. Juan and Lydia both work, file a joint return, and have one qualifying child. They have AGI of $16,000. What is their EIC?

    a. $0.

    b. $457.

    c. $1,971.

    d. $3,043.

LO 8 40. Thomas and Stephani are married with four qualifying children. Their AGI is $25,000. How much is their EIC?

    a. $3,043.

    b. $4,903.

    c. $5,028.

    d. $5,657.

LO 9 41. Which of the following credits is *never* a refundable credit?

    a. EIC.

    b. Foreign Tax Credit.

    c. Child tax credit.

    d. First-time homebuyers credit.

Problems

LO 1 42. Tim and Martha paid $7,900 in qualified employment-related expenses for their three young children who live with them in their household. Martha received $1,800 of dependent care assistance from her employer, which was properly excluded from gross income. The couple had $57,000 of AGI earned equally by Tim and Martha. What amount of child and dependent care tax credit can they claim on their Form 1040? How would your answer differ (if at all) if the couple had AGI of $36,000 that was entirely earned by Tim?

_____

_____

_____

_____

_____

_____

LO 1 43. Adrienne is a single mother with a 6-year-old daughter who lived with her during the entire year. Adrienne paid $2,900 in child care expenses so that she would be able to work. Of this amount, $500 was paid to Adrienne's mother, whom Adrienne cannot claim as a dependent. Adrienne earned $1,900 from her job as a freelance writer and received alimony payments of $21,000 from her ex-husband. What amount, if any, of child and dependent care tax credit can Adrienne claim?

_____

_____

_____

_____

_____

LO 2 44. What is the AGI limit above which each of the following taxpayers would *not* be eligible to receive a credit for persons who are elderly or disabled?

   a. A single taxpayer eligible for the credit who receives $1,000 of nontaxable social security benefits.

   b. Taxpayers filing a joint return for which one taxpayer is eligible for the credit, and the taxpayers have received no taxable social security benefits.

   c. Taxpayers filing a joint return, and both are eligible for the credit and received $2,000 of nontaxable social security benefits.

_____

_____

_____

_____

_____

_____

LO 2 45. Assuming that an AGI limitation does not apply, what amount of credit for people who are elderly or disabled would be permitted in each of the instances in Problem 44?

_____

_____

_____

_____

_____

LO 3 46. In each of the following cases, certain qualifying educational expenses were paid during the tax year for individuals who were the taxpayer, spouse, or dependent. The taxpayer has a tax liability and no other credits. Determine the amount of Hope credit and/or lifetime learning credit that should be taken in each instance:

a. A single individual with modified AGI of $32,900 and expenses of $3,300 for a child who is a full-time college freshman.

b. A single individual with modified AGI of $44,500 and expenses of $3,800 for a child who is a full-time college junior.

c. A couple, married filing jointly, with modified AGI of $79,300 and expenses of $8,000 for a child who is a full-time graduate student.

_____

_____

_____

_____

_____

_____

LO 3 47. Walt and Deloris have two dependent children, Bill and Tiffany. Bill is a freshman at State University, and Tiffany is working on her graduate degree. The couple paid qualified expenses of $3,900 for Bill (who is a half-time student) and $7,800 for Tiffany. What are the amount and type of educational tax credits that Walt and Deloris can take, assuming they have no modified AGI limitation?

_____

_____

_____

_____

_____

_____

LO 3 48. Use the information in Problem 47. What educational tax credits are available if Walt and Deloris report modified AGI of $84,300? Does your answer change if Tiffany is taking one class a semester (is less than a half-time student) and not taking classes in a degree program? Why or why not?

_____

_____

_____

_____

_____

_____

LO 3 49. Jeremy and Celeste paid the following amounts for their daughter, Alyssa, to attend the University of Colorado during 2009. Alyssa was in her first year of college and attended full-time.

Tuition and fees (for fall semester 2009)	$1,950
Tuition and fees (for spring semester 2010)	1,000
Books	600
Room and board	1,200

The spring semester at the University of Colorado begins in January. In addition to the above, Alyssa's Uncle Devin sent $800 for her tuition directly to the university.

Jeremy and Celeste have modified AGI of $165,000. What is the amount of qualifying expenses for the purposes of the Hope credit? What is the amount of the Hope credit that Jeremy and Celeste can claim based on their AGI?

LO 4 50. A taxpayer reported foreign income tax of $1,326 on foreign income of $8,112. Her worldwide taxable income was $91,400, and her U.S. tax liability was $23,000. What is the amount of foreign tax credit allowed? What would be the allowed credit if her worldwide taxable income was $19,900 and her U.S. tax liability was $2,200?

LO 5 51. Determine the amount of the child tax credit in each of the following cases:
   a. A single parent with modified AGI of $43,400 and two children.
   b. A single parent with modified AGI of $76,058 and three children.
   c. A married couple with modified AGI of $107,933 and one child.

LO 6 52. Determine the retirement savings contributions credit in each of the following cases:
   a. A married couple filing jointly with modified AGI of $37,000 and an IRA contribution of $1,500.
   b. A married couple filing jointly with modified AGI of $19,000 and an IRA contribution of $1,500.
   c. A married couple filing jointly with modified AGI of $52,000 and an IRA contribution of $1,500.
   d. A married couple filing jointly with modified AGI of $33,000 and an IRA contribution of $2,000.
   e. A single taxpayer with modified AGI of $12,000 and an IRA contribution of $1,000.

LO 7 53. Niles and Marsha adopted a child. They paid $6,000 in 2008, and $7,700 in 2009 for adoption-related expenses. The adoption was finalized in late 2009. Marsha received $3,000 of employer-provided adoption benefits in 2009. For question *a* assume that any adoption credit is not limited by modified AGI or by the amount of tax liability.

EXHIBIT 10-1

Form W-4 (2009)

Purpose. Complete Form W-4 so that your employer can withhold the correct federal income tax from your pay. Consider completing a new Form W-4 each year and when your personal or financial situation changes.

Exemption from withholding. If you are exempt, complete **only** lines 1, 2, 3, 4, and 7 and sign the form to validate it. Your exemption for 2009 expires February 16, 2010. See Pub. 505, Tax Withholding and Estimated Tax.

Note. You cannot claim exemption from withholding if (a) your income exceeds $950 and includes more than $300 of unearned income (for example, interest and dividends) and (b) another person can claim you as a dependent on their tax return.

Basic instructions. If you are not exempt, complete the **Personal Allowances Worksheet** below. The worksheets on page 2 further adjust your withholding allowances based on itemized deductions, certain credits, adjustments to income, or two-earner/multiple job situations.

Complete all worksheets that apply. However, you may claim fewer (or zero) allowances. For regular wages, withholding must be based on allowances you claimed and may not be a flat amount or percentage of wages.

Head of household. Generally, you may claim head of household filing status on your tax return only if you are unmarried and pay more than 50% of the costs of keeping up a home for yourself and your dependent(s) or other qualifying individuals. See Pub. 501, Exemptions, Standard Deduction, and Filing Information, for information.

Tax credits. You can take projected tax credits into account in figuring your allowable number of withholding allowances. Credits for child or dependent care expenses and the child tax credit may be claimed using the **Personal Allowances Worksheet** below. See Pub. 919, How Do I Adjust My Tax Withholding, for information on converting your other credits into withholding allowances.

Nonwage income. If you have a large amount of nonwage income, such as interest or

dividends, consider making estimated tax payments using Form 1040-ES, Estimated Tax for Individuals. Otherwise, you may owe additional tax. If you have pension or annuity income, see Pub. 919 to find out if you should adjust your withholding on Form W-4 or W-4P.

Two earners or multiple jobs. If you have a working spouse or more than one job, figure the total number of allowances you are entitled to claim on all jobs using worksheets from only one Form W-4. Your withholding usually will be most accurate when all allowances are claimed on the Form W-4 for the highest paying job and zero allowances are claimed on the others. See Pub. 919 for details.

Nonresident alien. If you are a nonresident alien, see the Instructions for Form 8233 before completing this Form W-4.

Check your withholding. After your Form W-4 takes effect, use Pub. 919 to see how the amount you are having withheld compares to your projected total tax for 2009. See Pub. 919, especially if your earnings exceed $130,000 (Single) or $180,000 (Married).

Personal Allowances Worksheet (Keep for your records.)

A Enter "1" for **yourself** if no one else can claim you as a dependent . . . . **A** _____

B Enter "1" if:
- You are single and have only one job; or
- You are married, have only one job, and your spouse does not work; or
- Your wages from a second job or your spouse's wages (or the total of both) are $1,500 or less.

 B _____

C Enter "1" for your **spouse**. But, you may choose to enter "-0-" if you are married and have either a working spouse or more than one job. (Entering "-0-" may help you avoid having too little tax withheld.) . . . . **C** _____

D Enter number of **dependents** (other than your spouse or yourself) you will claim on your tax return . . . . . . **D** _____

E Enter "1" if you will file as **head of household** on your tax return (see conditions under **Head of household** above) . **E** _____

F Enter "1" if you have at least $1,800 of **child or dependent care expenses** for which you plan to claim a credit . . **F** _____
 (**Note.** Do **not** include child support payments. See Pub. 503, Child and Dependent Care Expenses, for details.)

G **Child Tax Credit** (including additional child tax credit). See Pub. 972, Child Tax Credit, for more information.
- If your total income will be less than $61,000 ($90,000 if married), enter "2" for each eligible child; then **less** "1" if you have three or more eligible children.
- If your total income will be between $61,000 and $84,000 ($90,000 and $119,000 if married), enter "1" for each eligible child plus "1" **additional** if you have six or more eligible children. **G** _____

H Add lines A through G and enter total here. (**Note.** This may be different from the number of exemptions you claim on your tax return.) ▶ **H** _____

For accuracy, complete all worksheets that apply.
- If you plan to **itemize or claim adjustments to income** and want to reduce your withholding, see the **Deductions and Adjustments Worksheet** on page 2.
- If you have **more than one job** or are **married and you and your spouse both work** and the combined earnings from all jobs exceed $40,000 ($25,000 if married), see the **Two-Earners/Multiple Jobs Worksheet** on page 2 to avoid having too little tax withheld.
- If **neither** of the above situations applies, **stop here** and enter the number from line H on line 5 of Form W-4 below.

- - - - - - - - - **Cut here and give Form W-4 to your employer. Keep the top part for your records.** - - - - - - - - -

Form W-4
Department of the Treasury
Internal Revenue Service

Employee's Withholding Allowance Certificate

▶ Whether you are entitled to claim a certain number of allowances or exemption from withholding is subject to review by the IRS. Your employer may be required to send a copy of this form to the IRS.

OMB No. 1545-0074

2009

1 Type or print your first name and middle initial.	Last name	2 Your social security number

Home address (number and street or rural route)	3 ☐ Single ☐ Married ☐ Married, but withhold at higher Single rate. **Note.** If married, but legally separated, or spouse is a nonresident alien, check the "Single" box.
City or town, state, and ZIP code	4 If your last name differs from that shown on your social security card, check here. You must call 1-800-772-1213 for a replacement card. ▶ ☐

5 Total number of allowances you are claiming (from line **H** above **or** from the applicable worksheet on page 2) **5** _____

6 Additional amount, if any, you want withheld from each paycheck . . . . **6** $ _____

7 I claim exemption from withholding for 2009, and I certify that I meet **both** of the following conditions for exemption.
- Last year I had a right to a refund of **all** federal income tax withheld because I had **no** tax liability **and**
- This year I expect a refund of **all** federal income tax withheld because I expect to have **no** tax liability.

If you meet both conditions, write "Exempt" here . . . . ▶ **7** _____

Under penalties of perjury, I declare that I have examined this certificate and to the best of my knowledge and belief, it is true, correct, and complete.

Employee's signature (Form is not valid unless you sign it.) ▶ _____ Date ▶ _____

8 Employer's name and address (Employer: Complete lines 8 and 10 only if sending to the IRS.)	9 Office code (optional)	10 Employer identification number (EIN)

For Privacy Act and Paperwork Reduction Act Notice, see page 2. Cat. No. 10220Q Form **W-4** (2009)

EXHIBIT 10-1   *(concluded)*

Deductions and Adjustments Worksheet

Note. Use this worksheet *only* if you plan to itemize deductions, claim certain credits, adjustments to income, or an additional standard deduction

1   Enter an estimate of your 2009 itemized deductions. These include qualifying home mortgage interest, charitable contributions, state and local taxes, medical expenses in excess of 7.5% of your income, and miscellaneous deductions. (For 2009, you may have to reduce your itemized deductions if your income is over $166,800 ($83,400 if married filing separately). See *Worksheet 2* in Pub. 919 for details.)   **1** $ _____

2   Enter: { $11,400 if married filing jointly or qualifying widow(er) / $ 8,350 if head of household / $ 5,700 if single or married filing separately }   **2** $ _____

3   **Subtract** line 2 from line 1. If zero or less, enter "-0-"   **3** $ _____

4   Enter an estimate of your 2009 adjustments to income and any additional standard deduction. (Pub. 919)   **4** $ _____

5   **Add** lines 3 and 4 and enter the total. (Include any amount for credits from *Worksheet 8* in Pub. 919.)   **5** $ _____

6   Enter an estimate of your 2009 nonwage income (such as dividends or interest)   **6** $ _____

7   **Subtract** line 6 from line 5. If zero or less, enter "-0-"   **7** $ _____

8   **Divide** the amount on line 7 by $3,500 and enter the result here. Drop any fraction   **8** _____

9   Enter the number from the **Personal Allowances Worksheet, line H, page 1**   **9** _____

10   **Add** lines 8 and 9 and enter the total here. If you plan to use the **Two-Earners/Multiple Jobs Worksheet,** also enter this total on line 1 below. Otherwise, **stop here** and enter this total on Form W-4, line 5, page 1   **10** _____

Two-Earners/Multiple Jobs Worksheet (See *Two earners or multiple jobs* on page 1.)

Note. Use this worksheet *only* if the instructions under line H on page 1 direct you here.

1   Enter the number from line H, page 1 (or from line 10 above if you used the **Deductions and Adjustments Worksheet)**   **1** _____

2   Find the number in **Table 1** below that applies to the **LOWEST** paying job and enter it here. **However,** if you are married filing jointly and wages from the highest paying job are $50,000 or less, do not enter more than "3."   **2** _____

3   If line 1 is **more than or equal to** line 2, subtract line 2 from line 1. Enter the result here (if zero, enter "-0-") and on Form W-4, line 5, page 1. **Do not** use the rest of this worksheet   **3** _____

Note. If line 1 is *less than* line 2, enter "-0-" on Form W-4, line 5, page 1. Complete lines 4–9 below to calculate the additional withholding amount necessary to avoid a year-end tax bill.

4   Enter the number from line 2 of this worksheet   **4** _____

5   Enter the number from line 1 of this worksheet   **5** _____

6   **Subtract** line 5 from line 4   **6** _____

7   Find the amount in **Table 2** below that applies to the **HIGHEST** paying job and enter it here   **7** $ _____

8   **Multiply** line 7 by line 6 and enter the result here. This is the additional annual withholding needed   **8** $ _____

9   Divide line 8 by the number of pay periods remaining in 2009. For example, divide by 26 if you are paid every two weeks and you complete this form in December 2008. Enter the result here and on Form W-4, line 6, page 1. This is the additional amount to be withheld from each paycheck   **9** $ _____

| Table 1 | | | | Table 2 | | | |
| **Married Filing Jointly** | | **All Others** | | **Married Filing Jointly** | | **All Others** | |
If wages from **LOWEST** paying job are—	Enter on line 2 above	If wages from **LOWEST** paying job are—	Enter on line 2 above	If wages from **HIGHEST** paying job are—	Enter on line 7 above	If wages from **HIGHEST** paying job are—	Enter on line 7 above
$0 - $4,500	0	$0 - $6,000	0	$0 - $65,000	$550	$0 - $35,000	$550
4,501 - 9,000	1	6,001 - 12,000	1	65,001 - 120,000	910	35,001 - 90,000	910
9,001 - 18,000	2	12,001 - 19,000	2	120,001 - 185,000	1,020	90,001 - 165,000	1,020
18,001 - 22,000	3	19,001 - 26,000	3	185,001 - 330,000	1,200	165,001 - 370,000	1,200
22,001 - 26,000	4	26,001 - 35,000	4	330,001 and over	1,280	370,001 and over	1,280
26,001 - 32,000	5	35,001 - 50,000	5				
32,001 - 38,000	6	50,001 - 65,000	6				
38,001 - 46,000	7	65,001 - 80,000	7				
46,001 - 55,000	8	80,001 - 90,000	8				
55,001 - 60,000	9	90,001 - 120,000	9				
60,001 - 65,000	10	120,001 and over	10				
65,001 - 75,000	11						
75,001 - 95,000	12						
95,001 - 105,000	13						
105,001 - 120,000	14						
120,001 and over	15						

form to determine the appropriate number of withholding allowances to claim. The larger the number of allowances, the smaller the amount of tax withheld from each paycheck.

To aid in making a reasonable estimate, employees generally fill out the "personal allowances worksheet" on page 1 of Form W-4. In concept, employees report the necessary number of allowances so the amount of tax paid during the year closely approximates the amount of expected tax liability. This worksheet is appropriate in most situations and takes into account the tax effect of a working or nonworking spouse and the child tax credit. Taxpayers who work more than one job or who anticipate itemizing their deductions should complete the appropriate worksheets on page 2 of Form W-4 to more precisely match withholdings with expected tax liability.

Employers determine the amount of tax to withhold using either a percentage method or a wage bracket method with a withholding table.[3] Both methods require the employer to know the marital status of the employee, the number of exemptions claimed on Form W-4, and the pay period of the company (weekly, monthly, or the like). Because most payroll systems are computerized, the method most commonly used is the percentage method; see Examples 10-1 and 10-2. *Note:* For 2009 Publication 15-T is used for all withholding calculations.

To compute the amount of withholding with the percentage method, the employer first performs the following steps to determine the amount of wages subject to withholding.

1. Multiplies the number of allowances claimed by the employee (see Form W-4 in Exhibit 10-1) by the allowance amount shown in the following table.
2. Subtracts the amount calculated in step 1 from the employee's gross wages for the period.
3. Determines the amount of withholding using the tables provided by the IRS. These tables are located in the appendix to this chapter.

The 2009 Amount for One Withholding Allowance (Used in Step 1)

Pay Period	Allowance Amount
Daily	$ 14.04
Weekly	70.19
Biweekly	140.38
Semimonthly	152.08
Monthly	304.17
Quarterly	912.50
Semiannually	1,825.00
Annually	3,650.00

EXAMPLE 10-1

Audrey is single and earns $500 per week. She claimed two allowances on the W-4 she provided her employer. The amount of federal income tax withheld from Audrey's paycheck is as follows:

Gross pay	$500.00
Less allowances (2 × $70.19)	(140.38)
Wages subject to withholding	$359.62

Using the percentage method table from the appendix in this chapter, Audrey can calculate that the federal income tax withholding each pay period is

$$\$6.20 + [15\% \times (\$359.62 - 200.00)] = \$30.14$$

[3] IRC § 3402(b) and IRC § 3402(c).

EXAMPLE 10-2

Mauro is married and claimed five exemptions on his W-4. He is paid twice a month (semimonthly) and has gross wages of $3,900 each pay period. The proper amount of federal withholding is as follows:

Gross pay	$3,900.00
Less allowances (5 × $152.08)	(760.40)
Wages subject to withholding	$3,139.60

Using the percentage method table from the appendix in this chapter, the taxpayer can calculate that the federal income tax withholding each pay period is

$$\$36.30 + [15\% \times (\$3,139.60 - \$1,019.00)] = \$354.39$$

Note that the withholding tables are structured so that employers withhold approximately the same amount for a given annual income regardless of how often the employee is paid. See Example 10-3.

EXAMPLE 10-3

Louisa is married, earns $36,400 per year, and claims two withholding allowances.

- If Louisa's pay period is on a weekly basis, her gross wages are $700.00 ($36,400/52), and her wages in excess of the allowance would be $559.62. Using the percentage method of withholding, her withholdings on a weekly basis would be $30.14. Over the period of a year, her withholdings total is $1,567.28.
- If Louisa is paid on a monthly basis, her gross wages would be $3,033.33 per month, and her wages in excess of the allowance would be $2,424.99. Louisa's monthly check has tax withholdings of $130.55. For the year, her withholdings total $1,566.60.

When the wage bracket method is used, withholding allowances are *not* deducted before figuring the federal withholding amount. See Example 10-4 for an illustration of a wage bracket table. Notice that the amount of federal withholding is a whole amount based on a range of wages. This "averaging" accounts for differences in withholding using the percentage method.

EXAMPLE 10-4

Using the same information as in Example 10-1, Audrey's federal withholding will be $31 calculated as follows:

1. Find the wage bracket table for "Single persons—Weekly payroll period."
2. Go down the left side of the table and find the range of at least $500 but less than $510 in wages. Do not deduct any withholding allowances.
3. Go across this row until you find the withholding allowances column for two allowances.
4. The intersection is $31.

Note that when the percentage method is used, the amount of federal withholding is $30.14 and when the wage bracket is used the amount of federal withholding is $31. This is due to averaging between the range of gross wages ($500–$510).

Generally, the largest amount of federal income tax withholding occurs when an employee claims single with no exemption allowances. The more exemptions claimed, the less tax that is withheld and the higher the net paycheck. In such cases, that may not provide for sufficient withholding during the year if, for example, an individual works multiple jobs. The withholding tables are constructed under the assumption that an individual works only one job. Because the U.S. tax system is a *progressive tax system,* individuals with higher levels

of income are taxed at higher rates. If a single employee works one job and earns $25,000 per year, the marginal withholding rate is 15%. If that same person works two jobs paying $25,000 each, the second job is added to the first job for purposes of taxation. The second job causes the marginal withholding rate to be 25% (when both jobs are added together), yet each employer will withhold at a marginal 15% rate as though the individual works only one job.

Unless the employee requests one or both employers to withhold an amount in excess of the statutory requirement, the employee will likely be underwithheld and will be required to pay additional taxes when filing his or her return and could incur an underpayment penalty. On line 6 of Form W-4, an employee can ask the employer to withhold an additional amount from each paycheck to cover this potential shortfall.

Employees can also claim exemption from withholding on line 7 of Form W-4. An individual can do so only if he or she did not have a federal tax liability in the prior tax year and expects to have no federal tax liability in the current year.[4] Such individuals expect either to have low Adjusted Gross Income (AGI) or to have unusually high deductions and/or credits.

FICA Taxes—Social Security Tax and Medicare Tax Withholding

Employers must also withhold Federal Insurance Contributions Act (FICA) taxes from the paychecks of employees. There are two parts to FICA taxes. One is the old age, survivors, and disability insurance (OASDI), commonly referred to as *social security*.[5] The other is hospital insurance for the elderly and other specified individuals, called *Medicare*.[6]

Unlike income tax withholding, which is deducted entirely from the paycheck of the employee, social security and Medicare taxes are collected equally from the employee and the employer. The employer withholds the appropriate amount from the employee (as with income tax withholding), and that amount is added to an equal amount from the pocket of the employer. Thus the employer pays half of the total FICA liability and the employee pays the other half.

If a taxpayer works two jobs, both employers are required to withhold FICA and match the amounts withheld. A taxpayer who has overpaid the social security portion of the tax because his or her combined taxable income from both jobs exceeds the annual wage base is entitled to receive the excess amount back when he or she files Form 1040. The excess social security tax withheld is recorded on the second page of Form 1040 under the Payments section.

In 2009 the social security tax rate is 6.2% of taxable wages for both employee and employer up to an annual wage base of $106,800.[7] For Medicare taxes, the rate is 1.45% for each party on an unlimited wage base. Thus the total amount collected by the federal government is 15.3% (12.4% plus 2.9%) on the wages of an individual up to $106,800 and 2.9% on individual wages above that threshold.

EXAMPLE 10-5 Henrietta earned $52,300 during 2009. Without regard to federal income taxes, her employer will withhold $3,242.60 ($52,300 × 0.062) from her paycheck for social security taxes and $758.35 ($52,300 × 0.0145) for Medicare taxes, for a total of $4,000.95. Henrietta's employer will match that amount and will deposit a total of $8,001.90 with the federal government during the year.

EXAMPLE 10-6 Haito earned $112,800 during 2009. Her employer will withhold social security taxes of $6,621.60 (maximum wage base of $106,800 × 0.062) and Medicare taxes of $1,635.60 ($112,800 × 0.0145) for a total of $8,257.20. The employer matches that amount and sends the federal government $16,514.40 during the year for social security and Medicare taxes.

---

[4] IRC § 3402(n).

[5] IRC § 3101(a).

[6] IRC § 3101(b).

[7] This annual wage base is subject to annual inflation adjustment.

EXHIBIT 10-2

Form **4070** (Rev. August 2005) Department of the Treasury Internal Revenue Service	**Employee's Report of Tips to Employer**	OMB No. 1545-0074

Employee's name and address	Social security number

Employer's name and address (include establishment name, if different)	**1** Cash tips received
	2 Credit and debit card tips received
	3 Tips paid out

Month or shorter period in which tips were received from , , to ,	**4** Net tips (lines **1 + 2 - 3**)
Signature	Date

For Paperwork Reduction Act Notice, see the instructions on the back of this form.	Cat. No. 41320P	Form **4070** (Rev. 8-2005)

Tips

Employees at restaurants or other establishments may receive tips from customers for services performed. Employees are required to report cash tips to their employer by the 10th of the month after the month in which the employee receives the tips. If tips are less than $20 in a month, no withholding is required. Employees can use Form 4070 to report tips (see Exhibit 10-2). The report must include the employee's name, address, and social security number, the period the report covers, and the total amount of tips received during the period. The report includes tips known to the employer (from credit card charges, for example) and cash tips, and the employee must sign the report. If the tips in any one month from any one job are less than $20, no reporting is required. Employers must withhold income tax, social security, and Medicare taxes on the amount of employee tips.[8]

Large food and beverage establishments may be required to "allocate" tips to employees. A large establishment is one with more than 10 employees on a typical business day during the preceding year that provides food or beverages for consumption on the premises, and where tipping is customary.[9] In effect, if employees do not report tips in an amount of at least 8% of gross receipts, the employer must allocate the difference to the employees. Employers are required to report allocated tips to the IRS on Form 8027 (Exhibit 10-3).

CONCEPT CHECK 10-2—LO 2

1. Withholding and other employment taxes are levied only on cash wages and salaries paid to the employee. True or false?
2. The employer fills out Form W-4 to determine how many withholding allowances the employee is entitled to take. True or false?
3. Jim is single and earns $600 per week. He claimed two allowances on his W-4 form provided to the employer. What amount of federal withholding tax will be deducted from his gross compensation?
4. Jenny earns $108,475 in 2009. How much social security tax will be withheld from her compensation? How much Medicare tax will be withheld from her compensation?
5. Form 4070 is completed by tipped employees for any and all tips earned for the period. True or false?

[8] IRC § 3121(q) and IRC § 3402(k).
[9] IRC § 6053(c).

EXHIBIT 10-3

Form **8027**	**Employer's Annual Information Return of Tip Income and Allocated Tips**	OMB No. 1545-0714
Department of the Treasury Internal Revenue Service	► See separate instructions.	20**09**

Draft as of 06/22/2009

Name of establishment

Number and street (see instructions)

City or town, state, and ZIP code

Employer identification number

Type of establishment (check only one box)
- ☐ **1** Evening meals only
- ☐ **2** Evening and other meals
- ☐ **3** Meals other than evening meals
- ☐ **4** Alcoholic beverages

Employer's name (same name as on Form 941)

Number and street (P.O. box, if applicable)   Apt. or suite no.

Establishment number (see instructions)

City, state, and ZIP code (if a foreign address, see instructions)

Does this establishment accept credit cards, debit cards, or other charges?   ☐ Yes (lines 1 and 2 **must** be completed)   ☐ No

Check **if:** Amended Return ☐   Final Return ☐

Attributed Tip Income Program (ATIP). See Revenue Procedure 2006-30 . . . . ► ☐

1 Total charged tips for calendar year 2009. . . . . **1**

2 Total charge receipts showing charged tips (see instructions) **2**

3 Total amount of service charges of less than 10% paid as wages to employees. . . . **3**

4a Total tips reported by indirectly tipped employees **4a**

b Total tips reported by directly tipped employees **4b**
Note. Complete the **Employer's Optional Worksheet for Tipped Employees** on page 6 of the instructions to determine potential unreported tips of your employees.

c Total tips reported (add lines 4a and 4b) **4c**

5 Gross receipts from food or beverage operations (not less than line 2—see instructions) . **5**

6 Multiply line 5 by 8% (.08) or the lower rate shown here ►_____ granted by the IRS. (Attach a copy of the IRS determination letter to this return.) **6**
Note. If you have allocated tips using other than the calendar year (semimonthly, biweekly, quarterly, etc.), mark an **"X"** on line 6 and enter the amount of allocated tips from your records on line 7.

7 Allocation of tips. If line 6 is more than line 4c, enter the excess here **7**
► This amount must be allocated as tips to tipped employees working in this establishment. Check the box below that shows the method used for the allocation. (Show the portion, if any, attributable to each employee in box 8 of the employee's Form W-2.)

a Allocation based on hours-worked method (see instructions for restriction) . . . ☐
Note. If you marked the checkbox in line 7a, enter the average number of employee hours worked per business day during the payroll period. (see instructions) _____

b Allocation based on gross receipts method . . . . ☐

c Allocation based on good-faith agreement (Attach a copy of the agreement.). . . ☐

8 Enter the total number of directly tipped employees at this establishment during 2009 ►

Under penalties of perjury, I declare that I have examined this return, including accompanying schedules and statements, and to the best of my knowledge and belief, it is true, correct, and complete.

Signature ►   Title ►   Date ►

For Privacy Act and Paperwork Reduction Act Notice, see page 6 of the separate instructions.   Cat. No. 49989U   Form **8027** (2009)

✳ *Printed on recycled paper*

Employers must use one of the following methods to allocate tips:

1. Gross receipts per employee.
2. Hours worked per employee.
3. Good-faith agreement between the employee and employer.

Employers are *not* required to withhold income, social security, or Medicare taxes on allocated tips.

REPORTING AND PAYING PAYROLL TAXES
LO 3

Payment of Payroll Taxes

Employers are required to pay withheld taxes (income tax, social security, Medicare) to the federal government on a timely basis.[10] These payments are called *payroll tax deposits.* The frequency of the deposits depends, in large part, on the dollar amounts withheld or otherwise owed to the government. Generally employers make payroll tax deposits with a financial institution that is an authorized depository for federal taxes.[11] There is also an electronic deposit requirement in 2009 for employers who made more than $200,000 in total tax deposits in the two years before the current year or if the employer was required to use the Electronic Funds Transfer Payment Systems (EFTPS) in 2008 or any prior year.[12] The EFTPS is a free service provided by the Department of Treasury. This service is available for all employers. When the employer identification number (EIN) is requested from the IRS, the employer is preenrolled with instructions on how to activate the EFTPS account. For more information, go to www.eftps.gov.

Employers typically deposit taxes either monthly or semiweekly. New employers are deemed monthly schedule depositors, except in unusual circumstances. The deposit schedule is based on the total tax liability that the employer reported on Form 941 during a four-quarter lookback period. For 2009 the lookback period runs from the quarters starting July 1, 2007, through June 30, 2008. If the employer reported total payroll taxes of $50,000 or less during the lookback period, the employer is a monthly schedule depositor. If total taxes exceed $50,000, the employer is a semiweekly schedule depositor.[13]

| **EXAMPLE 10-7** | Smith Company is determining how often it needs to deposit payroll taxes for calendar year 2009. The company made quarterly payroll tax deposits during the lookback period as follows: |

Quarter July 1–September 30, 2007	$ 8,000
Quarter October 1–December 31, 2007	9,000
Quarter January 1–March 31, 2008	10,000
Quarter April 1–June 30, 2008	10,000
Total payroll taxes paid in lookback period	$37,000

Because the total payroll taxes deposited in the lookback period were less than $50,000, Smith Company will be a monthly payroll tax depositor during 2009.

Monthly depositors are required to deposit payroll taxes with the authorized depository on or before the 15th day of the following month. The taxes that must be deposited are the sum of (a) withheld income taxes, (b) social security and Medicare taxes withheld from the employee, and (c) the employer's matching amount for social security and Medicare taxes.

[10] IRC § 6302(a) and Reg. § 31.6302-1(a).
[11] IRC § 6302(c).
[12] Refer to Publication 15 under "How to Deposit."
[13] Reg. §31.6302-1(b).

EXAMPLE 10-8   XYZ Company is a monthly depositor. For payroll paid during the month of April, the company withheld $4,000 in income taxes and $2,500 in social security and Medicare taxes. The company is required to match the $2,500 amount and to deposit $9,000 with an authorized depository no later than May 15.

Semiweekly schedule depositors must remit payroll taxes more often. Payroll taxes associated with payrolls paid on a Wednesday, Thursday, or Friday must be deposited by the following Wednesday. For payrolls paid on Saturday, Sunday, Monday, or Tuesday, the semiweekly schedule depositor must deposit the taxes no later than the following Friday.

EXAMPLE 10-9   LMNO Company, which pays its employees every Friday, is a semiweekly schedule depositor. When the company paid its employees on Friday, it incurred a payroll tax liability of $19,000 on that date. LMNO must deposit applicable payroll taxes no later than Wednesday of the next week.

It is important to note that the applicable payroll date is the date the payroll is *paid*, not the end of the payroll period.

EXAMPLE 10-10   Nichols Company is a monthly schedule depositor that pays its employees on the first day of the month for the payroll period ending on the last day of the prior month. Payroll taxes withheld on June 1 are due no later than July 15 even though the payroll is for work performed by employees through May 31.

If the day on which taxes are due is a weekend or holiday, taxes are payable on the next banking day. Semiweekly schedule depositors have at least three banking days to make a deposit. Thus if a banking holiday means that an employer does not get three banking days, the payment date is extended.

EXAMPLE 10-11   LMNO Company (from Example 10-9) pays employees on Friday. The following Monday is a banking holiday. Because LMNO is a semiweekly schedule depositor, it must normally deposit applicable payroll taxes on the following Wednesday. Because Monday is a banking holiday, the company does not have at least three banking days to make its deposit. Thus the company has until Thursday to make its deposit.

Employers with a payroll tax liability of less than $2,500 at the end of any quarter can pay the payroll tax liability when they file their quarterly payroll tax reports rather than with an authorized depository.

Employers make deposits with the authorized depository using Form 8109-B (see Exhibit 10-4), the Federal Tax Deposit (FTD) Coupon. Employers indicate the amount of deposit and tax year, darken the oval for 941 type of tax, and darken the oval for the appropriate quarter. Once a company applies for a taxpayer ID number from the IRS and notifies the IRS that it will have employees, the company will receive a booklet of tax deposit coupons preprinted with the name, address, and ID number of the company.

The Internal Revenue Service encourages employers to make deposits using EFTPS and imposes a 10% failure-to-deposit penalty if an employer does not remit tax deposits using EFTPS as required. For EFTPS payments to be on time, the transaction must be initiated at least one business day before the date the deposit is due. If the employer fails to initiate the deposit transaction according to the rules, a deposit can be made using the Federal Reserve Electronic Tax Application (FR-ETA) process. FR-ETA allows the employer to initiate the transaction and have funds transferred from its financial institution on the same day. When the employer enrolls in EFTPS, it is automatically enrolled in FR-ETA. For more information refer to Publication 15.

EXHIBIT 10-4

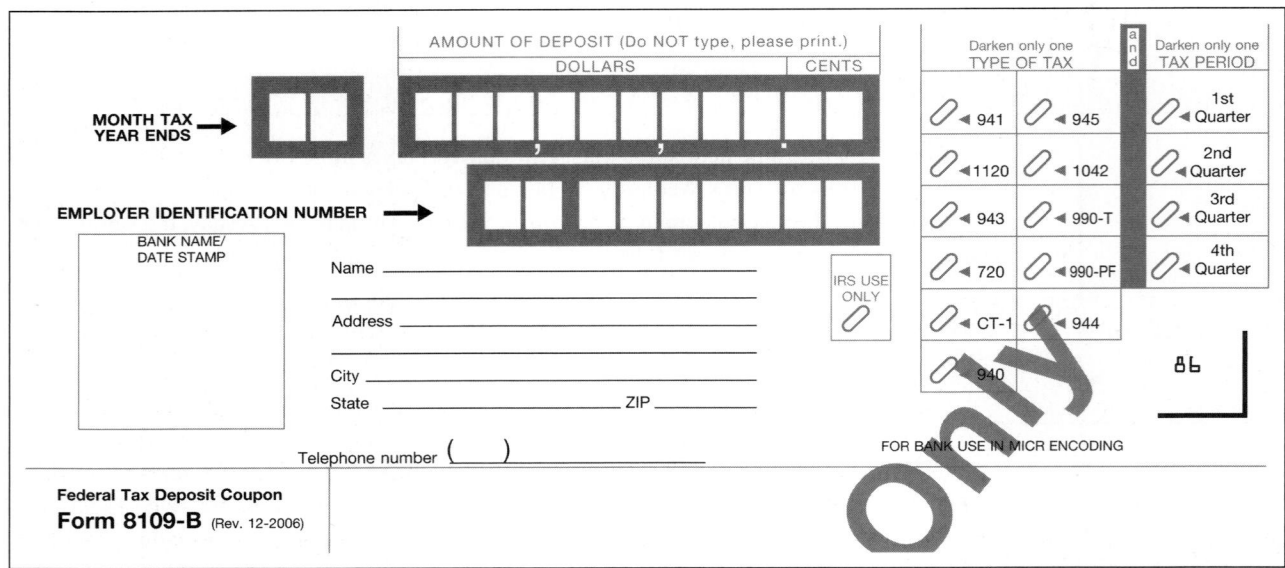

If an employer accumulates $100,000 or more in taxes on any day during a deposit period, it must deposit the tax by the next banking day, whether it is a monthly or semiweekly schedule depositor. This rule applies to a single day, and the taxes do not accumulate during the period. For example, if $100,000 of taxes are accumulated on a Monday, they must be deposited by Tuesday. If on that Tuesday, additional accumulated taxes are $90,000, the taxes are deposited by Friday. An employer who is a monthly schedule depositor and accumulates a $100,000 tax liability on any day becomes a semiweekly schedule depositor on the next day and remains so for at least the rest of the calendar year and for the following year.

EXAMPLE 10-12

Price and Company started its business on March 31, 2009. On April 10 it paid wages for the first time and accumulated a tax liability of $30,000. On Friday, April 24, Price paid wages and incurred a tax liability of $70,000, which brings the accumulated tax liability to $100,000. Because this is the first year of its business, the tax liability for its lookback period is zero, so the company would be a monthly schedule depositor. However, because Price accumulated $100,000 tax liability on April 24, it became a semiweekly schedule depositor on April 25. It will be a semiweekly schedule depositor for the remainder of 2009 and for 2010. In this example, Price and Company is required to deposit the $100,000 by Monday, April 27, the next banking day.

Deposit Penalties

If payroll taxes are not paid on a timely basis, the employer is subject to penalty. The penalty is based on the amount not properly or timely deposited. The penalties are as follows:

- 2% for deposits made 1 to 5 days late.
- 5% for deposits made 6 to 15 days late.
- 10% for deposits made 16 or more days late.
- 10% if electronic deposit is required but not used.
- 10% if deposits are paid directly to the IRS, or paid with the return, or paid to an unauthorized financial institution.
- 15% for amounts unpaid more than 10 days after the date of the first notice the IRS sent asking for the tax due.

Employers who withhold taxes from employee paychecks are holding the withheld taxes in trust for the employee. As such, employers have a high level of responsibility. Individuals may be personally responsible for unpaid payroll taxes. If the IRS determines that an individual is

responsible for collecting, accounting for, and paying payroll taxes and that the person acted willfully in not paying the taxes, the IRS can assess a penalty on the individual equal to the amount of tax due. Refer to Publication 15 under "Deposit Penalties" for additional rules.

Reporting Payroll Taxes and Form 941

In addition to depositing payroll taxes on a predetermined schedule, employers must also provide quarterly reports to the IRS on Form 941 (see Exhibit 10-5 for a filled-in illustration using Example 10-13). The report is due no later than the last day of the month following the end of the quarter. Form 941 is a reconciliation of the amount of payroll taxes that should be paid (lines 2 through 10) with the amount of payroll taxes deposited (line 11). If any balance is due, it is paid with the return using a Form 941-V payment voucher (Exhibit 10-6). The amounts appearing on Form 941 for the four quarters in the calendar year will be reconciled with the year-end form and given to employees on their W-2s.

Under the American Recovery and Reinvestment Act (ARRA) of 2009, Form 941 was revised to allow a credit against employment taxes for providing COBRA (Consolidated Omnibus Budget Reconciliation Act of 1985) premium assistance to qualified former employees, retirees, spouses, former spouses, and dependent children. COBRA was enacted to provide temporary continuation of health coverage at group rates. For detailed information regarding eligibility and income limitations, visit www.irs.gov and enter the keywords COBRA Health Insurance Continuation Premium Subsidy. The Department of Labor is another good source of information (www.dol.gov).

Any references to COBRA in this chapter are limited to completing Form 941. The ARRA allows a credit against payroll taxes for employers that provide COBRA premium assistance to eligible individuals. COBRA continuation coverage began after February 16, 2009. Under this legislation, a group health plan must treat an assistance-eligible individual as having paid the required COBRA continuation coverage premium if the individual elects COBRA coverage and the individual pays 35% of the amount of the premium. The continuation coverage period began September 1, 2008, and ends December 31, 2009, and must be due to the involuntary termination from employment during the period of a covered employee who elects COBRA coverage. The assistance for the coverage can last up to nine months.

The 65% of the premium not paid by the assistance-eligible individual is reimbursed to the employer that maintains the group health plan. The reimbursement is made through a credit against the employers' employment tax liabilities. This credit is treated as a deposit made on the first day of the return period and applied against the employer's deposit requirement. The credit calculation is included on lines 12a, 12b, and 13 of Form 941. The employer does not submit any additional information regarding the subsidy with Form 941. However, the employer is required to maintain supporting documentation for the credit claimed.

Note that because an individual can be eligible for the COBRA subsidy as late as December 31, 2009, and the subsidy can apply for up to nine months, it is expected that eligibility for the subsidy will be used up by the end of 2010, and Form 941 for the fourth quarter of 2010 will be the last time to take this credit.

For example, assume an employer is required to make deposits for the second quarter that total $40,000 without regard to the COBRA premium subsidy. The employer provides assistance to eligible individuals with a total of $5,000 during the quarter based on 35% of the premium payment received from the individuals during the quarter. The employer reports the $5,000 subsidy on line 12a of Form 941. The employer will be treated as having made a $5,000 payroll tax deposit on the first day of the quarter and will not be subject to a failure-to-deposit penalty for the quarter even if it reduces its deposits during the quarter by the amount of the subsidy. Once the deposit exceeds $5,000, the employer is required to make regularly required tax deposits. However, COBRA premium assistance credits are not taken into consideration for the $100,000 deposit rules because this rule applies to payroll tax liability and does not apply to the employer's deposit schedule rule.

EXHIBIT 10-5

Form **941 for 2009:** Employer's QUARTERLY Federal Tax Return

950109

(Rev. April 2009)   Department of the Treasury — Internal Revenue Service

OMB No. 1545-0029

(EIN) Employer identification number: 3 6 – 1 2 3 4 5 6 7

Name *(not your trade name)* Watson Company

Trade name *(if any)*

Address 123 Main Street
Number   Street   Suite or room number

Mason City   IA
City   State   ZIP code

Report for this Quarter of 2009
(Check one.)

[X] **1:** January, February, March
[ ] **2:** April, May, June
[ ] **3:** July, August, September
[ ] **4:** October, November, December

Read the separate instructions before you complete Form 941. Type or print within the boxes.

Part 1: Answer these questions for this quarter.

1   Number of employees who received wages, tips, or other compensation for the pay period including: *Mar. 12* (Quarter 1), *June 12* (Quarter 2), *Sept. 12* (Quarter 3), *Dec. 12* (Quarter 4)   **1**   6

2   Wages, tips, and other compensation   **2**   300,000.

3   Income tax withheld from wages, tips, and other compensation   **3**   24,000.

4   If no wages, tips, and other compensation are subject to social security or Medicare tax   [ ] Check and go to line 6.

5   Taxable social security and Medicare wages and tips:

	Column 1		Column 2
5a Taxable social security wages	300,000.	× .124 =	37,200.
5b Taxable social security tips	.	× .124 =	.
5c Taxable Medicare wages & tips	300,000.	× .029 =	8,700.

5d Total social security and Medicare taxes (*Column 2,* lines 5a + 5b + 5c = line 5d)   **5d**   45,900.

6   Total taxes before adjustments (lines 3 + 5d = line 6)   **6**   69,900.

7   **CURRENT QUARTER'S ADJUSTMENTS,** for example, a fractions of cents adjustment. See the instructions.

7a Current quarter's fractions of cents   .

7b Current quarter's sick pay   .

7c Current quarter's adjustments for tips and group-term life insurance   .

7d **TOTAL ADJUSTMENTS.** Combine all amounts on lines 7a through 7c   **7d**   0.

8   Total taxes after adjustments. Combine lines 6 and 7d   **8**   69,900.

9   Advance earned income credit (EIC) payments made to employees   **9**   .

10 Total taxes after adjustment for advance EIC (line 8 – line 9 = line 10)   **10**   69,900.

11 Total deposits for this quarter, including overpayment applied from a prior quarter and overpayment applied from Form 941-X or Form 944-X   63,800.

12a COBRA premium assistance payments (see instructions)   6,000.

12b Number of individuals provided COBRA premium assistance reported on line 12a   3

13 Add lines 11 and 12a   **13**   69,800.

14 **Balance due.** If line 10 is more than line 13, write the difference here   **14**   100.
For information on how to pay, see the instructions.

15 **Overpayment.** If line 13 is more than line 10, write the difference here   .   Check one [ ] Apply to next return. [ ] Send a refund.

► You **MUST** complete both pages of Form 941 and **SIGN** it.   Next ➡

For Privacy Act and Paperwork Reduction Act Notice, see the back of the Payment Voucher.   Cat. No. 17001Z   Form **941** (Rev. 4-2009)

EXHIBIT 10-5 *(continued)*

950209

Name *(not your trade name)*	**Employer identification number (EIN)**

Part 2: Tell us about your deposit schedule and tax liability for this quarter.

If you are unsure about whether you are a monthly schedule depositor or a semiweekly schedule depositor, see *Pub. 15 (Circular E),* section 11.

16 [I] [A]   Write the state abbreviation for the state where you made your deposits OR write "MU" if you made your deposits in *multiple* states.

17 Check one: ☐ **Line 10 is less than $2,500.** Go to Part 3.

☐ **You were a monthly schedule depositor for the entire quarter.** Enter your tax liability for each month. Then go to Part 3.

Tax liability: Month 1 [_____ . ___]

Month 2 [_____ . ___]

Month 3 [_____ . ___]

Total liability for quarter [_____ . ___] **Total must equal line 10.**

☐ **You were a semiweekly schedule depositor for any part of this quarter.** Complete *Schedule B (Form 941): Report of Tax Liability for Semiweekly Schedule Depositors,* and attach it to Form 941.

Part 3: Tell us about your business. If a question does NOT apply to your business, leave it blank.

18 If your business has closed or you stopped paying wages . . . . ☐ Check here, and

enter the final date you paid wages [__ / __ / __] .

19 If you are a seasonal employer and you do not have to file a return for every quarter of the year . . ☐ Check here.

Part 4: May we speak with your third-party designee?

Do you want to allow an employee, a paid tax preparer, or another person to discuss this return with the IRS? See the instructions for details.

☐ Yes. Designee's name and phone number [_____] [(___) ___ – ____]

Select a 5-digit Personal Identification Number (PIN) to use when talking to the IRS. ☐ ☐ ☐ ☐ ☐

☐ No.

Part 5: Sign here. You MUST complete both pages of Form 941 and SIGN it.

Under penalties of perjury, I declare that I have examined this return, including accompanying schedules and statements, and to the best of my knowledge and belief, it is true, correct, and complete. Declaration of preparer (other than taxpayer) is based on all information of which preparer has any knowledge.

X **Sign your name here** [_____]

Print your name here [_____]

Print your title here [_____]

Date [__ / __ / __]

Best daytime phone [(___) ___ – ____]

Paid preparer's use only Check if you are self-employed . . . . ☐

Preparer's name	Greg Oliver	Preparer's SSN/PTIN	
Preparer's signature		Date	/ /
Firm's name (or yours if self-employed)		EIN	
Address		Phone	( ) –
City		State	ZIP code

Page **2** Form **941** (Rev. 4-2009)

(continued)

EXHIBIT 10-5 *(concluded)*

Schedule B (Form 941):
Report of Tax Liability for Semiweekly Schedule Depositors
(Rev. February 2009)   Department of the Treasury — Internal Revenue Service

960309

OMB No. 1545-0029

(EIN)
Employer identification number   3 6 – 1 2 3 4 5 6 7

Name *(not your trade name)*   Watson Company

Calendar year   2 0 0 9   (Also check quarter)

Report for this Quarter ...
(Check one.)

[X] **1:** January, February, March

[ ] **2:** April, May, June

[ ] **3:** July, August, September

[ ] **4:** October, November, December

Use this schedule to show your TAX LIABILITY for the quarter; DO NOT use it to show your deposits. When you file this form with Form 941 (or Form 941-SS), DO NOT change your tax liability by adjustments reported on any Forms 941-X. You must fill out this form and attach it to Form 941 (or Form 941-SS) if you are a semiweekly schedule depositor or became one because your accumulated tax liability on any day was $100,000 or more. Write your daily tax liability on the numbered space that corresponds to the date wages were paid. See Section 11 in *Pub. 15 (Circular E), Employer's Tax Guide,* for details.

Month 1

#		#		#		#		Tax liability for Month 1
1		9		17		25		
2		10		18		26		23,300
3		11		19		27		
4		12		20		28		
5		13		21		29		
6		14		22		30		
7		15	11,650	23		31	11,650	
8		16		24				

Month 2

#		#		#		#		Tax liability for Month 2
1		9		17		25		
2		10		18		26		23,300
3		11		19		27		
4		12		20		28	11,650	
5		13		21		29		
6		14		22		30		
7		15	11,650	23		31		
8		16		24				

Month 3

#		#		#		#		Tax liability for Month 3
1		9		17		25		
2		10		18		26		23,300
3		11		19		27		
4		12		20		28		
5		13		21		29		
6		14		22		30		
7		15	11,650	23		31	11,650	
8		16		24				

Fill in your total liability for the quarter (Month 1 + Month 2 + Month 3) = Total tax liability for the quarter ▶
Total must equal line 10 on Form 941 (or line 8 on Form 941-SS).

Total liability for the quarter

69,900

For Paperwork Reduction Act Notice, see separate instructions.   Cat. No. 11967Q   Schedule B (Form 941) Rev. 2-2009

EXHIBIT 10-6

Form **941-V**	**Payment Voucher**	OMB No. 1545-0029
Department of the Treasury Internal Revenue Service	▶ Do not staple this voucher or your payment to Form 941.	2009

1 Enter your employer identification number (EIN).	2 Enter the amount of your payment. ▶	Dollars	Cents
36 ⋮ 1234567		100	00

3 Tax period		4 Enter your business name (individual name if sole proprietor).
⦸ 1st Quarter	⊘ 3rd Quarter	**Watson Company**
		Enter your address.
⊘ 2nd Quarter	⊘ 4th Quarter	**123 Main Street**
		Enter your city, state, and ZIP code.
		Mason City, IA

Schedule B is used to report an employer's payroll tax liability for each period and not for the amount of payroll tax deposits. Therefore, the amounts entered on Schedule B relate to the payroll tax liability for each month in the quarter. Using the previous example, if the amount of payroll tax liability is $40,000, this amount will be allocated according to the employer payroll periods on the schedule. Refer to Exhibit 10-5 and Example 10-13 for a filled-in Form 941 and Schedule B. Also new to Form 941 is the requirement that any return prepared by a paid preparer must be signed by the preparer; prior to 2009 this was optional.

Small business employers may have the option of filing these taxes on an annual basis. Form 944—Employer's Annual Federal Tax Return is for employers who have received written notification from the IRS that they qualify for the Form 944 program. Refer to Publication 15, Chapter 12—Filing Form 941 or Form 944 for a detailed explanation of qualification requirements.

EXAMPLE 10-13

Watson Company (EIN: 36-1234567), located at 123 Main Street, Mason City, IA, had the following payroll data for the first quarter, ended March 31, 2009:

Number of employees	6
Gross wages	$300,000
Total income tax withheld from wages	$ 24,000*
Social security wages	$300,000
Medicare wages	$300,000

* Assume $4,000 per pay period.

Assume that Watson Company pays wages on a semimonthly basis ($50,000 per pay period). Deposits for the quarter were $69,800. Exhibit 10-5 is the filled-in 941 (including Schedule B) for Watson Company for the first quarter of 2009. Exhibit 10-6 is a filled-in voucher coupon for the amount of additional tax due for the quarter. COBRA premium assistance payments totaled $6,000. The number of individuals provided COBRA premium assistance was 3. Greg Oliver is the paid preparer of Form 941.

The payroll tax liability per pay period is calculated as follows:

Social security tax	$50,000 x 12.4% =	$ 6,200
Medicare tax	$50,000 x 2.9% =	1,450
Federal income tax		4,000
Total tax liability per period		$11,650
Total tax liability for the quarter		$69,900
Deposits made for the quarter:		69,800
Deposit due with 941 return:		$ 100

**CONCEPT
CHECK 10-3—LO 3**

1. All new employers must use the semiweekly deposit system. True or false?
2. The deposit schedule for an employer is based on the total tax liability that the employer reported on Form 941 during the prior four quarters starting on July 1 and ending on March 31 of the next year. True or false?
3. Semiweekly schedule depositors remit taxes on the following Wednesday if the payroll is paid on a Wednesday, Thursday, or Friday. True or false?
4. The penalty for not paying the appropriate federal taxes on time is based on the total amount of the tax liability whether or not a partial payment was made on time. True or false?
5. Form 941 is prepared by the employer to record all federal taxes withheld, including federal withholding, social security, and Medicare taxes and amounts paid for these taxes. True or false?

SELF-EMPLOYMENT TAXES, UNEMPLOYMENT TAXES, FORM 940, TAXES FOR HOUSEHOLD EMPLOYEES, AND SCHEDULE H
LO 4

Self-Employment Tax

To this point, this chapter has covered the rules associated with payroll taxes derived from an employee–employer relationship. Self-employed individuals (those filing Schedule C or Schedule F) pay similar taxes, called *self-employment taxes*.

Self-employment taxes are based on net earnings (profit) generated by the business. Because the self-employed taxpayer acts, in effect, as an employee and an employer, the self-employed taxpayer pays both parts of social security and Medicare taxes. Thus these individuals pay 12.4% social security tax on net earnings from self-employment of up to $106,800 and a 2.9% Medicare tax on all net earnings without limit.[14] If net earnings from self-employment are less than $400, no self-employment tax is payable.[15] Self-employment tax is reported on Schedule SE.

Remember that self-employed taxpayers are allowed a 50% deduction for self-employment tax in determining adjusted gross income (line 27 on Form 1040). This deduction gives the sole proprietor a share of the employer tax expense that would be allowed for corporate businesses. The amount of net self-employment earnings subject to FICA taxes is first reduced by 7.65% before calculating the taxes. Remember from Chapter 6 that sole proprietors are not considered employees; therefore, there is no employer match of FICA taxes and no business expense allowed in reducing taxable income. To compensate self-employed individuals for this inability to take the employer share as a business deduction, they are permitted to reduce net self-employment earnings by 7.65% so that only 92.35% (100% − 7.65%) of net self-employment earnings are subject to FICA taxes. For 2009 self-employed individuals can reduce their quarterly estimated payments to get an advance benefit from the Making Work Pay Credit.

In some situations, a taxpayer is an employee of a company as well as a sole proprietor. For example, a taxpayer can work as a teacher and sell real estate as a part-time business. The school district withholds the teacher's FICA taxes while the teacher must pay FICA taxes on the net earnings generated by the real estate business. If the earnings from the teacher's Form W-2 and the net earnings from the real estate business are less than the ceiling for social security ($106,800 in 2009), there is no problem. What if both activities combined generate more than $106,800 in earnings? In this type of situation, wages subject to social security are deducted from the ceiling amount of $106,800. The balance is then compared with the earnings from self-employment. If the taxpayer in this situation earned

[14] IRC § 1401(a) and IRC § 1401(b).
[15] IRC § 1402(b).

EXHIBIT 10-8

Form **940 for 2009:** **Employer's Annual Federal Unemployment (FUTA) Tax Return** 850109
Department of the Treasury — Internal Revenue Service

OMB No. 1545-0028

(EIN)
Employer identification number   3 6 – 1 2 3 4 5 6 7

Name (not your trade name)   Boone Company

Trade name (if any)

Address   567 End Avenue
Number   Street   Suite or room number

Mason City   IA
City   State   ZIP code

Type of Return
(Check all that apply.)

☐ **a.** Amended
☐ **b.** Successor employer
☐ **c.** No payments to employees in 2009.
☐ **d.** Final: Business closed or stopped paying wages

Read the separate instructions before you fill out this form. Please type or print within the boxes.

Part 1: Tell us about your return. If any line does NOT apply, leave it blank.

1   If you were required to pay your state unemployment tax in ...

   1a One state only, write the state abbreviation . .   **1a** I A

   - OR -

   1b More than one state (You are a multi-state employer) . . . . . **1b** ☐ Check here. Fill out Schedule A.

2   If you paid wages in a state that is subject to **CREDIT REDUCTION** . . . . . **2** ☐ Check here. Fill out Schedule A (Form 940), Part 2.

Part 2: Determine your FUTA tax before adjustments for 2009. If any line does NOT apply, leave it blank.

3   Total payments to all employees . . . . **3**   82,000.

4   Payments exempt from FUTA tax . . . . **4**   0.

   Check all that apply: **4a** ☐ Fringe benefits   **4c** ☐ Retirement/Pension   **4e** ☐ Other
   4b ☐ Group-term life insurance   **4d** ☐ Dependent care

5   Total of payments made to each employee in excess of $7,000 . . . . **5**   65,000.

6   Subtotal (line 4 + line 5 = line 6) . . . . **6**   65,000.

7   Total taxable FUTA wages (line 3 – line 6 = line 7) . . . . **7**   17,000.

8   FUTA tax before adjustments (line 7 × .008 = line 8) . . . . . **8**   136.

Part 3: Determine your adjustments. If any line does NOT apply, leave it blank.

9   If ALL of the taxable FUTA wages you paid were excluded from state unemployment tax, multiply line 7 by .054 (line 7 × .054 = line 9). Then go to line 12 . . . . **9**   .

10 If SOME of the taxable FUTA wages you paid were excluded from state unemployment tax, OR you paid ANY state unemployment tax late (after the due date for filing Form 940), fill out the worksheet in the instructions. Enter the amount from line 7 of the worksheet . . . . **10**   .

11 If credit reduction applies, enter the amount from line 3 of Schedule A (Form 940) . . . . **11**   .

Part 4: Determine your FUTA tax and balance due or overpayment for 2009. If any line does NOT apply, leave it blank.

12 Total FUTA tax after adjustments (lines 8 + 9 + 10 + 11 = line 12) . . . . **12**   136.

13 FUTA tax deposited for the year, including any overpayment applied from a prior year . . **13**   0.

14 Balance due (If line 12 is more than line 13, enter the difference on line 14.)
   • If line 14 is more than $500, you must deposit your tax.
   • If line 14 is $500 or less, you may pay with this return. For more information on how to pay, see the separate instructions . . . . **14**   136.

15 Overpayment (If line 13 is more than line 12, enter the difference on line 15 and check a box below.) . . . . **15**   .

Check one: ☐ Apply to next return.
            ☐ Send a refund.

▶ You **MUST** fill out both pages of this form and **SIGN** it.

Next ➡

For Privacy Act and Paperwork Reduction Act Notice, see the back of Form 940-V, Payment Voucher.   Cat. No. 11234O   Form **940** (2009)

(continued)

EXHIBIT 10-8   *(concluded)*

860209

Name *(not your trade name)*	Employer identification number (EIN)

Part 5: Report your FUTA tax liability by quarter only if line 12 is more than $500. If not, go to Part 6.

16   Report the amount of your FUTA tax liability for each quarter; do NOT enter the amount you deposited. If you had no liability for a quarter, leave the line blank.

16a   **1st quarter** (January 1 – March 31) 16a

16b   **2nd quarter** (April 1 – June 30) 16b

16c   **3rd quarter** (July 1 – September 30) 16c

16d   **4th quarter** (October 1 – December 31) 16d

17   Total tax liability for the year (lines 16a + 16b + 16c + 16d = line 17) **17**   Total must equal line 12.

Part 6: May we speak with your third-party designee?

Do you want to allow an employee, a paid tax preparer, or another person to discuss this return with the IRS? See the instructions for details.

☐ **Yes.**   Designee's name and phone number   (   )   –

Select a 5-digit Personal Identification Number (PIN) to use when talking to IRS

☐ **No.**

Part 7: Sign here. You MUST fill out both pages of this form and SIGN it.

Under penalties of perjury, I declare that I have examined this return, including accompanying schedules and statements, and to the best of my knowledge and belief, it is true, correct, and complete, and that no part of any payment made to a state unemployment fund claimed as a credit was, or is to be, deducted from the payments made to employees. Declaration of preparer (other than taxpayer) is based on all information of which preparer has any knowledge.

✗ **Sign your name here**   Print your name here

Print your title here

Date   /   /   Best daytime phone   (   )   –

Paid preparer's use only   Check if you are self-employed . . . ☐

Preparer's name		Preparer's SSN/PTIN
Preparer's signature		Date / /
Firm's name (or yours if self-employed)		EIN
Address		Phone ( ) –
City	State	ZIP code

and are under the direction of the employer. Independent contractors are likely to work for many individuals. For example, you may have someone clean your house every two weeks. That person may clean houses for 40 other people. It is likely that your household worker is an independent contractor, not an employee. Thus you would not need to withhold taxes from the individual.

Instead of filing Form 941 and Form 940, individuals who employ household workers report employment taxes on Schedule H (see Exhibit 10-9 for a filled-in illustration of Example 10-16). The form is not filed separately but is attached to Form 1040. The amount of tax due on line 27 of Schedule H is carried forward to line 62 of Form 1040. Thus the employment taxes due for household employees are paid when Form 1040 is filed or extended.

A taxpayer who has nonhousehold workers (that is, a taxpayer with a business) and household workers can elect to account for and report the latter according to the rules pertaining to his or her regular employees.

EXHIBIT 10-9

SCHEDULE H (Form 1040)	**Household Employment Taxes**	OMB No. 1545-1971

SCHEDULE H (Form 1040)

Department of the Treasury
Internal Revenue Service (99)

Household Employment Taxes

(For Social Security, Medicare, Withheld Income, and Federal Unemployment (FUTA) Taxes)

▶ Attach to Form 1040, 1040NR, 1040-SS, or 1041.
▶ See separate instructions.

OMB No. 1545-1971

2009

Attachment Sequence No. **44**

Name of employer

Max and Abigail Jones

Social security number

Employer identification number

A Did you pay **any one** household employee cash wages of $1,700 or more in 2009? (If any household employee was your spouse, your child under age 21, your parent, or anyone under age 18, see the line A instructions on page H-4 before you answer this question.)

☒ **Yes.** Skip lines B and C and go to line 1.
☐ **No.** Go to line B.

B Did you withhold federal income tax during 2009 for any household employee?

☐ **Yes.** Skip line C and go to line 5.
☐ **No.** Go to line C.

C Did you pay **total** cash wages of $1,000 or more in **any** calendar **quarter** of 2008 or 2009 to **all** household employees? (**Do not** count cash wages paid in 2008 or 2009 to your spouse, your child under age 21, or your parent.)

☐ **No.** Stop. Do not file this schedule.
☐ **Yes.** Skip lines 1-9 and go to line 10 on the back. (Calendar year taxpayers having no household employees in 2009 **do not** have to complete this form for 2009.)

Part I Social Security, Medicare, and Federal Income Taxes

1	Total cash wages subject to social security taxes (see page H-4)	**1**	4,800	
2	Social security taxes. Multiply line 1 by 12.4% (.124)	**2**		595
3	Total cash wages subject to Medicare taxes (see page H-4)	**3**	4,800	
4	Medicare taxes. Multiply line 3 by 2.9% (.029)	**4**		139
5	Federal income tax withheld, if any	**5**		0
6	**Total social security, Medicare, and federal income taxes.** Add lines 2, 4, and 5	**6**		734
7	Advance earned income credit (EIC) payments, if any	**7**		0
8	**Net taxes** (subtract line 7 from line 6)	**8**		734

9 Did you pay **total** cash wages of $1,000 or more in **any** calendar **quarter** of 2008 or 2009 to **all** household employees? (**Do not** count cash wages paid in 2008 or 2009 to your spouse, your child under age 21, or your parent.)

☐ **No.** Stop. Include the amount from line 8 above on Form 1040, line 59, and check box **b** on that line. If you are not required to file Form 1040, see the line 9 instructions on page H-4.

☒ **Yes.** Go to line 10 on the back.

For Privacy Act and Paperwork Reduction Act Notice, see page H-7 of the instructions.   Cat. No. 12187K   **Schedule H (Form 1040) 2009**

(continued)

EXHIBIT 10-9   *(concluded)*

Schedule H (Form 1040) 2009   Page **2**

Part II   Federal Unemployment (FUTA) Tax

		Yes	No
10	Did you pay unemployment contributions to only one state? (If you paid contributions to XXXXX, check "No.") **10**	X	
11	Did you pay all state unemployment contributions for 2009 by April 15, 2010? Fiscal year filers, see page H-4 **11**	X	
12	Were all wages that are taxable for FUTA tax also taxable for your state's unemployment tax? **12**	X	

Next: If you checked the **"Yes"** box on **all** the lines above, complete Section A.
     If you checked the **"No"** box on **any** of the lines above, skip Section A and complete Section B.

Section A

13	Name of the state where you paid unemployment contributions ▶	NM	
14	State reporting number as shown on state unemployment tax return ▶	J1234	
15	Contributions paid to your state unemployment fund (see page H-5) . **15** 480		
16	Total cash wages subject to FUTA tax (see page H-5) **16**	4,800	
17	**FUTA tax.** Multiply line 16 by .008. Enter the result here, skip Section B, and go to line 26 . . . **17**	38	

Section B

18 Complete all columns below that apply (if you need more space, see page H-5):

(a) Name of state	(b) State reporting number as shown on state unemployment tax return	(c) Taxable wages (as defined in state act)	(d) State experience rate period From	To	(e) State experience rate	(f) Multiply col. (c) by .054	(g) Multiply col. (c) by col. (e)	(h) Subtract col. (g) from col. (f). If zero or less, enter -0-.	(i) Contributions paid to state unemployment fund

19	Totals **19**		
20	Add columns (h) and (i) of line 19 . . . . **20**		
21	Total cash wages subject to FUTA tax (see the line 16 instructions on page H-5) **21**		
22	Multiply line 21 by 6.2% (.062) **22**		
23	Multiply line 21 by 5.4% (.054) **23**		
24	Enter the **smaller** of line 20 or line 23		
	(XXXX employers must use the worksheet in the separate instructions and check here) . . . . ☐ **24**		
25	**FUTA tax.** Subtract line 24 from line 22. Enter the result here and go to line 26 . . . . . . **25**		

Part III   Total Household Employment Taxes

26	Enter the amount from line 8. If you checked the "Yes" box on line C of page 1, enter -0- **26**	734
27	Add line 17 (or line 25) and line 26 (see page H-5) **27**	772
28	Are you required to file Form 1040?	

    ☒ **Yes. Stop.** Include the amount from line 27 above on Form 1040, line 59, and check box **b** on that line. **Do not** complete Part IV below.

    ☐ **No.** You may have to complete Part IV. See page H-5 for details.

Part IV   Address and Signature— Complete this part **only** if required. See the line 28 instructions on page H-5.

Address (number and street) or P.O. box if mail is not delivered to street address	Apt., room, or suite no.

City, town or post office, state, and ZIP code

Under penalties of perjury, I declare that I have examined this schedule, including accompanying statements, and to the best of my knowledge and belief, it is true, correct, and complete. No part of any payment made to a state unemployment fund claimed as a credit was, or is to be, deducted from the payments to employees. Declaration of preparer (other than taxpayer) is based on all information of which preparer has any knowledge.

▶ Employer's signature	▶ Date	

Paid Preparer's Use Only	Preparer's signature ▶	Date	Check if self-employed ☐	Preparer's SSN or PTIN
	Firm's name (or yours if self-employed), address, and Zip code ▶		EIN	
			Phone no.	

Schedule H (Form 1040) 2009

EXAMPLE 10-16   Max and Abigail Jones employed a household worker for the entire year. They paid the household worker $400 per month for a total of $4,800 for the year. For purposes of this example, assume they live in New Mexico, have a state reporting number of J1234, and have paid $480 of state unemployment taxes for this worker.

Max and Abigail paid cash wages of $4,800 for the year and answered yes to Question A on Schedule H.

Part I Calculations

Social security tax	$4,800 × 12.4% =	$595
Medicare tax	$4,800 × 2.9% =	139
Total taxes		$734

Part II Calculations

Answer yes to Questions 10, 11, and 12 and enter NM, J1234, and $480 on lines 13, 14, and 15, respectively.

Lines 16 and 17 are the total wages subject to FUTA tax (in this situation the total is $4,800) and the total FUTA tax due of $38.40 ($38 rounded) ($4,800 × 0.8%).

Part III Calculations

Add the FUTA tax and the FICA taxes for a total amount due and reportable on Form 1040 line 62.

**CONCEPT CHECK
10-4—LO 4**

1. A self-employed taxpayer is treated both as an employee and an employer and thus pays a combined total of 15.3% for FICA taxes. True or false?
2. What is the effective tax rate for FUTA, provided that employers pay into their state SUTA programs on a timely basis?
   a. 0.8%
   b. 6.2%
   c. 5.4%
   d. 10%
3. Who can use Schedule H? _____
4. Taxpayers who employ household workers are subject to payroll taxes under what conditions?
   _____
   _____

EMPLOYER PAYROLL REPORTING REQUIREMENTS INCLUDING FORMS W-2 AND W-3

LO 5

Employer Payroll Reporting to Employees

Employers must annually report payroll-related information to employees and to the IRS.[19] The information is reported to both parties on Form W-2, Wage and Tax Statement.

The W-2 is a multipart form labeled Copy A, B, C, D, 1, and 2. Each labeled part is used for a different purpose. The employer sends the employee Copies 1 and 2 (filed with the employee's state and local tax returns), Copy B (filed with the employee's federal tax return—see Exhibit 10-10), and Copy C (retained by the employee). The employer retains Copy D. The employee uses the information from the W-2 to prepare his or her federal and state income tax returns. The employer must mail each employee his or her W-2 copies no later than January 31.

The employer must send Copy A of Form W-2 for each employee to the Social Security Administration (SSA) no later than February 28 or the next business day if February 28 falls

---

[19] IRC § 6051.

EXHIBIT 10-10

		a Employee's social security number		Safe, accurate, FAST! Use	Visit the IRS website at *www.irs.gov/efile*.

			OMB No. 1545-0008		

b Employer identification number (EIN)

1 Wages, tips, other compensation	**2** Federal income tax withheld

c Employer's name, address, and ZIP code

3 Social security wages	**4** Social security tax withheld
5 Medicare wages and tips	**6** Medicare tax withheld
7 Social security tips	**8** Allocated tips

d Control number

9 Advance EIC payment	**10** Dependent care benefits

e Employee's first name and initial   Last name   Suff.

11 Nonqualified plans	**12a** See instructions for box 12
13 Statutory employee / Retirement plan / Third-party sick pay	**12b**
14 Other	**12c**
	12d

f Employee's address and ZIP code

15 State Employer's state ID number	**16** State wages, tips, etc.	**17** State income tax	**18** Local wages, tips, etc.	**19** Local income tax	**20** Locality name

Form **W-2** **Wage and Tax Statement**   **2009**   Department of the Treasury—Internal Revenue Service

Copy B—To Be Filed With Employee's FEDERAL Tax Return.
This information is being furnished to the Internal Revenue Service.

on a weekend. The SSA uses Copy A to track wages for social security purposes. The SSA also transmits the W-2 information to the IRS. Employers with 250 or more employees file their W-2s electronically. The employer completes Form 4419, Application for Filing Information Returns Electronically (not shown here), and files it with the IRS.

Form W-3 (Transmittal of Wage and Tax Statements) accompanies the W-2s sent by the employer (see Exhibit 10-11). The W-3 summarizes the information contained on the attached W-2s. The totals on the W-3 must equal the accumulated amounts on the W-2s. Recording payroll and preparing the governmental forms is time-consuming, so many employers use accountants or payroll services to provide these services and to prepare year-end W-2 and W-3 information in a timely manner.

An employer prepares a Form W-2C (Statement of Corrected Income and Tax Amounts) to correct a W-2 and provides appropriate copies to the employee. The employer files Copy A with the Social Security Administration, and a Form W-3C (Transmittal of Corrected Income and Tax Statements) accompanies Copy A to the Social Security Administration. These forms can be accessed through the IRS Web site.

The following penalties are imposed on employers for incorrect or late filing of W-2s:

- A W-2 filed within 30 days of the due date: $15 per return ($75,000 maximum penalty/$25,000 for small businesses).
- A W-2 filed between 30 days late and August 1: $30 per return ($150,000 maximum penalty/$50,000 for small businesses).
- A W-2 filed after August 1: $50 per return ($250,000 maximum penalty/$100,000 for small businesses).

EXHIBIT 10-11

33333	a Control number	For Official Use Only ▶ OMB No. 1545-0008	

b Kind of Payer	941 ☐ Military ☐ 943 ☐ 944 ☐ CT-1 ☐ Hshld. emp. ☐ Medicare govt. emp. ☐ Third-party sick pay ☐	1 Wages, tips, other compensation	2 Federal income tax withheld
		3 Social security wages	4 Social security tax withheld
c Total number of Forms W-2	d Establishment number	5 Medicare wages and tips	6 Medicare tax withheld
e Employer identification number (EIN)		7 Social security tips	8 Allocated tips
f Employer's name		9 Advance EIC payments	10 Dependent care benefits
		11 Nonqualified plans	12 Deferred compensation
		13 For third-party sick pay use only	
		14 Income tax withheld by payer of third-party sick pay	
g Employer's address and ZIP code			
h Other EIN used this year			
15 State Employer's state ID number		16 State wages, tips, etc.	17 State income tax
		18 Local wages, tips, etc.	19 Local income tax
Contact person		Telephone number ( )	For Official Use Only
Email address		Fax number ( )	

Under penalties of perjury, I declare that I have examined this return and accompanying documents, and, to the best of my knowledge and belief, they are true, correct, and complete.

Signature ▶ _____ Title ▶ _____ Date ▶ _____

Form **W-3** Transmittal of Wage and Tax Statements   **2009**   Department of the Treasury Internal Revenue Service

- Penalty of $100 per return or, if higher, 10% of the amount to be reported correctly for intentional disregard of filing requirements, providing payees with incorrect statements, or reporting incorrect information (no maximum penalty).
- The filing of W-2s containing mismatched names and social security numbers: $50 per form.

CONCEPT CHECK 10-5—LO 5

1. The employee uses the information from a W-2 to prepare his or her federal, state, and local (if applicable) tax returns. True or false?
2. Where and when must the employer send Copy A of the W-2 form?
3. Explain the process by which an employer corrects an employee's W-2.
4. What are the maximum penalty amounts per return imposed on a company that prepares incorrect W-2s?

SUPPLEMENTAL WAGE PAYMENTS, BACKUP WITHHOLDING, FORM W-9, ESTIMATED TAX PAYMENTS, AND FORM 1040-ES

LO 6

Supplemental Wage Payments

Supplemental wages are compensation paid in addition to an employee's regular wages and include vacation pay, commissions, bonuses, accumulated sick pay, severance pay, taxable fringe benefits, and expense allowances paid under a nonaccountable plan. The amount

withheld from these supplemental payments depends on whether the employer accounts for the payment separately from regular wages.

Supplemental wages can be combined with regular wages, and the total amount will be taxed as if it were a single payment for a regular payroll period. If the supplemental payments are identified separately from regular wages, the federal income tax withholding method depends on whether the employer withholds income tax from the employee's regular wages.

1. Method 1: If taxes are withheld from the employee's wages:
   a. Withhold a flat 25% (no other percentage is allowed), or
   b. Add the supplemental and regular wages for the period and figure the income tax withholding as if the total was a single payment. Subtract the tax already withheld from regular wages. Withhold the remaining tax from the supplemental wages.
2. Method 2: If taxes are not withheld from the employee's wages:
   a. Add the supplemental and regular wages and calculate the withholding tax as in part b of method 1. (This could occur when the value of the employee's withholding allowances claimed on the W-4 is more than the wages.)

Regardless of the method used to withhold income tax on supplemental wages, the wages are subject to social security, Medicare, and FUTA taxes as well as state withholding (if applicable) and SUTA.

EXAMPLE 10-17   Monique's base salary is $2,000, and she is paid on the first of the month. She is single and claims one withholding allowance. On June 1, 2009, she is paid $2,000, and $151.22 (using the percentage method) is withheld from her earnings. In July 2009 she receives a commission of $1,000, which is included in her regular wages. The amount of withholding is based on a total of $3,000. The amount withheld from her wages is $301.22 (using the percentage method).

EXAMPLE 10-18   Riva is paid a base salary of $2,000 on the first of each month. She is single and claims one withholding allowance. For the pay period of August 1, 2009, the amount of tax withheld (using the percentage method) is $151.22. On August 19, 2009, she receives a bonus of $1,000. Using method 1b, the amount subject to withholding is $3,000. The amount of withholding on the combined $3,000 is $301.22 Subtract the amount already withheld for the month of $151.22. The difference of $150.00 is the amount to be withheld from the bonus payment.

EXAMPLE 10-19   Using the information from Example 10-18, the employer elects to use a flat rate of 25% of withholding on the bonus. In this situation, the amount of withholding on the bonus is $1,000 × 25% = $250.00.

Backup Withholding

Generally an employer must withhold 28% of certain taxable payments if the payee fails to furnish the employer with a correct taxpayer identification number (TIN). Payments subject to backup withholding include interest, dividends, rents, royalties, commissions, nonemployee compensation, and certain other payments made in the course of a trade or business. In addition, certain payments made by brokers and barter exchanges and certain payments made by fishing boat operators are subject to backup withholding.[20]

Payments a taxpayer receives are subject to backup withholding under these circumstances:

• The taxpayer does not furnish a TIN to the requester.
• The IRS tells the requester that a taxpayer has furnished an incorrect TIN.

[20] Publication 15, page 5.

- The IRS informs the payee that he or she is subject to backup withholding due to nonreporting of any interest and dividends on a tax return.
- The payee did not certify to the requester that he or she was not subject to backup withholding.

Backup withholding does not apply to wages, pensions, annuities, IRAs, Section 404(k) distributions from an employee stock ownership plan (ESOP), medical savings accounts, health savings accounts, long-term care benefits, and real estate transactions. The IRS lists specific payees exempt from backup withholding as well as specific types of payments that are exempt from backup withholding. To avoid this backup withholding, payees must furnish a correct TIN to the payer via Form W-9.

Form W-9

Anyone who is required to file an information return with the IRS must supply the payer a correct TIN to report transactions such as income paid to the taxpayer, a real estate transaction, any mortgage interest the taxpayer paid, and contributions to an IRA. The form used to report this information to the payer is a Form W-9.

A U.S. person (or resident alien) uses Form W-9 to

- Certify that the TIN the taxpayer is giving is correct.
- Certify that the taxpayer is not subject to backup withholding.
- Claim exemption from backup withholding if the taxpayer is a U.S. exempt payee.

For federal purposes, a U.S. person includes but is not limited to

- An individual who is a citizen or resident of the United States.
- A partnership, corporation, company, or association created or organized in the United States or under the laws of the United States.
- Any estate (other than a foreign estate) or trust.

Special rules apply to partnerships, corporations, associations, and estates. There are 15 provisions for exemption from backup withholding; refer to the W-9 instructions located at the IRS Web site (www.irs.gov) for a complete list. Failure to furnish a correct TIN to a requester can result in a penalty of $50 for each failure unless the failure is due to reasonable cause, not willful neglect. If a taxpayer makes a false statement with no reasonable basis that results in no backup withholding, the taxpayer is subject to a $500 penalty. Willfully falsifying certifications may subject the taxpayer to criminal penalties including fines and imprisonment.[21] See Exhibit 10-12 for the W-9 form.

Estimated Tax Payments and Form 1040-ES

Estimated tax is the method individuals use to pay tax on income that is taxable but not subject to payroll withholding such as earnings from self-employment, interest, dividends, rents, and alimony. In most cases, a taxpayer must make estimated tax payments if he or she expects to owe at least $1,000 in tax and the taxpayer expects his or her withholding and credits to be less than the smaller of

- 90% of the tax shown on the taxpayer's current return.
- 100% of the tax shown on the taxpayer's prior year tax return if the AGI shown on that return is less than or equal to $150,000 or, if married filing separately, is less than or equal to $75,000.
- 110% of the tax shown on the taxpayer's prior year tax return if the adjusted gross income shown on that return is more than $150,000 or, if married filing separately, is more than $75,000.

[21] IRS instructions for Requester of Form W-9 and Form W-9.

EXHIBIT 10-12

| Form **W-9** (Rev. October 2007) Department of the Treasury Internal Revenue Service | **Request for Taxpayer Identification Number and Certification** | **Give form to the requester. Do not send to the IRS.** |

Print or type — See Specific Instructions on page 2.

Name (as shown on your income tax return)

Business name, if different from above

Check appropriate box: ☐ Individual/Sole proprietor ☐ Corporation ☐ Partnership
☐ Limited liability company. Enter the tax classification (D=disregarded entity, C=corporation, P=partnership) ▶ _____
☐ Other (see instructions) ▶

☐ Exempt payee

Address (number, street, and apt. or suite no.)

Requester's name and address (optional)

City, state, and ZIP code

List account number(s) here (optional)

Part I   Taxpayer Identification Number (TIN)

Enter your TIN in the appropriate box. The TIN provided must match the name given on Line 1 to avoid backup withholding. For individuals, this is your social security number (SSN). However, for a resident alien, sole proprietor, or disregarded entity, see the Part I instructions on page 3. For other entities, it is your employer identification number (EIN). If you do not have a number, see *How to get a TIN* on page 3.

Note. If the account is in more than one name, see the chart on page 4 for guidelines on whose number to enter.

Social security number

or

Employer identification number

Part II   Certification

Under penalties of perjury, I certify that:

1. The number shown on this form is my correct taxpayer identification number (or I am waiting for a number to be issued to me), and
2. I am not subject to backup withholding because: (a) I am exempt from backup withholding, or (b) I have not been notified by the Internal Revenue Service (IRS) that I am subject to backup withholding as a result of a failure to report all interest or dividends, or (c) the IRS has notified me that I am no longer subject to backup withholding, and
3. I am a U.S. citizen or other U.S. person (defined below).

Certification instructions. You must cross out item 2 above if you have been notified by the IRS that you are currently subject to backup withholding because you have failed to report all interest and dividends on your tax return. For real estate transactions, item 2 does not apply. For mortgage interest paid, acquisition or abandonment of secured property, cancellation of debt, contributions to an individual retirement arrangement (IRA), and generally, payments other than interest and dividends, you are not required to sign the Certification, but you must provide your correct TIN. See the instructions on page 4.

Sign Here | Signature of U.S. person ▶ | Date ▶

If a taxpayer meets one of the percentage criteria just noted, it is said that he or she has met the "safe harbor" rule. Safe harbor is a term used to describe a provision of the IRC that protects a taxpayer from penalty.

The estimated tax payments can be paid in total by April 15 (provided this date is a business day—otherwise the next business day) or in four equal amounts by the following dates:

- 1st payment—April 15, 2009.
- 2nd payment—June 16, 2009.
- 3rd payment—September 15, 2009.
- 4th payment—January 15, 2010.

Taxpayers make estimated payments using Form 1040-ES (see Exhibit 10-13). The taxpayer submits the coupon for the appropriate period. It is important to remember to include the correct taxpayer identification number (social security number) and remit the payment to the address given in the instructions. This form is also accessible on the IRS Web site. Using information from Example 10-20, Form 1040-ES is completed in Exhibit 10-13. It shows the first-quarter estimated payment due from Ramon. The total amount of all the estimated payments appears on line 65 of Form 1040 in the Payments section.

EXHIBIT 10-13

Form **1040-ES** Department of the Treasury Internal Revenue Service	**2009 Estimated Tax**	**Payment Voucher 1** OMB No. 1545-0074
File only if you are making a payment of estimated tax by check or money order. Mail this voucher with your check or money order payable to the **"United States Treasury."** Write your social security number and "2009 Form 1040-ES" on your check or money order. Do not send cash. Enclose, but do not staple or attach, your payment with this voucher.		**Calendar year—Due April 15, 2009**

Amount of estimated tax you are paying by check or money order.

	Dollars	Cents
	441	25

Print or type	Your first name and initial **Ramon**	Your last name **Juarez**	Your social security number
	If joint payment, complete for spouse		
	Spouse's first name and initial	Spouse's last name	Spouse's social security number
	Address (number, street, and apt. no.)		
	City, state, and ZIP code. (If a foreign address, enter city, province or state, postal code, and country.)		

EXAMPLE 10-20

Ramon Juarez works as a professor at a local college. He also sells real estate as a part-time business. During 2009 Ramon earned $87,500 from the college. He also earned $15,000 in commissions for selling real estate. He operates his real estate business as a sole proprietorship. Ramon estimates that he will owe $1,765 more in taxes for 2009. He will make an estimated tax payment of $1,765 using Form 1040-ES. Assuming his self-employment earnings are consistent throughout the year, he would make estimated tax payments based on the commissions he earned each period. In this case, if he earned $3,750 in commissions each period, he could remit $441.25 ($1,765/4) to the IRS on each of the due dates.

CONCEPT CHECK 10-6—LO 6

1. Describe the two methods that are available to calculate the withholding from supplemental payments.
2. Payments subject to backup withholding are withheld at a flat tax rate of 28% if the payee fails to furnish the payer with a correct TIN. True or false?
3. What is a Form W-9?
4. What is the penalty for failing to furnish a correct TIN to a requester?
5. Taxpayers use Form 1040-ES to remit additional amounts to the IRS so that they receive a refund when they file Form 1040. True or false?

Summary

LO 1: Explain the tax issues associated with payroll and Form 1040.

• Withholding taxes are imposed on taxpayers to help fund government operations using a "pay-as-you-go" system.
• Form W-2 is the starting point for Form 1040.

LO 2: Calculate federal income tax withholding, social security, and Medicare taxes on wages and tips.

• Withholding of taxes is an approximation of the proportionate share of total tax liability the employee will owe to the federal government.
• A W-4 form is completed by the employee to list filing status and claim withholding allowances. This information is used by the employer to calculate withholding.
• Two withholding methods are allowed: the wage bracket method and the percentage method.
• FICA taxes encompass social security taxes and Medicare taxes.
• Social security tax withholding is 6.2% of each employee's wages up to a maximum of $106,800 of wages for 2009. Medicare withholding is 1.45% of all wages.
• The employer must pay an additional amount equal to the amount withheld from employees.

LO 3: Describe the rules for reporting and paying payroll taxes including deposit penalties and Form 941.

- Employers must make payroll tax deposits of amounts withheld from employees' wages.
- Employers typically deposit taxes monthly or semiweekly. A lookback period generally determines the frequency of required deposits.
- Employers must make timely deposits to an authorized federal depository bank using Form 8109-B or through the Electronic Federal Tax Payment System (EFTPS).
- Payroll taxes not paid on a timely basis are subject to deposit penalties that range from 2% to 15%.
- Form 941 is used to report amounts withheld for income, social security, and Medicare taxes for the quarter. It is due by the end of the month following the end of a quarter.
- With IRS permission, Form 944 can be filed for small business employers.

LO 4: Calculate self-employment taxes, unemployment taxes, Form 940, taxes for household employees, and Schedule H.

- Self-employment taxes are based on net earnings of $400 or more generated by a sole proprietor taxpayer. The rate paid is based on both the employee and employer portions.
- 50% of self-employment taxes are permitted *for* AGI deduction on Form 1040.
- The federal unemployment tax (FUTA) is 6.2% of wages up to $7,000. The maximum credit for state unemployment taxes (SUTA) is 5.4%, reducing the amount due to the IRS to 0.8%.
- Form 940 is filed annually by the employer to report and reconcile FUTA liabilities and payments.
- Household workers are considered employees subject to federal income, social security, Medicare, and FUTA taxes.
- Schedule H reports tax information for household workers. It is filed with Form 1040.

LO 5: Determine employer payroll reporting requirements, including Forms W-2 and W-3.

- Employers report wages earned and taxes withheld to employees on Form W-2.
- A Form W-2 must be given to each employee no later than January 31 with a copy to the Social Security Administration by February 28 (February 29 in a leap year).
- Form W-3 is a transmittal form that summarizes all employee W-2s prepared by a company.

LO 6: Explain supplemental wage payments, backup withholding, Form W-9, estimated tax payments, and Form 1040-ES.

- Supplemental wages are compensation paid in addition to an employee's regular wages.
- Withholding on supplemental wages can be calculated using one of two methods: using a flat tax rate of 25% or combining the supplemental wages with regular wages.
- Anyone required to file an information return with the IRS must supply the payer a correct taxpayer ID number (TIN) using Form W-9.
- Failure of a taxpayer to furnish a TIN to a requester can result in a $50 penalty. A taxpayer making a false statement that results in no backup withholding is subject to a civil penalty of $500.
- Failure to provide a correct TIN can result in 28% withholding on certain taxable payments.
- Form 1040-ES is used when a taxpayer must make tax payments for estimated taxes due.
- Estimated payments are required if unpaid tax liability >= $1,000 and withholding and credits do not meet certain "safe harbor" thresholds.
- Estimated taxes are due April 15, June 15, September 15, and January 15 or on the next business day if any of these dates falls on a weekend or holiday.

Discussion Questions

LO 2   1.   What type of compensation is subject to employer withholding?

_____

_____

_____

LO 2   2.   Who completes Form W-4 , and what is its purpose? What information does it provide to employers?

_____

_____

_____

LO 2   3.   If a taxpayer makes $30,000 per year, will the annual withholding differ depending on whether the taxpayer is paid weekly, semimonthly, or monthly? Explain.

_____

_____

_____

LO 2   4.   If a taxpayer works more than one job, will the withholding from the various jobs necessarily cover his or her tax liability? Explain.

_____

_____

_____

LO 2   5.   In addition to federal tax withholding, what other taxes are employers required to withhold from an employee's paycheck? How are the calculations made?

_____

_____

_____

LO 2   6.   Who pays FICA? What are the percentages and limits on the payments?

_____

_____

_____

LO 2   7.   When are employees required to report tips to their employer? Are tips subject to the same withholding requirements as regular salary?

_____

_____

_____

LO 2   8.   What are the tip reporting requirements for large food and beverage establishments?

_____

_____

_____

LO 3   9.   When must employers make payroll tax deposits?

_____

_____

_____

LO 3   10. What is a *lookback* period?

_____

_____

_____

LO 3   11. When must monthly and semiweekly schedule depositors make their deposits? What taxes must be deposited?

_____

_____

_____

LO 3   12. What are the penalties for not making timely payroll deposits?

_____

_____

_____

LO 3   13. If a business fails to make payroll deposits, who is held responsible?

_____

_____

_____

LO 3   14. How often must employers report payroll taxes to the IRS? What form must the employer file?

_____

_____

_____

LO 3   15. What are the rules for deducting COBRA assistance payments on Form 941 for the 2009 tax year?

_____

_____

_____

LO 4   16. What is the FUTA tax, and at what percentage is it assessed?

_____

_____

_____

LO 4   17. What individuals are subject to the payroll taxes on household employees?

_____

_____

_____

LO 4   18. How are household payroll taxes reported? When are they due?

_____

_____

_____

LO 5   19. How does an employer report wages to the employee, the federal government, and the Social Security Administration? When is this notification due?

_____

_____

_____

LO 5   20. What are the penalties imposed on employers for filing incorrect W-2s?

_____

_____

_____

LO 6   21. What are supplemental wage payments?

_____

_____

_____

LO 6   22. Explain the two methods for income tax withholding on supplemental wage payments.

_____

_____

_____

LO 6   23. Explain the provisions of backup withholding and the conditions under which an employer must comply with these provisions.

_____

_____

_____

LO 6   24. What is a Form W-9? Why must this form be filed?

_____

_____

_____

LO 6   25. Explain the purpose of Form 1040-ES. Under what conditions are taxpayers required to file 1040-ES? When is Form 1040-ES filed?

_____

_____

_____

Multiple-Choice Questions

LO 2   26. Employees claim withholding allowances on Form W-4. Each withholding allowance claimed lowers their annual withholding base by what amount for calendar year 2009?

a. $3,500.

b. $3,550.

c. $3,600.

d. $3,650.

LO 2   27. Iesiah is single and is paid $1,154 per week and claims one allowance. What is the amount of federal income tax withheld on Iesiah's gross wages for the week? Use the wage bracket table in the appendix at the end of the chapter.

   a. $175.

   b. $178.

   c. $180.

   d. $195.

LO 2   28. Latrice is married, is paid $2,685 semimonthly, and claims four withholding allowances. What is the amount of federal income tax withheld on Latrice's gross wages for the semimonthly period? Use the wage bracket table in the appendix at the end of the chapter.

   a. $193.

   b. $196.

   c. $199.

   d. $216.

LO 2   29. Erica earned $95,700 during 2009. How much will her employer withhold from her, in total, for FICA taxes?

   a. $7,244.55.

   b. $7,321.05.

   c. $7,432.65.

   d. $7,458.75.

LO 2   30. Doris has two jobs and earned $98,000 from her first job and $18,000 from her second job. How much total FICA taxes will Doris have withheld from her wages from working two jobs?

   a. $7,466.00.

   b. $8,669.40.

   c. $8,843.00.

   d. $8,874.00.

LO 2   31. Carlos earned a total of $150,000 for 2009. How much in FICA tax will his employer be required to withhold in his name?

   a. $6,621.60 in social security and $1,548.60 in Medicare.

   b. $6,621.60 social security and $2,175.00 in Medicare.

   c. $9,300.00 in social security and $2,175.00 in Medicare.

   d. $9,300.00 in social security and $1,548.60 in Medicare.

LO 2   32. Ken has two jobs, and both employers withheld FICA tax. From his first job, he earned $85,000, and from his second job, he earned $25,000. How much can Ken claim as an additional payment on his Form 1040 as excess social security paid in 2009?

   a. $0.

   b. $86.80.

   c. $198.40.

   d. $248.00.

LO 2   33. Sheila earned $75 in tips in September. When must she inform her employer of her tips on Form 4070 for federal income tax and FICA withholding purposes?

   a. By September 30.

   b. By October 10.

c. By October 31.

d. She is not subject to payroll taxes on tips of less than $80 in any one month.

LO 2 34. In a large food or beverage establishment, any tip shortfall from a directly tipped employee is recorded on the employee's W-2 as

    a. W-2 box 1—Wages, tips, other compensation.

    b. W-2 box 14—Other.

    c. W-2 box 8—Allocated tips.

    d. W-2 box 7—Social security tips.

LO 2 35. Employers with a payroll tax liability of less than $2,500 at the end of any quarter must pay their tax liability

    a. Directly to the authorized depository after the end of the quarter when Form 941 is filed.

    b. Directly to the authorized depository on the same day the Form 941 is mailed.

    c. Directly to the Internal Revenue Service when they file Form 941.

    d. Directly only if they use the EFTPS form of payment before Form 941 is filed.

LO 3 36. Lauer Company started its business on June 30, 2009. On July 10 it paid wages for the first time and accumulated a tax liability of $48,000. On Friday, July 24, it incurred a tax liability of $52,000. How is Lauer Company treated as a depositor?

    a. Monthly because new companies do not have a lookback period.

    b. Semiweekly because its accumulated tax liability is $100,000.

    c. Monthly because its accumulated tax liability is not more than $100,000 on any one day.

    d. Semiweekly for this pay period only and then monthly for the remainder of the year.

LO 3 37. What is the penalty for sending a required tax payment (unless specifically excluded) directly to the Internal Revenue Service?

    a. 2%.

    b. 5%.

    c. 10%.

    d. 15%.

LO 3 38. A semiweekly schedule depositor's payroll period ends and is paid on Friday, June 26. The depositor (employer) must deposit the federal taxes for this pay period on or before

    a. June 30.

    b. June 26.

    c. The following Wednesday.

    d. The following Friday.

LO 3 39. To what amount of employer tax accumulation does the one-day deposit rule apply?

    a. $75,000.

    b. $100,000.

    c. More than $100,000.

    d. An amount between $75,000 and $99,999.

LO 4 40. Employers are required to deposit FUTA taxes when their liability exceeds

    a. $100.

    b. $500.

  c. $1,000.

  d. $1,500.

LO 4   41. Household employees are subject to FICA withholding if they are paid at least what amount during 2009?

  a. $1,000.

  b. $1,500.

  c. $1,600.

  d. $1,700.

LO 4   42. Employers pay a maximum unemployment tax of 6.2% on how much of an employee's taxable wages for 2009?

  a. $1,000.

  b. $1,500.

  c. $3,200.

  d. $7,000.

LO 2, 4   43. Carlos has two jobs; he is an attorney (not a partner) in a law firm and he has a small legal practice (sole proprietorship) providing real estate legal services. How does he compute his federal income tax for the year?

  a. His wages from the law firm are taxed as an employee, as are his wages from the private practice.

  b. His wages from the law firm are considered self-employment, as are the earnings from his private practice.

  c. His wages from the law firm are taxed as an employee, and his earnings from his private practice are taxed as a self-employed proprietor.

  d. His wages from the law firm are taxed as an employee, and his earnings from self-employment are taxed up to the maximum for social security only.

LO 4   44. Adrienne is a self-employed attorney. She has net earnings (profit) from her practice of $80,500. Her self-employment taxes for the year are

  a. $9,982.00.

  b. $11,374.29.

  c. $12,919,12.

  d. $12,316.50.

LO 4   45. Carol works for ABC Company and earned $63,000 for 2009. How much in FUTA tax is her employer required to withhold in her name? Assume that the employer receives the maximum credit for state unemployment taxes.

  a. $0.

  b. $56.

  c. $378.

  d. $434.

LO 4   46. On January 2, 2009, Jane employed a part-time household worker in her home. She paid the household worker $300 per month for 2009. What amount of FICA tax is Jane required to record on Schedule H?

  a. $168.30.

  b. $275.40.

   c. $336.60.

   d. $550.80.

LO 6   47. A taxpayer with 2009 AGI of $238,000 has no income tax withholding and is required to pay estimated taxes. The taxpayer can avoid an underpayment penalty by paying

   a. At least 90% of the 2009 tax liability ratably over four quarterly payments.

   b. At least 100% of the 2008 tax liability ratably over four quarterly payments.

   c. At least 90% of the 2008 tax liability ratably over four quarterly payments.

   d. 100% of the 2009 tax liability ratably over four quarterly payments.

LO 6   48. Henry received a bonus of $4,400 from his employer. Which one of the following federal income withholding tax amounts is not in accordance with IRS rules regarding supplemental wage payments? Henry earns biweekly wages of $3,500, is single, and claims one allowance. Assume his employer uses the percentage method of withholding.

   a. $1,286.13 on his bonus if taxes were already withheld from his regular pay.

   b. $1,637.80 if his bonus and wages are paid at the same time during the pay period.

   c. $1,777.12 if his bonus is taxed at the supplemental wage percentage and added to his regular wages paid in the same period.

   d. $1,963.25 if his bonus and wages are paid at the same time during the pay period.

Problems   **LO 2**   49. Allison is paid $500 per week. What is the amount of federal income tax withheld from Allison's paycheck under the following conditions? Use the percentage method table in the appendix to this chapter.

   a. Allison is single and claims three withholding allowances.

   _____

   b. Allison is married and claims three withholding allowances.

   _____

   c. Allison is single and claims one withholding allowance.

   _____

LO 2   50. Martin is married and claims five exemptions on his W-4. What is his federal income tax withholding under the following conditions? Use the percentage method table in the appendix to this chapter.

   a. Martin is paid semimonthly, and his gross pay is $2,300 per paycheck.

   _____

   b. Martin is paid monthly, and his gross pay is $2,800 per paycheck.

   _____

   c. Martin is paid weekly, and his gross pay is $3,300 per paycheck.

   _____

LO 2   51. Lisa earns $48,000 per year. She is married and claims two allowances. Use the wage bracket tables available online or the percentage method tables in the appendix to this chapter.

   a. If she is paid weekly, what is her withholding per paycheck?

   _____

   b. If she is paid monthly, what is her withholding per paycheck?

   _____

    c. If she is paid semimonthly, what is her withholding per paycheck?

    d. In each of these circumstances, should the annual withholding differ? Explain.

LO 2   52. Henry, who earned $58,500 during 2009, is paid on a monthly basis, is married, and claims four allowances.

    a. What is Henry's federal tax withholding?

    b. What is Henry's FICA withholding?

    53. Roberto's salary is $107,000 in 2009. Roberto is paid on a semimonthly basis, is single, and claims one allowance.

    a. What is Roberto's federal tax withholding per pay period?

    b. What is Roberto's FICA withholding per pay period before he reaches the social security limit?

    c. What is Roberto's FICA withholding per pay period after he reaches the social security limit?

LO 3   54. Baker Company is trying to determine how often it needs to deposit payroll taxes for calendar year 2009. The company made the following quarterly payroll tax deposits during the last two years:

Quarter beginning January 1, 2007	$10,000
Quarter beginning April 1, 2007	10,000
Quarter beginning July 1, 2007	11,000
Quarter beginning October 1, 2007	12,000
Quarter beginning January 1, 2008	12,000
Quarter beginning April 1, 2008	12,000
Quarter beginning July 1, 2008	11,000
Quarter beginning October 1, 2008	12,000

    a. What is the lookback period and amount?

    b. In 2009 how often must Baker Company make payroll deposits?

LO 4   55. CFG Company has the following employees:

	Wages Paid
Eddie	$12,000
Melanie	8,000
Shelly	22,000

CFG receives the maximum credit for state unemployment taxes. Calculate the FUTA tax that CFG Company would owe for the year.

_____

_____

LO 4   56. Jacob Turner hired Jen Hatcher to clean his house starting on January 2 at $55 per week. Jacob does not withhold any federal taxes. Assume that Jen does not clean houses for anyone else. Assume Jacob paid $1,000 in wages for the 4th quarter of 2008.

a. How much in payroll taxes should Jacob pay?

_____

b. Complete the Schedule H that Jacob must file.

c. When should Schedule H be filed?

_____

LO 2, 4   57. Jones Company has the following employees on payroll:

	Semimonthly Payroll	Withholding Allowances	Marital Status
Heather	$1,500	4	Married
Keith	$1,700	3	Married
Thad	$3,100	1	Single
Abbie	$3,500	2	Married

Calculate the payroll for the end of February. Include in your calculations federal withholding, FICA, and FUTA. Assume that Jones Company received the maximum credit for state unemployment taxes.

_____

_____

_____

_____

Tax Return Problems

These problems are intended to be completed manually. Go to the IRS Web site at www.irs.gov to obtain 2009 forms.

Tax Return Problem 1   Use the information from Problem 57. Prepare the Form 941 including Schedule B for the first quarter of 2009. Assume that the payroll is consistent every pay period beginning in January through March 31 and that all tax deposits were made on a timely basis as required. Jones Company's Employer Identification Number (EIN) is 36-1238975, and its address is 1825 Elkhart Way, Columbus, GA 31904. Assume Jones paid $2,400 in COBRA assistance payments for two individuals for the quarter.

Tax Return Problem 2   Use the information from Problem 57. Prepare the Form 940 for 2009. Assume that Jones Company has timely paid all amounts due to the state unemployment fund (assume a total amount of $3,471) and that the payroll was consistent throughout the entire year. No FUTA deposits were made during the year.

Tax Return Problem 3   Use the information from Problem 57. Prepare a Form W-2 for Abbie Cooper. Her SSN is 123-45-6789 and her address is 988 Main Street, Midland, GA 31820. The EIN for Jones Company is 36-1238975, and its address is 1825 Elkhart Way, Columbus, GA 31904.

We have provided selected filled-in source documents on our Web site at www.mhhe.com/cruz2010.

Appendix

PARTIAL WAGE BRACKET METHOD WITHHOLDING

Tables for Percentage Method of Withholding
(For Wages Paid Through December 2009)

TABLE 1—WEEKLY Payroll Period

(a) SINGLE person (including head of household)—

If the amount of wages (after subtracting withholding allowances) is:

The amount of income tax to withhold is:

Not over $138 . . . . $0

Over—	But not over—		of excess over—
$138	—$200	. . . 10%	—$138
$200	—$696	. . . $6.20 plus 15%	—$200
$696	—$1,279	. . . $80.60 plus 25%	—$696
$1,279	—$3,338	. . . $226.35 plus 28%	—$1,279
$3,338	—$7,212	. . . $802.87 plus 33%	—$3,338
$7,212	. . . .	$2,081.29 plus 35%	—$7,212

(b) MARRIED person—

If the amount of wages (after subtracting withholding allowances) is:

The amount of income tax to withhold is:

Not over $303 . . . . $0

Over—	But not over—		of excess over—
$303	—$470	. . . 10%	—$303
$470	—$1,455	. . . $16.70 plus 15%	—$470
$1,455	—$2,272	. . . $164.45 plus 25%	—$1,455
$2,272	—$4,165	. . . $368.70 plus 28%	—$2,272
$4,165	—$7,321	. . . $898.74 plus 33%	—$4,165
$7,321	. . . .	$1,940.22 plus 35%	—$7,321

TABLE 2—BIWEEKLY Payroll Period

(a) SINGLE person (including head of household)—

If the amount of wages (after subtracting withholding allowances) is:

The amount of income tax to withhold is:

Not over $276 . . . . $0

Over—	But not over—		of excess over—
$276	—$400	. . . 10%	—$276
$400	—$1,392	. . . $12.40 plus 15%	—$400
$1,392	—$2,559	. . . $161.20 plus 25%	—$1,392
$2,559	—$6,677	. . . $452.95 plus 28%	—$2,559
$6,677	—$14,423	. . . $1,605.99 plus 33%	—$6,677
$14,423	. . . .	$4,162.17 plus 35%	—$14,423

(b) MARRIED person—

If the amount of wages (after subtracting withholding allowances) is:

The amount of income tax to withhold is:

Not over $606 . . . . $0

Over—	But not over—		of excess over—
$606	—$940	. . . 10%	—$606
$940	—$2,910	. . . $33.40 plus 15%	—$940
$2,910	—$4,543	. . . $328.90 plus 25%	—$2,910
$4,543	—$8,331	. . . $737.15 plus 28%	—$4,543
$8,331	—$14,642	. . . $1,797.79 plus 33%	—$8,331
$14,642	. . . .	$3,880.42 plus 35%	—$14,642

TABLE 3—SEMIMONTHLY Payroll Period

(a) SINGLE person (including head of household)—

If the amount of wages (after subtracting withholding allowances) is:

The amount of income tax to withhold is:

Not over $299 . . . . $0

Over—	But not over—		of excess over—
$299	—$433	. . . 10%	—$299
$433	—$1,508	. . . $13.40 plus 15%	—$433
$1,508	—$2,772	. . . $174.65 plus 25%	—$1,508
$2,772	—$7,233	. . . $490.65 plus 28%	—$2,772
$7,233	—$15,625	. . . $1,739.73 plus 33%	—$7,233
$15,625	. . . .	$4,509.09 plus 35%	—$15,625

(b) MARRIED person—

If the amount of wages (after subtracting withholding allowances) is:

The amount of income tax to withhold is:

Not over $656 . . . . $0

Over—	But not over—		of excess over—
$656	—$1,019	. . . 10%	—$656
$1,019	—$3,152	. . . $36.30 plus 15%	—$1,019
$3,152	—$4,922	. . . $356.25 plus 25%	—$3,152
$4,922	—$9,025	. . . $798.75 plus 28%	—$4,922
$9,025	—$15,863	. . . $1,947.59 plus 33%	—$9,025
$15,863	. . . .	$4,204.13 plus 35%	—$15,863

TABLE 4—MONTHLY Payroll Period

(a) SINGLE person (including head of household)—

If the amount of wages (after subtracting withholding allowances) is:

The amount of income tax to withhold is:

Not over $598 . . . . $0

Over—	But not over—		of excess over—
$598	—$867	. . . 10%	—$598
$867	—$3,017	. . . $26.90 plus 15%	—$867
$3,017	—$5,544	. . . $349.40 plus 25%	—$3,017
$5,544	—$14,467	. . . $981.15 plus 28%	—$5,544
$14,467	—$31,250	. . . $3,479.59 plus 33%	—$14,467
$31,250	. . . .	$9,017.98 plus 35%	—$31,250

(b) MARRIED person—

If the amount of wages (after subtracting withholding allowances) is:

The amount of income tax to withhold is:

Not over $1,313 . . . . $0

Over—	But not over—		of excess over—
$1,313	—$2,038	. . . 10%	—$1,313
$2,038	—$6,304	. . . $72.50 plus 15%	—$2,038
$6,304	—$9,844	. . . $712.40 plus 25%	—$6,304
$9,844	—$18,050	. . . $1,597.40 plus 28%	—$9,844
$18,050	—$31,725	. . . $3,895.08 plus 33%	—$18,050
$31,725	. . . .	$8,407.83 plus 35%	—$31,725

TABLES

SINGLE Persons—WEEKLY Payroll Period
(For Wages Paid Through December 2009)

If the wages are—		And the number of withholding allowances claimed is—										
At least	But less than	0	1	2	3	4	5	6	7	8	9	10
		The amount of income tax to be withheld is—										
$0	$145	$0	$0	$0	$0	$0	$0	$0	$0	$0	$0	$0
145	150	1	0	0	0	0	0	0	0	0	0	0
150	155	1	0	0	0	0	0	0	0	0	0	0
155	160	2	0	0	0	0	0	0	0	0	0	0
160	165	2	0	0	0	0	0	0	0	0	0	0
165	170	3	0	0	0	0	0	0	0	0	0	0
170	175	3	0	0	0	0	0	0	0	0	0	0
175	180	4	0	0	0	0	0	0	0	0	0	0
180	185	4	0	0	0	0	0	0	0	0	0	0
185	190	5	0	0	0	0	0	0	0	0	0	0
190	195	5	0	0	0	0	0	0	0	0	0	0
195	200	6	0	0	0	0	0	0	0	0	0	0
200	210	7	0	0	0	0	0	0	0	0	0	0
210	220	8	1	0	0	0	0	0	0	0	0	0
220	230	10	2	0	0	0	0	0	0	0	0	0
230	240	11	3	0	0	0	0	0	0	0	0	0
240	250	13	4	0	0	0	0	0	0	0	0	0
250	260	14	5	0	0	0	0	0	0	0	0	0
260	270	16	6	0	0	0	0	0	0	0	0	0
270	280	17	7	0	0	0	0	0	0	0	0	0
280	290	19	8	1	0	0	0	0	0	0	0	0
290	300	20	10	2	0	0	0	0	0	0	0	0
300	310	22	11	3	0	0	0	0	0	0	0	0
310	320	23	13	4	0	0	0	0	0	0	0	0
320	330	25	14	5	0	0	0	0	0	0	0	0
330	340	26	16	6	0	0	0	0	0	0	0	0
340	350	28	17	7	0	0	0	0	0	0	0	0
350	360	29	19	8	1	0	0	0	0	0	0	0
360	370	31	20	10	2	0	0	0	0	0	0	0
370	380	32	22	11	3	0	0	0	0	0	0	0
380	390	34	23	13	4	0	0	0	0	0	0	0
390	400	35	25	14	5	0	0	0	0	0	0	0
400	410	37	26	16	6	0	0	0	0	0	0	0
410	420	38	28	17	7	0	0	0	0	0	0	0
420	430	40	29	19	8	1	0	0	0	0	0	0
430	440	41	31	20	10	2	0	0	0	0	0	0
440	450	43	32	22	11	3	0	0	0	0	0	0
450	460	44	34	23	13	4	0	0	0	0	0	0
460	470	46	35	25	14	5	0	0	0	0	0	0
470	480	47	37	26	16	6	0	0	0	0	0	0
480	490	49	38	28	17	7	0	0	0	0	0	0
490	500	50	40	29	19	8	1	0	0	0	0	0
500	510	52	41	31	20	10	2	0	0	0	0	0
510	520	53	43	32	22	11	3	0	0	0	0	0
520	530	55	44	34	23	13	4	0	0	0	0	0
530	540	56	46	35	25	14	5	0	0	0	0	0
540	550	58	47	37	26	16	6	0	0	0	0	0
550	560	59	49	38	28	17	7	0	0	0	0	0
560	570	61	50	40	29	19	8	1	0	0	0	0
570	580	62	52	41	31	20	10	2	0	0	0	0
580	590	64	53	43	32	22	11	3	0	0	0	0
590	600	65	55	44	34	23	13	4	0	0	0	0
600	610	67	56	46	35	25	14	5	0	0	0	0
610	620	68	58	47	37	26	16	6	0	0	0	0
620	630	70	59	49	38	28	17	7	0	0	0	0
630	640	71	61	50	40	29	19	8	1	0	0	0
640	650	73	62	52	41	31	20	10	2	0	0	0
650	660	74	64	53	43	32	22	11	3	0	0	0
660	670	76	65	55	44	34	23	13	4	0	0	0
670	680	77	67	56	46	35	25	14	5	0	0	0
680	690	79	68	58	47	37	26	16	6	0	0	0
690	700	80	70	59	49	38	28	17	7	0	0	0
700	710	83	71	61	50	40	29	19	8	1	0	0
710	720	85	73	62	52	41	31	20	10	2	0	0
720	730	88	74	64	53	43	32	22	11	3	0	0
730	740	90	76	65	55	44	34	23	13	4	0	0
740	750	93	77	67	56	46	35	25	14	5	0	0
750	760	95	79	68	58	47	37	26	16	6	0	0
760	770	98	80	70	59	49	38	28	17	7	0	0
770	780	100	83	71	61	50	40	29	19	8	1	0

SINGLE Persons—WEEKLY Payroll Period
(For Wages Paid Through December 2009)

If the wages are—		And the number of withholding allowances claimed is—										
At least	But less than	0	1	2	3	4	5	6	7	8	9	10
		The amount of income tax to be withheld is—										
$780	$790	$103	$85	$73	$62	$52	$41	$31	$20	$10	$2	$0
790	800	105	88	74	64	53	43	32	22	11	3	0
800	810	108	90	76	65	55	44	34	23	13	4	0
810	820	110	93	77	67	56	46	35	25	14	5	0
820	830	113	95	79	68	58	47	37	26	16	6	0
830	840	115	98	80	70	59	49	38	28	17	7	0
840	850	118	100	83	71	61	50	40	29	19	8	1
850	860	120	103	85	73	62	52	41	31	20	10	2
860	870	123	105	88	74	64	53	43	32	22	11	3
870	880	125	108	90	76	65	55	44	34	23	13	4
880	890	128	110	93	77	67	56	46	35	25	14	5
890	900	130	113	95	79	68	58	47	37	26	16	6
900	910	133	115	98	80	70	59	49	38	28	17	7
910	920	135	118	100	83	71	61	50	40	29	19	8
920	930	138	120	103	85	73	62	52	41	31	20	10
930	940	140	123	105	88	74	64	53	43	32	22	11
940	950	143	125	108	90	76	65	55	44	34	23	13
950	960	145	128	110	93	77	67	56	46	35	25	14
960	970	148	130	113	95	79	68	58	47	37	26	16
970	980	150	133	115	98	80	70	59	49	38	28	17
980	990	153	135	118	100	83	71	61	50	40	29	19
990	1,000	155	138	120	103	85	73	62	52	41	31	20
1,000	1,010	158	140	123	105	88	74	64	53	43	32	22
1,010	1,020	160	143	125	108	90	76	65	55	44	34	23
1,020	1,030	163	145	128	110	93	77	67	56	46	35	25
1,030	1,040	165	148	130	113	95	79	68	58	47	37	26
1,040	1,050	168	150	133	115	98	80	70	59	49	38	28
1,050	1,060	170	153	135	118	100	83	71	61	50	40	29
1,060	1,070	173	155	138	120	103	85	73	62	52	41	31
1,070	1,080	175	158	140	123	105	88	74	64	53	43	32
1,080	1,090	178	160	143	125	108	90	76	65	55	44	34
1,090	1,100	180	163	145	128	110	93	77	67	56	46	35
1,100	1,110	183	165	148	130	113	95	79	68	58	47	37
1,110	1,120	185	168	150	133	115	98	80	70	59	49	38
1,120	1,130	188	170	153	135	118	100	83	71	61	50	40
1,130	1,140	190	173	155	138	120	103	85	73	62	52	41
1,140	1,150	193	175	158	140	123	105	88	74	64	53	43
1,150	1,160	195	178	160	143	125	108	90	76	65	55	44
1,160	1,170	198	180	163	145	128	110	93	77	67	56	46
1,170	1,180	200	183	165	148	130	113	95	79	68	58	47
1,180	1,190	203	185	168	150	133	115	98	80	70	59	49
1,190	1,200	205	188	170	153	135	118	100	82	71	61	50
1,200	1,210	208	190	173	155	138	120	103	85	73	62	52
1,210	1,220	210	193	175	158	140	123	105	87	74	64	53
1,220	1,230	213	195	178	160	143	125	108	90	76	65	55
1,230	1,240	215	198	180	163	145	128	110	92	77	67	56
1,240	1,250	218	200	183	165	148	130	113	95	79	68	58

$1,250 and over Use Table 1(a) for a **SINGLE person** on page 5. Also see the instructions on page 3.

Buzzwords

Annuity: Series of payments made pursuant to a contract usually between an individual and an insurance company, brokerage firm, or bank. Payments are normally uniformly spaced (monthly, quarterly, or annually).

Beneficiary: Person(s) entitled to receive the benefits from a plan.

Contributions: Amounts deposited into the tax-deferred plan by the donor. Contributions may or may not be tax-deductible, depending on the plan. When making a contribution to the plan, the donor is said to have "funded" the plan.

Distributions: Amounts withdrawn from the tax-deferred plan. Distributions are made to, or for the benefit of, the beneficiary and must be made in accordance with applicable tax rules. Distributions may or may not be taxable, depending on the plan.

Donor: Person(s) or entity(ies) responsible for making contributions to a plan. The donor and the beneficiary can be, and often are, the same individual.

Taxability of plan earnings: Except in unusual circumstances, earnings derived from the investment of plan assets are not taxed in the year earned.

Tax-deferred retirement plan: Account held by a trustee to accumulate and invest assets to be distributed to a beneficiary during retirement.

Tax-deferred plans for other purposes: Account held by a trustee to accumulate and invest assets to pay for a specific purpose such as health care or education.

Trustee: Entity—often a bank, brokerage firm, or insurance company—legally responsible to ensure that a plan's contributions and distributions follow legal and tax rules.

will be taxed; if the plan is funded with already-taxed dollars, some or all of the distributions will not be taxed. This rule of thumb is not always true, but it is a good place to start.

In this chapter, we also discuss the tax rules pertaining to distributions from an *annuity*, which is a series of payments made pursuant to a contract. The contract is usually between an individual and an insurance company, a financial services company, or an employer. Annuities often arise in conjunction with the payout phase of a retirement plan. The primary tax issue associated with an annuity payment is how much of each payment is taxable.

Payments to a tax-advantaged retirement plan are often tax-deductible and are shown as a *for AGI* deduction on Form 1040, line 32 (for an IRA) or 28 (for Keogh, SEP, or SIMPLE plans). Form 1040A accommodates only IRA contributions (line 17). Deductible payments made by employers (with respect to pension plans and 401(k) plans) are reported on the employer's tax return. Distributions from retirement plans and annuities are usually taxable, at least in part, and are found on Form 1040, lines 15 and 16, or Form 1040A, lines 11 and 12.

CONCEPT CHECK 11-1—LO 1	1. Tax-deferred retirement accounts are essentially tax-free accounts. True or false?
	2. The period in which accumulated assets are paid to plan beneficiaries is known as the _____ period.
	3. A Keogh plan is an example of an individual-based retirement plan. True or false?
	4. Two examples of employer-based retirement plans are _____ and _____.
	5. Distributions from pension plans are taxable if the contributions were made using dollars that were not previously taxed. True or false?

EMPLOYER-SPONSORED RETIREMENT PLANS
LO 2

Qualified Pension Plans

A *qualified pension plan* provides systematic and definite payments to employees and their beneficiaries after retirement. Individuals receive payments over a period of years, often for life. Most often, the payments are made monthly. The *retirement benefit* amount is determined

using factors such as years of employee service and compensation received.[2] The amount of payment must be "definitely determinable" using actuarial assumptions in a manner not subject to employer discretion.[3]

A qualified pension plan must meet strict requirements including (1) not discriminating in favor of highly compensated employees, (2) formation and operation for the exclusive benefit of employees or their beneficiaries, (3) having certain vesting and funding requirements, and (4) having certain minimum participation standards.[4]

A qualified pension plan provides significant tax benefits to both employers and employees. The primary benefits follow:

- The employer gets an immediate deduction for contributions.[5]
- Employer contributions are not compensation to the employee.
- Earnings from investments held by the plan are not taxable when earned.[6]
- Plan assets or earnings are not taxable to employees until the amounts are distributed.[7]

Qualified pension plans may be noncontributory or contributory. In a noncontributory plan, only the employer (not the employee) contributes. In a contributory plan, the employee can choose to contribute beyond employer contributions. The employer can require employee contributions as long as the plan is nondiscriminatory toward highly paid individuals.

A pension plan can also be a qualified profit-sharing plan. Contributions are not required on an annual basis, and it does not matter whether the employer has positive income in a contribution year.[8] Profit-sharing plans must have a definite, predetermined formula for allocating plan contributions to participants and for establishing benefit payments. Note that the required formula applies to the allocation of those contributions once made, not to the amount of the contributions.

Qualified plans may be either a defined contribution plan or a defined benefit plan. *Defined contribution plans* establish the contribution but do not establish the amount of retirement benefits. These plans provide an individual account for each participant and pay benefits based on those accounts.[9] Thus the amount of eventual retirement benefits is unknown. *Defined benefit plans* are those plans that are not defined contribution plans.[10] These defined benefit plans provide a stream of definitely determinable retirement benefits. Defined benefit plans are often deemed to be "less risky" to beneficiaries because, by design, they provide greater certainty as to the amount and timing of future benefits.

TAX YOUR BRAIN

Are qualified pension plans likely to be defined contribution or defined benefit plans? Which are qualified profit-sharing plans likely to be?

ANSWER

Pension plans are more likely to be defined benefit plans, and profit-sharing plans are more likely to be defined contribution plans. By their very nature, defined benefit plans require a more precisely defined stream of inputs (contributions) to enable them to provide a precisely defined stream of outputs (benefits). Contributions to profit-sharing plans are more variable, which makes it less likely there will be a "stream of definitely determinable benefits."

[2] An example is a pension plan that pays each retired employee an annual pension (payable on a monthly basis) equal to 3% of the employee's final salary for each year of service to the company. Thus an employee who worked 20 years for the company would receive an annual pension equal to 60% of his or her final annual salary.

[3] IRC § 401(a)(25).

[4] IRC § 401(a).

[5] IRC § 404.

[6] IRC § 501(a).

[7] IRC § 402.

[8] IRC § 401(a)(27).

[9] IRC § 414(i).

[10] IRC § 414(j).

Normally a bank, insurance company, or financial services company administers a trust that receives the contributions made to pension or profit-sharing plans. One reason for the trust arrangement is that, in the event that the business has financial difficulties or declares bankruptcy, creditors cannot attach the assets set aside for the benefit of the employees. From a practical matter, few companies are in the business of running a pension plan.

To obtain and retain qualified status, a pension or profit-sharing plan must meet complex rules, including the following:

- Be for the exclusive benefit of the employees and their beneficiaries.[11]

- Not discriminate in favor of highly compensated employees—employees who either (a) own more than 5% of the corporation's stock in the current or prior year or (b) received more than $110,000 compensation in the previous year and were in the top 20% of employees based on compensation.[12]

- Have adequate coverage for rank-and-file employees. In general, the plan must benefit at least 70% of those employees who are not highly compensated.[13] A defined benefit plan must also meet certain minimum participation requirements.[14]

- Meet certain minimum vesting standards.[15] *Vesting* occurs when an employee obtains a nonforfeitable right to his or her benefits. Employee contributions must vest immediately. Employer contributions must fully vest after five years of service or must vest 20% in the third year of service and increase 20% per year thereafter until fully vested after seven years of service.

TAX YOUR BRAIN   Why would Congress require vesting rules for employer contributions?

ANSWER

It did so for at least two reasons. First, by design, pension plans provide benefits to participants during retirement. By requiring vesting, Congress ensured that participants will receive payments because the payments cannot go to others or back to the company. Second, qualified plans give employers an immediate tax deduction for contributions. With vesting, Congress has reasonable assurance that the employer deductions are valid in the long run.

Qualified plans must also meet certain limitations on contributions and benefits. Annual per employee additions to a defined contribution plan cannot exceed the lower of $49,000 or 100% of the employee's compensation.[16] Annual additions include employer contributions, employee contributions, and forfeitures (for employees leaving the company before full vesting).

Defined benefit plans have no restrictions on contributions. However, these plans are restricted to annual benefits to a participant equal to the lower of $195,000 or 100% of average compensation of the participant for the highest three years.[17]

For profit-sharing plans, employers can take a maximum annual deduction of 25% of compensation paid.[18]

---

[11] IRC § 401(a).

[12] IRC §414(q). The 20% criterion is effective only if the taxpayer elects. The $110,000 amount is subject to annual inflation adjustment.

[13] IRC § 410(b).

[14] IRC § 401 (a)(26).

[15] IRC § 411(a).

[16] IRC § 415(c)(1). The contribution limit is subject to annual inflation adjustment.

[17] IRC § 415(b)(1). The contribution limit is subject to annual inflation adjustment.

[18] IRC § 404(a)(3)(A).

401(k) Plans

An employer can provide a 401(k) plan (named after the IRC section from which it comes) in addition to, or in the place of, a qualified pension or profit-sharing plan. A 401(k) plan is a qualified profit-sharing plan under which an employee can choose to receive a specified portion of her or his wages directly in cash or can elect to have the employer pay the amount on the employee's behalf into a qualified trust for the benefit of the employee on retirement.[19] Trust payments are made with pretax dollars. A 403(b) plan (again named after the IRC section that created it) is equivalent to a 401(k) plan but is for employees of educational and certain tax-exempt organizations.

An employee may elect to defer up to $16,500 under a 401(k) plan.[20] Employees age 50 or over can defer an additional $5,500. Any excess contributions must either be returned to the employee by April 15 of the following year or be included in the employee's gross income.

EXAMPLE 11-1

Fouad earns $80,000 in taxable wages. His employer establishes a 401(k) plan in which he participates. Fouad elects to have 3% of his wages paid into the 401(k) plan. For the year, his employer withholds $2,400 ($80,000 × 3%) from his paychecks on a pretax basis and deposits the amount in trust on Fouad's behalf. As a result, Fouad's taxable wages for the year are $77,600 ($80,000 − $2,400).

A 401(k) plan must meet all of the qualification rules established for pension and profit-sharing plans. In addition, amounts held in the trust cannot be distributed except in the case of termination of the plan or the employee's (a) separation from service, death, or disability, (b) attainment of the age of 59½, or (c) hardship.[21] Hardship distributions are permitted if the employee has an "immediate heavy financial need" that can be met with the distribution and that cannot be relieved by alternative sources such as loans or insurance.[22] Additional nondiscrimination rules apply to 401(k) plans as enumerated in IRC § 401(k)(3).

Keogh Plans

Self-employed individuals are not employees, so they cannot participate in a qualified pension or profit-sharing plan established by an employer. However, they can establish an individual Keogh plan, which is subject to the same contribution and benefit limitations as pension or profit-sharing plans. For defined contribution Keogh plans, self-employed individuals can contribute the lower of $49,000 or 25% of earned income from self-employment.[23] For purposes of the calculation, earned income cannot exceed $245,000.[24] Earned income from self-employment is determined after the deduction for one-half of the self-employment taxes paid and after the amount of the Keogh contribution.

EXAMPLE 11-2

Walter is a self-employed architect. In 2009 his earnings, before the Keogh deduction but after deduction for one-half the self-employment tax, are $60,000. His Keogh deduction for purposes of the 25% calculation is

$$\$60,000 - 0.25X = X$$

$$\text{Thus } X = \$48,000$$

where X is the amount of self-employment income after the Keogh deduction.

Walter is entitled to contribute the lower of $49,000 or $12,000 (25% of $48,000). Thus his maximum Keogh contribution is $12,000.

---

[19] IRC § 401(k)(2).

[20] IRC § 402(g)(1). The contribution limit is subject to annual inflation adjustment.

[21] IRC § 401(k)(2).

[22] Reg. § 1.401(k)-1(d)(2).

[23] IRC § 415(c). The contribution limit is subject to annual inflation adjustment.

[24] IRC § 404(l). The earned income limit is subject to annual inflation adjustment.

Defined benefit Keogh plans are subject to the $195,000/100% funding rules given previously for qualified defined benefit plans. Keogh plans must be established by the end of the tax year (once established, the plan continues from year to year). Contributions are required no later than the due date of the return, including extensions.[25]

If a self-employed individual has employees, the Keogh plan must also cover full-time employees under the same nondiscrimination, vesting, and other rules established for qualified plans. Contributions for these employees are deductible by the self-employed individual on Schedule C of his or her tax return.

Simplified Employee Pensions

Qualified pension and profit-sharing plans are complex and can be difficult to establish and administer. Small businesses can establish a *Simplified Employee Pension* (SEP).[26] With a SEP, an employer contributes to IRA accounts of its employees, up to a specified maximum contribution. SEPs must conform to the following rules:

- All employees who have reached the age of 21, who have worked for the employer for at least three of the preceding five years, and who received at least $550 in compensation must be covered.[27]
- Contributions cannot discriminate in favor of highly compensated employees.
- Annual deductible contributions cannot exceed the lower of 25% of the employee's compensation (with a maximum of $245,000) or the $49,000 limitation for defined contribution plans.[28]
- The employer cannot restrict the employee's withdrawals.[29]

Initial SEP adoption must be effective no later than the due date of the employer's return, including extensions. Most small employers adopt an SEP by using Form 5305-SEP. Contributions to the SEP are required no later than the due date of the return of the employer, including extensions.

Self-employed individuals can create and contribute to an SEP. Contribution limits are determined in the same manner as for Keogh plans.

SIMPLE Plans

Employers with 100 or fewer employees who do not have a qualified pension or profit-sharing plan can establish a *SIMPLE retirement plan* for their employees.[30] Under a SIMPLE plan, the employer creates an IRA or a 401(k) account for each employee. Eligible employees are those who earned at least $5,000 during any two preceding years and who are reasonably expected to earn at least $5,000 in the current year. Employees are not required to contribute. SIMPLE plans are not subject to the nondiscrimination rules that apply to other qualified plans. Thus there is no requirement that a certain number or percentage of employees must participate in the SIMPLE plan.

Employees can elect to contribute an employer-specified percentage (or dollar amount if the employer agrees) of their pretax wages with a maximum annual contribution of $11,500.[31] Employees age 50 or older can elect to make additional contributions of up to $2,500 (for a maximum of $14,000).

[25] IRC § 404(a)(6).

[26] IRC § 408(k).

[27] IRC § 408(k)(2). The $550 compensation amount is subject to annual inflation adjustment.

[28] Both dollar amounts are subject to annual inflation adjustment.

[29] IRC § 408(k)(4)(B).

[30] IRC 408(p).

[31] IRC § 408(p)(2)(A)(ii). The maximum contribution is subject to annual inflation adjustment.

From Shoebox to Software

Contributions to qualified plans, Keogh plans, SEPs, and SIMPLE plans are deductible as a *for* AGI deduction to the extent contributed by the individual. The portion contributed by the employer is not deductible (remember that the employer contribution is not taxable to the employee in the first place).

In tax software, employee contributions to these plans are generally reported on a worksheet. You enter the amount of the deductible contribution in the appropriate box, and that amount carries forward to Form 1040, line 28.

The plan's trustee will report for an individual covered by an SEP or SIMPLE plan the amount of employee contribution in box 8 or 9 of Form 5498 (see Exhibit 11-1).

The trustees of qualified pension plans report employee contributions to employees on a similar form.

Employers either must make a matching contribution of up to 3% (in most instances) of the employee's compensation or must make a nonelective contribution of 2% of compensation for each employee eligible to participate (whether or not the employee actually participates). Contributions to a SIMPLE plan fully and immediately vest to the employee.

EXAMPLE 11-3	Acme Corporation established a SIMPLE plan for its 10 eligible employees, each of whom earned over $5,000 in the current and prior years. Seven employees elect to contribute 5% of their pretax wages while the other three decline to participate. Acme can choose to make either matching contributions of 3% of wages for the seven employees who elected to participate or a contribution of 2% of wages for all 10 employees.

EXHIBIT 11-1

☐ CORRECTED (if checked)			
TRUSTEE'S or ISSUER'S name, street address, city, state, and ZIP code	**1** IRA contributions (other than amounts in boxes 2-4, 8-10, 13a, 14a, and 15a) $	OMB No. 1545-0747 20**09** Form **5498**	**IRA Contribution Information**
	2 Rollover contributions $		
	3 Roth IRA conversion amount $	**4** Recharacterized contributions $	**Copy B** **For** **Participant**
TRUSTEE'S or ISSUER'S federal identification no. PARTICIPANT'S social security number	**5** Fair market value of account $	**6** Life insurance cost included in box 1 $	
PARTICIPANT'S name	**7** IRA ☐ SEP ☐ SIMPLE ☐ Roth IRA ☐		This information is being provided to the Internal Revenue Service.
	8 SEP contributions $	**9** SIMPLE contributions $	
Street address (including apt. no.)	**10** Roth IRA contributions $	**11** Check if RMD for 2010 ☐	
	12a RMD date	**12b** RMD amount $	
City, state, and ZIP code	**13a** Postponed contribution $	**13b** Year	**13c** Code
	14a Repayments $	**14b** Code	
Account number (see instructions)	**15a** Other contributions $	**15b** Code	

Form **5498**   (keep for your records)   Department of the Treasury - Internal Revenue Service

Employers establish a SIMPLE plan using Form 5305-S or 5305-SA. The employer retains the form and does not file it with the IRS. Employers must initially adopt the plan between January 1 and October 1. The employer must make contributions no later than the due date of the employer's return, including extensions.

CONCEPT CHECK 11-2—LO 2

1. Qualified pension plans are either defined _____ plans or defined _____ plans.
2. Employees must make contributions to qualified pension plans. True or false?
3. The maximum contribution to a 401(k) plan is _____ for individuals under age 50.
4. A Keogh plan can be used by self-employed individuals. True or false?
5. A SIMPLE plan can be used by employers with 100 or fewer employees who also meet other requirements. True or false?

INDIVIDUAL-SPONSORED RETIREMENT PLANS
LO 3

Individual-sponsored retirement plans are Individual Retirement Accounts (IRAs). There are two types: a traditional IRA and a Roth IRA. Although the accounts sound similar, they have significant differences.

Traditional IRA

A traditional IRA is a tax-deferred retirement account for individuals with earned income (employees and self-employed individuals). Qualified individuals can make IRA contributions and take a *for* AGI deduction equal to the lower of $5,000 or the amount of compensation for the year.[32] Individuals who are age 50 or older as of the end of the tax year can contribute the lower of $6,000 or the amount of annual compensation. Earnings on invested contributions grow tax-deferred until distribution.

A qualified individual is someone who is not an active participant and whose spouse is not an active participant in an employer-sponsored retirement plan (qualified pension or profit-sharing plan, Keogh, 401(k), SEP, SIMPLE). Even if an individual (or spouse) is an active participant, she or he can make a deductible IRA contribution if her or his AGI is below certain limits. The allowed IRA deduction begins to be phased out for active participants when AGI exceeds certain amounts, depending on the filing status of the taxpayer.[33] For joint filers, the amount is $89,000, for single or head of household filers the amount is $55,000, and for married filing separately the amount is zero.[34]

Once AGI reaches the indicated amounts, the taxpayer can use the following formula to determine the disallowed portion of the IRA deduction:

$$\frac{\text{AGI} - \text{Applicable limit}}{\$10,000 \text{ or } 20,000} \times \$\,5,000 = \text{Disallowed deduction}$$

The denominator of the fraction is $10,000 for taxpayers filing as single or head of household and $20,000 for married filing jointly. For taxpayers over 50 years old, the $5,000 figure is $6,000.

---

[32] IRC § 219(b)(1).
[33] IRC § 219(g)(3)(B).
[34] These amounts increase each year in accordance with an IRC schedule.

EXAMPLE 11-4	Teresa, age 31, is single and reported AGI of $56,200 in tax year 2009. She is an active participant in her employer's pension plan. Her disallowed deduction is $600 ([$56,200 − $55,000] / $10,000 × $5,000). Thus, she would be entitled to make a deductible IRA contribution of $4,400 ($5,000 − $600). If Teresa's AGI exceeded $65,000, her deductible contribution would be zero. If her employer did not have a pension plan, her deductible contribution would be $5,000.

Special rules apply to married taxpayers. If both spouses are employed and neither is covered by an employer plan, each spouse can make a deductible contribution to separate IRA accounts, subject to the lower of $5,000 or earned income limits.

EXAMPLE 11-5	Earl and Amanda are both under age 50 and file a joint return. Neither is covered under an employer plan. Each of them contributed equally to their AGI of $93,000. Both Earl and Amanda are entitled to make a deductible $5,000 contribution to an IRA (total of $10,000). Note that the AGI limitations do not affect the calculations because neither spouse was covered under an employer plan.

If only one spouse is employed, and that spouse is not covered under an employer plan (or his or her AGI is less than the phaseout limitation), the working spouse and the nonworking spouse may *each* make a deductible $5,000 contribution toward an IRA. This result is also true if the "nonworking" spouse earned less than $5,000 as long as the couple's *combined* earned income is at least $10,000. This is an exception to the general rule that contributions are permitted only when the taxpayer has earned income.

If one spouse is covered under an employer-sponsored plan but the other spouse is not covered, the noncovered spouse may contribute up to $5,000 toward a deductible IRA.[35] The deduction is phased out for joint AGI between $166,000 and $176,000.

A taxpayer who is not eligible to make a deductible contribution to an IRA because he or she is an active participant in an employer plan and earns too much can make a designated *non*deductible IRA contribution.[36] The contribution is limited to the lower of $5,000 or 100% of compensation ($6,000 for those age 50 or over) but must be reduced by the amount of any deductible contribution allowed.[37] Even though the contribution may be nondeductible, the earnings of the IRA will grow tax-deferred until withdrawn.

EXAMPLE 11-6	Bonnie is an active participant in an employer plan. Because of AGI limitations, her deductible IRA contribution is limited to $1,200. She can make a nondeductible IRA contribution of up to $3,800. If Bonnie's AGI were high enough that she was ineligible to make any *deductible* contribution, she would be permitted a $5,000 *nondeductible* contribution.

The IRA trust account must be established and contributions, both deductible and nondeductible, must be made no later than the due date of the taxpayer's income tax return, not including extensions (April 15 for most taxpayers). Contributions made after January 1 and before April 15 may be treated as a deduction in the prior year. No form or statement is filed with the tax return for the year the traditional IRA is established.

Deductible contributions are *not* permitted once a taxpayer reaches age 70½. Taxpayers can make deductible and nondeductible contributions to the same IRA, although determining the taxability of distributions becomes problematic.

Contributions in excess of the amount allowable are subject to a 6% excise tax,[38] which is reported on Form 5329.

[35] IRC § 219(g)(7).

[36] IRC § 408(o).

[37] Thus, a maximum contribution of $5,000 can be made, whether deductible or not deductible.

[38] IRC § 4973(a).

Roth IRA

With a traditional IRA, contributions are deductible (assuming eligibility requirements are met), the account grows tax-deferred, and distributions are fully taxable. With a Roth IRA, contributions are not deductible, the account grows tax-free, and distributions are not taxable. In effect, when choosing between traditional and Roth IRAs, taxpayers are trading the nondeductibility of contributions for the nontaxability of distributions.

A *Roth IRA* is an IRA designated as a Roth when it is established.[39] Taxpayers can make nondeductible contributions to a Roth IRA in an amount equal to the lower of $5,000 or 100% of compensation, reduced by the amount of contributions for the year to other IRAs (not including SEP or SIMPLE plans).[40] Taxpayers who are age 50 or over at the end of the year are permitted a contribution of $6,000 or 100% of compensation. Permitted contributions are phased out ratably starting when AGI reaches $166,000 for joint returns, $105,000 for those filing single or head of household, and $0 for married filing separately.[41] The phaseout range is $15,000 for single and head of household and $10,000 for joint filers. The formulas to determine the disallowed contribution in the phaseout range follow.

Use this formula for joint returns:

$$\frac{\text{AGI} - \text{Applicable limit}}{\$10,000} \times \$5,000 = \text{Disallowed contribution}$$

Use this formula for single or head of household returns:

$$\frac{\text{AGI} - \text{Applicable limit}}{\$15,000} \times \$5,000 = \text{Disallowed contribution}$$

For taxpayers age 50 or older, the $5,000 figure is $6,000.

AGI limits do not include any income resulting from the conversion of a traditional IRA to a Roth IRA.

Roth IRAs, like traditional ones, are established with a trustee and must be established and funded no later than the due date of the return for the contribution year, not including extensions.[42] Taxpayers use Form 5305-R (or -RA or -RB) to set up the account. This form is not filed with the taxpayer's return. Unlike traditional IRAs, contributions to a Roth IRA are permitted after age 70½ subject to normal funding rules.

Excess contributions to a Roth IRA are subject to a 6% excise tax under the rules applicable to a traditional IRA.

Roth 401(k) plans are permitted. A Roth 401(k) has the funding characteristics of a 401(k) (can defer up to $16,500 or $22,000 if age 50 or over) and the tax characteristics of a Roth IRA (contributions are not deductible and distributions are not taxable).

CONCEPT CHECK 11-3—LO 3

1. Two types of individual-sponsored retirement plans are _____ and _____ .
2. A single individual, age 58, with wages of $30,000 can make a tax-deductible contribution of up to $_____ to a traditional IRA.
3. A married couple with earned income of $200,000 is ineligible to make a deductible contribution to a traditional IRA. True or false?
4. Generally distributions from a Roth IRA are not taxable. True or false?

---

[39] IRC § 408A(b).
[40] IRC § 408A(c)(2)(B) and § 408A(f)(2).
[41] IRC § 408A(c)(3).
[42] IRC § 408A(c)(7) and § 219(f)(3).

From Shoebox to Software

Qualified individuals can make deductible contributions to a traditional IRA. Trustees report contributions on Form 5498 (see Exhibit 11-1).

In your software, you generally enter information concerning IRA contributions on a worksheet or directly on Form 5498. If the requirements to make a deductible contribution are met, the amount in box 1 of Form 5498 is entered as a contribution at the top of the form. It is important to realize that the amount in box 1 is only the amount *contributed*—the trustee makes no determination as to whether the amount is deductible. It is the responsibility of the taxpayer or preparer to report the proper deduction.

Information from the worksheet is carried forward to Form 1040, line 32, or Form 1040A, line 17.

If you open the tax return file for Jose and Maria Ramirez and then open the IRA summary sheet, you will see that the maximum allowable IRA contribution for Jose is zero. This is so because he was covered by a retirement plan at work and he earned in excess of the income limitation.

Contributions to a Roth IRA are in box 10 of Form 5498. You record this amount in the appropriate place on the IRA worksheet or the form.

TAX-DEFERRED NONRETIREMENT PLANS
LO 4

The two major types of tax-deferred nonretirement plans are health-related plans and education-related plans. In Chapter 4, we discussed health savings accounts. Here we describe the Coverdell Education Savings Account.

Coverdell Education Savings Account

Taxpayers who meet AGI limitations can contribute to a Coverdell Education Savings Account (CESA) exclusively to pay the qualified elementary, secondary, or higher education expenses of the beneficiary.[43] CESAs are similar to Roth IRAs in that contributions are not deductible, earnings accumulate tax-free, and distributions are not taxable (if used for their intended purpose).

Contributions are limited to $2,000 per year per beneficiary, must be in cash, and must be made before the beneficiary turns 18.[44]

Subject to limitations as to the amount, any person can contribute to a CESA for any person (themselves included). The contributor is not required to report a certain amount of earned income, nor must the contributor be related to the beneficiary. A contributor (or contributors) can establish multiple CESAs for multiple beneficiaries, and an individual can be the beneficiary of multiple CESAs. However, for any given tax year, the aggregate contributions to all CESAs for a specific individual beneficiary cannot exceed $2,000.

EXAMPLE 11-7   Roger and Shelly have one child, Caroline. They established a CESA for Caroline. Shelly's parents can establish a separate CESA for Caroline or can contribute to the CESA already established. The total permitted contributions to all CESAs for which Caroline is the beneficiary cannot exceed $2,000. Thus, if Caroline's parents contribute $1,500 to her CESA in 2009, the grandparents can contribute a maximum of $500 in 2009.

Permitted contributions begin to phase out ratably when the contributor's AGI reaches $190,000 for joint returns or $95,000 for single and head of household returns.[45] When AGI

[43] IRC § 530(b)(1).

[44] IRC § 530(b)(1)(A).

[45] AGI is increased by foreign income excluded from AGI under IRC § 911, 931, and 933.

exceeds $220,000 for married taxpayers or $110,000 for single or head of household taxpayers, no CESA contribution is allowed. The formulas to determine the disallowed contribution in the phaseout range are as follows.

Use this formula for joint returns:

$$\frac{\text{AGI} - \text{Applicable limit}}{\$30,000} \times \$2,000 = \text{Disallowed contribution}$$

Use this formula for single or head of household returns:

$$\frac{\text{AGI} - \text{Applicable limit}}{\$15,000} \times \$2,000 = \text{Disallowed contribution}$$

EXAMPLE 11-8	Vance and Martha file a joint return showing AGI of $196,300. Their disallowed CESA contribution is $420 ([$196,300 − $190,000] / [$30,000 × $2,000]), so their permitted contribution is $1,580 ($2,000 − $420). If their AGI was over $220,000, Vance and Martha would not be permitted to make a CESA contribution.

Taxpayers establish the trust using a Form 5305-E or 5305-EA. As with the Roth IRA, the form is not filed with the taxpayer's return but is retained in the tax files. The trustee must be a bank or other entity or person who will administer the account properly.[46]

You can find additional information about CESAs in Chapter 7 of IRS Publication 970—Tax Benefits for Education.

CONCEPT CHECK 11-4—LO 4	1. Contributions to Coverdell Education Savings Accounts (CESAs) are not deductible. True or false? 2. The maximum annual contribution to a CESA is $_____. 3. Contributions to CESA accounts begin to be phased out when AGI reaches $_____ for a single taxpayer.

DISTRIBUTIONS FROM TAX-DEFERRED PENSION PLANS
LO 5

General

All pension plans have an accumulation period when contributions are received and invested and a distribution period when assets are paid to owners or beneficiaries. Individuals with pension plan assets normally withdraw those assets during their retirement. The payments received during retirement are *distributions* or *withdrawals*.

Recall that a defined benefit plan provides a retiree certain specified distributions over a specified period or for life. Normally retirees receive fixed distributions (often with inflation adjustments) on a regular basis (such as monthly or quarterly). Many large corporations and unions have defined benefit plans. Retirees do not have an ownership interest in any portion of the plan assets; they are simply entitled to a stream of payments (called an *annuity*).

The second category of pension plans is a defined contribution plan. These plans accumulate assets from contributions and earnings that belong to a specific individual but that are not predetermined as to the value upon retirement. An IRA is an example of a defined contribution plan. While the retiree worked, he or she contributed to the IRA and invested those contributions. The IRA assets belong to the retiree, but there is no guarantee as to

[46] IRC § 530(b)(1)(B).

either their value at retirement or the date the assets will be exhausted once withdrawals commence. Because assets in defined contribution plans belong to the retiree, he or she usually can specify the amount and timing of plan withdrawals.

To reduce the chance of living beyond the point that their pension plan assets are exhausted, beneficiaries of defined contribution plans sometimes choose to buy an annuity contract using some or all of the plan assets. In doing so, the beneficiary is trading a lump sum for a stream of payments. Effectively, the beneficiary becomes a participant in a defined benefit plan to the extent of the annuity.

You can find additional information pertaining to distributions from tax-deferred pension plans in IRS Publication 575—Pension and Annuity Income.

Distributions from Qualified Pension Plans

A distribution from a qualified pension plan (pension and profit-sharing plan, Keogh, 401(k), 403(b), IRA, SEP, SIMPLE) may be fully taxable, nontaxable, or a combination of both. Generally proceeds are tax-free if they are attributable to contributions made with taxed dollars (a nondeductible contribution), and proceeds are taxable if they are attributable to contributions made with untaxed dollars (a deduction was allowed or income was excluded) or if they are attributable to tax-deferred earnings. The annuity provisions govern taxability of distributions from qualified employer retirement plans.[47]

To apply the simplified method of taxing payments from a qualified plan, the taxpayer must first determine the amount that she or he contributed to the plan with previously taxed dollars. The previously taxed investment is divided by the number of anticipated future payments (see the following table). The resulting fraction represents the proportion of each payment that will be tax-free. The remainder of the annuity payment is taxable as ordinary income. If the employee contributed nothing to the plan, the entire payment is taxable.

If the annuity is payable over the life of a single individual, the number of anticipated payments is determined as of the starting date of the payments as follows:

Age of the Individual	Number of Anticipated Monthly Payments
55 or under	360
56–60	310
61–65	260
66–70	210
71 or over	160[48]

If the annuity is payable over the life of more than one individual (the lives of a retiree and his or her spouse), the number of anticipated payments is determined as of the starting date of the payments as follows:

Combined Ages of the Individuals	Number of Anticipated Monthly Payments
110 or under	410
111–120	360
121–130	310
131–140	260
141 or over	210[49]

[47] Specifically, the simplified rules under IRC § 72(d).

[48] IRC § 72(d)(1)(B)(iii).

[49] IRC § 72(d)(1)(B)(iv).

EXAMPLE 11-9

Zeke is entitled to monthly payments of $2,000 over his life from his employer's qualified pension plan. He contributed $97,500 to the plan prior to his retirement at age 64. Zeke would be able to exclude $375 ($97,500 / 260) from each payment as a nontaxable return of his contributions. The remaining $1,625 would be taxable at ordinary income rates.

EXAMPLE 11-10

Instead of taking $2,000 a month over his life, Zeke chose to receive monthly payments of $1,800 a month over his life and that of his 62-year-old wife. The combined ages of Zeke and his wife are 126. Thus, Zeke would be permitted to exclude $314.52 ($97,500/310) from each payment with the remaining $1,485.48 being taxable.

The anticipated payment tables assume monthly payments. If payments are received other than monthly, appropriate adjustments are made. For example, the number of anticipated monthly payments for an individual age 55 or under is 360. If the actual payments are made quarterly, the number of anticipated quarterly payments will be 90 (360/4). This would be the number used in the denominator to determine the exclusion amount.

Retirement plans (other than Roth IRAs) must make required distributions.[50] For many plans (especially qualified pension and profit-sharing plans), the plan administrator determines the required distribution rules. Such determination is not a concern to the recipient. However, especially in the case of a traditional IRA, the taxpayer may be required to make the appropriate required minimum distribution calculations.

Generally, distributions from a retirement plan can be taken without penalty once the owner (the person who made the contributions) reaches age 59½. However, it is usually good tax planning to defer withdrawals for as long as practical so that the account balance can continue to grow tax-deferred. Tax-deferral cannot continue indefinitely—the tax code mandates certain minimum withdrawals. These minimum withdrawals commence once the plan owner reaches age 70½.

The required minimum distribution (RMD) for a year is equal to the account balance at the end of the prior year divided by the minimum distribution period. The minimum distribution period is determined in accordance with life expectancy tables provided by the IRS in Publication 590. Some of these tables are provided in the appendix to this chapter. Table III is the one used by owners of the retirement plan who are either unmarried or whose spouse is not more than 10 years younger. Table I is used by the beneficiary of a retirement plan after the original owner has died. Table II (not provided but available in Publication 590) is used by owners whose spouse is more than 10 years younger. When referring to the tables, the age used is the age of the taxpayer as of the end of the year for which the distribution is calculated.

EXAMPLE 11-11

Arlene is age 77 and must determine her required minimum distribution for tax year 2009. She would use the balance in her retirement account as of the end of 2008 and would refer to the proper life expectancy table using her age as of the end of 2009.

EXAMPLE 11-12

Mort is unmarried and has been receiving distributions from his retirement plan. He must determine his required minimum distribution for 2009. He is age 76 at the end of 2009. At the end of 2008 his plan had a balance of $110,000. Using Table III, his life expectancy is 22.0 years. Mort must receive at least $5,000 ($110,000/22.0) from his retirement plan in 2009. If Mort were married and the age difference between Mort and his spouse was 10 years or less, the answer to this question would be the same. If the age difference were more than 10 years, Mort would need to use Table II in IRS Publication 590 to determine the appropriate life expectancy.

[50] IRC § 401(a)(9).

Once a plan owner reaches age 70½, there are special rules associated with determining and distributing the very first payment.

Plans can distribute each employee's interest either (1) in a lump sum on the required *beginning date* or (2) in payments starting on the required beginning date, over the life expectancy of the employee or of the employee and a designated beneficiary. The required beginning date is April 1 of the calendar year following the year in which the taxpayer reaches age 70½.[51]

Note that the first distribution is calculated for the tax year in which the taxpayer reaches age 70½. However, that first distribution does not need to be made until April 1 of the tax year after the taxpayer reaches age 70½.

EXAMPLE 11-13	Taxpayer A's 70th birthday was February 1, 2009, so the taxpayer reaches age 70½ on August 1, 2009. The distribution calculated for 2009 must be distributed to the taxpayer no later than April 1, 2010. Taxpayer B's 70th birthday was November 1, 2009, so the taxpayer is 70½ on May 1, 2010. There is no required distribution for 2009. The distribution calculated for 2010 must be distributed to the taxpayer no later than April 1, 2011.

EXAMPLE 11-14	Mort is unmarried. His 70th birthday was March 1, 2009. Thus he reached age 70½ on September 1, 2009, and his required beginning date is April 1, 2010. At the end of 2008, the balance in his retirement plan was $300,000. He needs to calculate his tax year 2009 required minimum distribution (2009 is the year he turned 70½). At the end of 2009 he will be 70 years old. Using Table III, the life expectancy to use in the calculations is 27.4 years. Thus he must receive at least $10,949 ($300,000/27.4) from his retirement plan no later than April 1, 2010.

EXAMPLE 11-15	Assume Mort's 70th birthday was November 1, 2008. Thus he reached age 70½ on May 1, 2009, and his required beginning date is April 1, 2010. At the end of 2008, the balance in his retirement plan was $550,000. He needs to calculate his tax year 2009 required minimum distribution (2009 is the year he turned 70½). At the end of 2009 he will be 71 years old. Using Table III, the life expectancy to use in the calculations is 26.5 years. Thus he must receive at least $20,755 ($550,000/26.5) from his retirement plan no later than April 1, 2010.

When the owner of a retirement plan dies, special rules apply. These rules depend on whether the beneficiary of the plan (the person who inherits the plan assets) is the spouse or someone else. If the sole beneficiary is the spouse, he or she can elect to be treated as the owner. If so, the beneficiary would account for the retirement plan using the rules just indicated. If the beneficiary is not the spouse (or if the spouse does not make the election to be treated as the owner), the beneficiary generally determines the required minimum distribution for the year of death using his or her age with reference to Table I. For each subsequent year, that factor is reduced by 1. There are special rules for beneficiaries that are not individuals.

EXAMPLE 11-16	Conrad died in 2009 at age 80. His nephew Arnold was the sole beneficiary and was age 67. Using Table I, Arnold would use 19.4 as the appropriate factor in 2009, 18.4 in 2010, and so forth.

Caution: The distribution rules for beneficiaries can be complex. Refer to the Internal Revenue Code and to IRS Publication 590 for additional information.

If required minimum distributions are not made properly, the taxpayer is subject to a nondeductible excise tax equal to 50% of the shortfall.[52] The penalty is reported on Form 5329.

---

[51] In the case of non-IRA accounts, it is the later of 70½ or the year in which the employee retires.
[52] IRC § 4974(a).

TAX YOUR BRAIN   Why are minimum withdrawal provisions required?

ANSWER

Recall that, for the most part, funds in a pension plan have never been taxed. If there were no minimum distribution standards, the assets could remain in the account and continue to accumulate tax-free indefinitely. In an effort to ensure eventual taxation of contributions and earnings, Congress enacted the minimum withdrawal provisions.

Special RMD Rule for 2009 Only

In late 2008 stock and bond markets fell considerably. The retirement account portfolios of many retirees were adversely affected. Partially in response to these significant losses, the Worker, Retiree, and Employer Recovery Act of 2008 (WRERA 2008) was passed by Congress and signed into law on December 23, 2008.

Under the law, required minimum distributions (RMDs) are suspended for calendar year 2009 (*only*) for all IRA, 401(k), 403(b), and most 457(b) plans. The suspension does *not* apply to taxpayers who reach age 70½ in 2008 and who are required to make their first withdrawal no later than April 1, 2009. In other words,

if an individual has been taking RMDs from a plan for a period of time, he or she will not be required to take a distribution in 2009. If, however, an individual's first withdrawal must be taken no later than April 1, 2009, that individual must make the withdrawal. Taxpayers can still elect to take voluntary withdrawals.

WRERA 2008 applies only to RMDs in 2009. The RMD rules will again be effective in 2010 and beyond. Thus, the discussion pertaining to RMD rules remains an important component of your understanding of tax-deferred retirement plans.

Retirement plan distributions that are includable in income are subject to a 10% additional tax unless the distributions meet *one* of the following exceptions:

- Distributed to an employee or retiree at or after age 59½.
- Made to a beneficiary or estate on or after the death of the employee.
- Paid attributable to a disability.
- Made to an employee over the age of 55 after separation from service (in the case of qualified pension and profit-sharing plans).
- Paid for deductible medical expenses (above the 7.5% threshold) whether or not the employee itemizes.
- Paid from an IRA to unemployed individuals for health insurance premiums.
- Paid from a CESA for higher education expenses.
- Paid from an IRA for "first home" purchases, with a $10,000 lifetime maximum.
- Paid from a qualified plan to an alternative payee under provisions of a qualified domestic relations order.
- Distributed to pay an IRS tax levy on the plan.
- Paid as part of a series of substantially equal periodic payments over the life expectancy of the employee (an annuity). In the case of qualified pension and profit-sharing plans, these payments can start only after separation from service.[53]

In the case of SIMPLE plans, distributions not meeting one or more of the preceding exceptions made during the first two years of participation are subject to a 25% additional tax, rather than 10%.

The purpose of the additional tax is to discourage withdrawals from retirement plans until the beneficiary retires unless the distribution is for one of the special purposes.

[53] IRC § 72(t)(1) through (8).

Taxpayers can choose to have the plan administrator withhold taxes on distributions. These withholdings are reported on Form 1099-R, box 4 (see Exhibit 11-3 later in this chapter).

CONCEPT CHECK 11-5—LO 5

1. A participant in a defined benefit plan is entitled to only a stream of payments. True or false?
2. Distributions from qualified pension plans may be taxable, nontaxable, or both. True or false?
3. The number of anticipated payments from a pension plan for a single individual, age 68, is _____.
4. The number of anticipated payments from a pension plan for a married couple aged 59 and 63 is _____.
5. Except in 2009, distributions are required from a traditional IRA. True or false?

Taxation of Traditional IRA Distributions

Distributions from traditional IRAs are fully taxable if the IRA was entirely funded with deductible contributions. If an IRA was funded partially with deductible contributions and partially with nondeductible contributions, a portion of each distribution is nontaxable. If such is the case, the taxpayer must first determine his or her tax basis in the IRA. The tax basis is equal to the sum of all nondeductible contributions made to the IRA minus the sum of all nontaxable distributions received as of the beginning of the year. Calculation of the tax-free portion is determined as follows:

$$\frac{\text{Tax basis in the IRA (i.e., after-tax contributions)}}{\text{End-of-year asset value} + \text{Distribution for the year}} \times \text{Distribution for the year} = \text{Nontaxable distribution}$$

EXAMPLE 11-17

Michael, age 65, retired in 2009. During the year, he received distributions of $7,000 from his IRA. He made nondeductible contributions of $10,000 to the IRA in prior years and has never received a nontaxable distribution. As of December 31, 2009, the value of his IRA was $100,000. The nontaxable portion of Michael's distribution is $654, calculated a follows:

$$[\$10,000 / (\$100,000 + \$7,000)] \times \$7,000 = \$654$$

Michael's taxable distribution is $6,346 ($7,000 − $654), and his tax basis carried forward to tax year 2010 is $9,346 ($10,000 − $654). This $9,346 figure will be used as the numerator of the fraction in 2010.

In tax year 2009, taxpayers who have reached the age of 70½ can make a distribution directly from a traditional IRA to a qualifying charity in an amount not to exceed $100,000 for the year. The distribution is not included in taxable income, and a deduction is not permitted for the contribution.

Distributions from IRAs with nondeductible contributions are reported on Form 8606, Part I (see Exhibit 11-2). The exclusion percentage is on line 10, and the nontaxable distribution is on line 13. The distribution and the taxable amount are carried forward to Form 1040, lines 15a and 15b, respectively.

Taxation of Roth IRA Distributions

Unlike traditional IRAs, no minimum withdrawal from a Roth IRA is required. Roth IRA withdrawals are not taxable when distributed unless they fail to meet a five-year holding period requirement.[54] Specifically, the distribution must be made after the five-tax-year period

[54] IRC § 408A(d)(1).

EXHIBIT 11-3

	☐ CORRECTED (if checked)		

| PAYER'S name, street address, city, state, and ZIP code | **1** Gross distribution
$ | OMB No. 1545-0119

2**0**09

Form **1099-R** | **Distributions From Pensions, Annuities, Retirement or Profit-Sharing Plans, IRAs, Insurance Contracts, etc.** |
| | **2a** Taxable amount
$ | | |

	2b Taxable amount not determined ☐	Total distribution ☐	**Copy B**
PAYER'S federal identification number	RECIPIENT'S identification number	**3** Capital gain (included in box 2a) $	**4** Federal income tax withheld $	**Report this income on your federal tax return. If this form shows federal income tax withheld in box 4, attach this copy to your return.**
RECIPIENT'S name		**5** Employee contributions /Designated Roth contributions or insurance premiums $	**6** Net unrealized appreciation in employer's securities $	
Street address (including apt. no.)		**7** Distribution code(s)	IRA/ SEP/ SIMPLE ☐	**8** Other $ %	This information is being furnished to the Internal Revenue Service.
City, state, and ZIP code		**9a** Your percentage of total distribution %	**9b** Total employee contributions $	
	1st year of desig. Roth contrib.	**10** State tax withheld $ $	**11** State/Payer's state no.	**12** State distribution $ $
Account number (see instructions)		**13** Local tax withheld $ $	**14** Name of locality	**15** Local distribution $ $

Form **1099-R**   Department of the Treasury - Internal Revenue Service

The expected return on an annuity that will last for a specified amount of time is easy to determine. If a contract will provide payments of $1,000 per month for five years, the expected return is $60,000 ($1,000 × 12 × 5). The expected return on a contract that will provide payments for the life of the contract owner is determined based on the life expectancy tables provided in IRS Publication 939. We have provided Table V, for single life annuities, in the appendix to this chapter. For dual life annuities, refer to Publication 939. The expected return is equal to the annual payout from the contract multiplied by the appropriate factor.

EXAMPLE 11-19   Bart is 57 years old and purchased a single life annuity contract that will pay him $5,000 per year for life. Bart paid $90,000 for the contract. The expected return on Bart's contract is $134,000 ($5,000 × 26.8).
   The exclusion ratio is 0.672 ($90,000/$134,000). Thus, each $5,000 annual payment will have a tax-free component of $3,360 (5,000 × 0.672) and a taxable component of $1,640 ($5,000 − $3,360).

EXAMPLE 11-20   Calvin is 60 years old and has purchased a single life annuity for $35,000. The annuity contract will provide Calvin payments of $300 per month for the rest of his life. Calvin's life expectancy from Table V in the appendix is 24.2 years. The expected return from the contract is $87,120 ($300 × 12 × 24.2). The exclusion ratio is 0.4017 ($35,000/$87,120). Thus, each $300 payment will have a tax-free component of $120.51 ($300 × 0.4017) and a taxable component of $179.49 ($300.00 − $120.51).

After the entire cost of the annuity has been recovered, all additional payments are fully taxable. If an individual dies before recovering the entire cost, the unrecovered cost can be used as an itemized deduction on the individual's final return.

TAX YOUR BRAIN Under what circumstances will the entire cost of an annuity be recovered?

ANSWER

In the case of an annuity that is payable for a fixed period, the entire cost will be recovered when the last payment is received. For annuities payable over the life of the recipient, the entire cost will be recovered if the annuitant lives exactly as long as the life expectancy used to determine the exclusion ratio. Mathematically, once the recipient reaches the life expectancy originally anticipated, the entire cost will have been recovered.

CONCEPT CHECK 11-7—LO 6

1. An annuity is a _____ of payments under a _____.
2. Annuity payments are always the same amount each period. True or false?
3. Annuity payments often have a taxable component and a nontaxable component. True or false?

Summary

LO 1. Discuss the basic tax and operational structure of tax-deferred plans and annuities.

- Specified retirement plans are encouraged and receive tax advantages.
- Important related terminology includes donor, beneficiary, contributions, distributions, annuity, and trustee.
- Tax-deferred does not mean tax-free.
- Generally, untaxed contributions are taxed on distribution but taxed contributions are not.
- Contributions to retirement plans can provide a tax deduction.

LO 2. Explain details about and contributions to employer-sponsored retirement plans.

- Employer-sponsored plans include qualified pension and profit-sharing, 401(k), 403(b), Keogh, SEP, and SIMPLE plans.
- Plans provide significant benefits to both employers and employees.
- Qualified plans are either defined contribution or defined benefit plans.
- All employer-sponsored plans have contribution limits that vary by plan.

LO 3. Describe the tax rules related to contributions to individual-sponsored retirement plans.

- Individual-sponsored IRAs include both traditional and Roth.
- Contributions are limited to the lower of $5,000 or 100% of compensation. Individuals over 50 can contribute up to $6,000.
- Special rules apply to compensation for married taxpayers and for individuals covered by employer-related plans.
- Contribution restrictions are based on AGI.
- Deductibility of contributions and taxability of distributions for traditional and Roth IRAs differ.

LO 4. Explain details about and contributions to tax-deferred nonretirement plans.

- A Coverdell Education Savings Account is a tax-deferred plan used for qualified elementary, secondary, or higher education expenses.
- The maximum annual contribution is $2,000, subject to AGI limitations.

LO 5. Apply the tax rules for distributions from tax-deferred plans and the tax treatment of those distributions.

- Generally, distributions are taxable if contributions were deductible.
- The simplified method is used to determine taxability of qualified plan distributions.
- Other retirement plans have required minimum distributions that must begin by April 1 of the year after the taxpayer reaches age 70½.
- Distributions are determined using life expectancy tables.
- Special rules apply to distributions in tax year 2009.
- Premature distributions are subject to 10% penalty; some exceptions apply.
- Rollovers are generally tax-free, but rollovers to a Roth IRA are subject to tax.

LO 6. Determine the tax treatment of annuity contracts.

- Normally, annuity payments are partially taxable and partially tax-free.
- The tax-free component is based on the cost of the annuity contract.
- Must determine expected return. The expected return is the amount the annuity recipient expects to receive from the contract. May need to refer to life expectancy tables.

Appendix

LIFE EXPECTANCY TABLES

Table I (Single Life Expectancy) (For Use by Beneficiaries)			
Age	**Life Expectancy**	**Age**	**Life Expectancy**
56	28.7	84	8.1
57	27.9	85	7.6
58	27.0	86	7.1
59	26.1	87	6.7
60	25.2	88	6.3
61	24.4	89	5.9
62	23.5	90	5.5
63	22.7	91	5.2
64	21.8	92	4.9
65	21.0	93	4.6
66	20.2	94	4.3
67	19.4	95	4.1
68	18.6	96	3.8
69	17.8	97	3.6
70	17.0	98	3.4
71	16.3	99	3.1
72	15.5	100	2.9
73	14.8	101	2.7
74	14.1	102	2.5
75	13.4	103	2.3
76	12.7	104	2.1
77	12.1	105	1.9
78	11.4	106	1.7
79	10.8	107	1.5
80	10.2	108	1.4
81	9.7	109	1.2
82	9.1	110	1.1
83	8.6	111 and over	1.0

Generally this table is to be used for IRAs by beneficiaries as a result of the death of the original IRA owner.

**Table III
(Uniform Lifetime)**

(For Use by:
- **Unmarried Owners,**
- **Married Owners Whose Spouses Are Not More Than 10 Years Younger, and**
- **Married Owners Whose Spouses Are Not the Sole Beneficiaries of Their IRAs)**

Age	Distribution Period	Age	Distribution Period
70	27.4	93	9.6
71	26.5	94	9.1
72	25.6	95	8.6
73	24.7	96	8.1
74	23.8	97	7.6
75	22.9	98	7.1
76	22.0	99	6.7
77	21.2	100	6.3
78	20.3	101	5.9
79	19.5	102	5.5
80	18.7	103	5.2
81	17.9	104	4.9
82	17.1	105	4.5
83	16.3	106	4.2
84	15.5	107	3.9
85	14.8	108	3.7
86	14.1	109	3.4
87	13.4	110	3.1
88	12.7	111	2.9
89	12.0	112	2.6
90	11.4	113	2.4
91	10.8	114	2.1
92	10.2	115 and over	1.9

Generally this table is to be used by the original owner of an IRA.

TABLE V—ORDINARY LIFE ANNUITIES
ONE LIFE—EXPECTED RETURN MULTIPLES

AGE	MULTIPLE	AGE	MULTIPLE	AGE	MULTIPLE
5	76.6	42	40.6	79	10.0
6	75.6	43	39.6	80	9.5
7	74.7	44	38.7	81	8.9
8	73.7	45	37.7	82	8.4
9	72.7	46	36.8	83	7.9
10	71.7	47	35.9	84	7.4
11	70.7	48	34.9	85	6.9
12	69.7	49	34.0	86	6.5
13	68.8	50	33.1	87	6.1
14	67.8	51	32.2	88	5.7
15	66.8	52	31.3	89	5.3
16	65.8	53	30.4	90	5.0
17	64.8	54	29.5	91	4.7
18	63.9	55	28.6	92	4.4
19	62.9	56	27.7	93	4.1
20	61.9	57	26.8	94	3.9
21	60.9	58	25.9	95	3.7
22	59.9	59	25.0	96	3.4
23	59.0	60	24.2	97	3.2
24	58.0	61	23.3	98	3.0
25	57.0	62	22.5	99	2.8
26	56.0	63	21.6	100	2.7
27	55.1	64	20.8	101	2.5
28	54.1	65	20.0	102	2.3
29	53.1	66	19.2	103	2.1
30	52.2	67	18.4	104	1.9
31	51.2	68	17.6	105	1.8
32	50.2	69	16.8	106	1.6
33	49.3	70	16.0	107	1.4
34	48.3	71	15.3	108	1.3
35	47.3	72	14.6	109	1.1
36	46.4	73	13.9	110	1.0
37	45.4	74	13.2	111	.9
38	44.4	75	12.5	112	.8
39	43.5	76	11.9	113	.7
40	42.5	77	11.2	114	.6
41	41.5	78	10.6	115	.5

This table is to be used by taxpayers with payments from an annuity not associated with a qualified pension or profit-sharing plan.

LO 2 53. Use the same information as in Problem 52. Answer the questions indicated, assuming that Ken is considering a SIMPLE plan.

LO 3 54. Under what circumstances is it advantageous for a taxpayer to make a nondeductible contribution to a traditional IRA rather than a contribution to a Roth IRA?

LO 3 55. April, who is under age 50, is considering investing in tax-free state government bonds or making a permitted tax-deductible contribution to a traditional IRA. Assume that the amounts are the same for either alternative and that she can reinvest the interest income from the government bonds indefinitely. What tax and nontax factors should she consider?

LO 3 56. Lance is single and has a traditional IRA into which he has made deductible contributions for several years. This year he changed employers and is now an active participant in his employer's pension plan. His AGI is $80,000. He wants to make a nondeductible contribution to his IRA in the current year. What advice would you give Lance?

LO 3, 5 57. What are the differences between a traditional IRA and a Roth IRA regarding the deductibility of contributions, taxability of IRA earnings, and taxability of distributions?

LO 5 58. Using the simplified method, determine the tax-free amount of the following distributions from a qualified pension plan. Contributions, if any, are made with previously taxed dollars.

    a. Person A, age 59, made no contributions to the pension plan and will receive a $500 monthly check for life.

    b. Person B, age 66, made contributions of $23,000 to the pension plan and will receive a monthly check of $1,300 for life.

    c. Person C, age 64, made contributions of $19,000 to the pension plan and will receive monthly payments of $1,200 over her life and the life of her 67-year-old husband.

    d. Person D, age 55, made contributions of $32,000 to the pension plan. He will receive quarterly payments of $5,000 over his life and the life of his 58-year-old wife.

_____

_____

_____

_____

_____

LO 5 59. Pablo and his wife Bernita are both age 45. Pablo works full-time, and Bernita works part-time. Their AGI is $90,000. Neither is a participant in an employer-sponsored retirement plan. They have been contributing to a traditional IRA for many years and have built up an IRA balance of $120,000. They are considering rolling the traditional IRA into a Roth IRA.

    a. Is the couple eligible to make the conversion? Why or why not?

    b. Assume that the couple does not make the conversion but, instead, establishes a separate Roth IRA in the current year and properly contributes $2,000 per year for four years, at which point the balance in the Roth is $21,000. At the end of four years, they withdraw $12,000 to pay for an addition to their house. What is the tax effect, if anything, of the withdrawal?

    c. Does your answer to (b) change if they withdraw $6,000? Why or why not?

    d. What if the $12,000 withdrawal is used to pay qualified education expenses for their daughter who is attending college?

_____

_____

_____

_____

_____

LO 6 60. Determine the tax-free amount of the monthly payment in each of the following instances. Use the life expectancy tables.

    a. Person A is age 57 and purchased an annuity for $82,000. The annuity pays $600 per month for life.

    b. Person B is 73 and purchased an annuity for $80,000. The annuity pays $950 per month for life.

    c. Person C is 68 and purchased an annuity for $40,000 that pays a monthly payment of $550 for 10 years.

_____

_____

_____

_____

_____

- Other securities or evidence of indebtedness or interest.
- Interests in a partnership.
- Certificates of trust or beneficial interests.

Note that because inventory does not qualify for like-kind treatment, a dealer cannot participate in a like-kind exchange on a trade-in.

EXAMPLE 12-2	Marius, a dealer in farm equipment, allows a trade-in of an old combine (large equipment used to harvest crops) toward the purchase of a new combine. He cannot use the like-kind rules to defer any taxable gain. However, the customer could use the like-kind rules to defer gain, assuming the customer is a farmer, not a dealer in farm equipment.

What Is a "Like-Kind" Asset?

The requirement that the property be like-kind does not require the asset received to be an exact duplicate of the property exchanged. To qualify as "like-kind," the property must be of the same nature or character. The grade or quality of the exchanged assets does not matter.[5]

EXAMPLE 12-3	Johnny exchanges a parcel of farm real property for city real property. Because both properties are real properties held for productive use, the exchange would qualify as a like-kind exchange.[6]

When a taxpayer exchanges business personal property, the property must be of the same depreciation class of property.[7] Thus the exchange of a five-year class asset for a seven-year class asset would *not* qualify for "like-kind" treatment.

Boot Property

When two taxpayers wish to exchange properties, the fair market values (FMVs) of the properties rarely are equal. Thus, to make an exchange a viable option, one participant gives extra consideration (usually cash or a note payable) to make the exchange values equitable. This extra consideration is called *boot,* defined as property given or received in a like-kind exchange that is *not* like-kind property. The receipt of boot property often triggers the recognition of gain. The following is the general rule concerning the receipt of boot:

When boot is received, the recognized gain is the **lesser** of

1. The FMV of the boot received; or,
2. The realized gain on the exchange.[8]

Gain or loss is determined by comparing the FMV received with the basis of the assets given. The receipt of boot causes the recognition of gain but not loss.[9] Giving boot does not trigger gain recognition.

[5] Reg. § 1.1031-1(b).
[6] Reg. § 1.1031(b).
[7] Rev. Proc. 87-56, 1987-2 CB 674; see Chapter 7 for a discussion of asset classes.
[8] IRC § 1031(b).
[9] IRC § 1031(c).

EXAMPLE 12-4

Sonja exchanges a machine used in business with Kelly for another machine. The basis of Sonja's old machine is $25,000, its FMV is $33,000, and she gives cash of $7,000. Kelly's basis in her machine is $35,000, and its FMV is $40,000.

	Sonja		Kelly
New machine—FMV	$40,000	Amount received	$40,000*
Basis of old	(25,000)	Basis of old	(35,000)
Cash given	(7,000)	Gain—recognized	$ 5,000
Gain—not recognized	$ 8,000		

* The amount received was the $33,000 FMV of Sonja's machine plus the $7,000 cash (boot).

Kelly recognizes the gain because she received boot in the transaction. The gain recognized is $5,000 because it is the lower of the boot received ($7,000 cash) or the gain realized ($5,000). Sonja defers her gain of $8,000.

Tax Basis of New Property Received

An important calculation in a nontaxable exchange is the basis calculation. The basis calculation is the method by which the taxpayer defers gain. Generally, the basis of the new property is calculated as follows:

Basis Calculation of the Property Received[10]	
	Adjusted basis of the property given up
+	Adjusted basis of the boot given
+	Gain recognized
−	FMV of boot received
−	Loss recognized
=	Adjusted basis of new asset

Alternatively, the taxpayer can calculate the adjusted basis by taking the FMV of the property received (like-kind asset) less the gain postponed (or plus the loss postponed).

TAX YOUR BRAIN

Why is the term *deferred* used instead of *excluded* when referring to the realized gain in a non-taxable exchange?

ANSWER

The gain is deferred because the unrecognized gain reduces the basis in the new asset received. Thus, the gain is deferred until the new asset is sold or disposed of. The reduced basis also causes less depreciation allowed on the new asset.

---

[10] IRC § 1031(d).

EXAMPLE 12-5

Assuming the same facts as in Example 12-4, what is the basis in the new properties for Sonja and Kelly?

	Sonja	Kelly
Adjusted basis of property given	$25,000	$35,000
+ Adjusted basis of boot given	7,000	–0–
+ Gain recognized	–0–	5,000
– FMV of boot received	–0–	7,000
– Loss recognized	–0–	–0–
Basis of new machine	$32,000	$33,000

Or	FMV of Property Received	–	Gain Postponed	+	Loss Postponed	=	Basis
Sonja	$40,000	–	$8,000	+	$–0–	=	$32,000
Kelly	33,000	–	–0–	+	–0–	=	33,000

In practice, the FMV is sometimes difficult to assess with used assets. If the item is large and valuable, it may be prudent to have the exchanged property appraised. For most businesses and most exchanges, the exchange is typically a trade-in of an old asset for a new asset. In this case, the new basis is the sales price of the new asset less any deferred gain (or plus any deferred loss).

The holding period used to determine any short-term or long-term treatment on the sale of the new asset includes the holding period of the old asset exchanged. Thus if a taxpayer exchanges a property held for 20 years for a new property, the new property has a holding period of 20 years plus the holding period of the new property.

Time Period for Finding Exchange Property

The taxpayer does not have an unlimited amount of time to find exchange property. After relinquishing his or her property, the taxpayer has 45 days to identify replacement property. In addition, the taxpayer must receive the replacement property within the earlier of 180 days after the property was given up or the due date for filing a return (including extensions) for the year of the transfer.

EXAMPLE 12-6

Dan transfers property to Joey, and Joey places cash with an escrow agent on December 10, 2009. Dan has until January 24, 2010 (45 days), to identify a replacement property and must receive the replacement property by April 15, 2010. If the tax return were extended, Dan would have 180 days from December 10 to receive the property.

Liabilities Assumed on the Exchange

The assumption or release of a liability adds complexity to a nontaxable exchange. When a taxpayer is released of a liability in an exchange, its release is considered boot received.[11] In other words, the taxpayer who assumes the debt is treated as having paid cash, and the taxpayer released of the debt is treated as having received cash. Because liabilities released are boot, the presence of a liability can trigger gain to the lesser of boot received or gain realized.

---

[11] IRC § 1031(d).

EXAMPLE 12-7

Jack exchanges land used in his business (FMV $200,000) for Dave's land (FMV $150,000). Jack's basis in the land is $75,000 and is subject to a liability of $50,000, which Dave assumes.

Proceeds	$200,000*
Basis	(75,000)
Realized gain	$125,000†

*The FMV of the land received of $150,000 plus the release of a liability of $50,000.
†The realized gain is $125,000, of which $50,000 is recognized (the lesser of boot received or gain realized). The released liability is boot. The basis in the new land is $75,000 (FMV of land received of $150,000 less the deferred gain of $75,000).

Exchanges between Related Parties

Exchanges between related parties are not like-kind exchanges if either party disposes of the property within two years of the exchange. Any gain realized on the exchange is recognized in the year of the subsequent sale.[12] A *related party* includes the taxpayer's spouse, child, grandchild, parent, brother, or sister; or a related corporation, S corporation, partnership, or trust. Death or involuntary conversions within the two-year period do not trigger the gain.[13]

TAX YOUR BRAIN

Why does the tax law disallow a nontaxable exchange between related parties if the property is sold within two years?

ANSWER

Suppose one brother was in the 35% tax bracket and the other brother was in the 15% tax bracket. The brothers could exchange gain property held by the high-bracket brother at no gain, and the low-bracket brother could sell the property and pay tax at a lower tax rate. Corporations and shareholders owning more than 50% of the stock are also related parties. Without the disallowance, the same type of transaction could occur between the corporation and a related shareholder.

Deferred Exchanges

One problem with a like-kind exchange is finding someone willing to exchange properties. However, with a properly executed like-kind exchange, the exchange can be nontaxable even if a seller of a property is unwilling to exchange properties. As noted, a like-kind exchange does not need to be simultaneous to be tax-free. The Ninth Circuit Court held that the contractual right to receive like-kind property is the same as the ownership rights themselves.[14] The court did not specify a time period, so Congress imposed the 45- and 180-day time requirements discussed earlier.

The most common arrangement for a deferred exchange occurs when the title to the property to be exchanged is placed in an escrow account with a custodian (usually an attorney or CPA). The custodian sells the property and places the cash in an escrow account. The taxpayer then has 45 days to identify like-kind property. When the property has been identified, the custodian purchases the new asset and distributes the title to the taxpayer. The main restriction is that the

[12] IRC § 1031(f).
[13] IRC § 1031(f)(2).
[14] *Starker v. US* (1979, CA9) 79-2 USTC 9541.

From Shoebox to Software

The reporting requirements for like-kind exchanges are not complex for single asset exchanges. The taxpayer is required to file Form 8824. On Form 8824, the taxpayer reports the FMV of property given up, the basis of the property given, and the gain or loss realized. The taxpayer compares the boot property to the realized gain to determine how much gain, if any, must be recognized. Exhibit 12-1 illustrates the reporting for the exchange in Example 12-7. Recall that Jack traded land with an FMV of $200,000 and a liability of $50,000 for land with an FMV of $150,000.[15] Because the gain of $50,000 is recognized on the like-kind exchange and the land was used in a business, the land is considered §1231 property. Thus, the gain transfers to page 1 of Form 4797.

taxpayer cannot, at any time, have actual or constructive receipt of the proceeds from the sale of old property. In other words, the taxpayer cannot touch or be able to use the cash proceeds; otherwise, the nontaxable exchange will be disqualified.[16]

EXAMPLE 12-8	On May 1, 2009, David offers to purchase real property from Zack for $100,000. However, David is unwilling to participate in a like-kind exchange. Thus, Zack enters into an exchange agreement with Carri (an attorney) to facilitate an exchange with respect to the real property. The exchange agreement between Zack and Carri provides that Zack will deliver a deed conveying real property to Carri, who, in turn, will deliver a deed conveying the real property to David in exchange for $100,000. The exchange agreement expressly limits Zack's rights to receive, pledge, borrow, or otherwise obtain benefits of the money or other property held by Carri. On May 17, 2009, Zack delivers to Carri a deed conveying the real property to Carri. On the same date, Carri delivers to David a deed conveying real property to him, and David deposits $100,000 in escrow. The escrow agreement provides that the money in escrow be used to purchase replacement property. On June 3, 2009 (within 45 days), Zack identifies replacement real property. On August 9, 2009, Carri uses $80,000 from the escrow to purchase the new real property. On the same date (within 180 days), Carri delivers to Zack a deed conveying new real property to him, and the escrow holder pays Zack $20,000, the balance of the escrow account (considered boot). Zack recognizes gain of the lesser of the realized gain or the boot received ($20,000).

CONCEPT CHECK 12-1—LO 1	1. With a correctly executed like-kind exchange, gain is never recognized unless the taxpayer receives boot. True or false? 2. For a transaction to qualify for a like-kind exchange, an exchange of assets must occur and the assets must be held for trade or business use or for investment and be like-kind assets. True or false? 3. A taxpayer has 180 days after relinquishing his or her property to identify a replacement property. True or false? 4. The basis in the replacement property is typically the FMV of the property received less the gain postponed. True or false?

INVOLUNTARY CONVERSIONS
LO 2

An *involuntary conversion* occurs when property is destroyed, stolen, condemned, or disposed of under the threat of condemnation and the taxpayer receives other property or payment such

---

[15] The dates included on the tax form were not given in the example.

[16] Reg. § 1.1031(k)-1(g). This regulation section gives safe harbor rules to protect against the actual or constructive receipt of the money.

EXHIBIT 12-1

Form **8824** Department of the Treasury Internal Revenue Service	**Like-Kind Exchanges** (and section 1043 conflict-of-interest sales) ▶ Attach to your tax return.	OMB No. 1545-1190 20**09** Attachment Sequence No. **109**

Name(s) shown on tax return
Jack A. Trade

Identifying number
123-45-6789

Part I   **Information on the Like-Kind Exchange**

Note: *If the property described on line 1 or line 2 is real or personal property located outside the United States, indicate the country.*

1 Description of like-kind property given up:
Land located at 519 Exchange Avenue, Anywhere, USA

2 Description of like-kind property received:
Land located at 321 Exchange Avenue, Anywhere, USA

3 Date like-kind property given up was originally acquired (month, day, year) . . . . . . **3** MM/ 10/15/08 /YY

4 Date you actually transferred your property to other party (month, day, year) . . . . . **4** MM/ 05/01/09 /YY

5 Date like-kind property you received was identified by written notice to another party (month, day, year). See instructions for 45-day written notice requirement . . . . **5** MM/ 05/01/09 /YY

6 Date you actually received the like-kind property from other party (month, day, year). See instructions **6** MM/ 05/01/09 /YY

7 Was the exchange of the property given up or received made with a related party, either directly or indirectly (such as through an intermediary)? See instructions. If "Yes," complete Part II. If "No," go to Part III . . . . ☐ **Yes** ☒ **No**

Part II   **Related Party Exchange Information**

8 Name of related party	Relationship to you	Related party's identifying number

Address (no., street, and apt., room, or suite no., city or town, state, and ZIP code)

9 During this tax year (and before the date that is 2 years after the last transfer of property that was part of the exchange), did the related party sell or dispose of any part of the like-kind property received from you (or an intermediary) in the exchange or transfer property into the exchange, directly or indirectly (such as through an intermediary), that became your replacement property? . . . . ☐ **Yes** ☐ **No**

10 During this tax year (and before the date that is 2 years after the last transfer of property that was part of the exchange), did you sell or dispose of any part of the like-kind property you received? . . . . ☐ **Yes** ☐ **No**

*If both lines 9 and 10 are "No" and this is the year of the exchange, go to Part III. If both lines 9 and 10 are "No" and this is **not** the year of the exchange, stop here. If either line 9 or line 10 is "Yes," complete Part III and report on this year's tax return the deferred gain or (loss) from line 24 **unless** one of the exceptions on line 11 applies.*

11 If one of the exceptions below applies to the disposition, check the applicable box:

a ☐ The disposition was after the death of either of the related parties.

b ☐ The disposition was an involuntary conversion, and the threat of conversion occurred after the exchange.

c ☐ You can establish to the satisfaction of the IRS that neither the exchange nor the disposition had tax avoidance as one of its principal purposes. If this box is checked, attach an explanation (see instructions).

For Paperwork Reduction Act Notice, see page 4 of the instructions.   Cat. No. 12311A   Form **8824** (2009)

EXHIBIT 12-1 *(continued)*

Form 8824 (2009)   Page **2**

Name(s) shown on tax return. Do not enter name and social security number if shown on other side.	Your social security number
Jack A. Trade	123-45-6789

Part III   **Realized Gain or (Loss), Recognized Gain, and Basis of Like-Kind Property Received**

Caution: *If you transferred* **and** *received* **(a)** *more than one group of like-kind properties or* **(b)** *cash or other (not like-kind) property, see* **Reporting of multi-asset exchanges** *in the instructions.*

Note: *Complete lines 12 through 14* **only** *if you gave up property that was not like-kind. Otherwise, go to line 15.*

12	Fair market value (FMV) of other property given up **12**	
13	Adjusted basis of other property given up **13**	
14	Gain or (loss) recognized on other property given up. Subtract line 13 from line 12. Report the gain or (loss) in the same manner as if the exchange had been a sale **14**	

Caution: *If the property given up was used previously or partly as a home, see* **Property used as home** *in the instructions.*

15	Cash received, FMV of other property received, plus net liabilities assumed by other party, reduced (but not below zero) by any exchange expenses you incurred (see instructions) **15**	50,000
16	FMV of like-kind property you received **16**	150,000
17	Add lines 15 and 16 **17**	200,000
18	Adjusted basis of like-kind property you gave up, net amounts paid to other party, plus any exchange expenses **not** used on line 15 (see instructions) **18**	75,000
19	**Realized gain or (loss).** Subtract line 18 from line 17 **19**	125,000
20	Enter the smaller of line 15 or line 19, but not less than zero **20**	50,000
21	Ordinary income under recapture rules. Enter here and on Form 4797, line 16 (see instructions) **21**	
22	Subtract line 21 from line 20. If zero or less, enter -0-. If more than zero, enter here and on Schedule D or Form 4797, unless the installment method applies (see instructions) **22**	50,000
23	**Recognized gain.** Add lines 21 and 22 **23**	50,000
24	Deferred gain or (loss). Subtract line 23 from line 19. If a related party exchange, see instructions **24**	75,000
25	**Basis of like-kind property received.** Subtract line 15 from the sum of lines 18 and 23 **25**	75,000

Part IV   **Deferral of Gain From Section 1043 Conflict-of-Interest Sales**

Note: *This part is to be used* **only** *by officers or employees of the executive branch of the Federal Government or judicial officers of the Federal Government (including certain spouses, minor or dependent children, and trustees as described in section 1043) for reporting nonrecognition of gain under section 1043 on the sale of property to comply with the conflict-of-interest requirements. This part can be used* **only** *if the cost of the replacement property is more than the basis of the divested property.*

26	Enter the number from the upper right corner of your certificate of divestiture. (**Do not** attach a copy of your certificate. Keep the certificate with your records.) ▶ _____ – _____	
27	Description of divested property ▶	
28	Description of replacement property ▶	
29	Date divested property was sold (month, day, year) **29**	MM/DD/YYYY
30	Sales price of divested property (see instructions) **30**	
31	Basis of divested property **31**	
32	**Realized gain.** Subtract line 31 from line 30 **32**	
33	Cost of replacement property purchased within 60 days after date of sale **33**	
34	Subtract line 33 from line 30. If zero or less, enter -0- **34**	
35	Ordinary income under recapture rules. Enter here and on Form 4797, line 10 (see instructions) **35**	
36	Subtract line 35 from line 34. If zero or less, enter -0-. If more than zero, enter here and on Schedule D or Form 4797 (see instructions) **36**	
37	**Deferred gain.** Subtract the sum of lines 35 and 36 from line 32 **37**	
38	**Basis of replacement property.** Subtract line 37 from line 33 **38**	

Form **8824** (2009)

Draft as of 12/17/2009

as an insurance or condemnation award. If the taxpayer receives other property for the converted property of similar or related use, the taxpayer recognizes no gain.[17]

EXAMPLE 12-9	The state of Alabama condemned 300 acres of Art's land. In payment to Art, the state awarded him 300 acres of similar land. In this case, Art recognizes no gain or loss, and the basis of his new land is the same as his old land.

A far more likely scenario is that the taxpayer receives cash either from the condemning authority or from an insurance policy (in the case of a casualty). In this case, the taxpayer must recognize any gain unless he or she elects the nonrecognition provisions.[18] This election provides that, in general, no gain will be recognized on an involuntary conversion if the taxpayer replaces the converted property with similar property of equal or greater value within a certain time.

EXAMPLE 12-10	A tornado destroyed Kelly's building used in a trade or business. Kelly purchased the building in 1980 for $100,000, and it is now fully depreciated (zero adjusted basis). She received $250,000 in insurance proceeds for the replacement cost. Unless Kelly elects to replace the property with similar-use property costing $250,000 or more, she must recognize the $250,000 gain on the sale of the building. To defer the entire gain, the replacement property must be purchased for an amount equal to or greater than the proceeds from the conversion. The gain is recognized at the lower of the gain realized or the proceeds *not* used for replacement. If, in this example, the replacement building costs only $240,000, Kelly would recognize $10,000 of the $250,000 realized gain.

The involuntary conversion provisions do not apply to losses. Losses are deducted without reference to the involuntary conversion rules and are allowed to the extent allowed by the casualty loss rules for either personal property (see Chapter 5) or business property (see Chapter 6).

Replacement Property

To postpone any gain, the taxpayer must purchase qualifying replacement property with the specific purpose of replacing the converted property. However, qualifying property depends on the type of property held prior to the involuntary conversion. If the property lost is anything other than real property, the replacement property must be "similar or related in service or use."[19] This test is more restrictive than the "like-kind" test.

EXAMPLE 12-11	A delivery van used in Chris's business was destroyed in an auto accident. The van was fully depreciated. Chris received $8,000 in insurance proceeds. To qualify as replacement property, Chris must replace the van with a vehicle of similar or related use.[20]

If the property destroyed or condemned is real property, the similar use restrictions are lowered. The replacement property for real property must be only "like-kind."[21]

[17] Section IRC § 1033(a)(1).
[18] Section IRC § 1033(2)(A).
[19] IRC § 1033(a)(2)(A).
[20] If the property was lost in a presidentially declared disaster zone, any tangible property held for productive use in the business qualifies. In this case, any tangible business property qualifies as replacement property.
[21] IRC § 1033(g)(1).

From Shoebox to Software

Because most post-1997 sales of residences produce gains of less than $250,000 for single taxpayers and $500,000 for married taxpayers, the reporting requirements involving the sale of a residence are minimal. If no gain is recognized on the sale of a residence, the taxpayer is not required to report the sale on any form or statement. If, however, the gain is larger than the allowed exclusion, the taxpayer is required to report the gain as a sale of a capital asset on Schedule D. When

the gain is partially excluded, the taxpayer should write the amount excluded on Schedule D. Exhibit 12-5 illustrates the presentation on Schedule D of a gain recognized on the sale of a residence when some of the gain is excluded.

Tax software usually performs the exclusion calculation for you. With most software programs, you go to the Schedule D Home Sale worksheet and fill in the house sale information.

Special Problems with Married Individuals

Married individuals can exclude up to $500,000 from the gain on a personal residence. However, what happens when one spouse is eligible for the exclusion and the other is not? In this case, each individual is treated separately.

EXAMPLE 12-19 Susan sold her personal residence on July 10, 2009, at a $190,000 gain. She excluded the gain. On August 15, 2009, she married Gus. He sold his house on December 12, 2009, at a gain of $480,000. Because Susan is not eligible for the exclusion (she sold a residence within two years of a previous sale), only $250,000 of the $480,000 gain is excluded from income.

Other special provisions for married individuals are summarized in Table 12-1.

TABLE 12-1
Provisions for Married Individuals

Source: IRS Publication 523, p. 16.

One spouse sells a home	The other spouse is still allowed an exclusion of gain up to $250,000.
Death of spouse before sale	The surviving spouse is deemed to have owned and lived in the property for any period when the decedent spouse owned and lived in the home. Starting in 2008, a surviving spouse can qualify for up to $500,000 if the sale of the residence occurs not later than two years after one spouse's death.
Home transferred from spouse	The transferee spouse is considered to have owned the residence for any period of time when the transferor spouse owned the residence.
Use of home after divorce	The taxpayer is considered to have used the house during any period when (1) the taxpayer owned it and (2) the spouse or former spouse is allowed to live in it under a divorce or separation agreement.

CONCEPT CHECK 12-4—LO 4

1. If married taxpayers live in their personal residence for more than two years, the couple can exclude the gain on the sale of their residence up to $500,000. True or false?
2. A taxpayer cannot exclude any gain on the sale of a residence if he or she has lived there less than two years. True or false?
3. Sharon and Johnny were recently married, and Sharon moved into Johnny's house. She then sold her home and took the exclusion. Because Sharon took the exclusion, Johnny must forfeit his exclusion if he were to sell his home within the next two years. True or false?

EXHIBIT 12-5

SCHEDULE D (Form 1040)	Capital Gains and Losses	OMB No. 1545-0074
Department of the Treasury Internal Revenue Service (99)	► Attach to Form 1040 or Form 1040NR. ► See Instructions for Schedule D (Form 1040). ► Use Schedule D-1 to list additional transactions for lines 1 and 8.	20**09** Attachment Sequence No. **12**

Name(s) shown on return: Rob Johnson

Your social security number: 123-45-6789

Part I   **Short-Term Capital Gains and Losses—Assets Held One Year or Less**

	(a) Description of property (Example: 100 sh. XYZ Co.)	(b) Date acquired (Mo., day, yr.)	(c) Date sold (Mo., day, yr.)	(d) Sales price (see page D-7 of the instructions)	(e) Cost or other basis (see page D-7 of the instructions)	(f) Gain or (loss) Subtract (e) from (d)
1						

2	Enter your short-term totals, if any, from Schedule D-1, line 2	**2**		
3	**Total short-term sales price amounts.** Add lines 1 and 2 in column (d)	**3**		
4	Short-term gain from Form 6252 and short-term gain or (loss) from Forms 4684, 6781, and 8824		**4**	
5	Net short-term gain or (loss) from partnerships, S corporations, estates, and trusts from Schedule(s) K-1		**5**	
6	Short-term capital loss carryover. Enter the amount, if any, from line 10 of your **Capital Loss Carryover Worksheet** on page D-7 of the instructions		**6**	( )
7	**Net short-term capital gain or (loss).** Combine lines 1 through 6 in column (f)		**7**	

Part II   **Long-Term Capital Gains and Losses—Assets Held More Than One Year**

	(a) Description of property (Example: 100 sh. XYZ Co.)	(b) Date acquired (Mo., day, yr.)	(c) Date sold (Mo., day, yr.)	(d) Sales price (see page D-7 of the instructions)	(e) Cost or other basis (see page D-7 of the instructions)	(f) Gain or (loss) Subtract (e) from (d)
8	Sale of Residence	04/05/09	05/05/09	470,000	325,000	145,000
	Section 121 Exclusion					(135,000)

9	Enter your long-term totals, if any, from Schedule D-1, line 9	**9**		
10	**Total long-term sales price amounts.** Add lines 8 and 9 in column (d)	**10**	470,000	
11	Gain from Form 4797, Part I; long-term gain from Forms 2439 and 6252; and long-term gain or (loss) from Forms 4684, 6781, and 8824		**11**	
12	Net long-term gain or (loss) from partnerships, S corporations, estates, and trusts from Schedule(s) K-1		**12**	
13	Capital gain distributions. See page D-2 of the instructions		**13**	
14	Long-term capital loss carryover. Enter the amount, if any, from line 15 of your **Capital Loss Carryover Worksheet** on page D-7 of the instructions		**14**	( )
15	**Net long-term capital gain or (loss).** Combine lines 8 through 14 in column (f). Then go to Part III on the back		**15**	10,000

For Paperwork Reduction Act Notice, see Form 1040 or Form 1040NR instructions.   Cat. No. 11338H   Schedule D (Form 1040) 2009

LO 1   51. Joshua owns undeveloped land that has an adjusted basis of $45,000. He exchanges it for other undeveloped land with a FMV of $70,000.

    a. What are his realized and recognized gain or loss on the exchange?

    _____

    _____

    _____

    b. What is his basis in the acquired land?

    _____

    _____

    _____

LO 2   52. Patti's garage (used to store business property) is destroyed by a fire. She decides not to replace it and uses the insurance proceeds to invest in her business. The garage had an adjusted basis of $50,000.

    a. If the insurance proceeds total $20,000, what is Patti's recognized gain or loss?

    _____

    _____

    _____

    b. If the insurance proceeds total $60,000, what is Patti's recognized gain or loss?

    _____

    _____

    _____

LO 2   53. Indicate whether the property acquired qualifies as replacement property for each of the following involuntary conversions:

    a. The Harts' personal residence is destroyed by a hurricane. They decide not to acquire a replacement residence but to invest the insurance proceeds in a house that they rent to tenants.

    _____

    _____

    _____

    b. Faiqa's personal residence is condemned. She uses the proceeds to invest in another personal residence.

    _____

    _____

    _____

    c. Tonya owns a storage warehouse used for business purposes. A flood destroys the building, and she decides to use the insurance proceeds to rebuild the warehouse in another state.

    _____

    _____

    _____

    d. Ramona owns an apartment building that is destroyed by a flood. She uses the insurance proceeds to build an apartment building nearby, which is out of the flood zone.

    _____

    _____

    _____

LO 2   54. Jessica's office building is destroyed by fire on November 15, 2009. The adjusted basis of the building is $410,000. She receives insurance proceeds of $550,000 on December 12, 2009.

    a. Calculate her realized and recognized gain or loss for the replacement property if she acquires an office building in December 2009 for $550,000.

_____

_____

_____

    b. Calculate her realized and recognized gain or loss for the replacement property if she acquires an office building in December 2009 for $495,000.

_____

_____

_____

    c. What is her basis for the replacement property in (*a*) and in (*b*)?

_____

_____

_____

    d. Calculate Jessica's realized and recognized gain or loss if she does not invest in replacement property.

_____

_____

_____

LO 2   55. Reid's personal residence is condemned on September 12, 2009, as part of a plan to add two lanes to the existing highway. His adjusted basis is $300,000. He receives condemnation proceeds of $340,000 on September 30, 2009. He purchases another personal residence for $325,000 on October 15, 2009. What are Reid's realized and recognized gain or loss?

_____

_____

_____

_____

LO 3   56. Pedro sells investment land on September 1, 2009. Information pertaining to the sale follows:

Adjusted basis	$25,000
Selling price	90,000
Selling expenses	1,500
Down payment	12,000
Four installment payments	15,000
Mortgage assumed by the buyer	18,000

Each installment payment is due on September 1 of 2010, 2011, 2012, and 2013 (ignore interest). Determine the tax consequences in 2009, 2010, 2011, 2012, and 2013.

_____

_____

_____

_____

LO 4 57. Virginia is an accountant for a global CPA firm. She is being temporarily transferred from the Raleigh, North Carolina, office to Tokyo. She will leave Raleigh on October 7, 2009, and will be out of the country for four years. She sells her personal residence on September 30, 2009, for $250,000 (her adjusted basis is $190,000). Upon her return to the United States in 2013, she purchases a new residence in Los Angeles for $220,000, where she will continue working for the same firm.

    a. What are Virginia's realized and recognized gain or loss?

         _____

         _____

         _____

    b. What is Virginia's basis in the new residence?

         _____

         _____

         _____

LO 4 58. On February 1, 2009, a 39-year-old widow buys a new residence for $150,000. Three months later, she sells her old residence for $310,000 (adjusted basis of $120,000). Selling expenses totaled $21,000. She lived in the old house for 15 years.

    a. What are the widow's realized and recognized gain or loss?

         _____

         _____

         _____

    b. What is her basis in the new residence?

         _____

         _____

         _____

LO 4 59. Dominique is a manager for a regional bank. He is being relocated several states away to act as a temporary manager while a new branch is interviewing for a permanent manager. He will leave on May 1, 2009, and will be at the new location for less than one year. He sells his personal residence on April 15, 2009, for $123,000 (adjusted basis $95,000). Upon completion of the assignment, he purchases a new residence for $200,000.

    a. What are Dominique's realized and recognized gain or loss?

         _____

         _____

         _____

    b. What is Dominique's basis in the new residence?

         _____

         _____

         _____

    c. Assume that Dominique is transferred out of state and sells his new residence for $230,000 two months later (he is single). What is the realized and recognized gain?

         _____

         _____

         _____

LO 5 60. Crystal owns 150 shares of Carson Inc. stock that has an adjusted basis of $100,000. On December 18, 2009, she sells the 150 shares for FMV ($88,000). On January 7, 2010, she purchases 200 shares of Carson stock for $127,500.

    a. What are Crystal's realized and recognized gain or loss on the sale of the 150 shares sold on December 18, 2009?

_____

_____

_____

    b. What is Crystal's adjusted basis for the 200 shares purchased on January 7, 2010?

_____

_____

_____

    c. How would your answers in (*a*) and (*b*) change if she purchased only 100 shares for $98,000 in January?

_____

_____

_____

LO 5   61. On January 1, 2009, Myron sells stock that has a $50,000 FMV on the date of the sale (basis $75,000) to his son Vernon. On October 21, 2009, Vernon sells the stock to an unrelated party. In each of the following, determine the tax consequences of these transactions to Myron and Vernon:

    a. Vernon sells the stock for $40,000.

_____

_____

_____

    b. Vernon sells the stock for $80,000.

_____

_____

_____

    c. Vernon sells the stock for $65,000.

_____

_____

_____

LO 5   62. Harold owns 130 shares of stock in Becker Corporation. His adjusted basis for the stock is $210,000. On December 15, 2009, he sells the stock for $180,000. He purchases 200 shares of Becker Corporation stock on January 12, 2010, for $195,000.

    a. What are Harold's realized and recognized gain or loss on the sale?

_____

_____

_____

    b. What is Harold's adjusted basis for the 200 shares purchased on January 12, 2010?

_____

_____

_____

    c. How would your answers in (*a*) and (*b*) change if he purchased only 100 shares for $95,000 in January?

_____

_____

_____

LO 5 63. Lewis owns 200 shares of stock in Modlin Corporation. His adjusted basis for the stock is $180,000. On December 15, 2009, he sells the stock for $170,000. He purchases 200 shares of Modlin Corporation stock on January 8, 2010, for $170,000.

a. What are Lewis's realized and recognized gain or loss on the sale?

b. What is Lewis's adjusted basis for the 200 shares purchased on January 8, 2010?

c. How would your answers in (a) and (b) change if he purchased only 100 shares for $105,000 in January?

d. What tax treatment is Lewis trying to achieve?

Tax Return Problems

Use your tax software to complete the following problems. If you are manually preparing the tax returns, the problem indicates the forms or schedules you will need.

Tax Return Problem 1

Wendy O'Neil (SSN 444-44-4444), who is single, worked full-time as the director at a local charity. She resides at 1501 Front Street, Highland, AZ 98765. For the year, she had the following reported on her W-2:

Wages	$46,200
Federal withholding	6,930
Social security wages	46,200
Social security withholding	2,864
Medicare withholding	670
State withholding	2,310

Other information follows:

1099-INT New Bank	$ 300
1099-DIV Freeze, Inc. Ordinary dividends	400
Qualified dividends	400

Wendy had the following itemized deductions:

State income tax withholding	$ 2,310
State income tax paid with the 2008 return	100
Real estate tax	2,600
Mortgage interest	8,060

Wendy inherited a beach house in North Carolina (rental only) on October 4, 2008, from her father. The FMV at the father's death was $850,000. He had purchased the house 20 years earlier for $100,000.

Summer rental income	$45,000
Repairs	2,500
Real estate taxes	6,500
Utilities	2,400
Depreciation	(Calculate)

On November 12, 2009, Wendy properly conducted a like-kind exchange for rental real estate located at 128 Lake Blvd., Hot Town, Arizona. She received rental property with a FMV of $950,000 and $20,000 cash in exchange for the North Carolina beach house. The Arizona property did not produce any income until 2010.

Prepare Form 1040 for Wendy for 2009. You will also need Schedule A, Schedule B, Schedule D, Schedule E, Form 4562, and Form 8824.

Tax Return Problem 2

Dave (SSN 455-55-5555) and Alicia Stanley (SSN 343-43-3434) are married and retired at age 50. The couple's income consists of rental property, stock investments, and royalties from an invention. They sold their large house that they had purchased six years ago for $580,000 on October 18, 2009, for $1 million. They now live in a condo at 101 Magnolia Lane, Suite 15, High Park, Florida 12345.

The rental property is an apartment complex (building cost $1.5 million and was purchased January 5, 2009) with 30 units that rent for $27,000 per month and are at 90% occupancy.

Rental income	$291,600
Salaries	115,000
Payroll taxes	8,798
Real estate taxes	18,750
Interest	45,000
Repairs and maintenance	29,000
Depreciation	(Calculate)

The following information is also for the year:

1099-INT	Old Bank	$ 22,000
1099-DIV	Dell, Inc. Ordinary dividends	15,250
	Qualified dividends	15,250
1099-DIV	IBM, Inc. Ordinary dividends	8,650
	Qualified dividends	8,650
1099-DIV	Pepsi, Inc. Ordinary dividends	18,785
	Qualified dividends	18,785
1099-MISC	Box 2 royalties	152,300

	Purchased	Sold	Sale Price	Basis	Gain/Loss
Dell (held 9 mo.)	12/01/08	09/01/09	$15,000	$ 9,000	$ 6,000
Pepsi (held 4 mo.)	09/01/09	12/29/09	17,000	25,000	(8,000)
IBM (held 30 mo.)	06/05/07	12/05/09	38,000	20,000	18,000

On January 3, 2010, Dave repurchased the exact number of shares he sold on 12/29/09. The Stanleys paid $13,000 each quarter (four payments) in federal estimated income taxes.

Prepare Form 1040 for the Stanleys. You will also need Schedule B, Schedule D, Schedule E, and Form 4562.

We have provided selected filled-in source documents on our Web site at www.mhhe.com/cruz2010.

PASSIVE ACTIVITY LOSSES
LO 2

The goal of the passive activity loss (PAL) rules is to restrict deductibility of tax losses created from activities that are not the taxpayer's primary source of income. The PAL rules supplement the at-risk rules. The loss must first be allowed under the at-risk rules and then must pass through PAL rule filters to ultimately be deductible and reduce taxable income.

Definition of Passive Activity

A *passive activity* is one in which the taxpayer does not materially participate. The IRC defines material participation by the taxpayer as participating in the activity on a regular, continuous, and substantial basis.[12]

Most rental activities and limited partnership interests are, by definition, passive activities. An additional potential passive activity is a trade or business in which the taxpayer does not materially participate. Table 13-2 summarizes passive activities.

TABLE 13-2
Passive Activities

Most rental properties
Any ownership interests as a limited partner
Any trade or business in which the taxpayer does not materially participate

TAX YOUR BRAIN   What constitutes regular, continuous, and substantial participation in an activity?

ANSWER
The IRS issued temporary regulations that list seven tests to determine material participation. It is clear, however, that investor-only participation is not sufficient to be classified as a material participant in an activity.

Temporary regulations provide seven tests to help determine whether a taxpayer materially participates in an activity.[13] A taxpayer materially participates if he or she meets any of the following seven tests.

Test 1: The 500-Hour Test
The individual participates in the activity for more than 500 hours. This test is the general test for most activities. The main premise is that if a taxpayer participates more than 500 hours in an activity, that taxpayer is more than a mere investor. Any work normally completed in the activity counts toward the 500-hour requirement.

Test 2: Sole Participant
The individual's participation in the activity for the taxable year constitutes all of the participation in such activity of all individuals (including individuals who are not owners of interest in the activity) for such year. If no one else works in the activity, the taxpayer must be a material participant. This rule is pertinent to many small sole proprietorships that operate cyclical or seasonal businesses.

EXAMPLE 13-8   Nidar is the sole owner and operator of a small coffee and hot chocolate shop in the mountains. The shop is open only in the winter during high-traffic times such as weekends and holidays. Even though Nidar works fewer than 500 hours in the activity, the work is not a passive activity because he is the only one who participates in the business.

[12] IRC § 469(h).
[13] IRS Reg. § 1.469-5T(a).

Test 3: More Than 100 Participation Hours

The individual participates in the activity for more than 100 hours during the tax year, and the individual's participation is not less than any other individual for the year.

EXAMPLE 13-9	Assume the same facts as in Example 13-8, but Nidar hires several part-time employees to help run the coffee and hot chocolate shop. If he works more than 100 hours and none of the other employees works more hours, the activity is not a passive activity.

Test 4: Aggregate Significant Participation

The activity is a significant participation activity (participation more than 100 hours) for the tax year, and the individual's aggregate participation in all significant participation activities during such year exceeds 500 hours. Test 4 is important to taxpayers who own and operate several businesses during the year but participate fewer than 500 hours in any one of them.

EXAMPLE 13-10	Let's assume that Nidar operates his coffee and hot chocolate shop in the mountains for 130 hours in the winter, operates a daiquiri shop at the beach for 200 hours in the summer, and works in a landscaping business of which he is a part owner for 250 hours during the year. All of these businesses are significant participation activities because Nidar worked more than 100 hours in each. Furthermore, in aggregate, his participation in all significant participation activities is more than 500 hours. Thus he is a material participant in all three activities.

Test 5: History of Material Participation

The individual materially participated in the activity for any 5 taxable years during the 10 taxable years immediately preceding the current taxable year.

Test 6: Personal Service Activity

The activity is a personal service activity, and the individual materially participated in it for any three taxable years (whether or not consecutive) preceding the taxable year.

Tests 5 and 6 are extremely important to individuals who cease to work in the activity (because of retirement, disability, or otherwise) but retain an ownership interest.

EXAMPLE 13-11	Tom is part owner in a furniture store with his son but retired from working in the business last year. Assuming that Tom worked more than 500 hours for 5 of the last 10 years, the current profit or loss from the activity is not passive. If Tom and his son operated a personal service activity such as a CPA firm, Tom needs to have been a material participant for only any three taxable years preceding the current year.

Test 7: Facts and Circumstances

Based on all of the facts and circumstances, the individual participates in the activity on a regular, continuous, and substantial basis during the tax year.

Test 7 is a catchall for taxpayers who do not meet one of the first six tests. However, the temporary regulations are silent about the conditions required to meet Test 7. Based on the lack of guidance in the regulations regarding Test 7, it would be prudent to rely on Tests 1 through 6 in determining material participation.

Passive Activity Losses: General Rule

Taxpayers subject to PAL rules include any individual, estate, trust, closely held C corporation, or any personal service corporation.[14] The general rule for passive activities generating

---

[14] IRC § 469(a)(2). In this text, the focus is exclusively on the individual taxpayer. However, these same PAL rules also apply to the other entity types.

a loss is that a taxpayer can deduct the passive loss to the extent of passive income. The PAL rules are applied on an individual-by-individual basis.

TAX YOUR BRAIN

Can two partners in a passive activity with identical passive losses from the activity be treated differently concerning the deductibility of the losses?

ANSWER

Yes, one of the partners who has passive income from another source can deduct the passive loss while the partner with no other passive activity cannot. Remember that PAL rules are applied on an individual basis, and any losses are allowed only to the extent of passive income.

EXAMPLE 13-12

Suppose Edna has an ownership interest in three passive activities. In the current tax year, the activities had the following income and losses:

Partnership A	$10,000
Partnership B	(8,000)
Partnership C	(6,000)

Edna can deduct passive losses only to the extent of passive income. Here she can deduct $10,000 of the $14,000 in passive losses. This assumes that Edna is at-risk for each of the loss activities. The excess $4,000 loss would be suspended and carried forward to future tax years until Edna has additional passive income (or until the activity is sold).

The IRC separates all income/loss items into three categories:[15]

1. **Active income/loss:** includes wages and profit or loss from a trade or business with material participation.
2. **Portfolio income:** includes interest, dividends, royalties, and capital gains.
3. **Passive income/loss:** includes any income or loss from a trade or business in which the taxpayer did not materially participate. It also includes income or loss from most rental activities whether or not there was material participation.[16]

Net passive losses cannot offset portfolio income or active income. In other words, all passive activities are first appropriately combined. If the result is net passive income, the income is reported. If the result is a net passive loss, the loss is suspended until additional passive income is generated.

Rental Activities

A *rental activity* is any activity in which a taxpayer receives payments principally for the use of tangible property. In general, rental activities are passive activities. One exception concerns real estate professionals. A rental business can qualify for active treatment if more than one-half of the personal services performed in a business during the year are performed in a real property trade or business and the taxpayer performs more than 750 hours of services in the activity.[17]

EXAMPLE 13-13

Richard owns and operates several rental houses and apartment complexes in a college town. This is his only business activity, and he works full-time in the venture. In this case, Richard meets the exception as a real estate professional, and the rental income and losses are not passive activities.

---

[15] IRC § 469(e).

[16] The sale of an asset (such as a piece of equipment) used in the passive activity would be considered passive. This does not include gains on investment property (that is, capital gains or losses).

[17] IRC 469(c)(7)(B).

From Shoebox to Software

EXAMPLE 13-14   Assume that Jose Ramirez (from the earlier chapters) received a K-1 (shown in Exhibit 13-3) from College Repairs Limited Partnership.

Upon reviewing the K-1, you know that the partnership is a passive activity because the limited partner box is checked (Question I on Schedule K-1). If the general partner box is checked, you must apply one of the seven material participation tests to determine whether the activity is passive. The interest and dividends ($500 and $200, respectively) are portfolio income, which you report on Schedule B. The $1,200 capital gain transfers to Schedule D. However, the $3,523 loss is a passive loss and is deductible on Schedule E only if Jose had passive income from another passive activity.

In Chapter 8, you entered information from a K-1 on Jose Ramirez's return. However, Jose materially participated in that partnership. In the College Repairs partnership, Jose is a limited partner, and thus the activity is passive.

In your tax software, open the Ramirez file and open a new K-1. Enter the information from the College Repairs LP from Exhibit 13-3. Assume that Jose is at-risk for this activity. After completing the K-1 information, the tax software transfers the information to Schedule B, Schedule D, and Form 8582. Note that the allowed loss on Form 8582 is zero because Jose had no other passive income. Also note that Schedule E, page 2, shows the College Repairs LP, but zero loss is allowed. Form 8582 is shown in Exhibit 13-4.

In addition to the real estate professional exception to the PAL rules, rental activities are not passive activities in six other cases.[18]

Case 1: Average Rental Period Fewer Than Seven Days

The average period for customer use is fewer than seven days. Businesses that rent or lease tangible property for short periods are active (nonpassive) activities. For example, businesses that rent automobiles, tools, or DVDs are not passive activities.

Case 2: Average Rental Period 30 or Fewer Days with Significant Personal Services

The average period of customer use is 30 or fewer days, and the owner provides significant personal services. An example meeting this exception for nonpassive classification would be the rental of a large crane for a construction site. If the average use were more than 7 days but fewer than 30 days and the rental company provided the crane operator, the rental would qualify as an active activity.

Case 3: Extraordinary Personal Services

The owner provides extraordinary personal services in connection with the rental of tangible property. The most common rental property meeting this exception includes hospitals and university dormitories. Dorm rooms and hospital rooms are essentially rented, but the extraordinary services provided (the education or medical care) qualify the business for active treatment.

Case 4: Incidental Rental Activity

The rental activity is incidental to a nonrental activity. This occurs if the property was predominantly used in a trade or business for at least two of the last five tax years. The gross rental income must be less than 2% of the lower of the basis of the property or its FMV. For example, suppose that a farmer leases a portion of his rice farm for duck hunting over the winter. If the rent received is less than 2% of the lower of basis or FMV, the rent is incidental to the farming activity.

[18] Reg. § 1.469-1T(e)(3).

EXHIBIT 13-3

651109

☐ Final K-1	☐ Amended K-1 OMB No. 1545-0099

Schedule K-1
(Form 1065)   20**09**

Department of the Treasury
Internal Revenue Service

For calendar year 2009, or tax
year beginning _____ , 2009
ending _____ , 20 ____

Partner's Share of Income, Deductions,
Credits, etc.   ► See back of form and separate instructions.

Part I	**Information About the Partnership**

A Partnership's employer identification number
52-7234562

B Partnership's name, address, city, state, and ZIP code

College Repairs, L.P.
123 University Drive
State University, NC 12345

C IRS Center where partnership filed return
Cincinnati, OH

D ☐ Check if this is a publicly traded partnership (PTP)

Part II	**Information About the Partner**

E Partner's identifying number
222-22-2222

F Partner's name, address, city, state, and ZIP code

Jose Ramirez
1234 West Street
Mytown, GA 33333

G ☐ General partner or LLC   ☒ Limited partner or other LLC
member-manager   member

H ☐ Domestic partner   ☐ Foreign partner

I What type of entity is this partner? Individual

J Partner's share of profit, loss, and capital (see instructions):

	Beginning	Ending
Profit	%	5.0 %
Loss	%	5.0 %
Capital	%	5.0 %

K Partner's share of liabilities at year end:
Nonrecourse . . . . . . $ _____
Qualified nonrecourse financing . $ _____
Recourse . . . . $ 7,000

L Partner's capital account analysis:
Beginning capital account . . . $ _____
Capital contributed during the year $ _____
Current year increase (decrease) . $ _____
Withdrawals & distributions . . $ (_____)
Ending capital account . . . . $ _____

☒ Tax basis   ☐ GAAP   ☐ Section 704(b) book
☐ Other (explain)

M Did the partner contribute property with a built-in gain or loss?
☐ Yes   ☒ No
If "Yes", attach statement (see instructions)

Part III	**Partner's Share of Current Year Income,**
	Deductions, Credits, and Other Items

1	Ordinary business income (loss)	15	Credits
	(3,523)		
2	Net rental real estate income (loss)		
3	Other net rental income (loss)	16	Foreign transactions
4	Guaranteed payments		
5	Interest income		
	500		
6a	Ordinary dividends		
	200		
6b	Qualified dividends		
	200		
7	Royalties		
8	Net short-term capital gain (loss)		
9a	Net long-term capital gain (loss)	17	Alternative minimum tax (AMT) items
	1,200		
9b	Collectibles (28%) gain (loss)		
9c	Unrecaptured section 1250 gain		
10	Net section 1231 gain (loss)	18	Tax-exempt income and nondeductible expenses
11	Other income (loss)		
		19	Distributions
12	Section 179 deduction		
13	Other deductions	20	Other information
14	Self-employment earnings (loss)		

*See attached statement for additional information.

For IRS Use Only

EXHIBIT 13-4

Form **8582**	**Passive Activity Loss Limitations**	OMB No. 1545-1008
Department of the Treasury Internal Revenue Service (99)	► See separate instructions. ► **Attach to Form 1040 or Form 1041.**	**2009** Attachment Sequence No. **88**

Name(s) shown on return	Identifying number
Jose and Maria Ramirez	222-22-2222

Part I 2009 Passive Activity Loss
Caution: *Complete Worksheets 1, 2, and 3 on page 2 before completing Part I.*

Rental Real Estate Activities With Active Participation (For the definition of active participation, see **Special Allowance for Rental Real Estate Activities** on page 3 of the instructions.)

1a	Activities with net income (enter the amount from Worksheet 1, column (a))	1a	
b	Activities with net loss (enter the amount from Worksheet 1, column (b))	1b (	)
c	Prior years unallowed losses (enter the amount from Worksheet 1, column (c))	1c (	)
d	Combine lines 1a, 1b, and 1c	1d	

Commercial Revitalization Deductions From Rental Real Estate Activities

2a	Commercial revitalization deductions from Worksheet 2, column (a)	2a (	)
b	Prior year unallowed commercial revitalization deductions from Worksheet 2, column (b)	2b (	)
c	Add lines 2a and 2b	2c (	)

All Other Passive Activities

3a	Activities with net income (enter the amount from Worksheet 3, column (a))	3a	
b	Activities with net loss (enter the amount from Worksheet 3, column (b))	3b (3,523	)
c	Prior years unallowed losses (enter the amount from Worksheet 3, column (c))	3c (	)
d	Combine lines 3a, 3b, and 3c	3d	(3,523)
4	Combine lines 1d, 2c, and 3d. If the result is net income or zero, all losses are allowed, including any prior year unallowed losses entered on line 1c, 2b, or 3c. **Do not** complete Form 8582. Report the losses on the forms and schedules normally used	4	(3,523)

If line 4 is a loss and: • Line 1d is a loss, go to Part II.

• Line 2c is a loss (and line 1d is zero or more), skip Part II and go to Part III.

• Line 3d is a loss (and lines 1d and 2c are zero or more), skip Parts II and III and go to line 15.

Caution: *If your filing status is married filing separately and you lived with your spouse at any time during the year,* **do not** *complete Part II or Part III. Instead, go to line 15.*

Part II Special Allowance for Rental Real Estate Activities With Active Participation
Note: *Enter all numbers in Part II as positive amounts. See page 8 of the instructions for an example.*

5	Enter the **smaller** of the loss on line 1d or the loss on line 4	5	
6	Enter $150,000. If married filing separately, see page 8	6	
7	Enter modified adjusted gross income, but not less than zero (see page 8)	7	

Note: *If line 7 is greater than or equal to line 6, skip lines 8 and 9, enter -0- on line 10. Otherwise, go to line 8.*

8	Subtract line 7 from line 6	8	
9	Multiply line 8 by 50% (.5). **Do not** enter more than $25,000. If married filing separately, see page 8	9	
10	Enter the **smaller** of line 5 or line 9	10	

If line 2c is a loss, go to Part III. Otherwise, go to line 15.

Part III Special Allowance for Commercial Revitalization Deductions From Rental Real Estate Activities
Note: *Enter all numbers in Part III as positive amounts. See the example for Part II on page 8 of the instructions.*

11	Enter $25,000 reduced by the amount, if any, on line 10. If married filing separately, see instructions	11	
12	Enter the loss from line 4	12	
13	Reduce line 12 by the amount on line 10	13	
14	Enter the **smallest** of line 2c (treated as a positive amount), line 11, or line 13	14	

Part IV Total Losses Allowed

15	Add the income, if any, on lines 1a and 3a and enter the total	15	
16	**Total losses allowed from all passive activities for 2009.** Add lines 10, 14, and 15. See page 10 of the instructions to find out how to report the losses on your tax return	16	0

For Paperwork Reduction Act Notice, see page 12 of the instructions. Cat. No. 63704F Form **8582** (2009)

EXHIBIT 13-7

Form **8582**	**Passive Activity Loss Limitations**	OMB No. 1545-1008
Department of the Treasury Internal Revenue Service (99)	▶ See separate instructions. ▶ Attach to Form 1040 or Form 1041.	20**09** Attachment Sequence No. **88**

Name(s) shown on return: Lori Doe   Identifying number: 487-65-4321

(Draft as of 06/24/2009 watermark)

Part I   2009 Passive Activity Loss
Caution: *Complete Worksheets 1, 2, and 3 on page 2 before completing Part I.*

Rental Real Estate Activities With Active Participation (For the definition of active participation, see **Special Allowance for Rental Real Estate Activities** on page 3 of the instructions.)

- 1a Activities with net income (enter the amount from Worksheet 1, column (a)) **1a**
- b Activities with net loss (enter the amount from Worksheet 1, column (b)) **1b** (10,000)
- c Prior years unallowed losses (enter the amount from Worksheet 1, column (c)) .... **1c** (   )
- d Combine lines 1a, 1b, and 1c **1d** (10,000)

Commercial Revitalization Deductions From Rental Real Estate Activities

- 2a Commercial revitalization deductions from Worksheet 2, column (a) . **2a** (   )
- b Prior year unallowed commercial revitalization deductions from Worksheet 2, column (b) .... **2b** (   )
- c Add lines 2a and 2b .... **2c** (   )

All Other Passive Activities

- 3a Activities with net income (enter the amount from Worksheet 3, column (a)) **3a** 60,000
- b Activities with net loss (enter the amount from Worksheet 3, column (b)) **3b** (90,000)
- c Prior years unallowed losses (enter the amount from Worksheet 3, column (c)) .... **3c** (   )
- d Combine lines 3a, 3b, and 3c **3d** (30,000)

4 Combine lines 1d, 2c, and 3d. If the result is net income or zero, all losses are allowed, including any prior year unallowed losses entered on line 1c, 2b, or 3c. **Do not** complete Form 8582. Report the losses on the forms and schedules normally used **4** (40,000)

If line 4 is a loss and:
- Line 1d is a loss, go to Part II.
- Line 2c is a loss (and line 1d is zero or more), skip Part II and go to Part III.
- Line 3d is a loss (and lines 1d and 2c are zero or more), skip Parts II and III and go to line 15.

Caution: *If your filing status is married filing separately and you lived with your spouse at any time during the year, **do not** complete Part II or Part III. Instead, go to line 15.*

Part II   Special Allowance for Rental Real Estate Activities With Active Participation
Note: *Enter all numbers in Part II as positive amounts. See page 8 of the instructions for an example.*

5 Enter the **smaller** of the loss on line 1d or the loss on line 4 .... **5** 10,000
6 Enter $150,000. If married filing separately, see page 8 .... **6** 150,000
7 Enter modified adjusted gross income, but not less than zero (see page 8) **7** 80,003

Note: *If line 7 is greater than or equal to line 6, skip lines 8 and 9, enter -0- on line 10. Otherwise, go to line 8.*

8 Subtract line 7 from line 6 .... **8** 69,997
9 Multiply line 8 by 50% (.5). **Do not** enter more than $25,000. If married filing separately, see page 8 **9** 25,000
10 Enter the **smaller** of line 5 or line 9 .... **10** 10,000

If line 2c is a loss, go to Part III. Otherwise, go to line 15.

Part III   Special Allowance for Commercial Revitalization Deductions From Rental Real Estate Activities
Note: *Enter all numbers in Part III as positive amounts. See the example for Part II on page 8 of the instructions.*

11 Enter $25,000 reduced by the amount, if any, on line 10. If married filing separately, see instructions **11**
12 Enter the loss from line 4 .... **12**
13 Reduce line 12 by the amount on line 10 .... **13**
14 Enter the **smallest** of line 2c (treated as a positive amount), line 11, or line 13 .... **14**

Part IV   Total Losses Allowed

15 Add the income, if any, on lines 1a and 3a and enter the total **15** 60,000
16 **Total losses allowed from all passive activities for 2009.** Add lines 10, 14, and 15. See page 10 of the instructions to find out how to report the losses on your tax return **16** 70,000

For Paperwork Reduction Act Notice, see page 12 of the instructions. Cat. No. 63704F Form **8582** (2009)

EXHIBIT 13-8

Version A, Cycle 1

Schedule E (Form 1040) 2009 — Attachment Sequence No. **13** — Page **2**

Name(s) shown on return. Do not enter name and social security number if shown on other side.

Lori Doe

Your social security number: 487-65-4321

Caution. The IRS compares amounts reported on your tax return with amounts shown on Schedule(s) K-1.

Part II Income or Loss From Partnerships and S Corporations **Note.** If you report a loss from an at-risk activity for which **any** amount is **not** at risk, you **must** check the box in column **(e)** on line 28 and attach **Form 6198.** See page E-1.

27 Are you reporting any loss not allowed in a prior year due to the at-risk or basis limitations, a prior year unallowed loss from a passive activity (if that loss was not reported on Form 8582), or unreimbursed partnership expenses? If you answered "Yes," see page E-7 before completing this section. ☐ Yes ☐ No

28	(a) Name	(b) Enter P for partnership; S for S corporation	(c) Check if foreign partnership	(d) Employer identification number	(e) Check if any amount is not at risk
A	Partnership A	P	☐	56-1234567	☐
B	Partnership B	P	☐	56-7654321	☐
C	Partnership C	P	☐	56-4444444	☐
D	Partnership D	P	☐	56-5555555	☐

	Passive Income and Loss		Nonpassive Income and Loss		
	(f) Passive loss allowed (attach Form 8582 if required)	(g) Passive income from Schedule K-1	(h) Nonpassive loss from Schedule K-1	(i) Section 179 expense deduction from Form 4562	(j) Nonpassive income from Schedule K-1
A		60,000			
B	40,000				
C	20,000				
D	10,000				
29a Totals		60,000			
b Totals	70,000				

30 Add columns (g) and (j) of line 29a ... 30 | 60,000
31 Add columns (f), (h), and (i) of line 29b ... 31 | (70,000)
32 **Total partnership and S corporation income or (loss).** Combine lines 30 and 31. Enter the result here and include in the total on line 41 below ... 32 | (10,000)

Part III Income or Loss From Estates and Trusts

33	(a) Name	(b) Employer identification number
A		
B		

	Passive Income and Loss		Nonpassive Income and Loss	
	(c) Passive deduction or loss allowed (attach Form 8582 if required)	(d) Passive income from Schedule K-1	(e) Deduction or loss from Schedule K-1	(f) Other income from Schedule K-1
A				
B				
34a Totals				
b Totals				

35 Add columns (d) and (f) of line 34a ... 35
36 Add columns (c) and (e) of line 34b ... 36 ( )
37 **Total estate and trust income or (loss).** Combine lines 35 and 36. Enter the result here and include in the total on line 41 below ... 37

Part IV Income or Loss From Real Estate Mortgage Investment Conduits (REMICs)—Residual Holder

38	(a) Name	(b) Employer identification number	(c) Excess inclusion from Schedules Q, line 2c (see page E-7)	(d) Taxable income (net loss) from Schedules Q, line 1b	(e) Income from Schedules Q, line 3b

39 Combine columns (d) and (e) only. Enter the result here and include in the total on line 41 below ... 39

Part V Summary

40 Net farm rental income or (loss) from **Form 4835.** Also, complete line 42 below ... 40
41 **Total income or (loss).** Combine lines 26, 32, 37, 39, and 40. Enter the result here and on Form 1040, line 17, or Form 1040NR, line 18 ▶ 41 | (10,000)
42 **Reconciliation of farming and fishing income.** Enter your **gross** farming and fishing income reported on Form 4835, line 7; Schedule K-1 (Form 1065), box 14, code B; Schedule K-1 (Form 1120S), box 17, code T; and Schedule K-1 (Form 1041), line 14, code F (see page E-8) | 42
43 **Reconciliation for real estate professionals.** If you were a real estate professional (see page E-2), enter the net income or (loss) you reported anywhere on Form 1040 or Form 1040NR from all rental real estate activities in which you materially participated under the passive activity loss rules ... 43

Schedule E (Form 1040) 2009

Reason for Change: The committee believes that the minimum tax should serve one overriding objective: to ensure that no taxpayer with substantial economic income can avoid significant tax liability by using exclusions, deductions, and credits. Although these provisions may provide incentives for worthy goals, they become counterproductive when taxpayers are allowed to use them to avoid virtually all tax liability. The ability of high-income individuals and highly profitable corporations to pay little or no tax undermines respect for the entire tax system and, thus, for the incentive provisions themselves. In addition, even aside from public perceptions, the committee believes that it is inherently unfair for high-income individuals and highly profitable corporations to pay little or no tax due to their ability to utilize various tax preferences.[23]

The AMT rules are based on the notion of alternative minimum taxable income (AMTI). To determine AMTI, the taxpayer starts with regular taxable income calculated in accordance with the laws discussed throughout this text. The taxpayer then makes adjustments to regular taxable income to arrive at AMTI, which is used to calculate the minimum tax liability using an AMT tax rate of 26% or 28%. The AMT for an individual taxpayer is reported on Form 6251.

AMT Formula

The base formula for calculating AMT is this:[24]

Regular taxable income		
	+	Personal/dependency exemptions and standard deduction if the taxpayer does not itemize.[a]
	+ / −	Adjustment items[b]
	+	Tax preference items[c]
	=	Alternative minimum taxable income (AMTI)
	−	AMT exemption amount[d]
	=	Alternative minimum tax base
	×	Tax rate of either 26% (or 28% less $3,500[e])
	=	Tentative minimum tax
	−	Regular tax
	=	Alternative minimum tax

[a] IRC Section 56(b)(1)(E).
[b] IRC Section 56.
[c] IRC Section 57.
[d] IRC Section 55(d)(1).
[e] IRC Section 55(b)(1)(A).

It is important to note that a taxpayer does not owe any AMT unless the AMT calculation results in an amount greater than the regular tax. Also note that the AMT tax rate is either 26% or 28%. If the taxpayer's AMTI is $175,000 or less, the AMT rate is 26%. If the AMTI amount is more than $175,000, the AMT rate is 28%; $3,500 is then subtracted from the resulting AMT tax calculation.

AMT Adjustment Items

Adjustments to regular income to arrive at AMTI can be either positive or negative.[25] The adjustments could reduce AMTI to the point that a taxpayer will not be subject to AMT. However, most adjustments increase AMTI. Table 13-3 lists the primary AMT adjustments.[26]

Only those adjustments affecting numerous taxpayers are covered in detail in this section. For more obscure adjustments, see the instructions for Form 6251 and IRC Section 56.

[23] Senate Report No. 99-313 (P.L. 99-514), 1986-3 CB (Part 3), p. 518. The Senate Report accompanied the Tax Reform Act of 1986.

[24] The format on Form 6251 is somewhat different, but the calculation is the same. On Form 6251, the preference items and adjustments are on the first part of the form and regular taxable income is added in Part II.

[25] A positive adjustment increases AMTI, and a negative adjustment decreases AMTI. Thus a negative adjustment is good for the taxpayer.

[26] IRC § 56.

TABLE 13-3
Adjustments to AMT

Standard deduction and personal/dependency exemptions not allowed.
Limitations on itemized deductions.
Depreciation placed in service after 1986 and before 1999.
Depreciation exceeding 150% declining balance for some assets placed in service after 1998.
Adjustments to gains and losses on the sale of assets (different gains are caused by different depreciation methods).
Treatment of incentive stock options.
Passive activities (differences in regular tax passive loss and AMT passive loss allowed).
Beneficiaries of estates and trusts (differences in regular income or loss and amount of AMT income or loss).
Treatment of long-term contracts.
Others.

Standard Deduction, Exemptions, and Itemized Deduction Limits

If the taxpayer does not itemize and takes the standard deduction for regular tax purposes, the standard deduction is added back as a positive adjustment to AMTI. Likewise, the personal exemptions are also added as a positive adjustment.[27]

EXAMPLE 13-20

Roland is married, files a joint return, and has two children. Because he rents his home (pays no mortgage interest) and lives in Florida (has no state income tax), he does not itemize his deductions but takes the standard deduction. Roland would have the following positive adjustments for AMTI:

Standard deduction	$11,400
Personal exemptions (4 × $3,650)	14,600*
	$26,000

*Because only high-income taxpayers are usually subject to AMT, the personal exemption may not be an adjustment because it is phased out as AGI reaches certain thresholds.

Limitations on Itemized Deductions

Several itemized deductions are either limited or disallowed in determining AMTI. For example, the AGI floor for medical expenses increases from 7.5% of AGI to 10% of AGI. Any itemized deduction for taxes or miscellaneous itemized deductions are totally disallowed for AMT purposes.[28] The itemized deduction for mortgage interest is also modified for AMTI because only mortgage interest used to build, buy, or substantially improve the taxpayer's home or second home is allowed. Interest expense from a home equity loan to purchase an auto or other asset (qualified housing interest) is disallowed for AMT purposes and causes a positive AMT adjustment. This qualified housing interest is treated like investment interest and is deductible only to the extent of investment income. All other itemized deductions are allowed as AMT deductions.

Table 13-4 summarizes the AMT adjustments for itemized deductions.

Depreciation Adjustment for AMT

Nearly every taxpayer who calculates depreciation on his or her tax return will have a depreciation adjustment for AMT purposes. For most assets, depreciation must be recalculated using methods allowable for AMT. The method and life used vary depending on when the asset was placed in service and the type of property (real property or personal property).

Real Property Placed in Service after 1986 and before 1999

Depreciation (for regular tax purposes) on all depreciable real property placed in service after 1986 and before 1999 is calculated using the straight-line method. The only difference is the depreciation life of 27.5 years for residential real property and 39 years for nonresidential real

[27] IRC § 56(b)(1)(E).
[28] IRC § 56(b)(1)(A).

TABLE 13-4
Summary of AMT Adjustments for Itemized Deductions

Medical	AGI floor increases from 7.5% to 10%.
Taxes	Not allowed for AMT.
Mortgage interest	Allowed for AMT only if the interest is to build, buy, or substantially improve the taxpayer's residence.
Gifts to charity	Allowed for AMT subject to the same limitations as regular tax.
Casualty and theft losses	Allowed for AMT subject to the same limitations as regular tax.
Miscellaneous itemized deductions	Not allowed for AMT.
High-income limitation of itemized deductions	Not applicable to AMT; any limitation for regular tax purposes creates a negative adjustment.

EXAMPLE 13-21

Suppose that Jergen had the Schedule A shown in Exhibit 13-9 for his regular tax return. The mortgage interest is all qualified mortgage interest to purchase his personal residence.

For AMT purposes, Jergen has the following adjustments:

Itemized Deduction	Regular Tax	Permitted AMT Deduction	AMT Adjustment
Medical	$59,300	$53,150	$ 6,150
Taxes	49,350	–0–	49,350
Mortgage interest	15,400	15,400	–0–
Charitable contributions	12,800	12,800	–0–
Miscellaneous deductions	1,880	–0–	1,880
2%/80% limit (1% in 2009)	(792)	–0–	(792)
Total AMT adjustment for itemized deductions			$56,588

Jergen's itemized deductions are limited for regular tax purposes because of his income level. One positive item concerning AMT is that the regular tax itemized deduction limitation does not apply to AMT itemized deductions. Additionally, because taxes are not allowed as an AMT deduction, any income from tax refunds included in regular taxable income results in a negative AMT adjustment.[29]

property.[30] For AMT purposes, the depreciation life is 40 years for *all* real property (straight-line and midmonth conventions stay the same). Table 13 in Revenue Procedure 87-57 is the appropriate table to use for the depreciation calculation for real property under the AMT rules. Table 13 is reproduced in the appendix to this chapter (Table 13A-1).

EXAMPLE 13-22

Alex purchased a warehouse for $310,000 in August 1998. The regular depreciation and AMT depreciation for 2009 are calculated as follows:

Regular Tax Depreciation (Table 6A-8—Chapter 6)	AMT Depreciation (Appendix Table 13A-1)	Adjustment
$310,000 × 2.564% = $7,948	$310,000 × 2.5% = $7,750	$198

The depreciation adjustment is only $198 for this asset. This is a small adjustment because the depreciation lives are virtually the same: 39 years for regular taxes compared to 40 years for AMT purposes.

[29] A negative AMT adjustment reduces the AMT income subject to tax. Recall that tax refunds are included in income only if the taxpayer deducted the taxes in a prior year.

[30] For assets placed in service prior to 1986, the difference in depreciation is called a *tax preference item* rather than an *adjustment* and thus is discussed in the preference section. Also, nonresidential real property purchased between December 31, 1986, and May 13, 1993, has a depreciable life of 31.5 years.

EXHIBIT 13-9

SCHEDULE A (Form 1040)	Itemized Deductions	OMB No. 1545-0074
Department of the Treasury Internal Revenue Service (99)	► **Attach to Form 1040.** ► **See Instructions for Schedule A (Form 1040).**	2009 Attachment Sequence No. **07**

Name(s) shown on Form 1040	Your social security number
Jergen Trade	487-65-4321

Medical and Dental Expenses	**Caution.** Do not include expenses reimbursed or paid by others.		
	1 Medical and dental expenses (see page A-1)	**1** 77,750	
	2 Enter amount from Form 1040, line 38 **2** 246,000		
	3 Multiply line 2 by 7.5% (.075)	**3** 18,450	
	4 Subtract line 3 from line 1. If line 3 is more than line 1, enter -0-	**4**	59,300
Taxes You Paid (See page A-2.)	**5** State and local **(check only one box):**		
	a ☒ Income taxes, **or**	**5** 40,300	
	b ☐ General sales taxes		
	6 Real estate taxes (see page A-5)	**6** 7,900	
	7 New motor vehicle taxes from line 11 of the worksheet on back. Skip this line if you checked box 5b	**7** 1,150	
	8 Other taxes. List type and amount ►	**8**	
	9 Add lines 5 through 8	**9**	49,350
Interest You Paid (See page A-5.) **Note.** Personal interest is not deductible.	**10** Home mortgage interest and points reported to you on Form 1098	**10** 15,400	
	11 Home mortgage interest not reported to you on Form 1098. If paid to the person from whom you bought the home, see page A-6 and show that person's name, identifying no., and address ►	**11**	
	12 Points not reported to you on Form 1098. See page A-6 for special rules	**12**	
	13 Qualified mortgage insurance premiums (see page A-6)	**13**	
	14 Investment interest. Attach Form 4952 if required. (See page A-6.)	**14**	
	15 Add lines 10 through 14	**15**	15,400
Gifts to Charity If you made a gift and got a benefit for it, see page A-7.	**16** Gifts by cash or check. If you made any gift of $250 or more, see page A-7	**16** 12,800	
	17 Other than by cash or check. If any gift of $250 or more, see page A-8. You **must** attach Form 8283 if over $500	**17**	
	18 Carryover from prior year	**18**	
	19 Add lines 16 through 18	**19**	12,800
Casualty and Theft Losses	**20** Casualty or theft loss(es). Attach Form 4684. (See page A-8.)	**20**	
Job Expenses and Certain Miscellaneous Deductions (See page A-9.)	**21** Unreimbursed employee expenses—job travel, union dues, job education, etc. Attach Form 2106 or 2106-EZ if required. (See page A-9.) ►	**21** 6,000	
	22 Tax preparation fees	**22** 800	
	23 Other expenses—investment, safe deposit box, etc. List type and amount ►	**23**	
	24 Add lines 21 through 23	**24** 6,800	
	25 Enter amount from Form 1040, line 38 **25** 246,000		
	26 Multiply line 25 by 2% (.02)	**26** 4,920	
	27 Subtract line 26 from line 24. If line 26 is more than line 24, enter -0-	**27**	1,880
Other Miscellaneous Deductions	**28** Other—from list on page A-10. List type and amount ►	**28**	0
Total Itemized Deductions	**29** Is Form 1040, line 38, over $166,800 (over $83,400 if married filing separately)?		
	☐ **No.** Your deduction is not limited. Add the amounts in the far right column for lines 4 through 28. Also, enter this amount on Form 1040, line 40a. ►	**29**	137,938
	☒ **Yes.** Your deduction may be limited. See page A-10 for the amount to enter.		
	30 If you elect to itemize deductions even though they are less than your standard deduction, check here ► ☐		

For Paperwork Reduction Act Notice, see Form 1040 instructions.	Cat. No. 17145C	Schedule A (Form 1040) 2009

EXAMPLE 13-23   Assume the same facts as in Example 13-22, but the property is an apartment building instead of a warehouse.

Regular Tax Depreciation (Table 6A-6 Chapter 6)	AMT Depreciation (Appendix Table 13A-1)	Adjustment
$310,000 × 3.636% = $ 11,272	$310,000 × 2.5% = $ 7,750	$ 3,522

In Example 13-23, the adjustment of $3,522 is higher because the depreciable lives are 27.5 years for regular tax purposes and 40 years for AMT purposes.

Real Property Placed in Service after 1998

Congress changed the law for real property placed in service after 1998. Because the depreciation difference affected only the depreciation life and the difference was only one year in the case of nonresidential real property, Congress eliminated this adjustment. For real property placed in service after 1998, there is no adjustment for depreciation.

Personal Property Placed in Service after 1986 and before 1999

For personal property, both the depreciation method and the class life are different under AMT rules. Regular MACRS depreciation for personal property is 200% declining balance (DB), and the life is determined under the general depreciation system (GDS). However, only 150% declining balance is allowed for AMT, and the life is determined under the alternative depreciation system (ADS). Both Revenue Procedure 87-56 and IRS Publication 946 present the different depreciation systems and corresponding lives.

See Exhibit 13-10 for a reproduction of page 98 of IRS Publication 946. The GDS shows the GDS class life for regular tax purposes; the last column gives the ADS life for AMT calculations. The AMT lives are almost always longer (*never* shorter) than the regular tax lives. Longer lives and a less aggressive depreciation method (150% DB versus 200% DB) ensure that a positive AMTI adjustment results for personal property. This adjustment is becoming less important because most of these assets were fully depreciated for regular tax purposes during the 2006 tax year.

TAX YOUR BRAIN   Will the AMT depreciation adjustment for these assets be larger or smaller as the years progress?

ANSWER

It will be smaller. Because a higher amount of depreciation is taken in the early years with accelerated methods, the 200% declining balance depreciation will decline more rapidly than the 150% declining balance as the assets get older. Thus the difference between the two numbers will narrow. The adjustment will actually become negative in the last years of depreciation.

Personal Property Placed in Service after 1998

In an attempt to simplify AMT calculations, Congress again changed the treatment of AMT depreciation for personal property. For any personal assets placed in service after 1998, the depreciation lives for AMT purposes are the same as for regular taxes (both will use the GDS life). The method still differs (150% DB for AMT and 200% DB for MACRS) for assets placed in service before then. Until all personal property placed in service between 1986 and 1998 is fully depreciated for both regular and AMT purposes, taxpayers must still be concerned with the calculations previously discussed.

EXHIBIT 13-10   Excerpt from Publication 946

Table B-1. Table of Class Lives and Recovery Periods

Asset class	Description of assets included	Class Life (in years)	GDS (MACRS)	ADS
	*SPECIFIC DEPRECIABLE ASSETS USED IN ALL BUSINESS ACTIVITIES, EXCEPT AS NOTED:*			
00.11	**Office Furniture, Fixtures, and Equipment:** Includes furniture and fixtures that are not a structural component of a building. Includes such assets as desks, files, safes, and communications equipment. Does not include communications equipment that is included in other classes.	10	7	10
00.12	**Information Systems:** Includes computers and their peripheral equipment used in administering normal business transactions and the maintenance of business records, their retrieval and analysis. Information systems are defined as: 1) Computers: A computer is a programmable electronically activated device capable of accepting information, applying prescribed processes to the information, and supplying the results of these processes with or without human intervention. It usually consists of a central processing unit containing extensive storage, logic, arithmetic, and control capabilities. Excluded from this category are adding machines, electronic desk calculators, etc., and other equipment described in class 00.13. 2) Peripheral equipment consists of the auxiliary machines which are designed to be placed under control of the central processing unit. Nonlimiting examples are: Card readers, card punches, magnetic tape feeds, high speed printers, optical character readers, tape cassettes, mass storage units, paper tape equipment, keypunches, data entry devices, teleprinters, terminals, tape drives, disc drives, disc files, disc packs, visual image projector tubes, card sorters, plotters, and collators. Peripheral equipment may be used on-line or off-line. Does not incude equipment that is an integral part of other capital equipment that is included in other classes of economic activity, i.e., computers used primarily for process or production control, switching, channeling, and automating distributive trades and services such as point of sale (POS) computer systems. Also, does not include equipment of a kind used primarily for amusement or entertainment of the user.	6	5	5
00.13	**Data Handling Equipment; except Computers:** Includes only typewriters, calculators, adding and accounting machines, copiers, and duplicating equipment.	6	5	6
00.21	**Airplanes (airframes and engines), except those used in commercial or contract carrying of passengers or freight, and all helicopters (airframes and engines)**	6	5	6
00.22	**Automobiles, Taxis**	3	5	5
00.23	**Buses**	9	5	9
00.241	**Light General Purpose Trucks:** Includes trucks for use over the road (actual weight less than 13,000 pounds)	4	5	5
00.242	**Heavy General Purpose Trucks:** Includes heavy general purpose trucks, concrete ready mix-trucks, and ore trucks, for use over the road (actual unloaded weight 13,000 pounds or more)	6	5	6
00.25	**Railroad Cars and Locomotives, except those owned by railroad transportation companies**	15	7	15
00.26	**Tractor Units for Use Over-The-Road**	4	3	4
00.27	**Trailers and Trailer-Mounted Containers**	6	5	6
00.28	**Vessels, Barges, Tugs, and Similar Water Transportation Equipment, except those used in marine construction**	18	10	18
00.3	**Land Improvements:** Includes improvements directly to or added to land, whether such improvements are section 1245 property or section 1250 property, provided such improvements are depreciable. Examples of such assets might include sidewalks, roads, canals, waterways, drainage facilities, sewers (not including municipal sewers in Class 51), wharves and docks, bridges, fences, landscaping shrubbery, or radio and television transmitting towers. Does not include land improvements that are explicitly included in any other class, and buildings and structural components as defined in section 1.48-1(e) of the regulations. Excludes public utility initial clearing and grading land improvements as specified in Rev. Rul. 72-403, 1972-2 C.B. 102.	20	15	20
00.4	**Industrial Steam and Electric Generation and/or Distribution Systems:** Includes assets, whether such assets are section 1245 property or 1250 property, providing such assets are depreciable, used in the production and/or distribution of electricity with rated total capacity in excess of 500 Kilowatts and/or assets used in the production and/or distribution of steam with rated total capacity in excess of 12,500 pounds per hour for use by the taxpayer in its industrial manufacturing process or plant activity and not ordinarily available for sale to others. Does not include buildings and structural components as defined in section 1.48-1(e) of the regulations. Assets used to generate and/or distribute electricity or steam of the type described above, but of lesser rated capacity, are not included, but are included in the appropriate manufacturing equipment classes elsewhere specified. Also includes electric generating and steam distribution assets, which may utilize steam produced by a waste reduction and resource recovery plant, used by the taxpayer in its industrial manufacturing process or plant activity. Steam and chemical recovery boiler systems used for the recovery and regeneration of chemicals used in manufacturing, with rated capacity in excess of that described above, with specifically related distribution and return systems are not included but are included in appropriate manufacturing equipment classes elsewhere specified. An example of an excluded steam and chemical recovery boiler system is that used in the pulp and paper manufacturing equipment classes elsewhere specified. An example of an excluded steam and chemical recovery boiler system is that used in the pulp and paper manufacturing industry.	22	15	22

LO 2   8. What are the differences between material participation, active participation, and significant participation?

_____

_____

_____

_____

LO 2   9. When a passive activity is sold or otherwise disposed of, what happens to any suspended losses from that activity?

_____

_____

_____

_____

LO 3   10. When must Form 6198 and Form 8582 be filed? Does the taxpayer file more than one Form 6198 or Form 8582?

_____

_____

_____

_____

LO 3   11. How do the passive loss rules and the at-risk rules work in conjunction to limit losses?

_____

_____

_____

_____

LO 4   12. Discuss the AMT formula and how it relates to the regular income tax. Include in your discussion factors that cause AMT to be assessed.

_____

_____

_____

_____

LO 4   13. What AMT adjustment items are likely to affect all taxpayers who itemize their deductions? Give examples.

_____

_____

_____

_____

LO 4   14. Are medical expenses treated differently for AMT purposes than for regular tax purposes? If so, explain.

_____

_____

_____

_____

LO 4   15. Are the depreciation lives the same for AMT purposes as for regular tax purposes? If not, how are the lives determined for AMT?

_____

_____

_____

_____

LO 4   16. Discuss the tax basis calculation adjustment. Why is the gain or loss on the sale of depreciable assets different for AMT purposes than for regular tax purposes?

_____

_____

_____

_____

Multiple-Choice Questions

LO 1   17. Which of the following increase(s) a taxpayer's at-risk amount?
   a. Cash and the adjusted basis of property contributed to the activity.
   b. Borrowed amounts used in the activity for which the taxpayer is personally liable.
   c. Income from the activity.
   d. All of the above.

LO 1   18. Which of the following increases a taxpayer's at-risk amount?
   a. Cash distributions.
   b. Property distributions.
   c. Increased share of liabilities.
   d. Loss items.

LO 1   19. In 2009 Kirsten invested $20,000 for a 10% partnership interest (not a passive activity). The partnership has losses of $150,000 in 2009 and $250,000 in 2010. Kirsten's share of the partnership's losses is $15,000 in 2009 and $25,000 in 2010. How much of the losses from the partnership can Kirsten deduct?
   a. $0 in 2009 and $0 in 2010.
   b. $15,000 in 2009 and $5,000 in 2010.
   c. $15,000 in 2009 and $25,000 in 2010.
   d. $20,000 in 2009 and $0 in 2010.

LO 1   20. Leonard invests $10,000 cash in an equipment-leasing activity for a 15% share in the business. The 85% owner is Rebecca, who contributes $10,000 and borrows $75,000 to put in the business. Only Rebecca is liable for repayment of the loan. The partnership incurs a loss of $125,000 during the year. What amount of the loss is deductible currently by Leonard and Rebecca (ignore passive loss rules)?
   a. $0 by Leonard and $0 by Rebecca.
   b. $10,000 by Leonard and $85,000 by Rebecca.
   c. $18,750 by Leonard and $106,250 by Rebecca.
   d. $21,250 by Leonard and $73,750 by Rebecca.

LO 1   21. Myer owns a 20% interest in a partnership (not involved in real estate) in which his at-risk amount was $50,000 at the beginning of the year. During the year, he receives a $40,000

a. $88,000.

b. $91,650.

c. $93,700.

d. $97,350.

LO 4 32. Which of the following itemized deductions is *not* allowed for AMT?

a. Medical expenses.

b. Taxes.

c. Charitable contributions.

d. Interest on loan to purchase principal residence.

LO 4 33. Which of the following statements is correct with regard to the medical expense deduction?

a. Medical expenses are not deductible for AMT.

b. The medical expense deduction is decreased for AMT.

c. The medical expense deduction is increased for AMT.

d. The same amount of medical expenses that is deductible for regular tax purposes is deductible for AMT.

LO 4 34. Paul reported the following itemized deductions on his 2009 tax return. His AGI for 2009 was $65,000. The mortgage interest is all qualified mortgage interest to purchase his personal residence. For AMT, compute his total adjustment for itemized deductions.

Medical expenses (after the 7.5% of AGI floor)	$ 6,000
State income taxes	3,600
Home mortgage interest	11,500
Charitable contributions	3,200
Miscellaneous itemized deductions (after the 2% of AGI floor)	1,800

a. $ 3,425.

b. $ 5,225.

c. $ 7,025.

d. $18,525.

LO 4 35. After computing all tax preferences and AMT adjustments, Phillip and his wife Carmin have AMTI of $210,000. If Phillip and Carmin file a joint tax return, what exemption amount can they claim for AMT for 2009?

a. $0.

b. $46,700.

c. $55,950.

d. $70,950.

Problems **LO 1** 36. In year 2009 Andrew contributes equipment with an adjusted basis of $20,000 and a FMV of $18,000 to Construction Limited Partnership (CLP) in return for a 3% limited partnership interest. Andrew's shares of CLP income and losses for the year were as follows:

Interest	$ 500
Dividends	300
Capital gains	900
Ordinary loss	(4,325)

CLP had no liabilities. What are Andrew's initial basis, allowed losses, and ending at-risk amount?

_____

_____

_____

_____

LO 1   37. Cindy, Casey, and Kara each invested $30,000 in a real estate venture. The partnership borrowed $200,000 and purchased a warehouse for $290,000. The note was secured by the building; there was no personal recourse against the partners. What is each partner's beginning at-risk amount in the venture?

_____

_____

_____

_____

LO 2   38. During the current year, Joshua worked 1,300 hours as a tax consultant and 450 hours as a real estate agent. His one other employee (his wife) worked 300 hours in the real estate business. Joshua earned $50,000 as a tax consultant, and together the couple lost $20,000 in the real estate business. How should Joshua treat the loss on his federal income tax return?

_____

_____

_____

_____

LO 2   39. Donald has two investments in activities that are considered nonrental passive activities. He acquired Activity A six years ago, and it was profitable until the current year. He acquired Activity B in the current year. His share of the loss from Activity A in the current year is $15,000, and his share of the loss from Activity B is $4,000. What is the total of Donald's suspended losses from these activities as of the end of the current year?

_____

_____

_____

_____

LO 2   40. Darrell acquired an activity eight years ago. The loss from it in the current year was $65,000. The activity involves residential rental real estate in which he is an active participant. Calculate Darrell's AGI after considering that Darrell's AGI was $100,000 before including any potential loss.

_____

_____

_____

_____

LO 2   41. Evelyn has rental income of $48,000 and passive income of $18,000. She also has $148,000 of losses from a real estate rental activity in which she actively participates.

Chapter Fourteen

Partnership Taxation

In this chapter, we discuss taxation of partnerships. As noted earlier in this text, the partnership itself does not pay income tax. However, a partnership must annually report each partner's share of its income or loss and other items on a Schedule K-1. This chapter presents the tax consequences of the partnership entity, from formation to liquidation. We also examine Form 1065, the annual information tax return filed by partnerships.

Learning Objectives

When you have completed this chapter, you should understand the following learning objectives (LO):

LO 1. Explain the rules dealing with the formation of a partnership.

LO 2. Be able to report partnership ordinary income or loss.

LO 3. Determine separately stated items.

LO 4. Calculate partner basis.

LO 5. Apply the rules for partnership distributions.

LO 6. Correctly report partnership liquidations and dispositions.

INTRODUCTION

Taxpayers are increasingly using the partnership organizational form for tax purposes. The partnership form allows substantial flexibility in terms of contributions and distributions. A partnership is subject to tax only at the partner level. In contrast to a corporation that pays a corporate tax, and then the individual shareholder is subject to tax on the dividends (double taxation), a partnership's income flows through to its partners, and the partnership pays no income tax at the entity level.

A historic disadvantage of a general partnership has been a lack of limited liability; all general partners are individually liable for partnership actions and liabilities. With the increasing availability of limited liability companies (LLCs), limited liability partnerships (LLPs), and limited partnerships (LPs), all of which are taxed as partnerships for federal purposes and which also limit the liability of at least some partners, this disadvantage has been eliminated. The discussions in this chapter encompass each of these organizational forms under the generic term *partnerships*.

FORMATION OF A PARTNERSHIP
LO 1

Generally, a partner recognizes no gain or loss on the formation of a partnership.[1] The most common way to form a partnership is for two or more partners (individuals or entities) to contribute cash, property, or services in exchange for a partnership interest.

[1] IRC §721.

EXAMPLE 14-1	Jason and Spence form a partnership to perform lawn care and landscaping. Each contributes $25,000 and receives a 50% interest in J&S Landscaping. No gain or loss is recognized in this transaction.

Beginning Partner Basis

The concept of *basis* is extremely important when dealing with partnerships. A partnership has two types of tax basis. One is the *outside basis,* which is the basis of the partnership interest in the hands of the partner. The second type is *inside basis,* the partner's share of the basis of the individual assets in the partnership.

When a partner contributes property to a partnership, the basis of the property carries over to the partnership (inside basis), and the partner's basis increases by the basis of the property contributed (outside basis).[2] This concept is known as *basis in, basis out.*

EXAMPLE 14-2	Bart and Alan form an LLC to construct personal residences. Each is a 50% partner in sharing income and loss items. Bart contributes the following assets to the partnership:

	Basis	FMV
Undeveloped land	$55,000	$100,000
Equipment	35,000	50,000
Total	$90,000	$150,000

Alan contributes the following assets to the partnership:

	Basis	FMV
Cash	$ 90,000	$ 90,000
Office equipment	30,000	40,000
Truck	5,000	20,000
Total	$125,000	$150,000

Bart's outside basis in his partnership interest is $90,000, the sum of the contributed assets' basis. Alan's outside basis in his partnership interest is $125,000, the sum of his contributed assets' basis.

In Example 14-2, Bart's partnership basis is only $90,000 while Alan's basis is $125,000, yet both own a 50% interest in the partnership. This happens because Bart's contributed assets had higher unrecognized gains. If Bart were to sell his partnership interest for its fair market value of $150,000, he would recognize a $60,000 gain—the same gain he deferred upon contributing the assets to the partnership.

In summary, a partner's basis in his or her partnership interest (outside basis) is the sum of any money contributed plus the adjusted basis of property contributed.

| TAX YOUR BRAIN  | Dave and Alisa form a law partnership. Dave gave $100,000 cash to the partnership, and Alisa gave $100,000 of unrealized accounts receivable from her cash basis sole proprietorship. What is the basis of the partnership interest for each partner?

ANSWER

Dave has a partnership basis of $100,000. Alisa, on the other hand, has a zero basis in her partnership interest. Even though she gave something of value for a 50% interest in the partnership, her basis is zero because the accounts receivable have a zero basis due to the fact that her sole proprietorship uses the cash basis of accounting. As these receivables are collected, Alisa's partnership basis will increase. |
| --- | --- |

---

[2] IRC §722.

EXHIBIT 14-1

Form **1065**		**U.S. Return of Partnership Income**		OMB No. 1545-0099

Form **1065**
Department of the Treasury
Internal Revenue Service

U.S. Return of Partnership Income

For calendar year 2009, or tax year beginning _____, 2009, ending _____, 20 _____.
► See separate instructions.

OMB No. 1545-0099

2009

A Principal business activity	Use the IRS label. Otherwise, print or type.	Name of partnership	D Employer identification number
B Principal product or service		Number, street, and room or suite no. If a P.O. box, see the instructions.	E Date business started
C Business code number		City or town, state, and ZIP code	F Total assets (see the instructions) $

G Check applicable boxes: **(1)** ☐ Initial return **(2)** ☐ Final return **(3)** ☐ Name change **(4)** ☐ Address change **(5)** ☐ Amended return
  (6) ☐ Technical termination - also check (1) or (2)
H Check accounting method: **(1)** ☐ Cash **(2)** ☐ Accrual **(3)** ☐ Other (specify) ► _____
I Number of Schedules K-1. Attach one for each person who was a partner at any time during the tax year ► _____
J Check if Schedules C and M-3 are attached . . . . ☐

Caution. *Include **only** trade or business income and expenses on lines 1a through 22 below. See the instructions for more information.*

Income	1a	Gross receipts or sales	1a	
	b	Less returns and allowances	1b	1c
	2	Cost of goods sold (Schedule A, line 8)		2
	3	Gross profit. Subtract line 2 from line 1c		3
	4	Ordinary income (loss) from other partnerships, estates, and trusts *(attach statement)* . .		4
	5	Net farm profit (loss) *(attach Schedule F (Form 1040))*		5
	6	Net gain (loss) from Form 4797, Part II, line 17 *(attach Form 4797)*		6
	7	Other income (loss) *(attach statement)*		7
	8	**Total income (loss).** Combine lines 3 through 7		8
Deductions (see the instructions for limitations)	9	Salaries and wages (other than to partners) (less employment credits)		9
	10	Guaranteed payments to partners		10
	11	Repairs and maintenance		11
	12	Bad debts		12
	13	Rent		13
	14	Taxes and licenses		14
	15	Interest		15
	16a	Depreciation *(if required, attach Form 4562)*	16a	
	b	Less depreciation reported on Schedule A and elsewhere on return	16b	16c
	17	Depletion **(Do not deduct oil and gas depletion.)**		17
	18	Retirement plans, etc.		18
	19	Employee benefit programs		19
	20	Other deductions *(attach statement)*		20
	21	**Total deductions.** Add the amounts shown in the far right column for lines 9 through 20.		21
	22	**Ordinary business income (loss).** Subtract line 21 from line 8		22

Sign Here

Under penalties of perjury, I declare that I have examined this return, including accompanying schedules and statements, and to the best of my knowledge and belief, it is true, correct, and complete. Declaration of preparer (other than general partner or limited liability company member manager) is based on all information of which preparer has any knowledge.

► _____ _____
Signature of general partner or limited liability company member manager Date

May the IRS discuss this return with the preparer shown below (see instructions)? ☐ **Yes** ☐ **No**

Paid Preparer's Use Only	Preparer's signature		Date	Check if self-employed ► ☐	Preparer's SSN or PTIN
	Firm's name (or yours if self-employed), address, and ZIP code	►		EIN ►	
					Phone no.

For Privacy Act and Paperwork Reduction Act Notice, see separate instructions.   Cat. No. 11390Z   Form **1065** (2009)

(continued)

EXHIBIT 14-1   *(continued)*

Form 1065 (2009)   Page **2**

Schedule A	**Cost of Goods Sold** (see the instructions)		
1	Inventory at beginning of year	**1**	
2	Purchases less cost of items withdrawn for personal use	**2**	
3	Cost of labor	**3**	
4	Additional section 263A costs *(attach statement)*	**4**	
5	Other costs *(attach statement)*	**5**	
6	**Total.** Add lines 1 through 5	**6**	
7	Inventory at end of year	**7**	
8	**Cost of goods sold.** Subtract line 7 from line 6. Enter here and on page 1, line 2	**8**	

9a Check all methods used for valuing closing inventory:

    (i) ☐ Cost as described in Regulations section 1.471-3

    (ii) ☐ Lower of cost or market as described in Regulations section 1.471-4

    (iii) ☐ Other (specify method used and attach explanation) ▶

    b Check this box if there was a writedown of "subnormal" goods as described in Regulations section 1.471-2(c) . . . ▶ ☐

    c Check this box if the LIFO inventory method was adopted this tax year for any goods *(if checked, attach Form 970)* . . ▶ ☐

    d Do the rules of section 263A (for property produced or acquired for resale) apply to the partnership? . . . . ☐ Yes ☐ No

    e Was there any change in determining quantities, cost, or valuations between opening and closing inventory? . . ☐ Yes ☐ No
       If "Yes," attach explanation.

Schedule B	**Other Information**		Yes	No
1	What type of entity is filing this return? Check the applicable box:			

    a ☐ Domestic general partnership   **b** ☐ Domestic limited partnership

    c ☐ Domestic limited liability company   **d** ☐ Domestic limited liability partnership

    e ☐ Foreign partnership   **f** ☐ Other ▶

2 At any time during the tax year, was any partner in the partnership a disregarded entity, a partnership (including an entity treated as a partnership), a trust, an S corporation, an estate (other than an estate of a deceased partner), or a nominee or similar person?

3 At the end of the tax year:

    a Did any foreign or domestic corporation, partnership (including any entity treated as a partnership), trust, or tax-exempt organization own, directly or indirectly, an interest of 50% or more in the profit, loss, or capital of the partnership? For rules of constructive ownership, see instructions. If "Yes," attach Schedule B-1, Information on Partners Owning 50% or More of the Partnership

    b Did any individual or estate own, directly or indirectly, an interest of 50% or more in the profit, loss, or capital of the partnership? For rules of constructive ownership, see instructions. If "Yes," attach Schedule B-1, Information on Partners Owning 50% or More of the Partnership

4 At the end of the tax year, did the partnership:

    a Own directly 20% or more, or own, directly or indirectly, 50% or more of the total voting power of all classes of stock entitled to vote of any foreign or domestic corporation? For rules of constructive ownership, see instructions. If "Yes," complete (i) through (iv) below

(i) Name of Corporation	**(ii)** Employer Identification Number (if any)	**(iii)** Country of Incorporation	**(iv)** Percentage Owned in Voting Stock

    b Own directly an interest of 20% or more, or own, directly or indirectly, an interest of 50% or more in the profit, loss, or capital in any foreign or domestic partnership (including an entity treated as a partnership) or in the beneficial interest of a trust? For rules of constructive ownership, see instructions. If "Yes," complete (i) through (v) below .

(i) Name of Entity	**(ii)** Employer Identification Number (if any)	**(iii)** Type of Entity	**(iv)** Country of Organization	**(v)** Maximum Percentage Owned in Profit, Loss, or Capital

Form **1065** (2009)

EXHIBIT 14-1 *(continued)*

		Yes	No
	Form 1065 (2009) Page **3**		
5	Did the partnership file Form 8893, Election of Partnership Level Tax Treatment, or an election statement under section 6231(a)(1)(B)(ii) for partnership-level tax treatment, that is in effect for this tax year? See Form 8893 for more details		
6	Does the partnership satisfy **all four** of the following conditions?		
a	The partnership's total receipts for the tax year were less than $250,000.		
b	The partnership's total assets at the end of the tax year were less than $1 million.		
c	Schedules K-1 are filed with the return and furnished to the partners on or before the due date (including extensions) for the partnership return.		
d	The partnership is not filing and is not required to file Schedule M-3 . . . . If "Yes," the partnership is not required to complete Schedules L, M-1, and M-2; Item F on page 1 of Form 1065; or Item L on Schedule K-1.		
7	Is this partnership a publicly traded partnership as defined in section 469(k)(2)?		
8	During the tax year, did the partnership have any debt that was cancelled, was forgiven, or had the terms modified so as to reduce the principal amount of the debt?		
9	Has this partnership filed, or is it required to file, Form 8918, Material Advisor Disclosure Statement, to provide information on any reportable transaction?		
10	At any time during calendar year 2009, did the partnership have an interest in or a signature or other authority over a financial account in a foreign country (such as a bank account, securities account, or other financial account)? See the instructions for exceptions and filing requirements for Form TD F 90-22.1, Report of Foreign Bank and Financial Accounts. If "Yes," enter the name of the foreign country. ▶ _____		
11	At any time during the tax year, did the partnership receive a distribution from, or was it the grantor of, or transferor to, a foreign trust? If "Yes," the partnership may have to file Form 3520, Annual Return To Report Transactions With Foreign Trusts and Receipt of Certain Foreign Gifts. See instructions		
12a	Is the partnership making, or had it previously made (and not revoked), a section 754 election? . . . . . . See instructions for details regarding a section 754 election.		
b	Did the partnership make for this tax year an optional basis adjustment under section 743(b) or 734(b)? If "Yes," attach a statement showing the computation and allocation of the basis adjustment. See instructions		
c	Is the partnership required to adjust the basis of partnership assets under section 743(b) or 734(b) because of a substantial built-in loss (as defined under section 743(d)) or substantial basis reduction (as defined under section 734(d))? If "Yes," attach a statement showing the computation and allocation of the basis adjustment. See instructions.		
13	Check this box if, during the current or prior tax year, the partnership distributed any property received in a like-kind exchange or contributed such property to another entity (other than entities wholly-owned by the partnership throughout the tax year) . . . . ▶ ☐		
14	At any time during the tax year, did the partnership distribute to any partner a tenancy-in-common or other undivided interest in partnership property?		
15	If the partnership is required to file Form 8858, Information Return of U.S. Persons With Respect To Foreign Disregarded Entities, enter the number of Forms 8858 attached. See instructions ▶ _____		
16	Does the partnership have any foreign partners? If "Yes," enter the number of Forms 8805, Foreign Partner's Information Statement of Section 1446 Withholding Tax, filed for this partnership. ▶ _____		
17	Enter the number of Forms 8865, Return of U.S. Persons With Respect to Certain Foreign Partnerships, attached to this return. ▶ _____		

Designation of Tax Matters Partner (see instructions)
Enter below the general partner designated as the tax matters partner (TMP) for the tax year of this return:

Name of designated TMP ▶ _____ Identifying number of TMP ▶ _____

If the TMP is an entity, name of TMP representative ▶ _____ Phone number of TMP ▶ _____

Address of designated TMP ▶ _____

Form **1065** (2009)

(continued)

EXHIBIT 14-1 *(continued)*

Form 1065 (2009) Page **4**

Schedule K		Partners' Distributive Share Items		Total amount	

Income (Loss)

	1	Ordinary business income (loss) (page 1, line 22)	1	
	2	Net rental real estate income (loss) (*attach Form 8825*)	2	
	3a	Other gross rental income (loss)	3a	
	b	Expenses from other rental activities (*attach statement*)	3b	
	c	Other net rental income (loss). Subtract line 3b from line 3a	3c	
	4	Guaranteed payments	4	
	5	Interest income	5	
	6	Dividends: a Ordinary dividends	6a	
		b Qualified dividends	6b	
	7	Royalties	7	
	8	Net short-term capital gain (loss) (*attach Schedule D (Form 1065)*)	8	
	9a	Net long-term capital gain (loss) (*attach Schedule D (Form 1065)*)	9a	
	b	Collectibles (28%) gain (loss)	9b	
	c	Unrecaptured section 1250 gain (*attach statement*)	9c	
	10	Net section 1231 gain (loss) (*attach Form 4797*)	10	
	11	Other income (loss) (*see instructions*) Type ▶	11	

Deductions

	12	Section 179 deduction (*attach Form 4562*)	12	
	13a	Contributions	13a	
	b	Investment interest expense	13b	
	c	Section 59(e)(2) expenditures: (1) Type ▶ (2) Amount ▶	13c(2)	
	d	Other deductions (*see instructions*) Type ▶	13d	

Self-Employment

	14a	Net earnings (loss) from self-employment	14a	
	b	Gross farming or fishing income	14b	
	c	Gross nonfarm income	14c	

Credits

	15a	Low-income housing credit (section 42(j)(5))	15a	
	b	Low-income housing credit (other)	15b	
	c	Qualified rehabilitation expenditures (rental real estate) (*attach Form 3468*)	15c	
	d	Other rental real estate credits (*see instructions*) Type ▶	15d	
	e	Other rental credits (*see instructions*) Type ▶	15e	
	f	Other credits (*see instructions*) Type ▶	15f	

Foreign Transactions

	16a	Name of country or U.S. possession ▶		
	b	Gross income from all sources	16b	
	c	Gross income sourced at partner level	16c	
		Foreign gross income sourced at partnership level		
	d	Passive category ▶ e General category ▶ f Other ▶	16f	
		Deductions allocated and apportioned at partner level		
	g	Interest expense ▶ h Other ▶	16h	
		Deductions allocated and apportioned at partnership level to foreign source income		
	i	Passive category ▶ j General category ▶ k Other ▶	16k	
	l	Total foreign taxes (check one): ▶ Paid ☐ Accrued ☐	16l	
	m	Reduction in taxes available for credit (*attach statement*)	16m	
	n	Other foreign tax information (*attach statement*)		

Alternative Minimum Tax (AMT) Items

	17a	Post-1986 depreciation adjustment	17a	
	b	Adjusted gain or loss	17b	
	c	Depletion (other than oil and gas)	17c	
	d	Oil, gas, and geothermal properties—gross income	17d	
	e	Oil, gas, and geothermal properties—deductions	17e	
	f	Other AMT items (*attach statement*)	17f	

Other Information

	18a	Tax-exempt interest income	18a	
	b	Other tax-exempt income	18b	
	c	Nondeductible expenses	18c	
	19a	Distributions of cash and marketable securities	19a	
	b	Distributions of other property	19b	
	20a	Investment income	20a	
	b	Investment expenses	20b	
	c	Other items and amounts (*attach statement*)		

Form **1065** (2009)

EXHIBIT 14-1 *(concluded)*

Form 1065 (2009)   Page **5**

Analysis of Net Income (Loss)

1 Net income (loss). Combine Schedule K, lines 1 through 11. From the result, subtract the sum of Schedule K, lines 12 through 13d, and 16l **1**

2 Analysis by partner type:	(i) Corporate	(ii) Individual (active)	(iii) Individual (passive)	(iv) Partnership	(v) Exempt organization	(vi) Nominee/Other
a General partners						
b Limited partners						

Schedule L — Balance Sheets per Books

	Assets	Beginning of tax year (a)	(b)	End of tax year (c)	(d)
1	Cash				
2a	Trade notes and accounts receivable				
b	Less allowance for bad debts				
3	Inventories				
4	U.S. government obligations				
5	Tax-exempt securities				
6	Other current assets (attach statement)				
7	Mortgage and real estate loans				
8	Other investments (attach statement)				
9a	Buildings and other depreciable assets				
b	Less accumulated depreciation				
10a	Depletable assets				
b	Less accumulated depletion				
11	Land (net of any amortization)				
12a	Intangible assets (amortizable only)				
b	Less accumulated amortization				
13	Other assets (attach statement)				
14	Total assets				
	Liabilities and Capital				
15	Accounts payable				
16	Mortgages, notes, bonds payable in less than 1 year				
17	Other current liabilities (attach statement)				
18	All nonrecourse loans				
19	Mortgages, notes, bonds payable in 1 year or more				
20	Other liabilities (attach statement)				
21	Partners' capital accounts				
22	Total liabilities and capital				

Schedule M-1 — Reconciliation of Income (Loss) per Books With Income (Loss) per Return

Note. Schedule M-3 may be required instead of Schedule M-1 (see instructions).

1 Net income (loss) per books

2 Income included on Schedule K, lines 1, 2, 3c, 5, 6a, 7, 8, 9a, 10, and 11, not recorded on books this year (itemize): _____

3 Guaranteed payments (other than health insurance)

4 Expenses recorded on books this year not included on Schedule K, lines 1 through 13d, and 16l (itemize):

a Depreciation $_____
b Travel and entertainment $_____

5 Add lines 1 through 4

6 Income recorded on books this year not included on Schedule K, lines 1 through 11 (itemize):

a Tax-exempt interest $_____

7 Deductions included on Schedule K, lines 1 through 13d, and 16l, not charged against book income this year (itemize):

a Depreciation $_____

8 Add lines 6 and 7

9 Income (loss) (Analysis of Net Income (Loss), line 1). Subtract line 8 from line 5

Schedule M-2 — Analysis of Partners' Capital Accounts

1 Balance at beginning of year
2 Capital contributed: **a** Cash   **b** Property
3 Net income (loss) per books
4 Other increases (itemize): _____
5 Add lines 1 through 4

6 Distributions: **a** Cash   **b** Property
7 Other decreases (itemize): _____
8 Add lines 6 and 7
9 Balance at end of year. Subtract line 8 from line 5

Form **1065** (2009)

Depreciation

A partnership calculates depreciation following the same rules as a sole proprietorship using Schedule C. Form 4562 must be completed and attached. One major exception concerns the §179 expense deduction. A partnership can use the §179 expense deduction, but the deduction cannot reduce the partnership ordinary income. Section 179 expense must be reported separately to each partner.

TAX YOUR BRAIN   Why must §179 expense be reported separately to each partner?

ANSWER

If you recall, each individual is allowed to deduct a maximum of $250,000 of §179 expense in tax year 2009. If the partnership deducts the §179 expense and does not separately state it to partners, an individual could set up numerous partnerships for his or her businesses and, effectively, have an unlimited §179 expense (up to $250,000 for each partnership).

Partner Health Premiums

Most employees can exclude from income the cost of employer-provided health and accident insurance. For employees of a partnership, this is certainly the case. However, because partners are not employees, partners cannot exclude from income the cost of their health insurance premiums paid by the partnership. The partnership treats the premiums as guaranteed payments to the partner, and the partner can deduct the premiums as a *for* AGI deduction on Form 1040.

CONCEPT CHECK 14-2—LO 2

1. A partnership can deduct which of the following in determining partnership ordinary income or loss?
   a. All ordinary and necessary expenses.
   b. Guaranteed payments.
   c. Depreciation.
   d. All of the above.

2. What tax form is a partnership required to file each year?
   a. Form 1120.
   b. Form 1040.
   c. Form 1065.
   d. Form 1120S.

3. A payment made to a partner that is calculated without regard to partnership income is a
   a. Partner salary.
   b. Partner withdrawal.
   c. Loan to a partner.
   d. Guaranteed payment.

SEPARATELY STATED ITEMS
LO 3

As noted earlier, a partnership must allocate income and expense items between ordinary items and separately stated items. The general rule regarding income and expense items of a partnership and their classification follows:

> All income and expense items of a partnership that may be treated differently at the partner level must be separately stated.

EXAMPLE 14-18

Bailey contributes land to a partnership with a basis of $8,000 and a FMV of $12,000 in 2007. In 2009, when the FMV of the land is $14,000, the partnership distributes the land to Jessica, another partner. The distribution triggers a precontribution gain of $4,000 to Bailey. Jessica has no gain or loss on the distribution and would have a basis of $12,000 in the land ($8,000 carryover basis plus the $4,000 gain recognized by Bailey).

Basis of Distributed Property

When property is distributed to a partner from a partnership, neither the partner nor the partnership recognizes any gain. The basis and the holding period of the distributed property carry over to the partner.[19] Hence, the partner steps into the shoes of the partnership. The only exception to the carryover basis rule occurs when the basis in the distributed property exceeds the basis in the partnership interest. The basis of the distributed property is limited to the basis of the partnership interest. Recall that the partner recognizes a gain only if the distribution exceeds basis and the distribution consists only of money and marketable securities.[20]

EXAMPLE 14-19

Fonda has a partnership basis of $6,000. She receives, from the partnership, a distribution of equipment with a basis to the partnership of $8,000 and a FMV of $5,000. The basis in the equipment to Fonda after the distribution is limited to her basis in the partnership of $6,000. Fonda recognizes no gain or loss and has a zero basis in her partnership interest after the distribution.

EXAMPLE 14-20

Assume the same facts as in Example 14-19 except that Fonda receives a $2,000 cash distribution and the equipment. In this case, she would first reduce her partnership basis by the $2,000 cash distribution. Fonda still does not recognize any gain but now has a basis of $4,000 in the equipment.

CONCEPT CHECK 14-5—LO 5

1. Which of the following is true concerning the recognition of gain on a distribution from a partnership?
   a. Gain is recognized if the partner receives property with a basis higher than his or her partnership interest basis.
   b. Gain is recognized if the partner receives cash in excess of his or her basis.
   c. The partner never recognizes a gain on a partnership distribution.
   d. The partner always recognizes a gain on a partnership distribution.

2. Nelson has a partnership basis of $12,000. He receives, from the partnership, a distribution of furniture with a basis to the partnership of $16,000 and a FMV of $10,000. Nelson's basis in the furniture after the distribution from the partnership is
   a. $10,000.
   b. $12,000.
   c. $16,000.
   d. None of the above.

3. Assume the same facts as in Question 2. However, Nelson receives a cash distribution of $4,000 with the furniture. The basis in the furniture after the distributions is
   a. $8,000.
   b. $10,000.
   c. $12,000.
   d. $16,000.

[19] See IRC §732(a) for the basis and IRC §735(b) for the holding period.
[20] This is assuming there is no triggered precontribution gain.

DISPOSAL OR LIQUIDATION OF A PARTNERSHIP INTEREST
LO 6

The most common way to dispose of a partnership interest is either through partnership liquidation or by selling the interest.[21]

Liquidation of a Partnership Interest

Liquidation occurs when a partner's entire interest is redeemed by the partnership. Most of the rules concerning nonliquidating distributions (discussed previously) also apply to liquidating distributions. Thus, a distribution of money in excess of basis causes a capital gain. If property is received in the liquidating distribution, no gain is recognized, and the basis of the property is adjusted as shown in Example 14-19.

One substantial difference in the liquidation rules and regular distribution rules is that a loss can be recognized on liquidating distributions. A loss occurs when the amounts received in liquidation are less than the partner's outside basis. One major caveat is that the loss can be recognized only after the final payment is received from the partnership and when only money, receivables, and/or inventory is/are distributed.

EXAMPLE 14-21   Cassandra has $20,000 basis in her partnership interest when she receives liquidating distributions from the partnership. She receives cash of $12,000 and equipment with a basis to the partnership of $6,000. Cassandra recognizes no gain or loss on the liquidating distribution. The equipment will have a basis to her of $8,000 ($20,000 partnership basis minus cash received of $12,000).

EXAMPLE 14-22   Assume the same facts as in Example 14-21 except that Cassandra receives cash of $12,000 and inventory with a basis to the partnership of $6,000. Cassandra recognizes a loss of $2,000 on the liquidation (cash and inventory basis of $18,000 minus the $20,000 partnership basis); the inventory will have a basis to her of $6,000.

If several assets are distributed in liquidation and the partner does not have outside basis to cover the basis in the partnership assets distributed, the outside basis is allocated among the distributed assets as follows:

1. The partnership basis is first reduced by money distributions.
2. Any remaining basis covers the basis in receivables and inventory distributed.
3. Any remaining basis is allocated to the other assets distributed in proportion to each asset's basis.[22]

EXAMPLE 14-23   Kelsey has a basis in her partnership interest of $10,000. She receives the following assets in complete liquidation of the partnership interest:

Cash	$3,000
Inventory (basis)	2,000
Equipment (basis)	2,000
Land (basis)	4,000

---

[21] Of course, a partnership interest could be disposed of through inheritance or by gift, but these disposals have limited income tax effects to the partner. There may be estate tax issues or gift tax considerations, but these are beyond the scope of this text.

[22] Reg. §1.732-1(c).

Kelsey has no recognized gain or loss, and her $10,000 outside basis is allocated to the assets as follows:

Cash	$3,000
Inventory	2,000
Equipment ($5,000 × $2,000/$6,000)	1,667
Land ($5,000 × $4,000/$6,000)	3,333

Sale of a Partnership Interest

The sale of a partnership interest is similar to the sale of any capital asset. The partner determines the amount realized from the sale and subtracts the basis of the partnership interest at the date of sale. The gain or loss is a capital item, and, assuming that the partner is an individual, he or she reports the transaction on Schedule D of Form 1040.

EXAMPLE 14-24

Bart purchased a 30% partnership interest for $23,000 in February 2007. His share of partnership income in subsequent years was $12,000 in 2007, $15,000 in 2008, and $8,000 in 2009. He made no additional contributions to, or withdrawals from, the partnership. On December 18, 2009, Bart sold his partnership interest for $74,000. His long-term capital gain is $16,000.

Amount realized		$74,000
Basis: Beginning	$23,000	
2007 income	+12,000	
2008 income	+15,000	
2009 income	+ 8,000	(58,000)
Long-term capital gain		$16,000

The partner may be subject to ordinary income from the sale if the partnership has substantially appreciated inventory or accounts receivable.[23] If the partnership sold or collected these items, ordinary income would result, and the partner would share in that ordinary income. A partner who is allowed capital gain treatment on the sale of the partnership interest would effectively convert the ordinary income to capital gain income and benefit from the preferential capital gain rates. IRC §751 prevents this conversion.

EXAMPLE 14-25

Assume the same facts as in Example 14-24. However, the partnership has uncollected accounts receivable with a FMV of $20,000 and a basis of $0.[24] Because Bart's share in the receivables is $6,000 (30% interest × $20,000), $6,000 of the $16,000 gain is ordinary, and the remaining $10,000 is capital gain.

CONCEPT CHECK 14-6—LO 6

1. Shelly has a basis in her partnership interest of $30,000. She receives the following assets in complete liquidation of the partnership interest:

Cash	$ 9,000
Inventory (basis)	6,000
Equipment (basis)	8,000
Land (basis)	12,000

   a. What is Shelly's recognized gain?
   b. What is Shelly's basis in each of the assets distributed?

(continued)

---

[23] IRC §751.

[24] Typically, a cash basis partnership will have a zero basis in accounts receivable because income is not recognized until the partnership collects the cash.

2. Callie purchased a 60% partnership interest for $55,000 in March 2008. She had income of $18,000 from the partnership in 2008 and $26,000 in 2009. She made no additional contributions to, or withdrawals from, the partnership. On December 30, 2009, Callie sold her partnership interest for $107,000.
   a. What is Callie's basis before the sale?
   b. What is Callie's gain or loss?
   c. Is the gain or loss (if any) capital or ordinary?

Comprehensive Example

Shafer and Jones Consulting, LLC, is a partnership formed on January 1, 2006, to perform business consulting services. The business is located at 1482 Jones Business Complex, Anywhere, North Carolina 27858. Its Employer ID is 92-1234567; it uses the tax/cash basis of accounting, is not subject to partnership audit procedures, has no foreign interests, and is not a tax shelter.

The home address for David A. Shafer (SSN 453-34-4444) is 103 Flower Rd., Anywhere, North Carolina 27858. He is a 60% partner. Robert B. Jones (SSN 555-33-3333) lives at 534 Bates Rd., Anywhere, North Carolina 27858. He is a 40% partner.

In 2009, David received a distribution of $60,000, and Robert received a $40,000 distribution. Both of these distributions are in addition to the guaranteed payments.

SHAFER AND JONES CONSULTING, LLC
Comparative Balance Sheet
As of December 31, 2008, and December 31, 2009

	12/31/08	12/31/09
Assets		
Cash	$ 29,452	$ 35,452
Investments	153,345	105,480
Office equipment	123,000	143,800
Accumulated depreciation (equipment)	(68,880)	(71,852)
Building	245,600	245,600
Accumulated depreciation (building)	(18,616)	(24,913)
Total assets	$463,901	$433,567
Liabilities and equity		
Notes payable	$233,800	$228,333
Capital accounts		
Capital, Shafer	138,061	123,140
Capital, Jones	92,040	82,094
Total liabilities and equity	$463,901	$433,567

SHAFER AND JONES CONSULTING, LLC
Income Statement
For the Year Ending December 31, 2009

Revenue	
Consulting income	$554,897
Interest income	1,231
Dividend income (qualified)	3,234
Long-term capital losses	(12,435)
Total revenue	$546,927

Expenses	
Salaries and wages (nonpartners)	$153,000
Guaranteed payments	
Shafer	100,000
Jones	96,000
Depreciation (MACRS—includes $5,000 §179 expense)	31,448
Interest expense	15,983
Taxes and licenses	15,548
Utilities	12,132
Travel	11,458
Meals and entertainment (100%)	11,345
Auto	9,880
Insurance (nonpartner health)	5,000
Accounting and legal	4,800
Repairs	3,200
Charitable contributions	1,500
Payroll penalties	500
Total expenses	$471,794
Net income	$ 75,133

See Table 14-4 for a spreadsheet of partnership ordinary income and separately stated items. Exhibits 14-3 and 14-4 show the presentation of Form 1065 and Schedule K-1s for Shafer and Jones Consulting. Form 4562 (depreciation), Schedule D (capital gains and losses), and a statement listing other deductions (line 20 of Form 1065) are omitted from the example.

TABLE 14-4

SHAFER AND JONES CONSULTING, LLC

Income Statement
For the Year Ending December 31, 2009

	Adjustments	Ordinary	Separately Stated
Consulting income		554,897	
Interest income			1,231
Dividend income (qualified)			3,234
Long-term capital losses			(12,435)
Expenses			
Salaries and wages (nonpartners)		153,000	
Guaranteed payments			
Shafer		100,000	100,000
Jones		96,000	96,000
Depreciation (MACRS—includes $5,000			
§179 expense)		26,448	5,000
Interest expense		15,983	
Taxes and licenses		15,548	
Utilities		12,132	
Travel		11,458	
Meals and entertainment (100%)	(5,673)*	5,672*	
Auto		9,880	
Insurance (nonpartner health)		5,000	
Accounting and legal		4,800	
Repairs		3,200	
Charitable contributions			1,500
Payroll penalties	(500)†		
Net income	$ 75,133	$ 95,776	

* Only 50% of meals and entertainment expenses are allowed.
† Penalties are not deductible.

EXHIBIT 14-3

Form **1065**		**U.S. Return of Partnership Income**				OMB No. 1545-0099

Form **1065**
Department of the Treasury
Internal Revenue Service

U.S. Return of Partnership Income
For calendar year 2009, or tax year beginning _____ , 2009, ending _____ , 20 _____ .
▶ See separate instructions.

OMB No. 1545-0099

2009

A Principal business activity	Use the IRS label. Other-wise, print or type.	Name of partnership	**D** Employer identification number
Consulting		Shafer and Jones Consulting, LLC	92-1234567
B Principal product or service		Number, street, and room or suite no. If a P.O. box, see the instructions.	**E** Date business started
Consulting		1482 Jones Business Complex	01/01/2006
C Business code number		City or town, state, and ZIP code	**F** Total assets (see the instructions)
541600		Anywhere, NC 27858	$ 433,567

(Watermark: Draft as of 06/23/2009)

G Check applicable boxes: **(1)** ☐ Initial return **(2)** ☐ Final return **(3)** ☐ Name change **(4)** ☐ Address change **(5)** ☐ Amended return
  (6) ☐ Technical termination - also check (1) or (2)
H Check accounting method: **(1)** ☒ Cash **(2)** ☐ Accrual **(3)** ☐ Other (specify) ▶ _____
I Number of Schedules K-1. Attach one for each person who was a partner at any time during the tax year ▶ 2
J Check if Schedules C and M-3 are attached ☐

Caution. Include **only** trade or business income and expenses on lines 1a through 22 below. See the instructions for more information.

Income	**1a**	Gross receipts or sales	**1a**	554,897		
	b	Less returns and allowances	**1b**		**1c**	554,897
	2	Cost of goods sold (Schedule A, line 8)			**2**	
	3	Gross profit. Subtract line 2 from line 1c			**3**	554,897
	4	Ordinary income (loss) from other partnerships, estates, and trusts *(attach statement)*			**4**	
	5	Net farm profit (loss) *(attach Schedule F (Form 1040))*			**5**	
	6	Net gain (loss) from Form 4797, Part II, line 17 *(attach Form 4797)*			**6**	
	7	Other income (loss) *(attach statement)*			**7**	
	8	**Total income (loss).** Combine lines 3 through 7			**8**	554,897
Deductions (see the instructions for limitations)	**9**	Salaries and wages (other than to partners) (less employment credits)			**9**	153,000
	10	Guaranteed payments to partners			**10**	196,000
	11	Repairs and maintenance			**11**	3,200
	12	Bad debts			**12**	
	13	Rent			**13**	
	14	Taxes and licenses			**14**	15,548
	15	Interest			**15**	15,983
	16a	Depreciation (*if required, attach Form 4562*)	**16a**	26,448		
	b	Less depreciation reported on Schedule A and elsewhere on return	**16b**		**16c**	26,448
	17	Depletion **(Do not deduct oil and gas depletion.)**			**17**	
	18	Retirement plans, etc.			**18**	
	19	Employee benefit programs			**19**	
	20	Other deductions *(attach statement)*			**20**	48,942
	21	**Total deductions.** Add the amounts shown in the far right column for lines 9 through 20			**21**	459,121
	22	**Ordinary business income (loss).** Subtract line 21 from line 8			**22**	95,776

Sign Here

Under penalties of perjury, I declare that I have examined this return, including accompanying schedules and statements, and to the best of my knowledge and belief, it is true, correct, and complete. Declaration of preparer (other than general partner or limited liability company member manager) is based on all information of which preparer has any knowledge.

▶ _____
Signature of general partner or limited liability company member manager

▶ _____
Date

May the IRS discuss this return with the preparer shown below (see instructions)? ☐ Yes ☐ No

Paid Preparer's Use Only

Preparer's signature		Date	Check if self-employed ▶ ☐	Preparer's SSN or PTIN
Firm's name (or yours if self-employed), address, and ZIP code			EIN ▶	
			Phone no.	

For Privacy Act and Paperwork Reduction Act Notice, see separate instructions. Cat. No. 11390Z Form **1065** (2009)

EXHIBIT 14-4

651109

☐ Final K-1   ☐ Amended K-1   OMB No. 1545-0099

Schedule K-1
(Form 1065)

2009

Department of the Treasury
Internal Revenue Service

For calendar year 2009, or tax
year beginning _____, 2009
ending _____, 20 ____

**Partner's Share of Income, Deductions,
Credits, etc.** ▶ See back of form and separate instructions.

Part I	**Information About the Partnership**

A Partnership's employer identification number
92-1234567

B Partnership's name, address, city, state, and ZIP code

Shafer and Jones Consulting, LLC
1482 Jones Business Complex
Anywhere, NC 27858

C IRS Center where partnership filed return
Cincinnati, OH

D ☐ Check if this is a publicly traded partnership (PTP)

Part II	**Information About the Partner**

E Partner's identifying number
453-34-4444

F Partner's name, address, city, state, and ZIP code

David A. Shafer
103 Flower Road
Anywhere, NC 27858

G ☐ General partner or LLC member-manager   ☒ Limited partner or other LLC member

H ☐ Domestic partner   ☐ Foreign partner

I What type of entity is this partner? Individual

J Partner's share of profit, loss, and capital (see instructions):

	Beginning	Ending
Profit	%	60 %
Loss	%	60 %
Capital	%	60 %

K Partner's share of liabilities at year end:

Nonrecourse	$ _____
Qualified nonrecourse financing	$ _____
Recourse	$ 137,000

L Partner's capital account analysis:

Beginning capital account	$ 138,061
Capital contributed during the year	$ _____
Current year increase (decrease)	$ 45,080
Withdrawals & distributions	$ (60,000)
Ending capital account	$ 123,140

☒ Tax basis   ☐ GAAP   ☐ Section 704(b) book
☐ Other (explain)

M Did the partner contribute property with a built-in gain or loss?
☐ Yes   ☒ No
If "Yes", attach statement (see instructions)

Part III	**Partner's Share of Current Year Income, Deductions, Credits, and Other Items**

1	Ordinary business income (loss) 57,466	15	Credits
2	Net rental real estate income (loss)		
3	Other net rental income (loss)	16	Foreign transactions
4	Guaranteed payments 100,000		
5	Interest income 739		
6a	Ordinary dividends 1,940		
6b	Qualified dividends 1,940		
7	Royalties		
8	Net short-term capital gain (loss)		
9a	Net long-term capital gain (loss) (7,461)	17	Alternative minimum tax (AMT) items
9b	Collectibles (28%) gain (loss)		
9c	Unrecaptured section 1250 gain		
10	Net section 1231 gain (loss)	18	Tax-exempt income and nondeductible expenses
11	Other income (loss)	C	3,704
		19	Distributions
12	Section 179 deduction 3,000	A	60,000
13	Other deductions		
A	900	20	Other information
14	Self-employment earnings (loss)		
A	154,466		

*See attached statement for additional information.

For IRS Use Only

For Paperwork Reduction Act Notice, see Instructions for Form 1065.   Cat. No. 11394R   **Schedule K-1 (Form 1065) 2009**

EXHIBIT 14-4 *(concluded)*

651109

☐ Final K-1 ☐ Amended K-1	OMB No. 1545-0099

Schedule K-1
(Form 1065)
2009

Department of the Treasury
Internal Revenue Service

For calendar year 2009, or tax

year beginning _____, 2009

ending _____, 20 _____

Partner's Share of Income, Deductions, Credits, etc. ► See back of form and separate instructions.

Part I	Information About the Partnership

A Partnership's employer identification number
92-1234567

B Partnership's name, address, city, state, and ZIP code

Shafer and Jones Consulting, LLC
1482 Jones Business Complex
Anywhere, NC 27858

C IRS Center where partnership filed return
Cincinnati, OH

D ☐ Check if this is a publicly traded partnership (PTP)

Part II	Information About the Partner

E Partner's identifying number
555-33-3333

F Partner's name, address, city, state, and ZIP code

Robert B. Jones
534 Bates Road
Anywhere, NC 27858

G ☐ General partner or LLC member-manager   ☒ Limited partner or other LLC member

H ☐ Domestic partner   ☐ Foreign partner

I What type of entity is this partner? Individual

J Partner's share of profit, loss, and capital (see instructions):

	Beginning	Ending
Profit	%	40 %
Loss	%	40 %
Capital	%	40 %

K Partner's share of liabilities at year end:

Nonrecourse	$	
Qualified nonrecourse financing	$	
Recourse	$	91,333

L Partner's capital account analysis:

Beginning capital account	$	92,040
Capital contributed during the year	$	
Current year increase (decrease)	$	30,053
Withdrawals & distributions	$ (	40,000)
Ending capital account	$	82,094

☒ Tax basis   ☐ GAAP   ☐ Section 704(b) book
☐ Other (explain)

M Did the partner contribute property with a built-in gain or loss?
☐ Yes   ☒ No
If "Yes", attach statement (see instructions)

Part III	Partner's Share of Current Year Income, Deductions, Credits, and Other Items

1	Ordinary business income (loss)	38,310	15	Credits
2	Net rental real estate income (loss)			
3	Other net rental income (loss)		16	Foreign transactions
4	Guaranteed payments	96,000		
5	Interest income	492		
6a	Ordinary dividends	1,294		
6b	Qualified dividends	1,294		
7	Royalties			
8	Net short-term capital gain (loss)			
9a	Net long-term capital gain (loss)	(4,974)	17	Alternative minimum tax (AMT) items
9b	Collectibles (28%) gain (loss)			
9c	Unrecaptured section 1250 gain			
10	Net section 1231 gain (loss)		18	Tax-exempt income and nondeductible expenses
11	Other income (loss)		C	2,469
			19	Distributions
12	Section 179 deduction	2,000	A	40,000
13	Other deductions A	600	20	Other information
14	Self-employment earnings (loss) A	132,310		

*See attached statement for additional information.

For IRS Use Only

For Paperwork Reduction Act Notice, see Instructions for Form 1065.   Cat. No. 11394R   Schedule K-1 (Form 1065) 2009

Summary

LO 1. Explain the rules dealing with the formation of a partnership.	• Generally there is no gain or loss on formation.
	• Basis determination is very important.
	• *Outside basis* is the tax basis of the partnership interest to the partner.
	• *Inside basis* is the partner's share of the basis of partnership assets.
	• The partnership holding period carries over from the contributing partner.
	• The FMV of services is income to the contributing partner.
	• Property contributed with liabilities may trigger a gain to the contributing partner.
LO 2. Be able to report partnership ordinary income or loss.	• The partnership files an annual information return, Form 1065.
	• Partnership income is separated into ordinary income or loss and separately stated items.
	• Income or loss is reported to partners on Schedule K-1.
	• Ordinary income is calculated as for a Schedule C business.
	• Guaranteed payments are an expense to the partnership.
	• The §179 depreciation expense deduction must be separately stated.
	• Partner health insurance premiums are treated as a guaranteed payment.
LO 3. Determine separately stated items.	• Separately stated items are income or expense items that may be treated differently at the partner level.
	• Examples of separately stated items include interest, capital gains, charitable contributions, and self-employment income.
LO 4. Calculate partner basis.	• In general, partner basis is equal to the basis of property contributed, plus or minus income or loss, plus or minus separately stated items, plus partner share of liabilities.
LO 5. Apply the rules for partnership distributions.	• In general, no gain or loss is recorded on a nonliquidating distribution.
	• Distributions reduce basis.
	• Partner basis of property received generally equals the partnership basis.
LO 6. Correctly report partnership liquidations and dispositions.	• Generally no gain or loss occurs on partnership liquidation.
	• Exceptions exist if amount in liquidation is less than basis and the distribution is only cash, receivables, or inventory.
	• Sale of partnership interest is sale of a capital asset.
	• If a partnership holds appreciated inventory or accounts receivable, part of the gain may be ordinary.

Discussion Questions

LO 1   1. Discuss the formation of a partnership. Is any gain or loss recognized? Explain.

_____

_____

_____

LO 1   2. What entity forms are considered partnerships for federal income tax purposes?

_____

_____

_____

LO 1   3. How does taxation for the corporate form and taxation for the partnership form differ?

_____

_____

_____

LO 1   4. What is the concept of *basis?* In your discussion, differentiate between outside basis and inside basis.

_____

_____

_____

LO 1   5. Elaborate on the term *basis-in, basis-out*. What does that phrase mean in the context of a partnership formation?

_____

_____

_____

LO 1   6. How can two partners, each with a 50% interest in a partnership, have different amounts of outside basis at the formation of a partnership? Shouldn't the two partners contribute the same amount to have the same interest?

_____

_____

_____

LO 1   7. When a partnership receives an asset from a partner, does the partnership ever recognize a gain? What is the basis of the asset in the hands of the partnership after contribution?

_____

_____

_____

LO 1   8. Discuss the concept of *steps into the shoes*. Does this concept pertain to the partnership, the partners, or both?

_____

_____

_____

LO 2   9. Why would smaller partnerships (and other businesses for that matter) use only the tax basis of accounting, which does not follow GAAP?

_____

_____

_____

LO 2   10. How is depreciation calculated by the partnership when a partner contributes a business asset?

_____

_____

_____

LO 2 11. Discuss the concepts of ordinary income and separately stated items concerning partnerships. When must a partnership item of income or loss be separately stated, and why?

_____

_____

_____

LO 2 12. Can a partner have a salary from a partnership? Why? What is a *guaranteed payment?*

_____

_____

_____

LO 2 13. Are guaranteed payments treated as ordinary items or as separately stated items?

_____

_____

_____

LO 2 14. Is the §179 expense deduction allowed for partnerships? If so, is §179 an ordinary income item or a separately stated item? Why?

_____

_____

_____

LO 3 15. If a partner owns a 20% interest, does that necessarily mean that he or she will receive 20% of the net income from the partnership? Explain.

_____

_____

_____

LO 3 16. Is partnership income considered self-employment income? If so, how is it calculated?

_____

_____

_____

LO 3 17. Why must some income and gain items be separately stated in a partnership?

_____

_____

_____

LO 4 18. Explain why nontaxable income and nondeductible expenses increase or reduce outside basis.

_____

_____

_____

LO 4 19. When is it mandatory that a partner calculate his or her partner interest basis (outside basis)? What items affect the outside basis of a partner?

_____

_____

_____

LO 4   20. How does a partner's share of partnership liabilities affect his or her outside basis?

_____

_____

_____

LO 5   21. The general rule is that partners do not recognize any gain when they receive a distribution. In what circumstances might a partner recognize a gain on a current distribution?

_____

_____

_____

LO 5   22. Define *precontribution gain.* What causes a partner to recognize it?

_____

_____

_____

LO 5   23. Describe the rules concerning the basis of property distributed to a partner. How does the concept of *basis-in, basis-out* apply to partnership distributions?

_____

_____

_____

LO 6   24. How can a partnership interest be disposed of? Which disposal method is more likely to produce a gain or loss? How is the gain or loss calculated?

_____

_____

_____

LO 6   25. How is the outside basis of a partner allocated to assets in a liquidation of the partnership interest? Include in your answer the effects of distributing cash, ordinary assets, §1231 assets, and capital assets.

_____

_____

_____

Multiple-Choice Questions

LO 1   26. Carmin performs services in exchange for a 25% interest in Real Estate Rental Partnership. The services were worth $15,000. The tax implications to Carmin are

  a. No taxable income and a partnership interest with a basis of $0.

  b. No taxable income and a partnership interest with a basis of $15,000.

  c. $15,000 of taxable income and a partnership interest with a basis of $0.

  d. $15,000 of taxable income and a partnership interest with a basis of $15,000.

LO 1   27. Billy contributes land with a FMV of $7,000 and a basis of $3,000 to a partnership in return for a 5% partnership interest in ABCD Partnership. Billy's basis in the partnership

  a. Is $0.

  b. Is $3,000.

  c. Is $7,000.

  d. Cannot be determined.

LO 1   49. On June 1 of the current year, Patti contributes equipment with a $45,000 basis and a $35,000 FMV in exchange for a partnership interest. She purchased the equipment three years ago.

     a. What is Patti's basis in her partnership interest?

     b. What is Patti's holding period of her partnership interest?

     c. What is the basis of the equipment in the hands of the partnership?

     d. What is the holding period of the equipment in the hands of the partnership?

     e. How will the partnership depreciate the equipment in the year of contribution?

_____

_____

_____

_____

LO 1 & 4   50. Dennis, Suzy, and Katherine form a partnership. Dennis and Suzy give equipment and a building, respectively. Katherine agrees to perform all of the accounting and office work in exchange for a 10% interest.

	FMV	Basis	Partnership Percentage
Dennis's equipment	$100,000	$10,000	45%
Suzy's building	100,000	45,000	45
Katherine's services	–0–	–0–	10

     a. Do any of the partners recognize any gain? If so, how much and why?

     b. What is the basis for each partner in his or her partnership interest?

     c. What is the basis to the partnership of each asset?

_____

_____

_____

_____

LO 1 & 4   51. Moe, Johnny, and Raymond form a partnership and contribute the following assets:

	FMV	Basis	Partnership Percentage
Moe's inventory	$ 50,000	$10,000	33.3%
Johnny's building	$110,000	$80,000	33.3%
Raymond's cash	$ 50,000	$50,000	33.3%

Johnny's building has a mortgage of $60,000, which the partnership assumes.

     a. Do any of the partners recognize any gain? If so, how much and why?

     b. What is the basis for each partner in his partnership interest?

     c. What is the basis to the partnership in each asset?

     d. How would your answer change with respect to Johnny if the basis in the building were $45,000?

_____

_____

_____

_____

LO 2 52. Barry and Kurt are equal partners in the BK Partnership. Barry receives a guaranteed payment of $55,000. In addition to the guaranteed payment, Barry withdraws $10,000 from the partnership. The partnership has $24,000 in ordinary income during the year.

    a. How much income must Barry report from BK Partnership?

    b. What is the effect on Barry's partnership basis?

_____

_____

_____

_____

_____

LO 2 53. Kerry is a partner in the Kerry, Davis, Smith & Jones Partnership. Kerry owned 25% from January 1, 2009, to June 30, 2009, when he bought Jones's 25% interest. He owned 50% for the rest of the year. The partnership had ordinary income of $146,000 and $15,000 in long-term capital gains. Barring any special allocations in a partnership agreement, what is Kerry's share of income?

_____

_____

_____

_____

_____

LO 2 & 3 54. Wade has a beginning basis in a partnership of $23,000. His share of income and expense from the partnership consists of the following amounts:

Ordinary income	$43,000
Guaranteed payment	12,000
Long-term capital gain	15,500
§1231 gain	4,300
Charitable contributions	2,000
§179 expense	18,000
Cash distribution	6,000

    a. What is Wade's self-employment income?

    b. Calculate Wade's basis at the end of the year.

_____

_____

_____

_____

LO 2 & 3 55. Bryan and Gayle are equal partners in BG Partnership. The partnership reports the following items of income and expense:

Ordinary income from operations	$13,000
Interest income	5,000
Long-term capital gains	23,000
§179 expense	55,000
Charitable contributions	3,000

    a. Which of these items are considered separately stated items? On what form will these items be reported to the partners?

    b. Where will these amounts be reported by the partners?

_____

_____

_____

_____

_____

LO 4 & 5 56. Kim has a basis in her partnership interest of $12,000 when she receives a distribution from the partnership of $6,000 cash and equipment with a basis of $8,000 ($12,000 FMV).

    a. How much gain or loss must Kim recognize on the distribution?

    b. What is Kim's ending partnership basis?

    c. What is Kim's basis in the equipment?

_____

_____

_____

_____

_____

LO 4 & 5 57. Zach contributed land with a FMV of $25,000 and a basis of $14,000 to a partnership on April 5, 2003. On June 6, 2009, the partnership distributed the land to Art, a partner in the same partnership. At distribution, the land had a FMV of $29,000.

    a. What is the effect of the distribution to Zach, if any?

    b. What is the effect of the distribution to Art?

_____

_____

_____

_____

_____

LO 5 58. Roberto has a basis of $6,000 in a partnership at the beginning of the year. He receives $7,000 in cash distributions, his distributive share of income is $3,500, and he receives a land distribution with a basis of $6,000 (FMV $12,000).

    a. Is Roberto required to recognize any gain? If so, how much is the gain?

    b. What is Roberto's basis in the land?

    c. What is Roberto's ending basis in his partnership interest?

_____

_____

_____

_____

_____

LO 5 59. Rhonda has a basis of $8,000 in a partnership at the beginning of the year. She receives $12,000 in cash distributions, and her distributive share of income is $2,500.

    a. Is Rhonda required to recognize any gain? If so, how much?

b. What is Rhonda's ending basis in her partnership interest?

_____

_____

_____

_____

_____

LO 6   60. Rebecca has a $40,000 basis in her partnership interest when she receives liquidating distributions from the partnership. She receives cash of $24,000 and equipment with a $12,000 basis to the partnership. What are the tax consequences of the liquidating distributions to Rebecca?

_____

_____

_____

_____

_____

LO 6   61. Calvin purchased a 40% partnership interest for $43,000 in February 2007. His share of partnership income in 2007 was $22,000, in 2008 was $25,000, and in 2009 was $12,000. He made no additional contributions to or withdrawals from the partnership. On December 18, 2009, Calvin sold his partnership interest for $103,000. What is his gain or loss on the sale of his partnership interest?

_____

_____

_____

_____

_____

Tax Return Problems

Tax Return Problem 1   Paul and Wayne equally own PW Partnership. Paul's basis was $30,000 and Wayne's basis was $22,000 at the beginning of the year. PW Partnership had the following income and expense items:

Sales	$330,000
Cost of goods sold	220,000
Guaranteed payment to Paul	40,000
Rent expense	24,000
Depreciation	33,000
Interest expense	4,000
Tax-exempt income	3,000
Health insurance premiums for Paul	3,600
Health insurance premiums for Wayne	3,600

a. Prepare page 1 and page 4 of Form 1065—ordinary income and separately stated items for the partnership.

b. Calculate Paul's basis in his partnership interest.

c. Calculate Wayne's basis in his partnership interest.

EXHIBIT 15-1   *(concluded)*

Form 1120 (2009)   Page **5**

Schedule L	Balance Sheets per Books	Beginning of tax year		End of tax year	
	Assets	**(a)**	**(b)**	**(c)**	**(d)**
1	Cash				
2a	Trade notes and accounts receivable				
b	Less allowance for bad debts	(	)	(	)
3	Inventories				
4	U.S. government obligations				
5	Tax-exempt securities (see instructions)				
6	Other current assets (attach schedule)				
7	Loans to shareholders				
8	Mortgage and real estate loans				
9	Other investments (attach schedule)				
10a	Buildings and other depreciable assets				
b	Less accumulated depreciation	(	)	(	)
11a	Depletable assets				
b	Less accumulated depletion	(	)	(	)
12	Land (net of any amortization)				
13a	Intangible assets (amortizable only)				
b	Less accumulated amortization	(	)	(	)
14	Other assets (attach schedule)				
15	Total assets				
	Liabilities and Shareholders' Equity				
16	Accounts payable				
17	Mortgages, notes, bonds payable in less than 1 year				
18	Other current liabilities (attach schedule)				
19	Loans from shareholders				
20	Mortgages, notes, bonds payable in 1 year or more				
21	Other liabilities (attach schedule)				
22	Capital stock: **a** Preferred stock				
	b Common stock				
23	Additional paid-in capital				
24	Retained earnings—Appropriated (attach schedule)				
25	Retained earnings—Unappropriated				
26	Adjustments to shareholders' equity (attach schedule)				
27	Less cost of treasury stock		(	)	(	)
28	Total liabilities and shareholders' equity				

Schedule M-1	Reconciliation of Income (Loss) per Books With Income per Return

Note: Schedule M-3 required instead of Schedule M-1 if total assets are $10 million or more—see instructions

1	Net income (loss) per books		7	Income recorded on books this year not included on this return (itemize):
2	Federal income tax per books			Tax-exempt interest $ _____
3	Excess of capital losses over capital gains			
4	Income subject to tax not recorded on books this year (itemize): _____		8	Deductions on this return not charged against book income this year (itemize):
	_____		a	Depreciation $ _____
5	Expenses recorded on books this year not deducted on this return (itemize):		b	Charitable contributions $ _____
a	Depreciation $ _____			
b	Charitable contributions $ _____			
c	Travel and entertainment $ _____		9	Add lines 7 and 8
6	Add lines 1 through 5		10	Income (page 1, line 28)—line 6 less line 9

Schedule M-2	Analysis of Unappropriated Retained Earnings per Books (Line 25, Schedule L)

1	Balance at beginning of year		5	Distributions: **a** Cash
2	Net income (loss) per books			**b** Stock
3	Other increases (itemize): _____			**c** Property
	_____		6	Other decreases (itemize): _____
	_____		7	Add lines 5 and 6
4	Add lines 1, 2, and 3		8	Balance at end of year (line 4 less line 7)

Form **1120** (2009)

> **EXAMPLE 15-1**
> Marty and Sara decide to form Boone Company. Marty transfers $1,000 cash in exchange for 100 shares of stock, and Sara transfers a bond with a fair market value (FMV) of $1,000 (basis of $800) for 100 shares. They are the only two shareholders of Boone Company. Because they control 80% or more of Boone immediately after the exchange, the transaction is tax-free.

Even when the 80% rule is met, a stockholder could be required to recognize a gain in two cases. The first is when the individual transfers property subject to a liability and the relief of liability is greater than the transferor's basis in the property. The gain is equal to the excess of liability over basis.

> **EXAMPLE 15-2**
> Gina transfers an apartment building to GGG Company in exchange for all of the stock in the company. The building has a basis of $100,000, a FMV of $500,000, and debt (assumed by the company) of $300,000. Even though Gina controls more than 80% of the company immediately after the exchange, the transaction is taxable because she has debt relief in excess of basis. She has a gain of $200,000 (relief of debt of $300,000 minus building basis of $100,000).

The second case involves an individual who contributes cash or property and receives, in return, stock plus other cash or property (this extra cash or property is called *boot,* discussed in an earlier chapter). In this case, the taxable gain is the lower of the FMV of the property received or the realized gain (the FMV of property contributed less the tax basis of the property contributed).

> **EXAMPLE 15-3**
> Ernie receives all of the stock of EBU Company in exchange for contributing a machine with a basis of $15,000 and a FMV of $25,000. Ernie also receives $3,000 cash from the company. The gain on transfer is $10,000 (the difference between the basis and FMV of the machine). The gain Ernie must report is $3,000, the lower of gain or cash received.

To the corporate entity, the basis of the cash or property received is equal to the basis in the hands of the shareholder plus any gain recognized by the shareholder. The basis of the stock in the hands of the shareholder is equal to the basis of the property contributed plus any gain recognized, minus any boot received (boot includes relief of liability). The amount of inside and outside basis for the stockholders in each of the three previous examples are as follows:

	Reported Gain	Stock Basis to Shareholder (Outside)	Property Basis to Corporation (Inside)
Marty	$ –0–	$ 1,000	$ 1,000
Sara	–0–	800	800
Gina	200,000	–0–	300,000
Ernie	3,000	15,000	18,000

Shareholders do not recognize losses as a result of the formation of a corporation when the 80% test is met.

If an individual provides services in exchange for stock upon the formation of a corporation, the individual will recognize ordinary income equal to the FMV of the services.

Unless a C corporation stockholder increases or decreases his or her proportionate ownership (buys or sells stock), there is generally no adjustment to the outside basis over time.

CONCEPT CHECK 15-2—LO 2	1. When forming a corporation, if the transferors control at least 80% of the corporate entity, the formation is generally tax-free. True or false? 2. The basis to the corporation of property received is equal to _____. 3. Arturo contributed land with a FMV of $100,000 and basis of $40,000 to a newly formed corporation in exchange for 90% of the stock. Arturo's basis in the stock is _____.

TAXABLE INCOME AND TAX LIABILITY
LO 3

Corporate taxable income is generally determined using the same operating rules as a trade or business that we discussed in Chapter 6. The general formula to determine corporate taxable income and tax liability follows. The line numbers pertain to Form 1120 in Exhibit 15-1.

Gross receipts or sales (line 1c)
− Cost of goods sold (line 2)

Gross profit (line 3)
+ Interest, dividends, capital gains, other income (lines 4–10)

Total income (line 11)
− Ordinary and necessary trade or business expenses (lines 12–27)

Taxable income before special deductions (line 28)
− Net operating loss deduction (line 29a)
− Dividends received deduction (line 29b)

= Taxable income (line 30)
× Applicable tax rates

= Tax liability (line 31)
− Tax payments during the tax year and tax credits (line 32h)

= Refund or tax due with return (line 34 or 35)

In corporate taxation, the notion of Adjusted Gross Income (AGI) does not exist.

As mentioned, determination of corporate taxable income generally follows the trade or business rules discussed in Chapter 6. A few differences pertaining to corporations—capital gains and losses, charitable contributions, the dividends received deduction, and some miscellaneous differences—must be noted.

Capital Gains and Losses (Form 1120, line 8)

As we discussed in Chapter 7, individuals (or other noncorporate taxpayers) include capital gains and losses in income. If capital losses exceed capital gains, individuals recognize a net capital loss of up to $3,000 with any excess being carried forward indefinitely. C corporations are not permitted to report any net capital losses. Thus capital losses can only offset capital gains.[6] In other words, the amount on line 8 must be either positive or zero; it cannot be negative.

[6] IRC § 1211(a).

Corporations are permitted to carry back excess capital losses three preceding years (starting with the earliest year) and then forward five years if any loss remains.[7] Corporations can use the carryback and carryforward amounts only against net capital gains in the years noted.

EXAMPLE 15-4

ABC Company, a C corporation, was formed in 2005 and reported net income in each year of its operation. The company had net capital gains and losses as follows:

2005	$ 7,000 gain
2006	10,000 gain
2007	1,000 gain
2008	5,000 gain
2009	21,000 loss

The 2009 capital loss must be carried back three years starting with the earliest year. Thus ABC Company will first apply the $21,000 loss from 2009 to tax year 2006, then to 2007, and finally to 2008. Because the total capital gains in those years were $16,000, ABC Company has a $5,000 capital loss to carry forward to tax years 2010 to 2014.

TAX YOUR BRAIN

Pirate Company was formed in 2004 and reported capital gains and losses, prior to any carryforwards and carrybacks, as follows:

2004	$ 2,000 loss
2005	7,000 gain
2006	10,000 gain
2007	16,000 loss
2008	5,000 gain
2009	14,000 loss

What is the proper tax treatment of the capital gain carryforwards and carrybacks, and what is the resulting net capital gain or loss for each year indicated?

ANSWER

Work from the oldest date to the present. The 2004 loss is carried forward to 2005 resulting in a $5,000 gain in 2005. In 2006 the $10,000 gain will be reported. In 2007 the $16,000 loss will be carried back first to 2005 eliminating the remaining $5,000 gain, and then to 2006 eliminating the $10,000 gain. A $1,000 loss carryforward then remains from 2007. This carryforward will be applied to 2008 resulting in a $4,000 gain in 2008. Finally, the 2009 loss will be carried back to the remaining 2008 gain, giving Pirate Company a $10,000 loss carryforward to be used starting in 2010 and expiring in 2014.

If a corporation carries back a capital loss, it files an amended return for the prior year(s) and will receive a refund.

The other major difference between individual and corporate taxation of capital gains pertains to tax rates. Individuals pay tax on net capital gains at a rate lower than for ordinary income. For corporations, net capital gains are included in income and are taxed at the marginal corporate rate.

[7] IRC § 1212(a).

Charitable Contributions

Corporations are permitted charitable contributions to qualified charitable organizations. The deduction is limited to 10% of taxable income before any of the following:

- Charitable contributions.
- Dividends received deduction (described next).
- Net operating loss carryback.
- Capital loss carryback.[8]

Any contributions in excess of the permitted amount are carried forward for five years, are added to the charitable contributions in that year, and are subject to the 10% limitation. In future years, current contributions are deducted first.[9]

EXAMPLE 15-5	Szabo Company reported $50,000 of taxable income before charitable contributions. The company had charitable contributions of $8,000. Szabo's charitable contributions are limited to $5,000 ($50,000 × 10%). Thus, Szabo's taxable income will be $45,000, and its charitable contributions carryforward is $3,000.

In general, if a corporation contributes ordinary income property, the deduction is limited to the corporation's basis in the property.[10] Ordinary income property is property that, if sold, would produce a gain other than a long-term capital gain. An example is inventory held by a corporation.

Taxpayers use carryforward information to determine any charitable contributions limitation but ignore carryback information. In effect, taxpayers use all information available when the return is filed but do not make changes for information that could become available in the future.

Dividends Received Deduction

C corporations are permitted a tax deduction for a portion of the dividends they receive from other domestic corporations. The dividends received deduction (DRD) is a percentage of the dividend and varies depending on the percentage ownership in the dividend-paying corporation:[11]

Ownership Percentage	Deduction Percentage
Less than 20%	70%
20% to less than 80%	80%
80% or more	100%

EXAMPLE 15-6	Duck Corporation owns 15% of Rose Company. Duck received a $10,000 dividend from Rose and is entitled to a $7,000 dividends received deduction. The deduction means that $3,000 of the dividend is included in Duck's taxable income. If Duck owned 40% of Rose, the DRD would have been $8,000, and only $2,000 of the dividend would have been taxable to Duck.

---

[8] IRC § 170(b)(2).

[9] IRC § 170(d)(2).

[10] In IRC § 170(e) there are three limited cases in which the deduction can exceed basis.

[11] IRC § 246(b)(3).

The DRD can be limited. If taxable income (before DRD or any capital loss carryback) is between 100% of the dividend and 70% (or 80% as appropriate) of the dividend, the DRD is limited to taxable income multiplied by the appropriate percentage.

EXAMPLE 15-7	Sylva Silverware owns 30% of Fredonia Flatware. Fredonia paid a $20,000 dividend to Sylva. Sylva's taxable income, before the DRD, was $50,000. Sylva's DRD is $16,000 ($20,000 × 80%).

EXAMPLE 15-8	Use the information from the previous example except that Sylva's taxable income, before the DRD, was $5,000. Sylva's taxable income is not between 80% of the dividend ($16,000) and 100% of the dividend ($20,000). Thus, the DRD is not limited.

EXAMPLE 15-9	Use the information from Example 15-7 except that Sylva's taxable income before the DRD was $18,000. In this case, Sylva's taxable income is in the limitation area (between $16,000 and $20,000). Thus, Sylva's DRD is limited to 80% of taxable income before the DRD, or $14,400 ($18,000 × 80%).

In Examples 15-7 through 15-9, if Sylva owned less than 20% of Fredonia, the applicable percentage would have been 70% and the lower dollar limit for purposes of the limitation would have been $14,000 (the $20,000 dividend × 70%).

Other Differences

Except for closely held C corporations, the passive loss rules (refer to Chapter 13) do not apply to corporations.[12] A *closely held C corporation* is one in which more than 50% of the value of its outstanding stock is owned, directly or indirectly, by not more than five individuals.[13]

Corporations normally incur various organizational expenses at the time of legal formation. These costs can include legal fees, incorporation fees, and filing fees. In general, capitalized costs are deductible over their useful life. Because the life of a corporation is theoretically indefinite, organizational expenses are recorded as a nonamortizable asset and are not deductible. However, the IRC permits corporations to elect to deduct organizational expenses in an amount equal to the lower of (1) the amount of organizational expenses or (2) $5,000.[14] If total organizational expenses exceed $50,000, then the $5,000 amount is reduced to zero on a dollar-for-dollar basis. Thus, when organizational expenses exceed $55,000, no immediate deduction is permitted. Any remaining organizational expenses are deductible over a 180-month period beginning with the month the corporation begins business. Expenditures must be incurred before the end of the fiscal year in which the corporation begins business, and the election must be filed with the first tax return. Expenditures associated with issuing or selling stock are not deductible.

Organizational expenses are different from *start-up expenses,* which are incurred prior to the time the corporation begins to produce income. If the enterprise is operating as a business, the expenses would be deductible as ordinary and necessary business expenses. However, the business is not yet active and is not earning income; thus the expenses are not deductible and must be capitalized. Corporations can elect to treat the expenses as deferred expenses and deduct them initially and/or over a 180-month period in a manner similar to that described for organizational expenses.[15] The 180-month period begins in the month in which the active trade or business begins. The election must be filed with the tax return for the corporation's first year. The calculations and limitations are determined separately for organizational expenses and for start-up expenses.

[12] IRC § 469(a)(2).
[13] IRC § 542(a)(2).
[14] IRC § 248(a).
[15] IRC § 195(b).

Corporate Tax Rates

Once corporate taxable income is determined, the amount of tax liability can be calculated with reference to a tax rate table. Tax rates for C corporations[16] are as follows:

Corporate Tax Rates			
Taxable Income Over	But Not Over	The Tax Is	Of the Amount Over
$ 0	$ 50,000	15%	$ –0–
50,000	75,000	$ 7,500 + 25%	50,000
75,000	100,000	13,750 + 34%	75,000
100,000	335,000	22,250 + 39%	100,000
335,000	10,000,000	113,900 + 34%	335,000
10,000,000	15,000,000	3,400,000 + 35%	10,000,000
15,000,000	18,333,333	5,150,000 + 38%	15,000,000
18,333,333	—	35% of taxable income	18,333,333

Corporate tax rates follow a progressive tax structure, but the rates "wobble around" as income increases. Technically, the tax rate for incomes between $75,000 and $10,000,000 is 34% and the rate above $10,000,000 is 35%.[17] However, the IRC also recaptures the benefit of reduced rates for those taxpayers with higher incomes. In other words, a corporate taxpayer with $60,000 of taxable income pays tax of 15% on the first $50,000 and 25% on the remaining $10,000. A corporate taxpayer with taxable income of $60,000,000 does not get the benefit of lower rates and pays tax at a 35% flat rate on every dollar of income. The tax rate tables are structured to eliminate the benefit of the lower brackets.

EXAMPLE 15-10 Beaufort Company has taxable income of $1,200,000. Its tax liability is $408,000 {calculated as $113,900 + [($1,200,000 – $335,000) × 34%] = $408,000}. You will get the same answer if you multiply taxable income by 34%.

Estimated Payments

A corporation must pay *estimated taxes*. The required annual payment is the lower of (1) 100% of the tax due for the year or (2) 100% of the tax due for the prior year.[18] Estimated payments can be made in four installments on the 15th day of the 4th, 6th, 9th, and 12th months of the corporation's fiscal year. For calendar year corporations, the due dates are April 15, June 15, September 15, and December 15. Estimated payments are reported on Form 1120, line 32b.

Large corporations (those with taxable income in excess of $1 million in any of the three preceding years) cannot use the prior year safe harbor except for the first quarterly installment payment. These corporations must base the final three quarterly payments on their estimate of current year tax due.

The corporate underpayment penalty is based on the same interest rate schedule used for individuals. The penalty is not deductible in any year.

Net Operating Losses

If a corporation has a net operating loss (NOL), it can carry the loss back two years and forward 20 years.[19] The corporation can affirmatively elect to waive the carryback period and only carry the loss forward.[20] The election is irrevocable for the tax year.

[16] IRC § 11(b).

[17] IRC § 11(b)(1)(C) and IRC § 11(b)(1)(D).

[18] IRC § 6655.

[19] IRC § 172 and IRC § 172(b)(1).

[20] IRC § 172(b)(3).

In general, a net operating loss occurs when the corporate entity has negative taxable income for the year.

TAX YOUR BRAIN

Under what circumstances would a corporation choose to forgo the carryback period for a net operating loss and elect to only carry the loss forward?

ANSWER

If tax rates will be higher in the future and if the corporation expects to earn money in the future, it may make sense to only carry the NOL forward. For example, if tax rates in prior years were 30% and are expected to be 40% in the future, the corporation would receive an additional 10 cents for each dollar of NOL if the loss were only carried forward.

CONCEPT CHECK 15-3—LO 3

1. Corporations follow the same tax rules for capital gains as do individuals. True or false?
2. The tax liability of a corporation with taxable income of $520,000 is _____.
3. A corporation reported taxable income of $390,000 before charitable contributions. The corporation made charitable contributions of $50,000. Its permitted deduction for charitable contributions in the current tax year is _____.
4. Organizational expenses are automatically deductible over 180 months. True or false?
5. Corporate net operating losses from 2009 can be carried back _____ years and forward _____ years.

If an eligible small business (ESB) realizes a net operating loss in 2008 (only), special carryback rules apply. In such cases, the ESB can affirmatively elect a carryback period of three, four, or five years rather than the normal two-year period. An ESB is defined as a corporation or partnership with average gross receipts (for the three years ending in 2008) of $15 million or less. If the ESB does not make the election, the normal two-year carryback rules will apply. For more information, see Rev. Proc. 2009-19 and Rev. Proc. 2009-26.

TRANSACTIONS WITH SHAREHOLDERS
LO 4

Dividends and Distributions

Corporations can pay cash or property (called *distributions*) to their shareholders. To the extent that distributions are from the earnings and profits of the corporation, the distribution is a *dividend*.[21] The corporation cannot deduct the cost of the dividend, and the shareholder reports taxable income in an amount equal to the fair market value of the property received.[22]

Earnings and profits (E&P) are conceptually similar to retained earnings except that they are calculated on the basis of tax law, not financial accounting standards.

Distributions paid in excess of earnings and profits are nontaxable to the extent of the stockholder's basis in her or his stock. The excess of a distribution over the stockholder's basis is treated as a capital gain (assuming the stock is a capital asset in the hands of the stockholder).[23]

If a corporation makes a distribution of property (not cash) that has a basis less than the fair market value (that is, appreciated property), the corporation is treated as selling the property at its fair market value. Thus the corporation recognizes a gain on the distribution of appreciated property.

EXAMPLE 15-11

Sasha received a $500 cash distribution from the E&P of Alpha Company. The dividend is fully taxable to Sasha.

---

[21] IRC § 316.
[22] IRC § 301.
[23] IRC § 301(c)(2) and § 301(c)(3).

EXAMPLE 15-12	Assume that Sasha's distribution was in the form of property with a FMV of $500 and a basis to Alpha Company of $400. Alpha will record a $100 gain. Sasha will report dividend income of $500.

EXAMPLE 15-13	Quad Company has E&P of $5,000. It makes a $6,000 cash distribution to Quincy, its sole shareholder. Assuming that Quincy has a basis in his stock of at least $1,000, he will report dividend income of $5,000 and a nontaxable distribution of $1,000. Quincy will reduce the basis of his stock by $1,000.

EXAMPLE 15-14	Use the information from Example 15-13. Assume that the basis of Quincy's stock is $200. In this case, he would report a dividend of $5,000, a nontaxable return of capital of $200, and a capital gain of $800. Quincy will also reduce the basis of his stock to zero.

The preceding discussion assumed that the distribution was made to shareholders on a pro rata basis. In other words, each shareholder receives a distribution proportionate to his or her ownership. Corporations can also make a non–pro rata distribution by which one or more stockholders receive a distribution that is not in proportion to their ownership percentage. If the distribution is in appreciated property, the corporation again has a deemed sale and gain based on FMV. The shareholder reports dividend income equal to the FMV of the cash or property received.

A shareholder may receive a distribution in full liquidation of her or his ownership interest. For example, a shareholder may sell all of her or his stock back to the corporation for cash or property. In such case, he or she will have a capital gain or loss equal to the difference between the amount of the distribution and his or her basis in the stock.

Liquidation

A *corporate liquidation* occurs when a corporation decides to cease doing business and wind up its business affairs. The corporation pays debts and distributes remaining assets to shareholders. In the case of a complete liquidation, the corporation records all assets and liabilities at fair market value (with associated write-ups or write-downs). The shareholder reports a capital gain or loss equal to the difference between his or her basis in the stock and the FMV of the property received.

EXAMPLE 15-15	Tara received cash of $5,000 and other assets with a FMV of $7,000 as a result of the complete liquidation of Blue Corporation. Tara's basis in the stock of Blue was $10,000. Tara will report a return of capital (nontaxable) of $10,000 and a capital gain of $2,000.

CONCEPT CHECK 15-4—LO 4	1. Dividends are always taxable to a shareholder. True or false?
	2. If a corporation pays a dividend in property, the stockholder will have a dividend equal to the corporate basis in the property. True or false?
	3. A corporation has earnings and profits of $10,000 and makes a cash distribution to its sole shareholder in the amount of $11,000. The amount of taxable dividend to the shareholder is _____.

SCHEDULES L, M-1, AND M-3
LO 5

Corporations must provide a beginning and ending balance sheet on Form 1120, Schedule L, as well as a reconciliation of book income to taxable income on Form 1120, Schedule M-1. See page 5 of Form 1120 in Exhibit 15-1 for both schedules. If a corporation's total receipts and total assets are both less than $250,000, the two schedules are not required.

Preparation of Schedule L is straightforward. It is prepared in accordance with the accounting method the corporation uses to keep its financial accounting records (accrual, cash, or mixed model).

Schedule M-1 can be more complex. It reconciles net income per books (line 1) with net income per the tax return (line 10). In effect, this schedule sets out all book/tax differences for the year regardless of whether they are permanent or temporary differences.

It is important to note that Schedule M-1 reconciles from net income per books (financial accounting net income) to net income per the tax law, *not* the other way around. Let's examine each of the lines individually.

Line 2: Federal income tax is an expense for book purposes but is not deductible for tax purposes. The amount of federal income tax expense must be added back to book income. This number is the federal income tax expense deduction on the income statement—*not* the tax expense on page 1 of the tax return.

Line 3: For book purposes, excess capital losses qualify as an expense. For tax purposes, recall that corporate capital losses are deductible only to the extent of capital gains. Thus, any excess of capital losses over capital gains must be added back to book income.

Line 4: Certain income may be taxable but may be properly excluded from book income. Examples include the last month's rent collected at lease signing by a landlord or the installment sale income reported in full on the books in a prior year. These items must be added to book income to arrive at taxable income.

Line 5: Certain expenses can be recorded on the books but are not deductible on the tax return. These items include the difference between accelerated depreciation taken on the books and straight-line depreciation for taxes in the early years of an asset's life; the difference between the book and tax deductions if charitable contributions are limited on the tax return; and 50% of travel and entertainment expenses that are not deductible on the tax return.

Line 7: Some income is reported on the books but is not reported on the tax return. Examples include life insurance proceeds that can be excluded for taxes but must be included for book purposes; prepayment of the last month of rent that will be included on the tax return at the beginning of the lease but on the books at the end of the lease; and interest from tax-exempt bonds.

Line 8: Deductions can be taken on the tax return but are not deductible in the financial records. Tax return depreciation in excess of book depreciation is an example. Another is the tax deduction for previously disallowed charitable contributions. These were deducted on the financial statements in a prior year.

EXAMPLE 15-16	Martin Company had book income of $50,000 for the year. It also had the following differences between book income and tax income:

Charitable contributions carryforward used in current year	$2,000
Excess depreciation on tax return	6,000

In addition, the company incurred $10,000 of travel and entertainment expense, only 50% of which is deductible for taxes. Martin Company's taxable income is $47,000 ($50,000 − $2,000 − $6,000 + [$10,000 × 50%]). A completed Schedule M-1 is shown in Exhibit 15-2.

EXHIBIT 15-2

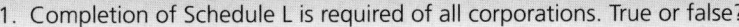

Schedule M-1	Reconciliation of Income (Loss) per Books With Income per Return		
	Note: Schedule M-3 required instead of Schedule M-1 if total assets are $10 million or more—see instructions		

1	Net income (loss) per books	50,000	7	Income recorded on books this year not included on this return (itemize):		
2	Federal income tax per books			Tax-exempt interest $		
3	Excess of capital losses over capital gains					
4	Income subject to tax not recorded on books this year (itemize):		8	Deductions on this return not charged against book income this year (itemize):		
5	Expenses recorded on books this year not deducted on this return (itemize):		a	Depreciation . . . $	6,000	
a	Depreciation $		b	Charitable contributions $	2,000	
b	Charitable contributions $					
c	Travel and entertainment $ 5,000					8,000
		5,000	9	Add lines 7 and 8		8,000
6	Add lines 1 through 5	55,000	10	Income (page 1, line 28)—line 6 less line 9		47,000

Corporations with total assets of $10 million or more must complete a separate Schedule M-3. This schedule is, in effect, an extremely detailed reconciliation of book income with taxable income. Thus it is an expanded version of Schedule M-1 for large corporations. You can locate a Schedule M-3 on the IRS Web site (www.irs.gov).

CONCEPT CHECK 15-5—LO 5

1. Completion of Schedule L is required of all corporations. True or false?
2. Schedule M-1 reconciles book income to taxable income. True or false?
3. A corporation's depreciation expense is lower on the financial statements than it is on the tax return. Would this difference be a negative or positive item on Schedule M-1?

OTHER CORPORATE ISSUES INCLUDING ALTERNATIVE MINIMUM TAX
LO 6

Corporations can be part of a controlled group. The most common of these groups are parent–subsidiary groups or brother–sister groups, which we discuss here, in addition to corporate alternative minimum tax.

Parent–Subsidiary Groups

Parent–subsidiary groups are those for which a common parent corporation owns, directly or indirectly, at least 80% of one or more other corporations. The ownership can be one or more chains of corporations connected through stock ownership with the parent corporation.

EXAMPLE 15-17

Garner Corporation owns 90% of Harnett Company. The two corporations are part of a parent–subsidiary group. The relationship holds as long as Garner owns at least 80% of Harnett.

EXAMPLE 15-18

Garner Corporation also owns 95% of Iona Company. Iona, in turn, owns 85% of Jasper Corporation. The entire Garner/Iona/Jasper chain of corporations is part of a parent–subsidiary group.

Parent–subsidiary corporations can elect to file a consolidated tax return. Form 1122 is attached to the first consolidated return for each of the subsidiaries of the group.[24] An appropriate officer

[24] Reg. § 1.1502-75(b).

of the subsidiary signs the form, thereby consenting to be included in the group. All members of the parent–subsidiary group must be included. Subsidiaries no longer file separate returns. In subsequent years, Form 851, which is an affiliation schedule listing the corporations that are part of the consolidated return, is attached to the consolidated return.

Electing to file as a consolidated entity has certain advantages. For example, a consolidated return allows the entity to offset losses from one corporation against profits of another. In addition, profits from intercompany sales are deferred. There are potential disadvantages as well. The election is binding on future tax years, losses on intercompany sales cannot be immediately recognized, and elections made by the parent are binding on all subsidiaries.

Brother–Sister Groups

A *brother–sister group* may exist if five or fewer persons own two or more corporations. The group exists if both of the following tests are met:

- **Total ownership test**: The shareholder group owns stock representing at least 80% of the voting shares of stock or at least 80% of the total value of all shares.
- **Common ownership test**: The shareholder group has common (identical) ownership of more than 50% of the voting power or more than 50% of the value of all shares.

At first glance, the tests seem to be the same with different percentages, but such is not the case. The 80% test examines ownership of an individual corporation. The 50% test, in effect, is based on the smallest common percentage across all of the corporations evaluated.

EXAMPLE 15-19

Three individuals have ownership interests in four different corporations as follows:

	Corporations				Identical Ownership
	A	B	C	D	
Reed	60%	20%	30%	30%	20%
Smith	30	65	30	40	30
Thomas	10	15	40	20	10
Totals	100%	100%	100%	90%	60%

The Identical Ownership column represents the smallest number reading across the column. In other words, it is the identical ownership across all of the corporations. So, for example, Reed owns at least 20% of each of the corporations.

The total ownership test is met because the three individuals own at least 80% of each of the four corporations (in this example for corporations A, B, and C, they actually own all the stock). The common ownership test is met because the common (identical) ownership is more than 50% (it is 60% in this example). Thus the four corporations are all part of a brother–sister group.

TAX YOUR BRAIN

In Example 15-19, if Reed sold half of her ownership in Corporation B to an unrelated third party, would the corporations remain as a brother–sister group?

ANSWER

No, by reducing her ownership in Corporation B to 10% of the total, Reed now has an identical common ownership across the four corporations of 10%. Thus, the sum of the common ownership for all three individuals is exactly 50%. The common ownership test must be more than 50%. Thus, the entities are no longer a brother–sister group.

One way to think about the two tests is that the 80% test is a "vertical test" (does the group own at least 80% of a specific individual corporation?) whereas the 50% test is a "horizontal test" (what is the smallest percentage that an individual owns across the various corporations?).

LO 1   26. A corporation has a fiscal year-end of June. If the corporation does not receive an automatic extension of time to file its return, the return will be due on the 15th of

    a. August.

    b. September.

    c. October.

    d. November.

LO 2   27. Two individuals form a corporation and own all of its stock. One individual contributes cash, and the other contributes property encumbered by a mortgage. The new corporation assumes the mortgage. Which of the following statements is true with respect to the individual who contributes the property?

    a. Because the 80% test is met, no gain or loss will be recognized.

    b. Gain is recognized to the extent of relief of liability.

    c. Gain is recognized to the extent of relief of liability in excess of the basis of property contributed.

    d. Gain is recognized to the extent the fair market value of the stock exceeds the basis of the property contributed.

LO 2   28. Tameka and Janelle form a corporation in which each will own 50% of the stock. Tameka contributes $50,000 in cash. Janelle contributes property with a basis of $30,000 and a FMV of $60,000. She receives $10,000 of inventory from the corporation. Which of the following statements is true?

    a. Janelle will report a gain of $10,000.

    b. Janelle will report a gain of $30,000.

    c. Tameka will report a gain of $10,000.

    d. Neither Tameka nor Janelle will report a gain or loss as a result of these transactions.

LO 2   29. Svetlana forms a corporation in which she is the sole shareholder. She contributes a vehicle with a basis of $15,000 and a FMV of $8,000 in exchange for stock. She also contributes cash of $2,000. Svetlana will recognize

    a. A $5,000 loss.

    b. A $7,000 loss.

    c. A $10,000 loss.

    d. Neither a gain nor loss.

LO 2   30. Annabelle forms a corporation in which she is the sole shareholder. She transfers $20,000 cash plus land with a $100,000 adjusted basis and a $160,000 FMV in exchange for all the stock of the corporation. The corporation assumes the $140,000 mortgage on the land. What is her basis in the stock, and what is the gain she must report (if any)?

    a. No gain; stock basis is $120,000.

    b. Gain of $20,000; stock basis is $120,000.

    c. No gain; stock basis is $100,000.

    d. Gain of $20,000; stock basis is zero.

LO 3   31. Mountain Company owns 10% of Valley Company. Both are domestic corporations. Valley pays a $60,000 dividend to Mountain. What amount of dividend income will be included in the taxable income of Mountain Company?

    a. $6,000.

    b. $12,000.

       c. $18,000.

       d. $60,000.

LO 3   32. For Subchapter C corporations, which of the following statements is true?

       a. Capital losses can be carried back three years and then carried forward five years.

       b. Corporations can elect to forgo the carryback period for capital losses and only carry the losses forward.

       c. Capital losses can be carried back 2 years and then carried forward 20 years.

       d. Capital losses are permitted up to $3,000 per year.

LO 1, 3   33. Which of the following statements is false?

       a. A corporation with average sales in excess of $5,000,000 must use the accrual method of accounting.

       b. The charitable contributions of a corporation may be limited.

       c. A corporation may be entitled to a deduction for dividends received from other domestic corporations.

       d. Passive loss rules apply to corporations.

LO 3   34. A calendar year corporate taxpayer must make its final estimated tax payment on the 15th of which month?

       a. November.

       b. December.

       c. January.

       d. February.

LO 4   35. Which, if any, of the following statements concerning the shareholders of a Subchapter C corporation is correct?

       a. Shareholders are taxed on their proportionate share of earnings and profits as they are earned.

       b. Shareholders are taxed on distributions from corporate earnings and profits.

       c. Shareholders are never taxed on earnings and profits or distributions from the corporation.

       d. None of these statements are correct.

LO 4   36. Parker Company has earnings and profits of $8,000. It distributes capital gain property with a basis of $2,000 and FMV of $9,000 to Gertrude Parker, its sole shareholder. Gertrude has a basis of $10,000 in her stock. Which of the following statements is true with respect to this transaction?

       a. Gertrude will report dividend income of $2,000 and a capital gain of $7,000.

       b. Gertrude will report dividend income of $8,000.

       c. Gertrude will report dividend income of $8,000 and a nontaxable distribution of $1,000.

       d. Gertrude will report dividend income of $9,000.

LO 5   37. Which of the following is a negative adjustment on Schedule M-1?

       a. Federal income tax.

       b. Charitable contributions in excess of the 10% limit.

       c. Depreciation for books in excess of depreciation for taxes.

       d. Tax-exempt interest income.

LO 5 38. Which of the following is a positive adjustment on Schedule M-1?

    a. Excess of capital losses over capital gains.

    b. Excess of capital gains over capital losses.

    c. Charitable contribution carryover to the current year.

    d. Depreciation for taxes in excess of depreciation for books.

LO 6 39. Banana Company is widely held. It owns 85% of Strawberry Corporation. Two individuals hold the remaining 15%. Which of the following statements is true?

    a. Banana and Strawberry must file a consolidated tax return.

    b. Banana and Strawberry can elect to file a consolidated tax return.

    c. Banana and Strawberry can file a consolidated tax return if the other owners of Strawberry agree.

    d. Banana and Strawberry are brother–sister corporations.

LO 6 40. What missing dollar amounts are correct in the following sentence? The AMT exemption is $_____ for corporations with AMT income of $_____ or less.

    a. $40,000; $150,000.

    b. $40,000; $310,000.

    c. $150,000; $310,000.

    d. This question cannot be answered with the information given.

LO 7 41. Which of the following items increase basis for a stockholder of a Subchapter S corporation?

    a. Capital contributions.

    b. Charitable contributions.

    c. Net losses.

    d. Distributions from the corporation.

LO 7 42. Which of the following statements is incorrect?

    a. An S corporation can own stock of a C corporation.

    b. A C corporation can own stock of an S corporation.

    c. An S corporation can be a partner in a partnership.

    d. An estate can own stock of an S corporation.

LO 7 43. Which, if any, of the following statements concerning the shareholders of a Subchapter S corporation is correct?

    a. Shareholders are taxed on their proportionate share of earnings that are distributed.

    b. Shareholders are taxed on the distributions from the corporation.

    c. Shareholders are taxed on their proportionate share of earnings whether or not distributed.

    d. None of these statements are correct.

LO 4, 7 44. Chen received a $10,000 dividend from a Subchapter C corporation. He also owns a 50% interest in a Subchapter S corporation that reported $100,000 of taxable income. He received a distribution of $20,000 from the Subchapter S corporation. How much income will Chen report as a result of these events?

a. $30,000.

b. $40,000.

c. $60,000.

d. $80,000.

Problems

LO 2 45. When a corporation is formed, in certain cases the transferor may report a gain. What are the instances in which a gain would be reported? In these cases, what is the basis of the stock held by the transferor?

_____

_____

_____

_____

_____

_____

LO 2 46. An individual contributes property with a FMV in excess of basis to a corporation in exchange for stock. The property is subject to a mortgage. In each of the following instances, determine the basis of the stock in the hands of the shareholder and the basis of the property contributed in the hands of the corporation. Assume that the 80% rule is met.

a. The property is subject to a mortgage that is less than basis, and the corporation assumes the mortgage.

b. The property is subject to a mortgage that is more than basis, and the corporation assumes the mortgage.

_____

_____

_____

_____

_____

_____

LO 2 47. Determine the basis of stock in the hands of the shareholder in each of the following instances. Assume that the 80% rule is met in all cases.

a. Contribution of property with a basis of $1,000 and a FMV of $1,400.

b. Contribution of property with a basis of $3,000 and a FMV of $3,800. The stockholder also received $500 cash from the corporation as part of the stock transaction.

c. Contribution of property with a basis of $8,200 and a FMV of $12,500. The stockholder also received property with a FMV of $1,700 from the corporation as part of the stock transaction.

d. Contribution of a building with a FMV of $200,000, a mortgage (assumed by the corporation) of $100,000, and a basis of $125,000.

e. Contribution of a building with a FMV of $1,700,000, a mortgage (assumed by the corporation) of $1,000,000, and a basis of $635,000.

_____

_____

_____

_____

_____

_____

Amended Tax Returns (Form 1040X)

Over 130 million individual income tax returns are filed each year. The vast majority of those returns are filed correctly. However, on occasion, the information on an already-filed tax return is determined to be incorrect.

There are literally hundreds of reasons why a previously filed return might be incorrect: a math error, a change of filing status, an additional or corrected informational tax form received, the basis or sales price on the sale of a capital asset initially reported incorrectly, a permitted itemized deduction omitted, and so on. There might be one error or multiple errors, and the changes might cause total tax liability to increase or decrease.

If a previously filed tax return is determined to be in error, the taxpayer must file an amended tax return on Form 1040X. On the amended return, the taxpayer provides numerical information concerning the tax return item(s) that is (are) being corrected plus a reconciliation between the original data and the correct data. The form also has a section where the taxpayer must explain the change.

Let us look at an example:

- Exhibit A-1 is the Form 1040 originally filed by Kim Watkins for tax year 2009. She had wage income and interest income, and she took the standard deduction. She originally received a refund of $252. After she had filed her return, she received a corrected Form 1099-INT from State Savings Bank. The corrected Form 1099-INT showed interest income in box 1 that was $250 greater than originally reported.

- As a result of receiving this corrected Form 1099-INT, Kim must file an amended tax return. The completed Form 1040X amended tax return is shown in Exhibit A-2.

- Column A of the amended return provides tax return information as it was originally filed. The information in column A comes from the data on the original Form 1040 in Exhibit A-1. Column B is used to indicate the numerical items that have changed. In this case, line 1, adjusted gross income, must increase by $250 to properly report the information on the corrected Form 1099-INT received by Kim. Column C represents the corrected totals.

- Because Kim's income increased by $250, she will owe additional tax of $62. That amount is reflected in column B starting on line 6. It also is the amount shown on line 21. When Kim files her amended Form 1040X, she must include a check for $62. Kim is in the 25% tax bracket. The additional tax represents the 25% income tax that is due on the additional $250 of income ($250 × 25% = $62.50, rounded to $62).

Only one item needed to be corrected in our example. If multiple changes are required, the taxpayer should clearly explain each item and provide a detailed summation and reconciliation.

Use the information from our previous example. Assume that Kim received two corrected 1099-INT forms, one from State Savings Bank that increased her interest income by $250 and another from State Bank and Trust that decreased her interest income by $100. In this

case, the amount on line 1, column B, of Form 1040X would be $150, the net difference. The explanation on page 2 needs to clearly explain the change. Here is how Part II, Explanation of Changes, might appear:

Taxpayer received two corrected Forms 1099-INT. One was from State Savings Bank. It showed corrected interest income $250 greater than originally reported. The other was from State Bank and Trust. It showed corrected interest income $100 less than originally reported. The amount on line 1, column B, is $150 determined as follows:

Change from corrected Form 1099-INT from State Savings Bank.............	$250
Change from corrected Form 1099-INT from State Bank and Trust.......	(100)
Net change to Form 1040X, line 1, column B....................................	$ 150

It is extremely important to note that the amended return must be prepared using the tax rules in effect for the year of the original return. For example, if we were preparing an amended return for Kim Watkins for tax year 2008, the standard deduction on line 2 of the 1040X would be $5,450 and the personal exemption on line 4 would be $3,500 because those were the correct amounts for tax year 2008. We would also use the tax tables or tax rate schedules for 2008, not 2009.

Generally a 1040X must be filed within three years after the date the original return was filed or within two years after the date the taxpayer paid the tax due on the original return, whichever is later.

Appendix B

Comprehensive Problems

In this appendix, we provide a series of comprehensive tax return problems. In the text, the scope of the tax return problems is generally limited to the subject matter of the chapter. The comprehensive problems in this appendix require integration of tax materials across multiple chapters. Each problem does have a primary focus area—Schedule A, C, D, or E. We provide two problems for Schedules A, C, and D. In each case, the first problem is a bit easier than the second.

The problems can be completed using the TaxACT software provided with this text or can be completed using the tax forms found on the IRS Web site (www.irs.gov).

COMPREHENSIVE PROBLEM #1

With Emphasis on Schedule A

James and Esther Johnson live at 45678 S.W. 112th Street, Homestead, Florida 33157. James, who is 66 years old, is retired receiving social security benefits and Esther, who is 65 years old, is also retired but working on a part-time basis. Their social security numbers are 200-00-0010 and 200-01-0011, respectively.

Annual social security income for Jim is $18,000 (SSA-1099, box 5) and for Esther is $10,800 (SSA-1099, box 5).

Interest received by them from Central Bank is $2,545 (1099-INT, box 1). No income tax withholding was made. The economic recovery payment received by James and Esther in 2009 was $500.

Esther is working part-time as an interior decorator as an employee of Decorating House, a corporation. Her Form W-2 shows the following information:

$$\text{Wages} = \$ 15,000.00$$
$$\text{Federal W/H} = \$ \ \ 1,500.00$$
$$\text{Social security wages} = \$ 15,000.00$$
$$\text{Social security W/H} = \$ \ \ \ \ \ 930.00$$
$$\text{Medicare wages} = \$ 15,000.00$$
$$\text{Medicare W/H} = \$ \ \ \ \ \ 217.50$$

Their itemized deductions are as follows:

1. Mortgage interest on their main home, $6,400. This is from a second mortgage of $120,000 that they obtained from the bank.
2. Real estate taxes, $5,700; use 7% for the state/local sales tax rate for sales taxes.
3. Doctors' expenses unreimbursed by insurance, $4,300.
4. Medical insurance premiums for the year, $2,400.
5. Prescribed medicine, $1,885.

6. Vitamins, $300.

7. Contributions to their church, $570.

8. Tax preparation fees for their 2008 return, $325, paid in 2009.

9. Lottery tickets bought by Esther during the year, $750. Winnings received, $940 (W-2G, box 1). Income tax withholding on winnings, $35 (W-2G, box 2).

Required:

Prepare their individual income tax return using the appropriate forms. They do not want to contribute to the presidential election campaign and do not want anyone to be a third-party designee. For any missing information, make reasonable assumptions.

COMPREHENSIVE PROBLEM #2

With Emphasis on Schedule A

Jamie and Cecilia Reyes are husband and wife and file a joint return. They live at 5677 Apple Cove Rd., Boise, Idaho. Their respective social security numbers are 444-33-2222 and 444-44-3333. Both are under 65 years of age. They provide more than half of the support of their daughter, Carmen (age 23), social security number 555-44-3333, who is a full-time veterinarian school student. Carmen received a $3,200 scholarship covering her room and board at college. They furnish all of the support of Maria (Jamie's grandmother), social security number 222-11-0000, who is age 70 and lives in a nursing home. They also have a son, Gustavo (age 4), social security number 777-66-5555.

During 2009 Jamie had the following transactions:

Salary	$145,625
(Federal income tax withholding was $26,213. Social security and Medicare withholding were appropriate for his income. State income tax withholding was $8,738.)	
Dividends (all qualified dividends)	2,500

Other receipts for the couple were as follows:

Interest income:	
Union Bank	$ 220
State of Idaho—interest on tax refund	22
City of Boise school bonds	1,250
Interest from U.S. savings bonds	410
2008 federal income tax refund received in 2009	2,007
2008 state income tax refund received in 2009	218
Idaho lottery winnings	1,100
Casino slot machine winnings	2,250
Gambling losses at casino	6,500

Other information that the Reyes provided for the 2009 tax year:

Mortgage interest on personal residence	$15,081
Interest on motor home	5,010
Doctor's fee for a face-lift for Mrs. Reyes	6,800
Dentist's fee for a new dental bridge for Mr. Reyes	2,500
Prescribed vitamins for the entire family	110

Property taxes paid	$ 7,025
DMV fees on motor home (tax portion)	1,044
DMV fees on family autos (tax portion)	436
Doctors' bills for grandmother	3,960
Nursing home for grandmother	12,200
Wheelchair for grandmother	1,030
Property taxes on boat	134
Interest on personal credit card	550
Interest on loan to buy school bonds	270
Cash contributions to church	5,100
Cash contribution to man at bottom of freeway off-ramp	10
Contribution of furniture to Goodwill—cost basis	4,000
Contribution of furniture to Goodwill—fair market value	410
Tax return preparation fee for 2008 taxes	525

Required:

Prepare a Form 1040, Schedule A, and other required forms and schedules necessary for the completion of the Reyeses' tax return. They do not want to contribute to the presidential election campaign and do not want anyone to be a third-party designee. For any missing information, make reasonable assumptions.

COMPREHENSIVE PROBLEM #3

With Emphasis on Schedule C

Christian Everland (SS# 555-55-5555) is single and resides at 3554 Arrival Road, Apt. 6E, Buckhead, Georgia 12345.

Last year Christian started his own landscaping business. He now has two employees and had the following business results in 2009:

Revenue	$63,500
Expenses	
Wages	$12,500
Payroll taxes	956
Fuel	3,500
Repairs	2,345
Assets	

Truck, used 100% for business. Original cost of $12,000. Purchased used on 03/01/09.
Mower #1. Original cost of $4,500. Purchased new on 01/05/09.
Mower #2. Leased for $200 per month for all of 2009.
Other business equipment. Original cost of $4,000. Purchased new on 01/05/09.

Christian has no other income, does not itemize, and has no dependents. Christian paid four quarterly federal tax estimates of $1,000 each.

Required:

Prepare Christian's 2009 Form 1040 and supplemental schedules. Schedule C, Form 4562, and Schedule SE are required. He wants to contribute to the presidential election campaign and does not want anyone to be a third-party designee. For any missing information, make reasonable assumptions.

COMPREHENSIVE PROBLEM #4

With Emphasis on Schedule C

Shelly Beaman (SS# 444-33-4848) is single and resides at 540 Front Street, Ashland, North Carolina 27898.

Shelly's W-2 wages	$55,800
Federal withholding	10,044
Social security wages	55,800
Social security withholding	3,460
Medicare withholding	809
State withholding	3,348
1099-INT New Bank	532
1099-DIV XYZ, Inc.	
Ordinary dividends	258
Qualified dividends	258

Shelly had the following itemized deductions:

State income tax withholding (from W-2)	$ 3,348
State income tax paid with 2008 return	600
Real estate tax	4,200
Mortgage interest	11,800
Charitable contributions	2,500

Shelly also started her own home design consulting business in March 2009. The results of her business operations for 2009 follow:

Gross receipts from clients		$154,000
Vehicle mileage	20,369 business miles	
	32,000 total miles during the year	
	2005 Chevy Suburban	
	Placed in service 03/01/09	
Postage		(750)
Office supplies		(1,500)
State license fees		(155)
Supplies		(5,300)
Professional fees		(2,500)
Design software		(1,000)
Professional education programs (registration)		(550)
Travel to education program		
Airplane		(350)
Lodging $119/night × 3 nights		
Meals per diem $39 × 3 days		

Business Assets	Date Purchased	Cost
Laptop	6/08/09	$ 2,500
Computer	3/05/09	5,700
Printer	3/01/09	1,800
Copier	6/02/09	1,700
Furniture	4/01/09	5,000
Building	3/01/09	175,000

Phone	(600)
Internet service	(450)
Rent	(8,300)
Insurance	(1,700)

Concept Check Answers

CHAPTER 1

Concept Check 1-1

1. Progressive, proportional, regressive.
2. Proportional.
3. Progressive.

Concept Check 1-2

1. True.
2. 25%. For a married couple, the marginal rate is 25% for taxable income between $67,901 and $137,050.
3. False. The average tax rate is the percentage that a taxpayer pays in tax given a certain amount of taxable income. The marginal tax rate represents the proportion of tax that he or she pays on the next dollar of taxable income.
4. False. All tax returns conform to the basic formula.

Concept Check 1-3

1. False. Only taxpayers with a simple tax structure who meet six criteria can file Form 1040EZ.
2. False. To file Form 1040EZ, a taxpayer must be under age 65.
3. True. With the fact pattern provided, Erma meets the six criteria and can file Form 1040EZ.

Concept Check 1-4

1. Wages, unemployment compensation, and interest. The category wages includes salary and tips.
2. Form 1099-G.
3. Single, married filing jointly.

Concept Check 1-5

1. True. Taxpayers must use the tax tables if their income is under $100,000. If taxpayers are eligible to use Form 1040EZ, they must have income under $100,000 (otherwise they would not be eligible to use the form).
2. $14,694.
3. $14,690.50.

Concept Check 1-6

1. False. Taxpayers pay an estimate of their tax liability during the year with income tax withholdings or quarterly estimated tax payments.
2. Refund, $608.
3. False. An Earned Income Credit is subtracted from the tax liability.

Concept Check 1-7

1. Ways and Means.
2. The Internal Revenue Code.
3. True. For any action to become law, both houses of Congress and the president must agree.

Concept Check 1-8

1. False. Statutory tax authority (the law) takes precedence over all other types of tax authority.
2. False. Revenue Procedures are issued by the IRS for use by all taxpayers.
3. IRS Treasury Regulations. See Table 1-6.

Concept Check 1-9

1. False. Tax cases can be appealed to the U.S. Supreme Court.
2. False. The taxpayer can file a suit with the Tax Court, the district court, or the Court of Federal Claims.
3. Tax. The advantage of using the Tax Court is that the taxpayer does not need to pay the IRS's proposed assessment prior to trial.

CHAPTER 2

Concept Check 2-1

1. False. A taxpayer should use the simplest form that is appropriate for his or her situation. This approach will save the taxpayer and the IRS time and money.
2. True. Adjusted Gross Income (AGI) is an important concept because several deductions and credits are dependent on the AGI amount. Some examples are the medical deduction and earned income credit.

Concept Check 2-2

1. True. Yes, couples in the process of obtaining a divorce (where the divorce is not yet final) can file a joint return.
2. True. The social security number and full name of the spouse must be shown on the return.
3. False. The surviving spouse must also meet another rule that states the household needs to be the principal place of abode for the entire year (except for temporary absences) of both the taxpayer and a child, stepchild, or adopted child who can be claimed as a dependent by the taxpayer.

Concept Check 2-3

1. True. The amount of the personal exemption is $3,650 for 2009. On a joint return, the taxpayer is entitled to two personal exemptions: one exemption for himself or herself and another one for his or her spouse, for a total of $7,300.

Concept Check 2-4

1. In addition to the dependent taxpayer test, joint return test, and citizen or resident test, a qualifying child must meet the following five tests: relationship test, age test, residency test, support test, and special test for qualifying child of more than one taxpayer.
2. The child must be under 19 years of age, or under 24 years of age and a full-time student. Beginning in 2009, the child must be younger than the person claiming the dependency.

Concept Check 2-5

1. False. A taxpayer must meet all of the four tests in order to be a qualifying relative.
2. False. A qualifying relative cannot earn an amount equal to or greater than the exemption amount, which is $3,650.

Concept Check 2-6

1. The amount of the standard deduction is
   a. Taxpayer is single, 41 years of age, and blind = $7,100 ($5,700 + $1,400).
   b. Taxpayer is head of household, 35 years of age, and not blind = $8,350.
   c. Taxpayers are married filing jointly, the husband is 67 and the wife is 61 years of age, and not blind = $12,500 ($11,400 + $1,100).

Concept Check 2-7

1. Tax for the single taxpayer is $4,844 and for the married taxpayers is $9,324.
2. The limitation for FICA (social security) for the year 2009 is $106,800.

Concept Check 2-8

1. The failure to file a tax return penalty does not apply because the taxpayer filed an extension before his or her return was due. However, the failure to pay does apply. The amount is $45 [($3,000 × .5%) 3 months].
2. True. The IRS can assess criminal penalties in addition to civil penalties. The former are applicable to tax evasion, willful failure to collect or pay tax, and willful failure to file a return.

CHAPTER 3

Concept Check 3-1

1. In general, an individual must recognize income on his or her tax return if a transaction meets all of the following three conditions: There must be an economic benefit; there must actually be a transaction that has reached a conclusion; and the income must not be tax-exempt income.
2. True. Certain income is statutorily excluded from taxation and will not be included in gross income even though the other two conditions are met. An example is tax-exempt interest.

Concept Check 3-2

1. True. According to Reg. 1.61-1(a), income may be realized in any form, whether in money, property, or services.
2. True. Receipt of property or services serves to trigger income recognition. Furthermore, taxpayers recognize income even if they receive it indirectly.

Concept Check 3-3

1. False. Interest is taxable if received from state or local bonds issued for private activities, such as convention centers, industrial parks, or stadiums.
2. False. A Schedule B is required if an individual receives *over* $1,500 of interest for the tax year.

Concept Check 3-4

1. True. Qualified dividends (1) are made from the earnings and profits of the payer corporation and (2) are from domestic corporations or qualified foreign corporations.
2. False. Corporations normally pay dividends in the form of cash, but they may pay them in property or anything of economic value. The basis of the property received as a dividend in the hands of the shareholder is the property's fair market value at the date of distribution.

Concept Check 3-5

1. The amount is $27,750 (22,000 + 4,500 + 1,250).

Concept Check 3-6

1. Items such as jury duty and gambling winnings are listed under line 21 of the Form 1040.

Concept Check 3-7

1. False. It is not taxable. This is an example of a *de minimis* benefit whose value is so small that keeping track of which employees received the benefit is administratively impractical.
2. True. It is not taxable. The individual must be a degree-seeking student at an educational institution and must use the proceeds for qualified tuition and related expenses (tuition, fees, books, supplies, and equipment). If the scholarship or fellowship payment exceeds permitted expenses, the excess is taxable income.

Concept Check 3-8

1. True. The law limits the ability of taxpayers to create debt instruments with interest rates that materially vary from market rates on the date the instrument is created. Imputing interest will reallocate payments such that more of the payment will be interest and less principal.

2. True. If someone purchases a debt instrument (such as a bond) from an issuer for an amount less than par, the transaction creates original issue discount (OID). The initial OID is equal to the difference between the acquisition price and the maturity value.

CHAPTER 4

Concept Check 4-1

1. At least half-time at an eligible educational institution.
2. Tuition and fees.
3. $120,000.

Concept Check 4-2

1. Self-employed.
2. Nontaxable.
3. Form 8889 and Form 1040.

Concept Check 4-3

1. False. Under current IRS regulations, moving expenses can be deducted only as a *for AGI,* or *above-the-line,* deduction.
2. False. In order to deduct moving expenses, taxpayers must meet both tests.
3. True. To the extent that the employer reimburses the employee for moving costs, those costs cannot be deducted.

Concept Check 4-4

1. Net earnings.
2. 7.65%

Concept Check 4-5

1. False. For self-employed individuals, the deduction is 100% of the costs.
2. False. The limitation on this deduction is that taxpayers cannot deduct the cost of premiums that exceeds *net* earnings from self-employment.
3. True. If the taxpayer is entitled to participate in any subsidized health plan maintained by any employer of the taxpayer or of the taxpayer's spouse, a deduction is not allowed.

Concept Check 4-6

1. Form 1040; as an *above-the-line* deduction.
2. Form 1099-INT.

Concept Check 4-7

1. False. Alimony payments can be made only in cash. If the payment consists of property, it is a property settlement.
2. False. As long as the couple is legally separated and there is a written agreement requiring payments, it will be classified as alimony.
3. True. If alimony payments decrease sharply in the second or third year of payment, this is a signal that the nature of the payments might be a property settlement, not alimony.

Concept Check 4-8

1. 900 hours.
2. $500.
3. Home schooling and nonathletic supplies.

Concept Check 4-9

1. True.
2. False.

CHAPTER 5

Concept Check 5-1

1. 7.5 % of AGI.
2. Actually paid. Payment by credit card meets this standard.
3. Insurance reimbursement.
4. Age.

Concept Check 5-2

1. True. In addition, the two other criteria are that it must be on personal property and the property must be assessed, at a minimum, on an annual basis.
2. False. When property is sold during the year, both the buyer and the seller receive a deduction for a portion of the real estate tax paid according to the number of days each owner held the property.
3. False. The tax benefit rule states that if you receive a refund of that expense, you are required to include that refund in income when it is received.
4. True. But generally most taxpayers receive a greater benefit by taking the credit.

Concept Check 5-3

1. Acquire, construct, or substantially improve.
2. $1,000,000.
3. Net investment.
4. 1%.

Concept Check 5-4

1. False. Charitable contributions can be taken only as an itemized deduction.
2. False. The overall limitation on the deductibility of charitable contributions is 50% of AGI. The 30% limit relates to the contribution of capital gain property.
3. True. If noncash gifts are worth over $500, the taxpayer must file Form 8283.

Concept Check 5-5

1. Sudden, unexpected, or unusual nature.
2. Form 4684 and then carried to the Form 1040.
3. Two; $500.
4. 10%.

Concept Check 5-6

1. False. The threshold is 2% of AGI.
2. True. The amount calculated there carries over to Form 1040.
3. False. The law does allow a deduction for uniforms required for employment as long as they would not usually be worn away from work. The accountant's blue suit would not fall into this category.

Concept Check 5-7

1. $166,800.
2. Indexed.

CHAPTER 6

Concept Check 6-1

1. False. Schedule C is used only for an activity in which the individual is self-employed and not an employee.
2. False. Any income received by the self-employed taxpayer is taxable and should be included on Schedule C.

Concept Check 12-3

1. A. The gross profit percentage is calculated by dividing the gross profit by the gross sales prices ($10,000/$30,000 = 33.3%).
2. B. The income recognized is $1,667 (the amount received in 2009 of $5,000 × 33.3% gross profit percentage).

Concept Check 12-4

1. True. The maximum gain exclusion is $500,000 for married taxpayers who file a joint return.
2. False. If the move is caused by an employment change or for health reasons, a taxpayer is eligible for some reduced exclusion. The exclusion is calculated by taking a ratio of the number of days used as a personal residence and dividing it by 730 days.
3. False. Johnny would still be allowed to exclude his gain but only to the maximum exclusion of $250,000.

Concept Check 12-5

1. $0. Because Leslie sold the stock to her brother, the related-party rules disallow any loss deduction on the sale by Leslie.
2. a. Leslie could deduct $2,000 in capital losses. In order for a corporation (or other entity) to be considered a related party, Leslie would have to have control of the corporation (greater than 50% ownership).

    b. $0. Because Leslie now has control of the corporation, she is considered a related party and the loss would be disallowed.
3. The purpose of the wash sale rules is to disallow a tax loss where the ownership of a company is not reduced. Thus if a taxpayer buys similar stock within 30 days of a stock sale (before or after), any loss on the sale is disallowed.

CHAPTER 13

Concept Check 13-1

1. D. All of the above increase the at-risk of a taxpayer. See Table 13-1 for all of the increases and decreases of at-risk.
2. A. Nonrecourse debt does not increase the taxpayer's at-risk. Nonrecourse debt is debt that the taxpayer is not personally liable for.

3. C. The loss is indefinitely carried forward and can be deducted once the taxpayer gets additional at-risk.

Concept Check 13-2

1. True. The only way a rental property is not a passive activity is when the taxpayer is a real estate professional. A rental business can qualify for nonpassive treatment if more than one-half of the personal services performed in a business during the year are performed in a real property trade or business and the taxpayer performs more than 750 hours of services in the activity.
2. True. Passive losses are allowed only to the extent of passive income. One exception is the $25,000 offset for rental properties.
3. False. The $25,000 offset is limited to $25,000 and is phased out after a taxpayer's AGI reaches $100,000.
4. True. Any suspended passive losses are allowed when the activity is sold.

Concept Check 13-3

1. In order for a loss to be deducted, it must first be allowed under the at-risk rules. Once the loss is allowed under the at-risk rules, the passive loss rules are applied.
2. The main reason is that passive losses are allowed when an activity is sold or disposed of. Thus if a taxpayer were considering the sale of a passive activity, he or she could lump all suspended passive losses on one activity and sell it. All of the losses would then be allowed. The allocation to all loss activities stops this potential abuse.
3. The taxpayer is eligible for the $25,000 offset for rental losses. However, the $25,000 limit is phased out once the taxpayer's AGI reaches $100,000 [($105,000 − $100,000) × ½ = $2,500]. Thus only $22,500 of the rental loss would be allowed.

Concept Check 13-4

1. False. The AGI floor for medical expenses is 10% for AMT purposes (as opposed to 7.5% for regular tax).
2. True. No taxes are allowed as a deduction for AMT. Any taxes deducted on the regular return are added back as a positive adjustment for AMT.
3. True. Personal exemptions are added as a positive adjustment for AMT purposes.
4. True. If AMTI is greater than $175,000, the AMT rate is 28%.

CHAPTER 14

Concept Check 14-1

1. True. The only time gain is recognized by a contributing partner is when the partner receives an interest for services or when he or she is released of a liability in excess of basis.
2. True. The basis of the assets typically carries over from the partner to the partnership.
3. False. The basis is dependent on the basis of the assets the individual partners contributed to the partnership. One partner could have a $0 basis while the other partner might have $100,000, yet both share 50% in the profit and loss of the partnership.
4. False. Gain must be recognized to the extent of the FMV of the partnership interest received for services.
5. True. An increase or decrease in partnership liabilities is treated as a cash contribution or cash distribution and thus increases or decreases partnership basis.

Concept Check 14-2

1. d. All of the above can be deducted from partnership income to determine the net income or loss from the partnership.
2. c. Any form of partnership files a Form 1065 informational return each year.
3. d. A guaranteed payment is a payment, usually for services, that is determined without regard to partnership income and is deductible by the partnership.

Concept Check 14-3

1. All income and expense items of a partnership that may be treated differently at the partner level must be "separately stated." Rental income/loss, capital gains/losses, and charitable contributions all can be treated differently at the partner level. For example, an individual partner can take up to $3,000 of capital losses against ordinary income while a corporate partner in the same partnership cannot.
2. A partner is not an employee of the partnership. Thus income received by the partner from the partnership has no social security or Medicare withheld by the partnership.

Concept Check 14-4

1. True. These are two of the uses of basis. Basis is also used to determine the basis (or whether a gain is recognized) of property distributed.

2. False. If the basis is not increased by tax-exempt income, then the exempt income will eventually be taxed when the partnership interest is sold. The lower basis will cause a higher gain upon sale.
3. False. The basis is first reduced by all adjustments except for losses, then money distributed, and then the basis of any property distributed. After those items, any basis remaining is used to determine the deductibility of losses.
4. False. The basis is always increased by the partner's share of recourse debt.

Concept Check 14-5

1. b. If a cash distribution or a release of liabilities exceeds basis, the partner will have a gain on a distribution from the partnership.
2. b. $12,000—the furniture would be reduced to the basis left in the partnership.
3. a. $8,000—the basis in the partnership is first reduced by the cash distribution. That leaves $8,000 for the furniture.

Concept Check 14-6

1. a. Shelly's recognized gain would be $0. She did not receive cash in excess of her basis.
   b. Shelly's basis in the assets would be as follows:

Cash	$9,000
Inventory	$6,000
Equipment ($15,000 × $8,000/$20,000)	$6,000
Land ($15,000 × $12,000/$20,000)	$9,000

2. a. $99,000 ($55,000 beginning basis + $18,000 + $26,000)
   b. $8,000 ($107,000 sales price − $99,000 basis)
   c. Because the partnership interest is a capital asset and there was no mention of inventory or receivables in the partnership, the gain would be a long-term capital gain.

CHAPTER 15

Concept Check 15-1

1. False. Some corporations are prohibited from using the cash basis. Corporations with average annual revenues over $5 million must use the accrual basis. Corporations with inventory must use the accrual basis at least for sales and cost of goods sold.

2. 2 ½ months after the end of the fiscal year. Note that the answer is NOT March 15. That is the proper answer for calendar year corporations but not for any others.

3. False. In the first year of operation, a corporation establishes its tax year. Although many corporations choose December 31, that date is not required.

Concept Check 15-2

1. True. Although an exchange of cash or property can be taxable, if the 80% rule is met, the formation activities are generally tax-free.

2. The basis in the hands of the shareholder plus any gain recognized by the shareholder.

3. $40,000. His basis in the stock is his carryover basis in the land.

Concept Check 15-3

1. False. Corporations cannot report a net capital loss whereas individuals can take up to $3,000 in capital losses in any tax year.

2. $176,800. Tax liability is equal to $113,900 plus 34% of the amount of taxable income over $335,000.

3. $39,000. A corporation can take a charitable contribution in an amount not to exceed 10% of taxable income before charitable contribution.

4. False. Although organizational expenses are deductible over 180 months or more, the corporation must make an affirmative election in its first tax return in order to do so.

5. 2, 20.

Concept Check 15-4

1. True. By definition, a dividend is a distribution from the earnings and profits of a corporation. Dividends are taxable to the shareholder. If a distribution is in excess of the earnings and profits of the corporation, it is not a dividend. It may or may not be taxable depending on the stockholder's basis in his or her stock.

2. False. Property dividends are taxed on the fair value of the property received by the stockholder.

3. $10,000. The amount of the dividend cannot exceed the earnings and profits of the corporation.

Concept Check 15-5

1. False. Corporations with total receipts and total assets under $250,000 are not required to complete Schedule L.

2. True.

3. Negative. Schedule M-1 reconciles from book income to tax income. There is more depreciation on the tax return than on the books. That means book income needs to be reduced to arrive at taxable income.

Concept Check 15-6

1. 80%.

2. Five.

3. $40,000.

Concept Check 15-7

1. False. Not only must a corporation meet tests in addition to the 100 shareholder limit, the corporation must also affirmatively elect Subchapter S status.

2. True. While there are some differences, the tax treatments of a partnership and a Subchapter S corporation are similar.

3. 1120S.

4. Not taxable. Subchapter S dividends are not taxable to a shareholder.

5. False. Corporate debt does not affect shareholders' basis in their stock.

2009 Tax Table

See the instructions for line 44 that begin on page 37 to see if you must use the Tax Table below to figure your tax.

Example. Mr. and Mrs. Brown are filing a joint return. Their taxable income on Form 1040, line 43, is $25,300. First, they find the $25,300–25,350 taxable income line. Next, they find the column for married filing jointly and read down the column. The amount shown where the taxable income line and filing status column meet is $2,964. This is the tax amount they should enter on Form 1040, line 44.

Sample Table

At least	But less than	Single	Married filing jointly *	Married filing separately	Head of a house-hold
			Your tax is—		
25,200	25,250	3,383	2,981	3,383	3,211
25,250	25,300	3,390	2,989	3,390	3,219
25,300	25,350	3,398	(2,996)	3,398	3,226
25,350	25,400	3,405	3,004	3,405	3,234

If line 43 (taxable income) is—		And you are—			
At least	But less than	Single	Married filing jointly *	Married filing separately	Head of a house-hold
			Your tax is—		
0	5	0	0	0	0
5	15	1	1	1	1
15	25	2	2	2	2
25	50	4	4	4	4
50	75	6	6	6	6
75	100	9	9	9	9
100	125	11	11	11	11
125	150	14	14	14	14
150	175	16	16	16	16
175	200	19	19	19	19
200	225	21	21	21	21
225	250	24	24	24	24
250	275	26	26	26	26
275	300	29	29	29	29
300	325	31	31	31	31
325	350	34	34	34	34
350	375	36	36	36	36
375	400	39	39	39	39
400	425	41	41	41	41
425	450	44	44	44	44
450	475	46	46	46	46
475	500	49	49	49	49
500	525	51	51	51	51
525	550	54	54	54	54
550	575	56	56	56	56
575	600	59	59	59	59
600	625	61	61	61	61
625	650	64	64	64	64
650	675	66	66	66	66
675	700	69	69	69	69
700	725	71	71	71	71
725	750	74	74	74	74
750	775	76	76	76	76
775	800	79	79	79	79
800	825	81	81	81	81
825	850	84	84	84	84
850	875	86	86	86	86
875	900	89	89	89	89
900	925	91	91	91	91
925	950	94	94	94	94
950	975	96	96	96	96
975	1,000	99	99	99	99

1,000

At least	But less than	Single	Married filing jointly *	Married filing separately	Head of a house-hold
1,000	1,025	101	101	101	101
1,025	1,050	104	104	104	104
1,050	1,075	106	106	106	106
1,075	1,100	109	109	109	109
1,100	1,125	111	111	111	111
1,125	1,150	114	114	114	114
1,150	1,175	116	116	116	116
1,175	1,200	119	119	119	119
1,200	1,225	121	121	121	121
1,225	1,250	124	124	124	124
1,250	1,275	126	126	126	126
1,275	1,300	129	129	129	129

If line 43 (taxable income) is—		And you are—			
At least	But less than	Single	Married filing jointly *	Married filing separately	Head of a house-hold
			Your tax is—		
1,300	1,325	131	131	131	131
1,325	1,350	134	134	134	134
1,350	1,375	136	136	136	136
1,375	1,400	139	139	139	139
1,400	1,425	141	141	141	141
1,425	1,450	144	144	144	144
1,450	1,475	146	146	146	146
1,475	1,500	149	149	149	149
1,500	1,525	151	151	151	151
1,525	1,550	154	154	154	154
1,550	1,575	156	156	156	156
1,575	1,600	159	159	159	159
1,600	1,625	161	161	161	161
1,625	1,650	164	164	164	164
1,650	1,675	166	166	166	166
1,675	1,700	169	169	169	169
1,700	1,725	171	171	171	171
1,725	1,750	174	174	174	174
1,750	1,775	176	176	176	176
1,775	1,800	179	179	179	179
1,800	1,825	181	181	181	181
1,825	1,850	184	184	184	184
1,850	1,875	186	186	186	186
1,875	1,900	189	189	189	189
1,900	1,925	191	191	191	191
1,925	1,950	194	194	194	194
1,950	1,975	196	196	196	196
1,975	2,000	199	199	199	199

2,000

At least	But less than	Single	Married filing jointly *	Married filing separately	Head of a house-hold
2,000	2,025	201	201	201	201
2,025	2,050	204	204	204	204
2,050	2,075	206	206	206	206
2,075	2,100	209	209	209	209
2,100	2,125	211	211	211	211
2,125	2,150	214	214	214	214
2,150	2,175	216	216	216	216
2,175	2,200	219	219	219	219
2,200	2,225	221	221	221	221
2,225	2,250	224	224	224	224
2,250	2,275	226	226	226	226
2,275	2,300	229	229	229	229
2,300	2,325	231	231	231	231
2,325	2,350	234	234	234	234
2,350	2,375	236	236	236	236
2,375	2,400	239	239	239	239
2,400	2,425	241	241	241	241
2,425	2,450	244	244	244	244
2,450	2,475	246	246	246	246
2,475	2,500	249	249	249	249
2,500	2,525	251	251	251	251
2,525	2,550	254	254	254	254
2,550	2,575	256	256	256	256
2,575	2,600	259	259	259	259
2,600	2,625	261	261	261	261
2,625	2,650	264	264	264	264
2,650	2,675	266	266	266	266
2,675	2,700	269	269	269	269

If line 43 (taxable income) is—		And you are—			
At least	But less than	Single	Married filing jointly *	Married filing separately	Head of a house-hold
			Your tax is—		
2,700	2,725	271	271	271	271
2,725	2,750	274	274	274	274
2,750	2,775	276	276	276	276
2,775	2,800	279	279	279	279
2,800	2,825	281	281	281	281
2,825	2,850	284	284	284	284
2,850	2,875	286	286	286	286
2,875	2,900	289	289	289	289
2,900	2,925	291	291	291	291
2,925	2,950	294	294	294	294
2,950	2,975	296	296	296	296
2,975	3,000	299	299	299	299

3,000

At least	But less than	Single	Married filing jointly *	Married filing separately	Head of a house-hold
3,000	3,050	303	303	303	303
3,050	3,100	308	308	308	308
3,100	3,150	313	313	313	313
3,150	3,200	318	318	318	318
3,200	3,250	323	323	323	323
3,250	3,300	328	328	328	328
3,300	3,350	333	333	333	333
3,350	3,400	338	338	338	338
3,400	3,450	343	343	343	343
3,450	3,500	348	348	348	348
3,500	3,550	353	353	353	353
3,550	3,600	358	358	358	358
3,600	3,650	363	363	363	363
3,650	3,700	368	368	368	368
3,700	3,750	373	373	373	373
3,750	3,800	378	378	378	378
3,800	3,850	383	383	383	383
3,850	3,900	388	388	388	388
3,900	3,950	393	393	393	393
3,950	4,000	398	398	398	398

4,000

At least	But less than	Single	Married filing jointly *	Married filing separately	Head of a house-hold
4,000	4,050	403	403	403	403
4,050	4,100	408	408	408	408
4,100	4,150	413	413	413	413
4,150	4,200	418	418	418	418
4,200	4,250	423	423	423	423
4,250	4,300	428	428	428	428
4,300	4,350	433	433	433	433
4,350	4,400	438	438	438	438
4,400	4,450	443	443	443	443
4,450	4,500	448	448	448	448
4,500	4,550	453	453	453	453
4,550	4,600	458	458	458	458
4,600	4,650	463	463	463	463
4,650	4,700	468	468	468	468
4,700	4,750	473	473	473	473
4,750	4,800	478	478	478	478
4,800	4,850	483	483	483	483
4,850	4,900	488	488	488	488
4,900	4,950	493	493	493	493
4,950	5,000	498	498	498	498

* This column must also be used by a qualifying widow(er).

(Continued on page D-2)

2009 Tax Table–*Continued*

If line 43 (taxable income) is—		And you are—			
At least	But less than	Single	Married filing jointly *	Married filing separately	Head of a household
		Your tax is—			

5,000

At least	But less than	Single	Married filing jointly	Married filing separately	Head of a household
5,000	5,050	503	503	503	503
5,050	5,100	508	508	508	508
5,100	5,150	513	513	513	513
5,150	5,200	518	518	518	518
5,200	5,250	523	523	523	523
5,250	5,300	528	528	528	528
5,300	5,350	533	533	533	533
5,350	5,400	538	538	538	538
5,400	5,450	543	543	543	543
5,450	5,500	548	548	548	548
5,500	5,550	553	553	553	553
5,550	5,600	558	558	558	558
5,600	5,650	563	563	563	563
5,650	5,700	568	568	568	568
5,700	5,750	573	573	573	573
5,750	5,800	578	578	578	578
5,800	5,850	583	583	583	583
5,850	5,900	588	588	588	588
5,900	5,950	593	593	593	593
5,950	6,000	598	598	598	598

6,000

At least	But less than	Single	Married filing jointly	Married filing separately	Head of a household
6,000	6,050	603	603	603	603
6,050	6,100	608	608	608	608
6,100	6,150	613	613	613	613
6,150	6,200	618	618	618	618
6,200	6,250	623	623	623	623
6,250	6,300	628	628	628	628
6,300	6,350	633	633	633	633
6,350	6,400	638	638	638	638
6,400	6,450	643	643	643	643
6,450	6,500	648	648	648	648
6,500	6,550	653	653	653	653
6,550	6,600	658	658	658	658
6,600	6,650	663	663	663	663
6,650	6,700	668	668	668	668
6,700	6,750	673	673	673	673
6,750	6,800	678	678	678	678
6,800	6,850	683	683	683	683
6,850	6,900	688	688	688	688
6,900	6,950	693	693	693	693
6,950	7,000	698	698	698	698

7,000

At least	But less than	Single	Married filing jointly	Married filing separately	Head of a household
7,000	7,050	703	703	703	703
7,050	7,100	708	708	708	708
7,100	7,150	713	713	713	713
7,150	7,200	718	718	718	718
7,200	7,250	723	723	723	723
7,250	7,300	728	728	728	728
7,300	7,350	733	733	733	733
7,350	7,400	738	738	738	738
7,400	7,450	743	743	743	743
7,450	7,500	748	748	748	748
7,500	7,550	753	753	753	753
7,550	7,600	758	758	758	758
7,600	7,650	763	763	763	763
7,650	7,700	768	768	768	768
7,700	7,750	773	773	773	773
7,750	7,800	778	778	778	778
7,800	7,850	783	783	783	783
7,850	7,900	788	788	788	788
7,900	7,950	793	793	793	793
7,950	8,000	798	798	798	798

8,000

At least	But less than	Single	Married filing jointly	Married filing separately	Head of a household
8,000	8,050	803	803	803	803
8,050	8,100	808	808	808	808
8,100	8,150	813	813	813	813
8,150	8,200	818	818	818	818
8,200	8,250	823	823	823	823
8,250	8,300	828	828	828	828
8,300	8,350	833	833	833	833
8,350	8,400	839	838	839	838
8,400	8,450	846	843	846	843
8,450	8,500	854	848	854	848
8,500	8,550	861	853	861	853
8,550	8,600	869	858	869	858
8,600	8,650	876	863	876	863
8,650	8,700	884	868	884	868
8,700	8,750	891	873	891	873
8,750	8,800	899	878	899	878
8,800	8,850	906	883	906	883
8,850	8,900	914	888	914	888
8,900	8,950	921	893	921	893
8,950	9,000	929	898	929	898

9,000

At least	But less than	Single	Married filing jointly	Married filing separately	Head of a household
9,000	9,050	936	903	936	903
9,050	9,100	944	908	944	908
9,100	9,150	951	913	951	913
9,150	9,200	959	918	959	918
9,200	9,250	966	923	966	923
9,250	9,300	974	928	974	928
9,300	9,350	981	933	981	933
9,350	9,400	989	938	989	938
9,400	9,450	996	943	996	943
9,450	9,500	1,004	948	1,004	948
9,500	9,550	1,011	953	1,011	953
9,550	9,600	1,019	958	1,019	958
9,600	9,650	1,026	963	1,026	963
9,650	9,700	1,034	968	1,034	968
9,700	9,750	1,041	973	1,041	973
9,750	9,800	1,049	978	1,049	978
9,800	9,850	1,056	983	1,056	983
9,850	9,900	1,064	988	1,064	988
9,900	9,950	1,071	993	1,071	993
9,950	10,000	1,079	998	1,079	998

10,000

At least	But less than	Single	Married filing jointly	Married filing separately	Head of a household
10,000	10,050	1,086	1,003	1,086	1,003
10,050	10,100	1,094	1,008	1,094	1,008
10,100	10,150	1,101	1,013	1,101	1,013
10,150	10,200	1,109	1,018	1,109	1,018
10,200	10,250	1,116	1,023	1,116	1,023
10,250	10,300	1,124	1,028	1,124	1,028
10,300	10,350	1,131	1,033	1,131	1,033
10,350	10,400	1,139	1,038	1,139	1,038
10,400	10,450	1,146	1,043	1,146	1,043
10,450	10,500	1,154	1,048	1,154	1,048
10,500	10,550	1,161	1,053	1,161	1,053
10,550	10,600	1,169	1,058	1,169	1,058
10,600	10,650	1,176	1,063	1,176	1,063
10,650	10,700	1,184	1,068	1,184	1,068
10,700	10,750	1,191	1,073	1,191	1,073
10,750	10,800	1,199	1,078	1,199	1,078
10,800	10,850	1,206	1,083	1,206	1,083
10,850	10,900	1,214	1,088	1,214	1,088
10,900	10,950	1,221	1,093	1,221	1,093
10,950	11,000	1,229	1,098	1,229	1,098

11,000

At least	But less than	Single	Married filing jointly	Married filing separately	Head of a household
11,000	11,050	1,236	1,103	1,236	1,103
11,050	11,100	1,244	1,108	1,244	1,108
11,100	11,150	1,251	1,113	1,251	1,113
11,150	11,200	1,259	1,118	1,259	1,118
11,200	11,250	1,266	1,123	1,266	1,123
11,250	11,300	1,274	1,128	1,274	1,128
11,300	11,350	1,281	1,133	1,281	1,133
11,350	11,400	1,289	1,138	1,289	1,138
11,400	11,450	1,296	1,143	1,296	1,143
11,450	11,500	1,304	1,148	1,304	1,148
11,500	11,550	1,311	1,153	1,311	1,153
11,550	11,600	1,319	1,158	1,319	1,158
11,600	11,650	1,326	1,163	1,326	1,163
11,650	11,700	1,334	1,168	1,334	1,168
11,700	11,750	1,341	1,173	1,341	1,173
11,750	11,800	1,349	1,178	1,349	1,178
11,800	11,850	1,356	1,183	1,356	1,183
11,850	11,900	1,364	1,188	1,364	1,188
11,900	11,950	1,371	1,193	1,371	1,193
11,950	12,000	1,379	1,198	1,379	1,199

12,000

At least	But less than	Single	Married filing jointly	Married filing separately	Head of a household
12,000	12,050	1,386	1,203	1,386	1,206
12,050	12,100	1,394	1,208	1,394	1,214
12,100	12,150	1,401	1,213	1,401	1,221
12,150	12,200	1,409	1,218	1,409	1,229
12,200	12,250	1,416	1,223	1,416	1,236
12,250	12,300	1,424	1,228	1,424	1,244
12,300	12,350	1,431	1,233	1,431	1,251
12,350	12,400	1,439	1,238	1,439	1,259
12,400	12,450	1,446	1,243	1,446	1,266
12,450	12,500	1,454	1,248	1,454	1,274
12,500	12,550	1,461	1,253	1,461	1,281
12,550	12,600	1,469	1,258	1,469	1,289
12,600	12,650	1,476	1,263	1,476	1,296
12,650	12,700	1,484	1,268	1,484	1,304
12,700	12,750	1,491	1,273	1,491	1,311
12,750	12,800	1,499	1,278	1,499	1,319
12,800	12,850	1,506	1,283	1,506	1,326
12,850	12,900	1,514	1,288	1,514	1,334
12,900	12,950	1,521	1,293	1,521	1,341
12,950	13,000	1,529	1,298	1,529	1,349

13,000

At least	But less than	Single	Married filing jointly	Married filing separately	Head of a household
13,000	13,050	1,536	1,303	1,536	1,356
13,050	13,100	1,544	1,308	1,544	1,364
13,100	13,150	1,551	1,313	1,551	1,371
13,150	13,200	1,559	1,318	1,559	1,379
13,200	13,250	1,566	1,323	1,566	1,386
13,250	13,300	1,574	1,328	1,574	1,394
13,300	13,350	1,581	1,333	1,581	1,401
13,350	13,400	1,589	1,338	1,589	1,409
13,400	13,450	1,596	1,343	1,596	1,416
13,450	13,500	1,604	1,348	1,604	1,424
13,500	13,550	1,611	1,353	1,611	1,431
13,550	13,600	1,619	1,358	1,619	1,439
13,600	13,650	1,626	1,363	1,626	1,446
13,650	13,700	1,634	1,368	1,634	1,454
13,700	13,750	1,641	1,373	1,641	1,461
13,750	13,800	1,649	1,378	1,649	1,469
13,800	13,850	1,656	1,383	1,656	1,476
13,850	13,900	1,664	1,388	1,664	1,484
13,900	13,950	1,671	1,393	1,671	1,491
13,950	14,000	1,679	1,398	1,679	1,499

* This column must also be used by a qualifying widow(er).

(Continued on page D-3)

14,000

If line 43 (taxable income) is—		And you are—			
At least	But less than	Single	Married filing jointly *	Married filing separately	Head of a house-hold
		Your tax is—			
14,000	14,050	1,686	1,403	1,686	1,506
14,050	14,100	1,694	1,408	1,694	1,514
14,100	14,150	1,701	1,413	1,701	1,521
14,150	14,200	1,709	1,418	1,709	1,529
14,200	14,250	1,716	1,423	1,716	1,536
14,250	14,300	1,724	1,428	1,724	1,544
14,300	14,350	1,731	1,433	1,731	1,551
14,350	14,400	1,739	1,438	1,739	1,559
14,400	14,450	1,746	1,443	1,746	1,566
14,450	14,500	1,754	1,448	1,754	1,574
14,500	14,550	1,761	1,453	1,761	1,581
14,550	14,600	1,769	1,458	1,769	1,589
14,600	14,650	1,776	1,463	1,776	1,596
14,650	14,700	1,784	1,468	1,784	1,604
14,700	14,750	1,791	1,473	1,791	1,611
14,750	14,800	1,799	1,478	1,799	1,619
14,800	14,850	1,806	1,483	1,806	1,626
14,850	14,900	1,814	1,488	1,814	1,634
14,900	14,950	1,821	1,493	1,821	1,641
14,950	15,000	1,829	1,498	1,829	1,649

15,000

At least	But less than	Single	Married filing jointly *	Married filing separately	Head of a house-hold
15,000	15,050	1,836	1,503	1,836	1,656
15,050	15,100	1,844	1,508	1,844	1,664
15,100	15,150	1,851	1,513	1,851	1,671
15,150	15,200	1,859	1,518	1,859	1,679
15,200	15,250	1,866	1,523	1,866	1,686
15,250	15,300	1,874	1,528	1,874	1,694
15,300	15,350	1,881	1,533	1,881	1,701
15,350	15,400	1,889	1,538	1,889	1,709
15,400	15,450	1,896	1,543	1,896	1,716
15,450	15,500	1,904	1,548	1,904	1,724
15,500	15,550	1,911	1,553	1,911	1,731
15,550	15,600	1,919	1,558	1,919	1,739
15,600	15,650	1,926	1,563	1,926	1,746
15,650	15,700	1,934	1,568	1,934	1,754
15,700	15,750	1,941	1,573	1,941	1,761
15,750	15,800	1,949	1,578	1,949	1,769
15,800	15,850	1,956	1,583	1,956	1,776
15,850	15,900	1,964	1,588	1,964	1,784
15,900	15,950	1,971	1,593	1,971	1,791
15,950	16,000	1,979	1,598	1,979	1,799

16,000

At least	But less than	Single	Married filing jointly *	Married filing separately	Head of a house-hold
16,000	16,050	1,986	1,603	1,986	1,806
16,050	16,100	1,994	1,608	1,994	1,814
16,100	16,150	2,001	1,613	2,001	1,821
16,150	16,200	2,009	1,618	2,009	1,829
16,200	16,250	2,016	1,623	2,016	1,836
16,250	16,300	2,024	1,628	2,024	1,844
16,300	16,350	2,031	1,633	2,031	1,851
16,350	16,400	2,039	1,638	2,039	1,859
16,400	16,450	2,046	1,643	2,046	1,866
16,450	16,500	2,054	1,648	2,054	1,874
16,500	16,550	2,061	1,653	2,061	1,881
16,550	16,600	2,069	1,658	2,069	1,889
16,600	16,650	2,076	1,663	2,076	1,896
16,650	16,700	2,084	1,668	2,084	1,904
16,700	16,750	2,091	1,674	2,091	1,911
16,750	16,800	2,099	1,681	2,099	1,919
16,800	16,850	2,106	1,689	2,106	1,926
16,850	16,900	2,114	1,696	2,114	1,934
16,900	16,950	2,121	1,704	2,121	1,941
16,950	17,000	2,129	1,711	2,129	1,949

17,000

At least	But less than	Single	Married filing jointly *	Married filing separately	Head of a house-hold
17,000	17,050	2,136	1,719	2,136	1,956
17,050	17,100	2,144	1,726	2,144	1,964
17,100	17,150	2,151	1,734	2,151	1,971
17,150	17,200	2,159	1,741	2,159	1,979
17,200	17,250	2,166	1,749	2,166	1,986
17,250	17,300	2,174	1,756	2,174	1,994
17,300	17,350	2,181	1,764	2,181	2,001
17,350	17,400	2,189	1,771	2,189	2,009
17,400	17,450	2,196	1,779	2,196	2,016
17,450	17,500	2,204	1,786	2,204	2,024
17,500	17,550	2,211	1,794	2,211	2,031
17,550	17,600	2,219	1,801	2,219	2,039
17,600	17,650	2,226	1,809	2,226	2,046
17,650	17,700	2,234	1,816	2,234	2,054
17,700	17,750	2,241	1,824	2,241	2,061
17,750	17,800	2,249	1,831	2,249	2,069
17,800	17,850	2,256	1,839	2,256	2,076
17,850	17,900	2,264	1,846	2,264	2,084
17,900	17,950	2,271	1,854	2,271	2,091
17,950	18,000	2,279	1,861	2,279	2,099

18,000

At least	But less than	Single	Married filing jointly *	Married filing separately	Head of a house-hold
18,000	18,050	2,286	1,869	2,286	2,106
18,050	18,100	2,294	1,876	2,294	2,114
18,100	18,150	2,301	1,884	2,301	2,121
18,150	18,200	2,309	1,891	2,309	2,129
18,200	18,250	2,316	1,899	2,316	2,136
18,250	18,300	2,324	1,906	2,324	2,144
18,300	18,350	2,331	1,914	2,331	2,151
18,350	18,400	2,339	1,921	2,339	2,159
18,400	18,450	2,346	1,929	2,346	2,166
18,450	18,500	2,354	1,936	2,354	2,174
18,500	18,550	2,361	1,944	2,361	2,181
18,550	18,600	2,369	1,951	2,369	2,189
18,600	18,650	2,376	1,959	2,376	2,196
18,650	18,700	2,384	1,966	2,384	2,204
18,700	18,750	2,391	1,974	2,391	2,211
18,750	18,800	2,399	1,981	2,399	2,219
18,800	18,850	2,406	1,989	2,406	2,226
18,850	18,900	2,414	1,996	2,414	2,234
18,900	18,950	2,421	2,004	2,421	2,241
18,950	19,000	2,429	2,011	2,429	2,249

19,000

At least	But less than	Single	Married filing jointly *	Married filing separately	Head of a house-hold
19,000	19,050	2,436	2,019	2,436	2,256
19,050	19,100	2,444	2,026	2,444	2,264
19,100	19,150	2,451	2,034	2,451	2,271
19,150	19,200	2,459	2,041	2,459	2,279
19,200	19,250	2,466	2,049	2,466	2,286
19,250	19,300	2,474	2,056	2,474	2,294
19,300	19,350	2,481	2,064	2,481	2,301
19,350	19,400	2,489	2,071	2,489	2,309
19,400	19,450	2,496	2,079	2,496	2,316
19,450	19,500	2,504	2,086	2,504	2,324
19,500	19,550	2,511	2,094	2,511	2,331
19,550	19,600	2,519	2,101	2,519	2,339
19,600	19,650	2,526	2,109	2,526	2,346
19,650	19,700	2,534	2,116	2,534	2,354
19,700	19,750	2,541	2,124	2,541	2,361
19,750	19,800	2,549	2,131	2,549	2,369
19,800	19,850	2,556	2,139	2,556	2,376
19,850	19,900	2,564	2,146	2,564	2,384
19,900	19,950	2,571	2,154	2,571	2,391
19,950	20,000	2,579	2,161	2,579	2,399

20,000

At least	But less than	Single	Married filing jointly *	Married filing separately	Head of a house-hold
20,000	20,050	2,586	2,169	2,586	2,406
20,050	20,100	2,594	2,176	2,594	2,414
20,100	20,150	2,601	2,184	2,601	2,421
20,150	20,200	2,609	2,191	2,609	2,429
20,200	20,250	2,616	2,199	2,616	2,436
20,250	20,300	2,624	2,206	2,624	2,444
20,300	20,350	2,631	2,214	2,631	2,451
20,350	20,400	2,639	2,221	2,639	2,459
20,400	20,450	2,646	2,229	2,646	2,466
20,450	20,500	2,654	2,236	2,654	2,474
20,500	20,550	2,661	2,244	2,661	2,481
20,550	20,600	2,669	2,251	2,669	2,489
20,600	20,650	2,676	2,259	2,676	2,496
20,650	20,700	2,684	2,266	2,684	2,504
20,700	20,750	2,691	2,274	2,691	2,511
20,750	20,800	2,699	2,281	2,699	2,519
20,800	20,850	2,706	2,289	2,706	2,526
20,850	20,900	2,714	2,296	2,714	2,534
20,900	20,950	2,721	2,304	2,721	2,541
20,950	21,000	2,729	2,311	2,729	2,549

21,000

At least	But less than	Single	Married filing jointly *	Married filing separately	Head of a house-hold
21,000	21,050	2,736	2,319	2,736	2,556
21,050	21,100	2,744	2,326	2,744	2,564
21,100	21,150	2,751	2,334	2,751	2,571
21,150	21,200	2,759	2,341	2,759	2,579
21,200	21,250	2,766	2,349	2,766	2,586
21,250	21,300	2,774	2,356	2,774	2,594
21,300	21,350	2,781	2,364	2,781	2,601
21,350	21,400	2,789	2,371	2,789	2,609
21,400	21,450	2,796	2,379	2,796	2,616
21,450	21,500	2,804	2,386	2,804	2,624
21,500	21,550	2,811	2,394	2,811	2,631
21,550	21,600	2,819	2,401	2,819	2,639
21,600	21,650	2,826	2,409	2,826	2,646
21,650	21,700	2,834	2,416	2,834	2,654
21,700	21,750	2,841	2,424	2,841	2,661
21,750	21,800	2,849	2,431	2,849	2,669
21,800	21,850	2,856	2,439	2,856	2,676
21,850	21,900	2,864	2,446	2,864	2,684
21,900	21,950	2,871	2,454	2,871	2,691
21,950	22,000	2,879	2,461	2,879	2,699

22,000

At least	But less than	Single	Married filing jointly *	Married filing separately	Head of a house-hold
22,000	22,050	2,886	2,469	2,886	2,706
22,050	22,100	2,894	2,476	2,894	2,714
22,100	22,150	2,901	2,484	2,901	2,721
22,150	22,200	2,909	2,491	2,909	2,729
22,200	22,250	2,916	2,499	2,916	2,736
22,250	22,300	2,924	2,506	2,924	2,744
22,300	22,350	2,931	2,514	2,931	2,751
22,350	22,400	2,939	2,521	2,939	2,759
22,400	22,450	2,946	2,529	2,946	2,766
22,450	22,500	2,954	2,536	2,954	2,774
22,500	22,550	2,961	2,544	2,961	2,781
22,550	22,600	2,969	2,551	2,969	2,789
22,600	22,650	2,976	2,559	2,976	2,796
22,650	22,700	2,984	2,566	2,984	2,804
22,700	22,750	2,991	2,574	2,991	2,811
22,750	22,800	2,999	2,581	2,999	2,819
22,800	22,850	3,006	2,589	3,006	2,826
22,850	22,900	3,014	2,596	3,014	2,834
22,900	22,950	3,021	2,604	3,021	2,841
22,950	23,000	3,029	2,611	3,029	2,849

* This column must also be used by a qualifying widow(er).

(Continued on page D-4)

2009 Tax Table–*Continued*

If line 43 (taxable income) is— At least	But less than	Single	Married filing jointly *	Married filing separately	Head of a household
23,000					
23,000	23,050	3,036	2,619	3,036	2,856
23,050	23,100	3,044	2,626	3,044	2,864
23,100	23,150	3,051	2,634	3,051	2,871
23,150	23,200	3,059	2,641	3,059	2,879
23,200	23,250	3,066	2,649	3,066	2,886
23,250	23,300	3,074	2,656	3,074	2,894
23,300	23,350	3,081	2,664	3,081	2,901
23,350	23,400	3,089	2,671	3,089	2,909
23,400	23,450	3,096	2,679	3,096	2,916
23,450	23,500	3,104	2,686	3,104	2,924
23,500	23,550	3,111	2,694	3,111	2,931
23,550	23,600	3,119	2,701	3,119	2,939
23,600	23,650	3,126	2,709	3,126	2,946
23,650	23,700	3,134	2,716	3,134	2,954
23,700	23,750	3,141	2,724	3,141	2,961
23,750	23,800	3,149	2,731	3,149	2,969
23,800	23,850	3,156	2,739	3,156	2,976
23,850	23,900	3,164	2,746	3,164	2,984
23,900	23,950	3,171	2,754	3,171	2,991
23,950	24,000	3,179	2,761	3,179	2,999
24,000					
24,000	24,050	3,186	2,769	3,186	3,006
24,050	24,100	3,194	2,776	3,194	3,014
24,100	24,150	3,201	2,784	3,201	3,021
24,150	24,200	3,209	2,791	3,209	3,029
24,200	24,250	3,216	2,799	3,216	3,036
24,250	24,300	3,224	2,806	3,224	3,044
24,300	24,350	3,231	2,814	3,231	3,051
24,350	24,400	3,239	2,821	3,239	3,059
24,400	24,450	3,246	2,829	3,246	3,066
24,450	24,500	3,254	2,836	3,254	3,074
24,500	24,550	3,261	2,844	3,261	3,081
24,550	24,600	3,269	2,851	3,269	3,089
24,600	24,650	3,276	2,859	3,276	3,096
24,650	24,700	3,284	2,866	3,284	3,104
24,700	24,750	3,291	2,874	3,291	3,111
24,750	24,800	3,299	2,881	3,299	3,119
24,800	24,850	3,306	2,889	3,306	3,126
24,850	24,900	3,314	2,896	3,314	3,134
24,900	24,950	3,321	2,904	3,321	3,141
24,950	25,000	3,329	2,911	3,329	3,149
25,000					
25,000	25,050	3,336	2,919	3,336	3,156
25,050	25,100	3,344	2,926	3,344	3,164
25,100	25,150	3,351	2,934	3,351	3,171
25,150	25,200	3,359	2,941	3,359	3,179
25,200	25,250	3,366	2,949	3,366	3,186
25,250	25,300	3,374	2,956	3,374	3,194
25,300	25,350	3,381	2,964	3,381	3,201
25,350	25,400	3,389	2,971	3,389	3,209
25,400	25,450	3,396	2,979	3,396	3,216
25,450	25,500	3,404	2,986	3,404	3,224
25,500	25,550	3,411	2,994	3,411	3,231
25,550	25,600	3,419	3,001	3,419	3,239
25,600	25,650	3,426	3,009	3,426	3,246
25,650	25,700	3,434	3,016	3,434	3,254
25,700	25,750	3,441	3,024	3,441	3,261
25,750	25,800	3,449	3,031	3,449	3,269
25,800	25,850	3,456	3,039	3,456	3,276
25,850	25,900	3,464	3,046	3,464	3,284
25,900	25,950	3,471	3,054	3,471	3,291
25,950	26,000	3,479	3,061	3,479	3,299
26,000					
26,000	26,050	3,486	3,069	3,486	3,306
26,050	26,100	3,494	3,076	3,494	3,314
26,100	26,150	3,501	3,084	3,501	3,321
26,150	26,200	3,509	3,091	3,509	3,329
26,200	26,250	3,516	3,099	3,516	3,336
26,250	26,300	3,524	3,106	3,524	3,344
26,300	26,350	3,531	3,114	3,531	3,351
26,350	26,400	3,539	3,121	3,539	3,359
26,400	26,450	3,546	3,129	3,546	3,366
26,450	26,500	3,554	3,136	3,554	3,374
26,500	26,550	3,561	3,144	3,561	3,381
26,550	26,600	3,569	3,151	3,569	3,389
26,600	26,650	3,576	3,159	3,576	3,396
26,650	26,700	3,584	3,166	3,584	3,404
26,700	26,750	3,591	3,174	3,591	3,411
26,750	26,800	3,599	3,181	3,599	3,419
26,800	26,850	3,606	3,189	3,606	3,426
26,850	26,900	3,614	3,196	3,614	3,434
26,900	26,950	3,621	3,204	3,621	3,441
26,950	27,000	3,629	3,211	3,629	3,449
27,000					
27,000	27,050	3,636	3,219	3,636	3,456
27,050	27,100	3,644	3,226	3,644	3,464
27,100	27,150	3,651	3,234	3,651	3,471
27,150	27,200	3,659	3,241	3,659	3,479
27,200	27,250	3,666	3,249	3,666	3,486
27,250	27,300	3,674	3,256	3,674	3,494
27,300	27,350	3,681	3,264	3,681	3,501
27,350	27,400	3,689	3,271	3,689	3,509
27,400	27,450	3,696	3,279	3,696	3,516
27,450	27,500	3,704	3,286	3,704	3,524
27,500	27,550	3,711	3,294	3,711	3,531
27,550	27,600	3,719	3,301	3,719	3,539
27,600	27,650	3,726	3,309	3,726	3,546
27,650	27,700	3,734	3,316	3,734	3,554
27,700	27,750	3,741	3,324	3,741	3,561
27,750	27,800	3,749	3,331	3,749	3,569
27,800	27,850	3,756	3,339	3,756	3,576
27,850	27,900	3,764	3,346	3,764	3,584
27,900	27,950	3,771	3,354	3,771	3,591
27,950	28,000	3,779	3,361	3,779	3,599
28,000					
28,000	28,050	3,786	3,369	3,786	3,606
28,050	28,100	3,794	3,376	3,794	3,614
28,100	28,150	3,801	3,384	3,801	3,621
28,150	28,200	3,809	3,391	3,809	3,629
28,200	28,250	3,816	3,399	3,816	3,636
28,250	28,300	3,824	3,406	3,824	3,644
28,300	28,350	3,831	3,414	3,831	3,651
28,350	28,400	3,839	3,421	3,839	3,659
28,400	28,450	3,846	3,429	3,846	3,666
28,450	28,500	3,854	3,436	3,854	3,674
28,500	28,550	3,861	3,444	3,861	3,681
28,550	28,600	3,869	3,451	3,869	3,689
28,600	28,650	3,876	3,459	3,876	3,696
28,650	28,700	3,884	3,466	3,884	3,704
28,700	28,750	3,891	3,474	3,891	3,711
28,750	28,800	3,899	3,481	3,899	3,719
28,800	28,850	3,906	3,489	3,906	3,726
28,850	28,900	3,914	3,496	3,914	3,734
28,900	28,950	3,921	3,504	3,921	3,741
28,950	29,000	3,929	3,511	3,929	3,749
29,000					
29,000	29,050	3,936	3,519	3,936	3,756
29,050	29,100	3,944	3,526	3,944	3,764
29,100	29,150	3,951	3,534	3,951	3,771
29,150	29,200	3,959	3,541	3,959	3,779
29,200	29,250	3,966	3,549	3,966	3,786
29,250	29,300	3,974	3,556	3,974	3,794
29,300	29,350	3,981	3,564	3,981	3,801
29,350	29,400	3,989	3,571	3,989	3,809
29,400	29,450	3,996	3,579	3,996	3,816
29,450	29,500	4,004	3,586	4,004	3,824
29,500	29,550	4,011	3,594	4,011	3,831
29,550	29,600	4,019	3,601	4,019	3,839
29,600	29,650	4,026	3,609	4,026	3,846
29,650	29,700	4,034	3,616	4,034	3,854
29,700	29,750	4,041	3,624	4,041	3,861
29,750	29,800	4,049	3,631	4,049	3,869
29,800	29,850	4,056	3,639	4,056	3,876
29,850	29,900	4,064	3,646	4,064	3,884
29,900	29,950	4,071	3,654	4,071	3,891
29,950	30,000	4,079	3,661	4,079	3,899
30,000					
30,000	30,050	4,086	3,669	4,086	3,906
30,050	30,100	4,094	3,676	4,094	3,914
30,100	30,150	4,101	3,684	4,101	3,921
30,150	30,200	4,109	3,691	4,109	3,929
30,200	30,250	4,116	3,699	4,116	3,936
30,250	30,300	4,124	3,706	4,124	3,944
30,300	30,350	4,131	3,714	4,131	3,951
30,350	30,400	4,139	3,721	4,139	3,959
30,400	30,450	4,146	3,729	4,146	3,966
30,450	30,500	4,154	3,736	4,154	3,974
30,500	30,550	4,161	3,744	4,161	3,981
30,550	30,600	4,169	3,751	4,169	3,989
30,600	30,650	4,176	3,759	4,176	3,996
30,650	30,700	4,184	3,766	4,184	4,004
30,700	30,750	4,191	3,774	4,191	4,011
30,750	30,800	4,199	3,781	4,199	4,019
30,800	30,850	4,206	3,789	4,206	4,026
30,850	30,900	4,214	3,796	4,214	4,034
30,900	30,950	4,221	3,804	4,221	4,041
30,950	31,000	4,229	3,811	4,229	4,049
31,000					
31,000	31,050	4,236	3,819	4,236	4,056
31,050	31,100	4,244	3,826	4,244	4,064
31,100	31,150	4,251	3,834	4,251	4,071
31,150	31,200	4,259	3,841	4,259	4,079
31,200	31,250	4,266	3,849	4,266	4,086
31,250	31,300	4,274	3,856	4,274	4,094
31,300	31,350	4,281	3,864	4,281	4,101
31,350	31,400	4,289	3,871	4,289	4,109
31,400	31,450	4,296	3,879	4,296	4,116
31,450	31,500	4,304	3,886	4,304	4,124
31,500	31,550	4,311	3,894	4,311	4,131
31,550	31,600	4,319	3,901	4,319	4,139
31,600	31,650	4,326	3,909	4,326	4,146
31,650	31,700	4,334	3,916	4,334	4,154
31,700	31,750	4,341	3,924	4,341	4,161
31,750	31,800	4,349	3,931	4,349	4,169
31,800	31,850	4,356	3,939	4,356	4,176
31,850	31,900	4,364	3,946	4,364	4,184
31,900	31,950	4,371	3,954	4,371	4,191
31,950	32,000	4,379	3,961	4,379	4,199

* This column must also be used by a qualifying widow(er).

(Continued on page D-5)

If line 43 (taxable income) is—		And you are—			
At least	But less than	Single	Married filing jointly *	Married filing separately	Head of a household
		Your tax is—			

32,000

At least	But less than	Single	Married filing jointly *	Married filing separately	Head of a household
32,000	32,050	4,386	3,969	4,386	4,206
32,050	32,100	4,394	3,976	4,394	4,214
32,100	32,150	4,401	3,984	4,401	4,221
32,150	32,200	4,409	3,991	4,409	4,229
32,200	32,250	4,416	3,999	4,416	4,236
32,250	32,300	4,424	4,006	4,424	4,244
32,300	32,350	4,431	4,014	4,431	4,251
32,350	32,400	4,439	4,021	4,439	4,259
32,400	32,450	4,446	4,029	4,446	4,266
32,450	32,500	4,454	4,036	4,454	4,274
32,500	32,550	4,461	4,044	4,461	4,281
32,550	32,600	4,469	4,051	4,469	4,289
32,600	32,650	4,476	4,059	4,476	4,296
32,650	32,700	4,484	4,066	4,484	4,304
32,700	32,750	4,491	4,074	4,491	4,311
32,750	32,800	4,499	4,081	4,499	4,319
32,800	32,850	4,506	4,089	4,506	4,326
32,850	32,900	4,514	4,096	4,514	4,334
32,900	32,950	4,521	4,104	4,521	4,341
32,950	33,000	4,529	4,111	4,529	4,349

33,000

At least	But less than	Single	Married filing jointly *	Married filing separately	Head of a household
33,000	33,050	4,536	4,119	4,536	4,356
33,050	33,100	4,544	4,126	4,544	4,364
33,100	33,150	4,551	4,134	4,551	4,371
33,150	33,200	4,559	4,141	4,559	4,379
33,200	33,250	4,566	4,149	4,566	4,386
33,250	33,300	4,574	4,156	4,574	4,394
33,300	33,350	4,581	4,164	4,581	4,401
33,350	33,400	4,589	4,171	4,589	4,409
33,400	33,450	4,596	4,179	4,596	4,416
33,450	33,500	4,604	4,186	4,604	4,424
33,500	33,550	4,611	4,194	4,611	4,431
33,550	33,600	4,619	4,201	4,619	4,439
33,600	33,650	4,626	4,209	4,626	4,446
33,650	33,700	4,634	4,216	4,634	4,454
33,700	33,750	4,641	4,224	4,641	4,461
33,750	33,800	4,649	4,231	4,649	4,469
33,800	33,850	4,656	4,239	4,656	4,476
33,850	33,900	4,664	4,246	4,664	4,484
33,900	33,950	4,671	4,254	4,671	4,491
33,950	34,000	4,681	4,261	4,681	4,499

34,000

At least	But less than	Single	Married filing jointly *	Married filing separately	Head of a household
34,000	34,050	4,694	4,269	4,694	4,506
34,050	34,100	4,706	4,276	4,706	4,514
34,100	34,150	4,719	4,284	4,719	4,521
34,150	34,200	4,731	4,291	4,731	4,529
34,200	34,250	4,744	4,299	4,744	4,536
34,250	34,300	4,756	4,306	4,756	4,544
34,300	34,350	4,769	4,314	4,769	4,551
34,350	34,400	4,781	4,321	4,781	4,559
34,400	34,450	4,794	4,329	4,794	4,566
34,450	34,500	4,806	4,336	4,806	4,574
34,500	34,550	4,819	4,344	4,819	4,581
34,550	34,600	4,831	4,351	4,831	4,589
34,600	34,650	4,844	4,359	4,844	4,596
34,650	34,700	4,856	4,366	4,856	4,604
34,700	34,750	4,869	4,374	4,869	4,611
34,750	34,800	4,881	4,381	4,881	4,619
34,800	34,850	4,894	4,389	4,894	4,626
34,850	34,900	4,906	4,396	4,906	4,634
34,900	34,950	4,919	4,404	4,919	4,641
34,950	35,000	4,931	4,411	4,931	4,649

35,000

At least	But less than	Single	Married filing jointly *	Married filing separately	Head of a household
35,000	35,050	4,944	4,419	4,944	4,656
35,050	35,100	4,956	4,426	4,956	4,664
35,100	35,150	4,969	4,434	4,969	4,671
35,150	35,200	4,981	4,441	4,981	4,679
35,200	35,250	4,994	4,449	4,994	4,686
35,250	35,300	5,006	4,456	5,006	4,694
35,300	35,350	5,019	4,464	5,019	4,701
35,350	35,400	5,031	4,471	5,031	4,709
35,400	35,450	5,044	4,479	5,044	4,716
35,450	35,500	5,056	4,486	5,056	4,724
35,500	35,550	5,069	4,494	5,069	4,731
35,550	35,600	5,081	4,501	5,081	4,739
35,600	35,650	5,094	4,509	5,094	4,746
35,650	35,700	5,106	4,516	5,106	4,754
35,700	35,750	5,119	4,524	5,119	4,761
35,750	35,800	5,131	4,531	5,131	4,769
35,800	35,850	5,144	4,539	5,144	4,776
35,850	35,900	5,156	4,546	5,156	4,784
35,900	35,950	5,169	4,554	5,169	4,791
35,950	36,000	5,181	4,561	5,181	4,799

36,000

At least	But less than	Single	Married filing jointly *	Married filing separately	Head of a household
36,000	36,050	5,194	4,569	5,194	4,806
36,050	36,100	5,206	4,576	5,206	4,814
36,100	36,150	5,219	4,584	5,219	4,821
36,150	36,200	5,231	4,591	5,231	4,829
36,200	36,250	5,244	4,599	5,244	4,836
36,250	36,300	5,256	4,606	5,256	4,844
36,300	36,350	5,269	4,614	5,269	4,851
36,350	36,400	5,281	4,621	5,281	4,859
36,400	36,450	5,294	4,629	5,294	4,866
36,450	36,500	5,306	4,636	5,306	4,874
36,500	36,550	5,319	4,644	5,319	4,881
36,550	36,600	5,331	4,651	5,331	4,889
36,600	36,650	5,344	4,659	5,344	4,896
36,650	36,700	5,356	4,666	5,356	4,904
36,700	36,750	5,369	4,674	5,369	4,911
36,750	36,800	5,381	4,681	5,381	4,919
36,800	36,850	5,394	4,689	5,394	4,926
36,850	36,900	5,406	4,696	5,406	4,934
36,900	36,950	5,419	4,704	5,419	4,941
36,950	37,000	5,431	4,711	5,431	4,949

37,000

At least	But less than	Single	Married filing jointly *	Married filing separately	Head of a household
37,000	37,050	5,444	4,719	5,444	4,956
37,050	37,100	5,456	4,726	5,456	4,964
37,100	37,150	5,469	4,734	5,469	4,971
37,150	37,200	5,481	4,741	5,481	4,979
37,200	37,250	5,494	4,749	5,494	4,986
37,250	37,300	5,506	4,756	5,506	4,994
37,300	37,350	5,519	4,764	5,519	5,001
37,350	37,400	5,531	4,771	5,531	5,009
37,400	37,450	5,544	4,779	5,544	5,016
37,450	37,500	5,556	4,786	5,556	5,024
37,500	37,550	5,569	4,794	5,569	5,031
37,550	37,600	5,581	4,801	5,581	5,039
37,600	37,650	5,594	4,809	5,594	5,046
37,650	37,700	5,606	4,816	5,606	5,054
37,700	37,750	5,619	4,824	5,619	5,061
37,750	37,800	5,631	4,831	5,631	5,069
37,800	37,850	5,644	4,839	5,644	5,076
37,850	37,900	5,656	4,846	5,656	5,084
37,900	37,950	5,669	4,854	5,669	5,091
37,950	38,000	5,681	4,861	5,681	5,099

38,000

At least	But less than	Single	Married filing jointly *	Married filing separately	Head of a household
38,000	38,050	5,694	4,869	5,694	5,106
38,050	38,100	5,706	4,876	5,706	5,114
38,100	38,150	5,719	4,884	5,719	5,121
38,150	38,200	5,731	4,891	5,731	5,129
38,200	38,250	5,744	4,899	5,744	5,136
38,250	38,300	5,756	4,906	5,756	5,144
38,300	38,350	5,769	4,914	5,769	5,151
38,350	38,400	5,781	4,921	5,781	5,159
38,400	38,450	5,794	4,929	5,794	5,166
38,450	38,500	5,806	4,936	5,806	5,174
38,500	38,550	5,819	4,944	5,819	5,181
38,550	38,600	5,831	4,951	5,831	5,189
38,600	38,650	5,844	4,959	5,844	5,196
38,650	38,700	5,856	4,966	5,856	5,204
38,700	38,750	5,869	4,974	5,869	5,211
38,750	38,800	5,881	4,981	5,881	5,219
38,800	38,850	5,894	4,989	5,894	5,226
38,850	38,900	5,906	4,996	5,906	5,234
38,900	38,950	5,919	5,004	5,919	5,241
38,950	39,000	5,931	5,011	5,931	5,249

39,000

At least	But less than	Single	Married filing jointly *	Married filing separately	Head of a household
39,000	39,050	5,944	5,019	5,944	5,256
39,050	39,100	5,956	5,026	5,956	5,264
39,100	39,150	5,969	5,034	5,969	5,271
39,150	39,200	5,981	5,041	5,981	5,279
39,200	39,250	5,994	5,049	5,994	5,286
39,250	39,300	6,006	5,056	6,006	5,294
39,300	39,350	6,019	5,064	6,019	5,301
39,350	39,400	6,031	5,071	6,031	5,309
39,400	39,450	6,044	5,079	6,044	5,316
39,450	39,500	6,056	5,086	6,056	5,324
39,500	39,550	6,069	5,094	6,069	5,331
39,550	39,600	6,081	5,101	6,081	5,339
39,600	39,650	6,094	5,109	6,094	5,346
39,650	39,700	6,106	5,116	6,106	5,354
39,700	39,750	6,119	5,124	6,119	5,361
39,750	39,800	6,131	5,131	6,131	5,369
39,800	39,850	6,144	5,139	6,144	5,376
39,850	39,900	6,156	5,146	6,156	5,384
39,900	39,950	6,169	5,154	6,169	5,391
39,950	40,000	6,181	5,161	6,181	5,399

40,000

At least	But less than	Single	Married filing jointly *	Married filing separately	Head of a household
40,000	40,050	6,194	5,169	6,194	5,406
40,050	40,100	6,206	5,176	6,206	5,414
40,100	40,150	6,219	5,184	6,219	5,421
40,150	40,200	6,231	5,191	6,231	5,429
40,200	40,250	6,244	5,199	6,244	5,436
40,250	40,300	6,256	5,206	6,256	5,444
40,300	40,350	6,269	5,214	6,269	5,451
40,350	40,400	6,281	5,221	6,281	5,459
40,400	40,450	6,294	5,229	6,294	5,466
40,450	40,500	6,306	5,236	6,306	5,474
40,500	40,550	6,319	5,244	6,319	5,481
40,550	40,600	6,331	5,251	6,331	5,489
40,600	40,650	6,344	5,259	6,344	5,496
40,650	40,700	6,356	5,266	6,356	5,504
40,700	40,750	6,369	5,274	6,369	5,511
40,750	40,800	6,381	5,281	6,381	5,519
40,800	40,850	6,394	5,289	6,394	5,526
40,850	40,900	6,406	5,296	6,406	5,534
40,900	40,950	6,419	5,304	6,419	5,541
40,950	41,000	6,431	5,311	6,431	5,549

* This column must also be used by a qualifying widow(er).

(Continued on page D-6)

2009 Tax Table—Continued

If line 43 (taxable income) is—		And you are—			
At least	But less than	Single	Married filing jointly *	Married filing separately	Head of a household
		Your tax is—			

41,000

At least	But less than	Single	MFJ	MFS	HoH
41,000	41,050	6,444	5,319	6,444	5,556
41,050	41,100	6,456	5,326	6,456	5,564
41,100	41,150	6,469	5,334	6,469	5,571
41,150	41,200	6,481	5,341	6,481	5,579
41,200	41,250	6,494	5,349	6,494	5,586
41,250	41,300	6,506	5,356	6,506	5,594
41,300	41,350	6,519	5,364	6,519	5,601
41,350	41,400	6,531	5,371	6,531	5,609
41,400	41,450	6,544	5,379	6,544	5,616
41,450	41,500	6,556	5,386	6,556	5,624
41,500	41,550	6,569	5,394	6,569	5,631
41,550	41,600	6,581	5,401	6,581	5,639
41,600	41,650	6,594	5,409	6,594	5,646
41,650	41,700	6,606	5,416	6,606	5,654
41,700	41,750	6,619	5,424	6,619	5,661
41,750	41,800	6,631	5,431	6,631	5,669
41,800	41,850	6,644	5,439	6,644	5,676
41,850	41,900	6,656	5,446	6,656	5,684
41,900	41,950	6,669	5,454	6,669	5,691
41,950	42,000	6,681	5,461	6,681	5,699

42,000

At least	But less than	Single	MFJ	MFS	HoH
42,000	42,050	6,694	5,469	6,694	5,706
42,050	42,100	6,706	5,476	6,706	5,714
42,100	42,150	6,719	5,484	6,719	5,721
42,150	42,200	6,731	5,491	6,731	5,729
42,200	42,250	6,744	5,499	6,744	5,736
42,250	42,300	6,756	5,506	6,756	5,744
42,300	42,350	6,769	5,514	6,769	5,751
42,350	42,400	6,781	5,521	6,781	5,759
42,400	42,450	6,794	5,529	6,794	5,766
42,450	42,500	6,806	5,536	6,806	5,774
42,500	42,550	6,819	5,544	6,819	5,781
42,550	42,600	6,831	5,551	6,831	5,789
42,600	42,650	6,844	5,559	6,844	5,796
42,650	42,700	6,856	5,566	6,856	5,804
42,700	42,750	6,869	5,574	6,869	5,811
42,750	42,800	6,881	5,581	6,881	5,819
42,800	42,850	6,894	5,589	6,894	5,826
42,850	42,900	6,906	5,596	6,906	5,834
42,900	42,950	6,919	5,604	6,919	5,841
42,950	43,000	6,931	5,611	6,931	5,849

43,000

At least	But less than	Single	MFJ	MFS	HoH
43,000	43,050	6,944	5,619	6,944	5,856
43,050	43,100	6,956	5,626	6,956	5,864
43,100	43,150	6,969	5,634	6,969	5,871
43,150	43,200	6,981	5,641	6,981	5,879
43,200	43,250	6,994	5,649	6,994	5,886
43,250	43,300	7,006	5,656	7,006	5,894
43,300	43,350	7,019	5,664	7,019	5,901
43,350	43,400	7,031	5,671	7,031	5,909
43,400	43,450	7,044	5,679	7,044	5,916
43,450	43,500	7,056	5,686	7,056	5,924
43,500	43,550	7,069	5,694	7,069	5,931
43,550	43,600	7,081	5,701	7,081	5,939
43,600	43,650	7,094	5,709	7,094	5,946
43,650	43,700	7,106	5,716	7,106	5,954
43,700	43,750	7,119	5,724	7,119	5,961
43,750	43,800	7,131	5,731	7,131	5,969
43,800	43,850	7,144	5,739	7,144	5,976
43,850	43,900	7,156	5,746	7,156	5,984
43,900	43,950	7,169	5,754	7,169	5,991
43,950	44,000	7,181	5,761	7,181	5,999

44,000

At least	But less than	Single	MFJ	MFS	HoH
44,000	44,050	7,194	5,769	7,194	6,006
44,050	44,100	7,206	5,776	7,206	6,014
44,100	44,150	7,219	5,784	7,219	6,021
44,150	44,200	7,231	5,791	7,231	6,029
44,200	44,250	7,244	5,799	7,244	6,036
44,250	44,300	7,256	5,806	7,256	6,044
44,300	44,350	7,269	5,814	7,269	6,051
44,350	44,400	7,281	5,821	7,281	6,059
44,400	44,450	7,294	5,829	7,294	6,066
44,450	44,500	7,306	5,836	7,306	6,074
44,500	44,550	7,319	5,844	7,319	6,081
44,550	44,600	7,331	5,851	7,331	6,089
44,600	44,650	7,344	5,859	7,344	6,096
44,650	44,700	7,356	5,866	7,356	6,104
44,700	44,750	7,369	5,874	7,369	6,111
44,750	44,800	7,381	5,881	7,381	6,119
44,800	44,850	7,394	5,889	7,394	6,126
44,850	44,900	7,406	5,896	7,406	6,134
44,900	44,950	7,419	5,904	7,419	6,141
44,950	45,000	7,431	5,911	7,431	6,149

45,000

At least	But less than	Single	MFJ	MFS	HoH
45,000	45,050	7,444	5,919	7,444	6,156
45,050	45,100	7,456	5,926	7,456	6,164
45,100	45,150	7,469	5,934	7,469	6,171
45,150	45,200	7,481	5,941	7,481	6,179
45,200	45,250	7,494	5,949	7,494	6,186
45,250	45,300	7,506	5,956	7,506	6,194
45,300	45,350	7,519	5,964	7,519	6,201
45,350	45,400	7,531	5,971	7,531	6,209
45,400	45,450	7,544	5,979	7,544	6,216
45,450	45,500	7,556	5,986	7,556	6,224
45,500	45,550	7,569	5,994	7,569	6,234
45,550	45,600	7,581	6,001	7,581	6,246
45,600	45,650	7,594	6,009	7,594	6,259
45,650	45,700	7,606	6,016	7,606	6,271
45,700	45,750	7,619	6,024	7,619	6,284
45,750	45,800	7,631	6,031	7,631	6,296
45,800	45,850	7,644	6,039	7,644	6,309
45,850	45,900	7,656	6,046	7,656	6,321
45,900	45,950	7,669	6,054	7,669	6,334
45,950	46,000	7,681	6,061	7,681	6,346

46,000

At least	But less than	Single	MFJ	MFS	HoH
46,000	46,050	7,694	6,069	7,694	6,359
46,050	46,100	7,706	6,076	7,706	6,371
46,100	46,150	7,719	6,084	7,719	6,384
46,150	46,200	7,731	6,091	7,731	6,396
46,200	46,250	7,744	6,099	7,744	6,409
46,250	46,300	7,756	6,106	7,756	6,421
46,300	46,350	7,769	6,114	7,769	6,434
46,350	46,400	7,781	6,121	7,781	6,446
46,400	46,450	7,794	6,129	7,794	6,459
46,450	46,500	7,806	6,136	7,806	6,471
46,500	46,550	7,819	6,144	7,819	6,484
46,550	46,600	7,831	6,151	7,831	6,496
46,600	46,650	7,844	6,159	7,844	6,509
46,650	46,700	7,856	6,166	7,856	6,521
46,700	46,750	7,869	6,174	7,869	6,534
46,750	46,800	7,881	6,181	7,881	6,546
46,800	46,850	7,894	6,189	7,894	6,559
46,850	46,900	7,906	6,196	7,906	6,571
46,900	46,950	7,919	6,204	7,919	6,584
46,950	47,000	7,931	6,211	7,931	6,596

47,000

At least	But less than	Single	MFJ	MFS	HoH
47,000	47,050	7,944	6,219	7,944	6,609
47,050	47,100	7,956	6,226	7,956	6,621
47,100	47,150	7,969	6,234	7,969	6,634
47,150	47,200	7,981	6,241	7,981	6,646
47,200	47,250	7,994	6,249	7,994	6,659
47,250	47,300	8,006	6,256	8,006	6,671
47,300	47,350	8,019	6,264	8,019	6,684
47,350	47,400	8,031	6,271	8,031	6,696
47,400	47,450	8,044	6,279	8,044	6,709
47,450	47,500	8,056	6,286	8,056	6,721
47,500	47,550	8,069	6,294	8,069	6,734
47,550	47,600	8,081	6,301	8,081	6,746
47,600	47,650	8,094	6,309	8,094	6,759
47,650	47,700	8,106	6,316	8,106	6,771
47,700	47,750	8,119	6,324	8,119	6,784
47,750	47,800	8,131	6,331	8,131	6,796
47,800	47,850	8,144	6,339	8,144	6,809
47,850	47,900	8,156	6,346	8,156	6,821
47,900	47,950	8,169	6,354	8,169	6,834
47,950	48,000	8,181	6,361	8,181	6,846

48,000

At least	But less than	Single	MFJ	MFS	HoH
48,000	48,050	8,194	6,369	8,194	6,859
48,050	48,100	8,206	6,376	8,206	6,871
48,100	48,150	8,219	6,384	8,219	6,884
48,150	48,200	8,231	6,391	8,231	6,896
48,200	48,250	8,244	6,399	8,244	6,909
48,250	48,300	8,256	6,406	8,256	6,921
48,300	48,350	8,269	6,414	8,269	6,934
48,350	48,400	8,281	6,421	8,281	6,946
48,400	48,450	8,294	6,429	8,294	6,959
48,450	48,500	8,306	6,436	8,306	6,971
48,500	48,550	8,319	6,444	8,319	6,984
48,550	48,600	8,331	6,451	8,331	6,996
48,600	48,650	8,344	6,459	8,344	7,009
48,650	48,700	8,356	6,466	8,356	7,021
48,700	48,750	8,369	6,474	8,369	7,034
48,750	48,800	8,381	6,481	8,381	7,046
48,800	48,850	8,394	6,489	8,394	7,059
48,850	48,900	8,406	6,496	8,406	7,071
48,900	48,950	8,419	6,504	8,419	7,084
48,950	49,000	8,431	6,511	8,431	7,096

49,000

At least	But less than	Single	MFJ	MFS	HoH
49,000	49,050	8,444	6,519	8,444	7,109
49,050	49,100	8,456	6,526	8,456	7,121
49,100	49,150	8,469	6,534	8,469	7,134
49,150	49,200	8,481	6,541	8,481	7,146
49,200	49,250	8,494	6,549	8,494	7,159
49,250	49,300	8,506	6,556	8,506	7,171
49,300	49,350	8,519	6,564	8,519	7,184
49,350	49,400	8,531	6,571	8,531	7,196
49,400	49,450	8,544	6,579	8,544	7,209
49,450	49,500	8,556	6,586	8,556	7,221
49,500	49,550	8,569	6,594	8,569	7,234
49,550	49,600	8,581	6,601	8,581	7,246
49,600	49,650	8,594	6,609	8,594	7,259
49,650	49,700	8,606	6,616	8,606	7,271
49,700	49,750	8,619	6,624	8,619	7,284
49,750	49,800	8,631	6,631	8,631	7,296
49,800	49,850	8,644	6,639	8,644	7,309
49,850	49,900	8,656	6,646	8,656	7,321
49,900	49,950	8,669	6,654	8,669	7,334
49,950	50,000	8,681	6,661	8,681	7,346

* This column must also be used by a qualifying widow(er).

(Continued on page D-7)

50,000

At least	But less than	Single	Married filing jointly*	Married filing separately	Head of a household
50,000	50,050	8,694	6,669	8,694	7,359
50,050	50,100	8,706	6,676	8,706	7,371
50,100	50,150	8,719	6,684	8,719	7,384
50,150	50,200	8,731	6,691	8,731	7,396
50,200	50,250	8,744	6,699	8,744	7,409
50,250	50,300	8,756	6,706	8,756	7,421
50,300	50,350	8,769	6,714	8,769	7,434
50,350	50,400	8,781	6,721	8,781	7,446
50,400	50,450	8,794	6,729	8,794	7,459
50,450	50,500	8,806	6,736	8,806	7,471
50,500	50,550	8,819	6,744	8,819	7,484
50,550	50,600	8,831	6,751	8,831	7,496
50,600	50,650	8,844	6,759	8,844	7,509
50,650	50,700	8,856	6,766	8,856	7,521
50,700	50,750	8,869	6,774	8,869	7,534
50,750	50,800	8,881	6,781	8,881	7,546
50,800	50,850	8,894	6,789	8,894	7,559
50,850	50,900	8,906	6,796	8,906	7,571
50,900	50,950	8,919	6,804	8,919	7,584
50,950	51,000	8,931	6,811	8,931	7,596

51,000

At least	But less than	Single	Married filing jointly*	Married filing separately	Head of a household
51,000	51,050	8,944	6,819	8,944	7,609
51,050	51,100	8,956	6,826	8,956	7,621
51,100	51,150	8,969	6,834	8,969	7,634
51,150	51,200	8,981	6,841	8,981	7,646
51,200	51,250	8,994	6,849	8,994	7,659
51,250	51,300	9,006	6,856	9,006	7,671
51,300	51,350	9,019	6,864	9,019	7,684
51,350	51,400	9,031	6,871	9,031	7,696
51,400	51,450	9,044	6,879	9,044	7,709
51,450	51,500	9,056	6,886	9,056	7,721
51,500	51,550	9,069	6,894	9,069	7,734
51,550	51,600	9,081	6,901	9,081	7,746
51,600	51,650	9,094	6,909	9,094	7,759
51,650	51,700	9,106	6,916	9,106	7,771
51,700	51,750	9,119	6,924	9,119	7,784
51,750	51,800	9,131	6,931	9,131	7,796
51,800	51,850	9,144	6,939	9,144	7,809
51,850	51,900	9,156	6,946	9,156	7,821
51,900	51,950	9,169	6,954	9,169	7,834
51,950	52,000	9,181	6,961	9,181	7,846

52,000

At least	But less than	Single	Married filing jointly*	Married filing separately	Head of a household
52,000	52,050	9,194	6,969	9,194	7,859
52,050	52,100	9,206	6,976	9,206	7,871
52,100	52,150	9,219	6,984	9,219	7,884
52,150	52,200	9,231	6,991	9,231	7,896
52,200	52,250	9,244	6,999	9,244	7,909
52,250	52,300	9,256	7,006	9,256	7,921
52,300	52,350	9,269	7,014	9,269	7,934
52,350	52,400	9,281	7,021	9,281	7,946
52,400	52,450	9,294	7,029	9,294	7,959
52,450	52,500	9,306	7,036	9,306	7,971
52,500	52,550	9,319	7,044	9,319	7,984
52,550	52,600	9,331	7,051	9,331	7,996
52,600	52,650	9,344	7,059	9,344	8,009
52,650	52,700	9,356	7,066	9,356	8,021
52,700	52,750	9,369	7,074	9,369	8,034
52,750	52,800	9,381	7,081	9,381	8,046
52,800	52,850	9,394	7,089	9,394	8,059
52,850	52,900	9,406	7,096	9,406	8,071
52,900	52,950	9,419	7,104	9,419	8,084
52,950	53,000	9,431	7,111	9,431	8,096

53,000

At least	But less than	Single	Married filing jointly*	Married filing separately	Head of a household
53,000	53,050	9,444	7,119	9,444	8,109
53,050	53,100	9,456	7,126	9,456	8,121
53,100	53,150	9,469	7,134	9,469	8,134
53,150	53,200	9,481	7,141	9,481	8,146
53,200	53,250	9,494	7,149	9,494	8,159
53,250	53,300	9,506	7,156	9,506	8,171
53,300	53,350	9,519	7,164	9,519	8,184
53,350	53,400	9,531	7,171	9,531	8,196
53,400	53,450	9,544	7,179	9,544	8,209
53,450	53,500	9,556	7,186	9,556	8,221
53,500	53,550	9,569	7,194	9,569	8,234
53,550	53,600	9,581	7,201	9,581	8,246
53,600	53,650	9,594	7,209	9,594	8,259
53,650	53,700	9,606	7,216	9,606	8,271
53,700	53,750	9,619	7,224	9,619	8,284
53,750	53,800	9,631	7,231	9,631	8,296
53,800	53,850	9,644	7,239	9,644	8,309
53,850	53,900	9,656	7,246	9,656	8,321
53,900	53,950	9,669	7,254	9,669	8,334
53,950	54,000	9,681	7,261	9,681	8,346

54,000

At least	But less than	Single	Married filing jointly*	Married filing separately	Head of a household
54,000	54,050	9,694	7,269	9,694	8,359
54,050	54,100	9,706	7,276	9,706	8,371
54,100	54,150	9,719	7,284	9,719	8,384
54,150	54,200	9,731	7,291	9,731	8,396
54,200	54,250	9,744	7,299	9,744	8,409
54,250	54,300	9,756	7,306	9,756	8,421
54,300	54,350	9,769	7,314	9,769	8,434
54,350	54,400	9,781	7,321	9,781	8,446
54,400	54,450	9,794	7,329	9,794	8,459
54,450	54,500	9,806	7,336	9,806	8,471
54,500	54,550	9,819	7,344	9,819	8,484
54,550	54,600	9,831	7,351	9,831	8,496
54,600	54,650	9,844	7,359	9,844	8,509
54,650	54,700	9,856	7,366	9,856	8,521
54,700	54,750	9,869	7,374	9,869	8,534
54,750	54,800	9,881	7,381	9,881	8,546
54,800	54,850	9,894	7,389	9,894	8,559
54,850	54,900	9,906	7,396	9,906	8,571
54,900	54,950	9,919	7,404	9,919	8,584
54,950	55,000	9,931	7,411	9,931	8,596

55,000

At least	But less than	Single	Married filing jointly*	Married filing separately	Head of a household
55,000	55,050	9,944	7,419	9,944	8,609
55,050	55,100	9,956	7,426	9,956	8,621
55,100	55,150	9,969	7,434	9,969	8,634
55,150	55,200	9,981	7,441	9,981	8,646
55,200	55,250	9,994	7,449	9,994	8,659
55,250	55,300	10,006	7,456	10,006	8,671
55,300	55,350	10,019	7,464	10,019	8,684
55,350	55,400	10,031	7,471	10,031	8,696
55,400	55,450	10,044	7,479	10,044	8,709
55,450	55,500	10,056	7,486	10,056	8,721
55,500	55,550	10,069	7,494	10,069	8,734
55,550	55,600	10,081	7,501	10,081	8,746
55,600	55,650	10,094	7,509	10,094	8,759
55,650	55,700	10,106	7,516	10,106	8,771
55,700	55,750	10,119	7,524	10,119	8,784
55,750	55,800	10,131	7,531	10,131	8,796
55,800	55,850	10,144	7,539	10,144	8,809
55,850	55,900	10,156	7,546	10,156	8,821
55,900	55,950	10,169	7,554	10,169	8,834
55,950	56,000	10,181	7,561	10,181	8,846

56,000

At least	But less than	Single	Married filing jointly*	Married filing separately	Head of a household
56,000	56,050	10,194	7,569	10,194	8,859
56,050	56,100	10,206	7,576	10,206	8,871
56,100	56,150	10,219	7,584	10,219	8,884
56,150	56,200	10,231	7,591	10,231	8,896
56,200	56,250	10,244	7,599	10,244	8,909
56,250	56,300	10,256	7,606	10,256	8,921
56,300	56,350	10,269	7,614	10,269	8,934
56,350	56,400	10,281	7,621	10,281	8,946
56,400	56,450	10,294	7,629	10,294	8,959
56,450	56,500	10,306	7,636	10,306	8,971
56,500	56,550	10,319	7,644	10,319	8,984
56,550	56,600	10,331	7,651	10,331	8,996
56,600	56,650	10,344	7,659	10,344	9,009
56,650	56,700	10,356	7,666	10,356	9,021
56,700	56,750	10,369	7,674	10,369	9,034
56,750	56,800	10,381	7,681	10,381	9,046
56,800	56,850	10,394	7,689	10,394	9,059
56,850	56,900	10,406	7,696	10,406	9,071
56,900	56,950	10,419	7,704	10,419	9,084
56,950	57,000	10,431	7,711	10,431	9,096

57,000

At least	But less than	Single	Married filing jointly*	Married filing separately	Head of a household
57,000	57,050	10,444	7,719	10,444	9,109
57,050	57,100	10,456	7,726	10,456	9,121
57,100	57,150	10,469	7,734	10,469	9,134
57,150	57,200	10,481	7,741	10,481	9,146
57,200	57,250	10,494	7,749	10,494	9,159
57,250	57,300	10,506	7,756	10,506	9,171
57,300	57,350	10,519	7,764	10,519	9,184
57,350	57,400	10,531	7,771	10,531	9,196
57,400	57,450	10,544	7,779	10,544	9,209
57,450	57,500	10,556	7,786	10,556	9,221
57,500	57,550	10,569	7,794	10,569	9,234
57,550	57,600	10,581	7,801	10,581	9,246
57,600	57,650	10,594	7,809	10,594	9,259
57,650	57,700	10,606	7,816	10,606	9,271
57,700	57,750	10,619	7,824	10,619	9,284
57,750	57,800	10,631	7,831	10,631	9,296
57,800	57,850	10,644	7,839	10,644	9,309
57,850	57,900	10,656	7,846	10,656	9,321
57,900	57,950	10,669	7,854	10,669	9,334
57,950	58,000	10,681	7,861	10,681	9,346

58,000

At least	But less than	Single	Married filing jointly*	Married filing separately	Head of a household
58,000	58,050	10,694	7,869	10,694	9,359
58,050	58,100	10,706	7,876	10,706	9,371
58,100	58,150	10,719	7,884	10,719	9,384
58,150	58,200	10,731	7,891	10,731	9,396
58,200	58,250	10,744	7,899	10,744	9,409
58,250	58,300	10,756	7,906	10,756	9,421
58,300	58,350	10,769	7,914	10,769	9,434
58,350	58,400	10,781	7,921	10,781	9,446
58,400	58,450	10,794	7,929	10,794	9,459
58,450	58,500	10,806	7,936	10,806	9,471
58,500	58,550	10,819	7,944	10,819	9,484
58,550	58,600	10,831	7,951	10,831	9,496
58,600	58,650	10,844	7,959	10,844	9,509
58,650	58,700	10,856	7,966	10,856	9,521
58,700	58,750	10,869	7,974	10,869	9,534
58,750	58,800	10,881	7,981	10,881	9,546
58,800	58,850	10,894	7,989	10,894	9,559
58,850	58,900	10,906	7,996	10,906	9,571
58,900	58,950	10,919	8,004	10,919	9,584
58,950	59,000	10,931	8,011	10,931	9,596

* This column must also be used by a qualifying widow(er).

(Continued on page D-8)

2009 Tax Table–Continued

59,000 / 60,000 / 61,000

If line 43 (taxable income) is— At least	But less than	Single	Married filing jointly *	Married filing separately *	Head of a household
59,000					
59,000	59,050	10,944	8,019	10,944	9,609
59,050	59,100	10,956	8,026	10,956	9,621
59,100	59,150	10,969	8,034	10,969	9,634
59,150	59,200	10,981	8,041	10,981	9,646
59,200	59,250	10,994	8,049	10,994	9,659
59,250	59,300	11,006	8,056	11,006	9,671
59,300	59,350	11,019	8,064	11,019	9,684
59,350	59,400	11,031	8,071	11,031	9,696
59,400	59,450	11,044	8,079	11,044	9,709
59,450	59,500	11,056	8,086	11,056	9,721
59,500	59,550	11,069	8,094	11,069	9,734
59,550	59,600	11,081	8,101	11,081	9,746
59,600	59,650	11,094	8,109	11,094	9,759
59,650	59,700	11,106	8,116	11,106	9,771
59,700	59,750	11,119	8,124	11,119	9,784
59,750	59,800	11,131	8,131	11,131	9,796
59,800	59,850	11,144	8,139	11,144	9,809
59,850	59,900	11,156	8,146	11,156	9,821
59,900	59,950	11,169	8,154	11,169	9,834
59,950	60,000	11,181	8,161	11,181	9,846
60,000					
60,000	60,050	11,194	8,169	11,194	9,859
60,050	60,100	11,206	8,176	11,206	9,871
60,100	60,150	11,219	8,184	11,219	9,884
60,150	60,200	11,231	8,191	11,231	9,896
60,200	60,250	11,244	8,199	11,244	9,909
60,250	60,300	11,256	8,206	11,256	9,921
60,300	60,350	11,269	8,214	11,269	9,934
60,350	60,400	11,281	8,221	11,281	9,946
60,400	60,450	11,294	8,229	11,294	9,959
60,450	60,500	11,306	8,236	11,306	9,971
60,500	60,550	11,319	8,244	11,319	9,984
60,550	60,600	11,331	8,251	11,331	9,996
60,600	60,650	11,344	8,259	11,344	10,009
60,650	60,700	11,356	8,266	11,356	10,021
60,700	60,750	11,369	8,274	11,369	10,034
60,750	60,800	11,381	8,281	11,381	10,046
60,800	60,850	11,394	8,289	11,394	10,059
60,850	60,900	11,406	8,296	11,406	10,071
60,900	60,950	11,419	8,304	11,419	10,084
60,950	61,000	11,431	8,311	11,431	10,096
61,000					
61,000	61,050	11,444	8,319	11,444	10,109
61,050	61,100	11,456	8,326	11,456	10,121
61,100	61,150	11,469	8,334	11,469	10,134
61,150	61,200	11,481	8,341	11,481	10,146
61,200	61,250	11,494	8,349	11,494	10,159
61,250	61,300	11,506	8,356	11,506	10,171
61,300	61,350	11,519	8,364	11,519	10,184
61,350	61,400	11,531	8,371	11,531	10,196
61,400	61,450	11,544	8,379	11,544	10,209
61,450	61,500	11,556	8,386	11,556	10,221
61,500	61,550	11,569	8,394	11,569	10,234
61,550	61,600	11,581	8,401	11,581	10,246
61,600	61,650	11,594	8,409	11,594	10,259
61,650	61,700	11,606	8,416	11,606	10,271
61,700	61,750	11,619	8,424	11,619	10,284
61,750	61,800	11,631	8,431	11,631	10,296
61,800	61,850	11,644	8,439	11,644	10,309
61,850	61,900	11,656	8,446	11,656	10,321
61,900	61,950	11,669	8,454	11,669	10,334
61,950	62,000	11,681	8,461	11,681	10,346

62,000 / 63,000 / 64,000

If line 43 (taxable income) is— At least	But less than	Single	Married filing jointly *	Married filing separately *	Head of a household
62,000					
62,000	62,050	11,694	8,469	11,694	10,359
62,050	62,100	11,706	8,476	11,706	10,371
62,100	62,150	11,719	8,484	11,719	10,384
62,150	62,200	11,731	8,491	11,731	10,396
62,200	62,250	11,744	8,499	11,744	10,409
62,250	62,300	11,756	8,506	11,756	10,421
62,300	62,350	11,769	8,514	11,769	10,434
62,350	62,400	11,781	8,521	11,781	10,446
62,400	62,450	11,794	8,529	11,794	10,459
62,450	62,500	11,806	8,536	11,806	10,471
62,500	62,550	11,819	8,544	11,819	10,484
62,550	62,600	11,831	8,551	11,831	10,496
62,600	62,650	11,844	8,559	11,844	10,509
62,650	62,700	11,856	8,566	11,856	10,521
62,700	62,750	11,869	8,574	11,869	10,534
62,750	62,800	11,881	8,581	11,881	10,546
62,800	62,850	11,894	8,589	11,894	10,559
62,850	62,900	11,906	8,596	11,906	10,571
62,900	62,950	11,919	8,604	11,919	10,584
62,950	63,000	11,931	8,611	11,931	10,596
63,000					
63,000	63,050	11,944	8,619	11,944	10,609
63,050	63,100	11,956	8,626	11,956	10,621
63,100	63,150	11,969	8,634	11,969	10,634
63,150	63,200	11,981	8,641	11,981	10,646
63,200	63,250	11,994	8,649	11,994	10,659
63,250	63,300	12,006	8,656	12,006	10,671
63,300	63,350	12,019	8,664	12,019	10,684
63,350	63,400	12,031	8,671	12,031	10,696
63,400	63,450	12,044	8,679	12,044	10,709
63,450	63,500	12,056	8,686	12,056	10,721
63,500	63,550	12,069	8,694	12,069	10,734
63,550	63,600	12,081	8,701	12,081	10,746
63,600	63,650	12,094	8,709	12,094	10,759
63,650	63,700	12,106	8,716	12,106	10,771
63,700	63,750	12,119	8,724	12,119	10,784
63,750	63,800	12,131	8,731	12,131	10,796
63,800	63,850	12,144	8,739	12,144	10,809
63,850	63,900	12,156	8,746	12,156	10,821
63,900	63,950	12,169	8,754	12,169	10,834
63,950	64,000	12,181	8,761	12,181	10,846
64,000					
64,000	64,050	12,194	8,769	12,194	10,859
64,050	64,100	12,206	8,776	12,206	10,871
64,100	64,150	12,219	8,784	12,219	10,884
64,150	64,200	12,231	8,791	12,231	10,896
64,200	64,250	12,244	8,799	12,244	10,909
64,250	64,300	12,256	8,806	12,256	10,921
64,300	64,350	12,269	8,814	12,269	10,934
64,350	64,400	12,281	8,821	12,281	10,946
64,400	64,450	12,294	8,829	12,294	10,959
64,450	64,500	12,306	8,836	12,306	10,971
64,500	64,550	12,319	8,844	12,319	10,984
64,550	64,600	12,331	8,851	12,331	10,996
64,600	64,650	12,344	8,859	12,344	11,009
64,650	64,700	12,356	8,866	12,356	11,021
64,700	64,750	12,369	8,874	12,369	11,034
64,750	64,800	12,381	8,881	12,381	11,046
64,800	64,850	12,394	8,889	12,394	11,059
64,850	64,900	12,406	8,896	12,406	11,071
64,900	64,950	12,419	8,904	12,419	11,084
64,950	65,000	12,431	8,911	12,431	11,096

65,000 / 66,000 / 67,000

If line 43 (taxable income) is— At least	But less than	Single	Married filing jointly *	Married filing separately *	Head of a household
65,000					
65,000	65,050	12,444	8,919	12,444	11,109
65,050	65,100	12,456	8,926	12,456	11,121
65,100	65,150	12,469	8,934	12,469	11,134
65,150	65,200	12,481	8,941	12,481	11,146
65,200	65,250	12,494	8,949	12,494	11,159
65,250	65,300	12,506	8,956	12,506	11,171
65,300	65,350	12,519	8,964	12,519	11,184
65,350	65,400	12,531	8,971	12,531	11,196
65,400	65,450	12,544	8,979	12,544	11,209
65,450	65,500	12,556	8,986	12,556	11,221
65,500	65,550	12,569	8,994	12,569	11,234
65,550	65,600	12,581	9,001	12,581	11,246
65,600	65,650	12,594	9,009	12,594	11,259
65,650	65,700	12,606	9,016	12,606	11,271
65,700	65,750	12,619	9,024	12,619	11,284
65,750	65,800	12,631	9,031	12,631	11,296
65,800	65,850	12,644	9,039	12,644	11,309
65,850	65,900	12,656	9,046	12,656	11,321
65,900	65,950	12,669	9,054	12,669	11,334
65,950	66,000	12,681	9,061	12,681	11,346
66,000					
66,000	66,050	12,694	9,069	12,694	11,359
66,050	66,100	12,706	9,076	12,706	11,371
66,100	66,150	12,719	9,084	12,719	11,384
66,150	66,200	12,731	9,091	12,731	11,396
66,200	66,250	12,744	9,099	12,744	11,409
66,250	66,300	12,756	9,106	12,756	11,421
66,300	66,350	12,769	9,114	12,769	11,434
66,350	66,400	12,781	9,121	12,781	11,446
66,400	66,450	12,794	9,129	12,794	11,459
66,450	66,500	12,806	9,136	12,806	11,471
66,500	66,550	12,819	9,144	12,819	11,484
66,550	66,600	12,831	9,151	12,831	11,496
66,600	66,650	12,844	9,159	12,844	11,509
66,650	66,700	12,856	9,166	12,856	11,521
66,700	66,750	12,869	9,174	12,869	11,534
66,750	66,800	12,881	9,181	12,881	11,546
66,800	66,850	12,894	9,189	12,894	11,559
66,850	66,900	12,906	9,196	12,906	11,571
66,900	66,950	12,919	9,204	12,919	11,584
66,950	67,000	12,931	9,211	12,931	11,596
67,000					
67,000	67,050	12,944	9,219	12,944	11,609
67,050	67,100	12,956	9,226	12,956	11,621
67,100	67,150	12,969	9,234	12,969	11,634
67,150	67,200	12,981	9,241	12,981	11,646
67,200	67,250	12,994	9,249	12,994	11,659
67,250	67,300	13,006	9,256	13,006	11,671
67,300	67,350	13,019	9,264	13,019	11,684
67,350	67,400	13,031	9,271	13,031	11,696
67,400	67,450	13,044	9,279	13,044	11,709
67,450	67,500	13,056	9,286	13,056	11,721
67,500	67,550	13,069	9,294	13,069	11,734
67,550	67,600	13,081	9,301	13,081	11,746
67,600	67,650	13,094	9,309	13,094	11,759
67,650	67,700	13,106	9,316	13,106	11,771
67,700	67,750	13,119	9,324	13,119	11,784
67,750	67,800	13,131	9,331	13,131	11,796
67,800	67,850	13,144	9,339	13,144	11,809
67,850	67,900	13,156	9,346	13,156	11,821
67,900	67,950	13,169	9,356	13,169	11,834
67,950	68,000	13,181	9,369	13,181	11,846

* This column must also be used by a qualifying widow(er).

(Continued on page D-9)

68,000

At least	But less than	Single	Married filing jointly*	Married filing separately	Head of a household
68,000	68,050	13,194	9,381	13,194	11,859
68,050	68,100	13,206	9,394	13,206	11,871
68,100	68,150	13,219	9,406	13,219	11,884
68,150	68,200	13,231	9,419	13,231	11,896
68,200	68,250	13,244	9,431	13,244	11,909
68,250	68,300	13,256	9,444	13,256	11,921
68,300	68,350	13,269	9,456	13,269	11,934
68,350	68,400	13,281	9,469	13,281	11,946
68,400	68,450	13,294	9,481	13,294	11,959
68,450	68,500	13,306	9,494	13,306	11,971
68,500	68,550	13,319	9,506	13,319	11,984
68,550	68,600	13,331	9,519	13,333	11,996
68,600	68,650	13,344	9,531	13,347	12,009
68,650	68,700	13,356	9,544	13,361	12,021
68,700	68,750	13,369	9,556	13,375	12,034
68,750	68,800	13,381	9,569	13,389	12,046
68,800	68,850	13,394	9,581	13,403	12,059
68,850	68,900	13,406	9,594	13,417	12,071
68,900	68,950	13,419	9,606	13,431	12,084
68,950	69,000	13,431	9,619	13,445	12,096

69,000

At least	But less than	Single	Married filing jointly*	Married filing separately	Head of a household
69,000	69,050	13,444	9,631	13,459	12,109
69,050	69,100	13,456	9,644	13,473	12,121
69,100	69,150	13,469	9,656	13,487	12,134
69,150	69,200	13,481	9,669	13,501	12,146
69,200	69,250	13,494	9,681	13,515	12,159
69,250	69,300	13,506	9,694	13,529	12,171
69,300	69,350	13,519	9,706	13,543	12,184
69,350	69,400	13,531	9,719	13,557	12,196
69,400	69,450	13,544	9,731	13,571	12,209
69,450	69,500	13,556	9,744	13,585	12,221
69,500	69,550	13,569	9,756	13,599	12,234
69,550	69,600	13,581	9,769	13,613	12,246
69,600	69,650	13,594	9,781	13,627	12,259
69,650	69,700	13,606	9,794	13,641	12,271
69,700	69,750	13,619	9,806	13,655	12,284
69,750	69,800	13,631	9,819	13,669	12,296
69,800	69,850	13,644	9,831	13,683	12,309
69,850	69,900	13,656	9,844	13,697	12,321
69,900	69,950	13,669	9,856	13,711	12,334
69,950	70,000	13,681	9,869	13,725	12,346

70,000

At least	But less than	Single	Married filing jointly*	Married filing separately	Head of a household
70,000	70,050	13,694	9,881	13,739	12,359
70,050	70,100	13,706	9,894	13,753	12,371
70,100	70,150	13,719	9,906	13,767	12,384
70,150	70,200	13,731	9,919	13,781	12,396
70,200	70,250	13,744	9,931	13,795	12,409
70,250	70,300	13,756	9,944	13,809	12,421
70,300	70,350	13,769	9,956	13,823	12,434
70,350	70,400	13,781	9,969	13,837	12,446
70,400	70,450	13,794	9,981	13,851	12,459
70,450	70,500	13,806	9,994	13,865	12,471
70,500	70,550	13,819	10,006	13,879	12,484
70,550	70,600	13,831	10,019	13,893	12,496
70,600	70,650	13,844	10,031	13,907	12,509
70,650	70,700	13,856	10,044	13,921	12,521
70,700	70,750	13,869	10,056	13,935	12,534
70,750	70,800	13,881	10,069	13,949	12,546
70,800	70,850	13,894	10,081	13,963	12,559
70,850	70,900	13,906	10,094	13,977	12,571
70,900	70,950	13,919	10,106	13,991	12,584
70,950	71,000	13,931	10,119	14,005	12,596

71,000

At least	But less than	Single	Married filing jointly*	Married filing separately	Head of a household
71,000	71,050	13,944	10,131	14,019	12,609
71,050	71,100	13,956	10,144	14,033	12,621
71,100	71,150	13,969	10,156	14,047	12,634
71,150	71,200	13,981	10,169	14,061	12,646
71,200	71,250	13,994	10,181	14,075	12,659
71,250	71,300	14,006	10,194	14,089	12,671
71,300	71,350	14,019	10,206	14,103	12,684
71,350	71,400	14,031	10,219	14,117	12,696
71,400	71,450	14,044	10,231	14,131	12,709
71,450	71,500	14,056	10,244	14,145	12,721
71,500	71,550	14,069	10,256	14,159	12,734
71,550	71,600	14,081	10,269	14,173	12,746
71,600	71,650	14,094	10,281	14,187	12,759
71,650	71,700	14,106	10,294	14,201	12,771
71,700	71,750	14,119	10,306	14,215	12,784
71,750	71,800	14,131	10,319	14,229	12,796
71,800	71,850	14,144	10,331	14,243	12,809
71,850	71,900	14,156	10,344	14,257	12,821
71,900	71,950	14,169	10,356	14,271	12,834
71,950	72,000	14,181	10,369	14,285	12,846

72,000

At least	But less than	Single	Married filing jointly*	Married filing separately	Head of a household
72,000	72,050	14,194	10,381	14,299	12,859
72,050	72,100	14,206	10,394	14,313	12,871
72,100	72,150	14,219	10,406	14,327	12,884
72,150	72,200	14,231	10,419	14,341	12,896
72,200	72,250	14,244	10,431	14,355	12,909
72,250	72,300	14,256	10,444	14,369	12,921
72,300	72,350	14,269	10,456	14,383	12,934
72,350	72,400	14,281	10,469	14,397	12,946
72,400	72,450	14,294	10,481	14,411	12,959
72,450	72,500	14,306	10,494	14,425	12,971
72,500	72,550	14,319	10,506	14,439	12,984
72,550	72,600	14,331	10,519	14,453	12,996
72,600	72,650	14,344	10,531	14,467	13,009
72,650	72,700	14,356	10,544	14,481	13,021
72,700	72,750	14,369	10,556	14,495	13,034
72,750	72,800	14,381	10,569	14,509	13,046
72,800	72,850	14,394	10,581	14,523	13,059
72,850	72,900	14,406	10,594	14,537	13,071
72,900	72,950	14,419	10,606	14,551	13,084
72,950	73,000	14,431	10,619	14,565	13,096

73,000

At least	But less than	Single	Married filing jointly*	Married filing separately	Head of a household
73,000	73,050	14,444	10,631	14,579	13,109
73,050	73,100	14,456	10,644	14,593	13,121
73,100	73,150	14,469	10,656	14,607	13,134
73,150	73,200	14,481	10,669	14,621	13,146
73,200	73,250	14,494	10,681	14,635	13,159
73,250	73,300	14,506	10,694	14,649	13,171
73,300	73,350	14,519	10,706	14,663	13,184
73,350	73,400	14,531	10,719	14,677	13,196
73,400	73,450	14,544	10,731	14,691	13,209
73,450	73,500	14,556	10,744	14,705	13,221
73,500	73,550	14,569	10,756	14,719	13,234
73,550	73,600	14,581	10,769	14,733	13,246
73,600	73,650	14,594	10,781	14,747	13,259
73,650	73,700	14,606	10,794	14,761	13,271
73,700	73,750	14,619	10,806	14,775	13,284
73,750	73,800	14,631	10,819	14,789	13,296
73,800	73,850	14,644	10,831	14,803	13,309
73,850	73,900	14,656	10,844	14,817	13,321
73,900	73,950	14,669	10,856	14,831	13,334
73,950	74,000	14,681	10,869	14,845	13,346

74,000

At least	But less than	Single	Married filing jointly*	Married filing separately	Head of a household
74,000	74,050	14,694	10,881	14,859	13,359
74,050	74,100	14,706	10,894	14,873	13,371
74,100	74,150	14,719	10,906	14,887	13,384
74,150	74,200	14,731	10,919	14,901	13,396
74,200	74,250	14,744	10,931	14,915	13,409
74,250	74,300	14,756	10,944	14,929	13,421
74,300	74,350	14,769	10,956	14,943	13,434
74,350	74,400	14,781	10,969	14,957	13,446
74,400	74,450	14,794	10,981	14,971	13,459
74,450	74,500	14,806	10,994	14,985	13,471
74,500	74,550	14,819	11,006	14,999	13,484
74,550	74,600	14,831	11,019	15,013	13,496
74,600	74,650	14,844	11,031	15,027	13,509
74,650	74,700	14,856	11,044	15,041	13,521
74,700	74,750	14,869	11,056	15,055	13,534
74,750	74,800	14,881	11,069	15,069	13,546
74,800	74,850	14,894	11,081	15,083	13,559
74,850	74,900	14,906	11,094	15,097	13,571
74,900	74,950	14,919	11,106	15,111	13,584
74,950	75,000	14,931	11,119	15,125	13,596

75,000

At least	But less than	Single	Married filing jointly*	Married filing separately	Head of a household
75,000	75,050	14,944	11,131	15,139	13,609
75,050	75,100	14,956	11,144	15,153	13,621
75,100	75,150	14,969	11,156	15,167	13,634
75,150	75,200	14,981	11,169	15,181	13,646
75,200	75,250	14,994	11,181	15,195	13,659
75,250	75,300	15,006	11,194	15,209	13,671
75,300	75,350	15,019	11,206	15,223	13,684
75,350	75,400	15,031	11,219	15,237	13,696
75,400	75,450	15,044	11,231	15,251	13,709
75,450	75,500	15,056	11,244	15,265	13,721
75,500	75,550	15,069	11,256	15,279	13,734
75,550	75,600	15,081	11,269	15,293	13,746
75,600	75,650	15,094	11,281	15,307	13,759
75,650	75,700	15,106	11,294	15,321	13,771
75,700	75,750	15,119	11,306	15,335	13,784
75,750	75,800	15,131	11,319	15,349	13,796
75,800	75,850	15,144	11,331	15,363	13,809
75,850	75,900	15,156	11,344	15,377	13,821
75,900	75,950	15,169	11,356	15,391	13,834
75,950	76,000	15,181	11,369	15,405	13,846

76,000

At least	But less than	Single	Married filing jointly*	Married filing separately	Head of a household
76,000	76,050	15,194	11,381	15,419	13,859
76,050	76,100	15,206	11,394	15,433	13,871
76,100	76,150	15,219	11,406	15,447	13,884
76,150	76,200	15,231	11,419	15,461	13,896
76,200	76,250	15,244	11,431	15,475	13,909
76,250	76,300	15,256	11,444	15,489	13,921
76,300	76,350	15,269	11,456	15,503	13,934
76,350	76,400	15,281	11,469	15,517	13,946
76,400	76,450	15,294	11,481	15,531	13,959
76,450	76,500	15,306	11,494	15,545	13,971
76,500	76,550	15,319	11,506	15,559	13,984
76,550	76,600	15,331	11,519	15,573	13,996
76,600	76,650	15,344	11,531	15,587	14,009
76,650	76,700	15,356	11,544	15,601	14,021
76,700	76,750	15,369	11,556	15,615	14,034
76,750	76,800	15,381	11,569	15,629	14,046
76,800	76,850	15,394	11,581	15,643	14,059
76,850	76,900	15,406	11,594	15,657	14,071
76,900	76,950	15,419	11,606	15,671	14,084
76,950	77,000	15,431	11,619	15,685	14,096

* This column must also be used by a qualifying widow(er).

(*Continued on page D-10*)

2009 Tax Table–*Continued*

77,000

If line 43 (taxable income) is— At least	But less than	Single	Married filing jointly *	Married filing separately	Head of a household
77,000	77,050	15,444	11,631	15,699	14,109
77,050	77,100	15,456	11,644	15,713	14,121
77,100	77,150	15,469	11,656	15,727	14,134
77,150	77,200	15,481	11,669	15,741	14,146
77,200	77,250	15,494	11,681	15,755	14,159
77,250	77,300	15,506	11,694	15,769	14,171
77,300	77,350	15,519	11,706	15,783	14,184
77,350	77,400	15,531	11,719	15,797	14,196
77,400	77,450	15,544	11,731	15,811	14,209
77,450	77,500	15,556	11,744	15,825	14,221
77,500	77,550	15,569	11,756	15,839	14,234
77,550	77,600	15,581	11,769	15,853	14,246
77,600	77,650	15,594	11,781	15,867	14,259
77,650	77,700	15,606	11,794	15,881	14,271
77,700	77,750	15,619	11,806	15,895	14,284
77,750	77,800	15,631	11,819	15,909	14,296
77,800	77,850	15,644	11,831	15,923	14,309
77,850	77,900	15,656	11,844	15,937	14,321
77,900	77,950	15,669	11,856	15,951	14,334
77,950	78,000	15,681	11,869	15,965	14,346

78,000

At least	But less than	Single	Married filing jointly *	Married filing separately	Head of a household
78,000	78,050	15,694	11,881	15,979	14,359
78,050	78,100	15,706	11,894	15,993	14,371
78,100	78,150	15,719	11,906	16,007	14,384
78,150	78,200	15,731	11,919	16,021	14,396
78,200	78,250	15,744	11,931	16,035	14,409
78,250	78,300	15,756	11,944	16,049	14,421
78,300	78,350	15,769	11,956	16,063	14,434
78,350	78,400	15,781	11,969	16,077	14,446
78,400	78,450	15,794	11,981	16,091	14,459
78,450	78,500	15,806	11,994	16,105	14,471
78,500	78,550	15,819	12,006	16,119	14,484
78,550	78,600	15,831	12,019	16,133	14,496
78,600	78,650	15,844	12,031	16,147	14,509
78,650	78,700	15,856	12,044	16,161	14,521
78,700	78,750	15,869	12,056	16,175	14,534
78,750	78,800	15,881	12,069	16,189	14,546
78,800	78,850	15,894	12,081	16,203	14,559
78,850	78,900	15,906	12,094	16,217	14,571
78,900	78,950	15,919	12,106	16,231	14,584
78,950	79,000	15,931	12,119	16,245	14,596

79,000

At least	But less than	Single	Married filing jointly *	Married filing separately	Head of a household
79,000	79,050	15,944	12,131	16,259	14,609
79,050	79,100	15,956	12,144	16,273	14,621
79,100	79,150	15,969	12,156	16,287	14,634
79,150	79,200	15,981	12,169	16,301	14,646
79,200	79,250	15,994	12,181	16,315	14,659
79,250	79,300	16,006	12,194	16,329	14,671
79,300	79,350	16,019	12,206	16,343	14,684
79,350	79,400	16,031	12,219	16,357	14,696
79,400	79,450	16,044	12,231	16,371	14,709
79,450	79,500	16,056	12,244	16,385	14,721
79,500	79,550	16,069	12,256	16,399	14,734
79,550	79,600	16,081	12,269	16,413	14,746
79,600	79,650	16,094	12,281	16,427	14,759
79,650	79,700	16,106	12,294	16,441	14,771
79,700	79,750	16,119	12,306	16,455	14,784
79,750	79,800	16,131	12,319	16,469	14,796
79,800	79,850	16,144	12,331	16,483	14,809
79,850	79,900	16,156	12,344	16,497	14,821
79,900	79,950	16,169	12,356	16,511	14,834
79,950	80,000	16,181	12,369	16,525	14,846

80,000

At least	But less than	Single	Married filing jointly *	Married filing separately	Head of a household
80,000	80,050	16,194	12,381	16,539	14,859
80,050	80,100	16,206	12,394	16,553	14,871
80,100	80,150	16,219	12,406	16,567	14,884
80,150	80,200	16,231	12,419	16,581	14,896
80,200	80,250	16,244	12,431	16,595	14,909
80,250	80,300	16,256	12,444	16,609	14,921
80,300	80,350	16,269	12,456	16,623	14,934
80,350	80,400	16,281	12,469	16,637	14,946
80,400	80,450	16,294	12,481	16,651	14,959
80,450	80,500	16,306	12,494	16,665	14,971
80,500	80,550	16,319	12,506	16,679	14,984
80,550	80,600	16,331	12,519	16,693	14,996
80,600	80,650	16,344	12,531	16,707	15,009
80,650	80,700	16,356	12,544	16,721	15,021
80,700	80,750	16,369	12,556	16,735	15,034
80,750	80,800	16,381	12,569	16,749	15,046
80,800	80,850	16,394	12,581	16,763	15,059
80,850	80,900	16,406	12,594	16,777	15,071
80,900	80,950	16,419	12,606	16,791	15,084
80,950	81,000	16,431	12,619	16,805	15,096

81,000

At least	But less than	Single	Married filing jointly *	Married filing separately	Head of a household
81,000	81,050	16,444	12,631	16,819	15,109
81,050	81,100	16,456	12,644	16,833	15,121
81,100	81,150	16,469	12,656	16,847	15,134
81,150	81,200	16,481	12,669	16,861	15,146
81,200	81,250	16,494	12,681	16,875	15,159
81,250	81,300	16,506	12,694	16,889	15,171
81,300	81,350	16,519	12,706	16,903	15,184
81,350	81,400	16,531	12,719	16,917	15,196
81,400	81,450	16,544	12,731	16,931	15,209
81,450	81,500	16,556	12,744	16,945	15,221
81,500	81,550	16,569	12,756	16,959	15,234
81,550	81,600	16,581	12,769	16,973	15,246
81,600	81,650	16,594	12,781	16,987	15,259
81,650	81,700	16,606	12,794	17,001	15,271
81,700	81,750	16,619	12,806	17,015	15,284
81,750	81,800	16,631	12,819	17,029	15,296
81,800	81,850	16,644	12,831	17,043	15,309
81,850	81,900	16,656	12,844	17,057	15,321
81,900	81,950	16,669	12,856	17,071	15,334
81,950	82,000	16,681	12,869	17,085	15,346

82,000

At least	But less than	Single	Married filing jointly *	Married filing separately	Head of a household
82,000	82,050	16,694	12,881	17,099	15,359
82,050	82,100	16,706	12,894	17,113	15,371
82,100	82,150	16,719	12,906	17,127	15,384
82,150	82,200	16,731	12,919	17,141	15,396
82,200	82,250	16,744	12,931	17,155	15,409
82,250	82,300	16,757	12,944	17,169	15,421
82,300	82,350	16,771	12,956	17,183	15,434
82,350	82,400	16,785	12,969	17,197	15,446
82,400	82,450	16,799	12,981	17,211	15,459
82,450	82,500	16,813	12,994	17,225	15,471
82,500	82,550	16,827	13,006	17,239	15,484
82,550	82,600	16,841	13,019	17,253	15,496
82,600	82,650	16,855	13,031	17,267	15,509
82,650	82,700	16,869	13,044	17,281	15,521
82,700	82,750	16,883	13,056	17,295	15,534
82,750	82,800	16,897	13,069	17,309	15,546
82,800	82,850	16,911	13,081	17,323	15,559
82,850	82,900	16,925	13,094	17,337	15,571
82,900	82,950	16,939	13,106	17,351	15,584
82,950	83,000	16,953	13,119	17,365	15,596

83,000

At least	But less than	Single	Married filing jointly *	Married filing separately	Head of a household
83,000	83,050	16,967	13,131	17,379	15,609
83,050	83,100	16,981	13,144	17,393	15,621
83,100	83,150	16,995	13,156	17,407	15,634
83,150	83,200	17,009	13,169	17,421	15,646
83,200	83,250	17,023	13,181	17,435	15,659
83,250	83,300	17,037	13,194	17,449	15,671
83,300	83,350	17,051	13,206	17,463	15,684
83,350	83,400	17,065	13,219	17,477	15,696
83,400	83,450	17,079	13,231	17,491	15,709
83,450	83,500	17,093	13,244	17,505	15,721
83,500	83,550	17,107	13,256	17,519	15,734
83,550	83,600	17,121	13,269	17,533	15,746
83,600	83,650	17,135	13,281	17,547	15,759
83,650	83,700	17,149	13,294	17,561	15,771
83,700	83,750	17,163	13,306	17,575	15,784
83,750	83,800	17,177	13,319	17,589	15,796
83,800	83,850	17,191	13,331	17,603	15,809
83,850	83,900	17,205	13,344	17,617	15,821
83,900	83,950	17,219	13,356	17,631	15,834
83,950	84,000	17,233	13,369	17,645	15,846

84,000

At least	But less than	Single	Married filing jointly *	Married filing separately	Head of a household
84,000	84,050	17,247	13,381	17,659	15,859
84,050	84,100	17,261	13,394	17,673	15,871
84,100	84,150	17,275	13,406	17,687	15,884
84,150	84,200	17,289	13,419	17,701	15,896
84,200	84,250	17,303	13,431	17,715	15,909
84,250	84,300	17,317	13,444	17,729	15,921
84,300	84,350	17,331	13,456	17,743	15,934
84,350	84,400	17,345	13,469	17,757	15,946
84,400	84,450	17,359	13,481	17,771	15,959
84,450	84,500	17,373	13,494	17,785	15,971
84,500	84,550	17,387	13,506	17,799	15,984
84,550	84,600	17,401	13,519	17,813	15,996
84,600	84,650	17,415	13,531	17,827	16,009
84,650	84,700	17,429	13,544	17,841	16,021
84,700	84,750	17,443	13,556	17,855	16,034
84,750	84,800	17,457	13,569	17,869	16,046
84,800	84,850	17,471	13,581	17,883	16,059
84,850	84,900	17,485	13,594	17,897	16,071
84,900	84,950	17,499	13,606	17,911	16,084
84,950	85,000	17,513	13,619	17,925	16,096

85,000

At least	But less than	Single	Married filing jointly *	Married filing separately	Head of a household
85,000	85,050	17,527	13,631	17,939	16,109
85,050	85,100	17,541	13,644	17,953	16,121
85,100	85,150	17,555	13,656	17,967	16,134
85,150	85,200	17,569	13,669	17,981	16,146
85,200	85,250	17,583	13,681	17,995	16,159
85,250	85,300	17,597	13,694	18,009	16,171
85,300	85,350	17,611	13,706	18,023	16,184
85,350	85,400	17,625	13,719	18,037	16,196
85,400	85,450	17,639	13,731	18,051	16,209
85,450	85,500	17,653	13,744	18,065	16,221
85,500	85,550	17,667	13,756	18,079	16,234
85,550	85,600	17,681	13,769	18,093	16,246
85,600	85,650	17,695	13,781	18,107	16,259
85,650	85,700	17,709	13,794	18,121	16,271
85,700	85,750	17,723	13,806	18,135	16,284
85,750	85,800	17,737	13,819	18,149	16,296
85,800	85,850	17,751	13,831	18,163	16,309
85,850	85,900	17,765	13,844	18,177	16,321
85,900	85,950	17,779	13,856	18,191	16,334
85,950	86,000	17,793	13,869	18,205	16,346

* This column must also be used by a qualifying widow(er).

(Continued on page D-11)

2009 Tax Table–*Continued*

If line 43 (taxable income) is—		And you are—			
At least	But less than	Single	Married filing jointly *	Married filing sepa-rately	Head of a house-hold
		Your tax is—			
86,000					
86,000	**86,050**	17,807	13,881	18,219	16,359
86,050	**86,100**	17,821	13,894	18,233	16,371
86,100	**86,150**	17,835	13,906	18,247	16,384
86,150	**86,200**	17,849	13,919	18,261	16,396
86,200	**86,250**	17,863	13,931	18,275	16,409
86,250	**86,300**	17,877	13,944	18,289	16,421
86,300	**86,350**	17,891	13,956	18,303	16,434
86,350	**86,400**	17,905	13,969	18,317	16,446
86,400	**86,450**	17,919	13,981	18,331	16,459
86,450	**86,500**	17,933	13,994	18,345	16,471
86,500	**86,550**	17,947	14,006	18,359	16,484
86,550	**86,600**	17,961	14,019	18,373	16,496
86,600	**86,650**	17,975	14,031	18,387	16,509
86,650	**86,700**	17,989	14,044	18,401	16,521
86,700	**86,750**	18,003	14,056	18,415	16,534
86,750	**86,800**	18,017	14,069	18,429	16,546
86,800	**86,850**	18,031	14,081	18,443	16,559
86,850	**86,900**	18,045	14,094	18,457	16,571
86,900	**86,950**	18,059	14,106	18,471	16,584
86,950	**87,000**	18,073	14,119	18,485	16,596
87,000					
87,000	**87,050**	18,087	14,131	18,499	16,609
87,050	**87,100**	18,101	14,144	18,513	16,621
87,100	**87,150**	18,115	14,156	18,527	16,634
87,150	**87,200**	18,129	14,169	18,541	16,646
87,200	**87,250**	18,143	14,181	18,555	16,659
87,250	**87,300**	18,157	14,194	18,569	16,671
87,300	**87,350**	18,171	14,206	18,583	16,684
87,350	**87,400**	18,185	14,219	18,597	16,696
87,400	**87,450**	18,199	14,231	18,611	16,709
87,450	**87,500**	18,213	14,244	18,625	16,721
87,500	**87,550**	18,227	14,256	18,639	16,734
87,550	**87,600**	18,241	14,269	18,653	16,746
87,600	**87,650**	18,255	14,281	18,667	16,759
87,650	**87,700**	18,269	14,294	18,681	16,771
87,700	**87,750**	18,283	14,306	18,695	16,784
87,750	**87,800**	18,297	14,319	18,709	16,796
87,800	**87,850**	18,311	14,331	18,723	16,809
87,850	**87,900**	18,325	14,344	18,737	16,821
87,900	**87,950**	18,339	14,356	18,751	16,834
87,950	**88,000**	18,353	14,369	18,765	16,846
88,000					
88,000	**88,050**	18,367	14,381	18,779	16,859
88,050	**88,100**	18,381	14,394	18,793	16,871
88,100	**88,150**	18,395	14,406	18,807	16,884
88,150	**88,200**	18,409	14,419	18,821	16,896
88,200	**88,250**	18,423	14,431	18,835	16,909
88,250	**88,300**	18,437	14,444	18,849	16,921
88,300	**88,350**	18,451	14,456	18,863	16,934
88,350	**88,400**	18,465	14,469	18,877	16,946
88,400	**88,450**	18,479	14,481	18,891	16,959
88,450	**88,500**	18,493	14,494	18,905	16,971
88,500	**88,550**	18,507	14,506	18,919	16,984
88,550	**88,600**	18,521	14,519	18,933	16,996
88,600	**88,650**	18,535	14,531	18,947	17,009
88,650	**88,700**	18,549	14,544	18,961	17,021
88,700	**88,750**	18,563	14,556	18,975	17,034
88,750	**88,800**	18,577	14,569	18,989	17,046
88,800	**88,850**	18,591	14,581	19,003	17,059
88,850	**88,900**	18,605	14,594	19,017	17,071
88,900	**88,950**	18,619	14,606	19,031	17,084
88,950	**89,000**	18,633	14,619	19,045	17,096

If line 43 (taxable income) is—		And you are—			
At least	But less than	Single	Married filing jointly *	Married filing sepa-rately	Head of a house-hold
		Your tax is—			
89,000					
89,000	**89,050**	18,647	14,631	19,059	17,109
89,050	**89,100**	18,661	14,644	19,073	17,121
89,100	**89,150**	18,675	14,656	19,087	17,134
89,150	**89,200**	18,689	14,669	19,101	17,146
89,200	**89,250**	18,703	14,681	19,115	17,159
89,250	**89,300**	18,717	14,694	19,129	17,171
89,300	**89,350**	18,731	14,706	19,143	17,184
89,350	**89,400**	18,745	14,719	19,157	17,196
89,400	**89,450**	18,759	14,731	19,171	17,209
89,450	**89,500**	18,773	14,744	19,185	17,221
89,500	**89,550**	18,787	14,756	19,199	17,234
89,550	**89,600**	18,801	14,769	19,213	17,246
89,600	**89,650**	18,815	14,781	19,227	17,259
89,650	**89,700**	18,829	14,794	19,241	17,271
89,700	**89,750**	18,843	14,806	19,255	17,284
89,750	**89,800**	18,857	14,819	19,269	17,296
89,800	**89,850**	18,871	14,831	19,283	17,309
89,850	**89,900**	18,885	14,844	19,297	17,321
89,900	**89,950**	18,899	14,856	19,311	17,334
89,950	**90,000**	18,913	14,869	19,325	17,346
90,000					
90,000	**90,050**	18,927	14,881	19,339	17,359
90,050	**90,100**	18,941	14,894	19,353	17,371
90,100	**90,150**	18,955	14,906	19,367	17,384
90,150	**90,200**	18,969	14,919	19,381	17,396
90,200	**90,250**	18,983	14,931	19,395	17,409
90,250	**90,300**	18,997	14,944	19,409	17,421
90,300	**90,350**	19,011	14,956	19,423	17,434
90,350	**90,400**	19,025	14,969	19,437	17,446
90,400	**90,450**	19,039	14,981	19,451	17,459
90,450	**90,500**	19,053	14,994	19,465	17,471
90,500	**90,550**	19,067	15,006	19,479	17,484
90,550	**90,600**	19,081	15,019	19,493	17,496
90,600	**90,650**	19,095	15,031	19,507	17,509
90,650	**90,700**	19,109	15,044	19,521	17,521
90,700	**90,750**	19,123	15,056	19,535	17,534
90,750	**90,800**	19,137	15,069	19,549	17,546
90,800	**90,850**	19,151	15,081	19,563	17,559
90,850	**90,900**	19,165	15,094	19,577	17,571
90,900	**90,950**	19,179	15,106	19,591	17,584
90,950	**91,000**	19,193	15,119	19,605	17,596
91,000					
91,000	**91,050**	19,207	15,131	19,619	17,609
91,050	**91,100**	19,221	15,144	19,633	17,621
91,100	**91,150**	19,235	15,156	19,647	17,634
91,150	**91,200**	19,249	15,169	19,661	17,646
91,200	**91,250**	19,263	15,181	19,675	17,659
91,250	**91,300**	19,277	15,194	19,689	17,671
91,300	**91,350**	19,291	15,206	19,703	17,684
91,350	**91,400**	19,305	15,219	19,717	17,696
91,400	**91,450**	19,319	15,231	19,731	17,709
91,450	**91,500**	19,333	15,244	19,745	17,721
91,500	**91,550**	19,347	15,256	19,759	17,734
91,550	**91,600**	19,361	15,269	19,773	17,746
91,600	**91,650**	19,375	15,281	19,787	17,759
91,650	**91,700**	19,389	15,294	19,801	17,771
91,700	**91,750**	19,403	15,306	19,815	17,784
91,750	**91,800**	19,417	15,319	19,829	17,796
91,800	**91,850**	19,431	15,331	19,843	17,809
91,850	**91,900**	19,445	15,344	19,857	17,821
91,900	**91,950**	19,459	15,356	19,871	17,834
91,950	**92,000**	19,473	15,369	19,885	17,846

If line 43 (taxable income) is—		And you are—			
At least	But less than	Single	Married filing jointly *	Married filing sepa-rately	Head of a house-hold
		Your tax is—			
92,000					
92,000	**92,050**	19,487	15,381	19,899	17,859
92,050	**92,100**	19,501	15,394	19,913	17,871
92,100	**92,150**	19,515	15,406	19,927	17,884
92,150	**92,200**	19,529	15,419	19,941	17,896
92,200	**92,250**	19,543	15,431	19,955	17,909
92,250	**92,300**	19,557	15,444	19,969	17,921
92,300	**92,350**	19,571	15,456	19,983	17,934
92,350	**92,400**	19,585	15,469	19,997	17,946
92,400	**92,450**	19,599	15,481	20,011	17,959
92,450	**92,500**	19,613	15,494	20,025	17,971
92,500	**92,550**	19,627	15,506	20,039	17,984
92,550	**92,600**	19,641	15,519	20,053	17,996
92,600	**92,650**	19,655	15,531	20,067	18,009
92,650	**92,700**	19,669	15,544	20,081	18,021
92,700	**92,750**	19,683	15,556	20,095	18,034
92,750	**92,800**	19,697	15,569	20,109	18,046
92,800	**92,850**	19,711	15,581	20,123	18,059
92,850	**92,900**	19,725	15,594	20,137	18,071
92,900	**92,950**	19,739	15,606	20,151	18,084
92,950	**93,000**	19,753	15,619	20,165	18,096
93,000					
93,000	**93,050**	19,767	15,631	20,179	18,109
93,050	**93,100**	19,781	15,644	20,193	18,121
93,100	**93,150**	19,795	15,656	20,207	18,134
93,150	**93,200**	19,809	15,669	20,221	18,146
93,200	**93,250**	19,823	15,681	20,235	18,159
93,250	**93,300**	19,837	15,694	20,249	18,171
93,300	**93,350**	19,851	15,706	20,263	18,184
93,350	**93,400**	19,865	15,719	20,277	18,196
93,400	**93,450**	19,879	15,731	20,291	18,209
93,450	**93,500**	19,893	15,744	20,305	18,221
93,500	**93,550**	19,907	15,756	20,319	18,234
93,550	**93,600**	19,921	15,769	20,333	18,246
93,600	**93,650**	19,935	15,781	20,347	18,259
93,650	**93,700**	19,949	15,794	20,361	18,271
93,700	**93,750**	19,963	15,806	20,375	18,284
93,750	**93,800**	19,977	15,819	20,389	18,296
93,800	**93,850**	19,991	15,831	20,403	18,309
93,850	**93,900**	20,005	15,844	20,417	18,321
93,900	**93,950**	20,019	15,856	20,431	18,334
93,950	**94,000**	20,033	15,869	20,445	18,346
94,000					
94,000	**94,050**	20,047	15,881	20,459	18,359
94,050	**94,100**	20,061	15,894	20,473	18,371
94,100	**94,150**	20,075	15,906	20,487	18,384
94,150	**94,200**	20,089	15,919	20,501	18,396
94,200	**94,250**	20,103	15,931	20,515	18,409
94,250	**94,300**	20,117	15,944	20,529	18,421
94,300	**94,350**	20,131	15,956	20,543	18,434
94,350	**94,400**	20,145	15,969	20,557	18,446
94,400	**94,450**	20,159	15,981	20,571	18,459
94,450	**94,500**	20,173	15,994	20,585	18,471
94,500	**94,550**	20,187	16,006	20,599	18,484
94,550	**94,600**	20,201	16,019	20,613	18,496
94,600	**94,650**	20,215	16,031	20,627	18,509
94,650	**94,700**	20,229	16,044	20,641	18,521
94,700	**94,750**	20,243	16,056	20,655	18,534
94,750	**94,800**	20,257	16,069	20,669	18,546
94,800	**94,850**	20,271	16,081	20,683	18,559
94,850	**94,900**	20,285	16,094	20,697	18,571
94,900	**94,950**	20,299	16,106	20,711	18,584
94,950	**95,000**	20,313	16,119	20,725	18,596

* This column must also be used by a qualifying widow(er).

(Continued on page D-12)

2009 Tax Table–*Continued*

95,000

If line 43 (taxable income) is—		And you are—			
At least	But less than	Single	Married filing jointly*	Married filing separately	Head of a household
		Your tax is—			
95,000	95,050	20,327	16,131	20,739	18,609
95,050	95,100	20,341	16,144	20,753	18,621
95,100	95,150	20,355	16,156	20,767	18,634
95,150	95,200	20,369	16,169	20,781	18,646
95,200	95,250	20,383	16,181	20,795	18,659
95,250	95,300	20,397	16,194	20,809	18,671
95,300	95,350	20,411	16,206	20,823	18,684
95,350	95,400	20,425	16,219	20,837	18,696
95,400	95,450	20,439	16,231	20,851	18,709
95,450	95,500	20,453	16,244	20,865	18,721
95,500	95,550	20,467	16,256	20,879	18,734
95,550	95,600	20,481	16,269	20,893	18,746
95,600	95,650	20,495	16,281	20,907	18,759
95,650	95,700	20,509	16,294	20,921	18,771
95,700	95,750	20,523	16,306	20,935	18,784
95,750	95,800	20,537	16,319	20,949	18,796
95,800	95,850	20,551	16,331	20,963	18,809
95,850	95,900	20,565	16,344	20,977	18,821
95,900	95,950	20,579	16,356	20,991	18,834
95,950	96,000	20,593	16,369	21,005	18,846

96,000

At least	But less than	Single	Married filing jointly*	Married filing separately	Head of a household
96,000	96,050	20,607	16,381	21,019	18,859
96,050	96,100	20,621	16,394	21,033	18,871
96,100	96,150	20,635	16,406	21,047	18,884
96,150	96,200	20,649	16,419	21,061	18,896
96,200	96,250	20,663	16,431	21,075	18,909
96,250	96,300	20,677	16,444	21,089	18,921
96,300	96,350	20,691	16,456	21,103	18,934
96,350	96,400	20,705	16,469	21,117	18,946
96,400	96,450	20,719	16,481	21,131	18,959
96,450	96,500	20,733	16,494	21,145	18,971
96,500	96,550	20,747	16,506	21,159	18,984
96,550	96,600	20,761	16,519	21,173	18,996
96,600	96,650	20,775	16,531	21,187	19,009
96,650	96,700	20,789	16,544	21,201	19,021
96,700	96,750	20,803	16,556	21,215	19,034
96,750	96,800	20,817	16,569	21,229	19,046
96,800	96,850	20,831	16,581	21,243	19,059
96,850	96,900	20,845	16,594	21,257	19,071
96,900	96,950	20,859	16,606	21,271	19,084
96,950	97,000	20,873	16,619	21,285	19,096

97,000

If line 43 (taxable income) is—		And you are—			
At least	But less than	Single	Married filing jointly*	Married filing separately	Head of a household
		Your tax is—			
97,000	97,050	20,887	16,631	21,299	19,109
97,050	97,100	20,901	16,644	21,313	19,121
97,100	97,150	20,915	16,656	21,327	19,134
97,150	97,200	20,929	16,669	21,341	19,146
97,200	97,250	20,943	16,681	21,355	19,159
97,250	97,300	20,957	16,694	21,369	19,171
97,300	97,350	20,971	16,706	21,383	19,184
97,350	97,400	20,985	16,719	21,397	19,196
97,400	97,450	20,999	16,731	21,411	19,209
97,450	97,500	21,013	16,744	21,425	19,221
97,500	97,550	21,027	16,756	21,439	19,234
97,550	97,600	21,041	16,769	21,453	19,246
97,600	97,650	21,055	16,781	21,467	19,259
97,650	97,700	21,069	16,794	21,481	19,271
97,700	97,750	21,083	16,806	21,495	19,284
97,750	97,800	21,097	16,819	21,509	19,296
97,800	97,850	21,111	16,831	21,523	19,309
97,850	97,900	21,125	16,844	21,537	19,321
97,900	97,950	21,139	16,856	21,551	19,334
97,950	98,000	21,153	16,869	21,565	19,346

98,000

At least	But less than	Single	Married filing jointly*	Married filing separately	Head of a household
98,000	98,050	21,167	16,881	21,579	19,359
98,050	98,100	21,181	16,894	21,593	19,371
98,100	98,150	21,195	16,906	21,607	19,384
98,150	98,200	21,209	16,919	21,621	19,396
98,200	98,250	21,223	16,931	21,635	19,409
98,250	98,300	21,237	16,944	21,649	19,421
98,300	98,350	21,251	16,956	21,663	19,434
98,350	98,400	21,265	16,969	21,677	19,446
98,400	98,450	21,279	16,981	21,691	19,459
98,450	98,500	21,293	16,994	21,705	19,471
98,500	98,550	21,307	17,006	21,719	19,484
98,550	98,600	21,321	17,019	21,733	19,496
98,600	98,650	21,335	17,031	21,747	19,509
98,650	98,700	21,349	17,044	21,761	19,521
98,700	98,750	21,363	17,056	21,775	19,534
98,750	98,800	21,377	17,069	21,789	19,546
98,800	98,850	21,391	17,081	21,803	19,559
98,850	98,900	21,405	17,094	21,817	19,571
98,900	98,950	21,419	17,106	21,831	19,584
98,950	99,000	21,433	17,119	21,845	19,596

99,000

If line 43 (taxable income) is—		And you are—			
At least	But less than	Single	Married filing jointly*	Married filing separately	Head of a household
		Your tax is—			
99,000	99,050	21,447	17,131	21,859	19,609
99,050	99,100	21,461	17,144	21,873	19,621
99,100	99,150	21,475	17,156	21,887	19,634
99,150	99,200	21,489	17,169	21,901	19,646
99,200	99,250	21,503	17,181	21,915	19,659
99,250	99,300	21,517	17,194	21,929	19,671
99,300	99,350	21,531	17,206	21,943	19,684
99,350	99,400	21,545	17,219	21,957	19,696
99,400	99,450	21,559	17,231	21,971	19,709
99,450	99,500	21,573	17,244	21,985	19,721
99,500	99,550	21,587	17,256	21,999	19,734
99,550	99,600	21,601	17,269	22,013	19,746
99,600	99,650	21,615	17,281	22,027	19,759
99,650	99,700	21,629	17,294	22,041	19,771
99,700	99,750	21,643	17,306	22,055	19,784
99,750	99,800	21,657	17,319	22,069	19,796
99,800	99,850	21,671	17,331	22,083	19,809
99,850	99,900	21,685	17,344	22,097	19,821
99,900	99,950	21,699	17,356	22,111	19,834
99,950	100,000	21,713	17,369	22,125	19,846

$100,000 or over — use the Tax Computation Worksheet on page 49

* This column must also be used by a qualifying widow(er)

2009 IRS Tax Forms

Included in this appendix are copies of select IRS tax forms that are used throughout *Fundamentals of Taxation*. All of these forms are also available for download from the IRS Web site: www.irs.gov.

Form **1040**

Department of the Treasury—Internal Revenue Service

U.S. Individual Income Tax Return 2009   (99)   IRS Use Only—Do not write or staple in this space.

OMB No. 1545-0074

For the year Jan. 1–Dec. 31, 2009, or other tax year beginning _____, 2009, ending _____, 20__

Label
(See instructions on page 14.)

Use the IRS label.

Otherwise, please print or type.

L A B E L - H E R E

Your first name and initial | Last name | Your social security number

If a joint return, spouse's first name and initial | Last name | Spouse's social security number

Home address (number and street). If you have a P.O. box, see page 14. | Apt. no.

City, town or post office, state, and ZIP code. If you have a foreign address, see page 14.

▲ You **must** enter your SSN(s) above. ▲

Checking a box below will not change your tax or refund.

Presidential Election Campaign ► Check here if you, or your spouse if filing jointly, want $3 to go to this fund (see page 14) ► ☐ You ☐ Spouse

Filing Status
Check only one box.

1 ☐ Single
2 ☐ Married filing jointly (even if only one had income)
3 ☐ Married filing separately. Enter spouse's SSN above and full name here. ►
4 ☐ Head of household (with qualifying person). (See page 15.) If the qualifying person is a child but not your dependent, enter this child's name here. ►
5 ☐ Qualifying widow(er) with dependent child (see page 16)

Exemptions

6a ☐ **Yourself.** If someone can claim you as a dependent, **do not** check box 6a
b ☐ **Spouse**
c Dependents:

(1) First name Last name | (2) Dependent's social security number | (3) Dependent's relationship to you | (4) ✓ if qualifying child for child tax credit (see page 17)

If more than four dependents, see page 17 and check here ► ☐

d Total number of exemptions claimed

Boxes checked on 6a and 6b
No. of children on 6c who:
• lived with you
• did not live with you due to divorce or separation (see page 18)
Dependents on 6c not entered above
Add numbers on lines above ►

Income

Attach Form(s) W-2 here. Also attach Forms W-2G and 1099-R if tax was withheld.

If you did not get a W-2, see page 22.

Enclose, but do not attach, any payment. Also, please use **Form 1040-V.**

7 Wages, salaries, tips, etc. Attach Form(s) W-2 | 7
8a **Taxable** interest. Attach Schedule B if required | 8a
b Tax-exempt interest. **Do not** include on line 8a | 8b
9a Ordinary dividends. Attach Schedule B if required | 9a
b Qualified dividends (see page 22) | 9b
10 Taxable refunds, credits, or offsets of state and local income taxes (see page 23) | 10
11 Alimony received | 11
12 Business income or (loss). Attach Schedule C or C-EZ | 12
13 Capital gain or (loss). Attach Schedule D if required. If not required, check here ► ☐ | 13
14 Other gains or (losses). Attach Form 4797 | 14
15a IRA distributions 15a | b Taxable amount (see page 24) | 15b
16a Pensions and annuities 16a | b Taxable amount (see page 25) | 16b
17 Rental real estate, royalties, partnerships, S corporations, trusts, etc. Attach Schedule E | 17
18 Farm income or (loss). Attach Schedule F | 18
19 Unemployment compensation in excess of $2,400 per recipient (see page 27) | 19
20a Social security benefits 20a | b Taxable amount (see page 27) | 20b
21 Other income. List type and amount (see page 29) | 21
22 Add the amounts in the far right column for lines 7 through 21. This is your **total income** ► | 22

Adjusted Gross Income

23 Educator expenses (see page 29) | 23
24 Certain business expenses of reservists, performing artists, and fee-basis government officials. Attach Form 2106 or 2106-EZ | 24
25 Health savings account deduction. Attach Form 8889 | 25
26 Moving expenses. Attach Form 3903 | 26
27 One-half of self-employment tax. Attach Schedule SE | 27
28 Self-employed SEP, SIMPLE, and qualified plans | 28
29 Self-employed health insurance deduction (see page 30) | 29
30 Penalty on early withdrawal of savings | 30
31a Alimony paid b Recipient's SSN ► | 31a
32 IRA deduction (see page 31) | 32
33 Student loan interest deduction (see page 34) | 33
34 Tuition and fees deduction. Attach Form 8917 | 34
35 Domestic production activities deduction. Attach Form 8903 | 35
36 Add lines 23 through 31a and 32 through 35 | 36
37 Subtract line 36 from line 22. This is your **adjusted gross income** ► | 37

For Disclosure, Privacy Act, and Paperwork Reduction Act Notice, see page 87.   Cat. No. 11320B   Form **1040** (2009)

Form **2106**

Department of the Treasury
Internal Revenue Service (99)

Employee Business Expenses

▶ See separate instructions.

▶ Attach to Form 1040 or Form 1040NR.

OMB No. 1545-0074

2009

Attachment Sequence No. **129**

Your name	Occupation in which you incurred expenses	Social security number

Part I   Employee Business Expenses and Reimbursements

Step 1 Enter Your Expenses

		Column A Other Than Meals and Entertainment	Column B Meals and Entertainment
1	Vehicle expense from line 22 or line 29. (Rural mail carriers: See instructions.)	**1**	
2	Parking fees, tolls, and transportation, including train, bus, etc., that **did not** involve overnight travel or commuting to and from work	**2**	
3	Travel expense while away from home overnight, including lodging, airplane, car rental, etc. **Do not** include meals and entertainment	**3**	
4	Business expenses not included on lines 1 through 3. **Do not** include meals and entertainment	**4**	
5	Meals and entertainment expenses (see instructions)	**5**	
6	**Total expenses.** In Column A, add lines 1 through 4 and enter the result. In Column B, enter the amount from line 5	**6**	

Note: *If you were not reimbursed for any expenses in Step 1, skip line 7 and enter the amount from line 6 on line 8.*

Step 2 Enter Reimbursements Received From Your Employer for Expenses Listed in Step 1

7	Enter reimbursements received from your employer that were **not** reported to you in box 1 of Form W-2. Include any reimbursements reported under code "L" in box 12 of your Form W-2 (see instructions)	**7**	

Step 3 Figure Expenses To Deduct on Schedule A (Form 1040 or Form 1040NR)

8	Subtract line 7 from line 6. If zero or less, enter -0-. However, if line 7 is greater than line 6 in Column A, report the excess as income on Form 1040, line 7 (or on Form 1040NR, line 8)	**8**	
	Note: If **both columns** of line 8 are zero, you cannot deduct employee business expenses. Stop here and attach Form 2106 to your return.		
9	In Column A, enter the amount from line 8. In Column B, multiply line 8 by 50% (.50). (Employees subject to Department of Transportation (DOT) hours of service limits: Multiply meal expenses incurred while away from home on business by 80% (.80) instead of 50%. For detail, see instructions.)	**9**	
10	Add the amounts on line 9 of both columns and enter the total here. **Also, enter the total on Schedule A (Form 1040), line 21** (or on **Schedule A (Form 1040NR), line 9**). (Armed Forces reservists, qualified performing artists, fee-basis state or local government officials, and individuals with disabilities: See the instructions for special rules on where to enter the total.) ▶	**10**	

For Paperwork Reduction Act Notice, see instructions.   Cat. No. 11700N   Form **2106** (2009)

(continued)

(concluded)

Form 2106 (2009)   **Page 2**

Part II Vehicle Expenses

Section A—General Information (You must complete this section if you are claiming vehicle expenses.)

		(a) Vehicle 1	**(b)** Vehicle 2
11	Enter the date the vehicle was placed in service	11 / /	/ /
12	Total miles the vehicle was driven during 2009	12 miles	miles
13	Business miles included on line 12	13 miles	miles
14	Percent of business use. Divide line 13 by line 12	14 %	%
15	Average daily roundtrip commuting distance	15 miles	miles
16	Commuting miles included on line 12	16 miles	miles
17	Other miles. Add lines 13 and 16 and subtract the total from line 12	17 miles	miles
18	Was your vehicle available for personal use during off-duty hours?		☐ Yes ☐ No
19	Do you (or your spouse) have another vehicle available for personal use?		☐ Yes ☐ No
20	Do you have evidence to support your deduction?		☐ Yes ☐ No
21	If "Yes," is the evidence written?		☐ Yes ☐ No

Section B—Standard Mileage Rate (See the instructions for Part II to find out whether to complete this section or Section C.)

22	Multiply line 13 by 55¢ (.55). Enter the result here and on line 1	22	

Section C—Actual Expenses

			(a) Vehicle 1	**(b)** Vehicle 2
23	Gasoline, oil, repairs, vehicle insurance, etc.	23		
24a	Vehicle rentals	24a		
b	Inclusion amount (see instructions)	24b		
c	Subtract line 24b from line 24a	24c		
25	Value of employer-provided vehicle (applies only if 100% of annual lease value was included on Form W-2—see instructions)	25		
26	Add lines 23, 24c, and 25	26		
27	Multiply line 26 by the percentage on line 14	27		
28	Depreciation (see instructions)	28		
29	Add lines 27 and 28. Enter total here and on line 1	29		

Section D—Depreciation of Vehicles (Use this section only if you owned the vehicle and are completing Section C for the vehicle.)

			(a) Vehicle 1	**(b)** Vehicle 2
30	Enter cost or other basis (see instructions)	30		
31	Enter section 179 deduction and special allowance (see instructions)	31		
32	Multiply line 30 by line 14 (see instructions if you claimed the section 179 deduction or special allowance)	32		
33	Enter depreciation method and percentage (see instructions)	33		
34	Multiply line 32 by the percentage on line 33 (see instructions)	34		
35	Add lines 31 and 34	35		
36	Enter the applicable limit explained in the line 36 instructions	36		
37	Multiply line 36 by the percentage on line 14	37		
38	Enter the **smaller** or line 35 or line 37. If you skipped lines 36 and 37, enter the amount from line 35. Also enter this amount on line 28 above	38		

Form **2106** (2009)

Form **4562**

Department of the Treasury
Internal Revenue Service   (99)

Depreciation and Amortization
(Including Information on Listed Property)
▶ See separate instructions.   ▶ Attach to your tax return.

OMB No. 1545-0172

2009

Attachment
Sequence No. **67**

Name(s) shown on return	Business or activity to which this form relates	Identifying number

Part I   **Election To Expense Certain Property Under Section 179**
Note: *If you have any listed property, complete Part V before you complete Part I.*

1	Maximum amount. See the instructions for a higher limit for certain businesses	**1** $250,000
2	Total cost of section 179 property placed in service (see instructions)	**2**
3	Threshold cost of section 179 property before reduction in limitation (see instructions)	**3** $800,000
4	Reduction in limitation. Subtract line 3 from line 2. If zero or less, enter -0-	**4**
5	Dollar limitation for tax year. Subtract line 4 from line 1. If zero or less, enter -0-. If married filing separately, see instructions	**5**

6	**(a)** Description of property	**(b)** Cost (business use only)	**(c)** Elected cost

7	Listed property. Enter the amount from line 29 . . . . **7**	
8	Total elected cost of section 179 property. Add amounts in column (c), lines 6 and 7	**8**
9	Tentative deduction. Enter the **smaller** of line 5 or line 8	**9**
10	Carryover of disallowed deduction from line 13 of your 2008 Form 4562	**10**
11	Business income limitation. Enter the smaller of business income (not less than zero) or line 5 (see instructions) . . .	**11**
12	Section 179 expense deduction. Add lines 9 and 10, but do not enter more than line 11	**12**
13	Carryover of disallowed deduction to 2010. Add lines 9 and 10, less line 12 ▶ **13**	

Note: *Do not use Part II or Part III below for listed property. Instead, use Part V.*

Part II   **Special Depreciation Allowance and Other Depreciation (Do not** include listed property.**)** (See instructions.)

14	Special depreciation allowance for qualified property (other than listed property) placed in service during the tax year (see instructions)	**14**
15	Property subject to section 168(f)(1) election	**15**
16	Other depreciation (including ACRS)	**16**

Part III   **MACRS Depreciation (Do not** include listed property.**)** (See instructions.)

Section A

17	MACRS deductions for assets placed in service in tax years beginning before 2009	**17**
18	If you are electing to group any assets placed in service during the tax year into one or more general asset accounts, check here . . . . ▶ ☐	

Section B—Assets Placed in Service During 2009 Tax Year Using the General Depreciation System

(a) Classification of property	**(b)** Month and year placed in service	**(c)** Basis for depreciation (business/investment use only—see instructions)	**(d)** Recovery period	**(e)** Convention	**(f)** Method	**(g)** Depreciation deduction
19a 3-year property						
b 5-year property						
c 7-year property						
d 10-year property						
e 15-year property						
f 20-year property						
g 25-year property			25 yrs.		S/L	
h Residential rental property			27.5 yrs.	MM	S/L	
			27.5 yrs.	MM	S/L	
i Nonresidential real property			39 yrs.	MM	S/L	
				MM	S/L	

Section C—Assets Placed in Service During 2009 Tax Year Using the Alternative Depreciation System

20a Class life					S/L	
b 12-year			12 yrs.		S/L	
c 40-year			40 yrs.	MM	S/L	

Part IV   **Summary** (See instructions.)

21	Listed property. Enter amount from line 28	**21**
22	**Total.** Add amounts from line 12, lines 14 through 17, lines 19 and 20 in column (g), and line 21. Enter here and on the appropriate lines of your return. Partnerships and S corporations—see instructions	**22**
23	For assets shown above and placed in service during the current year, enter the portion of the basis attributable to section 263A costs **23**	

For Paperwork Reduction Act Notice, see separate instructions.   Cat. No. 12906N   Form **4562** (2009)

(continued)

(concluded)

Form 4562 (2009) Page **2**

Part V   Listed Property (Include automobiles, certain other vehicles, cellular telephones, certain computers, and property used for entertainment, recreation, or amusement.)

Note: *For any vehicle for which you are using the standard mileage rate or deducting lease expense, complete only 24a, 24b, columns (a) through (c) of Section A, all of Section B, and Section C if applicable.*

Section A—Depreciation and Other Information (Caution: *See the instructions for limits for passenger automobiles.*)

24a Do you have evidence to support the business/investment use claimed? ☐ Yes ☐ No   **24b** If "Yes," is the evidence written? ☐ Yes ☐ No

(a) Type of property (list vehicles first)	(b) Date placed in service	(c) Business/ investment use percentage	(d) Cost or other basis	(e) Basis for depreciation (business/investment use only)	(f) Recovery period	(g) Method/ Convention	(h) Depreciation deduction	(i) Elected section 179 cost
25 Special depreciation allowance for qualified listed property placed in service during the tax year and used more than 50% in a qualified business use (see instructions) . . . **25**								
26 Property used more than 50% in a qualified business use:								
		%						
		%						
		%						
27 Property used 50% or less in a qualified business use:								
		%			S/L –			
		%			S/L –			
		%			S/L –			

28 Add amounts in column (h), lines 25 through 27. Enter here and on line 21, page 1 . . .   **28**

29 Add amounts in column (i), line 26. Enter here and on line 7, page 1 . . . .   **29**

Section B—Information on Use of Vehicles

Complete this section for vehicles used by a sole proprietor, partner, or other "more than 5% owner," or related person. If you provided vehicles to your employees, first answer the questions in Section C to see if you meet an exception to completing this section for those vehicles.

	(a) Vehicle 1		(b) Vehicle 2		(c) Vehicle 3		(d) Vehicle 4		(e) Vehicle 5		(f) Vehicle 6	
30 Total business/investment miles driven during the year (**do not** include commuting miles)												
31 Total commuting miles driven during the year												
32 Total other personal (noncommuting) miles driven												
33 Total miles driven during the year. Add lines 30 through 32												
34 Was the vehicle available for personal use during off-duty hours?	Yes	No	Yes	No	Yes	No	Yes	No	Yes	No	Yes	No
35 Was the vehicle used primarily by a more than 5% owner or related person?												
36 Is another vehicle available for personal use?												

Section C—Questions for Employers Who Provide Vehicles for Use by Their Employees

Answer these questions to determine if you meet an exception to completing Section B for vehicles used by employees who **are not** more than 5% owners or related persons (see instructions).

	Yes	No
37 Do you maintain a written policy statement that prohibits all personal use of vehicles, including commuting, by your employees?		
38 Do you maintain a written policy statement that prohibits personal use of vehicles, except commuting, by your employees? See the instructions for vehicles used by corporate officers, directors, or 1% or more owners . . .		
39 Do you treat all use of vehicles by employees as personal use?		
40 Do you provide more than five vehicles to your employees, obtain information from your employees about the use of the vehicles, and retain the information received?		
41 Do you meet the requirements concerning qualified automobile demonstration use? (See instructions.) . .		

Note: *If your answer to 37, 38, 39, 40, or 41 is "Yes," do not complete Section B for the covered vehicles.*

Part VI   Amortization

(a) Description of costs	(b) Date amortization begins	(c) Amortizable amount	(d) Code section	(e) Amortization period or percentage	(f) Amortization for this year
42 Amortization of costs that begins during your 2009 tax year (see instructions):					

43 Amortization of costs that began before your 2009 tax year **43**

44 Total. Add amounts in column (f). See the instructions for where to report **44**

Form **4562** (2009)

Form **4797**

Department of the Treasury
Internal Revenue Service   (99)

Sales of Business Property
(Also Involuntary Conversions and Recapture Amounts
Under Sections 179 and 280F(b)(2))
▶ Attach to your tax return.   ▶ See separate instructions.

OMB No. 1545-0184

2009

Attachment
Sequence No. **27**

Name(s) shown on return

Identifying number

| 1 | Enter the gross proceeds from sales or exchanges reported to you for 2009 on Form(s) 1099-B or 1099-S (or substitute statement) that you are including on line 2, 10, or 20 (see instructions) . . . . | **1** | |

Part I   **Sales or Exchanges of Property Used in a Trade or Business and Involuntary Conversions From Other Than Casualty or Theft—Most Property Held More Than 1 Year** (see instructions)

2	(a) Description of property	(b) Date acquired (mo., day, yr.)	(c) Date sold (mo., day, yr.)	(d) Gross sales price	(e) Depreciation allowed or allowable since acquisition	(f) Cost or other basis, plus improvements and expense of sale	(g) Gain or (loss) Subtract (f) from the sum of (d) and (e)

3	Gain, if any, from Form 4684, line 43	**3**	
4	Section 1231 gain from installment sales from Form 6252, line 26 or 37	**4**	
5	Section 1231 gain or (loss) from like-kind exchanges from Form 8824	**5**	
6	Gain, if any, from line 32, from other than casualty or theft.	**6**	
7	Combine lines 2 through 6. Enter the gain or (loss) here and on the appropriate line as follows:	**7**	

Partnerships (except electing large partnerships) and S corporations. Report the gain or (loss) following the instructions for Form 1065, Schedule K, line 10, or Form 1120S, Schedule K, line 9. Skip lines 8, 9, 11, and 12 below.

Individuals, partners, S corporation shareholders, and all others. If line 7 is zero or a loss, enter the amount from line 7 on line 11 below and skip lines 8 and 9. If line 7 is a gain and you did not have any prior year section 1231 losses, or they were recaptured in an earlier year, enter the gain from line 7 as a long-term capital gain on the Schedule D filed with your return and skip lines 8, 9, 11, and 12 below.

| 8 | Nonrecaptured net section 1231 losses from prior years (see instructions) . . . . | **8** | |
| 9 | Subtract line 8 from line 7. If zero or less, enter -0-. If line 9 is zero, enter the gain from line 7 on line 12 below. If line 9 is more than zero, enter the amount from line 8 on line 12 below and enter the gain from line 9 as a long-term capital gain on the Schedule D filed with your return (see instructions) . . . . | **9** | |

Part II   **Ordinary Gains and Losses** (see instructions)

10	Ordinary gains and losses not included on lines 11 through 16 (include property held 1 year or less):						

11	Loss, if any, from line 7	**11**	( )
12	Gain, if any, from line 7 or amount from line 8, if applicable	**12**	
13	Gain, if any, from line 31	**13**	
14	Net gain or (loss) from Form 4684, lines 35 and 42a	**14**	
15	Ordinary gain from installment sales from Form 6252, line 25 or 36	**15**	
16	Ordinary gain or (loss) from like-kind exchanges from Form 8824.	**16**	
17	Combine lines 10 through 16	**17**	

18	For all except individual returns, enter the amount from line 17 on the appropriate line of your return and skip lines a and b below. For individual returns, complete lines a and b below:		
a	If the loss on line 11 includes a loss from Form 4684, line 39, column (b)(ii), enter that part of the loss here. Enter the part of the loss from income-producing property on Schedule A (Form 1040), line 28, and the part of the loss from property used as an employee on Schedule A (Form 1040), line 23. Identify as from "Form 4797, line 18a." See instructions . .	**18a**	
b	Redetermine the gain or (loss) on line 17 excluding the loss, if any, on line 18a. Enter here and on Form 1040, line 14	**18b**	

For Paperwork Reduction Act Notice, see separate instructions.   Cat. No. 13086I   Form **4797** (2009)

(continued)

(concluded)

Form 4797 (2009)   Page **2**

Part III   Gain From Disposition of Property Under Sections 1245, 1250, 1252, 1254, and 1255
(see instructions)

19	(a) Description of section 1245, 1250, 1252, 1254, or 1255 property:		**(b)** Date acquired (mo., day, yr.)	**(c)** Date sold (mo., day, yr.)
A				
B				
C				
D				

	These columns relate to the properties on lines 19A through 19D. ▶		**Property A**	**Property B**	**Property C**	**Property D**
20	Gross sales price (**Note:** *See line 1 before completing.*)	20				
21	Cost or other basis plus expense of sale	21				
22	Depreciation (or depletion) allowed or allowable	22				
23	Adjusted basis. Subtract line 22 from line 21	23				
24	Total gain. Subtract line 23 from line 20	24				
25	**If section 1245 property:**					
a	Depreciation allowed or allowable from line 22	25a				
b	Enter the **smaller** of line 24 or 25a	25b				
26	**If section 1250 property:** If straight line depreciation was used, enter -0- on line 26g, except for a corporation subject to section 291.					
a	Additional depreciation after 1975 (see instructions)	26a				
b	Applicable percentage multiplied by the **smaller** of line 24 or line 26a (see instructions)	26b				
c	Subtract line 26a from line 24. If residential rental property **or** line 24 is not more than line 26a, skip lines 26d and 26e	26c				
d	Additional depreciation after 1969 and before 1976	26d				
e	Enter the **smaller** of line 26c or 26d	26e				
f	Section 291 amount (corporations only)	26f				
g	Add lines 26b, 26e, and 26f	26g				
27	**If section 1252 property:** Skip this section if you did not dispose of farmland or if this form is being completed for a partnership (other than an electing large partnership).					
a	Soil, water, and land clearing expenses	27a				
b	Line 27a multiplied by applicable percentage (see instructions)	27b				
c	Enter the **smaller** of line 24 or 27b	27c				
28	**If section 1254 property:**					
a	Intangible drilling and development costs, expenditures for development of mines and other natural deposits, mining exploration costs, and depletion (see instructions)	28a				
b	Enter the **smaller** of line 24 or 28a	28b				
29	**If section 1255 property:**					
a	Applicable percentage of payments excluded from income under section 126 (see instructions)	29a				
b	Enter the **smaller** of line 24 or 29a (see instructions)	29b				

Summary of Part III Gains. Complete property columns A through D through line 29b before going to line 30.

30	Total gains for all properties. Add property columns A through D, line 24	30	
31	Add property columns A through D, lines 25b, 26g, 27c, 28b, and 29b. Enter here and on line 13	31	
32	Subtract line 31 from line 30. Enter the portion from casualty or theft on Form 4684, line 37. Enter the portion from other than casualty or theft on Form 4797, line 6	32	

Part IV   Recapture Amounts Under Sections 179 and 280F(b)(2) When Business Use Drops to 50% or Less
(see instructions)

			(a) Section 179	**(b)** Section 280F(b)(2)
33	Section 179 expense deduction or depreciation allowable in prior years	33		
34	Recomputed depreciation (see instructions)	34		
35	Recapture amount. Subtract line 34 from line 33. See the instructions for where to report	35		

Form **4797** (2009)

SCHEDULE A (Form 1040)	Itemized Deductions	OMB No. 1545-0074

SCHEDULE A (Form 1040)

Department of the Treasury
Internal Revenue Service (99)

Itemized Deductions

► **Attach to Form 1040.**   ► **See Instructions for Schedule A (Form 1040).**

OMB No. 1545-0074

2009

Attachment Sequence No. **07**

Name(s) shown on Form 1040

Your social security number

Medical and Dental Expenses	**Caution.** Do not include expenses reimbursed or paid by others.		
	1 Medical and dental expenses (see page A-1)	1	
	2 Enter amount from Form 1040, line 38 **2**		
	3 Multiply line 2 by 7.5% (.075)	3	
	4 Subtract line 3 from line 1. If line 3 is more than line 1, enter -0-		4

Taxes You Paid (See page A-2.)	5 State and local **(check only one box):**
	    a ☐ Income taxes, **or**
	    b ☐ General sales taxes
		5	

	6 Real estate taxes (see page A-5)	6	
	7 New motor vehicle taxes from line 11 of the worksheet on back. Skip this line if you checked box 5b	7	
	8 Other taxes. List type and amount ► _____	8	
	9 Add lines 5 through 8		9
Interest You Paid (See page A-5.) **Note.** Personal interest is not deductible.	10 Home mortgage interest and points reported to you on Form 1098	10	
	11 Home mortgage interest not reported to you on Form 1098. If paid to the person from whom you bought the home, see page A-6 and show that person's name, identifying no., and address ► _____ _____	11	
	12 Points not reported to you on Form 1098. See page A-6 for special rules	12	
	13 Qualified mortgage insurance premiums (see page A-6) .	13	
	14 Investment interest. Attach Form 4952 if required. (See page A-6.)	14	
	15 Add lines 10 through 14		15
Gifts to Charity If you made a gift and got a benefit for it, see page A-7.	16 Gifts by cash or check. If you made any gift of $250 or more, see page A-7	16	
	17 Other than by cash or check. If any gift of $250 or more, see page A-8. You **must** attach Form 8283 if over $500 . . .	17	
	18 Carryover from prior year	18	
	19 Add lines 16 through 18		19
Casualty and Theft Losses	20 Casualty or theft loss(es). Attach Form 4684. (See page A-8.)		20
Job Expenses and Certain Miscellaneous Deductions (See page A-9.)	21 Unreimbursed employee expenses—job travel, union dues, job education, etc. Attach Form 2106 or 2106-EZ if required. (See page A-9.) ►	21	
	22 Tax preparation fees	22	
	23 Other expenses—investment, safe deposit box, etc. List type and amount ► _____ _____	23	
	24 Add lines 21 through 23	24	
	25 Enter amount from Form 1040, line 38 **25**		
	26 Multiply line 25 by 2% (.02)	26	
	27 Subtract line 26 from line 24. If line 26 is more than line 24, enter -0-		27
Other Miscellaneous Deductions	28 Other—from list on page A-10. List type and amount ► _____ _____		28
Total Itemized Deductions	29 Is Form 1040, line 38, over $166,800 (over $83,400 if married filing separately)? ☐ **No.** Your deduction is not limited. Add the amounts in the far right column for lines 4 through 28. Also, enter this amount on Form 1040, line 40a. ☐ **Yes.** Your deduction may be limited. See page A-10 for the amount to enter. ►		29
	30 If you elect to itemize deductions even though they are less than your standard deduction, check here . . . . ► ☐		

For Paperwork Reduction Act Notice, see Form 1040 instructions.   Cat. No. 17145C   Schedule A (Form 1040) 2009

(continued)

(concluded)

Schedule A (Form 1040) 2009   Page **2**

Worksheet for Line 7— New motor vehicle tax deduction

Use this worksheet to figure the amount to enter on line 7.

(Keep a copy for your records.)

Before you begin: ✓ You cannot take this deduction if the amount on Form 1040, line 38, is equal to or greater than $135,000 ($260,000 if married filing jointly).

✓ See the instructions for line 7 that begin on page A-6.

1. Enter the state or local sales or excise taxes you paid in 2009 for the purchase of a new motor vehicle **after** February 16, 2009 . . . . **1**

2. Enter the purchase price (before taxes) of the new motor vehicles **2**

3. Is the amount on line 2 more than $49,500?
   ☐ **No.** Enter the amount from line 1.
   ☐ **Yes.** Enter the portion of the tax from line 1 that is attributable to the first $49,500 of the purchase price of each new motor vehicle (see instructions).   **3**

4. Enter the amount from Form 1040, line 38 . . . . **4**

5. Enter the total of any—
   • Amounts from Form 2555, lines 45 and 50; Form 2555-EZ, line 18; and Form 4563, line 15, and
   • Exclusion of income from Puerto Rico   **5**

6. Add lines 4 and 5 . . . . **6**

7. Enter $125,000 ($250,000 if married filing jointly) **7**

8. Is the amount on line 6 more than the amount on line 7?
   ☐ **No.** Enter the amount from line 3 above on Schedule A, line 7. **Do not** complete the rest of this worksheet.
   ☐ **Yes.** Subtract line 7 from line 6 . . . . **8**

9. Divide line 8 by $10,000. Enter the result as a decimal (rounded to at least three places). If the result is 1.000 or more, enter 1.000 . . . . **9**

10. Multiply line 3 by line 9 . . . . **10**

11. **Deduction for new motor vehicle taxes.** Subtract line 10 from line 3. Enter the result here and on Schedule A, line 7 . . . . **11**

Schedule A (Form 1040) 2009

SCHEDULE B	Interest and Ordinary Dividends	OMB No. 1545-0074

SCHEDULE B
(Form 1040A or 1040)

Department of the Treasury
Internal Revenue Service (99)

Interest and Ordinary Dividends

► **Attach to Form 1040A or 1040.**   ► **See instructions on back.**

OMB No. 1545-0074

20**09**

Attachment
Sequence No. **08**

Name(s) shown on return

Your social security number

Part I
Interest

(See instructions on back and the instructions for Form 1040A, or Form 1040, line 8a.)

Note. If you received a Form 1099-INT, Form 1099-OID, or substitute statement from a brokerage firm, list the firm's name as the payer and enter the total interest shown on that form.

1 List name of payer. If any interest is from a seller-financed mortgage and the buyer used the property as a personal residence, see instructions on back and list this interest first. Also, show that buyer's social security number and address ►

Amount

1

2 Add the amounts on line 1 . . . .   **2**

3 Excludable interest on series EE and I U.S. savings bonds issued after 1989. Attach Form 8815 . . . .   **3**

4 Subtract line 3 from line 2. Enter the result here and on Form 1040A, or Form 1040, line 8a . . . . ►   **4**

Note. If line 4 is over $1,500, you must complete Part III.

Part II
Ordinary
Dividends

(See instructions on back and the instructions for Form 1040A, or Form 1040, line 9a.)

Note. If you received a Form 1099-DIV or substitute statement from a brokerage firm, list the firm's name as the payer and enter the ordinary dividends shown on that form.

5 List name of payer ►

Amount

5

6 Add the amounts on line 5. Enter the total here and on Form 1040A, or Form 1040, line 9a . . . . ►   **6**

Note. If line 6 is over $1,500, you must complete Part III.

Part III
Foreign
Accounts
and Trusts

(See instructions on back.)

You must complete this part if you **(a)** had over $1,500 of taxable interest or ordinary dividends; **(b)** had a foreign account; or **(c)** received a distribution from, or were a grantor of, or a transferor to, a foreign trust.

	Yes	No

7a At any time during 2009, did you have an interest in or a signature or other authority over a financial account in a foreign country, such as a bank account, securities account, or other financial account? See instructions on back for exceptions and filing requirements for Form TD F 90-22.1 . . . .

b If "Yes," enter the name of the foreign country ►

8 During 2009, did you receive a distribution from, or were you the grantor of, or transferor to, a foreign trust? If "Yes," you may have to file Form 3520. See instructions on back . . . . . .

For Paperwork Reduction Act Notice, see Form 1040A or 1040 instructions.   Cat. No. 17146N   **Schedule B (Form 1040A or 1040) 2009**

(continued)

(concluded)

General Instructions

Section references are to the Internal Revenue Code unless otherwise noted.

What's New

Form 1040A. Form 1040A filers will now file Schedule B to report interest and ordinary dividends. Schedule 1 (Form 1040A), Interest and Ordinary Dividends for Form 1040A Filers, is now obsolete. For any prior year returns (before 2009) that need to be filed, still use Schedule 1.

Schedule A. Schedule A, Itemized Deductions, is no longer associated with Schedule B. Schedules A and B are now separate schedules.

Purpose of Form

Use Schedule B if any of the following applies.

• You had over $1,500 of taxable interest or ordinary dividends.

• You received interest from a seller-financed mortgage and the buyer used the property as a personal residence.

• You have accrued interest from a bond.

• You are reporting original issue discount (OID) in an amount less than the amount shown on Form 1099-OID.

• You are reducing your interest income on a bond by the amount of amortizable bond premium.

• You are claiming the exclusion of interest from series EE or I U.S. savings bonds issued after 1989.

• You received interest or ordinary dividends as a nominee.

• You had a foreign account or you received a distribution from, or were a grantor of, or transferor to, a foreign trust. Part III of the schedule has questions about foreign accounts and trusts.

Specific Instructions

You can list more than one payer on each entry space for lines 1 and 5, but be sure to clearly show the amount paid next to the payer's name. Add the separate amounts paid by the payers listed on an entry space and enter the total in the "Amount" column. If you still need more space, attach separate statements that are the same size as the printed schedule. Use the same format as lines 1 and 5, but show your totals on Schedule B. Be sure to put your name and social security number (SSN) on the statements and attach them at the end of your return.

Part I. Interest

Line 1. Report on line 1 all of your taxable interest. Taxable interest should be shown on your Forms 1099-INT, Forms 1099-OID, or substitute statements. Include interest from series EE, H, HH, and I U.S. savings bonds. List each payer's name and show the amount. Do not report on this line any tax-exempt interest from box 8 or box 9 of Form 1099-INT. Instead, report the amount from box 8 on line 8b of Form 1040A or 1040. If an amount is shown in box 9 of Form 1099-INT, you generally must report it on line 13 of Form 6251. See the Instructions for Form 6251 for more details.

Seller-financed mortgages. If you sold your home or other property and the buyer used the property as a personal residence, list first any interest the buyer paid you on a mortgage or other form of seller financing. Be sure to show the buyer's name, address, and SSN. You must also let the buyer know your SSN. If you do not show the buyer's name, address, and SSN, or let the buyer know your SSN, you may have to pay a $50 penalty.

Nominees. If you received a Form 1099-INT that includes interest you received as a nominee (that is, in your name, but the interest actually belongs to someone else), report the total on line 1. Do this even if you later distributed some or all of this income to others. Under your last entry on line 1, put a subtotal of all interest listed on line 1. Below this subtotal, enter "Nominee Distribution" and show the total interest you received as a nominee. Subtract this amount from the subtotal and enter the result on line 2.

If you received interest as a nominee, you must give the actual owner a Form 1099-INT unless the owner is your spouse. You must also file a Form 1096 and a Form 1099-INT with the IRS.
For more details, see the General Instructions for Forms 1099, 1098, 3921, 3922, 5498, and W-2G and the Instructions for Forms 1099-INT and 1099-OID.

Accrued interest. When you buy bonds between interest payment dates and pay accrued interest to the seller, this interest is taxable to the seller. If you received a Form 1099 for interest as a purchaser of a bond with accrued interest, follow the rules earlier under *Nominees* to see how to report the accrued interest. But identify the amount to be subtracted as "Accrued Interest."

Original issue discount (OID). If you are reporting OID in an amount less than the amount shown on Form 1099-OID, follow the rules earlier under *Nominees* to see how to report the OID. But identify the amount to be subtracted as "OID Adjustment."

Amortizable bond premium. If you are reducing your interest income on a bond by the amount of amortizable bond premium, follow the rules earlier under *Nominees* to see how to report the interest. But identify the amount to be subtracted as "ABP Adjustment."

Line 3. If, during 2009, you cashed series EE or I U.S. savings bonds issued after 1989 and you paid qualified higher education expenses for yourself, your spouse, or your dependents, you may be able to exclude part or all of the interest on those bonds. See Form 8815 for details.

Part II. Ordinary Dividends

You may have to file Form 5471 if, in 2009, you were an officer or director of a foreign corporation. You may also have to file Form 5471 if, in 2009, you owned 10% or more of the total (a) value of a foreign corporation's stock, or (b) combined voting power of all classes of a foreign corporation's stock with voting rights. For details, see Form 5471 and its instructions.

Line 5. Report on line 5 all of your ordinary dividends. This amount should be shown in box 1a of your Forms 1099-DIV or substitute statements. List each payer's name and show the amount.

Nominees. If you received a Form 1099-DIV that includes ordinary dividends you received as a nominee (that is, in your name, but the ordinary dividends actually belong to someone else), report the total on line 5. Do this even if you later distributed some or all of this income to others. Under your last entry on line 5, put a subtotal of all ordinary dividends listed on line 5. Below this subtotal, enter "Nominee Distribution" and show the total ordinary dividends you received as a nominee. Subtract this amount from the subtotal and enter the result on line 6.

If you received dividends as a nominee, you must give the actual owner a Form 1099-DIV unless the owner is your spouse. You must also file a Form 1096 and a Form 1099-DIV with the IRS.
For more details, see the General Instructions for Forms 1099, 1098, 3921, 3922, 5498, and W-2G and the Instructions for Form 1099-DIV.

Part III. Foreign Accounts and Trusts

Line 7a. Check the "Yes" box on line 7a if either (1) or (2) below applies.

1. You own more than 50% of the stock in any corporation that owns one or more foreign bank accounts.

2. At any time during 2009 you had an interest in or signature or other authority over a financial account in a foreign country (such as a bank account, securities account, or other financial account).

For line 7a, item (2) does not apply to foreign securities held in a U.S. securities account.

Exceptions. Check the "No" box if any of the following applies to you.

• The combined value of the accounts was $10,000 or less during the whole year.

• The accounts were with a U.S. military banking facility operated by a U.S. financial institution.

• You were an officer or employee of a commercial bank that is supervised by the Comptroller of the Currency, the Board of Governors of the Federal Reserve System, or the Federal Deposit Insurance Corporation; the account was in your employer's name; and you did not have a personal financial interest in the account.

• You were an officer or employee of a domestic corporation with securities listed on national securities exchanges or with assets of more than $10 million and 500 or more shareholders of record; the account was in your employer's name; you did not have a personal financial interest in the account; and the corporation's chief financial officer has given you written notice that the corporation has filed a current report that includes the account.

See Form TD F 90-22.1 to find out if you are considered to have an interest in or signature or other authority over a financial account in a foreign country (such as a bank account, securities account, or other financial account). You can get Form TD F 90-22.1 by visiting the IRS website at www.irs.gov/pub/irs-pdf/f90221.pdf.

If you checked the "Yes" box on line 7a, file Form TD F 90-22.1 by June 30, 2010, with the Department of the Treasury at the address shown on that form. Do not attach it to Form 1040.

If you are required to file Form TD F 90-22.1 but do not do so, you may have to pay a penalty of up to $10,000 (more in some cases).

Line 7b. If you checked the "Yes" box on line 7a, enter the name of the foreign country or countries in the space provided on line 7b. Attach a separate statement if you need more space.

Line 8. If you received a distribution from a foreign trust, you must provide additional information. For this purpose, a loan of cash or marketable securities generally is considered to be a distribution. See Form 3520 for details.

If you were the grantor of, or transferor to, a foreign trust that existed during 2009, you may have to file Form 3520.

Do not attach Form 3520 to Form 1040. Instead, file it at the address shown in its instructions.

If you were treated as the owner of a foreign trust under the grantor trust rules, you are also responsible for ensuring that the foreign trust files Form 3520-A. Form 3520-A is due on March 15, 2010, for a calendar year trust. See the instructions for Form 3520-A for more details.

SCHEDULE C
(Form 1040)

Department of the Treasury
Internal Revenue Service (99)

Profit or Loss From Business
(Sole Proprietorship)

▶ Partnerships, joint ventures, etc., generally must file Form 1065 or 1065-B.

▶ Attach to Form 1040, 1040NR, or 1041.   ▶ See Instructions for Schedule C (Form 1040).

OMB No. 1545-0074

2009

Attachment
Sequence No. **09**

Name of proprietor | Social security number (SSN)

A	Principal business or profession, including product or service (see page C-3 of the instructions)		B Enter code from pages C-9, 10, & 11 ▶
C	Business name. If no separate business name, leave blank.		D Employer ID number (EIN), if any
E	Business address (including suite or room no.) ▶		
	City, town or post office, state, and ZIP code		
F	Accounting method: **(1)** ☐ Cash **(2)** ☐ Accrual **(3)** ☐ Other (specify) ▶		
G	Did you "materially participate" in the operation of this business during 2009? If "No," see page C-4 for limit on losses		☐ Yes ☐ No
H	If you started or acquired this business during 2009, check here . . . . ▶ ☐		

Part I Income

1	Gross receipts or sales. **Caution.** See page C-4 and check the box if:		
	• This income was reported to you on Form W-2 and the "Statutory employee" box on that form was checked, or		
	• You are a member of a qualified joint venture reporting only rental real estate income not subject to self-employment tax. Also see page C-4 for limit on losses.	▶ ☐	**1**
2	Returns and allowances		**2**
3	Subtract line 2 from line 1		**3**
4	Cost of goods sold (from line 42 on page 2)		**4**
5	**Gross profit.** Subtract line 4 from line 3		**5**
6	Other income, including federal and state gasoline or fuel tax credit or refund (see page C-4) .		**6**
7	**Gross income.** Add lines 5 and 6 . . . . ▶		**7**

Part II Expenses. Enter expenses for business use of your home **only** on line 30.

8	Advertising	**8**		18	Office expense	**18**	
9	Car and truck expenses (see page C-5)	**9**		19	Pension and profit-sharing plans .	**19**	
10	Commissions and fees .	**10**		20	Rent or lease (see page C-6):		
11	Contract labor (see page C-5)	**11**		a	Vehicles, machinery, and equipment	**20a**	
12	Depletion	**12**		b	Other business property . . .	**20b**	
13	Depreciation and section 179 expense deduction (not included in Part III) (see page C-5)	**13**		21	Repairs and maintenance . . .	**21**	
				22	Supplies (not included in Part III) .	**22**	
				23	Taxes and licenses	**23**	
				24	Travel, meals, and entertainment:		
				a	Travel	**24a**	
14	Employee benefit programs (other than on line 19) . .	**14**		b	Deductible meals and entertainment (see page C-7) . .	**24b**	
15	Insurance (other than health)	**15**		25	Utilities	**25**	
16	Interest:			26	Wages (less employment credits) .	**26**	
a	Mortgage (paid to banks, etc.)	**16a**		27	Other expenses (from line 48 on page 2)	**27**	
b	Other	**16b**					
17	Legal and professional services	**17**					

28	**Total expenses** before expenses for business use of home. Add lines 8 through 27 . . . . . ▶	**28**	
29	Tentative profit or (loss). Subtract line 28 from line 7	**29**	
30	Expenses for business use of your home. Attach **Form 8829**	**30**	
31	**Net profit or (loss).** Subtract line 30 from line 29.		
	• If a profit, enter on both **Form 1040, line 12,** and **Schedule SE, line 2,** or on **Form 1040NR, line 13** (if you checked the box on line 1, see page C-7). Estates and trusts, enter on **Form 1041, line 3.**	**31**	
	• If a loss, you **must** go to line 32.		
32	If you have a loss, check the box that describes your investment in this activity (see page C-8).		
	• If you checked 32a, enter the loss on both **Form 1040, line 12,** and **Schedule SE, line 2,** or on **Form 1040NR, line 13** (if you checked the box on line 1, see the line 31 instructions on page C-7). Estates and trusts, enter on **Form 1041, line 3.**	32a ☐ All investment is at risk.	
	• If you checked 32b, you **must** attach **Form 6198.** Your loss may be limited.	32b ☐ Some investment is not at risk.	

For Paperwork Reduction Act Notice, see page C-9 of the instructions.   Cat. No. 11334P   **Schedule C (Form 1040) 2009**

(continued)

(concluded)

Schedule C (Form 1040) 2009   Page **2**

Part III   Cost of Goods Sold (see page C-8)

33 Method(s) used to value closing inventory: **a** ☐ Cost   **b** ☐ Lower of cost or market   **c** ☐ Other (attach explanation)

34 Was there any change in determining quantities, costs, or valuations between opening and closing inventory? If "Yes," attach explanation . . . .   ☐ Yes   ☐ No

35 Inventory at beginning of year. If different from last year's closing inventory, attach explanation . . .	35	
36 Purchases less cost of items withdrawn for personal use	36	
37 Cost of labor. Do not include any amounts paid to yourself	37	
38 Materials and supplies	38	
39 Other costs	39	
40 Add lines 35 through 39	40	
41 Inventory at end of year	41	
42 **Cost of goods sold.** Subtract line 41 from line 40. Enter the result here and on page 1, line 4 . . .	42	

Part IV   Information on Your Vehicle. Complete this part **only** if you are claiming car or truck expenses on line 9 and are not required to file Form 4562 for this business. See the instructions for line 13 on page C-5 to find out if you must file Form 4562.

43 When did you place your vehicle in service for business purposes? (month, day, year) ▶ _____ / _____ / _____

44 Of the total number of miles you drove your vehicle during 2009, enter the number of miles you used your vehicle for:

   a Business _____   **b** Commuting (see instructions) _____   **c** Other _____

45 Was your vehicle available for personal use during off-duty hours? . . . .   ☐ Yes   ☐ No

46 Do you (or your spouse) have another vehicle available for personal use?. . . . .   ☐ Yes   ☐ No

47a Do you have evidence to support your deduction? . . . .   ☐ Yes   ☐ No

   b If "Yes," is the evidence written? . . . .   ☐ Yes   ☐ No

Part V   Other Expenses. List below business expenses not included on lines 8–26 or line 30.

--		
--		
--		
--		
--		
--		
--		
48 Total other expenses. Enter here and on page 1, line 27	48	

Schedule C (Form 1040) 2009

SCHEDULE D
(Form 1040)

Department of the Treasury
Internal Revenue Service (99)

Capital Gains and Losses

► **Attach to Form 1040 or Form 1040NR.**   ► **See Instructions for Schedule D (Form 1040).**
► **Use Schedule D-1 to list additional transactions for lines 1 and 8.**

OMB No. 1545-0074

2009

Attachment
Sequence No. **12**

Name(s) shown on return

Your social security number

Part I   Short-Term Capital Gains and Losses—Assets Held One Year or Less

	(a) Description of property (Example: 100 sh. XYZ Co.)	**(b)** Date acquired (Mo., day, yr.)	**(c)** Date sold (Mo., day, yr.)	**(d)** Sales price (see page D-7 of the instructions)	**(e)** Cost or other basis (see page D-7 of the instructions)	**(f) Gain or (loss)** Subtract (e) from (d)
1						

2 Enter your short-term totals, if any, from Schedule D-1, line 2 . . . . **2**

3 **Total short-term sales price amounts.** Add lines 1 and 2 in column (d) **3**

4 Short-term gain from Form 6252 and short-term gain or (loss) from Forms 4684, 6781, and 8824 . . . . . **4**

5 Net short-term gain or (loss) from partnerships, S corporations, estates, and trusts from Schedule(s) K-1 . . . . **5**

6 Short-term capital loss carryover. Enter the amount, if any, from line 10 of your **Capital Loss Carryover Worksheet** on page D-7 of the instructions . . . . **6** (   )

7 **Net short-term capital gain or (loss).** Combine lines 1 through 6 in column (f) **7**

Part II   Long-Term Capital Gains and Losses—Assets Held More Than One Year

	(a) Description of property (Example: 100 sh. XYZ Co.)	**(b)** Date acquired (Mo., day, yr.)	**(c)** Date sold (Mo., day, yr.)	**(d)** Sales price (see page D-7 of the instructions)	**(e)** Cost or other basis (see page D-7 of the instructions)	**(f) Gain or (loss)** Subtract (e) from (d)
8						

9 Enter your long-term totals, if any, from Schedule D-1, line 9 . . . . **9**

10 **Total long-term sales price amounts.** Add lines 8 and 9 in column (d) **10**

11 Gain from Form 4797, Part I; long-term gain from Forms 2439 and 6252; and long-term gain or (loss) from Forms 4684, 6781, and 8824 . . . . **11**

12 Net long-term gain or (loss) from partnerships, S corporations, estates, and trusts from Schedule(s) K-1 . . . . **12**

13 Capital gain distributions. See page D-2 of the instructions **13**

14 Long-term capital loss carryover. Enter the amount, if any, from line 15 of your **Capital Loss Carryover Worksheet** on page D-7 of the instructions . . . . **14** (   )

15 **Net long-term capital gain or (loss).** Combine lines 8 through 14 in column (f). Then go to Part III on the back **15**

For Paperwork Reduction Act Notice, see Form 1040 or Form 1040NR instructions.   Cat. No. 11338H   **Schedule D (Form 1040) 2009**

(continued)

(concluded)

Part III   **Summary**

16 Combine lines 7 and 15 and enter the result **16**

If line 16 is:
- A **gain**, enter the amount from line 16 on Form 1040, line 13, or Form 1040NR, line 14. Then go to line 17 below.
- A **loss**, skip lines 17 through 20 below. Then go to line 21. Also be sure to complete line 22.
- **Zero**, skip lines 17 through 21 below and enter -0- on Form 1040, line 13, or Form 1040NR, line 14. Then go to line 22.

17 Are lines 15 and 16 **both** gains?
☐ **Yes.** Go to line 18.
☐ **No.** Skip lines 18 through 21, and go to line 22.

18 Enter the amount, if any, from line 7 of the **28% Rate Gain Worksheet** on page D-8 of the instructions . . . . ▶   **18**

19 Enter the amount, if any, from line 18 of the **Unrecaptured Section 1250 Gain Worksheet** on page D-9 of the instructions . . . . ▶   **19**

20 Are lines 18 and 19 **both** zero or blank?
☐ **Yes.** Complete Form 1040 through line 43, or Form 1040NR through line 40. Then complete the **Qualified Dividends and Capital Gain Tax Worksheet** on page 38 of the Instructions for Form 1040 (or in the Instructions for Form 1040NR). **Do not** complete lines 21 and 22 below.
☐ **No.** Complete Form 1040 through line 43, or Form 1040NR through line 40. Then complete the **Schedule D Tax Worksheet** on page D-10 of the instructions. **Do not** complete lines 21 and 22 below.

21 If line 16 is a loss, enter here and on Form 1040, line 13, or Form 1040NR, line 14, the **smaller** of:
- The loss on line 16 or
- ($3,000), or if married filing separately, ($1,500)   . . . .   **21** (   )

Note. When figuring which amount is smaller, treat both amounts as positive numbers.

22 Do you have qualified dividends on Form 1040, line 9b, or Form 1040NR, line 10b?

☐ **Yes.** Complete Form 1040 through line 43, or Form 1040NR through line 40. Then complete the **Qualified Dividends and Capital Gain Tax Worksheet** on page 38 of the Instructions for Form 1040 (or in the Instructions for Form 1040NR).
☐ **No.** Complete the rest of Form 1040 or Form 1040NR.

SCHEDULE E
(Form 1040)

Department of the Treasury
Internal Revenue Service (99)

Supplemental Income and Loss

(From rental real estate, royalties, partnerships,
S corporations, estates, trusts, REMICs, etc.)

▶ **Attach to Form 1040, 1040NR, or Form 1041.**   ▶ **See Instructions for Schedule E (Form 1040).**

OMB No. 1545-0074

2009

Attachment
Sequence No. **13**

Name(s) shown on return

Your social security number

Part I   Income or Loss From Rental Real Estate and Royalties   **Note.** If you are in the business of renting personal property, use **Schedule C** or **C-EZ** (see page E-3). If you are an individual, report farm rental income or loss from **Form 4835** on page 2, line 40.

1   List the type and address of each **rental real estate property:**

A _____

B _____

C _____

2   For each rental real estate property listed on line 1, did you or your family use it during the tax year for personal purposes for more than the greater of:
• 14 days **or**
• 10% of the total days rented at fair rental value?
(See page E-3)

	Yes	No
A		
B		
C		

		Properties			Totals
Income:		A	B	C	(Add columns A, B, and C.)
3 Rents received	3				3
4 Royalties received	4				4
Expenses:					
5 Advertising	5				
6 Auto and travel (see page E-4)	6				
7 Cleaning and maintenance	7				
8 Commissions	8				
9 Insurance	9				
10 Legal and other professional fees	10				
11 Management fees	11				
12 Mortgage interest paid to banks, etc. (see page E-5)	12				12
13 Other interest	13				
14 Repairs	14				
15 Supplies	15				
16 Taxes	16				
17 Utilities	17				
18 Other (list) ▶ _____	18				
19 Add lines 5 through 18	19				19
20 Depreciation expense or depletion (see page E-5)	20				20
21 Total expenses. Add lines 19 and 20	21				
22 Income or (loss) from rental real estate or royalty properties. Subtract line 21 from line 3 (rents) or line 4 (royalties). If the result is a (loss), see page E-5 to find out if you must file **Form 6198**	22				
23 Deductible rental real estate loss. **Caution.** Your rental real estate loss on line 22 may be limited. See page E-5 to find out if you must file **Form 8582.** Real estate professionals **must** complete line 43 on page 2	23	( )	( )	( )	

24   **Income.** Add positive amounts shown on line 22. **Do not** include any losses | 24

25   **Losses.** Add royalty losses from line 22 and rental real estate losses from line 23. Enter total losses here | 25 ( )

26   **Total rental real estate and royalty income or (loss).** Combine lines 24 and 25. Enter the result here. If Parts II, III, IV, and line 40 on page 2 do not apply to you, also enter this amount on Form 1040, line 17, or Form 1040NR, line 18. Otherwise, include this amount in the total on line 41 on page 2 | 26

For Paperwork Reduction Act Notice, see page E-8 of the instructions.   Cat. No. 11344L   **Schedule E (Form 1040) 2009**

(continued)

Draft as of 06/23/2009

(concluded)

Version A, Cycle 1

Schedule E (Form 1040) 2009	Attachment Sequence No. **13**	Page **2**

Name(s) shown on return. Do not enter name and social security number if shown on other side. | **Your social security number**

Caution. The IRS compares amounts reported on your tax return with amounts shown on Schedule(s) K-1.

Part II   Income or Loss From Partnerships and S Corporations   Note. If you report a loss from an at-risk activity for which **any** amount is **not** at risk, you **must** check the box in column **(e)** on line 28 and attach **Form 6198**. See page E-1.

27   Are you reporting any loss not allowed in a prior year due to the at-risk or basis limitations, a prior year unallowed loss from a passive activity (if that loss was not reported on Form 8582), or unreimbursed partnership expenses? If you answered "Yes," see page E-7 before completing this section.   ☐ **Yes**   ☐ **No**

28

	(a) Name	(b) Enter **P** for partnership; **S** for S corporation	(c) Check if foreign partnership	(d) Employer identification number	(e) Check if any amount is not at risk
A			☐		☐
B			☐		☐
C			☐		☐
D			☐		☐

	Passive Income and Loss		Nonpassive Income and Loss		
	(f) Passive loss allowed (attach **Form 8582** if required)	(g) Passive income from **Schedule K–1**	(h) Nonpassive loss from **Schedule K–1**	(i) Section 179 expense deduction from **Form 4562**	(j) Nonpassive income from **Schedule K–1**
A					
B					
C					
D					
29a Totals					
b Totals					

30	Add columns (g) and (j) of line 29a	**30**	
31	Add columns (f), (h), and (i) of line 29b	**31** (	)
32	**Total partnership and S corporation income or (loss).** Combine lines 30 and 31. Enter the result here and include in the total on line 41 below	**32**	

Part III   Income or Loss From Estates and Trusts

33

	(a) Name	(b) Employer identification number
A		
B		

	Passive Income and Loss		Nonpassive Income and Loss	
	(c) Passive deduction or loss allowed (attach **Form 8582** if required)	(d) Passive income from **Schedule K–1**	(e) Deduction or loss from **Schedule K–1**	(f) Other income from **Schedule K–1**
A				
B				
34a Totals				
b Totals				

35	Add columns (d) and (f) of line 34a	**35**	
36	Add columns (c) and (e) of line 34b	**36** (	)
37	**Total estate and trust income or (loss).** Combine lines 35 and 36. Enter the result here and include in the total on line 41 below	**37**	

Part IV   Income or Loss From Real Estate Mortgage Investment Conduits (REMICs)—Residual Holder

38

(a) Name	(b) Employer identification number	(c) Excess inclusion from **Schedules Q**, line 2c (see page E-7)	(d) Taxable income (net loss) from **Schedules Q**, line 1b	(e) Income from **Schedules Q**, line 3b

39	Combine columns (d) and (e) only. Enter the result here and include in the total on line 41 below	**39**	

Part V   Summary

40	Net farm rental income or (loss) from **Form 4835**. Also, complete line 42 below	**40**	
41	**Total income or (loss).** Combine lines 26, 32, 37, 39, and 40. Enter the result here and on Form 1040, line 17, or Form 1040NR, line 18 ▶	**41**	

42   **Reconciliation of farming and fishing income.** Enter your **gross** farming and fishing income reported on Form 4835, line 7; Schedule K-1 (Form 1065), box 14, code B; Schedule K-1 (Form 1120S), box 17, code T; and Schedule K-1 (Form 1041), line 14, code F (see page E-8)   **42**

43   **Reconciliation for real estate professionals.** If you were a real estate professional (see page E-2), enter the net income or (loss) you reported anywhere on Form 1040 or Form 1040NR from all rental real estate activities in which you materially participated under the passive activity loss rules . .   **43**

Schedule E (Form 1040) 2009

SCHEDULE EIC
(Form 1040A or 1040)

Department of the Treasury
Internal Revenue Service (99)

Earned Income Credit

Qualifying Child Information

*Complete and attach to Form 1040A or 1040
only if you have a qualifying child.*

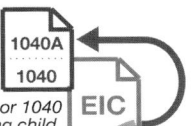

OMB No. 1545-0074

20**09**

Attachment
Sequence No. **43**

Name(s) shown on return

Your social security number

Before you begin:

- See the instructions for Form 1040A, lines 41a and 41b, or Form 1040, lines 64a and 64b, to make sure that **(a)** you can take the EIC, and **(b)** you have a qualifying child.
- Be sure the child's name on line 1 and social security number (SSN) on line 2 agree with the child's social security card. Otherwise, at the time we process your return, we may reduce or disallow your EIC. If the name or SSN on the child's social security card is not correct, call the Social Security Administration at 1-800-772-1213.

- If you take the EIC even though you are not eligible, you may not be allowed to take the credit for up to 10 years. See back of schedule for details.
- It will take us longer to process your return and issue your refund if you do not fill in all lines that apply for each qualifying child.

Qualifying Child Information	Child 1	Child 2	Child 3
1 Child's name If you have more than three qualifying children, you only have to list three to get the maximum credit.	First name Last name	First name Last name	First name Last name
2 Child's SSN The child must have an SSN as defined on page 43 of the Form 1040A instructions or page 50 of the Form 1040 instructions unless the child was born and died in 2009. If your child was born and died in 2009 and did not have an SSN, enter "Died" on this line and attach a copy of the child's birth certificate, death certificate, or hospital medical records.			
3 Child's year of birth	Year ___ ___ ___ *If born after 1990 and the child was younger than you, skip lines 4a and 4b; go to line 5.*	Year ___ ___ ___ *If born after 1990 and the child was younger than you, skip lines 4a and 4b; go to line 5.*	Year ___ ___ ___ *If born after 1990 and the child was younger than you, skip lines 4a and 4b; go to line 5.*
4 a Was the child under age 24 at the end of 2009, a student, and younger than you?	☐ Yes. ☐ No. *Go to line 5.* *Continue.*	☐ Yes. ☐ No. *Go to line 5.* *Continue.*	☐ Yes. ☐ No. *Go to line 5.* *Continue.*
b Was the child permanently and totally disabled during any part of 2009?	☐ Yes. ☐ No. *Continue.* The child is not a qualifying child.	☐ Yes. ☐ No. *Continue.* The child is not a qualifying child.	☐ Yes. ☐ No. *Continue.* The child is not a qualifying child.
5 Child's relationship to you (for example, son, daughter, grandchild, niece, nephew, foster child, etc.)			
6 Number of months child lived with you in the United States during 2009 • If the child lived with you for more than half of 2009 but less than 7 months, enter "7." • If the child was born or died in 2009 and your home was the child's home for the entire time he or she was alive during 2009, enter "12."	_____ months *Do not enter more than 12 months.*	_____ months *Do not enter more than 12 months.*	_____ months *Do not enter more than 12 months.*

For Paperwork Reduction Act Notice, see Form 1040A or 1040 instructions.

Cat. No. 13339M

Schedule EIC (Form 1040A or 1040) 2009

SCHEDULE SE (Form 1040) Department of the Treasury Internal Revenue Service (99)	**Self-Employment Tax** ▶ Attach to Form 1040. ▶ See Instructions for Schedule SE (Form 1040).	OMB No. 1545-0074 20**09** Attachment Sequence No. **17**

| Name of person with **self-employment** income (as shown on Form 1040) | Social security number of person
with **self-employment** income ▶ | |

Who Must File Schedule SE

You must file Schedule SE if:

- You had net earnings from self-employment from **other than** church employee income (line 4 of Short Schedule SE or line 4c of Long Schedule SE) of $400 or more, **or**
- You had church employee income of $108.28 or more. Income from services you performed as a minister or a member of a religious order **is not** church employee income (see page SE-1).

Note. Even if you had a loss or a small amount of income from self-employment, it may be to your benefit to file Schedule SE and use either "optional method" in Part II of Long Schedule SE (see page SE-4).

Exception. If your only self-employment income was from earnings as a minister, member of a religious order, or Christian Science practitioner **and** you filed Form 4361 and received IRS approval not to be taxed on those earnings, **do not** file Schedule SE. Instead, write "Exempt—Form 4361" on Form 1040, line 56.

May I Use Short Schedule SE or Must I Use Long Schedule SE?

Note. Use this flowchart **only if** you must file Schedule SE. If unsure, see *Who Must File Schedule SE,* above.

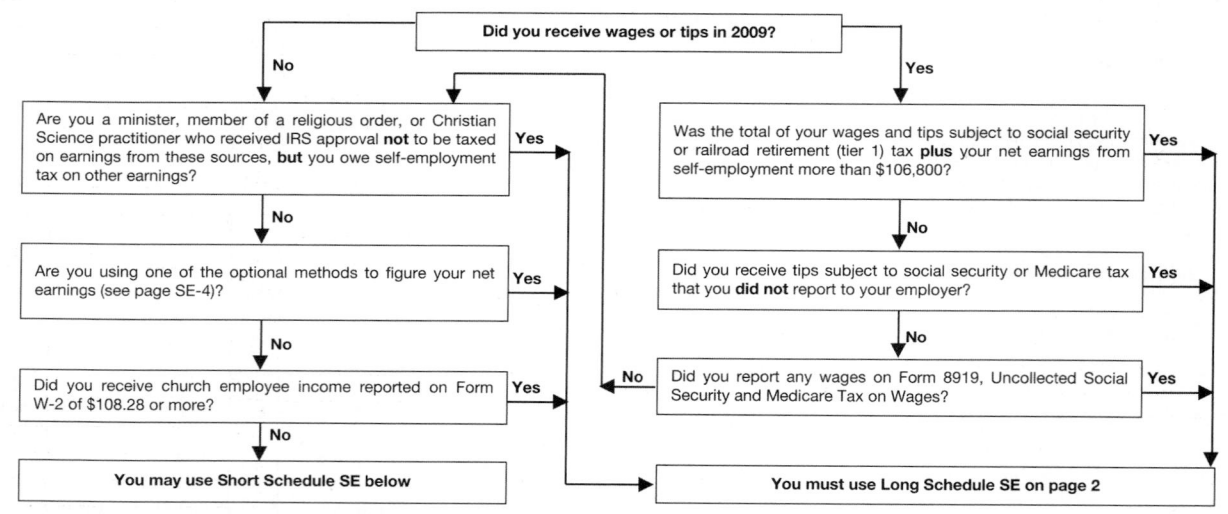

Section A—Short Schedule SE. Caution. Read above to see if you can use Short Schedule SE.

1a	Net farm profit or (loss) from Schedule F, line 36, and farm partnerships, Schedule K-1 (Form 1065), box 14, code A	**1a**
b	If you received social security retirement or disability benefits, enter the amount of Conservation Reserve Program payments included on Schedule F, line 6b, or listed on Schedule K-1 (Form 1065), box 20, code Y	**1b** ( )
2	Net profit or (loss) from Schedule C, line 31; Schedule C-EZ, line 3; Schedule K-1 (Form 1065), box 14, code A (other than farming); and Schedule K-1 (Form 1065-B), box 9, code J1. Ministers and members of religious orders, see page SE-1 for types of income to report on this line. See page SE-3 for other income to report	**2**
3	Combine lines 1a, 1b, and 2	**3**
4	**Net earnings from self-employment.** Multiply line 3 by 92.35% (.9235). If less than $400, **do not** file this schedule; you do not owe self-employment tax . . . . ▶	**4**
5	**Self-employment tax.** If the amount on line 4 is: • $106,800 or less, multiply line 4 by 15.3% (.153). Enter the result here and on **Form 1040, line 56.** • More than $106,800, multiply line 4 by 2.9% (.029). Then, add $13,243.20 to the result. Enter the total here and on **Form 1040, line 56.**	**5**
6	**Deduction for one-half of self-employment tax.** Multiply line 5 by 50% (.50). Enter the result here and on **Form 1040, line 27** **6**	

For Paperwork Reduction Act Notice, see Form 1040 instructions.	Cat. No. 11358Z	Schedule SE (Form 1040) 2009

Schedule SE (Form 1040) 2009 | Attachment Sequence No. **17** | Page **2**

| Name of person with **self-employment** income (as shown on Form 1040) | Social security number of person with **self-employment** income ▶ |

Section B—Long Schedule SE

Part I   Self-Employment Tax

Note. If your only income subject to self-employment tax is **church employee income,** skip lines 1 through 4b. Enter -0- on line 4c and go to line 5a. Income from services you performed as a minister or a member of a religious order **is not** church employee income. See page SE-1.

A   If you are a minister, member of a religious order, or Christian Science practitioner **and** you filed Form 4361, but you had $400 or more of **other** net earnings from self-employment, check here and continue with Part I . . . . . . ▶ ☐

1a Net farm profit or (loss) from Schedule F, line 36, and farm partnerships, Schedule K-1 (Form 1065), box 14, code A. **Note.** Skip lines 1a and 1b if you use the farm optional method (see page SE-4)	**1a**	
b If you received social security retirement or disability benefits, enter the amount of Conservation Reserve Program payments included on Schedule F, line 6b, or listed on Schedule K-1 (Form 1065), box 20, code Y	**1b** (	)
2 Net profit or (loss) from Schedule C, line 31; Schedule C-EZ, line 3; Schedule K-1 (Form 1065), box 14, code A (other than farming); and Schedule K-1 (Form 1065-B), box 9, code J1. Ministers and members of religious orders, see page SE-1 for types of income to report on this line. See page SE-3 for other income to report. **Note.** Skip this line if you use the nonfarm optional method (see page SE-4)	**2**	
3 Combine lines 1a, 1b, and 2	**3**	
4a If line 3 is more than zero, multiply line 3 by 92.35% (.9235). Otherwise, enter amount from line 3	**4a**	
b If you elect one or both of the optional methods, enter the total of lines 15 and 17 here . .	**4b**	
c Combine lines 4a and 4b. If less than $400, **stop;** you do not owe self-employment tax. **Exception.** If less than $400 and you had **church employee income,** enter -0- and continue ▶	**4c**	

5a Enter your **church employee income** from Form W-2. See page SE-1 for definition of church employee income. **5a**	**5a**	
b Multiply line 5a by 92.35% (.9235). If less than $100, enter -0-	**5b**	
6 **Net earnings from self-employment.** Add lines 4c and 5b	**6**	
7 Maximum amount of combined wages and self-employment earnings subject to social security tax or the 6.2% portion of the 7.65% railroad retirement (tier 1) tax for 2009	**7**	106,800 00

8a Total social security wages and tips (total of boxes 3 and 7 on Form(s) W-2) and railroad retirement (tier 1) compensation. If $106,800 or more, skip lines 8b through 10, and go to line 11 **8a**		
b Unreported tips subject to social security tax (from Form 4137, line 10) **8b**		
c Wages subject to social security tax (from Form 8919, line 10) **8c**		
d Add lines 8a, 8b, and 8c	**8d**	
9 Subtract line 8d from line 7. If zero or less, enter -0- here and on line 10 and go to line 11 . ▶	**9**	
10 Multiply the **smaller** of line 6 or line 9 by 12.4% (.124)	**10**	
11 Multiply line 6 by 2.9% (.029)	**11**	
12 **Self-employment tax.** Add lines 10 and 11. Enter here and on **Form 1040, line 56.** . . .	**12**	
13 **Deduction for one-half of self-employment tax.** Multiply line 12 by 50% (.50). Enter the result here and on **Form 1040, line 27** . **13**		

Part II   Optional Methods To Figure Net Earnings (see page SE-4)

Farm Optional Method. You may use this method **only** if **(a)** your gross farm income[1] was not more than $6,540, **or (b)** your net farm profits[2] were less than $4,721.

14 Maximum income for optional methods	**14**	4,360 00
15 Enter the **smaller** of: two-thirds (2/3) of gross farm income[1] (not less than zero) **or** $4,360. Also include this amount on line 4b above	**15**	

Nonfarm Optional Method. You may use this method **only** if **(a)** your net nonfarm profits[3] were less than $4,721 and also less than 72.189% of your gross nonfarm income,[4] **and (b)** you had net earnings from self-employment of at least $400 in 2 of the prior 3 years. **Caution.** You may use this method no more than five times.

16 Subtract line 15 from line 14	**16**	
17 Enter the **smaller** of: two-thirds (2/3) of gross nonfarm income[4] (not less than zero) **or** the amount on line 16. Also include this amount on line 4b above	**17**	

[1] From Sch. F, line 11, and Sch. K-1 (Form 1065), box 14, code B.

[2] From Sch. F, line 36, and Sch. K-1 (Form 1065), box 14, code A—minus the amount you would have entered on line 1b had you not used the optional method.

[3] From Sch. C, line 31; Sch. C-EZ, line 3; Sch. K-1 (Form 1065), box 14, code A; and Sch. K-1 (Form 1065-B), box 9, code J1.

[4] From Sch. C, line 7; Sch. C-EZ, line 1; Sch. K-1 (Form 1065), box 14, code C; and Sch. K-1 (Form 1065-B), box 9, code J2.

Schedule SE (Form 1040) 2009

Index